Human
Resources and
Labor Markets

Human Resources and Labor Markets

LABOR AND MANPOWER IN THE AMERICAN ECONOMY

Sar A. Levitan
GEORGE WASHINGTON UNIVERSITY

Garth L. Mangum
UNIVERSITY OF UTAH

Ray Marshall
UNIVERSITY OF TEXAS

HARPER & ROW, PUBLISHERS
New York, Evanston, San Francisco, London

HUMAN RESOURCES AND LABOR MARKETS: Labor and Manpower in the American Economy

Copyright © 1972 by **Sar A. Levitan, Garth L. Mangum,** and **Ray Marshall**

Standard Book Number: 06-043997-1

Library of Congress Catalog Card Number: 76-184938

Contents

EPILOGUE

Preface

Ten years of labor in the "vineyards" of manpower policy convinced us that the integration of human resource development, labor market economics, and economic theory had been too long neglected. This volume is an early step in that direction.

The days when textbook authors needed only a quill and parchment to prepare a manuscript are long gone. Scholarship does not flow without logistical support from research assistants, administrators, and secretaries. Financial support is vital. Our debts are many. Roger Davidson subjected himself to reading the complete draft and supplied a valuable critical commentary to the text. Ethel Brandwein, Vernon M. Briggs, Jr., Lowell Glenn, Laura Landakusic, Steve Markowitz, David Marwick, David Moewes, John Ostbo, and Robert Taggart III made major contributions and the authors did the rest. Audrey Barber, Evelyn McConkie, Neva Nielson, Illa Rowley, Ivis Steele, and Susie Turner moved the words from dictating machine or foolscap to manuscript, improving them in the process. Barbara Pease prepared the volume for publication. Recognition should go to all who have advised us or from whom we have adapted ideas, and to the government administrators who have borne our constant probing and querying, but their names are too many to list. Gratitude is also due to Harper & Row editors John W. Greenman and Anita Tarshish.

The Ford Foundation has been the major source of support for the activities of two of us over several years and a substantial supporter of the third. Most of the materials herein were gathered during the course of Foundation-funded evaluations of federal manpower programs. Much was gathered in projects funded by the Office of Research and Development and the Office of Evaluation of the U.S. Department of Labor, Manpower Administration. Though none of these institutions is in the business of subsidizing textbook writers, their support of other activities made this textbook possible. We offer our gratitude and absolve them of blame.

Ultimately, our greatest debt is to you the reader who will use the book. We trust that the experience will be beneficial to you.

The Authors

Labor Day, 1971

Human Resources and Labor Markets

Chapter 1
Human Resource Development in Perspective

Economists traditionally have identified three factors of production: land, capital, and labor. In the preindustrial society agriculture was the major source of wealth. Production was based on rudimentary skills passed from father to son, crude farming tools, and incremental improvements made by each generation on the "original and indestructable powers of the soil." Capital and labor were wedded to the land, and economic power belonged to those who could control its use.

With the Industrial Revolution, capital became the critical economic factor. It was capital that bought the machinery which, more than skill, accounted for rising productivity. The labor which operated the machines was relatively untrained and easily replaceable. Skill requirements increased as technology became more sophisticated, and by organizing workers gained more power, but capital remained the central factor in the mass-production economy. Government was concerned primarily with ensuring tranquil labor–management relations, and employers with maintaining a dependable labor force; neither displayed much concern with skill development.

In modern society, the role of labor as a factor of production is becoming increasingly important. The world in which the bulk of the labor force was devoted to the production of goods is fading, just as did the world in which agriculture dominated the economic scene. The shift from manufacturing to service and information-processing activities and the increasing pace of technological change are making manpower the key ingredient to the nation's well-being and growth. In a service-oriented era, the quality, quantity, and utilization of human resources become of central importance. Capital and natural resource endowments are vital factors in advanced countries, but it is the laborer—the human resource—who contributes most to the contemporary "wealth of nations." Thus expansion and improvement of the work force are the *sine qua non* of continued increases in this output. Labor is the major beneficiary of as well as the chief contributor to prosperity and growth: The bulk of the national product is distributed in wages and salaries to individual workers, and expansion of the total product has improved the welfare of these workers.

THE SCOPE

Manpower development is, therefore, central to modern society. It embraces a broad range of areas which are of vital concern to all citizens, not only social scientists and policy formulators. Five main categories of interest can be identified.

FACTORS AFFECTING THE SUPPLY OF AND DEMAND FOR LABOR   Demographic forces determine the total pool of available workers, as well as their age and, to a large extent, their distribution in the labor force. Cultural, economic, and military as well as demographic factors affect the rates of labor force participation—that is, the proportion of able-bodied persons who seek work. Even broader social factors affect the worker's level of commitment and the willingness of those outside the labor force to participate in the world of work.

ALLOCATION OF WORKERS AMONG JOBS AND JOBS AMONG WORKERS   Changes in the industrial and occupational distribution of employment such as the massive decline in the agricultural sector have important implications for the welfare of individuals and for public policy. In geographic areas or occupational categories where workers are in short supply, measures have to be taken to overcome shortages, and in areas or jobs characterized by an oversupply of workers, alternative opportunities may be needed. To the extent that any worker is "underemployed" in a job that does not fully utilize or develop his abilities, measures that would tap his potential would benefit not only the individual but also the whole economy.

PRODUCTIVITY OF THE WORK FORCE IN ITS VARIOUS ECONOMIC APPLICATIONS   The level of total output and the standard of living it will support depend on the skills and abilities of the labor force. In order to realize the full potential of our nation's human resources and to ensure that each worker reaps a just reward for his labors, it is vital to understand the impact of education, vocational training, work experience, and related factors on the productivity of workers.

EFFICIENCY OF LABOR MARKET INSTITUTIONS IN UTILIZING AVAILABLE HUMAN RESOURCES   Many workers may be trapped in jobs for which they are overqualified as the result of discrimination or arbitrary credentialing which qualifies workers for jobs on the basis of educational attainment that may be unrelated to performance. Other institutional imperfections may also limit the best match-up of supply and demand.

PUBLIC POLICY   Government plays an important role in the labor market. It regulates labor–management relations and participates actively through education, manpower, and other human resource policies. The goal of studying human resource development is to provide guidelines for public and private policy which will help develop and utilize the labor force as well as solve related problems such as poverty and racial discrimination.

THE SETTING

Because human resource development deals with such a broad range of subjects, its study requires an understanding of the massive tides of change which are transforming our society and economy. Among the most important of these, at least in terms of their impact on the availability and use of human resources, are the following:

First, continued gains in productivity have led to rising earnings and income which have been shared in some measure by almost all segments of the population. Affluence has significant implications for the utilization of human resources. For one thing, it means that monetary incentives are less powerful. The law of diminishing returns applies here as elsewhere, so that affluent workers can be expected to opt for leisure over work, to be less satisfied with wage gains alone, and to be unwilling to work in demeaning jobs. Affluence also means that society has greater opportunity and obligation to help those with special needs—to become concerned with the qualitative as well as quantitative aspects of life. As most people improve their incomes, poverty becomes less tolerable and increased welfare efforts more feasible. In turn, as the welfare floor is raised, the boundaries between work and dependence grow hazy, and low-wage earners may drop out of the work force if they can qualify for a more attractive income maintenance program.

A second major development is the accelerated pace of technological change. Many thousands of jobs are being eliminated annually as new techniques of production or new patterns of demand emerge and even more jobs are created. But such new jobs usually require a higher level of skill, so that workers displaced by technological change rarely qualify for the opportunities it creates. Overall, workers are increasingly pressed to demonstrate educational competence and flexibility in adapting to the job situation. But there persists a vast and probably growing number of repetitive and dull, though physically undemanding, jobs which have resulted from mechanization. Manpower policies can cushion the transitions of displaced workers and help provide the skills to meet new needs. Efforts can also be made to increase the attractiveness of employment or at least widen the opportunities for upward mobility.

A third significant development is the drastic redistribution of population and industry. Urbanization has proceeded at a rapid pace, so that over two-thirds of the U.S. population now reside in metropolitan areas. Rural outmigration continues as agricultural employment declines, and this adds relatively untrained workers to the urban labor forces. Racial and ethnic minorities tend to concentrate in the central cities, while the majority of people who have greater opportunities flee to the suburbs. Those who are locked in the central city by low income or racial discrimination face sustained job shortages. Manpower policy can recognize and deal with these locational changes, so that, as effectively as possible, workers can be matched with available jobs.

Fourth, the progress of racial minorities toward equal employment opportunity has been significant over the last decade, but continued pressure will be needed to finish the task. Blacks, Chicanos, Indians, and others are still denied the full measure of opportunities to develop their abilities and to compete freely in the labor market. Manpower programs and policies have played and can continue to play an important role in analyzing the problems of minorities and in implementing measures to assist them.

A final significant development is the rapid growth of government functions. Though questions may be raised about big government's accountability to the governed, there is little doubt that its responsibilities will continue to grow. Governmental support of programs designed to improve the employability and job opportunities of disadvantaged workers increased tenfold during the 1960s. So far, governmental manpower efforts have been largely experimental. Further expansion is likely over the coming years, as the millions who are left out of the economic mainstream continue to demand society's attention. If this occurs, manpower policies must necessarily be integrated with other economic policies. Human resource measures may become an increasingly significant factor alongside monetary and fiscal measures in determining economic policy.

HUMAN RESOURCES IN FLUX

These important transformations obviously affect the content and application of human resource development. It is likely that this will continue to be a "growth area" affecting economic policy and resource allocation, both private and public. Theory and evaluation must adjust as new needs are perceived and new manpower efforts initiated.

Experiences with the manpower programs of the last decade and with broader human resource questions have provided practical and theoretical lessons. We know a great deal about the factors determining the supply of labor and the institutions affecting its quality. Theories of labor markets, including an increased focus on the operations of "secondary" markets, explain the allocation of labor among industries, occupations, and individuals. The productivity of labor has been estimated in a number of ways, and efforts have been made to measure the gains from remedial education and training. Special efforts have been made to provide compensatory aid to victims of discrimination in order to expand their opportunities and raise their productivity. The broader implications of human resource development not only touch on blue-collar problems, military policies, and the persistence of poverty in an affluent society, but also affect the determination of national priorities and economic policy.

What further changes are likely in the nature of work and what do they imply for human resource development and labor market? Despite some increases in leisure and some decline of labor force participation for marginal groups, most Americans will continue to work for a living. Perhaps with rising female participation the proportion will rise. Goods are not free. The age of abundance has not arrived, and he who does not work is therefore a "free rider." Ours remains a work-achievement–oriented society. Even those who can afford to do otherwise are expected to contribute to the social welfare and to fulfill their own needs. The dropouts from society are few, although their number may be increasing. A study by the National Planning Association demonstrated that we lacked the manpower to achieve a set of broadly agreed and modest national goals established by a presidential commission. The challenge we face is not a redundancy of manpower but the "human use of human beings."

The most important task at present is to draw together these diverse experiences and insights, blending theory with practical wisdom. The foundations must be strengthened so that manpower economics can learn from the past in dealing with the future.

Part 1
Labor
Market
Dynamics

Chapter 2
Work Life, Work Time, and Mobility

There is a myth about the nature and work life of the American worker. It projects the picture of a male family breadwinner working at his bench or desk 40 hours a week, year round from the time he leaves school until he retires. But the male, year-round, full-time workers, though still the largest group in the American work force, are no longer in the majority.

For one thing, Americans are moving to a shorter work life. They stay in school longer, retire earlier, and live longer after they retire—somewhat over seven years, or double what it was at the turn of the century.

During the work life, leisure is assuming a greater role. Americans have decreased the number of hours they work weekly and annually, while real earnings continue to rise because of increased productivity (though inflation and rising taxes may take their toll). From one-third to two-fifths of the total rise in productivity during the present century has taken the form of increased leisure rather than higher wages.

Mobility has also been a characteristic of American working life. Part of the American dream is that, regardless of a person's origins, he can move up to jobs requiring more skill and responsibility and offering more prestige and income than the one he started with—or his father held. More than other industrialized nations, the United States has been, and continues to be, a land of much upward social and occupational mobility both of an intergenerational and intragenerational nature. Americans are also the most geographically mobile of industrial people.

9

WORK LIFE: START LATER, RETIRE EARLIER

Men: Shorter Work Life Despite Longer Life

Men and women differ not only in the number of years they can expect to live (life expectancy), but also, and much more significantly, in the length and pattern of their work lives.

Later entrance into the labor force and earlier retirement have arrested and reversed the long-term rise in the length of work life. The work-life expectancy of a man born at the turn of this century lengthened by nearly ten years during the following five decades, largely because average life expectancy rose from 48 to 67 years. The best measure of long-term work-life expectancy is gained by comparing the average number of years spent in the labor force by males reaching adulthood. Stuart H. Garfinkle of the U.S. Department of Labor has estimated that the average work-life expectancy for a 20-year-old man rose from 39 years in 1900 to 43 years by 1960 (Table 2–1). Since 1950, however, work-life expectancy has declined by half a year per decade.

TABLE 2–1   *Average Work-Life Expectancy for Men in the Labor Force, 1900–1960*

| | AVERAGE NUMBER OF YEARS REMAINING | | |
AGE AND YEAR	*Life Expectancy*	*Work-Life Expectancy*	*In Retirement*
Age 20			
1900	42.2	39.4	2.8
1940	46.8	41.3	5.5
1950	48.9	43.1	5.8
1960	49.6	42.6	7.0
Age 60			
1900	14.3	11.5	2.8
1940	15.1	9.2	5.9
1950	15.7	9.8	5.9
1960	15.8	8.5	7.3

SOURCE: Stuart H. Garfinkle, *The Length of Working Life for Males, 1900–1960,* U.S. Department of Labor, Manpower Administration, Manpower Report No. 8 (Washington, D.C.: U.S. Government Printing Office, 1963), p. 8.

Many factors have contributed to later entry into the labor force. One is the great decline in farming; farmers' children were put to work at an early age. Another is the impact of child labor laws and compulsory school attendance. To a large degree, these laws reflect the desire for a better life through more schooling, and the emphasis on longer schooling also has its roots in a practical payoff: Education is a good economic investment. In 1900, when about two-fifths of the work force was employed on farms, the average age of entry into the labor force was about 15. By midcentury, the average age for young men had risen to about 17.5 years, and currently it is almost 18.

Income support from Social Security and private pension plans and compulsory retirement programs have dramatically increased the tendency to retire at age 65 or even earlier. Almost one-fourth of the men in the labor force at age 64 retire during the next year. Retirement continues to be a more important reason than death for separation from the labor force for several years after age 65, although the tendency to retire declines very sharply after age 65. Those who continue to work often do so part time: In 1968, over half of the 65- to 69-year-old male jobholders worked less than 50 weeks. This part-time and part-year employment may reflect the greater incidence of health problems, reduced opportunities because of discrimination, and the ceiling that Social Security puts on the retirees' earnings if they are to qualify for full-benefit payments.

The number of years males spend outside the labor force has increased by over 50 percent during this century. A man born in 1900 spent, on the average, 16.1 years outside the labor force compared with the projected 25.2 years for one born in 1960. Despite later entry into the work force, the additional 9.1 years outside the labor force were added mostly at the end of life. Few could afford to retire at the turn of the century. In 1900, a man aged 20 had a life expectancy of 42 more years, of which he worked 39 years and spent 3 in retirement. In 1960, the 20-year-old could look forward to 50 more years, of which the last 7 would be in retirement.

Women: More Work and Longer Life Expectancy

Women have accounted for two of every three additions to the labor force in the past three decades.[1] Unlike men, women have quite varied work-life expectancies, depending on whether they stay single, marry, give birth to children, or become the head of household because of separation, divorce, or the death of their husbands (Table 2–2). Most women (95 out of 100) marry—and marry young. Half are married before they are 21, and more marry at age 18 than at any other age. Whether or not they marry, about 9 of 10 women work outside the home at some time. Marriage and the presence of children tend to curtail employment, while widowhood, divorce, and the decrease of family responsibilities tend to bring women back into the labor force. Women begin their careers at about the same age as men, usually after finishing high school. Frequently, they leave the work force a few years after they marry to have children; a growing proportion resume work before the children reach school age.

The small minority of women who never marry have the most con-

TABLE 2–2   *Average Work-Life Expectancy for Women in the Labor Force, by Marital Status and Age, 1960*

	AGE			
MARITAL STATUS	20	35	50	60
Single	45.3	31.2	17.1	10.0
Married, Husband Present, No Children	34.9	24.4	13.7	8.7
Married, Husband Present, in Labor Force After Birth of Last Child	a	23.8	11.9	6.9
Widowed	41.8	27.3	13.4	7.1
Divorced	43.3	28.8	15.5	8.4

a Amounts not significant.
SOURCE: Stuart H. Garfinkle, *Work Life Expectancy of Females,* U.S. Department of Labor, Manpower Administration, Manpower Report No. 12 (Washington, D.C.: U.S. Government Printing Office, 1967), p. 4.

tinuous and longest attachment to the labor force; their work-life pattern closely resembles that of men. The 20-year-old women who remain single will probably continue to work for about 45 years—slightly more than the average of 43 years for men. In general, however, women—especially those who can depend on their husband's income—tend to work fewer years and to retire earlier than men. The Social Security option of retirement at age 62 may also play a part in encouraging women to leave the work force.

The one married woman in ten who does not have children has a work-life expectancy of 35 years—10 years less than single women—if she enters the labor force by age 20. The working life of married women with children is less predictable because of the intermittent nature of their careers. The average woman has borne her last child by age 30; by her mid-30s all her children are in school and her family responsibilities are considerably diminished. If she returns under these conditions (usually after having been out of the labor force for about 8 to 10 years), her work-life expectancy is essentially the same as for a newly-married 20-year-old woman—24 more years. This means that a far greater portion of a woman's work life occurs *after* she has reared her children to school age and has reentered the labor force.

Because the care of young children is a major factor preventing women from working, the decline in birth rates since 1958 has made it possible for larger numbers of younger women to enter or remain in the labor force. The more children a married woman has, the shorter her work-life expectancy. It is estimated that the first child reduces work-life expectancy by about 10 years; each additional child reduces it by about 2 to 3 years. A relatively large percentage of widowed, separated, and divorced women return to the labor force, their work patterns often resembling those of men and single women.

WORK TIME: FEWER HOURS, MORE "LEISURE"

During his work life, today's worker has about 1,200 more hours of free time each year, or 3.3 hours each day, than did the worker at the turn of the century. This is in addition to the extra 9 years of nonwork time the male has gained because he starts work later, retires earlier, and lives longer.[2]

Shorter working hours do not necessarily improve the quality of a person's life or necessarily enlarge the amount of leisure time. Part of the increase in "nonworking" time is used up in longer hours of commuting; wrestling with do-it-yourself projects or balky "work-saving" appliances for which repairmen are hard to find and even more burdensome to pay; and/or holding two jobs because there is more "free" time (e.g., moonlighters with extra jobs or those who help their working wives with the housework). Similarly, household appliances, convenience foods, ready-made clothes, and smaller families made possible by birth-control technology have given housewives "free time" to take on paid jobs—and thus end up with the double load of work plus running the home and family.

The intrinsic value of leisure to a worker should, however, not be overlooked. Eli Ginzberg points out that workers have not lost their zeal to reduce working hours. They wish to minimize the hours spent under supervision "to be masters of their own souls for as much of the day as possible." [3] A recent study of assemblyline workers in the automobile industry supports this view. Younger workers, especially, expressed preference for free time (away from the rigid discipline of the production line which leaves no opportunity for personal business) rather than overtime work.[4] Nevertheless, during the 1960s, there was a stronger emphasis on raising income; only 8 percent of the rise in productivity was allocated to reducing work time, with the balance used to boost income.[5]

Whether future productivity increases will be adequate to provide a continuation of large increases in both leisure and standard of living remains questionable. The goods-producing sector of our economy is not now growing as rapidly as the service-producing sector in which productivity gains are smaller. Thus, past increases in leisure and standard of living cannot be sustained without technological breakthroughs in the service sector. The three-day or four-day workweek and a carefree abundance of goods are much further away than the prophets of cybernetics like to anticipate.[6]

The distribution of additional leisure time has taken several forms, and the emphasis has changed over the years from reduction in weekly hours of work to allocation of leisure time in blocks of days or weeks. Kreps and Spengler estimate that between 1890 and 1963 nonworking hours per year increased by 1,220, distributed as follows:

Reduction in workweek—1,100 hours (21.2 per week: from 61.9 to 40.7)

Increase in paid holidays—32 hours (4 days: from 2 to about 6 per year)

Increases in paid vacations—48 hours (6 days: to 1½ weeks per year)

Increase in paid sick leave—40 hours (1 week) [7]

Most of the drop in workweek came in the first two decades of this century as social, health, and fatigue factors were the main thrust for a reduction to 50 hours. Another sharp decline toward a statutory 40-hour week took place in the Great Depression of the 1930s under the National Industrial Recovery and Fair Labor Standards Acts. Overtime pay was required for longer workweeks to encourage the sharing of work opportunities and to reduce unemployment. During World War II, of course, longer hours were worked, but in the postwar period the average declined slowly from the 40-hour norm to 38 by 1969. In recent years, the decline in hours has averaged about 2 percent per decade—more because of increased part-time employment rather than a cutback in hours. Bureau of Labor Statistics (BLS) projections anticipate that the rate of decline in average hours paid for in all private industry will be cut in half during the 1970s.[8] The BLS projections assume nearly full employment; higher unemployment would intensify pressures for reductions in hours and other work-sharing devices.

Although interest in the shorter workweek has continued, preferences for leisure switched after World War II to paid vacations, especially in concentrated spells. Not only are more workers receiving vacations, but also the vacations are longer—4 weeks for workers with 20 years' service is not unusual. The United Steelworkers "sabbatical" plan negotiated in 1963, originally conceived of as a means of spreading work, allowed an extended vacation of 13 weeks, but the idea was not picked up by other industries during the 1960s. Paid holidays for wage earners were also a development of World War II and the postwar period: six a year for all workers (including farmers) is about average, with workers in metropolitan areas getting more (seven for plant workers, about eight for office workers). In the quest for more blocks of free time, even legal holidays were rescheduled. More three-day weekends became a reality in 1971, when Congress decreed that Washington's Birthday, Memorial Day, Veterans Day, and Columbus Day were to be celebrated on Mondays.

Juanita Kreps speculates that a large share of future growth in productivity will be allocated to blocks of leisure at the beginning and end of work life (especially the latter), in contrast to the earlier pattern of its absorption into shorter workweeks.[9] However, older workers might want to distribute their work and leisure differently, rearranging their total pool of work years so that they would not be forced to retire at a time when they might prefer to continue useful work. Whatever the individual preference, however, institutional arrangements and business conditions dictate the terms of nonwork time both at the beginning and end of work life. Part-time and part-year work opportunities for older and younger workers depend on the need for their services. Higher retirement benefits, however, would raise workers' options in choosing between work and leisure.

If given the choice, do workers prefer extra leisure or added income? It is difficult to generalize about this. Evidence seems to indicate that shorter hours are preferred by very young and very old workers, and by women, particularly if they are married and have household responsibilities. The bulk of part-time workers belong to these groups. About 90 percent of the 11 million people who worked part-time in 1969 did not want full-time employment or were not available for it. In fact, some might have not worked at all if required to work regular hours.[10]

However, men with growing family responsibilities tend to maximize income instead of leisure, and many moonlight to supplement their income.[11] Almost half of all moonlighters were men between 25 and 44, though this age group comprised only about two-fifths of all employed men. The primary motivation of all moonlighters appeared to be financial pressure, with four of ten working to meet regular expenses and one of ten working to pay off debts. Further, there was no significant inverse relationship between moonlighting and length of workweek; thus, among full-time workers, factors other than length of workweek determined whether they were moonlighting. While women represented more than one-third of all employed persons in 1969, they accounted for only about one-sixth of the total moonlighters.

Workers By-passed by Shorter Workweek

Despite the trend to shorter average working hours, a significant number of people—about one-seventh of all workers in 1970—are still working more than 49 hours a week. The bulk of these were persons with single jobs, not moonlighters with multiple jobs. Many of the long-hour workers genuinely enjoy their work or hold responsible positions and are either required or expected to work long hours; others who work long hours are paid low wages and frequently are not covered by minimum wage legislation requiring overtime pay after 40 hours.[12]

Leisure That Is Productive Work: Unpaid Volunteers

Free time is not synonymous with leisure. While much of the extra free time is consumed by coping with the more complicated mechanics of contemporary life, some is utilized in productive work that does not show up in national accounts. This is the contribution of volunteers doing "good works" for diverse social causes. Almost 22 million Americans—1 of every

6 adults—contribute free labor to some health, educational, religious, or welfare service. Their contribution is equivalent to the work performed by a full-time regular work force of over 900,000. Voluntarism is apparently a function of being part of the Establishment. For example, married people between the ages of 25 and 44—those with the most demanding responsibilities for raising families—accounted for half the volunteers. Three-fifths of the volunteers were women, and more than half also had paid jobs. The more schooling (and income) a person had, the more likely he was to do volunteer work.[13]

WORKERS' MOBILITY: THE AMERICAN DREAM OF MOVING UP THE JOB LADDER

Mobility has always been a characteristic of American working life, and few people hold just one job over a working lifetime. They change employers, though not necessarily the types of work they perform; or they may change jobs while staying with the same employer (sometimes by transferring to a different branch or plant). They move to new locations, though most employment shifts are within the same community or labor-market area. They shift in and out of the labor force in response to changing economic or personal conditions.[14]

Perhaps most important is workers' mobility up the occupational ladder. Quite properly, Americans persist in the belief that, regardless of one's origins, economic and social opportunity should be open to all. Social mobility is of importance not only to individuals but also to the efficiency and well-being of society as a whole. As Lloyd Reynolds has pointed out:

> Geographic movement is apt to be a painful necessity, costly to individuals and the community. Movement from employer to employer may be simply an aimless wandering from one mediocre job to another. Real progress comes only through movement to a new job involving more in the way of skill, responsibility, independence, and income.[15]

Upward Occupational Mobility

Occupational and social mobility may be analyzed either in terms of changes that occur within a worker's own lifetime (intragenerational) or in terms of changes from parent to offspring (intergenerational).[16] More than other industrialized nations, the United States is predominantly open and upwardly mobile. Extensive studies have documented that intergenerational and intragenerational upward occupational mobility have been and remain a fact of American economic life. In longitudinal studies of men between 45 and 59 years of age, Herbert Parnes discovered that almost three-fifths had moved into occupations with higher socioeconomic status than those in which they began their work careers.[17]

Most of the upward mobility involves relatively short social distances, rather than dramatic, long-distance, Horatio-Alger-type leaps. Blau and

TABLE 2–3   *Distribution of Business Executives by Family Status, 1900 and 1964*

ECONOMIC STATUS OF FATHER	1900	1925	1950	1964	1900–1964 DIFFERENCE
Wealthy	45.6%	36.6%	36.1%	10.5%	−35.1%
Medium	42.1	47.8	51.8	66.2	24.1
Poor	12.3	15.8	12.1	23.2	11.0

SOURCE: Joseph W. McGuire and Joseph A. Pichler, *Inequality: The Poor and Rich in America* (Belmont, Calif.: Wadsworth, 1969), p. 57.

Duncan found the usual move to be only 2 or 3 steps upward in their hierarchy of 17 occupational levels (ranging from farm laborers up to self-employed professionals).[18] Nonetheless, more of America's current business leaders have emerged from lower-class and middle-class origins than at the turn of the century (Table 2–3). Higher education appears to provide the ladder for upward mobility. But at the same time, a college education remains largely a function of family income. In 1968, it was twice as likely that a young person would attend college if his family's annual income exceeded $15,000 than if the income were between $5,000 and $7,500. The number of children who have to share a family's income also is a significant factor, and the steady trend toward family limitation should promote the chances of obtaining a college education.

Immigration and westward migration, and the continued growth of economic opportunities, have prevented locked-in social stratification in the United States. More American professionals have risen from the "lower" classes than in other nations. Blau and Duncan point out that about 10 percent of the sons of American manual workers moved into professional and technical occupations, compared with 7 percent for Japan and the Netherlands, 3.5 for Sweden, and 2.2 for Great Britain.[19] Comparing the United States, Great Britain, the Netherlands, and Japan, McGuire and Pichler concluded that there is more upward mobility into the middle class by craftsmen in the United States than in other industrial nations. They also found a lower rate of intergenerational downward mobility—from professional to skilled occupations—in America than in Great Britain and the Netherlands.[20]

The frustrations of blue-collar workers have received much public attention. One of their complaints is that men who start their careers as blue-collar workers have poorer chances of reaching a higher occupational status than those who start out in white-collar occupations (they already have achieved some status) or farm occupations (they are likely to benefit from the mobility because of a low starting point).

Ginzberg is more sanguine about the upward mobility of male blue-collar workers.[21] As a group these workers are relatively better off than their fathers—whether they be native-born whites from low-income farm families, or of foreign extraction, or blacks. Some advance to managerial or entrepreneurial ranks—as the carpenter who becomes a contractor or the truck driver who acquires a small fleet. Intergenerational upward mobility is enhanced by their children's greater access to a higher education at the mushrooming junior and community colleges.

Upward mobility among blue-collar workers is not universal, however. Ginzberg finds large groups of immobile and "vulnerable" workers in their ranks. Included in these sizable groups are men who hold blue-collar jobs similar to those held by their fathers, or who have even moved down the occupational scale; female heads of families who tend to be in low-paying, low-skill jobs; male heads unable to earn enough to allow their families to live much above the poverty level; and families whose children are unlikely to have access to college or other paths upward.

Just as blue-collar workers have difficulty moving up, so white-collar workers tend not to cross class boundaries into blue-collar jobs. White-collar workers who are unsuccessful in their occupations move into retail trade which, according to Blau and Duncan, still allows them to maintain white-collar status and to remain within the higher social scale, even though with relatively unskilled jobs.[22] Evidently, they prefer the status of a white-collar job, even though a job in coveralls or a hard-hat may pay better, have shorter hours, and require more skills.

Some blue-collar workers do shift to white-collar jobs. Johnson and Stern found that in the early 1960s one-fifth of the white-collar jobs in Milwaukee were filled by workers with at least a year's blue-collar experience. Though nearly two-thirds of the moves were into managerial, professional, and technical occupations, the "upward" mobility did not always involve an immediate financial gain and, indeed, sometimes meant reduced take-home pay because of lost overtime.[23] Most of the upward movement analyzed by Johnson and Stern involved job shifts within the same firm, and the initiative came primarily from the employers.

Government manpower programs have devoted few resources to upgrading workers, though much rhetoric has been devoted to developing "new careers" to help the disadvantaged. A more pragmatic approach might encourage lesser-skilled blue-collar workers to move into occupations that provide them "open" rather than "dead-end" jobs, so that the severely disadvantaged will have access to entry level jobs which will provide them a meaningful path to expanded upward mobility.

Upward Mobility for Blacks

The upward mobility of blacks was a central issue of the 1960s. Past discrimination and hurdles built into our institutional structure have prevented blacks from utilizing opportunities that lead other minority or ethnic groups such as immigrants and their children to upward mobility.

During the 1960s, however, extensive civil rights legislation and the widespread rejection by American society of discrimination in employment boosted the status of American blacks, though the gaps between whites and blacks were not eliminated. A broad and important segment of American blacks—3 million black men with families—not only received proportionately larger income boosts during the 1960s than whites, but also narrowed somewhat the gap between average annual income of blacks and whites.[24] In part, this is attributable to the fact that there has been a steady movement of blacks out of the lower occupational groups (especially marginal farmers and farm laborers) into the categories of craftsmen and operatives, so that, by 1969, three of every five black workers were in these latter categories. More striking is the fact that during the 1960s blacks also gained entry into the preferred craftsmen category, although the number of openings remained limited. Average annual family income also went up more for black than for white craftsmen (45 percent compared to 30), and this increase is not attributable only to the fact that increasing numbers of black wives went to work. Relatively more black than white wives were in the labor force both at the start and the end of the 1960s, and the increase in their median earnings was about four times that of white working wives. In absolute terms, however, a gap remains: Median earnings of black wives of blue-collar workers in 1969 were $2,828 compared with $3,465 for white wives.[25]

More than three-fifths of the increase in black employment between 1961 and 1969 was in professional, white-collar, and skilled occupations, while the lowest paid occupations—private household work and farm work—registered declines. Herbert Parnes and others have questioned the significance of these increases in black family income and occupational mobility. Parnes expected blacks to show upward occupational mobility because of their low starting position. His longitudinal studies, however, convinced him that the contrary occurred, and that the relative disadvantages of black men when they begin "their working lives have become more pronounced during their work careers." [26]

Geographical Mobility

About 1 of 14 Americans moves across county lines each year, with about half of these migrating into another state. Counting also those who move within a county, the ratio goes up to about one in six. The ratios show very little variation over the 22 years in which the Bureau of the Census has been measuring these changes.[27]

The character of geographic migration affecting labor mobility has changed. The flood of European immigrants has been curtailed, and western migration and the movement from the farm to the city have leveled off. A newer and more significant development is the movement from inner cities to the suburbs. There are now more people in the suburbs than in the inner cities. This flight, primarily of white residents to the suburban rings, has been coupled with a relocation of plants and, particularly, retail and service establishments. Unemployment and transportation problems thus are compounded for those left in the inner city, as well as for suburbanites who still work in the cities.

Removing Impediments to Mobility

Society's challenge is to create conditions that will both optimize upward mobility and facilitate the process of matching workers and jobs. This suggests policies that open opportunities for upward movement, have sufficient clout to discourage "wasteful" or misdirected mobility, and maintain freedom of individual choice.

Socially beneficial occupational mobility can be achieved by providing better opportunities for education, training, retraining, and upgrading, while placing less emphasis on formal "credentials." [28] Continued attacks on discrimination, and efforts to sustain and solidify the advances made in the last generation, must be an essential ingredient of any occupational mobility policy. In promoting occupational mobility, special provisions must be made for those left behind either because they are in depressed areas or are otherwise not mobile, or because they have been denied opportunities for upward mobility.

Discouraging "wasteful" mobility certainly involves reexamination of social values and the status of various occupations. A concerted effort is needed to overcome what Secretary of Labor James D. Hodgson has described as a "crisis in craftsmanship." [29] The quality of American life is not enhanced by worship of the diploma certifying that the recipient has completed a course in "higher education," while public and private services are deteriorating because society considers the providers of these services to be inferior.

NOTES

1. U.S. Department of Labor, *1969 Handbook on Women Workers,* Women's Bureau Bulletin 294 (Washington, D.C.: U.S. Government Printing Office, 1969), p. 7.

2. Juanita M. Kreps and Joseph J. Spengler, "The Leisure Component of Economic Growth," in National Commission on Technology, Automation, and Economic Progress, *The Employment Impact of Technological Change,* Appendix Vol. II (Washington, D.C.: U.S. Government Printing Office, February 1966), p. 355.

3. U.S. Congress, House Committee on Education and Labor, *Hearings on Hours of Work,* 88th Cong., 1st Sess. (Washington, D.C.: U.S. Government Printing Office, 1963), p. 220.

4. Judson Gooding, "Blue-Collar Blues on the Assembly Line," *Fortune* (July 1970), pp. 69 ff.

5. Geoffrey H. Moore and Janice Neipert Hedges, "Trends in Labor and Leisure," *Monthly Labor Review* (February 1971), pp. 3–11.

6. Victor R. Fuchs, ed., *Production and Productivity in Service Industries* (New York: National Bureau of Economic Research and Columbia University Press, 1969), p. 10.

7. Kreps and Spengler, *loc. cit.*

8. U.S. Department of Labor, Bureau of Labor Statistics, *The U.S. Economy in 1980: A Summary of BLS Projections,* Bulletin 1673 (Washington, D.C.: U.S. Government Printing Office, 1970), p. 4.

9. Juanita M. Kreps, "Time for Leisure, Time for Work," *Monthly Labor Review* (April 1969), pp. 60–61.

10. Paul O. Flaim and Paul M. Schwab, "Employment and Unemployment Developments in 1969," *Monthly Labor Review* (February 1970), p. 41.

11. Vera C. Perrella, "Moonlighters: Their Motivation and Characteristics," *Monthly Labor Review* (August 1970), pp. 57–64.

12. Peter Henle, "Leisure and the Long Work Week," *Monthly Labor Review* (July 1966), p. 721.

13. *Americans Volunteer,* U.S. Department of Labor, Manpower Administration, Manpower/Automation Research Monograph No. 10 (Washington, D.C.: U.S. Government Printing Office, April 1969).

14. Major research on labor mobility in the 1960s is summarized by Herbert S. Parnes, "Labor Force Participation and Labor Mobility," in *A Review of Industrial Relations Research,* Industrial Relations Research Association Series, Vol. 1 (Madison, Wisc.: The Association, 1970), pp. 33–78.

15. Lloyd G. Reynolds, *Labor Economics and Labor Relations* (Englewood Cliffs, N.J.: Prentice-Hall, 1964), 4th ed.; p. 390.

16. Joseph W. McGuire and Joseph A. Pichler, *Inequality: The Poor and Rich in America* (Belmont, Calif.: Wadsworth, 1969), pp. 48 ff.

17. Herbert Parnes et. al., *The Pre-Retirement Years,* Volume I, U.S. Department of Labor, Manpower Administration, Manpower Research Monograph No. 15 (Washington, D.C.: U.S. Government Printing Office, 1970), p. 127.

18. Peter M. Blau and Otis Dudley Duncan, *The American Occupational Structure* (New York: John Wiley, 1964), p. 420.

19. Blau and Duncan, *op. cit.,* p. 435.

20. McGuire and Pichler, *op. cit.,* p. 52.

21. Eli Ginzberg, "The Long View," in Sar A. Levitan, ed., *Blue-Collar Workers: A Symposium on Middle America* (New York: McGraw-Hill, 1971), Chap. 2.

22. Blau and Duncan, *op. cit.,* p. 421.

23. David B. Johnson and James L. Stern, "Why and How Workers Shift From Blue-Collar to White-Collar Jobs," *Monthly Labor Review* (October 1969), pp. 7–13.

24. Herman P. Miller, "A Profile of the Blue-Collar American" in Sar A. Levitan, ed., *Blue-Collar Workers: A Symposium on Middle America* (New York: McGraw-Hill, 1971), Chap. 3.

25. U.S. Bureau of the Census, *Current Population Reports,* Series P-60, No. 73, "Occupation and Earnings of Family Heads in 1969, 1965, and 1959," (Washington, D.C.: Government Printing Office, 1970), Tables 3, 9, and 10.

26. Herbert Parnes *et al., op. cit.,* p. 128.

27. U.S. Bureau of the Census, *Current Population Reports,* Series

P-20, No. 193, "Mobility of the Population of the United States, March 1968 to March 1969," (Washington, D.C.: U.S. Government Printing Office, 1969), p. 1.

28. S. M. Miller, *Breaking the Credentials Barrier* (New York: Ford Foundation, 1968).

29. U.S. Department of Labor, Release No. 11325, July 10, 1970.

Chapter 3
Labor Force Participation and Unemployment

Changing patterns of work life have been accompanied by dramatic shifts in labor force participation rates (the proportion of the working-age population employed or looking for work as opposed to working in the home, studying at school, or enjoying leisure) and in the composition of the work force. The key long-run shifts are greater participation of women and declining roles for younger and older workers. These shifts have resulted in an increased reliance on "peripheral" workers, whose work-life patterns are different from those of workers who are employed full-time throughout the year.[1]

Underlying the changed composition in the work force is the rising level of expectations, which outstrips the sustained but relatively modest rises in productivity. This means that millions of families now "need" more than the male breadwinner can earn and that the added worker is far more likely to be the wife than a son or daughter. Moreover, the growth of consumer purchases on credit has heightened pressure on family income to meet the payments. In the two decades after World War II, consumer indebtedness grew from $6 to $86 billion, or at an annual rate of over 14 percent—more than twice the growth rate of all financial assets. Thus, America is increasingly a nation of multiworker families "hooked" into working to maintain the desired standard of living.

Work, however, is no longer the only way to support a family. Income-support programs—including unemployment insurance, public and private retirement or disability benefits, and public assistance—provide money,

23

limited as it may be. Relief (and other income-support programs) and work are increasingly interdependent. This was reflected in the movement of the 1960s toward providing relief for parents who are capable of working but who are unemployed; traditionally, relief had been aimed exclusively at helping persons outside the labor force—mothers and dependent children, the indigent aged, and the disabled.

The labor market has its pathologies, however, and not all persons who want jobs are successful in getting them. Forced idleness falls disproportionately on blacks, Indians, Chicanos, and younger and older workers. The American economy has not been successful in eliminating the ups and downs of business cycles; after nearly a decade of continued growth in the 1960s, the economy once again experienced a contraction and unemployment rose to over 6 percent.

OVERALL SHIFTS IN LABOR FORCE

A key change has been the sharp increase in the number of working women—especially married women. During the 1960s women entered the labor force three times faster than men; for the first time, married men—the group that had previously constituted the bulk of the labor force—dropped to less than half of all workers. A large share of newly married women are working; an increasing number of married women return to work after their children have entered school or grown up and many do not wait that long. Since the beginning of the century, participation rates of married women have increased fivefold, and their share of the labor force has risen sixfold, to about one-fifth.[2]

Young people, however, have shown a long-term decline in their participation rate, in part, perhaps, because their mothers add to the family exchequer, but more often because they encounter economic and legal barriers to work. Thus, youngsters stay in school longer before starting their full-time work careers. Since the turn of the century, the participation rate for 14-to-19-year-old males has dropped by about a third, while their share of the labor force has been cut in half—from about 10 to about 5 percent. After the post-World War II "baby boom," however, the sheer numbers of young people increased despite a reduced participation rate. Young workers aged 16 to 24 accounted for more than half of the labor force increase in the 1960s, which raised their proportion in the labor force from one in five to one in four.

The early work years are characterized by much part-time work (often combined with school) and fairly frequent job changes. The pattern changes as persons mature. Adult men reach a peak participation rate of about 97 percent in their mid-20s, and this percentage remains relatively stable for some 30 years. Job stability increases as the worker matures: A 55-year-old man can be expected to stay on a job over 7 years, or about 1½ times longer than a man of 20.[3]

TABLE 3–1 *Participation Rates and Percentage Distribution of the Labor Force, 1947 and 1970*

AGE–SEX	1947 Participation Rate	1947 Percent of Labor Force	1970 Participation Rate	1970 Percent of Labor Force
TOTAL	58.9%	100.0%	61.3%	100.0%
Male	86.8	72.6	80.6	63.3
16–17	52.2	1.9	47.5	2.1
18–19	80.5	3.1	69.9	3.0
20–24	84.9	8.4	86.6	8.6
25–34	95.8	17.4	96.6	13.9
35–44	98.0	15.8	97.0	12.6
45–54	95.5	12.9	94.3	12.2
55–64	89.6	9.3	83.0	8.3
65 and over	47.8	3.9	26.8	2.5
Female	31.8	27.4	43.4	36.7
16–17	29.5	1.0	34.9	1.5
18–19	52.3	2.0	53.7	2.2
20–24	44.9	4.5	57.8	5.7
25–34	32.0	6.2	45.0	6.6
35–44	36.3	6.0	51.1	7.0
45–54	32.7	4.5	54.4	7.6
55–64	24.3	2.5	43.0	4.8
65 and over	8.1	0.7	9.7	1.2

NOTE: Detail may not add to totals due to rounding.
SOURCE: U.S. Department of Labor, *Manpower Report of the President* (Washington, D.C.: U.S. Government Printing Office, 1970), pp. 215–217, and *Employment and Earnings* (January 1971), Table A-2, pp. 117–118.

At the other end of the age spectrum, there has been a long-term decline in the participation rate of older males; for men over 65, the rate has dropped to less than half of what it was at the turn of the century. As in the case of youngsters, however, the sheer growth in the number of those 55 and older has offset their declining participation rate; there were more of these older workers in 1970 than a decade earlier.

These shifts have left overall labor force participation rates basically unchanged during the current century; the declines in some groups canceled out the increases in others. Since the end of World War II, annual labor force participation rates have ranged between 59 and 61 percent of the total noninstitutional population in the United States. During the same period, male rates declined steadily from 87 to 81 percent, while the comparable rates for women rose from 32 to 43 percent (Table 3–1).

Of the 140.2 million noninstitutional Americans aged 16 or older in 1970, an average of 85.9 million were in the labor force (Table 3–2).

TABLE 3–2 *Labor Force Participation by Sex and Color, 1970*

SEX AND COLOR	NUMBER (IN MILLIONS)	PARTICIPATION RATE	PERCENT OF LABOR FORCE
TOTAL LABOR FORCE (including armed forces)	85.9	61.3%	100.0%
Males			
White	48.8	81.0	56.8
Nonwhite	5.5	77.6	6.4
Females			
White	27.5	42.6	32.0
Nonwhite	4.0	49.5	4.7

SOURCE: U.S. Bureau of Labor Statistics, *Employment and Unemployment in 1970,* Special Labor Force Report 129 (Washington, D.C.: U.S. Government Printing Office, 1971), Table A-2.

Excluding the 3.2 million in the armed forces, the civilian labor force averaged 82.7 million, of whom 78.6 million were employed. This left 54.3 million outside the labor force—including full-time students, housewives (mostly with responsibilities for raising children), retired workers, and some potential workers who quit looking for work because jobs were not available. In addition to the unemployed, many of these who were "not in the labor force," as well as those who worked only part time, comprised part of the labor "reserves," some of whom (especially nonworking wives and mothers, if day-care facilities were provided) might be induced to work in a tight labor market.

MAJOR FACTORS

A host of economic, political, social, and demographic factors have contributed to the changing composition of the work force, as well as to its growth and size. These factors have been transforming the United States, first from a rural, farm-oriented to an urban, blue-collar, goods-producing society, and now to a suburban, white-collar, service-oriented people.

At the turn of the century, the United States was still largely a rural economy. Farm chores were thrust upon rural children at an early age, and schools closed in peak farm seasons to free students for work. Farmers worked through to their end, with little or no thought of "retirement." Wives (both on and off farms) were fully occupied with their household chores; they had few labor-saving devices or easy access to ready-made clothing, processed food, or other household items.

A dramatic decline in farming and a massive migration to the cities resulted from increased productivity and a changing technology which both reduced the need for manual and farm workers and created new or expanding industries and occupations, mostly in the cities. Greater opportunities for free education and increased levels of attainment equipped would-be workers for the growing numbers of jobs requiring higher skills and knowledge. At the same time, prolonged education (which reflected compulsory education as well as child labor laws) delayed the age of entering a full work career.

Improved productivity and technology also permitted shorter hours of work, and produced labor-saving devices (including more reliable birth-control methods—with no pun intended) and ready-made goods which made it easier for women to hold a job and run a home. The flexibility shown by management, especially in times of labor shortages or tight labor markets, tapped hitherto untouched sources of workers. To attract the potential labor "reserves," employers made many adjustments—for example, scheduling more convenient hours of work, restructuring jobs into less skilled components (especially starting in World War II), easing discriminatory barriers against women, blacks, and other minority groups, and hiring "marginal" workers.

Changing attitudes virtually eliminated the view that women and youngsters should work only in cases of financial necessity, or that young women should work only until Mr. Right came along and then quit to raise a family. World War II was the main turning point: Only one of every seven married women was in the labor force in 1940, compared with more than two of five now.

Labor force data do not support popular impressions that work is going out of fashion. While population nearly tripled between 1900 and 1969, the labor force grew at a slightly faster pace (from 28 million in a population of 76 million, to 86 of 205 million).

The high birth rates of the post-World War II "baby boom," following as they did the low birth rates of the depression and war years, resulted not only in a greater absolute number of youngsters, but also in their higher proportion in the population in the 1960s. In 1940, children under 10 accounted for one-sixth of the population; by 1960, one of every five persons was in that age group. As these youngsters reached work age in the mid-1960s, they swamped the labor market even though their participation rates had been—and still are—declining.

Because of lower infant mortality and better health conditions, life expectancy for male babies has risen by about 18 years since the turn of the century. The number of people 65 and over increased from 9 million (6.8 percent of total population) in 1940 to 16.4 million, or 8.4 percent, three decades later. Therefore, even though their participation rates had plummeted, the number of workers 65 and older actually increased, comprising a nearly constant proportion of the work force.

Immigration was an important source of labor through the first two decades of this century, but its role has declined since immigration was drastically curtailed in the 1920s. The heavy flow of Puerto Ricans to New

York City, Cubans to Florida and elsewhere, and Mexicans to the Southwest have been important exceptions since World War II.

Military requirements, including the draft law, have strongly affected labor force participation. Military needs remove large numbers of younger males as a source of civilian workers and generate demand for additional workers to produce goods to support the armed forces. At the peak of World War II, over 12 million persons were in the armed forces, and some 8 million of those who were unemployed in 1940 were absorbed into jobs. Thus, about 20 million more people were at work or in the armed forces in 1944 than were holding jobs four years earlier.

The Korean and Vietnam Wars affected the demand for and supply of labor, though to a lesser extent than World War II. The expanded military requirements in Vietnam kept about 1 million young men out of the civilian labor force during the second half of the 1960s (about 900,000 eighteen-to-25-year-olds plus an undetermined number of draft-deferred students who might not have enrolled in college in the absence of a draft). Vietnam-related increases in defense expenditures accounted for the creation of about 1.4 million new jobs in the private sector and an additional 200,000 government jobs for civilians between 1965 and 1968. Defense needs thus reversed the secular decline of blue-collar jobs which began after the Korean War.[4]

RISING EXPECTATIONS
AND MULTIWORKER FAMILIES

Rising expectations have significantly affected labor market behavior. It appears that when wages are high and jobs plentiful, leisure may be deemed too "expensive," especially if a still higher standard of living is sought. Thus, many "secondary" workers (wives and youngsters) are encouraged to work to enable the family to achieve the desired standard of living. Once the multiworker families get accustomed to a higher level of living, the added earners are, in effect, obliged to continue to work in order to maintain the desired level, with inflation adding extra impetus. In 1969, more than half of U.S. families had two or more gainfully employed workers—compared with about two-fifths in 1960 and less than one-third a decade earlier.

How are multiworker family members thus "hooked?" A standard of living clearly beyond the reach of the average wage earner is urged upon them, not only by manufacturers and retailers of consumer goods, but also by the government which publicizes appealing standards of living. The BLS city-worker's budget (spring 1969) for a moderate or "intermediate" standard of living (one with few luxuries) for a family of four required $10,273. The "higher" BLS budget for the same family, one perhaps more in line with the popular conception of American affluence, carried a price tag of $14,959. The BLS budgets apply to an urban family of four, husband aged 38, wife not working, son 13 years old and daughter 8. Average income for this particular type of family is estimated as adequate for the "intermediate" budget but not for the "higher" budget.[5] However, in 1969, the typical white, married blue-collar worker (craftsmen and operatives) earned a total of $8,025. His family could reach the "intermediate" standard of living only through his wife's work, which added an average of $3,394.

The contribution of wives' earnings to the rising standard of living is shown also by the fact that, for families with incomes above the median, the earnings of wives account for about a quarter of the family's total income. Among families with lower family income, wives' earnings account for about one-sixth. The share of family income contributed by wives reflects the amount of time they work as well as their rates of earnings. In 1968, the overall share earned by wives in all husband–wife families, regardless of time worked, was 27 percent (up from 20 percent in 1960); but the share ranged from 37 percent for wives working full time, year-round to only 13 percent for those who worked less than a full year or all year at part-time jobs. While the share of family income earned by wives working full time remained about the same throughout the 1960s, the share earned by wives working part time or part year more than doubled during the decade.[6]

"ADDITIONAL" WORKERS AND THE BUSINESS CYCLE

The ready availability of jobs and a high level of economic activity are major factors in increasing labor force participation and opening opportunities for multiworker families. The size of the labor force expands when jobs are plentiful, and persons who might otherwise not seek jobs enter the work force, a process facilitated by employers making various accommodations to the needs of "secondary" workers.

Just as workers are lured into the work force by high demand, they can become discouraged and drop out of the labor force when they cannot find jobs. The hypothesis that the labor force expands in depressions, as wives and children of unemployed or underemployed workers try to find jobs to replace lost income,[7] is not supported by evidence. While some additional workers enter the labor force during recessions to bolster sagging family income, more workers withdraw in discouragement.[8] The additional worker is more likely to be a low-income person than the discouraged worker.[9]

The additional-worker hypothesis was revived in 1970, when the nation was experiencing a combination of inflation and recession. The selective decline in economic activity still left job vacancies for secondary workers, especially married women, who might have sought employment to maintain family income eroded by inflation and reduced opportunities to work overtime. The net effect was an expansion of the labor force accompanied by rising unemployment rates. However, as the recession continued, the labor force participation rate declined and the labor force expansion reflected only population growth.

LABOR MARKET PATHOLOGIES: UNEMPLOYMENT, UNDEREMPLOYMENT, AND SHORTAGES

In the United States, labor demand has tended to fall short of the available labor supply, except in times of war. At the same time, there have been frequent sustained shortages of highly specialized labor. Some unemployment and some shortages are to be expected in any dynamic economy, regardless of the level of labor demand. Job changes, plant shutdowns, the search for a first job, and seasonal swings all cause some temporary joblessness and underemployment; innovations (e.g., widespread use of computers) or extremely large changes in demand (e.g., rapid expansion and contraction of the space program) may result in temporary shortages or surpluses of skilled personnel. As long as labor market imbalances remain brief and moderate, they are only of passing social concern—a small price to be paid for free market operations. Above and beyond some frictional minima, however, unemployment, underemployment, and labor shortages arising from longer-term imbalances have far-reaching implications for the well-being of individuals and for society as a whole.

The Historical Perspective

The levels of unemployment have varied widely over the past 40 years, encompassing long periods of massive waste of manpower and considerably shorter periods of general shortages of labor (Table 3–3). Experience has shown that most of those gyrations could have been avoided or at least minimized by responsible and compassionate public policy, though complete cures for the ailments that plague the labor market remain elusive. The disaster of the 1930s, which brought unemployment rates of 25 percent or more, was eventually diagnosed as a shortage of effective demand. The crisis apparently developed mainly because economists and politicians lacked a clear remedy for the malady and relied too long on the response of "automatic" market mechanisms. The massive infusion of labor demand caused by World War II solved the unemployment problem, but at a cost of debilitating inflation. The jobless rate declined to just over 1 percent, a condition that could only be characterized as minimal frictional unemployment caused by excessive labor demand and strong social pressures against "slackers" during a national emergency.

The Great Depression left deep scars, and the prevailing view during the mid-1940s was that the high unemployment would return once the war

TABLE 3–3   *Average Unemployment, 1929–1970*

YEAR	NUMBER (IN THOUSANDS)	PERCENT OF LABOR FORCE
1929	1,550	3.2%
1930	4,340	8.7
1931	8,020	15.9
1932	12,060	23.6
1933	12,830	24.9
1934	11,340	21.7
1935	10,610	20.1
1936	9,030	16.9
1937	7,700	14.3
1938	10,390	19.0
1939	9,480	17.2
1940	8,120	14.6
1941	5,560	9.9
1942	2,660	4.7
1943	1,070	1.9
1944	670	1.2
1945	1,040	1.9
1946	2,270	3.9
1947	2,311	3.9
1948	2,276	3.8
1949	3,637	5.9
1950	3,288	5.3
1951	2,055	3.3
1952	1,883	3.0
1953	1,834	2.9
1954	3,532	5.5
1955	2,852	4.4
1956	2,750	4.1
1957	2,859	4.3
1958	4,602	6.8
1959	3,740	5.5
1960	3,852	5.5
1961	4,714	6.7
1962	3,911	5.5
1963	4,070	5.7
1964	3,786	5.2
1965	3,366	4.5
1966	2,875	3.8
1967	2,975	3.8
1968	2,817	3.6
1969	2,831	3.5
1970	4,088	4.9

SOURCE: *Employment and Earnings* (January 1971), p. 23. Data include 14- and 15-year-olds prior to 1947.

was over. Congress responded by enacting the Employment Act of 1946, a legislative affirmation of the national goal of an economic climate which would provide job opportunities to all persons "able, willing, and seeking work." The expected high level of unemployment did not develop in the immediate postwar adjustment period, largely because labor demand was sustained at high levels by a big backlog of consumer spending.

In the 1950s, business contractions became more frequent and recovery after each recession grew less and less adequate, leaving joblessness progressively higher. Although mass unemployment was avoided in the late 1940s and 1950s, the persistent rise of unemployment raised fears of a progressive malaise which looked increasingly like secular stagnation. The policies of the federal government in the 1950s, primarily designed to aid and support normal market mechanisms, were not adequate in our increasingly complex, interdependent economy. In the 1960s, they were replaced by diverse efforts to combat unemployment—aid to depressed areas, stimulation of business investment and consumer demand, and special manpower programs aimed at improving the opportunities of the poor and unskilled to compete in the job market.

Policy orientation slowly shifted to the profound and continuing problems of persons who were particularly disadvantaged in the labor market and living in poverty. Confined to the low end of the employment ladder by a lack of skills or special personal problems and living largely in big-city ghettos and rural slums, a small portion of the work force was living through a continuing cycle of intermittent unemployment and underemployment at low-paying jobs. Ultimately, these measures, coupled with the escalation of the Vietnam War, generated high employment. As the economy moved into the 1970s on a downbeat, fears of "mass" unemployment were abated and concern turned to what John T. Dunlop had labeled, a decade earlier, "class" unemployment.[10]

Unemployment and Underemployment

Underutilized manpower resources may be divided into four distinct groups: the unemployed; persons outside the labor force who want or need work; persons who are working fewer hours than they would prefer because of economic reasons beyond their personal control; and persons employed at jobs that are below their actual or potential skill level. No reasonable estimate of the size of the last group exists, although it must be large indeed. Data for the first three groups for the high-employment year of 1969 and during the recession of 1961 are summarized in the following tabulation:

Type of Unemployment or Underemployment	Number	
	1969	1961
Unemployed	2,831,000	4,713,000
Outside labor force, but wanted work	574,000	n.a.
On reduced workweeks, economic reasons	2,056,000	3,141,000

The estimates for 1969 relate to a period of strong demand, when under-utilization was at one of the low points of the previous 25 years. When labor demand was weaker in 1961, underemployment and unemployment were commensurately higher.

The Causes of Unemployment

Total unemployment is primarily a function of the general economic environment and in large measure is responsive to policy actions. Identification of specific forms of unemployment and their causes may be helpful in the design of remedial policies for particular maladies. The causes of unemployment, in good times and bad, are reasonably clear and fall into four broad categories: cyclical, frictional, seasonal, and structural. Elements of each cause of joblessness usually can be found in each unemployment situation because they tend to reinforce and compound one another.

Cyclical Unemployment

Cyclical swings in business activity are the most commonly recognized (and probably most important) cause of unemployment and under-employment. The outstanding characteristic of cyclical unemployment in a modern economy is that the individual worker has little control over his fate. Since the end of World War II, business recessions have been mild and of short duration. In each, unemployment stayed quite low until the peak of business activity passed, then rose sharply as the recession grew progressively worse. For some time after the trough had passed, unemployment tended to continue high. Policy response to cyclical unemployment has taken two forms—income-protection plans and attempts at stabilization of demand and production. In a marked downturn, virtually no jobs at any pay level are available in the sore spots most affected by the turn of activity. During the downturn of 1970, for example, the unemployment rate in Seattle rose to depression proportions; aerospace workers with many years' seniority were laid off for extended periods and few other employers were hiring.

The economy has a basic productive potential which is a function of its resources—labor, capital, and natural resources—and the state of technology. A departure from the level of output appropriate to the existing resource base may result in continuing unemployment or overemployment, with neither being necessarily responsive to automatic correction by market mechanisms. Arthur Okun estimated that for each 1 percent shortfall in the level of real output (GNP) from potential output, the overall unemployment rate would be higher by about 0.3 percentage points.[11]

Policy prescriptions growing out of Okun's "gap" analysis are simple; they call for the stimulation or repression of consumer and business demand by the use of tax cuts or increases, higher government spending or retrenchment, and stimulation or restraint of the credit and monetary supply. Policies designed to stabilize the labor market at a high employment level are not always consistent with other economic goals of maximum price stability or minimum inflation, long-term growth, and a favorable balance of international trade and payments. Consequently, decisions often reflect goals other than high employment.

Other Types of Unemployment

The three remaining causes of unemployment—seasonal changes in activity, frictions in the job market, and structural imbalances—probably vary directly with cyclical joblessness and tend to be restricted to particular classes of workers.

Seasonal swings in activity—notably in outdoor work such as construction and agriculture—tend to result in temporary joblessness and contribute significantly to total unemployment. While precise measures are difficult—especially because a seasonal slack period may be extended by cyclical weakness or the slow obsolescence of an industry—the BLS estimated that seasonal unemployment accounted for about one-fourth of total forced idleness in the late 1950s; reexamination of comparable data for the late 1960s suggests a similar conclusion. In construction and agriculture, the proportion was estimated at more than 40 percent compared with 10 to 15 percent in transportation and trade.[12] If seasonal joblessness could be reduced appreciably, it would benefit all sectors of the economy.

Seasonal swings recur annually, making it possible to measure in great detail their characteristics and predict their timing, amplitude, and cause (weather, institutional factors, and custom). Because seasonality is predictable within a relatively narrow range, employment and unemployment statistics are adjusted for seasonality, permitting closer identification of cyclical and secular trends. This adjustment, however, should not obscure the very sizable economic loss associated with seasonality. Much can be done to minimize these costs.[13]

Frictional unemployment results from temporary difficulties in matching available workers with available jobs. It arises mainly from lack of knowledge of opportunities, and is marked by its relatively short duration. Such unemployment is unavoidable—as when women or younger workers enter the labor force, or when skilled workers voluntarily quit.

Seasonal and frictional unemployment overlap, making clearcut distinctions impossible. Each June and July, for example, thousands of young people enter the labor market in search of temporary or permanent jobs. This vast inflow is partly seasonal—arising from the institutionally determined school year—and partly frictional—reflecting the time necessary to scour the market and find employment. As time passes, some of this unemployment can become cyclical or structural—that is, demand is not strong enough to absorb all of them (as in the summer of 1970), or demand is strong enough, but they are not adequately prepared for the jobs available.

Structural unemployment is more complex than seasonal and frictional unemployment, and arises from basic changes in the composition of labor demand and failure of the labor supply to accommodate to new market conditions. Recent examples include large cutbacks in the space program; the decline of the railroads, which combined with the switch to diesel locomotives to displace thousands of skilled railroad workers; the decline of coal mining in Appalachia; and the relocation of the New England textile industry in the South. These and other transformations left many skilled and unskilled workers stranded in areas with job deficits and urgently needing to learn a new skill or to relocate in expanding labor markets.

Possibly a more subtle cause of structural unemployment is technological progress and automation. Productivity advances in agriculture displaced thousands of farmers; similar displacements have occurred in the durable goods sector of manufacturing, where automation has reduced the need for some skills and sharply modified others. Because the structurally unemployed generally have a large investment in their skill and location, they are less likely than mobile young workers to find new jobs quickly. Thus, structural unemployment tends to be of long duration and requires vigorous efforts at retraining or relocation.

Reflecting these kinds of problems, unemployment can be classified according to probable cause. The immediate causes of unemployment are divided into the three categories given below and are generally associated with the underlying initial causes shown in the right-hand column. As involuntary idleness persists beyond a month, the probability that it is frictional diminishes; after 15 weeks or more, it could no longer be considered seasonal, and a basic structural or cyclical problem becomes probable. The application of this analysis to 1969 unemployment may be broken down as follows:

Classification	Percent of Unemployment in 1969	Cause
Loss of job	36%	Seasonal or cyclical
Quit job	15	Largely frictional
Entered or reentered labor force	49	Largely frictional but some seasonal

Applying the preceding analysis and available data on the duration of unemployment, it is possible to classify the causes of unemployment in any given year. Assuming, for example, that there was no cyclical unemployment in 1969—a year of strong demand and low unemployment—Table 3–4 indicates one breakdown of the economic causes of unemployment. The data suggest that joblessness in a period of strong demand is essentially frictional and of short duration, though about one-eighth of the unemployment appears to have been structural. By the spring of 1971, as the reces-

TABLE 3–4   *Distribution of Unemployment by Duration and Cause,*
1969 and May 1971

INITIAL CLASSIFICATION	LESS THAN 5 WEEKS *Largely Frictional and Seasonal*		5–14 WEEKS *More Serious Problems Emerging*		15 WEEKS OR MORE *Structural or Cyclical*	
	1969	May 1971	1969	May 1971	1969	May 1971
TOTAL (all causes)	58%	42%	29%	28%	13%	30%
Lost job	51	32	32	29	18	39
Left job	61	47	28	27	12	26
Entered or reentered work force	62	53	28	28	11	19

NOTE: Details may not add to totals because of rounding.
SOURCE: Based on U.S. Bureau of Labor Statistics data.

sion deepened, the relative significance of frictional unemployment declined and long-term or cyclical unemployment became relatively much more significant (Table 3–4).

It is, of course, difficult to distinguish those unemployed because of seasonal employment patterns, those with serious labor market problems, and those who are making a fairly easy transition between jobs (or between entry into a full work career and retirement from it). Nearly 10 percent of those who held full-time jobs in 1969 were employed for 40 to 49 weeks. The "frictionally unemployed" are found among these 6.8 million workers who were idle as much as a fifth of the time, along with the 1.8 million peripheral part-time workers who had between 40 and 49 weeks of employment. The "structurally unemployed" have more deep-seated problems; there is little demand for their labor. They were found among the 14.5 million full-time and the 10.2 million part-time peripheral workers who held their jobs 39 weeks or less in 1969 (Table 5–1, p. 56).

Characteristics of the Unemployed

Employability is a function of workers' preparedness for work, as well as employers' needs and prejudices. Thus, the likelihood of being unemployed varies with workers' personal characteristics as well as with the more general economic factors that generate unemployment. Forced idleness is most likely to be visited upon those who are least able to cope with it—in general, the ill-prepared and the young. If the persons involved also happen to be black or female (or both), the likelihood of being jobless is multiplied by a factor of two or more.

There is a certain socioeconomic logic in the sequence of age–sex unemployment. Most Americans live in families in which the principal— although not only—breadwinner is an adult male with job experience and training. Most such men have a full-time, year-round commitment to the labor force, and even a short period of unemployment can be a very serious matter because of their family responsibilities. Although unemployment among male family heads is appreciably lower than the national average, it tends to be especially cyclically responsive, reflecting the heavy concentration of men in manufacturing and construction. In 1969, for example, male heads of households accounted for more than half of the labor force but for only about one-fourth of the unemployed. Wives and other relatives accounted for about two-thirds of total unemployment, while female heads of households accounted for about 8 percent.

The incidence of unemployment is higher among women, and is particularly severe for young workers even when high employment prevails (Figure 3–1). Frictional unemployment is higher for women and teenagers than for men, reflecting their greater likelihood of entering or leaving the labor force and the demands of school, military service, and marriage. These frictions are not the only explanations, however. Young workers and women are often restricted to entry-level jobs which are frequently sensitive to seasonal fluctuations or offer few opportunities for upward mobility. Employees have little to lose by giving up such jobs. The structural component of unemployment may also be important for younger workers and women. Mature women reentering the labor force after raising children may find their skills outmoded. Among younger workers, the steady erosion of unskilled entry-level jobs probably has been very important, especially for school dropouts whose unemployment rates may be more than twice those of their peers who graduated from high school.[14]

Unemployment varies with educational attainment, and this difference tends to be reflected in rates of unemployment by occupation. Professional and technical workers—many are college graduates—have averaged 2 percent or less unemployment in any year since occupational unemployment rates were first regularly measured in 1958. The rate for laborers— many of whom did not complete high school—has never averaged less than 6.5 percent and has been as high as 15.0 percent. The rate for laborers typically has been about five times greater than that for professional and technical workers and about two times greater than that for craftsmen. Obviously, inadequate preparation consigns a worker to the end of the employment queue and the top of the layoff list. The program implications are clear: Improved education and training can increase the supply of relatively skilled workers and rescue some of the unskilled from the cycle of recurring unemployment and underemployment.

In part, skill differentials and educational deficiencies are the cause of substantially higher levels of joblessness among blacks than among whites. Throughout the post-Korean War period, the jobless rates of blacks

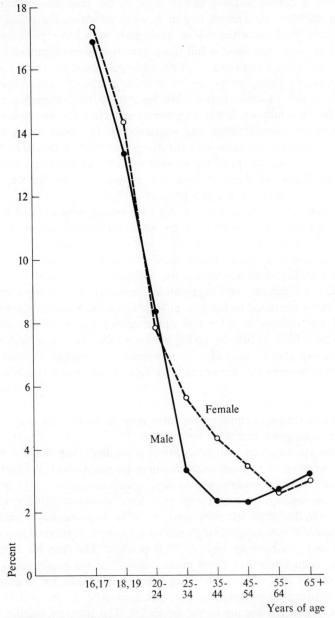

FIGURE 3–1.   *Rates of Unemployment by Age and Sex, 1969.*
SOURCE: *Employment and Earnings* (January 1971), p. 121.

have been about double the jobless rates of whites. Skill differentials are not the only explanation, however. Regardless of educational attainment, work experience, and sex, blacks are more likely than whites to be unemployed, to have extended periods of joblessness, and, when employed, to have lower levels of earnings. Discrimination doubtlessly accounts for a significant part of these differences.[15]

Discrimination also plays a role in the higher jobless rates of women and teenagers. A woman or teenager is more likely to be laid off than a man, more likely to be working part time for economic reasons, and less likely to be in a high-income, high-status occupation. Of course, higher unemployment among women and younger workers should be expected, given lack of seniority, initial entry to the labor force, tendency to seek new jobs, or relative lack of experience.

Association with particular industries is often a cause of high jobless levels. Construction and agriculture are subject to seasonal swings in activity, while durable-goods manufacturing is very sensitive to cyclical changes. These industries tend to have higher unemployment rates and to be particularly responsive to changes in the growth rate of the economy.

Unemployment is also a function of geography. Industrial concentrations are partly responsible for this. The declines in military-aerospace purchasing had a very distinct impact in the early 1970s on rising unemployment in Washington and southern California. Other areas have been subject to persistently high levels of joblessness and underutilization because of declining industries. The experiences of Appalachian soft-coal regions and former New England textile and leather towns have been well documented.

A more recent phenomenon is the high unemployment in central metropolitan areas, reflecting the great migration of population from backward rural areas to big-city slums and the flight of industry from the inner city. The contribution of migration to unemployment in central-city areas has not been measured; but whatever the causes, the incidence of unemployment is greater in central cities than in their surrounding rings. In the nation's 20 largest cities—which contain about one-third of all workers—the unemployment rate of central-city residents was 3.9 percent in 1969, compared with an average rate of 3.0 percent for suburban residents.[16]

When these data are further broken down to measure specific poverty areas, the unemployment gap and extent of employment problems grow progressively worse. A special report on the employment status of men in urban poverty areas showed that the unemployment rate for married men was two and one-half times as great as in other urban areas; that unemployed men had usually worked in semiskilled or unskilled jobs; that a disproportionate share of the unemployed were blacks; that their duration of unemployment was longer than average; and that they had more frequent spells of unemployment than their suburban neighbors.[17]

Area unemployment statistics may underestimate real forced idleness in depressed areas. When job opportunities are not available, workers may become discouraged about finding work and give up looking for jobs; hence, they are neither considered as being in the labor force nor counted as unemployed. A special survey showed that in 1968, a year of high employment, an estimated 670,000 "discouraged" workers were not in the labor force but would have welcomed work if jobs were available.[18]

Averages tend to understate the actual number of people hit by unemployment at some time during the year. Monthly average unemployment for 1969 was 2.8 million, but work-experience data show that 11.7 million persons were among the unemployed for at least one week during 1969.[19] The pressures of forced idleness on economic well-being, however, are greatest when unemployment extends over a long period or is repetitive. In 1969, for example, 2.3 million persons were unemployed for 15 weeks or more, many because of repeated spells of unemployment. Similar work-experience data for urban poverty areas in 1967 show that fewer adult men were in the work force; a smaller proportion of them had any work; of those who did work, fewer held full-time jobs; the incidence of unemployment was half again as high as for residents in nonpoverty neighborhoods; and nearly 30 percent of the men in poverty neighborhoods who were unemployed were out of work for a total of four months or more.[20]

Labor Shortages

While unemployment has been high for selected groups of workers, there have been continuing shortages of other kinds of workers—mainly those in the highly skilled, highly paid professions and those in the lowest-skilled, lowest-paid occupations. Amelioration of shortages in these groups is an important objective because manpower bottlenecks create dislocations and obstacles to balanced economic growth. High employment levels are often erroneously identified by employers as shortages of general labor, largely because a tight market increases labor turnover, may reduce the rate of productivity growth, and usually results in higher unit labor costs. These concerns have surfaced only on rare occasions, including the latter half of the 1960s.

A more important problem exists, however, with respect to shortages of highly skilled workers. It may require several years of specialized training, not to mention huge costs, to develop skilled professional personnel. Filling these gaps should be a first-line national priority. Shortages of most unskilled jobs can usually be cured with a bigger dose of income and a dollop of prestige.

Some shortages result from restrictive practices designed to provide selected groups of workers with strong bargaining power. Some unions and professional associations engage in restrictive practices designed to limit the supply of labor and raise income. Well-known examples include many construction craft unions, medical and dental associations, and university faculties which restrict the supply of new young Ph.Ds. These special-interest groups primarily restrict supply through arbitrary qualification standards for apprenticeship, unduly extended apprenticeships, limits on the number of apprentices per journeyman, artificially high licensing standards, and other techniques. Such practices are always defended as maintaining high standards to protect the public from the "untrained" and "inept." A reasonable distribution of employment opportunities will not be achieved unless restrictive practices are corrected.

NOTES

1. Herbert S. Parnes, "Labor Force Participation and Labor Mobility," in *A Review of Industrial Relations Research,* Industrial Relations Research Association Series, Vol. 1 (Madison, Wisc.: The Association, 1970), pp. 1–33.

2. William G. Bowen and T. Aldrich Finegan, *The Economics of Labor Force Participation* (Princeton, N.J.: Princeton University Press, 1969), pp. 559–565, esp. tables on pp. 561 and 565.

3. Stuart H. Garfinkle, *Job Changing and Manpower Training,* U.S. Department of Labor, Manpower Administration, Office of Manpower, Automation and Training, Manpower Report No. 10 (Washington, D.C.: U.S. Government Printing Office, 1964), p. 1.

4. Richard P. Oliver, "Increase in Defense-Related Employment During Vietnam Buildup," *Monthly Labor Review* (February 1970), pp. 3 ff.; and U.S. Congress, Senate Subcommittee on Employment, Manpower, and Poverty, *Hearings on Manpower Development and Training Legislation, 1970,* 91st Cong., 2d Sess. (Washington, D.C.: U.S. Government Printing Office, 1970), Part 3, pp. 1254 ff.

5. U.S. Department of Labor, Bureau of Labor Statistics, *Three Standards of Living for an Urban Family of Four Persons, Spring 1967,* BLS Bulletin 1570–5 (Washington, D.C.: U.S. Government Printing Office, 1969), p. 39.

6. Elizabeth Waldman, "Women at Work: Changes in the Labor Force Activity of Women," *Monthly Labor Review* (June 1970), p. 16.

7. W. S. Woytinsky, *Three Aspects of Labor Dynamics* (New York: Social Science Research Council, 1942), Part III.

8. Jacob Mincer, "Labor Force Participation and Unemployment: A Review of Recent Evidence," in Robert and Margaret Gordon, eds., *Prosperity and Unemployment* (New York: John Wiley, 1966), pp. 73 ff; and Bowen and Finegan, *op. cit.,* p. 483.

9. Glen G. Cain, *The Net Effect of Unemployment on Labor Force Participation of Secondary Workers* (Madison, Wisc.: Social Systems Research Institute, University of Wisconsin, October 1964).

10. John T. Dunlop, "Public Policy and Unemployment," in *Studies in Unemployment,* U.S. Congress, Senate Special Committee on Unemployment Problems, 86th Cong., 2d Sess. (Washington, D.C.: U.S. Government Printing Office, 1960), p. 3.

11. Arthur Okun, "Potential GNP: Its Measurement and Significance," *Proceedings of the Business and Economic Statistics Section of the American Statistical Association,* 1962, pp. 98–104.

12. Seymour Wolfbein, *Employment and Unemployment in the United States* (Chicago: Science Research Associates, 1962), p. 293.

13. Sol Swerdloff and Robert J. Myers, "Seasonality and Construction," *Monthly Labor Review* (September 1967), pp. 1–8.

14. Howard V. Hayghe, "Employment of High School Graduates and Dropouts," *Monthly Labor Review* (August 1970), pp. 35 ff.

15. James Gwartney, "Discrimination and Income Differentials," *American Economic Review* (June 1970), pp. 396–408.

16. Paul O. Flaim and Paul M. Schwab, "Geographic Aspects of Unemployment in 1969," *Employment and Earnings* (April 1970), pp. 5–25.

17. Hazel M. Willacy, "Men in Poverty Neighborhoods: A Status Report," *Monthly Labor Review* (February 1969), pp. 23–27.

18. Paul O. Flaim, "Persons Not in the Labor Force," *Monthly Labor Review* (July 1969), p. 11.

19. Howard V. Hayghe, "Work Experience of the Population in 1969," *Monthly Labor Review* (January 1971), pp. 45–52.

20. Forrest A. Bogan, "Work Experience of the Population in 1967," *Monthly Labor Review* (June 1969), pp. 44–50.

Chapter 4
Women
at Work

Women, especially wives and mothers, have played a key role in the changing composition of the labor force. Women workers are on the increase, not only in the percentage who work but also in their share of the labor force and in the variety of jobs they hold. Participation rates of women have doubled since 1900. With an average of 31.6 million women in the work force, women accounted for 36.7 percent of total workers in 1970. Since World War II, about two-thirds of the total increase in civilian employment has come from women workers. Increases in the number of working wives and mothers in this period have been most dramatic. The number of working mothers has increased almost eightfold since 1940, although the total number of women workers only doubled. In March 1969, 11.9 million mothers with children under 18 years were working or seeking work, or four of every ten mothers with children that age. In 1960, only three of ten such mothers were working, and less than one of ten in 1940.

Four of every ten married women were employed in 1970, compared with one of every three in 1960, and only one of 20 in 1900. The 17.6 million working wives accounted in 1969 for about one-fifth of the labor force. In addition, about one of every nine families was headed by a woman, and half of these women were in the labor force. In the 1960s, nearly half of the increase in the total labor force came from married women.[1]

FACTORS AFFECTING FEMALE WORK

American women of all classes have entered the labor market; black women and immigrants were the pioneers, followed by young single women, then "mature" wives. The latest influx has been of young mothers. The husbands' occupations seem to have little impact upon wives' employment: There is little variation in labor force participation among wives of blue-collar, clerical, or professional workers. The major variables affecting women's participation are husbands' earnings, marital status, availability of child-care facilities, educational attainment, and race.

Husbands' Earnings

The level of husbands' earnings affects the likelihood of wives being in the labor force. Except for older couples, about 45 percent of wives worked in 1969 if their husband made between $3,000 and $8,000. Wives' participation in the labor force drops with rising husbands' earnings—to 35 percent for those whose husbands' annual earnings were between $10,000 and $15,000, and only 18 percent for wives whose husbands earned more than $25,000.

Wives' earnings are important for achieving what many Americans deem a "good" living—say, $15,000 a year or more. The number of families at this income level would have been cut by half in 1968 if the families were to depend exclusively on the earnings of the husband alone, rather than the income of the entire family.[2]

However, sheer economic necessity, in the most basic meaning of the phrase, is the reason that more than half of the women in the labor force work. Of the 31 million women at work, about 41 percent are either single, divorced, separated, or widowed. Many of these women are the sole supporters not only of themselves but also of children or parents. In addition, almost 5 million working women are married to men who earn less than $5,000 annually. As Juanita Kreps has pointed out, these women do not have the luxury of choosing work at home over work in the market place.[3]

Female Family Heads

Women—5.6 million of them—head 1 of every 9 families. More than half of these women are in the labor force, rearing 8 million children and providing for an additional 5 million persons in their families. In 1970, 43 percent of female family heads were widows, 46 percent were divorced or separated, and 11 percent were single women who had never married—although a third of them had children.[4]

Female-headed families have been increasing faster over the past decade than families in general—24 percent compared with only 14 percent. They account, moreover, for a large and growing portion of the remaining poverty in the United States. In 1969, nearly half of poor families with children were headed by women. The growing number of female-headed families with children is one reason for the rise of welfare rolls in recent years.

The median income of female-headed families with children is only about one-third that of two-parent families. Only 38 percent of the families headed by women in 1969 had incomes over $5,000, and only 9 percent, over $10,000. By contrast, 55 percent of husband-wife families with children had incomes over $10,000.

Many female heads of families cannot work full time year-round, usually because of the presence of children. Although 70 percent of female family heads aged 16 to 44 worked at some time during the year in 1967, only 38 percent worked year-round at full-time jobs. Working only part time or part-year meant half of the families were poor. Nor was full-time work any guarantee of escaping poverty, for 16 percent of female family heads who worked full time year-round were poor.

The proportion of families headed by divorced women has gone up by almost half over the last decade—to about 2.2 percent (or 1.1 million) of all families. Families headed by separated women have also increased, but not as markedly. Our mores seem to require that the mother assume responsibility for caring for the children: Though the father is not relieved of economic responsibility, the brunt of the support usually falls on the mother. Divorced and separated women are thus more likely to be found in the labor force than are wives, widows, or even single women. The proportion of divorced women who worked in 1969 was 72 percent, compared with 40 percent for wives and 54 percent for separated women. Divorced and separated women are also more likely than wives to be employed in full-time jobs.[5] Further, the participation rates of divorced, widowed, or separated women with children under six are markedly higher than those of mothers with husbands present.

Marital Status of Working Mother with Children Under 6 Years	Participation Rate March 1969
TOTAL	30.4%
Married, husband present	28.5
Divorced	68.1
Separated	44.2
Widowed	34.5

High participation rates, coupled with the generally lower income of female-headed families, indicate that day-care facilities at reasonable cost are particularly important to this group of women.

Day-Care Facilities

Although the presence of children, especially preschoolers under six, greatly reduces the chances of a woman's working, an increasing number of younger mothers have entered the labor force. The number of working young mothers (aged 20 to 34 years) with children under six increased by 600,000 from 1964 to 1969, when about three of every ten were in the labor force (Table 4–1).

One-fourth of all wives with children under the age of three work, as do one-third of those whose youngest were between three and five, and one-half of those with school-age children. In 1948, only 13 percent of all mothers with children under six were in the labor force; the ratio rose to 30 percent by 1969. Estimates for the future show a continuing rising trend. As already indicated, a group of mothers with children under six who have particularly high participation rates are those who are divorced, widowed, or separated, and their numbers are increasing.

As the number of working mothers with young children rises, day-care facilities become increasingly important. However, the types and quality of day-care used by working mothers vary widely, with child-care centers

TABLE 4–1   *Labor Force Participation of Women 20 to 34 Years Old, March 1969*

AGE AND MARITAL STATUS	POPULATION: PERCENT DISTRIBUTION	LABOR FORCE PARTICIPATION RATE
20 to 24 Years		
TOTAL (8,040,000)	100.0%	56.6%
Single	35.4	69.4
Widowed, divorced, or separated	7.3	62.9
Married, husband present	57.2	47.9
With children under 6	35.5	33.3
No children under 6	21.7	71.8
25 to 34 Years		
TOTAL (12,285,00)	100.0	43.4
Single	8.7	80.9
Widowed, divorced, or separated	10.0	63.5
Married, husband present	81.3	36.9
With children under 6	53.9	27.2
No children under 6	27.3	56.0

NOTE: Detail may not add to totals due to rounding.
SOURCE: U.S. Department of Labor, *Manpower Report of the President* (Washington, D.C.: U.S. Government Printing Office, 1970), p. 48.

accounting only for a minute proportion of day care. Nearly half of all children under 14 whose mothers worked part or full time in 1964 were cared for in their own homes, usually by relatives; about 16 percent were maintained in someone else's home. Only 2 percent of all children, and 6 percent of children under six, were in child-care centers. The rest were provided for under other arrangements or left to shift for themselves—"latchkey" children.[6] A more recent study of Aid to Families With Dependent Children (AFDC) mothers who were enrolled in work-training programs shows that they make limited use of group-care facilities and tend to have their children cared for privately, usually by relatives.[7]

Although it has been estimated that several million children need day care in licensed centers and family homes, facilities in 1971 could accommodate only 780,000 children.[8] And these limited facilities had to be shared with children who needed care because their mothers were ill or physically handicapped or because the children were orphaned or abandoned.

Day-care facilities are run by a wide variety of sponsors—including private-for-profit groups and unions, churches, or other nonprofit community or governmental organizations. Limited federal funds are already being channeled into some of these facilities—for example, day care for children of migrant workers, and the Work Incentive Program for welfare mothers.[9] The cost of day care varies widely and depends on the services offered. Annual cost per child for group care averages about $400 for school-age children and $1,600 for preschoolers. The Department of Health, Education, and Welfare has estimated the annual cost per child of "acceptable" group day care (as distinct from "minimum" or "desirable" care) for three- to five-year-olds to be $1,862.

The fact that day-care facilities are relatively rare and costly has led to demands for further government outlays, not only to support more facilities but also to subsidize part of the costs to enable more working mothers to provide their children decent facilities. Of particular concern are working mothers who are heads of families and who raise their children alone, mothers on relief who want to break out of dependency through "workfare" instead of welfare, and other low-income mothers. Since the proportion of working mothers is highest among families in which the husband's income is under $7,000 a year, decent day-care facilities are beyond their reach if they are not subsidized by the government.

Education and Race

The more education a woman acquires, the more likely she is to work. Educational attainment is more a determinant of labor force participation for women than for men who, once out of school, tend to be in the labor force regardless of educational attainment. In 1969, the participation rate ranged from 30 percent for women with an elementary education to 54 percent for women with a college education. The participation rate for college-educated women aged 45 to 54 approached that of men, with nearly nine of every ten women in the labor force.[10]

Job opportunities for college-educated women have increased substantially. Better-educated women are in a better position to take advantage of rising demand in the expanding clerical and technical occupations; they may also be less satisfied with housekeeping. Women who have invested in a college education may also be reluctant to forgo the rewards from work in professional fields; their opportunity costs of staying at home are greater than for less-educated women. Married women with four or more years of college who worked full time year-round in 1968 earned twice as much as those with grade-school education.

Race is also an important determinant of female labor participation. Black married women have had a longer history of labor force participation than white women. Their earnings, though low, have been needed to supplement the comparatively lower earnings of their husbands and to support larger families. They also have higher participation rates and higher unemployment rates than whites.[11]

More black married women than white work at some point during the year; in 1966, 66 percent of blacks had work experience, compared with 46 percent of whites. Black women are more likely to be forced into idleness, primarily because of the kinds of jobs open to them. The incidence of unemployment among black wives—one of every five—was twice as high as among whites and their spells of joblessness were of longer duration (almost one-third of unemployed black women were out of jobs 15 or more weeks compared with one-fifth of whites).

Black women have lower levels of educational attainment than white women. But even where levels are the same, black women are less apt to break into the "better" occupations: In March 1967, among all employed women 18 years and over who had high-school diplomas, only half of the black women were in professional, managerial, clerical, and sales occupations, compared with four of five white women. One-third of black women were service workers but only one-tenth of whites.

Another factor contributing to the black wives' higher participation is that they are better educated than their husbands; the reverse is true for whites. With more education, earnings potential and attractive work opportunities increase. Although black wives who had some work experience in 1968 contributed only slightly more to family income than white wives did—29 percent compared with 27 percent—the share was much larger when family income was over $15,000; 12 percent of black wives earned at least half the family income compared with 5 percent among white wives. This indicates a greater role for Negro wives in helping their families reach middle-class status.

PATTERNS AND AGES OF WORK
FOR WOMEN

Wives and mothers more frequently move in and out of the labor market, either on a part-time or full-time basis, in response to their families' shifting needs, their own work desires, and labor market conditions. About half of all wives worked at some time during 1968, but only four of every ten workers were employed full time year-round. Since about three of every four employed married women work at full-time jobs, many did not work year-round. Many women prefer part-time employment; they accounted for two-thirds of all voluntary part-time employment experience in 1969.

The distribution of womens' employment by age is bimodal. This M-shaped curve (Figure 4–1) reflects two peak participation periods: one, in early adulthood when girls are just out of school or are young wives earning money at the start of married life; and the second when mature women return to work after their children have entered school or are grown.

For many years, 18- and 19-year-olds had the highest participation rates among women; these were premarriage and prechildren years. After World War II, many mature 45- to 54-year-old women entered and stayed in the job market, and the labor force participation rate of this group passed the younger group. But since 1964, participation rates of 20- to 24-year-old women have been rising most rapidly. In 1970, this age group had a participation rate of 58 percent, exceeding that of the older group. The younger women's increased participation rate may have resulted from the Vietnam War, higher levels of educational attainment, and lower birth rates.

DISCRIMINATION

The recent interest in the Women's Liberation Movement and the Equal Rights Amendment has again illuminated the discrimination against women in the job market. Not only do women earn less than men, but the gap has been widening. In 1955, the median wage for women who worked full time year-round was 64 percent of what men earned; in 1968, only 58 percent. The earning comparisons give some idea of the disparity between men and women, but they do not present a *prima facie* case of the "exploitation" of women. The female labor force is heavily weighted with married women whose attachment to the work force is not as committed as that of men. Even comparison by sex of earnings of full-time, year-round workers leaves much to be desired. For example, married women have less occupational choice because they frequently put convenience of location or flexibility of hours above earnings. Their family ties give them less geographic mobility than males, and some, indeed, give up good jobs to follow husbands who decide to accept jobs elsewhere. Nonetheless, there is strong

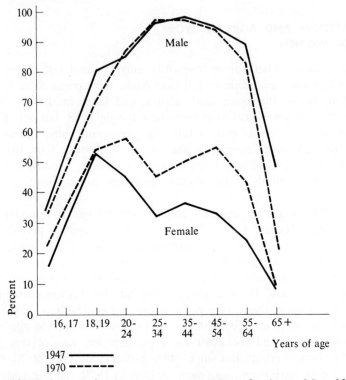

FIGURE 4–1. *Labor Force Participation Rates by Age and Sex, 1947–1970.*
SOURCE: U.S. Department of Labor, *Manpower Report of the President*
(Washington, D.C.: U.S. Government Printing Office, 1971), Table A–2,
pp. 216–217, and *Employment and Earnings* (January 1971), Table A–2,
pp. 117–118.

evidence that women are paid less than men for performing the same work,
laws to the contrary notwithstanding.

The maldistribution of occupations by sex is a better indicator of the
impact of discrimination (Table 4–2). The majority of women are in
clerical and service work (including domestic), retail sales, teaching, and
nursing. Even though women can now be found in virtually every occupation, most of the growth has been in these "women's" occupations, with the
result that the bulk of women are still concentrated there. According to one
estimate, almost half of the net increase in employed women between 1950
and 1960 occurred in occupations in which at least 70 percent of the workers were women, and almost 60 percent of the increase was registered in
occupations that had a majority of women.[12]

Women are forced to concentrate in jobs that tend to have lower levels
of responsibility and pay, while the better-paying jobs and occupations
offering opportunities for upward mobility are frequently foreclosed. Indeed,

TABLE 4–2   *Distribution of Employed Women by Occupation, 1940 and 1970*

MAJOR OCCUPATION GROUP	PERCENT OF WOMEN EMPLOYED		AS PERCENT OF BOTH SEXES EMPLOYED IN OCCUPATION	
	1970	1940	1970	1940
TOTAL				
Thousands	29,667	11,920	—	—
Percent	100.0	100.0	38.1	25.9
White-collar workers				
Professional, technical workers	14.5	13.2	38.5	45.4
Managers, officials, proprietors	4.5	3.8	15.9	11.7
Clerical workers	34.5	21.2	74.6	52.6
Sales workers	7.0	7.0	43.1	27.9
Blue-collar workers				
Craftsmen, foremen	1.0	0.9	3.3	2.1
Operatives	14.5	18.4	30.9	25.7
Nonfarm laborers	0.5	0.8	3.7	3.2
Service workers				
Private household workers	5.1	17.6	97.4	93.8
Service workers (except private household)	16.5	11.3	60.2	40.1
Farm workers				
All farm occupations	1.8	5.8	16.7	8.0

SOURCE: U.S. Department of Labor, *Manpower Report of the President* (Washington, D.C.: U.S. Government Printing Office, 1971), Table A-9.

women's share of professional and technical occupations has actually declined during the past three decades from 45 to 39 percent, even though the absolute numbers of professional and technical women workers more than doubled (Table 4–2). The relative decline, however, reflects a change in the mix of professional jobs. For example, the great increase in professionals included the spurt of engineering and related space-age occupations which are predominantly male. Whether this change in mix is a function of discrimination or unavailability of women to fill these positions is left to speculation.

As Elizabeth Waldman of the BLS has pointed out, the broad category of professional jobs is a "notorious example of a field divided along sexual lines." [13] Two-thirds of all professional women workers are either nurses or teachers, and women teachers are mostly confined to primary grades while men tend to teach in high school and college.

Many factors contribute to make women seek out, and remain in, low-paying, low-status "women's" jobs. Not only does society place a low value on women's market services, but also women themselves tend to base their job choices on short-run needs rather than on long-run career considerations. Thus, they are frequently willing to take these less desirable jobs because the hours and location are convenient, enabling them to combine family and job responsibilities more easily. Also, they forgo further training or long-run considerations for their own career aspirations in order to earn money—limited though it may be—to put husbands through school or to meet family bills.

The low value given to housewives' nonmarket homemaking duties is reflected in the fact that this productive work is not counted in the gross national product or other national accounts, although such services are counted if maids or others are paid to perform them! If, in 1964, the value of housewives' unpaid services had been counted in money terms—just using the wage rates of domestic workers—wives would have added about one-fourth to the GNP, or an additional $180 billion in 1971 dollars.[14]

IMPROVING THE EMPLOYMENT STATUS OF WOMEN

For many years, legislation dealing with women workers was confined to state "protective" laws regulating minimum wages, maximum hours, and other standards of work concerned with promoting the health and safety. In 1938, the Fair Labor Standards Act (FLSA) was adopted to provide federal standards on wages and hours for both men and women. More recently, the emphasis has shifted toward curbing sex discrimination and providing equal pay and employment opportunities. While many states adopted such laws, it was not until the 1960s that the federal government entered this field.

Among the major laws are the Equal Pay Act of 1963 and Title VII of the Civil Rights Act of 1964, which prohibits discrimination in employment based on sex as well as on race, color, religion, and national origin. In addition, Executive Order 11246, as amended in 1967, prohibits sex discrimination (as well as race, color, religion, and national origin) by federal contractors and subcontractors; and the age-discrimination section of the Employment Act of 1967 protects most individuals over age 40 until they reach 65, regardless of sex.

The mere passage of legislation, of course, does not guarantee equal employment opportunities. The laws leave much to be desired in coverage, scope, and sanctions, and little is done to insure compliance with existing provisions. For instance, the Equal Pay Act is an amendment to the FLSA and its coverage is limited generally to that of the federal minimum wage law, leaving out higher-paying executive, administrative, and professional positions—the very jobs where discrimination appears most rampant and its elimination is most crucial if women are to achieve an equal footing with men. And at the opposite end of the job spectrum, many women are not helped because they are concentrated in low-paying lesser-skill jobs in industries or establishments also not covered by the FLSA.[15]

The most publicized and controversial of the recent legislative attempts to improve the status of women is the proposed Equal Rights Amendment to the Constitution. It states that "equality of rights under the law shall not be denied or abridged by the United States or by any State on account of sex," and would make discriminatory laws unconstitutional. If it were adopted, women would presumably acquire the same "rights" as men in all areas of economic, social, and political life. However, many groups that favor improving the employment status of women oppose the amendment on the grounds that it would erode hard-won protective legislation. There also is concern, about drafting women for military service and changes in alimony and child-custody arrangements, although supporters challenge the validity of such arguments.

NOTES

1. Elizabeth Waldman, "Women at Work: Changes in the Labor Force Activity of Women," *Monthly Labor Review* (June 1970), p. 11.

2. Herman P. Miller, *Rich Man, Poor Man* (New York: Thomas Y. Crowell, 1971), Chap. XII.

3. Juanita M. Kreps, *Sex in the Market Place: American Women at Work* (Baltimore: Johns Hopkins, 1971).

4. Robert L. Stein, "The Economic Status of Families Headed by Women," *Monthly Labor Review* (December 1970), pp. 3 ff.

5. Elizabeth Waldman, "Marital and Family Characteristics of the U.S. Labor Force," *Monthly Labor Review* (May 1970), p. 21.

6. Seth Low and Pearl Spindler, U.S. Department of Labor and U.S. Department of Health, Education, and Welfare, *Child Care Arrangements of Working Mothers in the United States* (Washington, D.C.: U.S. Government Printing Office, 1968), pp. 15–16.

7. U.S. Department of Health, Education, and Welfare, Social and Rehabilitation Service, *Preliminary Report of Findings of 1969 AFDC Study* (Washington, D.C.: U.S. Government Printing Office, March 1970), Tables 30, 31, 32.

8. U.S. Department of Labor, Women's Bureau, "Day Care: An Employer's Plus," Women's Bureau Release 71-112, March 1971, p. 1.

9. U.S. Congress, House Committee on Ways and Means, *Hearings on Social Security and Welfare Proposals,* 91st Cong., 1st Sess. (Washington, D.C.: U.S. Government Printing Office, 1969), Part 1, pp. 288–294.

10. U.S. Department of Labor, Women's Bureau, *Trends in Educational Attainment of Women* (Washington, D.C.: U.S. Government Printing Office, October 1969), p. 17.

11. Vera C. Perrella, "Women and the Labor Force," *Monthly Labor Review* (February 1968), p. 10.

12. Valerie Kincade Oppenheimer, *The Female Labor Force in the United States,* Population Monograph Series No. 5 (Berkeley: University of California, 1970), p. 160.

13. Elizabeth Waldman, *op. cit.*, p. 12.

14. Ahmad Hussein Shamseddine, "GNP Imputations of the Value of Housewives' Services," *The Economic and Business Bulletin* of the School of Business Administration, Temple University (Summer 1968), pp. 53–61.

15. Robert D. Moran, "Reducing Discrimination: Role of the Equal Pay Act," *Monthly Labor Review* (June 1970), pp. 31 ff.

Chapter 5
Shifting Composition of Employment

The dramatic enlargement in the role of women in the work force has coincided with significant declines in the roles of older and younger males. Other changes in the economy have brought increased reliance upon "peripheral" workers whose work patterns differ from those who work full time year-round—namely, they are characterized by intermittent and part-time work as well as much movement in and out of the labor force. There have been important changes, too, in the type of work done—in the occupations and industries in which Americans are employed.

PERIPHERAL WORKERS

While the majority of workers still hold full-time, year-round jobs and account for the bulk of all hours worked, a very substantial number work intermittently. A total of 92.5 million persons were in the labor force during 1969, but only 57 percent were employed more than 35 hours per week (full time) for 50 weeks or more (year-round). Civilian employment averaged 77.9 million, or 14.6 million less than the total number of persons who worked during the year. There were 18.3 million part-time workers and 21.4 million who had full time jobs but worked 49 weeks or less. (Table 5–1).

These 40 million "peripheral" workers [1] include many different groups with diverse employment experiences, but they have much in common. They are usually marginal workers who enter and leave the labor force as

TABLE 5–1 *Work Experience of Persons 16 Years Old and Over, 1969*

	NUMBER (IN THOUSANDS)			PERCENT		
	Both Sexes	*Men*	*Women*	*Both Sexes*	*Men*	*Women*
TOTAL WHO WORKED DURING THE YEAR	92,477	54,390	38,087	100.0	100.0	100.0
Full time [a]	74,153	47,750	26,403	80.2	87.8	69.3
50–52 weeks	52,796	37,160	15,636	57.1	68.3	41.1
48–49 weeks	2,436	1,526	910	2.6	2.8	2.4
40–47 weeks	4,405	2,625	1,780	4.8	4.8	4.7
27–39 weeks	4,540	2,232	2,308	4.9	4.1	6.1
14–26 weeks	4,728	1,944	2,784	5.1	3.6	7.3
13 weeks or less	5,248	2,263	2,985	5.7	4.2	7.8
Part time	18,324	6,640	11,684	19.8	12.2	30.7
50–52 weeks	6,282	2,366	3,916	6.8	4.4	10.3
48–49 weeks	520	189	331	0.6	0.3	0.9
40–47 weeks	1,311	459	852	1.4	0.8	2.2
27–39 weeks	2,281	801	1,480	2.5	1.5	3.9
14–26 weeks	3,275	1,213	2,062	3.5	2.2	5.4
13 weeks or less	4,655	1,612	3,043	5.0	3.0	8.0

[a] Usually worked 35 hours or more a week.
SOURCE: U.S. Bureau of Labor Statistics, *Work Experience of the Population in 1969,* Special Labor Force Report 127, (Washington, D.C.: U.S. Government Printing Office, 1971), Table A-1.

secondary earners. And, for the most part, they toil in low-paying, dead-end jobs (Figure 5–1).

Voluntary Part-Time or Part-Year Work

Voluntary part-time workers deserve separate attention because their number has been growing at a rapid pace, from roughly one-eighth of average full-time workers in 1960 to one-seventh in 1969. This has not happened because of a shortage of full-time jobs, but rather because of a growth in part-time positions which are attractive to those who do not want to work full time.

More than two-thirds of the voluntary part-time workers are female; and three-fifths of these are married and living with their husbands. Overwhelmingly, their jobs are concentrated in the service and retail sectors which accounted for almost three-fourths of the voluntary part-time jobs in 1969. More and more employers are restructuring their operations to use part-time personnel, and married women are increasingly willing to combine part-time work with family care.

In addition to women, who often prefer part-time or part-year jobs,

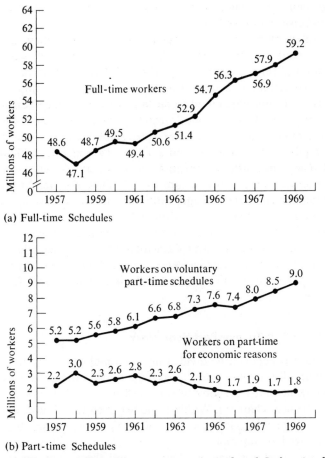

(a) Full-time Schedules

(b) Part-time Schedules

FIGURE 5–1. *Labor Force in Non-Agricultural Industries by Full-Time and Part-Time Status, 1957–1969 (annual averages).*

SOURCE: U.S. Department of Labor.

two other groups account for the bulk of the remaining peripheral workers. (1) Older persons in the process of leaving the labor force are often characterized by limited employability, alternative sources of income, and a desire for less demanding work. (2) And youths and college students are just entering the labor force, supplementing income while attending school, or unable to find full-time, year-round jobs.

Peripheral workers are generally employed in low-wage, low-skill, and low-status occupations. They are agricultural laborers, textile workers, hospital aides, maintenance personnel, and sales people. Their jobs are concentrated in the service and retail sectors with few paying more than the minimum wage, and many paying less. Even when worked full time, these jobs usually yield an income near or below poverty thresholds. Because of unattractive working conditions and low pay, they are characterized by high absenteeism and rapid turnover.

Peripheral workers and the marginal jobs for which they are hired constitute a "secondary labor market" which is different in many ways from the market for full-time, year-round workers. Intermittent work patterns are built into the secondary system. Employers act on the assumption that these employees are not committed to sustained work: Fringe benefits are minimized, little investment is made in training, and opportunities for advancement are closed off. On the other side, employees feel little attachment to their jobs and tend to quit on a moment's notice or without any notice at all. They have little interest in retirement plans or any long-range benefits because they expect their tenure to be limited; they tend to rely on job changes rather than advancements within the firm as a route upward.

This system has different effects on different people. It may fill the need of a wife to get out of the house several afternoons a week or of a college student to earn money over Christmas or during the school year. But it is inimical to the migrant workers and his family who cannot find year-round employment, or the ghetto family head who moves from one dead-end job to another.

Involuntary Part-Time or Part-Year Work

Peripheral workers can be divided into two major groups: those who are employed at full-time jobs interrupted by periods of forced idleness, and those who work at part-time jobs because full-time work is not available (discussed in the next chapter). Within these two groups are those who hold seasonal jobs where unemployment is predictable and regular, those who are underemployed or unemployed for a comparatively short time while searching or preparing for new employment, and those who have serious problems in finding and holding jobs throughout the year.

Certain occupations and industries, especially agriculture and contract construction, have largely seasonal employment patterns. Agriculture is highly seasonal, and though migration can usually extend the working period, unemployment is still frequent. In 1968, more than three-fourths of farm laborers and foremen worked less than 50 weeks, and 45 percent held jobs less than half the year. However, agricultural employment is declining; the number of farm laborers fell from 2.3 million in 1958 to 1.4 million in 1969. Thus, agriculture is becoming a less important factor affecting labor force behavior.

Many of the 43 percent of all workers who held part-year jobs during 1969 found their employment interrupted by periods of forced idleness. Many suffer from serious deficiencies and are unable to find or hold down continuous employment. A growing proportion, however, are those who seek part-time employment because of other interests or concerns.

The employment patterns of these peripheral workers are likely to continue in their recent trends. Seasonal unemployment will diminish as agricultural employment continues to decline, as construction becomes more stable through better planning and the introduction of industrialized methods, and as the number of teenagers looking for summer jobs levels off during the 1970s. Some inroads will probably be made against "frictional unemployment" through improved labor market services; and manpower programs may help those with the severe employment problems—though accelerating technological change could undo any gains which are made. However, part-time employment will probably continue to grow along with expansion of the service sector, not to mention increases in the number of married women seeking part-time work as birth rates remain low. It appears that employment patterns will become more flexible; and, hopefully, the impact of adverse economic factors will be reduced.

YOUTH

In the course of U.S. economic history, the threshold to the world of work has come later and later in life. Children once entered the work force before reaching their teens; today, some youth may reach their mid-20s before entering the labor force permanently. Increased affluence, the steady decline of family farming, and child protection laws have contributed importantly to this trend. These factors, in combination with technological and socioeconomic changes, also have made it much more complicated for young people to pass over the threshold and find a job that provides dignity, an adequate income, and reasonable economic security. And the transition from school to work is made more difficult because young people lack work experience, having devoted their lives to meeting the expanding educational requirements of contemporary jobs. Nor do government and business expend much effort to smooth the way. As a result, some youngsters—especially dropouts—never find the bridge and are doomed to lives of intermittent unemployment between low-pay, high-risk jobs.

Young men and women show divergent trends in labor force participation. Young men's participation has declined dramatically since the turn of the century, largely because of increased school enrollment.[2] Among young girls, participation rates have risen since the end of World War II, probably because of growing job opportunities for part-time workers in retail trade and services. Labor force participation rates of 16- to 24-year-old girls in 1947 and 1970 were as follows:

	Participation Rates	
Age	1947	1970
16–17	29.5%	34.9%
18–19	52.3	53.7
20–24	44.9	57.8

At the same time, the extremely high birth rates of the post-World War II era meant that in the 1960s the number of teenagers (aged 16 to 19) burgeoned from 10.6 million in 1960 to 14.1 million in 1968. As a result, their proportion of the total labor force remained at 4 percent or more, despite further declines in the participation rates of boys.

Pursuit of higher education to qualify for more complex jobs is the main reason for late entry into the labor force. However, some young men are simply discouraged; about 660,000 sixteen- to 21-year-olds, many of them school dropouts, were neither in the labor force nor enrolled in school in 1969. Overrepresented in this category were young black men, many of them living in city slums where the problems of drugs, delinquency, and crime have grown progressively worse in an atmosphere of idle hopelessness. Whatever their special job difficulties, these youngsters are prime candidates for lives of underemployment. Why are such youngsters outside the work force? Some believe that no one would hire them because they are too young.[3] And judging from the unemployment rates of their peers who are in the labor force, this is probably true. Others are waiting to begin military service; many employers will not hire youth who are eligible for the draft. Some have given up entirely or are engaged in illicit pursuits but are not counted among the unemployed, and some depend upon parental support and do not need or care to work.

Among the 16- to 21-year-old males going to school, a little over one-third were in the labor force—mostly working at, or seeking, part-time jobs. Many young men in school and not in the labor force—over 3 million in 1969—would probably like to have some additional income but feel that work is not available.

When employed, teenagers and men in their early 20s tend to be entry-level workers such as laborers, semiskilled operatives, and service workers. A large share work only part time. Teenagers are about three times more likely than mature men to be working in agriculture. The 1968 earnings of employed youth reflected their concentration in low-paying jobs:

Type of Income	All Males	16- to 19- Year-Olds	20- to 24- Year-Olds
Total money income	$6,626	$1,207	$3,896
Year-round, full-time workers' income	8,783	2,994	5,574

Joblessness and job turnover have always been relatively high among younger workers who are adjusting to the world of work. In 1969, a year of very strong demand and tight labor markets, the rate of unemployment for 16- to 24-year-olds averaged 8.4 percent, more than double the rate for persons aged 25 and over. The unemployment situation for black and other minority group youngsters was far worse; their rates ranged upward to levels approximating depression conditions. Obviously, high unemployment and undesirable jobs are critical factors keeping large numbers of young men outside the labor force, regardless of their school status.

In recent years, the younger workers' normal liabilities have been reinforced by the great increases in the numbers of such workers and the continuing erosion of unskilled, entry-level jobs.[4] The proportion of jobs in the less-skilled laborer, operative, and farming occupations has dropped substantially since the late 1940s—from over 4 of every 10 jobs to less than 3 in 10 by 1969. At the same time, the more demanding white-collar positions have risen to nearly 5 in 10 from 3½ in 10. However, this does not necessarily mean that youth employment opportunities have been adversely affected, because education has kept pace with the increased demand for higher skills. Since 1940, the proportion of workers with high-school diplomas has doubled, and the proportion with college degrees has tripled; the median number of school years completed has risen from 9.1 years to 12.3.

Economists disagree over the impact upon youth employment of rising federal minimum wages and broader coverage under the Fair Labor Standards Act. Arguments purporting to show that the FLSA contributed directly to a decline in employment opportunities for youth and that minimum wage provisions are therefore responsible for recent high youth joblessness are not persuasive; but proponents of higher minimum wages have not disproved the claims that statutory minimum wages may have exerted long-run impacts and slowed the growth of those sectors employing youth. Some have proposed, therefore, a dual minimum, with one rate for adults and a lower rate for new entrants into the labor force, under the assumption that the differential will encourage youth employment but still provide meaningful protection.

THE GOLDEN YEARS?

Older Americans, men and women alike, are faced with a bewildering and growing array of socioeconomic problems. Trained and educated in the pre-World War II years, many lack the skills necessary to compete in a highly technical world of work. As a result, many are employed at jobs below their potential skill level; and others have left the work force altogether. Our society takes pride in the recent increases in early retirement for what some call "The Golden Years." This pride is partly misplaced; a large number of older Americans do not have adequate income to sustain a decent standard of living, and many have been forced by unemployment into premature retirement.

Older workers' employment problems spring partly from the failure of employers to recognize the vast accumulation of skill and experience currently going unutilized. Recent estimates place the number of healthy males aged 65 and over at something over 2 million, and there were another half million men 45 to 64 outside the work force. Many of these men are voluntarily retired and have adequate incomes; however, many others have been forced out of the market and are living on substandard incomes.[5]

As with younger workers, sheer population growth among older Americans has offset declining participation rates since the turn of the century, and especially in the post-World War II years. The number of older Americans (aged 55 and over) has increased by more than 50 percent since the end of World War II, rising to about 38 million. High birth and immigration rates before the Great Depression account for much of the increase, but the rise also reflects a longer lifespan brought about by better living, health, and work conditions. These same factors might be expected to stimulate participation by older people, and women seem to have benefited from them. However, men apparently encounter offsetting factors, for the proportion working has declined sharply—especially after age 65, though declining rates are also evident in preretirement years, especially for reasons of poor health.[6] Older men account for a steadily declining proportion of the labor force, even though their percentage of the total population has held quite steady. About 9 million men aged 55 years and over were employed in 1969. They accounted for 11.6 percent of total employment, down from 12.6 percent in 1960 and 13.7 percent in 1947. The number of older persons is expected to increase dramatically to a total of 44 million in 1980—a 70 percent jump from 1950. This increase also should be accompanied by further improvements in health care, permitting an extension of working life.

These large numbers of nonworking retirees would not constitute a serious social and economic problem if they had enough income to assure an adequate standard of living. However, many retirement incomes are inadequate: Nearly 5 million older Americans (aged 65 and over) were living in poverty in 1969 and the income gap for these people seems to be widening.

The crucial retirement age is 65, reflecting the rapid development and liberalization of private and public pension plans. Many workers are retiring even earlier. More than half of those eligible are electing to draw Social Security benefits before age 65. Beyond that age, only one in four older men is in the labor force and, of those working, more than one-third hold part-time jobs. Although these older men usually work part time by choice, they are twice as likely to do so for economic reasons than men in their prime working years.

Older workers are less likely than young workers to move among jobs. The benefits that accrue to seniority (especially job security) are important to older workers, who usually have considerable training, experience, community ties, and company loyalty. In addition, age barriers limit their opportunities for changing jobs. In part because they are less mobile, older workers tend to be concentrated in declining occupations and industries. Many are farmers or self-employed. As a result of this uneven distribution of employment, there are great disparities in the earnings of older men. On the average, however, their earnings are lower than for the next youngest age cohort.[7] This difference is partly due to the tendency for some older workers to work only part-time or part-year; but there are also significant differences among full-time, year-round male workers, as shown in the following tabulation for 1969:

	Age in Years		
Classification	45–54	55–64	65 and over
Median total income, all persons with income	$8,619	$7,279	$2,828
Median income, full-time, year-round workers	9,307	8,399	6,581
Percent of total with incomes of less than $3,000	8.9	17.0	53.6

The unemployment problems of older workers are somewhat unique. Because they have long job tenure, they are less likely to lose their jobs through layoff.[8] But once set adrift from employment, they are apt to be shunted around among low-paying temporary jobs. Not only are there age barriers in hiring, but also older workers often lack adequate training for today's technical jobs. Older workers are thus much more likely than their middle-aged colleagues to have frequent spells of unemployment and to spend many more weeks of fruitless searching for employment (Table 5–2).[9] Faced with this experience, many older workers simply withdraw from the labor force, often without adequate income.[10]

TABLE 5–2   *Frequency and Duration of Unemployment of Persons with Work Experience by Age, 1969*

AGE	PERCENT WITH UNEMPLOYMENT IN 1969	PERCENT WITH		PERCENT UNEMPLOYED	
		2 Spells	3 or More Spells	15 to 26 Weeks	27 Weeks or More
25–34 years	12.4%	13.6%	16.1%	14.9%	5.9%
35–44 years	9.7	16.7	17.4	13.7	7.7
45–54 years	9.0	16.0	18.4	18.8	8.2
55–64 years	7.9	14.5	22.5	19.9	11.3
65 years and older	6.4	15.8	21.2	17.5	17.5

SOURCE: U.S. Bureau of Labor Statistics, *Work Experience of the Population in 1969*, Special Labor Force Report 127, (Washington, D.C.: U.S. Government Printing Office, 1971), Table C-1.

INDUSTRIAL AND OCCUPATIONAL SHIFTS

Shift to Service-Producing, White-Collar Employment

At the turn of the century, 70 percent of all workers were in industries producing physical goods—in agriculture, forestry, fishing, mining, manufacturing, and construction; the rest were in service-producing industries. Seven decades later, the relative importance of the two was nearly reversed, with more than 6 of every 10 workers employed in service-producing industries—wholesale and retail trade, personal and business services, government, transportation and public utilities, finance, insurance, and real estate.

The most notable change has been the persistent decline in farm employment, coupled with the burgeoning of service jobs. After 1950, farm employment declined by about 200,000 annually. In 1953, for the first time, the number of service workers—including cooks, janitors, barbers, practical nurses, firemen, and policemen—equaled the agricultural work force. The gap between the two continued to widen, and by 1970, there were more than three service workers for every farm worker.

The shift from goods-producing to service-producing industries was accompanied by a shift from blue-collar to white-collar occupations. In 1900, white-collar workers accounted for only 18 percent of employment. By 1956, white-collar workers for the first time outnumbered blue-collar workers; now they account for almost half of all employment. The rising demand for white-collar service workers reflects higher standards of living, including better health care, more government services, and more luxuries.

The occupational and industrial shifts were accompanied by pervasive changes that have broad implications for the economic and social structure of the nation. First, the shifts favored occupations requiring more extensive skills and educational attainment. Profound occupational changes have also occurred within the goods-producing industries. Technological and organizational changes have enhanced the importance of nonproduction workers—for example, the white-collar jobs of executives, sales personnel, office workers, engineers—as opposed to blue-collar positions. While there may be disagreements about the net effects of technological advances—whether they have created more jobs than they have eliminated—there is little dispute that the occupational shifts have emphasized higher skills, both at the manual and intellectual level—definitely away from heavy, arduous, unskilled labor. Well known are the examples of coal miners displaced by automatic digging machines, stevedores by hoisting machinery, clerks by automated billing and office machines, and many relatively unskilled hand functions by automated assembly lines.

Second, while the industrial shifts were made possible by increased productivity—fewer farmers, for example, were needed to produce ever increasing quantities of food—the evidence is mounting that the predominance of service industries cannot sustain past rates of growth in productivity. Goods-producing industries, which have large concentrations of blue-collar workers, were able to double their output between 1950 and 1970 with only a small increase of workers. Based on his extensive studies of the service industries, Victor Fuchs has concluded that the growth in productivity per worker since World War II in the goods-producing industries was twice as great as in the service industries; as the proportion of workers engaged in service industries increases, the total economic growth will necessarily decrease.[11]

The movement of millions of workers from goods-producing to service-producing has not slackened demand for labor. The fears or hopes of the prophets of cybernetics have not materialized, and instead of vast numbers of available but unneeded workers, the problem during the last half of the 1960s was more one of labor shortages in highly skilled occupations than surpluses.

Industrial Distribution

Despite the reduced relative importance of employment in goods-producing industries, manufacturing remains the largest single provider of jobs (Table 5–3). Its share of employment grew from 21 percent in 1900 to 30 percent in 1947. Since then the relative importance of manufacturing as a source of jobs has declined to 26 percent of total employment. Nevertheless, manufacturing employment reached an all-time peak in 1969 of over 20 million. The expansion occurred mostly in the durable goods industries, reflecting growing consumer demand for televisions, autos, and other consumer capital goods and, in the 1960s, the immense demands of the Vietnam War.

The major growth in employment occurred in the service-producing industries, with the government sector growing faster than any other major industry in the postwar period. State and local governments account for the largest share of public employees (three of four in 1969) and most of the growth. The federal payroll increased by less than half between 1947 and 1970, while state and local employment more than tripled to nearly 10 million. Two-thirds of the state and local gain during the past decade has been in education (schools account for half of total state and local workers).

Retail and wholesale trade, providing one of every five jobs in 1970, has doubled its share of employment since 1900. This growth has been an important source of employment for women and youth entering the labor force, and it came about despite the industry's increasing reliance on self-service techniques, automatic materials-handling equipment, and vending machines.

Employment in the hetereogenous service industry group—varied per-

TABLE 5–3   *Distribution of Employment by Industry, 1900, 1947, and 1970*

INDUSTRY	1900	1947	1970
TOTAL EMPLOYMENT [a]			
Thousands	26,278	51,772	74,106
Percent	100.0	100.0	100.0
Goods-producing industries	69.7	50.9	36.2
Manufacturing	20.8	30.0	26.2
Durable goods	—	16.2	15.1
Nondurable goods	—	13.8	11.1
Mining	2.4	1.8	0.8
Construction	4.4	3.8	4.5
Agriculture	42.1	15.2	4.7
Service-producing industries	30.2	49.1	63.8
Transportation and utilities	8.7	8.0	6.1
Trade	9.5	17.3	20.2
Wholesale	—	4.6	5.2
Retail	—	12.7	15.0
Finance, insurance, real estate	1.2	3.4	5.0
Services and miscellaneous	6.6	9.8	15.6
Government	4.2	10.6	17.0
Federal	—	3.7	3.7
State and local	—	6.9	13.3

NOTE: Detail may not add to totals due to rounding.
[a] Agriculture includes wage and salary, self-employed, and unpaid family workers. Data for other industries exclude self-employed and unpaid family workers.
SOURCE: Data for 1900 are from C. G. Williams, *Labor Economics* (New York: John Wiley, 1970), p. 1617; data for 1947 and 1970 are from *Employment and Earnings* (March 1971), pp. 21, 49.

sonal, business, health, and private educational services—more than doubled its share of total employment between 1900 and 1970. Private medical and health services experienced the largest gain, with private hospital employment accounting for about half that expansion; this reflects higher standards of health care and extension of private medical insurance plans as well as Medicare for the aged and Medicaid for those on welfare.

Occupational Distribution

Technological innovation, together with the shift from goods-producing to service-producing industries, caused significant occupational changes (Table 5–4). Employment growth in professional and technical occupations has outdistanced that of all other occupational groups in recent

TABLE 5–4   *Distribution of Employment by Occupation,[a] 1900, 1950, and 1970*

OCCUPATION	1900	1950	1970
TOTAL			
Thousands	29,030	58,999	78,627
Percent	100.0	100.0	100.0
White-collar workers	17.6	36.6	48.3
Professional and technical	4.3	8.6	14.2
Managers, officials and			
proprietors, except farm	5.8	8.7	10.5
Clerical	3.0	12.3	17.4
Sales	4.5	7.0	6.2
Blue-collar workers	35.8	41.1	35.3
Craftsmen and foremen	10.5	14.1	12.9
Operatives and kindred	12.8	20.4	17.7
Laborers, except farm and mine	12.5	6.6	4.7
Service workers	9.0	10.5	12.4
Private household	5.4	2.6	2.0
Service workers, except private			
household	3.6	7.9	10.4
Farm workers	37.5	11.8	4.0
Farmers and farm managers	19.9	7.4	2.2
Farm laborers and foremen	17.7	4.4	1.7

[a] Not directly comparable. Figures for 1970 are employed persons 16 years and older; for 1900, gainful workers; and for 1950, labor force figures.
SOURCE: U.S. Department of Labor, *Manpower Report of the President* (Washington, D.C.: U.S. Government Printing Office, 1970), p. 226 and *Employment Earnings* (January 1971), p. 127.

decades. Nearly all professional fields have registered gains, but increases have been especially large in teaching, accounting, the health professions, social and welfare work, engineering and scientific work, and computer-related occupations. To put these professions in perspective, teaching is the largest group with almost a quarter of all professionals, followed by engineering.

Clerical occupations are the largest employers of white-collar workers; and their share of total employment has increased almost sixfold since the turn of the century, compared with a threefold increase for all professional jobs. The increase occurred despite the labor-saving effects of computers and new office equipment—testifying to the mounting volume of paper work in business and government. Women hold about three-fourths of all clerical jobs, and about one-third of all employed women are clerical workers. The largest group of clerical workers are stenographers, secretaries, and typists —more than 95 percent of whom are women. Much of the expansion in clerical employment has been in part-time jobs, positions desired by many married women.

Despite fears that the advent of mass production and automation would reduce the need for skilled manual workers, blue-collar employment has continued to grow, with the largest increase among craftsmen and foremen. Manufacturing employs a greater number of craftsmen than any other industry group, but in construction craftsmen form a higher proportion of employees—one-half, compared with one-fifth in manufacturing and transportation, and fewer than one-tenth in other industries. Operatives and kindred workers, or semiskilled employees, remain the single largest occupational group, with about 14 million workers in 1970, or almost one-fifth of all employment. Operatives in factories account for three of five semiskilled workers; among the nonfactory operatives, the largest group are drivers of trucks, buses, and taxicabs. Over the first half of this century, operatives' employment increased sharply as technological innovations shifted industries to mass production processes which used this type of labor. As these processes became well established, more sophisticated advances—including automation—slowed down that employment growth.

Service occupations, except in private households, have grown faster in the past decade than total employment; protective (fire and police), health, and food service workers have registered the largest gains. The demand for service workers, as does the demand for service-producing industries, reflects increasing leisure and higher levels of income.

NOTES

1. Dean Morse, *The Peripheral Worker* (New York: Columbia University Press, 1969).

2. Jacob Mincer, "Labor Force Participation and Unemployment: A Review of Recent Evidence," in Robert and Margaret Gordon, eds., *Prosperity and Unemployment* (New York: John Wiley, 1966), pp. 73–112.

3. Robert Stein, "Reasons for Nonparticipation in the Labor Force," *Monthly Labor Review* (July 1967), p. 26.

4. Edward Kalachek, *The Youth Labor Market* (Ann Arbor, Mich.: Institute of Labor and Industrial Relations, University of Michigan, January 1969), p. 55.

5. National Council on the Aging's National Institute on Industrial Gerontology, *Employment Aspects of the Economics of Aging,* U.S. Senate Special Committee on Aging, 91st Cong., 1st Sess. (Washington, D.C.: U.S. Government Printing Office, December 1969).

6. Herbert Parnes, *et al., The Pre-Retirement Years,* U.S. Department of Labor, Manpower Administration, Manpower Research Monograph No. 15 (Washington, D.C.: U.S. Government Printing Office, 1970) [cf. p. 21, n. 17], Vol. II, p. 7.

7. U.S. Bureau of the Census, *Current Population Reports,* Series P-60, No. 75, "Income in 1969 of Families and Persons in the United States," (Washington, D.C.: U.S. Government Printing Office, 1970), Table 45.

8. Edward O'Boyle, "Job Tenure: How It Relates to Race and Age," *Monthly Labor Review* (September 1969), p. 18.

9. U.S. Bureau of Labor Statistics, *Work Experience of the Population in 1969,* Special Labor Force Report 127 (Washington, D.C.: U.S. Government Printing Office, 1971).

10. Lenore Bixby and Eleanor Rings, "Work Experience of Men Claiming Retirement Benefits in 1966," *Social Security Bulletin* (August 1969).

11. Victor R. Fuchs, *The Service Economy* (New York: National Bureau of Economic Research and Columbia University Press, 1968), p. 47.

Shifting Composition of Employment   69

8. Edward Kaplan, "Job Trends: More Polish, Less In-House, and Sign of ... by Labor Pools, September 1969, p. 14.

...

70

Chapter 6
Measurement
and Forecasting

Sophisticated measurement techniques and extensive data gathered over the years by governmental and private organizations have given us a clearer picture of the changing patterns of American work. As a nation we have been fortunate in having such extensive data, although there is room for improvement. The challenge is to interpret the data wisely and apply the lessons learned to achieve societal goals.

MEASUREMENT OF THE LABOR FORCE—
MANPOWER STATISTICS

The United States has the most comprehensive flow of labor market information of any nation. Each month the Bureau of Labor Statistics, working with other federal, state, and private organizations, collects and publishes a detailed history of the previous month's labor market activity.[1] These analyses and statistical reports include reliable estimates of (a) the size, marital status, and demographic composition of the population aged 16 years and over; (b) the number of workers by occupation, hours worked, age, sex, and color; (c) the number of filled jobs in nonfarm industries and average weekly hours and earnings for nonsupervisory personnel; (d) the total number of persons actively seeking work and the number drawing jobless pay; the extent of strike activity, recent collective bargaining settlements, and pending negotiations; and (e) trends in wages, productivity, and unit labor costs. The most recent addition to the list is a monthly report on job vacancies in manufacturing.

Other federal agencies provide information on (a) total income flow earned from both past and present work; (b) investments in training, especially formal education; (c) employment in select sectors of the economy (e.g., manufacturing) or by profession (e.g., scientific and technical personnel); and special analytical measures such as full-time equivalent employment and income.

Special data have been developed to supplement the recurring monthly and annual data. These special studies, which are designed mainly to portray labor market interactions at more detailed levels, include surveys of the poverty population (e.g., the Survey of Economic Opportunity) and longitudinal labor force participation and work-experience studies.

Because of the great expansion of labor market information and research in the past two decades, analysts can verify most labor market measures by comparison with an alternative, totally independent source. Until 1940, there were no reliable estimates of the current employment status of the population aside from the decennial censuses, and even that information had serious conceptual flaws for the analysis of labor market conditions.

This vast flow of manpower data, collected from thousands of homes and firms, comprises a keystone for the formulation and implementation of monetary and fiscal policies and federal, state, municipal, and private manpower programs. These same data figure prominently in business research and planning and in private research.

Major Data Sources

The manpower statistics now in wide use originate from three major sources: (a) *household interviews,* including decennial censuses, monthly current population surveys, and special household surveys; (b) *employer surveys,* including industry censuses, monthly payroll reports from individual firms, and special industrial studies; and (c) *documentary or administrative statistics* drawn from the operating records of the Social Security Administration, the Manpower Administration, the Office of Economic Opportunity, and various regulatory organizations such as the Interstate Commerce Commission. Each source has its own strengths, weaknesses, and unique conceptual and methodological properties. Together, however, these sources provide a network of manpower information which, while different in collection technique and concept, is unmatched in its detail which satisfies quantitative requirements for macroanalysis while providing a considerable body of microanalytical data.

Manpower Statistics Before World War II

The decennial census, required by the Constitution to help apportion representatives among states, was not intended to provide manpower information. It did, however, furnish data on population, the human resource base from which all manpower analysis departs. By the mid-1800s, tidbits of economic intelligence, notably industrial employment estimates, were beginning to be collected in the decennial censuses.[2] In each subsequent census, the volume of employment information was expanded and refined as new departments and agencies sought to cope with the problems of a growing nation. Designed for other purposes (mainly political apportionment and tax assessment), the censuses became a vehicle for the collection of manpower data and are virtually the only source of national socioeconomic information for the 1800s. Because of collection and definitional weaknesses, these early employment data are of very limited value in economic analysis.[3]

Employment figures gathered in the censuses of the early 1900s were based on the so-called gainful worker concept. Individuals were recorded as gainfully employed if they reported a trade (occupation) that provided money income or its equivalent. This concept had no time reference and therefore tended to exclude unemployment—most of the unemployed had held a job of one kind or another—and to inflate the employment figures further because those who had retired also had a gainful occupation. During the late 1930s, the gainful worker concept—which provided a useful inventory of occupational skills—was displaced by the more precise activity-oriented concept now in use.

SOCIAL PROBLEMS
AND STATISTICAL DEVELOPMENT

Most present-day manpower information systems were by-products of programs designed for other needs, or else thrown together in response to large-scale socioeconomic crises. As a result, available manpower information has grown erratically—almost haphazardly—and has taken a distinctly social rather than economic orientation. Major developments and improvements of manpower statistics closely followed and largely resulted from the Great Depression of the 1930s, the cumulative recessions of the 1950s, and the overriding concern of federal officials with the nature and origins of the poverty in the late 1960s.

The state of other arts also affected the evolution of the information network. Breakthroughs in communications, data processing, methods of statistical analysis, new methods of data collection, sampling techniques, and other factors played an important role in the growth of manpower data systems, as did the consolidation of the reporting and analysis of manpower information in the Department of Labor in the late 1950s.

There has always been a certain ambivalence in the collection and analysis of employment and unemployment statistics, arising from differences in the objectives of the users. Some analysts, concerned with the welfare implications which may be drawn from the statistics, focus attention on the conditions and availability of jobs, with special reference to the impact of unemployment. More recently, manpower data have been used extensively in analyzing resource use, with a special view to the elimination of labor bottlenecks and promotion of long-term growth. Oscillations between the two views have coincided with cyclical swings in unemployment.

Based on the old practice of blaming the messenger for the bad news, it was inevitable that the collectors of manpower statistics would be criticized by some when they reported unwelcome news. During the election of 1960, the credibility of the employment and unemployment figures came under severe analytical and political attack. After the election, President Kennedy appointed a panel of experts to appraise the employment and unemployment statistics.

The Gordon Committee

The presidential committee chaired by Professor R. A. Gordon— hence, the Gordon Committee—interpreted its mandate widely. It examined and reported on the concepts, techniques, prospects, and problems involved in all major manpower data series then in existence.[4] The Committee's report was significant mainly because it synthesized past statistical experience and clarified certain conceptual and methodological problems and recommendations for the future development of manpower information systems along resource-use lines. The report set the tone for the further development of labor market statistics in the 1960s and 1970s. Aside from its substantive contributions, the Gordon Committee gave the collectors of manpower data a clean bill of health and made special efforts to remove manpower data collection from further political disputes.

Concepts and Sources: Their Current Status

The concept of employment used in manpower statistics is based essentially on remuneration, not work. The labor force statistics therefore exclude the work of housewives, students, and volunteers. Also excluded from the manpower statistics are groups engaged in illicit occupations. The latter exclusions are based not on conceptual or moral objections, but rather on the difficulties in obtaining such data. Nonetheless, the unmeasured activities are important and result in serious gaps. The annual gross revenue accruing to organized crime is variously estimated at $10 to $60 billion, and some states, such as New York, are now moving to capture some of this income by legalizing and regulating gambling. The services of housewives are also vital, providing the minimum equivalent of $180 billion in unpaid domestic service annually. Volunteer work is also very important, involving during a typical period the equivalent of about 900,000 full-time, year-round workers. Because of the large outputs generated by these "nonemployment" activities, it is important to remember that employment figures used in manpower analysis are based on a definition that embraces mainly *reported* pay or profits.

EMPLOYMENT   The oldest continuous employment series is the *payroll employment* data, which date back to 1919. These data, which include all forms of wage and salary employment in private firms, government units and nonprofit organizations, are relatively easy and inexpensive to collect. It is a highly reliable count of all filled jobs—the numbers are taken directly from payroll records—and provides consistent national, regional, state, and city figures on the number of jobs in a wide variety of industries. This monthly series is the best source of information on trends in wage and salary employment and a major source of information on hours of work paid for, average hourly and weekly wages of production and nonsupervisory workers, and labor turnover (total hiring and total separations) in manufacturing. Compiled from mail questionnaires, the series covers a sample of firms employing about 30 million workers.

Some kinds of work do not fit in the "establishment" employment definitions because they do not appear on a "normal" payroll record. Included are the self-employed, domestics working in private homes, unpaid family workers, and agricultural workers. Employment estimates for these groups are drawn largely from household surveys and administrative statistics.

Wage and salary employment is also measured in the *monthly household survey* (Current Population Survey). Because of conceptual and methodological differences the count of persons with wage and salary *employment* differs from the number of jobs counted on payroll records.[5] The most important difference is multiple job holding—a person may hold two jobs but is only counted once in the household survey. There are also differences attributable to unpaid absences from work. If no payroll entry occurs for a person, then no payroll job is recorded in the survey of firms. However, he is counted as employed in the household survey if he is away on an unpaid vacation, personal business, on strike, or for similar reasons.

The household survey is wider in scope than the establishment data. It covers all forms of employment, including self-employment, unpaid family workers, private household workers, and agriculture—all of which are excluded from the industry employment estimates based on employer reports. Each of these sets of data makes a unique contribution to the understanding of employment trends. The industry survey is strong on industry and geographic detail, while the household data are strong on characteristics of the employed, including age, sex, education, and occupation.

UNEMPLOYMENT   The unemployment rate has an enormous impact on government policy and public opinion, but it is one of the least understood and most controversial statistics issued by the government. No single definition of what constitutes unemployment has ever been devised that is acceptable to all political and economic groups. The unemployment statistic used today is rooted in the Great Depression. When mass unemployment in the 1930s illuminated the need for reliable current statistics, experiments with household (or population) surveys were begun. These efforts were sound in design but lacked the necessary objectivity because the definition of unemployment was based on a person's reported willingness and ability to work. The concept was dependent on the interpretation and attitudes of both the interviewer and interviewee. A more objective and rigorous standard had to be devised. A small group of economists, statisticians, and sociologists in the Works Progress Administration developed a more objective measure based on actual activity during a specified week. Responsibility for the national sample survey (begun in 1940) was ultimately passed to the Bureau of the Census, and the survey (now the Current Population Survey) continues to utilize essentially the same concepts and methods today.

CURRENT POPULATION SURVEY (CPS)   Although technical in detail, the concepts and definitions used in the Current Population Survey are very simple. The labor force consists of all employed and unemployed persons who are at least 16 years old. For purposes of the survey, people are counted as employed if they worked during the survey week for pay or profit or worked 15 hours or more in a family enterprise. People who had regular jobs but were temporarily absent during the survey week for such reasons as vacation, illness, strikes, or bad weather are also counted as employed. Specifically excluded are those whose activity was confined to work around the house (mainly housewives) or to unpaid volunteer work for charitable organizations. Unemployed persons are those who were not working during the reference period, were available for work and had engaged in specific work-seeking activity within the prior four weeks, were waiting to be called back from layoff, or were waiting to report to a new job beginning within 30 days.

The CPS is limited to a very definite group composed of working-age (16 years and over) civilians who are not in institutions. Because it is useful to know the importance of defense demands on the manpower supply, official figures from the Department of Defense on the size of the armed forces are added to the civilian work force to provide an estimate of the total labor force. Persons who are neither employed nor unemployed—

mostly housewives, students, disabled, and retired workers—are considered "not in the labor force."

Monthly employment and unemployment data are obtained by skilled interviewers from a sample survey of about 50,000 households. At the Bureau of the Census, data from the sample households (for the calendar week including the nineteenth of the month) are then "blown up" to national totals. Most data from this CPS are cross-classified by demographic characteristics such as age, sex, color, marital status, occupation, hours of work, and duration of and reasons for unemployment. The survey also provides data on the characteristics and past work experience of those not in the labor force.

The CPS also yields information on topics of special interest through supplemental questions each month. In the various months, questions dealing with such matters as work experience in the prior year, income, marital and family status, and multiple job holding are explored. Most contemporary labor market analysis is based on material drawn from CPSs or the decennial census.[6]

ADMINISTRATIVE STATISTICS   Administrative statistics tend to reflect the peculiarities of the program for which they are collected and therefore cannot be conveniently lumped into a simple classification scheme. Important labor market data are derived from Social Security files and from insured unemployment coverage and claims records. Both programs are limited in coverage but provide detailed data of considerable analytical significance. The Social Security figures cover employment by size of firm, geographic location of employment, and some earnings data. Insured unemployment claims—persons reporting a week of unemployment under an unemployment insurance program—comprise a cyclically sensitive crosscheck of the total unemployment estimates and are available in considerable geographic detail. However, unemployment insurance data do not measure total unemployment because they exclude persons who have exhausted their benefit rights, who have not earned rights to unemployment insurance, and who have lost jobs not covered by unemployment insurance.

Program Needs

Despite improvements brought about by the Gordon Committee report and the recent introduction of new data series growing out of the concern with poverty, important gaps remain in our knowledge of labor market interactions. Possibly the most significant omissions are data on underemployment—which would provide insights on short workweeks, productivity and low earnings, the extent of employment below capabilities and, most important of all, some reasonable assessment of the real social and economic costs of underemployment. Such an effort would, of course, involve difficult statistical and definitional problems, and the potential use of the data to affect social policy is bound to raise controversy. Yet the costs of not fully assessing underutilized labor supplies may well be greater than currently supposed. The social disruptions that occurred in the 1960s strongly suggest that society cannot continue to ignore the inequities implicit in the highly unequal pattern of economic opportunity. Low national unemployment rates are no reason for complacency if that low rate coexists with substantial involuntary nonparticipation or underutilization of women, younger workers, older workers, and minority groups.

Data on worker motivation, while important, are largely absent from governmental labor market information. Attitudinal data directed at assessing the determinants of work-seeking activity, development of job skills, and the desire to achieve are increasingly important to adequate decision making and policy planning in our complex yet fragmented society. It may prove dangerous to ignore the ghettos and campuses, which are promoting attitudes and actions that seemingly divert sectors of the population from the mainstream of American life. Attitudinal studies should also recognize the pervading significance of industrial peace and provide employers and unions with a notion of the kinds of job restructuring, administrative changes, and reward systems necessary to give the worker a greater stake in his job and company. Obviously, such a departure from the traditional modes of labor market analysis and data collection would require fuller development of interdisciplinary research, drawing heavily on the training and techniques of psychologists, sociologists, and political scientists.

FORECASTING MANPOWER SUPPLIES AND REQUIREMENTS [7]

The Employment Act of 1946 stimulated interest in the size of the labor force for which jobs were to be provided "for all of those able, willing and seeking to work." In the 1950s, creeping unemployment, often attributed to a mismatch between available and demanded skills, intensified the need to foresee changes in manpower supply and demand. The development of new manpower programs in the mid-1960s increased demands for advance information about manpower changes. At its best, forecasting is a critical ingredient in advance planning, encouraging the realistic appraisal of the likely costs and benefits of differing programs to facilitate a reasonable distribution of scarce resources. It is also used for individual career planning, market research, policy evaluation, and analysis of socioeconomic objectives.

The Nature of Manpower Projections

Projections and forecasts are often differentiated, but in reality the difference lies in the confidence of the forecaster. After examining past trends, the projector develops a working model of the system. Assumptions about how the important variables are likely to behave in the future are developed and then applied to extend the past performance of relevant variables. Accuracy in projections is largely a function of the realism of the assumptions and the identification of all relevant variables; consequently, the cardinal sin of the projector is failure to make his assumptions explicit. Confusion also stems from failure to differentiate between descriptive projections (what is likely to be) and normative projections (what ought to be). Users of projections must take note of the underlying assumptions and appraise their validity; they should avoid reading into long-range forecasts an implied commitment to an imputed straight-line trend at intermediate points.

In the United States, projectors generally emphasize descriptions that may enable decision makers to make more rational decisions. As various forms of public planning become more accepted in the United States, policy makers will be forced into more serious consideration of the manpower implications of their decisions.

In summary, forecasts are based on implicit and explicit assumptions concerning the nature and direction of future trends. Because anticipated expectations are rarely met, forecasts should be regarded as "most likely" approximations. With all these caveats, competent long-range manpower supply and demand forecasts can nonetheless influence decision making because they (a) illuminate likely bottlenecks and imbalances in particular segments of the labor market, (b) indicate the likely consequences of instituting changes in existing programs or introducing new programs, and (c) provide an estimate of the total manpower resource "pie" by helping to "price out" societal goals in manpower terms, to choose among these goals when necessary, and to move them along the least-cost path.

Projecting Manpower Supplies and Requirements

Forecasts may be calculated in a wide variety of ways, ranging in complexity from simple linear extrapolation of past trends to complex econometric models. Each technique has its own special properties of detail, conditional restraints, and applicability to reality.[8] Because they are based on known population levels and long-standing trends in labor force participation, projections of the potential total labor supply are quite reliable. Unfortunately, no reliable base exists from which to project labor supplies by skill level or any qualitative element other than educational attainment. Thus, few attempts are made to project the supply of skills. However, this is not a serious loss, since few jobs have fixed skill requirements. Most employers vary their requirements to suit the state of the labor market, while the workers' mobility renders projections of supply by occupation and industry of little value.

Because employment levels in modern economies are in large part the consequence of public policy, levels of labor demand are subject to guess. Projectors have resorted to two major approaches, with little practical difference between them. One is to assume a level of unemployment based either on a normative or descriptive judgment. The other is to project GNP on the basis of assumed future growth rates and estimate the consequent employment. Neither method is very reliable, but in any event the purposes of the manpower analyst are usually best served by projections of the *structure* of labor demand rather than the *level* of total demand.

In projecting the structure of manpower requirements, total assumed GNP is distributed among industries on the basis of further assumptions as to national economic goals. These are translated into anticipated patterns of consumption, investment, and government spending. Projecting requirements is especially difficult because the priorities assigned to national goals may change radically. The unexpected appearance of Sputnik and the resulting massive mobilization of scientific and technical personnel in the space program in the 1960s illustrates a radical alteration of national priorities which affected the composition of manpower demand. In addition, goals are heavily determined by private units which may sharply and quickly change their demand patterns. Finally, innovations may alter the composition of labor demand and also modify the relative significance of different goals. Despite these difficulties, analysts are increasingly engaged in assessing the likely patterns of demand, relating these demands to manpower requirements, and measuring the requirements against the anticipated supply.

Overall manpower forecasts, therefore, usually involve a two-pronged effort. On one side, technicians—demographers, statisticians, and economists—develop detailed projections of the probable labor supply in its quantitative and even qualitative aspects. On the other side, policy makers articulate needs, specify goals, and establish a scheme of priorities. The broad estimates are then brought together, yielding a view of the likely future interaction of labor supply and demand.

Uses of Manpower Projections

A major concern of government is to avoid mismatches between manpower demands and supplies. Clearly, the minimum level of unemployment attainable with "tolerable" inflation and the speed with which its can be achieved are affected by the degree to which open jobs match the qualifications of available workers. This requires more detailed and reliable short-term and medium-term projections of the labor supply by age, sex, race, and skill than are currently available. In fact, usable projections are largely limited to long-term forecasts of the total supply of labor. These projections may also provide warning, however. For example, projected age, race, and sex characteristics of the labor force portend growing imbalances between manpower demand and supply unless traditional employment patterns are substantially altered.[9] If the rates at which younger workers and blacks are penetrating certain occupations fail to increase substantially, unemployment of these groups will be significantly worsened in the years ahead. Providing warnings of projected shortages (or surpluses) of teachers, medical personnel, or scientists and engineers also is a familiar use of these long-term projections.

Less familiar is the increasing demand for manpower projections created by three policy developments. First, welfare- and education-oriented programs require assessment of manpower requirements as well as dollar costs so that potential manpower bottlenecks can be noted and efforts made to avoid them. Second, the expanded role of government in the economy has increased the need to foresee the impact on manpower of government decisions, especially those involving defense and space efforts. Both civilian and federal employment declined with reduced Asian military involvement in 1970, creating substantial unemployment among skilled scientific and engineering personnel as well as among young men leaving the armed forces. Such cases illuminated the need for contingency plans to generate jobs for these diverse groups. Third, the threat of major technological change has aroused some interest in projections of regional, industrial, and occupational employment fluctuations. Such "early warning" signals might stimulate advance planning to ease the adjustment to change. The recession of 1970 indicated that little progress has been made in this area.

Educational planners, involved in decisions concerning physical facilities, finances, and curricula, are among those most persistently demanding projections of the manpower future. Fortunately, the required projections are not as difficult as might be assumed. Buildings have a long life, but they exercise little constraint on curriculum choices, and financial needs depend primarily on the number of students. Curriculum planning requires relatively little lead time or detail because curricula are relatively uniform in elementary schools and high schools and, even at the college levels, concentrations are sufficiently broad to require comparatively little detailed anticipation of occupational choices.

Vocational education and apprenticeship are oriented to specific occupations and thus require detailed projections of the employment outlook. But the number needed for replacement and industry expansion almost always exceeds the number trained, and the gap is flexibly filled by those who pick up the trade outside the formal channels. The more specific the occupational training required, of course, the greater the need for projections. But lack of projections is probably less of a barrier to planning than structural and institutional difficulties: (a) Budgetary constraints are more to blame than is lack of information for the oft-noted (but probably exaggerated) obsolescence of vocational-school equipment and curricula; (b) more information is available than is used; (c) there are no overwhelming obstacles to reasonably accurate two- to five-year projections of local manpower requirements; and (d) planning should not be based entirely on local projections—from a national viewpoint, for example, it would make sense to allocate expenditures in declining regions for vocational education deliberately aimed at providing training for future outmigrants.

Projection needs for counseling and guidance parallel those of educational planning. Persistent youth unemployment has caused dissatisfaction with the information available for counseling and making vocational choices. The standard source is the *Occupational Outlook Handbook,*[10] a BLS publication which projects, in terms of general trends, employment in nearly 700 specific occupations for roughly a decade ahead. The *Handbook* has gained wide acceptance by educational counselors.

Labor Supplies in 1980–1985

The working-age population (aged 16 years and over) will total about 166 million in 1980 and about 176 million in 1985. The projection that the labor force will reach 100 million in 1980 may be made with considerable confidence. This means an average annual increase in the labor force of 1.5 million throughout the 1970s, compared with average annual increases of about 1.3 million between 1960 and 1968.[11]

Labor force growth is expected to slow down after 1980 because the working-age population will increase by only 1.9 million annually between 1980 and 1985, compared with about 2.4 million annually prior to 1980. This slowing of population growth is definite because all the people who will reach working age between 1980 and 1985 have already been born. This anticipated growth in the work force also reflects changes in participation rates because total participation in the labor force tends to change relatively slowly, although population changes generally are more important over the longer run.[12]

The labor force changes constantly, renewing itself as older workers retire and are replaced by younger workers and reentrants. Achievement of the projected labor force growth by 1980 means that nearly 41 million workers will enter the labor force and over 26 million will retire, die, or quit working after 1968.[13] The gross increase will be accounted for mainly by new young workers seeking their first job, although about 15 percent of the increase will be reentrants, mainly women returning to the labor market after starting a family.

These gross flows will result in very large labor force increases for adults, both male and female. The number of teenagers in the labor force will rise much more slowly in the 1970s than in the 1960s, and, after 1980, the teenage labor force will actually decline, reflecting the slow rate of population growth of the 1960s. In the late 1950s, the BLS correctly projected rapid expansion in teenage work force and suggested a probable deterioration of their employment situation. The slow growth and ultimate decline in their labor force in the 1970s and 1980s may improve the job opportunities for teenagers. At the same time, however, the number of black youths will increase by over 40 percent. To a large degree, such youngsters have almost no suitable job opportunities in today's labor market. With labor force growth accelerating, much greater efforts must be mounted to draw such youngsters into the mainstream of economic activity.

The number of 20- to 24-year-olds—which increased very rapidly during the late 1960s—should also begin to slow appreciably by mid-decade, and the group is expected to remain virtually stable between 1980 and 1985. During the 1960s, young people under the age of 25 accounted for about half of total labor force expansion. In the 1970s, they are expected to account for about one-fourth of labor force growth, and between 1980 and 1985, their number in the work force will drop.

Labor force increases for persons just over 25 years of age are going to be one of the dramatic and productive labor force changes of the 1970s. The same persons who flooded labor markets as teenagers and young adults in the 1960s—and in many instances were not absorbed for a long time—will now appear as highly educated, full-time, year-round workers. In particular, the number of 25- to 34-year-old workers will increase enormously in the next decade—by about 800,000 a year, or nearly 50 percent, to more than 26 million in 1980. By 1980, one out of every four workers will be in this age group in comparison with about one in every five in 1969.

The number of workers aged 35–44 will show only a fractional increase prior to 1980 and then, reflecting the same World War II baby boom, will surge dramatically. During the 1970s, the supply of these workers will increase only moderately. The number of workers aged 45 years and over is expected to increase by only 1 million in the 1970s, compared to 3 million in the 1960s. This smaller rise reflects the comparatively few people born in the depths of the Great Depression. There is a problem here, of course, in the form of a potential large shortage of skilled senior managers and professionals. Younger workers will have to be advanced rapidly during the 1970s and groomed to take on greater responsibility earlier than their fathers and grandfathers—a development the younger workers are likely to welcome.

Dramatic changes are ordained in the average educational attainment of the labor force. The entrance of better-educated young workers at the same time that older, less-educated workers are retiring continues to tip the balance toward a higher and higher average educational attainment for the nation's working force. By 1980, more than seven in ten persons in the adult labor force (aged 25 years and over) will have graduated at least from high school, and more than one in six (about 13 million) will have completed four years or more of college work—compared with 36 percent high-school graduates and 14 percent college graduates or higher in the 1969 labor force. This increase in educational endowment is an important part of the expected rise in productivity in the years ahead.[14]

Labor force increases for blacks will probably continue to be relatively larger than for whites in the 1970s, especially among younger workers and adult males. The black labor force is expected to rise by more than one-fourth by 1980, compared with an increase of about one-sixth in the white labor force. The rapid rate of growth—which reflects a sharp population increase—raises the possibility of exacerbating the already high unemployment rates for nonwhite workers. However, higher levels of educational attainment and progress toward equal employment opportunities may combine to produce further improvements in the employment status of blacks.

Some Implications

The major conclusions of the new labor force projections are that (a) the rate of growth of the labor force in the 1970s will be about the same as during the preceding decade; (b) the teenage labor force, with its myriad of special problems, will grow much more slowly in the coming decade (the 20- to 24-year-olds will also increase by less than in the 1960s, so that the number of workers under 25 years of age will no longer show the largest and most rapid growth); and (c) young adults, aged 25–34, will grow at a dramatic rate, while the increase of workers 35 and over will be very small.

These projections have important implications. The expected overall growth of the labor force should provide more than an adequate manpower base for continued rapid expansion of national output, while the rising educational endowment of the labor force offers substantial potential for increasing productivity and the rate of economic growth. The increased supply of educated workers should help relieve skilled-worker and white-collar bottlenecks caused by a shortage of mature workers. Unemployment problems for the young should be reduced because fewer youths will compete for jobs, while opportunities for advancement by younger workers to higher levels may improve because the supply of mature workers is likely to be stretched thin. However, increased education and training do not automatically mean the end of skilled manpower shortages, or of youth unemployment. Sending more youngsters to college will not train the plumbers, electricians, or other skilled workers who are in short supply; overemphasis on college education for white-collar jobs—which may pay less, have longer hours, and require little preparation—presents the real possibility that some young people are being "overeducated." As a result, they may lack jobs commensurate with their education at the same time that skilled jobs go unfilled.

For the less educated, the number of jobs available may decline while their number in the labor force continues large. Moreover, with the supply of educated workers rising, entry-level job requirements may be adjusted up as employers perceive the rise of the educational endowment of the work force. Thus, despite their dwindling number, the nation cannot be complacent about the undereducated and untrained: Manpower and retraining programs will need to be expanded to correct these serious deficiencies.

National Goals

Stripped to the bare essentials, the national economic objectives include:

1. a high and rising standard of living for all citizens
2. continuing investment in productive equipment
3. investment in humans
   (a) education, including manpower training
   (b) health
   (c) income protection and personal economic safety
4. investment in public goods
   (a) transportation systems
   (b) housing, community development, and preservation of environment
   (c) public safety, including police and fire protection
   (d) research and exploration, including space
5. adequate national defense programs.

Leonard Lecht and other analysts working at the National Planning Association converted these general goals into manpower costs and related them to the likely configuration of the manpower supply in the years ahead. They concluded that full achievement of 15 goals (plus space exploration) specified by a presidential commission [15] would require about 12 percent more workers than are expected to be in the labor force in the mid-1970s.[16] Thus, even the large increases in the labor supply of the 1970s are likely to be inadequate to meet our expanding needs and desires. In a sense, this is fortunate because it implies that vigorous pursuit of national goals will yield a continuing strong demand for labor—with the favorable possibility of relatively full employment, upgrading of workers, and progress in eliminating discrimination.

Within the context of national economic aspirations and the output potential dictated by employment and productivity growth, it is possible to project the supply and demand estimates for various skills (Table 6–1). The latest estimates suggest that manpower requirements for professional and technical workers will increase by 37 percent between 1970 and 1980, with the strongest demands in the computer fields and health occupations. Shortages in the health occupations are likely to persist in the 1970s as the supply continues to grow more slowly than the demands. The demand for technicians is also expected to be strong, increasing about twice as rapidly as overall labor demand. This will reflect both the increasing sophis-

TABLE 6–1   *Projected Occupational Employment, 1980 (in thousands)*

OCCUPATION	1970	1980	PERCENT CHANGE
White collar	37,997	48,300	27.1%
Professional and technical	11,140	15,500	39.1
Managers, officials, and proprietors	8,289	9,500	14.6
Clerical workers	13,714	17,300	26.1
Sales workers	4,854	6,000	23.6
Blue collar	27,791	31,100	11.9
Craftsmen and foremen	10,158	12,200	20.1
Operatives	13,909	15,400	10.7
Nonfarm laborers	3,724	3,500	− 6.0
Service workers	9,712	13,100	34.9
Farm workers	3,126	2,600	−16.8

SOURCE: *Employment and Earnings* (January 1971), p. 126, and U.S. Bureau of Labor Statistics, *The U.S. Economy in 1980: A Summary of BLS Projections,* Bulletin 1673 (Washington, D.C.: U.S. Government Printing Office, 1970), p. 57.

tication of machinery and changes in the growth rates of various industries. In order to meet this demand, additional post-high-school training will have to be provided.[17] A similar analysis for teachers yields a different conclusion. The diminished birth rates of the 1960s, coupled with a sharp rise in the number of college graduates specializing in education, suggests an excess supply of teachers throughout most of the 1970s.

Skilled workers in the nonprofessional fields may also continue in short supply. Construction skills are in short supply in some areas, suggesting the need to reevaluate journeyman standards and the desirability of expanding apprenticeship programs. Auto mechanics and other skilled repairmen are also going to be in great demand in the 1970s, as autos and other consumer and business equipment grow increasingly complex.

Demands for semiskilled and unskilled workers are not expected to be particularly strong in the 1970s, as automated equipment and other innovations continue to replace repetitive chores performed by nonskilled workers. However, demand should continue quite strong in service occupations, reflecting the steady shift to a service-oriented economy and the relative slowness of technological breakthroughs in the service sector.

Demand for manpower in the 1970s should be strong, with the most significant barrier to the attainment of our national manpower goals the continued mismatching of manpower supply and demand. These projections illustrate the need to intensify and reorient both education and manpower training and retraining programs to better serve the interests and needs of America in the years ahead.

The State of the Art

National projections do not provide a blueprint of the future, but they do signal the warnings necessary for sound fiscal, monetary, and manpower policies. It was not for lack of knowledge that inadequate provisions were made for teachers and classrooms to serve the postwar baby boom or that insufficient jobs were generated to absorb veterans returning from Vietnam or engineers laid off in the aerospace industry. Employment policy that takes seriously the goal of "useful jobs for all of those able, willing and seeking to work" will pay more attention to the age, sex, and racial structure of the labor force for which jobs must be provided, but here too there is no lack of reliable knowledge. Demographic projections provide adequate guidance for 10 to 15 years ahead on growth potential, employment needs, and quantitative educational requirements. It would be useful to have more advance information concerning the qualitative characteristics of the labor supply, but provision of better education and broader skills is an adequate substitute for detailed projections.

At local and regional levels, projections are more difficult because changes are less likely to be washed out by crosscurrents. The first need, of course, is a consistent national policy of full employment to maximize opportunity and provide a solid base for local projections. The second is to proceed with a program of making projections, so that experience can be gained.

Educational planners have all the enrollment projections and information about their students' employment prospects that they need for planning general education. The shortages of elementary teachers in the 1950s, of high-school teachers in the early 1960s, and the excess supply of teachers emerging now were not difficult to foresee, given postwar birth rates and college enrollment figures for the 1960s. What was lacking was not forewarning, but sufficiently flexible institutions.

Planners of more employment-oriented types of education and training—apprenticeship and vocational, technical, and to a lesser extent graduate education—need more detailed projections. Counseling and guidance people have less information than they need, but, all too often, more than they use.

Serious obstacles to satisfactory adjustment to manpower changes are still posed by lack of knowledge concerning job content, skill requirements, and transferability of skills. Employers tend to require excessive education and training, in part because they do not know what skills a job actually requires. And without knowledge about the transferability of skills, neither the detail required of projections nor the appropriate content of training can be satisfactorily determined. Manpower planning by individual economic actors—workers and firms—is increasingly important. In the past, firms have planned production, investment, and expansion, but rarely their manpower needs. Some firms have discovered the road to high profits may lie in their ability to attract and hold good employees. Also, increasing sensitivity to human distress and to criticism for failure to avoid displacement brought some commitment to the principle of planning to adjust to reduced manpower needs through attrition.

On balance, although there is need for improvement in manpower projections, their deficiencies are not a serious limiting factor in program analysis and decision making. Methodological improvements can and should be made, but steps to improve the presentation and dissemination of available projections are probably more important. In the end, the manpower problems of the past few years cannot be blamed upon the lack of information concerning the manpower future. Action, not information, has been the absent factor.

Effort and resources might be invested in the development of manpower projections within the region, the locality, and the firm. Many organizations and individuals are involved in projecting, and all are not equally expert. The work of the BLS is the soundest available; less sophisticated agencies, usually involved in projections of specialized types of manpower, would be aided by government-wide projection guidelines. More intensive research effort needs to go into understanding skill requirements and transferability. In the end, however, the main burden is on the projection user: Accept the fact that even with the best of techniques, the future will remain opaque; use projections with patience and wisdom; and have faith in the far from perfect but reasonable flexibility of the labor market and the adaptability of human beings.

NOTES

1. Among the more important statistical publications are the *Monthly Labor Review, Employment and Earnings, Manpower Report of the President* (annual), *Current Wage Developments,* and *Unemployment Insurance Statistics.*

2. J. E. Morton, *On the Evolution of Manpower Statistics,* Studies in Employment and Unemployment Series (Kalamazoo, Mich.: Upjohn Institute for Employment Research, December 1969), pp. 36–51.

3. Stanley Lebergott, *Manpower in Economic Growth* (New York: McGraw-Hill, 1964).

4. The President's Committee to Appraise Employment and Unemployment Statistics, *Measuring Employment and Unemployment* (Washington, D.C.: U.S. Government Printing Office, 1962).

5. Gloria P. Green, "Comparing Employment Estimates from Household and Payroll Surveys," *Monthly Labor Review* (December 1969), pp. 9–20.

6. William G. Bowen and T. Aldrich Finegan, *The Economics of the Labor Force Participation* (Princeton, N.J.: Princeton University Press, 1969).

7. This section draws heavily on Garth L. Mangum and Arnold L. Nemore, "The Nature and Functions of Manpower Projections," *Industrial Relations* (May 1966), pp. 1–16.

8. Herman Stekler, *Economic Forecasting* (New York: Praeger, 1970), pp. 3–15, 92–102.

9. National Commission on Technology, Automation, and Economic Progress, *Technology and the American Economy* (Washington, D.C.: U.S. Government Printing Office, 1966), pp. 54–55.

10. U.S. Department of Labor, Bureau of Labor Statistics, *Occupational Outlook Handbook,* 1970–71 ed., Bulletin No. 1650 (Washington, D.C.: U.S. Government Printing Office, 1970).

11. Sophia C. Travis, "The U.S. Labor Force: Projections to 1985," *Monthly Labor Review* (May 1970), pp. 3–13.

12. Richard Easterlin, *Population, Labor Force and Long Swings in Economic Growth* (New York: Columbia University Press, 1968), pp. 141–182.

13. U.S. Department of Labor, Bureau of Labor Statistics, *The U.S. Economy in 1980: A Summary of BLS Projections,* Bulletin 1673 (Washington, D.C.: U.S. Government Printing Office, 1970), p. 27.

14. Denis F. Johnston, "Education of Adult Workers: Projections to 1985," *Monthly Labor Review* (August 1970), pp. 43 ff.

15. American Assembly, *Goals for Americans: The Report of the President's Commission on National Goals* (Englewood Cliffs, N.J.: Prentice-Hall, 1960).

16. Leonard Lecht, *Manpower Needs for National Goals in the 1970s* (New York: Praeger, 1969), pp. 10–11.

17. Michael F. Crowley, "Projected Requirements for Technicians in 1980," *Monthly Labor Review* (May 1970), pp. 13–17.

Part II
Preparation
for
Employment

Chapter 7
Education in Manpower Development

Ask what single characteristic most differentiates the steadily and well employed from those suffering sporadic or long-term unemployment or working at low wages; the answer will generally be "Education." Ask also what single factor has had the greatest influence on the U.S. economy's record for productivity and growth; more often than not, the answer will be the same.

The consensus on the importance of education is so overwhelming that several facts may be surprising: (a) Even the expectation of a tie between education and employability and economic growth is a new condition. (b) For most jobs, there is no clear substantive relationship between job content and school curricula. (c) Schools see employability as a goal of their efforts on behalf of only a minority of their students. (d) Some researchers doubt that education has much to do with productivity for most of the work force, and a few investigators have even suggested that education may be a detriment. (e) It is by no means clear whether the observed correlation between a nation's economic growth rates and its investment in education means that education creates wealth, or simply that wealthy nations can afford education; whether education results in higher incomes, or whether people capable of earning higher incomes pursue education.

This chapter assesses the role of formal education in developing productivity and opening employment opportunities. Chapters 9 and 10 focus on the specific roles of vocational education and the colleges while Chapter 11 examines on-the-job training.

MANPOWER DEVELOPMENT IN THE SCHOOLS:
A HISTORICAL PERSPECTIVE

Manpower development is the process of preparing people for a productive employment role. If people are an essential resource in the production process, then manpower development consists of seeing to it that people contribute their maximum potential in producing that combination of goods and services preferred by the society at given price relationships. Manpower development is also the process of preparing individuals for employment that will give them the optimum combination of income and other job satisfactions. Fortunately, there are some indications that these two goals are generally consistent, with the wage system acting as an equilibrating mechanism. Unfortunately, just as both objectives can be achieved simultaneously, both often fail of achievement—a problem explored by Chapter 12.

The Emergence of Education
as a Work Prerequisite

A hierarchy of the requirements for productivity and employability might include good mental and physical health, a commitment to work as the most appropriate source of income, acceptance of industrial discipline, good human relations skills, basic skills of communication and computation, technological familiarity, and job skills. The list hardly seems controversial, but a generation ago the last three items would have been included for only a minority of jobs. Compared to the current 12.3 years of educational attainment by the average member of the labor force, the average worker had only 8.7 years of schooling in 1940 and only 10.4 years in 1952 (the rise seems to be flattening; the 1980 projections are for 12.6 years). At the turn of the century, only 6 percent of the population remained in school after their seventeenth birthday, but it is doubtful that anyone would have blamed a person's unemployment on his lack of education.

At what point did education and formal training become a critical determinant of employability? It has not been many years since most lawyers learned their profession by "reading" law as clerks. Formal training for physicians is less than a century old. The designation of engineer gained educational connotations only in this century. Formal credentialing of school teachers is also of relatively recent date, and a few states still do not require a bachelor's degree. Beyond the professions, bookkeepers, accountants, stenographers, and clerks obviously were required to read, write, and cipher. Education had little relevance to employment for most of the labor force until after World War II.

The dramatic increase in the education of the American people surely is one of the most significant domestic developments of the past 25 years. In 1950, for example, 59 percent of the population 17 years of age and older had graduated from high school. By 1969, this proportion had risen to 80 percent. The proportion of high-school graduates who go to college has not fluctuated as much; it remained at about 50 percent during the 1960s. However, the proportion of college graduates who went to graduate school increased dramatically from one-sixth in 1961 to one-half in 1965. There have been equally large increases in expenditures on education in the United States. The total cost of education was about $9 billion in 1950, compared with about $66 billion in 1970.

This great increase in the importance of education can be explained by a number of factors, some short run and some long run. One of the long-run factors has been the prevailing attitude about education in the United States. This attitude stems in large measure from the conviction that one of the best ways to upward mobility is through education, a conviction that apparently became much stronger after the exhaustion of the frontier. The frontier had made formal education seem to be less important than an ability to deal with the immediate physical environment as a means of improving one's fortunes. With industrialization and the passing of the frontier, a more complex society required more formal education for successfully dealing with its environment.

The belief that education was a means of personal improvement and security undoubtedly was strengthened by the depression of the 1930s. Many of those who suffered unemployment during that period probably resolved to make themselves or their children "depression proof" in the future through education. Bakke, for example, in a study of unemployed workers during the 1930s, found that many of them felt they would not have been unemployed if they had gained more education during the boom period of the 1920s.[1] Arguing from Bakke's findings, Berg concludes that "no one can estimate how much the educational achievement of the population of forty to fifty today is attributable to the economic pressures generated in the 'dirty thirties' and perceived directly by them or transmitted to them by their parents." [2]

World War II is properly designated as the event that transformed education from a minor to a major qualification for employment. The war itself imposed demands for skilled training. A 12-million-man military force was extracted from the prime labor force age group at the same time that war production multiplied the demand for technical and craft skills. In addition to those who learned new skills on the job, 7.5 million were trained by the public vocational education system before the war's end. Where skills could not be supplied fast enough, jobs were broken down into simpler tasks which could be performed by unskilled and inexperienced workers. Although the emphasis on vocational and skill training did not continue into the postwar period, formal education quickly emerged as a requirement for employment.

The emphasis on technology was accelerated during the war by the development of nuclear weapons and was continued with the space race in the later postwar period. Much of the increased demand for college graduates following World War II was stimulated by the federal government, in part, as a consequence of the Cold War emphasis on national prestige derived from scientific and technical achievement, and the rate of economic development. America's development of the atomic bomb undoubtedly "persuaded" the Russians to bridge the nuclear gap and develop their space technology, which, in turn, prompted the United States to attempt greater scientific achievements. Sputnik clearly elicited federal support for higher education: There was a space race to be won. Cold War strategy also involved economic development: A major Soviet goal was to become Number One, and the competitive threat was an effective goal for the U.S. Studies by economists attributing a significant part of economic growth to education therefore strengthened federal support for education.

Postwar population developments also have influenced the demand for education. The college-age population declined during the 1950s because of the low birth rates during the depression of the 1930s and World War II. But elementary and secondary enrollments were swollen by the postwar baby boom. There were actually fewer 15 to 24-year-olds in 1950 than in 1930, even though the total population increased 45 percent during those years. Hence, there was only a slight increase in college enrollment in the 1950s, resulting mainly from an increase in the percentage of college-age people going to college, not from an increase in the number of people in the college-age group. During the 1960s, the number of college graduates increased greatly because of the coming of age of those born during the postwar baby boom. The number of bachelors or equivalent degrees increased from 187,000 in the 1940s to 287,000 in 1956 and 505,000 in 1965. The graduation of the postwar-baby-boom generation and the lower rate of population growth during the 1960s are expected to cause the demand for teachers to be lower during the 1970s and 1980s relative to the supply than was the case during the 1950s and 1960s.

The growth in the number of persons attending college after World War II also was stimulated by the GI Bill of Rights and to some extent by the practice of granting draft deferments or exemptions to college students during the 1960s. Draft deferments were based upon the belief that educated manpower was important in achieving national objectives.

Just why, in the post-World War II period, education became a widely accepted prerequisite for employment is a matter of controversy. Of course, as long as professional and white-collar occupations were expanding as a proportion of all employment, education was certain also to become a necessity for a growing percentage of workers. But the emphasis went far beyond that, until a high-school diploma was required for most apprenticeships, many semiskilled factory jobs, and even laborers' jobs at the bottom of a seniority ladder leading into semiskilled and skilled ranks. Perhaps these jobs, or at least those a few steps up the promotion ladder, were becoming more technical—and requiring an ability to comprehend written instructions, to reading and record of guages and graphs, and similar activities. But why assume that instructions are to be read and workmen are to keep records? In factories throughout much of the world, safety and other instructions are given on picture-signs, and clerks circulate to keep records. An alternative hypothesis is that as long as educated people were available employers preferred to hire them and emerging jobs were structured to fit them. The post-World War II GI Bill no doubt played an important role in kicking off a spiral in which the supply of educated manpower sparked the demand for it.

Table 7–1 compares educational attainment by occupation for 1952 and 1970. It is difficult to attribute to anything but supply the fact that 38 percent of laborers had a high-school education or better in 1970, compared with 16 percent 18 years earlier. Of course, the proportion of educated people in the labor force would of necessity expand to accompany the growth of professional, technical, and clerical jobs. But it has been estimated that this accounts for only 15 percent of the rise in educational attainment in the work force. The other 85 percent represents higher educational attainment within the same occupation. In many cases, the content of the job required more education. In others, the employer selected those with more education because they were available and because he assumed that education was likely to correlate positively with productivity and promotability. In still others, it was simply the fact that with educational attainment rising throughout the population, anyone hired at random was likely to have more education than his predecessor.

Education of the Labor Force:
Future Prospects

Bureau of Labor Statistics projections promise both a younger and a better-educated labor force to 1985. While the adult labor force is expected to increase about 30 percent, the number of high-school graduates will rise 60 percent and college graduates, 80 percent. In the process, the labor force will become much more homogeneous in educational attainment. Most of those who entered the labor force before World War II will have retired or died. The older workers will be the postwar GI Bill generation. Those born in the postwar baby boom will rise from 24 to 34 percent of the workers 25 and older. The younger adult workers will be only slightly better educated than in 1970. But the older workers will show a marked change. Even those 65 and over in the labor force will have a median educational attainment of 12.1 years, compared with 9.6 years in 1970. The gap in educational attainment between blacks and other workers will have shrunk to 0.3 years from the 3.3 years of three decades earlier. The traditional educational advantage of female over male workers will have disappeared.

Of course, there will still be those with less than adequate education— 20.1 million workers without high-school diplomas in 1985, compared to

TABLE 7-1 *The Changing Educational Pattern of Major Occupational Groups, 1952 and 1970 (percentage distribution)*

MAJOR OCCUPATIONAL GROUP	LESS THAN 8 YEARS		8–11 YEARS		12 YEARS		13–15 YEARS		16 YEARS OR MORE		MEDIAN SCHOOL YEARS COMPLETED
	1952	1970	1952	1970	1952	1970	1952	1970	1952	1970	1970
White collar											
Professional and technical	1%	a	7%	3%	16%	18%	21%	19%	55%	60%	16.3
Managerial and officials	10	3	32	18	34	39	13	20	11	20	12.7
Clerical and sales	4	1	25	16	50	57	15	20	7	7	12.6
Blue collar											
Craftsmen and foremen	18	10	48	37	27	43	6	9	1	2	12.1
Operatives	25	15	50	42	21	38	3	5	1	1	11.3
Laborers	43	23	41	39	14	30	2	7	1	1	10.5
Farm	43	25	38	39	14	27	4	7	2	2	9.3
Service and private household	31	14	43	39	20	36	4	10	2	1	11.6

a Less than 0.5%.
SOURCE: Derived from several U.S. Department of Labor sources.

24.7 million in 1970. Despite black gains, this group will still include a disproportionate number of those without a high-school education. If present attitudes persist, these educationally disadvantaged workers will face relatively worse job prospects. But the overwhelming fact will be the decline in the educational differentials which have persisted so long.

Does this outlook for educational attainment match the expected educational requirements of future jobs? The question may be answered differently depending upon whether the criterion is the objective requirements of job content or the preferences of employers. Occupational trends promise to continue the positive correlation between education and employment. Projections discussed in earlier chapters are repeated here to estimate the future relationship. White-collar workers increased from 20 percent of all workers at the turn of the century to 45 percent in 1968. They will comprise 50 percent of all workers in 1980. What links these occupations together is their reliance on intellectual and verbal rather than manual and manipulative skills. The fastest growing occupational group in the labor market will continue to be professional and technical workers. Computer systems analysts head the list followed by computer programmers, urban planners, recreation workers, social workers, economists, engineers, and paramedical workers. Clerical employees, always a growth category, will rise another 35 percent with computer operators, like computer systems analysts, more than doubling in number and office machine operators increasing by 40 percent or more. Sales workers and managers will increase but not as rapidly. The number of farm workers will continue its rapid downward trend; blue-collar workers will decrease slowly in number.

In the blue-collar category, only craftsmen and foremen will increase rapidly, with emphasis on those craft skills likely to require the most formal education. Business machine service will be one of the leading growth occupations with an increase of over 100 percent—and these machines are more likely to be electronic than mechanical. Electricians, plumbers, and appliance servicemen will require less formal education, as will cement masons, bricklayers, glaziers, operating engineers, roofers, and iron workers—the other growth crafts. Service occupations will grow with population, but the greatest growth will come in those with some educational content— police officers, hospital attendants, cosmetologists, and practical nurses.

Of all these, only the professional occupations require college degrees. The critical message these projections convey to the educational community is that less than one out of five jobs will require a college degree. As it happens, this is about the proportion of those entering the ninth grade who now complete college. However, the growth occupations have in common the need, if not the custom, of postsecondary but less than baccalaureate education. The half of all college entrants who drop out before graduation may help fill this need. The continued rapid expansion of two-year community colleges is probably a more functional approach. With 2.5 million enrollees, these institutions represent a doubling in colleges and a tripling of enrollments during the past decade. Five million students enrolled in 1225 two-year postsecondary institutions is the expectation for 1975.

EDUCATION AND EMPLOYABILITY

The higher a person's educational attainment, the more likely he is to be in the labor force, to avoid unemployment, to be unemployed only briefly when he enters or reenters the labor force or changes jobs, and to hold a better job. There is a positive and significant correlation between level of education and lifetime earnings. Studies have also shown that those nations that spend the highest proportions of their national income on education tend to experience the most rapid economic growth.

These should be strong testimonials to the value of education in developing the labor force and increasing the employment and earnings of people. But the relationship is far from simple. Because the educational attainment of the work force rose from 9.1 years in 1940 to 12.3 years in 1969, one might expect unemployment to have diminished in seriousness. In point of fact, of course, overall unemployment has fluctuated cyclically, with no evidence of upward or downward trend over time—except for an upward trend in teenage unemployment.

Similarly, a general shift toward the upper rungs of the occupational ladder might have been expected. Those occupations, which have always attracted people with the most education, have, in fact, expanded most rapidly. Yet the major effect of the rising educational attainment has been to raise the educational level within occupations. Therefore, it is not really clear whether individuals have climbed the occupational ladder as they achieved education or whether the steps in the ladder have become farther apart as better-educated people became available for the same jobs. If education were an antidote for unemployment, one would expect nations with lower levels of education to have higher unemployment levels. Yet the western European nations in which unemployment rarely rises to one-half the U.S. rate all have far lower educational levels.

People with more education earn substantially more over a working lifetime. Does this occur because their education prepares them for better jobs, because employers value and are willing to pay for their educational attainment, or because education has been pursued by those who possess more native ability, motivation, or labor market contacts? Do employers prefer the better-educated because job content requires such workers, because they are better disciplined or more promotable, because they have demonstrated persistence, or simply because employers have unrealistic views about the value of education? Does a better-educated labor force cause an economy to grow more rapidly, or is it that a more rapidly growing economy can afford the luxury of more education? What exactly is the contribution of education to employability? None of these questions can be satisfactorily answered, but they are worth exploring. Few of these questions would have been asked a few years ago. That they are being asked increasingly is evidence of a reaction against education's previously sacrosanct status.

Education, Employment, and Income

The independent contribution of education to employability could be measured only if certain experimental conditions were met. Youth of equal ability and socioeconomic background would have to undertake different levels of education accompanied by specified additional training before seeking jobs under prescribed circumstances from employers who are totally objective. Since the necessary studies have not been made, it is possible only to report the facts and speculate about their meaning. Whether jobs demand education or employers merely prefer it, years of educational attainment remain the best available predictor of wages and employment rates. Rising employment tends to be distributed more than proportionately to those with more education; falling employment impinges, with some lag, on those well educated. Those with more education not only tend to have lower unemployment rates, but they also tend to be unemployed for shorter periods when they are removed from work. The median years of school completed among men who in March 1967 had been unemployed 1 to 4 weeks was 11.6 years; for those unemployed 5 to 14 weeks the median was 11.1 years; for those unemployed 15 to 26 weeks, the median was 10.6 years.

While workers with diplomas tend to experience lower unemployment rates, the relationships are not consistent for dropouts—whether from elementary school, high school, or college. Persons with five to eight years of schooling are subject to about the same incidence of unemployment as those with one to three years of high school (Table 7–2). For high-school and college graduates, however, unemployment is reduced.

College graduates, in general, have encountered little serious difficulty in the labor market, either because their numbers were few or their skills great enough to be competitively attractive. In addition, higher education may have been selective enough to enroll and graduate those with the most potential or the best family or social connections. In the early 1970s, however, college graduates—especially those trained in elementary and secondary education—found themselves in trouble when an enlarged graduating class confronted the impact of falling birthrates and contracting school needs. Those in physics and related areas encountered a more temporary decrease in demand which resulted from curtailed federal research and defense expenditures.

TABLE 7–2 *Unemployment Rates, by Years of School Completed, March 1970*

PERCENT OF LABOR FORCE UNEMPLOYED

YEARS OF SCHOOL COMPLETED (BOTH SEXES)	Total, 18 Years Old and Over	18–19 Years	20–24 Years	25–34 Years	35–44 Years	45–54 Years	55–64 Years	65 Years and Over
Both Sexes								
TOTAL	4.2%	11.5%	7.2%	3.8%	3.3%	3.0%	3.0%	3.4%
Elementary								
Less than 5 years [a]	5.6	b	b	2.9	6.8	7.0	3.9	4.8
5 to 7 years	4.9	15.1	12.7	6.9	4.3	4.2	3.5	4.2
8 years	4.8	12.8	12.3	7.3	5.2	3.3	3.7	4.4
High school								
1 to 3 years	6.3	14.6	12.9	6.7	4.6	3.5	3.9	2.8
4 years	3.9	9.8	6.7	3.4	2.9	2.7	2.3	2.2
College								
1 to 3 years	3.9	9.6	5.9	2.8	3.1	2.7	2.8	2.0
4 years or more	1.5	b	3.3	1.5	0.8	1.4	1.3	1.0

[a] Includes persons reporting no school years completed.
[b] Not computed; base too small.
SOURCE: U.S. Bureau of Labor Statistics, *Educational Attainment of Workers, March 1969, 1970*, Special Labor Force Report 125 (Washington, D.C.: U.S. Government Printing Office, 1970), Table K.

Education and the Transition
from School to Work

People who attain the most education, of course, also have other advantages which would have been present without the added education. A young person's educational attainment, for example, is also highly correlated with the education of his parents.

The impact of family income is also relevant. Families with incomes under $3,000 produce, proportionately, twice as many high-school dropouts as graduates. Among youth who ranked in the highest ability quartile in a 1963 U.S. Labor Department study, 91 percent of the males and 76 percent of the females from the families of the highest socioeconomic class attended college, compared to only 52 percent of the males and 28 percent of the females in the lowest socioeconomic class. However, fewer dropouts gave economic reasons for leaving school than noted school-connected difficulties—for example, as lack of interest, poor grades, disciplinary difficulties.

The Labor Department study also found a relationship between amount of education and how jobs are sought and obtained. For one thing, those with higher education are more likely to have a job waiting for them when they leave school. And among those who look for employment, the better educated (particularly the college trained) find jobs sooner. Dropouts tend to rely on friends and relatives (with the more limited range of choices thus provided) than high-school graduates and those with some college training. These last two groups rely more on institutional sources such as schools and placement agencies. However, other studies have found that successful minority-group members use the public employment service simply because they have few friends and relatives through whom they can gain access to desirable jobs.

Vocational training and academic education are often viewed as alternative ways of preparing for employment. However, rather than compensating for lack of education, skill training and educational attainment are positively correlated, largely because vocational training ordinarily becomes available only during the last two years of high school. By this time, the compulsory school attendance age has been reached or passed and most who are likely to do so have dropped out.

The cooperative-work program, though still enrolling few students throughout the nation, is potentially useful in assisting the movement of high-school students into the labor force. Under this program, the student's day usually is split between school and part-time employment; special efforts are made to integrate the activities into a meaningful preparation for work. Because these opportunities also become available in the last years of high school, over twice as many graduates as dropouts have participated. Even of those high-school graduates who do not go on to college, three times as many undertake some form of postsecondary training as do the dropouts. The follow-up on the 1963 study conducted two years later found that one-fifth of the high-school graduates had returned to school compared with only one-twentieth of the dropouts. In addition, one-fourth of the graduates were participating in formal job training outside regular schools, compared with one-eighth of the dropouts.

Guidance from school or state employment service officials provides another bridge from school to job. But the 1963 survey of out-of-school youths noted that over half of the high-school graduates and less than one-fourth of the dropouts received such help. Because most guidance is directed to students during their senior year in high school, dropouts tend to be excluded from this experience.

The effectiveness of vocational guidance is partially demonstrated by the fact that dropouts who had been counseled were half again as likely to have jobs waiting for them when they left school as those who had not. However, vocational guidance seemed to make little difference in whether or not graduates were immediately employed.

Not all students receive vocational guidance, and studies have shown that it usually is directed at those who seemingly need it least. Kaufman found that academic students were more likely to receive guidance than vocational students.[3] Only one-half of vocational students, compared with three-fourths of academic students, recalled discussing the selection of their courses with a counselor. Actual discussion of job plans was even less frequent, with one-fifth of the vocational and one-third of the academic students receiving assistance. If academic students receive more exposure to placement services beyond high school and are generally better equipped to make decisions, then the order of priorities in high-school vocational guidance activities is obviously inverted.

Because the placement process is institutionalized, the college-to-work bridge seems to be a secure one for the approximately 700,000 young people who now cross it each year. However, it must be kept in mind that their first postgraduation job will rarely be their first work experience. The transition from school to work will have been underway for a number of years.

The one-half of youth who, on the average, enter but do not complete college have an unknown variety of experiences. Unfortunately, we know relatively little about the amount of schooling and training this group obtains, their reasons for failing to complete college, and their labor force experience. While those who complete a two- or three-year course probably find it a satisfactory bridge to their working career, those who fail to finish an intended four-year course are likely to be less well prepared for a specific occupation. It may be significant that those who have attended college but have not graduated, experience almost as much unemployment as high-school graduates.

Once most members of the labor force are high school graduates, a diploma offers little competitive advantage. At that point the quality of the education received becomes more significant. One of four high-school students was enrolled in vocational courses in 1966, but 60 percent of these were in home economics and agriculture. Office occupations enrolled another 25 percent. No data are available concerning relative quality or results. Overall, those who receive vocational education in high school appear to have the edge in employment and earnings during the first 6 to 10 years beyond high school; after that point, those from the general and academic curriculum catch up and begin to pass them. However, vocational enrollees tend to be of lower ability than others. When controlled for ability and socioeconomic status, high-school vocational training—even at its present quality and relevance—does seem to have significant employment and earnings advantages.

The increasingly small proportion who fail to complete high school, of course, find themselves at the rear of any labor market queue. If one is looking for a simple formula for success in the transition from school to work, therefore, the statistics would endorse "stay in school as long as possible," but observation of job content does not always explain why this is so.

Some degree of selectivity is doubtless at work; so that those who achieve the highest educational attainment tend to have the most native ability. Many with the ability to successfully complete college do not do so. We do not know whether their employability suffers compared with those with equal ability but greater educational attainment. It frequently is suggested that technological developments tend to require higher levels of education, though it is not clear whether this is attributable to change in job content or more rapid growth of higher-level jobs. The findings of the BLS appear to favor the latter explanation, with the educational upgrading within occupational classifications probably resulting more from the rising educational attainment of the labor force than from the requirements of jobs. It is to be expected, of course, that the availability of higher quality labor would, over time, encourage development of a technology attuned to its use. Finally, it may be that employers simply consider education a meaningful screening device and select those with the highest attainment.

THE CONSPICUOUS CONSUMPTION
OF EDUCATION

We have explored but not resolved the issue of whether educated people experience less unemployment because they are educated or whether those with the greatest ability and access to jobs are those who seek education. There is left the issue of employer bias. Do employers prefer better-educated people for subjective reasons and not for their potential productivity?

Berg, in an important exercise in iconoclasm (subtitled, appropriately, *The Great Training Robbery*), argues that education has little to do with productivity in many jobs, and is even a negative factor in some.[4] Relying primarily on secondary sources, he identifies numerous situations where employers have imposed educational requirements beyond the actual job needs. In these cases, he finds evidence of employee unrest and high turn-over, which, he asserts, occurs because workers become bored with assign-ments below their capability and expectations. He does not explore the likelihood that the employer may, in fact, be paying triply for his conspicu-ous consumption of educated people. In addition to the rate he would have paid for an individual with just enough capability to do the job, the em-ployer pays the added wage necessary to attract and meet the expectations of the overeducated employee. To this is added the cost of unrest and turn-over.

There are several possible explanations of this apparently irrational bias on the part of employers. Some, concerned about promotability, may be looking ahead to the requirements of the job at the top of a promotion ladder. But relying upon past education for skills required by a future job suggests little faith in a person's ability to learn on the job. Racial bias has also been suggested as a cause of inflated educational requirements. Know-ing that various minorities have lower than average educational attainment, employers may require education as a defensible shield for reducing the number of minority applicants. To the extent that education is a surrogate for all the advantages listed in the previous section, employers may be act-ing rationally and getting their money's worth.

Many employers undoubtedly share the current bias in favor of formal education. Berg's examples were primarily blue-collar and lower-level white-collar workers in repetitive jobs, but equally well known is the restlessness of graduate engineers who find themselves doing technician-level work in production settings. Similar overqualification and underemployment can be found throughout the labor market. The use of nurses' aides who assume some of the registered nurses' responsibilities is a partial solution to one such problem. The New Careers program described in Chapter 18 is an at-tempt to exploit such situations to provide employment for disadvantaged persons. Repetitive functions that require limited skills but are currently performed by professionals are identified. Undereducated, disadvantaged people are then trained to perform these subprofessional functions. Increas-ing the number of technicians per graduate engineer is a similar approach. This trend is opposed by professionals who are as jurisdiction-conscious as craft unionists. Various licensing and credentialing requirements, usually defended as necessary to protect the consumer, protect jurisdiction at the cost of overqualification.

There is no necessary inconsistency in arguing both that the jobs re-quiring formal education are growing more rapidly than any others and that overqualification is pervasive in U.S. labor markets. The less physical and the more intellectual the production processes, the greater the need for formal education. Manipulative skills such as typing that are generally applicable are taught more efficiently in the classroom than on the job. Given these trends, those without adequate formal education are at a technical disadvantage. Because education has purposes other than preparation for employment, the desire to consume education may lead to overqualification as a worker and overinvestment in the labor force.

The Educational Institutions for Manpower Development

Since manpower is defined as the productive capacity of human beings, every institution that affects our lives has an impact on manpower development. Consider the attributes of employability listed at the beginning of this chapter. The home is a key determinant of mental and physical health, commitment to work, acceptance of discipline, and human relations skills. The neighborhood and community are also involved. But because improvement in these basic institutions is difficult, schools and other institutions are asked to provide remedies for any deficiencies. Thus, elementary and secondary schools become the focus for the development not only of a general ability to understand and function in society but also of discipline and human relations skills, as well as basic skills in communications and computation.

Manpower experts sometimes express dismay because the schools do not generally recognize their role as manpower developers. They feel that basic manpower requirements would be better met if preparation for employment were specifically included among the priority objectives of education. Rupert Evans accuses American education of concentrating on "school for schooling's sake." The elementary schools prepare young people to go to high school which concentrates on getting them into college which has its eye fixed on graduate-school requirements. Only then, when the schooling potential is exhausted, is the emphasis vocational, but largely for education as a profession.[5]

The pattern began in the days when elementary schools were assigned the job of producing literate citizens and "Americanizing" immigrants. Only the college-bound enrolled in high school as a preparatory stage. Vocational education was established as a separate system to protect it from the disdain of the academic educator. But with the high schools providing mass education, and education a growing prerequisite for employment, many feel that education needs a change of signals. One indicator is the growing interest in a career-development system; another is the growth of community colleges. Finally, dissatisfaction with the way schools' fulfill their employment-preparation role is a factor in the growing political criticism of education.

Whether viewed as a vocalization of general education or a generalization of vocational education, their is growing interest in discovering techniques for integrating the two. The basic assumption is that preparation for a working career is among the most important of education's many objectives. Thus, no one without the requisites for employability, including a salable skill, can be considered educated. At the same time, skill preparation should neither supplant other general education objectives nor be so structured that the individual will not be able to realize his true potential. Some of the techniques for accomplishing this goal (discussed in Chapter 9) are elementary-school orientation to the world of work, information and training in occupational choice; integration of academic and vocational content so that each serves as a vehicle for the other; and a more active role for schools in the placement process.

Community colleges have almost doubled in numbers in ten years, while their enrollment has tripled. The title is significant. While the term "junior college" indicates a college-transfer emphasis and a desire to grow up to a senior college, the community college is committed to serve the community's education needs, whatever they might be. Most institutions that call themselves community colleges could have more honestly retained the "junior college" title. However, the generally recognized attributes, too often observed in the breach, are (a) a truly "open door" admissions policy for all persons over 18, regardless of past education, who can profit from instruction; (b) a service-oriented and student-centered philosophy which contrasts with the university's too often self-serving ambitions for a "community of scholars"; (c) a faculty that concentrates on teaching rather than research; (d) heavy emphasis on occupationally oriented two-year terminal programs; (e) a strong counseling and guidance program; (f) use of the campus as a community center for nonstudent activities and of the staff as a source of technical services to community institutions; and (g) an ambition to place one such institution within commuting distance of everyone in the population. At least two community colleges have incorporated skills centers financed by the Manpower Development and Training Act (discussed in Chapter 17) into their facilities; these centers offer remedial training and stipends to disadvantaged adults who are not stigmatized as "second-class citizens" by being shunted to separate and less than equal facilities. Many community colleges accept individual referrals or whole classes of manpower program enrollees on contract.

Universities are being pressured by state and local governments, and community leaders to give more attention to undergraduate teaching and community service. In fact, a general reaction to the overexpectations of the 1960s seems to be subjecting the entire educational system to unfamiliar criticism. Education has long been a "sacred cow," deliberately shielded from partisan politics, decentralized, and characterized by professional autonomy. The 1960s saw federal support for education rise from $2 billion to $8 billion while all U.S. expenditures on education rose from $25 billion to $66 billion. Whatever the ills of society—and many formerly unrecognized ills were uncovered during the period—more and better education was the prescription. Because the products of education are difficult to measure, education administrators tend to measure the output by the input.

Getting more education was simply a question of funding; quality was another matter.

Education reached a zenith of public support in 1965 with the Elementary and Secondary Education Act. Since then, there has been a rising crescendo of criticism. The legislation was designed to provide additional federal funds for school districts heavily impacted with poverty. Initially, much of the money was channeled to affluent school districts, and many schools spent their ESEA grants for "frills," ignoring more serious needs. Head Start was briefly the great hope for social rehabilitation. It soon became apparent that a short preschool experience was no panacea as long as the children were then dumped into the same old schools and remained in the same homes with the same old problems. There was increasing concern because students emerged from the schools at various exit points without salable skills. Manpower training programs were assailed because enrollees were trained for low-level jobs which, if available, left them in employed poverty. Too often the trained would-be worker discovered that problems of housing, transportation, isolation in a rural depressed area, or racial discrimination stood in the way of employment. Then, on top of it all, campus unrest persuaded many that college youth, the ultimate recipients of public largesse, were ungratefully "biting the hand that was feeding them."

Among the consequences of this disillusionment have been a rising rate of rejections in school bond elections and reduced generosity among legislators. Other public needs seem to take higher priority. For the first time, a president of the United States has found vetoing education appropriations less than threatening politically. There is a new demand for accountability. Granting a diploma is no evidence that education has done its job. Performance contracting in which public or private institutions are rewarded for demonstrated improvement in educational achievement has aroused considerable interest and some experimentation. The failure of our educational system to prepare noncollege-bound youth (and many college graduates) for successful working careers is an important factor in this discontent. At the same time, some more radical criticism charge that the schools are merely conveyor belts designed to put people in slots in the agri-business "machine." Such are the penalties for the American faith in education as a key to both social change and social stability.

RETURNS TO INVESTMENT
IN EDUCATION

Within the last ten years, the economics of education has become a major field for professional economists. For many, the subject consists of school finance. For most, however, the query has been, "Does education pay?" If so, how much of what kind for whom under what conditions?

The school-finance approach emerged as school enrollments mushroomed following the World War II GI Bill and the postwar baby boom.

Its emphasis was on how to get enough classrooms and teachers and funds to support them. The landmark in the education-as-investment approach was the American Economic Association presidential address of Theodore W. Schultz of the University of Chicago in December 1960.[6] Titling his address "Investment in Human Capital," he noted the failure of his fellow economists to subject expenditures on education to the same rigorous analyses applied to investments in machinery, factories, and other forms of capital. The economic fathers—Adam Smith, David Ricardo, Thomas Malthus, Karl Marx, and Alfred Marshall, to name a few—had mentioned the importance of education and training in the improvement of labor as a factor of production, but no one then or since had attempted to specify a rate of return.

Schultz had been attracted to the "riddle of economic growth." It had been supposed that adding greater accumulations of reproducible capital to a fixed supply of land and labor would result eventually in diminishing returns to such investments. When this did not occur in the United States, one logical explanation was that the supply of one or both of the other inputs must not be fixed. Improvement in the quality of human resources was a possible answer.

Related enigmas surrounded the persistent relatively large increases in the real earnings of workers and the unexplained residuals in economic growth. Economists involved in the postwar recovery of Europe had found economies growing more rapidly than could be explained by the aggregate inputs of manhours of labor, the stock and flows of reproducible capital, and natural resources. The residual had been explained as a product of technological change,[7] but the source had not been identified. A technological improvement could include any change in the quality of the inputs, including labor; hence, education, health care, or any other investment in human beings could be a factor in that technological change.

Had the answer to the question "Does education pay?" been negative, interest among academic researchers might have died at birth. Because the preliminary results supported the predispositions of academicians and politicians, and the self-interests of the former, an immense literature emerged during the 1960s exploring and applying the investment-in-human-capital concept. Only the broadest outlines can ge given here.

Measuring the Returns

Bowen has summarized the general approaches to measuring the return to investment in education.[8] One approach has been to correlate indexes of educational activity with some index of national economic activity. Examples are intercountry comparisons of the relationship between per capita educational expenditures and growth in GNP.[9] In general, among underdeveloped economies those with the highest levels of education expenditures experience the fastest growth. But does the country grow because of its investment in human resources, or does it buy education because its favorable growth rate enables it to indulge its philosophical commitments? Or is it because high-level workers demand better education for their children? Other studies have compared levels of education expenditure to period of country growth. The indications are supportive but leave the same question. Does the country grow because it invests or invest because it is growing and can afford it? Interindustry and interfirm comparisons have the same possibilities and shortcomings.

A number of researchers have attributed to investments in human beings the residual in economic growth rates unexplained by inputs of capital and land. Such approaches rarely show a direct cause-and-effect relationship to expenditures on education, on-the-job training, health care or any other investment in human productivity, but they give strong support to education as a major factor. Kendrick found that for the period 1889–1957 a combined index of all inputs increased at an average of 1.9 percent per year.[10] Because the output increased at 3.5 percent per year the residual of 1.6 percent per year was attributed to increased productivity of labor, of which 80 percent was credited to improvements in labor and 20 percent to additions to the stock of physical capital. Solow identified a residual equal to 90 percent of the increase in output per manhour in the U.S. economy between 1915 and 1955.[11] However, it is only judgment that attributes substantial portions of this unexplained growth to human capital investments.

Given the difficulties of identifying the national rates of return from human resource investments, it has become the standard practice to measure the direct returns of education—that is, to compare the lifetime earnings of those with more and less education. The difference can then be expressed as an annual rate of return on the costs of the education.

This straightforward approach too has its difficulties. As with any cost-benefit analysis, measurement of educational costs and benefits is not simple, and the choice of an appropriate discount rate can often predetermine the results. Most of the studies have looked at a cross section of people of different ages, races, education, and incomes and assumed that what was true of an age-income profile would be true of individuals over their life histories. Yet the many changes in educational costs and techniques, life expectancies, occupational structures, economic conditions, and other factors make this unlikely. However, these are only technical difficulties. The more serious ones are conceptual. Education is only partially approached as an investment by its purchasers (investors). It may be the parent who pays and makes the judgment of usefulness and purpose. Education, being a consumption good, may change the tastes of those who receive it, radically altering other consumption and investment decisions. At the elementary and secondary level, attendance is a matter of compulsion, not choice. Society has decided it has an interest in the education of its citizens in addition to the individual benefits. If left to their own discretion and asked to pay for their own education, people, it is assumed, would meet their individual needs, but there would be insufficient education for social purposes. Measurements of return must differentiate between private and social benefits but neglect neither. If education is left to individual investment, those who can afford it will have it while those who need it the most to rise above their present circumstances will not be able to afford it.

If aggregate incremental earnings are taken as a measure of the national return from investment in education, the problem of conspicuous consumption emerges. As pointed out earlier in the chapter, if the employer hires those with educational attainment greater than required for the job, he may add to employee earnings without getting a commensurate increase in productivity. The most important criticism has also been identified earlier: Insofar as there is a tendency for those with the greatest native ability and motivation to gain the most education, the education investment may be credited with what is really an economic rent on unusual ability. Other technical and conceptual difficulties with the returns-to-investment-in-education approach are discussed in Chapter 27.

Despite all of these handicaps, however, careful scholars have appraised the contribution of a wide variety of investments in human resources, including education and training. Becker has estimated the private return on a college education and on-the-job training.[12] Hansen has calculated the rate of return for all levels of education from the first year of grade school through college.[13] Weisbrod has appraised the returns to lower levels of education, to health care, and to a variety of other aspects of human resource development.[14] Ribich has examined antipoverty efforts and manpower programs from the investment viewpoint.[15] Hansen and Weisbrod together have appraised the California education system from the human capital viewpoint and found it guilty of an inverse redistribution of income.[16] These are only a few examples from a voluminous literature.

For the most part, the results have been favorable to education; they suggest a rate of return above that normally expected from investments in other forms of capital. In general, the prescriptive message has been "more." But as noted, Berg has criticized possible overly favorable biases based on the factors of conspicuous consumption and native ability.[17] Chamberlain has warned that education enthusiasts may be laying a trap for themselves in their unrestrained endorsement of the human capital approach.[18] After everyone becomes committed to justifying education by incremental earnings "accounting techniques," what happens if diminishing returns set in? Will other social advantages be neglected because of overemphasis on economic values?

In the polemics of the debate over returns to education, we must avoid the conclusions that (a) technical difficulties in establishing relationships imply that no relationships exist and (b) criticism of a particular educational institution or process implies that that process or institution does not make an important contribution to learning. Moreover, there can be little question that, however difficult it may be to measure precisely, "trained intelligence" is the main hope for solving the world's social, environmental, and economic problems. Moreover, trained intelligence clearly is an important factor in improving the production of goods and services. However, intelligence can be and is trained in places other than formal educational institutions, and various places, procedures, and institutions undoubtedly have advantages and disadvantages for various kinds of intelligence training. The task of the future is to identify the unique role of each process and to improve it.

SUMMARY

There is strong evidence that in the 1960s education was somewhat overemphasized as a necessary preparation for employment. If so, that overemphasis was only overreaction in rhetoric to a belatedly recognized new fact of life. It did not result in an excessive allocation of resources to education. It resulted in an unrealistic expectation of what education could do in the short run for problems of long standing, and probably generated exaggerations of the contribution of education to higher personal and national incomes. There was implied overpromise that was certain to be followed by frustration and a negative reaction.

One cause of the public disillusionment was the unrest among youth, which was only partly connected to their role as students. Another was an underestimation of the degree to which educational reform was needed and the difficulty of bringing it about. Even the nature of the changes needed was unknown.

What remains beyond question, however, is that the thrust of economic and technological forces is toward those occupations of greater intellectual content. Jobs that have the highest social content are those that require articulation of ideas, orally and in writing. Any job a machine can do will continue to be performed by men only as long as men are willing to work more cheaply than machines. For anyone who wants to avoid that form of slavery, more intellectual preparation is necessary.

The educational world is in ferment. Experiments are numerous. They are certain to lead to a less monolithic system with greater variety and choice. Examples are the Carnegie Foundation proposals for an open system with freedom of entry, exit, and reentry, both in youth and later life, and the beginnings of "noncampus colleges" which seek to make it possible for anyone to obtain college credit for his work and life experiences and his independent study. There must and will be a better meshing between the school and the "real" world outside. Included will be a greater merging and smoother transition between the school and the labor market. Through it all, education, in some and various forms, will remain and increasingly be a prerequisite to attractive employment.

NOTES

1. E. Wight Bakke, *The Unemployed Worker and Citizens Without Work* (New Haven, Conn.: Yale University Press, 1940).

2. Ivar Berg, *Education and Jobs: The Great Training Robbery* (New York: Praeger, 1970), pp. 4–5.

3. Jacob J. Kaufman et al., *The Role of the Secondary Schools in the Preparation of Youth for Employment* (University Park, Pa.: Institute for Research on Human Resources, Pennsylvania State University, 1967), pp. 12:5–6.

4. Berg, *op. cit.*, Ch. II.

5. Rupert N. Evans, "School for Schoolings Sake," in *The Transition from School to Work,* a report based on the Princeton Manpower Symposium, May 9–10, 1968 (Princeton, N.J.: Princeton University Press, 1963), pp. 189–209.

6. Theodore W. Schultz, "Investment in Human Capital," *American Economic Review* (March 1961), pp. 1–17.

7. Robert Solow, "Technical Change and the Aggregate Production Function," *Review of Economics and Statistics* (August 1957), pp. 312–320; B. F. Mossell, "Capital Formation and Technological Change in United States Manufacturing," *Review of Economics and Statistics* (May 1960), pp. 182–188.

8. William G. Bowen, *Economic Aspects of Education* (Princeton, N.J.: Industrial Relations Section, Princeton University, 1964).

9. Frederick Harbison and Charles A. Myers, *Education, Manpower and Economic Growth* (New York: McGraw-Hill, 1969).

10. John W. Kendrick, *Productivity Trends in the U.S.* (Princeton, N.J.: Princeton University Press, 1961).

11. Solow, *op. cit.*

12. Gary Becker, *Human Capital* (New York: National Bureau of Economic Research, 1964.

13. W. Lee Hansen, "Total and Private Rates of Return to Investment in Schooling," *Journal of Political Economy* (April 1963), pp. 128–137, 139–140.

14. Burton A. Weisbrod, *External Benefits of Public Education* (Princeton, N.J.: Industrial Relations Section, Princeton University, 1964), pp. 95–96.

15. Thomas I. Ribich, *Education and Poverty* (Washington, D.C.: Brookings Institution, 1968).

16. W. Lee Hansen and Burton A. Weisbrod, *Benefits, Costs and Finance of Public Higher Education* (Chicago: Markham, 1969).

17. Berg, *op. cit.*

18. Neil W. Chamberlain, "Some Second Thoughts on the Concept of Human Capital," in Industrial Relations Research Association, *Proceedings of the Twentieth Annual Winter Meeting,* pp. 4–13.

Chapter 8
Counseling and Guidance for Occupational Choice

Efficient allocation of manpower resources requires each individual to be in the job where he can be most productive; in general this will be the job where he will maximize his earnings. Providing jobs that offer the most intrinsic satisfaction is another goal of the manpower system. All these considerations involve the process of occupational choice. No subject in manpower is of greater complexity. A number of theories attempt to explain the process of choice, but each rests on remarkably little empirical data. The demand for school counselors, the government subsidies for the training of counselors, and the introduction of counseling into almost every manpower program illustrate the widespread assumptions that counseling and guidance are the keys to sound occupational choice. Yet there is little evidence about what counseling is, who should do it, and how effective it is.

Chief among the difficulties of describing occupational choice is the fact that it is not a simple one-time decision. Rather, it is a complex development process continuing over substantial periods of time. A career encompasses the long-run objectives and consequences of an individual's experiences in the labor market. Occupational choice is complex, in part because of the vastness and changeability of modern occupations and the fact that young people are usually unfamiliar with the world of work. Attitudes and values, often conflicting expressions of each person's unique background, enter into the process and add complications.

There has been surprisingly little empirical study of the processes by which occupational choices are made, how the process might be rationalized, and what assistance is most helpful in practice. Most of the research has emanated from the field of counseling and guidance. Generally, it assumes the value of these functions and is designed to test the particular notions about guidance held by various leaders in that field. The limited studies, usually concentrating on small numbers of college students, are useful for their own purposes, but they tell us little about how occupational choice occurs, how valid the choices are, what the social and economic costs of haphazard choice are, how choices could be improved, and whether the costs of assistance would be justified by the benefits. This chapter reviews various concepts about the process and occupational choice and assesses the contributions of the counseling and guidance profession from which available information and speculation emanates.

THE PROCESS OF CAREER DEVELOPMENT

Most of the thinking about the process of occupational choice has been contributed by education psychologists. From the beginning of the century through World War II, those interested in the subject had as their ideal the notion of matching men and jobs. It was assumed that the process could be a mechanical one of defining job requirements in terms of individual traits and through testing, determining who was best qualified for which position. After World War II, increased attention was devoted to the roles of self-concept, feeling, and motivation in determining vocational choice— to the "psychodynamics of vocational behavior." Currently, lifetime vocational development is emphasized.

Theories of Occupational Choice

RATIONAL APPROACHES   Psychological theories of vocational choice may be divided into four major groups. The first—rational approaches to career choice—is more a technique of guidance than a description of how vocational development occurs. Through tests and interviews, the individual's aptitudes, abilities, and interests are identified and matched with the objective requirements of occupations. The development of the first intelligence scale (1905) and of Army tests for classifying men for military service in World War I cemented such testing and measurement into educational psychology by the 1920s.

Conceiving the goal of vocational guidance to be ability to predict occupational success, the psychometricians developed a wide range of intelligence, aptitude, and achievement measures, and even looked forward to the construction of a machine that would furnish differential occupational predictions from an input of aptitude test data. Despite the faith invested in these techniques, the limitations of such a highly rationalized approach slowly became evident. Research proved that IQ scores do not remain constant for individuals over time, that many achievement test were not properly validated, and that a person could successfully prepare for more than one area of work. Nonetheless, the trait-and-factor approach, which dominated vocational counseling until the end of World War II, continues to be widely used, especially when the client's abilities, aptitudes, and interests fit into a sharply defined pattern.

PERSONALITY THEORIES   A second group of theories about occupational choice has been influenced by the growing interest in personality which was sparked by Freudian psychology and the mental health movement. Two predominant theories of behavior emerged: One attempts to demonstrate that occupational choice is determined by the structure and interests laid down in early childhood and by the quality of family relationships; the other holds that interests and vocational preferences are expressions of personality and specifically that various personality types tend to enter certain work environments. However, empirical studies have both failed to substantiate the importance of early family relationships and demonstrated again the complexity of vocational development.

Focusing on the higher professions and occupations, the second theory categorizes a person's attributes into six types. A typology of work environments corresponds to the six personality types, with each environment being dominated by the corresponding type of personality.

The personality approach appealed especially to school counselors who claimed that many students in the expanded schooling process could not be helped with vocational choice as long as school and personal problems stood in the way. The goal was self-acceptance and understanding, with the client retaining responsibility for guiding the direction of his life. Psychology sought to deal with all types of life adjustments, not just vocational aspects.

DEVELOPMENTAL THEORIES   A more recent approach conceives of work behavior as a function of a prolonged developmental process which begins in late childhood. Occupational choice is thought to be an irreversible process which takes place over a period of years and consists of a series of compromises between intraindividual abilities, interests, and aptitudes and environmental demands, pressures, and constraints. As an individual reaches maturity, he becomes increasingly concerned with the realistic opportunities of available work environments and makes the compromises that result in a final choice.

An alternative approach emphasizes the development of the self concept and its adaptation to society through the work role. The individual's self-concept and vocational preferences grow and change with time and experience. By consciously matching his attributes with the requirements of a particular occupation or filling a work role that provides personal satisfaction, a person translates his self-concept into occupational terms.

Another developmental concept views vocational choice as a sequence of decisions with regard to school, work, and life. The process is conceived of as a two-way interaction between career and identity, in which the emerging cognitive structure of the self develops in relation to the world.

SOCIOLOGICAL AND SITUATIONAL THEORIES   A final category among psychologically oriented theories might be called sociological, situational, or accident theories of vocational development. These approaches are similar in that each assumes that circumstances beyond the control of the individual contribute significantly to his career choices, and hence that the individual's principal task is to develop techniques to cope effectively with his environment.

Because of the American "tradition of opportunity," we often presume that individuals have more freedom in determining what they will do in life than they actually do. The environment has its effect in shaping the individual's personality and influencing his choices. This relationship has been noted in such findings as the tendency of youth from lower socioeconomic backgrounds to aspire to lower-level occupations than do middle-class youth, and the inclination of some persons to follow work activities passively, merely reacting to situations, while others pursue a career on an active basis.

The Economists' Approach

In contrast, economists usually examine only the potential net rewards from labor and assume that the normal, rational individual will choose that occupation that promises the optimum lifetime combination of pecuniary rewards (compensation which can purchase goods and services) and nonpecuniary benefits (e.g., prestige, working conditions, and convenience). He maximizes his utility (satisfaction or pleasure), given the constraints of his innate abilities, preferences, and financial resources to improve his abilities. For any job, the pecuniary and nonpecuniary benefits must be balanced against the various costs, including the compensation foregone (opportunity cost) of passing up the most lucrative opening available; actual outlays for training for the position and opportunities foregone, for both expenditures and time spent, during training; and work-related expenses. An individual will choose that job that offers the greatest excess of benefits over costs throughout his expected work life.

Economists and psychologists do not ignore each others' insights. The individual's psychological makeup—which dictates his preferences for types of work, styles of life, aspirations, or attitudes toward risk—can be included among the economists' nonpecuniary factors. So can the influence of parents, peer group, and broader cultural surroundings which may affect his preferences. A host of social and demographic factors—age, sex, race or ethnic group affiliation, religion, and marital status—may also shape his preferences, though this influence may not be observable in available measures of the individual's personality traits.

Despite recognition of the psychological factors, however, economists tend to concentrate on what they can measure and are trained to deal with —the comparative pecuniary returns from working in various occupations. Such considerations have an advantage over the psychological ones in that they are easily measured. The few empirical studies performed by economists support the concept of the "economic man." Relative salary changes are responded to by increases or decreases in the flow of new entrants to the affected occupations.

THE COMPLEXITY
OF CAREER DEVELOPMENT

In the past two decades, the study of occupational development has been motivated by a desire to find ways of improving vocational choice. Before programs can be instituted to teach adolescents how they can or should make decisions, it is necessary to have a fairly clear formulation of ways in which career decisions are actually made. However, empirically validated conceptions of the process have been slow in developing. Although various researchers have postulated fairly simple formulations, there have been few longitudinal studies involving a sizable number of subjects. In addition to simplifying personality, the theories have generally ignored factors outside the individual—for example, socioeconomic status, family aspirations, preferences, ethnic origin, ease of entry to some occupations and inaccessibility of others, notions about occupational prestige, the nature of the educational system, and the influence of peers and adults.

Researchers are now realizing that no simple model of career development will serve to explain how the process occurs for most people, yet some theory is necessary to guide counselors. Interest is rising in multidimensional and probabilistic models but, thus far, guidance counselors operate with little knowledge of the process of vocational choice.

A recent trend is to focus more on extra-individual factors. Eli Ginzberg, for example, has shifted from analysis of factors internal to the individual (the approach in an early book on vocational choice) to a consideration of the way different groups explore, become established, and progress in their work and careers.[1] Through interactions between what an individual seeks to accomplish and the available employment opportunities, certain basic work relationships are established:

1. peripheral—labor force attachment is less than full time, full year; included in this group are youths with part-time jobs and married women

2. market—characterized by workers in full-time jobs who have little opportunity for advancement and limited job security
3. organizational—includes employment in a wide array of employment structures, such as government, business firms, and structured labor markets; the career pattern of most males culminates in an organizational relationship
4. individualistic—includes self-employed professionals, scholars, independent businessmen; requires either professional education, a specialized talent or skill, or ability to take risks.

These relationships change, of course, as individuals move from one category to another—for example, a peripheral female worker who begins to work full time. Ginzberg maintains that guidance specialists should use this model as they counsel young, mature, and older clients. Because most people have limited control over their own work, they must respond to conditions of the organization or market. Counselors use the model, for example, to assist women to prepare for a shift from peripheral status to full-time work and to assist disadvantaged workers who wish to obtain employment within large organizations where their opportunities for advancement may be greater.

Currently, these views about occupational choice are best described as unproven hypotheses. However, a number of long-term longitudinal studies are now underway which should clarify the developmental processes of career choices.

GUIDANCE PERSONNEL
AND WHERE THEY WORK

The increasing number and complexity of occupations, the advent of manpower and antipoverty programs for the disadvantaged, rising school enrollments, and the concern for the development of human resources have all interacted to expand vastly the demand for guidance personnel. Currently, there are approximately 60,000 full-time counselors, of whom 40,000 are employed in elementary and secondary schools and junior colleges. Two other major federal-state programs, the employment service and rehabilitation agencies, account for about 6,000 counselors each. The remaining counselors are employed by colleges and universities, private and parochial secondary schools, voluntary agencies, commercial enterprises, and special governmental programs.

Utilization and Training of Counselors

The counseling relationship is a personal one, influenced by both client behavior and counselor effectiveness. The counselor's effectiveness depends upon his personality as well as his knowledge and techniques. For this reason, both the selection and training of guidance personnel is important. Historically, training has been haphazard, but it has become increasingly professionalized in recent years.

Training counselors is not as difficult as selecting persons likely to find success and satisfaction in the field. General characteristics of successful counselors include a basic level of intelligence and emotional stability, flexibility, freedom from dogmatism, and, most particularly, an ability to enter into personal relationships with other human beings. Paradoxically for such a profession, the problem of counselor selection is complicated by the fact that most of the standard personality tests do not seem to be significantly related to counseling effectiveness. Grades earned by trainees in their academic courses correlate very poorly with supervisors' ratings of effectiveness in actual counseling situations.

There are several levels of training for counseling personnel. Persons obtaining Ph.D. or Ed.D. degrees are frequently called counseling psychologists. Persons with this level of training are probably better able to carry out psychological research investigations and supervise counselor-training programs, but may not necessarily be more skillful counselors than those with master's level training. Master's level preparation is by far the most common, with 6,500 specialist certificates, 44,000 one-year master's degrees, 6,500 two-year master's degrees, and 3,800 doctorates awarded between 1966 and 1970.

Demand in the mid-1960s for increased counseling personnel to staff the new manpower programs was the impetus for a new concept of support personnel. The most extensive and controversial attempt to use personnel trained in a short special program was Project CAUSE (Counselor Adviser University Summer Education). During the summers of 1964 and 1965, eight-week training programs were provided to train personnel to be employed by the Employment Service in the new Youth Opportunity Centers. A comprehensive examination of this program gathered data from 1450 counselors and their supervisors. The findings indicate that it is feasible to teach trainees to understand the situation of the disadvantaged in short periods, but that it is more difficult to teach counseling techniques and to orient trainees to the employment service. CAUSE-trained counselors experienced a very high turnover—of the approximately 3300 graduates, only a few hundred remained by the fall of 1967.[2] The program was widely resented by professionals, but it forced consideration of the appropriate functions of aides.

Recently, leaders in the field of vocational guidance have advocated the establishment of differentiated staffing patterns in school settings, which would utilize the services of individuals with different training, skill levels, and interests. The new patterns would require changes in certification, counselor education, and other areas, but would remedy some current problems. One of the most serious of these is that guidance personnel are not equipped to accomplish all that is expected of them. Typical school counselors lack the background to provide the type of service specified in the Vocational Education Amendments of 1968.

Noting that much of the vocational guidance functions will have to be carried out in group settings, Kenneth Hoyt has proposed that vocational education and counselor education departments cooperate in the training of "guidance teachers" at the undergraduate level. They would be responsible mainly for teaching group guidance to prospective vocational students in junior-high-schools. The preparation of a variety of guidance technicians in two-year (or shorter) programs was also advocated: outreach specialists, trained in the recruitment of the disadvantaged; data gatherers, who would conduct local occupational surveys and maintain up-to-date information on job and other opportunities; test operators, trained in the assessment of student potential for success in vocational education; and researchers, who would conduct follow-up studies of vocational education graduates.

Settings in Which Counselors Work

The majority of counselors are found in school settings, primarily in secondary schools. In all states except Michigan, counselors are drawn from the ranks of teachers, the normal requirement being one to five years' teaching experience. Work experience other than teaching is also a fairly common requirement.

ELEMENTARY- AND JUNIOR-HIGH-SCHOOL COUNSELING   Despite strong advocacy and some progress, widespread introduction of counselors into elementary schools is not likely to occur: There are not enough trained personnel. Educational administrators, faced with tight budgets and pressures for accountability, are likely to prefer specialists such as psychologists and remedial speech and reading teachers to help the exceptional child. Moreover, the contribution of counselors to the educability of the child has never been proven. However, steps should be taken to ensure that elementary-school students are exposed to the values of a work-oriented society because attitudes formed in early childhood years are likely to be lasting. Elementary teachers are in a position to influence such attitudes, but they must first gain better understandings of the world of business and industry. There is particular need for social studies materials oriented toward the noncollege bound as well as the outlook for college graduates.

In junior high school, students are just beginning to get an idea of the kind of adult they would like to be and are having their first opportunity to elect some of the courses they will take. They must make educational decisions which will affect their vocational choice and development before they achieve vocational maturity. One study of the vocational maturity of ninth-grade boys found that more than half of them planned to enter occupations that appeared inappropriate for them in intellectual and educational requirements. Guidance activities in the junior high school must capitalize on the vocational readiness that is already there and encourage the student to engage in further vocational development activities. The use of group guidance procedures to introduce students to the world of work is becoming more commonplace in junior high schools.

SENIOR-HIGH-SCHOOL COUNSELING   Most counseling activity occurs at the high-school level. Although this period is of prime importance in career development, studies of vocational guidance at this level repeatedly point out its inadequacies. Only about 50 percent of American high schools provide any form of vocational guidance during a student's educational career.[3] Even students majoring in vocational areas receive little occupational guidance.

The lack of adequate attention to vocational counseling in the high school can be attributed primarily to the extent to which the high-school years have come to be regarded as a time of preparation for entering college. Counselor time and effort tend to be concentrated on helping students with college plans—on the emphasis demanded by the students' families, their teachers, and themselves. Noncollege-bound students tend to be neglected; those contemplating college—and their counselors—are so caught up in meeting future educational requirements that comparatively little thought is devoted to the decision making in these students lives. A recent national survey found secondary-school counselors spending twice as much time on college-related counseling as on vocational topics.[4]

Thus, the improvement of vocational guidance at the high-school level depends upon countering the influence of the "revolution of rising educational expectations." Overworked counselors understandably respond first to pressures for assistance with personal problems and second to plans for college education. They must not only become better prepared in the vocational aspects of guidance, counselors must also appreciate the importance of career development and understand that vocational problems are not less worthwhile than personal and educational ones. Vocational guidance can be improved through the provision of better local occupational information, provision of high-school placement services where there is sufficient demand, and utilization of the methods and media discussed later in the chapter.

COUNSELING WOMEN STUDENTS   Studies have shown vocational counseling to be more deficient for girls than for boys. However, the need for women to receive educational and vocational guidance is increasing. Women, including wives and mothers, are entering the labor force in large numbers. More women are also entering higher education. While those with more years of education are more prone to enter the labor force, women can look to their traditional field of teaching to absorb only part of the number of college-trained women. Large numbers of women must prepare themselves to enter such fields as medicine, law, and science. Counselors could contribute by advising women of their potential opportunities, but vocational guidance presently tends to discourage women from preparing for nontraditional fields.

There is no way to identify in elementary school or high school those women who will become committed to a career. At the same time, preparation for some fields must begin in high school. Required are timely guidance and educational planning for the choices available to them, including combinations of career and marriage and new fields that are opening up to them.

COUNSELING IN JUNIOR AND SENIOR COLLEGES   It is ironic that guidance services for the college bound are the central concern of high-school guidance, but that once in college the student is largely on his own. College counseling tends to be directed toward personal adjustment rather than educational and vocational decisions. Many college counselors report a lack of student interest in exploration of vocational abilities. In some colleges, the reputation of the counseling service as the place to go with emotional problems discourages its use for vocational assistance. Involvement in college may also become a means of postponing career commitment. Small incremental decisions, such as enrolling in a particular course, are likely to have more influence on eventual career choice than consideration of one's talents, interests, and opportunities. Vocational uncertainty may be among the prime reasons for the fact that one-half of those who enter college drop out.

EMPLOYMENT SERVICE COUNSELING   Employment Service counselors, for the most part, enter the scene after the individual's most important occupational decisions have been made, as often as not by default. Employment Service representatives visit approximately one-half of the high schools in the country each year to administer the General Aptitude Test Battery and to counsel those members of the graduating class not planning to attend college. School dropouts, of course, miss this service.

In addition, Employment Service counseling occurs when the individual applies at a local office for placement. Ordinarily, unless he is applying for only a part-time or summer job, his schooling is behind him and the possibilities for further preparation are limited. Little career counseling is given, if the individual is seeking only a part-time or temporary job. If jobs are available, the individual may be referred without any appreciable counseling. It is primarily when no job can be found for an individual that he enters the counseling process. There he may be counseled on ways to make himself more employable, guided into more realistic preferences, or referred to a manpower program to improve his prospects. If he is young enough, he may be counseled to return to school. But at best, his alternatives are likely to have been so limited or channeled by time, responsibilities, preparation, and past decisions that counseling can only help him make the best among existing choices.

Employment Service counselors are usually college graduates who have accumulated some graduate credits in guidance; approximately one in nine has a master's degree. In 1964, the United States Training and Employment Service specified levels of employment in counseling positions and detailed education and experience requirements and scope of work for each level.

MANPOWER PROGRAM COUNSELING   Manpower program counselors operate in a world quite different from that of school counselors. Their clients are all out of school. Most have entered or experimented with the labor market and found themselves in deep trouble. They are likely to be minority group members and almost certainly have multiple competitive handicaps.

Training-program administrators may attempt to saddle counselors with disciplinary responsibilities. Some believe the two roles—enrollee advocates *and* enforcers of rules and discipline—are incompatible. Others feel it is better for counselors than unsympathetic instructors or administrators to enforce discipline.

Counselor-enrollee ratios are much lower in manpower programs than in schools, but almost every enrollee has a problem. Thus, counseling tends to be limited to the worst cases. Manpower program counselors at their best are aggressive interventionists. They may find themselves providing bail or birth control information, appealing for cooperation from creditors, arranging for transportation or child care, or begging for free medical services and a variety of other support activities to keep the enrollee in the program.

Occupational choice is the least of the activities. Referrals to training programs are ordinarily made according to openings available in particular courses. Because resources are inadequate to take the enrollee from his present status to his full potential, he will be prepared for whatever entry-level jobs are available or will be referred to those that require no preparation. In such circumstances, occupational choice must usually be slighted.

VOCATIONAL REHABILITATION COUNSELING   The vocational rehabilitation counselor is likewise concerned with making the best of his clients' limited prospects. The obstacles, however, are more likely to be physical and mental, though there is a wide overlap with socioeconomic handicaps. Counseling in this setting consists of (a) evaluation of a client's prospects to detemine whether he is potentially employable; (b) development of a rehabilitation plan jointly with the client to determine the steps to and the objectives of rehabilitation; (c) purchase of the services necessary to rehabilitation (primarily health with little expenditure on training); and (d) placement in a sheltered workshop situation or work with employers to develop a job opportunity.

A special federally funded training program prepares vocational rehabilitation counselors for this activity which has little to do with occupational choice. The tendency to add services to the socioeconomically handicapped affects only the nature of the services purchased, not the techniques involved in the delivery of these services.

INFORMATION BASES FOR CAREER DECISIONS

Vocational choice as a rational process based on assessing the individual's abilities and matching them with the requirements of certain occupations has always been an attractive idea. But, experience has established that its implementation poses problems. There are some difficulties in precise measurement of abilities and more in communication of information to the individual and his use of it. Nor is there a single occupation for which an individual is best suited.

Use of Tests in Client Self-Knowledge

Tests are used in counseling and guidance to gain knowledge. In addition to what the client would like to find out about himself, there are three major criteria for test selection: The most important criterion is validity, or the extent to which the test measures what it purports to measure; second, adequate norms showing how certain groups of people perform on the test should be available to the counselor; and third, the test should be reliable, or reasonably free from chance errors affecting the scores.

In recent years, testing measures have increasingly come under attack from representatives of minority groups who claim that the instruments are biased in favor of children who come from middle-class backgrounds. These criticisms are particularly meaningful when directed toward intelligence and placement measures, which in effect determine what sort of educational and training opportunities will be open to the student in the future. Authorities on intelligence testing have recognized for some time that some degree of measurement error is present and that an enriched environment, particularly one free of conditions likely to cause emotional disturbances, may result in an increase in IQ score.

In using test information, counselors must pay particular attention to the reference group for which test norms were established. A child from a deprived urban environment cannot be expected to perform as well as middle-class children. In addition, most tests are related primarily to cognitive functions and do not record students' strengths and weaknesses in many other critical areas. In certain settings, work-sample tests, comprised of a group of increasingly difficult and varied work tasks, have been used successfully with persons who have difficulty establishing stable work patterns.

The counselor must explain test results in such a way as to make them intelligible to the client. To do this, the counselor must have a high degree of skill in analyzing test results and their strengths and limitations and must integrate test results with background materials on the client.

The process by which personal assessments is facilitated in counseling has been described by Ginzberg:

> What are the essential elements of a sound framework for personal assessment? Personal assessment is a process in which a counselee, seeking clarification of his career goals, reviews with his counselor his strengths and weaknesses and explores the answers to questions about which he is uncertain. Both counselee and counselor start with a fair amount of information about the counselee's personality, background, and performance to date. As the counselee interprets his own characteristics, the counselor has an opportunity to judge whether the interpretations are reasonable or to suggest alternative interpretations. Occasionally the counselee is encouraged to take a test to get some additional clues about his capacities or interest, and this becomes one more input. The counselor must interpret test results in terms of their incremental input, knowing that the new information will be relevant only if the counselee is helped to assimilate it into his decision-making. It is the counselee, not the counselor, who needs to become self-conscious in developing and implementing a career plan.[5]

The tests most useful in counseling are vocational-aptitude and vocational-interest tests. It is not possible to predict success on the basis of aptitude and interest measures. But, in general, low scores predict better than high and can often serve to rule out certain occupational areas.

There is some evidence that vocational counseling supported by tests produces better outcomes than interviewing alone. However, researchers have been distressed to find that a large proportion of students who have undergone testing of their abilities and interests come out of their counseling interviews with little understanding about their own characteristics.

Academic aptitude, personality pattern, social status, and similar factors have been shown to have no influence on a client's willingness to accept information from a counselor. Different arrangements for imparting test information have not been found to be crucial factors in improvement of the self-image. Group and individual situations have been shown to work about equally well.

Uses of Occupational Information

The counselor's function is to see that the most dependable knowledge available is presented to and used by the client in making vocational decisions. The counselor should put the counselee in touch with the best sources of information and point out the alternatives and their consequences, but leave choice to the counselee.

Occupational information should possess several essential characteristics. The first is accuracy. Government publications usually meet this criterion, but publications of private schools, business institutions, and other groups may be propaganda pieces rather than sources of objective information. The second criterion, recency, presents a special problem because of the complexity and rapid change now characteristic of the occupational arena. Availability is another criterion of good occupational sources. The U.S. Department of Labor's *Occupational Outlook Handbook* is an example of a source that meets these standards.[6]

A final criterion for materials is appropriateness. The reading level of most occupational materials tends to be too high for a large proportion of the groups for whom they are prepared. Resources tend to be concentrated in white-collar fields and directed toward persons intending to pursue higher education; only about one-fourth are directed toward terminal students, and these materials are also of the lowest quality. There has been a particular lack of information about training opportunities in technical and business schools.

Counselors should possess knowledge of trends in occupational structure and the paths by which youth enter into the realm of work. A particular problem for counselors is that youths often aspire to jobs beyond their abilities. While the counseling situation must serve to equilibrate aspirations with abilities, counselors also have the task of helping to identify talent and facilitate its development. A primary source concerning occupational trends is the *Occupational Outlook Handbook*. In addition to summarizing major trends, it gives detailed information about 700 occupations and 30 major industries. Revised editions, which are printed periodically, are supplemented by the *Occupational Outlook Quarterly*.

The increased interest in occupational requirements and manpower forecasting has produced projections of greater scope and validity. However, there is a serious lack of information available on posthigh-school training opportunities not geared toward higher education. Counselors' ignorance limits the usefulness of those surveys that are available.

Despite the rapid expansion in recent years of federal training programs, no government agency has distributed comprehensive information about these programs. Kenneth Hoyt and others are developing materials to provide up-to-date information about posthigh-school training opportunities in technical schools and private business colleges.

In general, there has been little effort to evaluate the effect of occupational information or indicate how it should be used. Information about occupations is often covered through special courses or through units in social studies or other classes. Such courses have proved to be of most value when integrated with the counseling process, giving the information personal meaning.

Methods and Technology Used
by Guidance Personnel

In response to the emphasis of the last several decades on counseling for personal adjustment, the one-to-one counseling relationship became the standard procedure. Group methods have, for the most part, been limited to administering tests and conducting classes on occupations. But recently counselors have found that the influence of peers in group situations is effective in handling certain personal and social problems. Moreover, new technologies such as television are finding new applications in vocational guidance. Television has the particular advantage that the individual can view occupations in action and imagine himself in those positions, but deliberate exploitation of its potential has been limited. The occupational roles in which individuals are even unintentionally depicted on television probably influence considerably the attitudes youngsters develop about various types of work. Recognizing this, feminists have protested that the only function of a female actress on the highly popular children's show "Sesame Street" was to make conversation and serve refreshments. In response, the producers transformed her into a nurse.

For a number of years corporations and industries have produced films about occupational opportunities. The usefulness of these films often has not been great because they were not integrated with other materials about occupations. With this and other forms of education technology, usefulness is dependent on the methods that guidance personnel use in stimulating students to seek and use occupational information.

As with many other areas in which information processing is an important component, there is currently considerable interest in the use of computers in career counseling. Since the late 1960s, the U.S. Department of Labor has funded the use of computers in Employment Service job placement applications in a few states. In most cases, their function is to store and recall all of the job orders available at a particular time. An experimental system in Utah, for instance, matches employer requirements with applicant characteristics over a wide range of criteria. A few private services perform a similar clearinghouse function for specialized occupations, and a few firms use computers in their personnel activities, storing and recalling the characteristics and experiences of employees as needed for technical assignments. All are for immediate placement and are not used to counsel applicants on the employment outlook or occupational choice.

There are now in various stages of development about a dozen computer-based vocational guidance systems for use of students. These systems operate at various levels of complexity and are designed to perform a variety of functions. Their basic purpose is to serve as a library of occupational and educational information which can be taped by counselors or by counselees. Several computer systems attempt to estimate the client's vocational maturity, to analyze his approach to decision making. The computer may also serve as a source of information and feedback throughout the learning process; the vocational guidance capability would become an integral part of the system. Career games are used to stimulate the process of occupational choice and demonstrate the ultimate results of alternative choices. It is too early to evaluate these techniques.

Implications of Counseling Technology for Vocational Guidance

The newer technological developments are concerned more with vocational guidance than with personal or educational guidance. The use of counseling technology must be approached cautiously. First, substantial commitment of funds may be required, especially in the case of computer applications. Expensive systems, once in place, may preclude the adoption of other systems in the future. Second, many of the applications require that the user sharply define values that previously were only vaguely determined. As a result questions of control and value become highly politicized. For instance, some educators fear that interest in homemaking may decline as computer-based life-career games, make girls more aware of alternative life styles. Third, there is considerable danger of overreliance on technology and misapplication of its uses, similar to the overdependence on tests during the 1930s and 1940s.

Computers clearly have the advantage of freeing counselors from much routine record keeping. But to be useful to the individual student, the computer must be programmed to answer the questions the students are likely to ask.

Most of the computer-based systems now under development have been funded by the government or by computer corporations. For computer systems to be economical, computerized vocational guidance would have to be a part of a total system of computer management of the learning process. Though costs and staffing problems may prevent computers from becoming widely adopted in the schools, they may serve as valuable tools in determining how the decision-making process occurs in the adolescent.

ISSUES IN OCCUPATIONAL CHOICE

In general, little is known about the processes through which occupational choices are made and the techniques by which they can be improved. That no set of decisions has a greater influence upon life patterns is clear. But we do not yet know whether and how the process of choice can be improved.

Several conclusions can be reached about current attempts to improve the process. Throughout the recent emphasis on personal adjustment, there was a nagging concern that vocational guidance, particularly for the noncollege bound, was being neglected. Counselors appear to find assistance with educational and emotional problems more familiar and interesting. Although there has been considerable interest in the process of career development during the last two decades, much of the research was designed to assess the value of theories based on simple formulations. An awareness is developing that a variety of intra- and extraindividual factors affect career development. Research is complicated by the fact that the decision-making process as it occurs in adolescents may differ considerably from the process as it occurs in adults. Improving the career development of individuals requires a knowledge of how decisions are made; hopefully, longitudinal studies now in progress will provide this information.

Counselors continue to be in short supply. Because subprofessionals have been shown to function effectively, particularly in dealing with disadvantaged persons, some guidance leaders advocate differentiated staffing patterns requiring different levels of preparation. Such salutory efforts would require changes in certification procedures and funding.

The American tradition of opportunity may arouse higher occupational expectations among youth than the marketplace can fulfill. Guidance counselors may contribute to these overexpectations, particularly by overemphasizing the higher education patterns most familiar to the counselor.

Though generally considered intrinsically "good," vocational guidance or other forms of counseling have been subject to little empirical evaluation. It should not be assumed a priori that guidance services should be expanded. For instance, expanded use of counselors in elementary schools has considerable advocacy but may not be a wise use of resources. In addition to concerted efforts to improve various aspects of counseling and guidance, there is a need for more empirical evidence on what works, how well, for whom, and under what conditions.

The counselor tends to view his role as helping with personal and emotional problems, while the public expects him to assist with vocational decisions. Some feel that the counselor's role should extend into participation in curriculum planning. Others advocate that, rather than helping people live in the system, counselors should become active in attempting to change the environment. Manpower experts would give priority to building the counselee's ability to function effectively in the labor market. There is no easy way to resolve these differences.

Personal adjustment counseling is now benefiting from the recent developments in behavior modification and learning theory, and vocational guidance should also. Vocational guidance needs an application of energy and ingenuity too seldom shown; required also are a flexibility and adaption to needs of the situation, and multimedia and technological operations can be useful if properly applied. Continued attendance in school can become only a means of postponing life's vocational decisions. An acceptance of the importance of vocational development should help.

The challenge remains that everyone believes in vocational guidance, few do it, and none know whether it helps. No two decisions are more vital in life than marital and occupational choice. Yet none are made with less rationality. Although both choices are often wrongly made, no one is certain that rational processes would be an improvement. We can at least suggest greater research and experiment in the realms of occupational choice.

NOTES

1. Eli Ginzberg, *Career Guidance: Who Needs It, Who Provides It, Who Can Improve It?* (New York: McGraw-Hill, 1971), p. 52 ff.

2. Charles A. Dailey, Glenn H. Carlson, and Michael R. McChesney, *The Projects CAUSE: An Evaluation* (Washington, D.C.: School of Business Administration, American University, 1968).

3. Howard Rosen, "Vocational Guidance: Room for Improvement," *Manpower* (August 1969), pp. 6–10.

4. Robert E. Campbell, *Vocational Guidance in Secondary Education: Results of a National Survey* (Columbus, Ohio: Center for Vocational and Technical Education, Ohio State University, 1968).

5. Ginzberg, *op. cit.*, p. 181.

6. U.S. Department of Labor, Bureau of Labor Statistics, *Occupational Outlook Handbook,* 1970–71 ed., Bulletin No. 1650 (Washington, D.C.: U.S. Government Printing Office, 1970).

Chapter 9
The Role of Vocational-Technical Education

As was explained in Chapter 7, manpower development is only one of the assigned objectives of the school system; yet nearly everything in the school experience contributes in some way to the preparation for employment. However, only vocational-technical education in the high schools and at the postsecondary level, and professional and graduate study in the universities are dedicated specifically to preparation for employment. In this chapter, we appraise the objectives, status, and achievements of occupational education—secondary and postsecondary but less than baccalaureate. Data are available only for that vocational-technical education supported in part by matching grants from federal vocational education appropriations. Programs offered by private and proprietary schools and by public schools not receiving federal vocational education support are significant and must be considered.

Public budgets not only represent sources of funding for public programs, they also indicate relative priorities between public and privately provided goods and services and among alternative public services. The total bill for public education in the United States is $55 billion annually. The $1.2 billion spent on vocational education in 1968 is an indication of the relatively low priority given to employment preparation. Another relevant contrast is provided by the $500 million a year spent on remedial manpower training for those already in the labor market and in trouble in job competition (discussed in Chapters 16–21).

LEGISLATIVE INTENT

To assess the role of vocational-technical education on the present manpower scene, it is necessary to be aware of the sharp change of direction mandated by Congress during the 1960s. Federal support for vocational education (as Chapter 16 recounts) emerged during World War I; it emphasized the limited skill needs of the labor market. Our "adolescent" industrial economy required comparatively few professionals and skilled workers; for most of the labor force, education and formal training were unnecessary for employment. Three broad occupational categories were identified—trades and industry, vocational agriculture, and home economics—and $7 million a year were appropriate for matching grants to encourage states to train young people in those areas. Other occupational groupings—distributive education, practical nursing, fishery occupations, and technical training—were added as years passed, and federal appropriations increased to $55 million a year by 1963. But the original philosophy prevailed until that year. Then rising youth employment, one of the byproducts of the postwar baby boom, struck the labor market and provided the impetus for the first basic reconsideration of the original philosophy. The relationship between education and jobs had shifted, as explained in Chapter 7, until education and training had become prerequisites to successful labor market participation.

After more than a year of deliberation, a presidential task force charged vocational education with two cardinal sins. It had been insensitive to (a) changes in the labor market and (b) the needs of various segments of the population.[1] Vocational courses enrolled only one in five high-school students and 2 percent of the postsecondary labor force—inadequate numbers in view of existing and projected needs. Low enrollments in urban centers were especially disturbing. Little was being done to serve youths whose socioeconomic or academic handicaps made it difficult for them to profit from the regular programs. Vocational education was neither retaining potential dropouts nor preparing them for employment.

Postsecondary programs were being neglected despite the higher skill and upgrading needs dictated by technological change. The range of occupations for which training was available was limited, and the content of the training was narrow. The distribution of enrollments did not relate rationally to the distribution of employment opportunities. Nearly two-thirds of vocational enrollments were in vocational agriculture and home economics. There was little training for women other than in home economics; office occupations did not qualify for federal support. Employment services and vocational schools were in separate worlds. All of the services related to instructional quality—including facilities and equipment, teacher education, counseling and guidance, curriculum materials, research and evaluation—were being neglected.

Investment in vocational education was declared to be "grossly incommensurate with the national interest and federal responsibilities"; financial support was not keeping pace with the needs for a trained labor force. The legislative "patchwork" and absence of long-range planning were censured.

Objectives of the Vocational Education Act of 1963

Congress responded to the report with little opposition, even though the legislation offered to remedy the situation represented a radical shift in philosophy. The objective of the Vocational Education Act of 1963 was to prepare specific groups of people for employment rather than to meet the skill needs of various occupational categories.

> . . . persons of all ages in all communities of the state—those in high school, those who have completed or discontinued their formal education and are preparing to enter the labor market, those who have already entered the labor market but need to upgrade their skills or learn new ones, and those with special education handicaps—will have ready access to vocational training or retraining which is of high quality, which is realistic in the light of actual or anticipated opportunities for gainful employment, and which is suited to their needs, interests, and ability to benefit from such training.[2]

Although Congress authorized training in any nonprofessional occupation and increased federal appropriations fivefold over a three-year period, it failed to require reorientation toward the new objectives. Funds no longer had to be spent in the limited number of occupational categories, but no different distribution was mandated. Except for home economics, neither "carrots" nor "sticks" were provided to influence expenditure patterns. Ten percent of existing home economics funds and all new funds for that category were to be spent in training for gainful employment. Vocational agriculture could—but need not—include training for occupations related to but outside of commercial agriculture. Despite rhetorical concern for those with academic, social, and economic handicaps which interfered with their ability to profit from regular vocational education problems, no specific expenditures or programs were required for them. All uses of federal vocational education funds, except research, were governed by a 50–50 federal-state matching formula.

The definition of vocational education was broadened to allow expenditures for guidance and counseling, teacher training, and instructional materials. The Act also opened the door to basic and general education where needed to facilitate skill training. Thus, new objectives were declared and funds were made available; but whether the objectives were pursued was left largely to state determination or Office of Education leadership.

The Impact of the 1963 Act

Results fell far short of expectations. Although expenditures tripled between 1964 and 1967, the new federal funds largely supported the old vocational categories—except for the addition of office occupations. Too little recognition had been given to new occupations, few innovative programs were undertaken, and there was little coordination between general and vocational education. It was not even certain that enrollments had increased much more than they would have in the absence of the legislation. Enrollment trends had been upward before 1963. Office occupations, which hitherto had not been eligible for federal support, accounted for four-fifths of the enrollment increase. How much was an actual increase in enrollments and how much was merely a transfer from state and local to federal financing? There was no way of knowing.

The Vocational Education Act of 1963 advocated two basic changes: (a) Vocational education was to serve the occupational needs of all people in the community through unified programs rather than train them in separate programs of selected occupational categories, and (b) emphasis was to be given to the needs of those persons who could not succeed in regular vocational education programs because of educational, socioeconomic, and other obstacles. Neither change occurred to any substantial degree during the Act's first four years. For instance, only 1 percent of the funds and enrollments had been specifically allocated to the disadvantaged.

There were two apparent explanations for the limited impact of the legislation. The first was its permissiveness. New objectives were prescribed and funds were provided, but the latter were not dependent upon the former. The new funds could be used to pursue old objectives as well as new ones. The second obstacle, allowed but not created by the permissiveness of the Act, was the lack of national leadership from the U.S. Office of Education. The agency had a long history of providing matching funds without prescribing objectives, establishing substantial guidelines, or evaluating state and local accomplishment. Its leadership was also more comfortable with higher and general education than vocational education. In the absence of federal leadership, normal lethargies ensured that business would be continued as usual.

The 1968 Amendments

Congressional dissatisfaction prompted passage of the Vocational Education Amendments of 1968. Hoping to apply leverage from outside of the system, Congress dictated the establishment of national and state advisory councils which were given independent budgets and staff and assigned monitoring and evaluation functions. An earmarking approach was introduced to assure expenditure of grant-in-aid funds according to congressional priorities. Specific allotments were made for training the disadvantaged and the handicapped. Postsecondary education and cooperative programs—wherein students spend part of their time in the classroom and part on the job, all under school supervision—were also recipients of specific allocations. Other funds were set aside for special innovative and exemplary programs. Home economics was redirected to give special attention to the homemaking needs of working wives and the poor. The definition of vocational education was broadened to include emerging as well as existing occupations. As part of experimental projects and programs for the disadvantaged vocational money could be spent in elementary schools. Finally, states could receive money only upon the U.S. Commissioner of Education's specific approval of an annually updated long-range plan. In effect, the intent was to move from a grant-in-aid to a proposal-review-and-approval process.

These and other changes were made to push vocational education forcibly into the directions it had failed to take under the more permissive legislation. Any sting was taken out of the implied criticism by raising the authorization to $910 million by 1972. Whether change would, in fact, follow was more than ever before dependent upon the foresight and political courage of the Commissioner of Education. If the Office of Education had in mind what it wanted vocational education to be, it was now in a good position to move the system toward those concepts. If it continued without objectives and without the ambition to achieve them, the 1968 legislation would prove only moderately more effective than that of 1963.

Initial budgetary history after 1968 made it apparent that vocational education was more popular in the legislative than the executive branch. In both the Johnson budget released in January 1969 and the Nixon version which followed a few months later, the 1968 amendments were, in effect, repealed even before they came into existence by the President's failure to recommend funds for the new proposals. This decision reflected no high-level policy determination. Office of Management and Budget staff (formerly Bureau of the Budget) were not as trusting as Congress. Since the 1963 Act had brought no significant changes in vocational education, what reason was there to think that additional moneys authorized by the 1968 legislation would be more effectively spent? Since the amendments earmarked certain proportions of the funds for special programs, the regular program would have to be cut considerably. General budgetary restraint reinforced the staff position.

Nonetheless, Congress responded to pressures from the well-organized vocational education lobby by appropriating, and repassing after a presidential veto, somewhat over half of the authorized increases. A similar scenario of low executive request, congressional increase, and presidential veto followed for the fiscal 1971 and 1972 budgets, with overriding of the vetoes as a significant change. The result was a total federal vocational education appropriation of $498 million, nearly double that of 1968 but considerably lower than the $870 million authorized in the Act for 1971.

The first few years following the 1968 amendments were not unlike those following the 1963 legislation. Reorientation of an established program is always difficult to achieve. State and national advisory councils expected to bring independent voices into vocational education planning appeared more likely to serve as additional lobbying bodies than as reformers. The Office of Education had been handicapped by an inability for political reasons to fill some of its major positions, and the firing of its commissioners by the President did not add to its decisiveness. Stung by criticisms that it had never made the state plan process meaningful by rejecting a deficient state plan, the Office of Education overreacted by sending most plans back for revision—but on minor technical grounds. No one yet knew what a good state plan would look like, or how to write regulations and guidelines for developing such plans. The basic question—How can people be best prepared for employment at the less than college level?—was asked as a new Commissioner of Education took office. Existing legislation had removed most of the legal obstacles to experimentation and innovation, but there was as yet no accepted answer.

THE STATUS OF VOCATIONAL EDUCATION

The fact that vocational education legislation in 1963 and 1968 failed initially to achieve substantial changes says nothing pro or con about the quality and accomplishments of vocational education. It only indicates that the objectives of the Acts were not fully endorsed or supported by vocational educators and by the federal Administrations. But while it is relatively easy to assess the extent to which the legislation wrought changes, evaluating the status and achievements of vocational education is not. Indications can be provided by reporting expenditures and enrollments and by summarizing the results of fragmentary studies concerning characteristics of enrollees, relevance of curricula, and results of vocational education. Some idea of future directions may be gained by examining innovative developments. Though present trends do not support sanguine estimates of the speed of their adoption, the 1968 amendments might eventually provide the necessary incentives.

Enrollments and Expenditures
in Vocational Education

The federal vocational education reporting system is slow and grossly deficient, with data both limited and at least two years old. Any evaluation of vocational education must depend upon the limited official data, fragmentary studies by various researchers, and personal observation and judgment.

Sparked by a nearly fourfold increase in total expenditures in five years, 8.8 million persons attended vocational education classes supported in part by federal grants during the 1969–1970 school year, the latest year for which data are available. This was a two-thirds increase over the 4.6 million of 1963–1964. However, aside from the office occupations, as explained previously, enrollment increases in the first three years following the implementation of the Act were no more rapid than during the preceding years.

The 1969–1970 enrollment exceeded that of the 1963–1964 by 140 percent for high-school students, increased almost sixfold for full-time postsecondary students, and increased 18 percent for adults attending part time. Numerically, however, only 842,000 postsecondary students and 411,000 adults were added. After a slow start, enrollment in courses designed specifically for those with special academic and socioeconomic handicaps, as required by the 1963 Act, had risen to 9 percent of the total enrollment in fiscal 1970.

Home economics, which had 44 percent of total enrollment in 1964, still accounted for 30 percent in fiscal 1970; and only 2 percent were listed as training for gainful occupations. Vocational agriculture enrollment fell slightly in the same period; in 1970, one-third were in related off-farm occupations rather than commercial agriculture. Home economics and vocational agriculture together still accounted for 40 percent of all vocational education enrollment. As low-cost programs, however, they absorbed little of the available funds.

Technical education enrollment increased only 23 percent between 1964 and 1970, and this rapidly growing area accounted for only 4 percent of total enrollment in the latter year. One-third were part-time adults and 56 percent were postsecondary students, indicating that most of the courses were at levels or durations beyond the reach of high schools. Health occupation enrollment increased fourfold in six years but still totaled only 200,000. Distributive occupations increased 59 percent, with part-time adults comprising only two-fifths of the total enrollment. Trade and industry enrollments increased 78 percent to nearly one-fourth of total 1970 enrollment. Only one-third of this category, which includes most of the skilled crafts, was made up of high-school students.

Examining enrollments by the service groups specified by the 1963 law indicates that, in 1970, 25 percent of high-school students were enrolled in vocational courses, 7 percent in on-farm and 4 percent in off-farm agriculture, 38 percent in home economics, and 26 percent in office occupations. The declining opportunities in agriculture are well known; home economics, with minor exceptions, does not train for jobs. Limited studies suggest that a high percentage of those obtaining typing, shorthand, and other office skills use them in employment. In general, however, the extent to which high-school students were being prepared for employment after four years of the 1963 law was unimpressive.

Postsecondary enrollments were more in accord with labor market trends, even though they comprised only 11 percent of vocational enrollments and involved less than 4 percent of the 18–24 age group. Eighty-five percent of postsecondary vocational students were being trained in office occupations, trade and industries, and health and technical programs—all in high demand. Adult enrollments were an impressive 30 percent of vocational enrollments, though only 3 percent of the 25–64 age group. Trade and industries enrolled one-third of this predominantly part-time group; another third was in home economics and agriculture. One-fourth of the disadvantaged group was in home economics, another one-fourth in office occupations, and one-fifth in trade and industry.

One intention of the 1968 amendments was to cause a significant increase in cooperative education; this was occurring. Enrollments in cooperative education programs in 1970 totaled 290,000—two-fifths in distributive education, one-quarter in office occupations and another quarter in trades and industry. Health occupations and off-farm agriculture accounted for the remainder.

The addition of office occupations to those specifically eligible for federal support was appropriate in view of employment trends and the deficiency of vocational education opportunities for women. The shift to off-farm, agriculturally related occupations while praiseworthy was of small magnitude. Home economics provided useful homemaking skills but probably made only a limited contribution to employability. Considering the growing demands, the efforts to develop training in such critically labor-short areas as health and technical occupations and some of the skilled trades have been surprisingly limited. However, all of the trends appear to be in the direction of improvement.

Projected Occupations and Training

Vocational education has ambitions not only to meet immediate manpower needs but also to prepare students for lifetime working careers. In a number of occupations, the vocational education system is turning out far too few graduates to fill the openings. Low enrollments in crafts such as the building trades and tool and die making are accounted for by reliance on apprenticeship in these jobs. The divergence between projected demand and vocational education output appears greatest for associate-degree nurses and nursing assistants, medical technologists, law enforcement officers, firemen, barbers, and most occupations for which postsecondary but less than college training is the customary preparation. Enrollment in health occupations and technical occupations is furthest below the demand levels.

In contrast, enrollments and completions for food service workers, general merchandise clerks, blacksmiths, auto body and fender repairmen, automobile mechanics, and those trained in the graphic arts appear to be excessive in relation to demand. Most of these trainees, however, are secondary-school students, relatively few of whom tend to become employed in the occupations for which they are trained. Familiar courses of long-standing popularity—such as automotive sales, finance and credit, real estate, transportation, stenography, typing, airplane mechanics, electrical skills, drafting, machine shop, sheet metal, and welding—all have enrollments which, in relation to average annual openings, would lead one to expect an oversupply were it not for the low completion rates.

These comparisons reflect a reasonably good fit for familiar occupations, general underenrollment for many emerging and expanding occupations, and possible overrapid expansion of some of the more exotic of the newer ones, such as those in the computer field. Even vocational agriculture enrollment does not exceed the number of openings, if off-farm occupations are included; nor does home economics enrollment exceed the number of potential housewives. The issue for these two categories is one of priorities. Given limited funds, how much should be spent on them, even though their per capita training costs are low? Health and technical occupations appear to be the major categories of deficient enrollment.

In addition, there are a few expanding occupations whose skill requirements are appropriate for vocational training but in which no vocational education courses were reported in 1967. Among them are environmental health occupations, various medical technologies, floristry, systems and budget analysis, quality control clerks, and traffic rate clerks.

Who Receives What in Vocational Education?

Two out of five American youths (one-half of those who finish high school) attend college, and half of these graduate. Although a remarkable accomplishment, four out of five still must obtain salable skills in high school, postsecondary technical or junior colleges, uncompleted college courses, apprenticeships or on the job training, or belatedly, remedial programs. Yet only about 15 percent of high-school students and 3 percent of adults receive vocational training. The fact that so few of the noncollege bound obtain meaningful occupational preparation is undoubtedly a major contribution to the demand for remedial manpower programs (discussed in Chapters 16–21).

Employment preparation can be gained in a variety of ways, including formal and informal on-the-job training. However, formal, in-school preparation is increasing in importance. In some cases, the rise is attributable to the requirements of the job content. In others, it is only the fact that educated people are available and employers rarely need to rely on others. How many of the perhaps two-thirds of the young people who currently neither attain a college education nor receive any meaningful vocational education need formal training can only be guessed. One can be certain that the proportion is large and increasing.

Official vocational education data provide no information on the socioeconomic background, ability, and role of enrollees. But fragmentary information suggests that high-school vocational students tend to have below-average ability and to be drawn from families of below-average socioeconomic environments. Blacks, American Indians, and Asian Americans all report higher proportions in vocational training relative to their weight in the population than white students.

Observation of vocational education programs suggests the poorest facilities, equipment, and teaching in urban slums, high quality but limited availability in wealthy suburbs, and limitation to agriculture, home economics, and some office occupations in rural areas. Quality and availability appears better in small-to-medium-sized cities, but enrollments are still low. The competence of vocational instructors is at least as good on the average as that of other teachers. However, school counselors appear less available to vocational than to other students, better informed about and overly oriented toward college preparatory work, and prone to direct minority group members toward traditional minority occupations.

Results of Vocational Education

Vocational education enrollments represent the inputs, not the output of the program. What counts, both for the individual and the labor market, is the number of people with marketable skills who have more successful working careers than would otherwise have been the case. Data on the long-term impact are severely limited, but there is considerable information on the number and proportion of students who find training-related jobs within a few months after graduation.

Vocational education dropout rates appear to be higher than those of other school programs, even when controlled for ability and socioeconomic status. Considering the high proportion of youth who delay entering the labor force for further schooling or military service or who flounder on the brink of the labor market, the fact that a low proportion make use of skills obtained in high-school vocational courses is not surprising. However, the smallness of the number using those skills reduces the impact on the labor market and suggests that many were either not seriously training for a career or have changed or will change their minds about their career choices.

Vocational students have relatively favorable short-run employment and earnings experience compared to graduates of academic and general curricula; but data are not available for long-run comparison. In 1969, 16–19-year-olds averaged 12.5 percent unemployment compared to 5.2 percent for vocationally trained youth. Only two out of three of those who completed secondary-level vocational training were available for placement, most of the rest having continued full-time school or entered the armed forces. Of those available for placement, 77 percent were employed in training-related jobs and 14 percent in nontraining-related employment. Graduates of vocational and technical high schools also have more stable employment and higher hourly earnings than other noncollege-trained persons during the first few posthigh-school years. The earnings progression of the average academically trained but noncollege high-school graduates tends to catch and pass those of the average vocational graduates after a few years, suggesting that in the long run the generally higher capability prevails over the initial training advantage. However, vocational students have a persistent advantage when adjustments are made for differences in ability.

Benefits cannot be realistically appraised without costs. Various studies indicate that with its expensive equipment and lower student-teacher ratios, per-pupil costs of vocational education exceed those of academic programs by from $200 to $600 per year. However, these costs vary widely by occupation.

Proprietory Vocational Education

This chapter thus far has been limited to vocational education in the public schools. However, some 7000 private schools offer vocational training to 1.5 million students.[3] As proprietory and, for the most part, profit-seeking schools, they sell their services to students in competition with subsidized public schools at tuition rates that cover costs plus a profit. Two out of five schools and slightly over half of the students are involved in trade and technical education. About one-fifth of the schools with 28 percent of the students are business schools, with cosmetology accounting for over one-third of the schools and 17 percent of the enrollments.

Most are small (240 students or less) and highly specialized. In the trade and technical schools, data processing, electronics, and medical services are the categories of largest enrollment. However, they, along with automobile maintenance, drafting, and radio-TV, account for less than 60 percent, with the remainder spread over some 230 occupations.

Little evaluative data is available on these schools. Perhaps the best indication is that these students are willing to pay the full cost of their training despite the availability, in most cases, of public schools. Federal manpower programs have also made liberal use of such schools.

NEW DIRECTIONS
IN VOCATIONAL EDUCATION

No aspect of American education has been so consistently under attack as that designed to prepare its students for employment. Perhaps the reason is that vocational education, having a specific measurable goal, finds it more difficult to hide its shortcomings. At times, the response to criticism has been met defensively. Vocational educators have tended to separate themselves organizationally from the rest of education and, in closed circles, to reassure themselves as to their achievements. The more academically oriented, unembarrassed by any test as objective as a placement rate, do not seem displeased to have a nearby group to consider inferior. However, many in both camps have responded more positively. Search for more effective techniques of employment preparation is widespread among vocational educators. A few general educators have recognized the key role of employment in American life and, therefore, the key role of employment preparation. The result has been considerable experimentation and a widening recognition of the value of certain principles and techniques.

Some of these projects are at the cutting edge of vocational education development. Their location, nature, and sponsorship vary widely, but they tend to have a number of characteristics in common: (a) They tend to opt for an earlier introduction to occupational concepts but to delay provision of specific occupational skills; (b) they endorse a blending of basic, general, and vocational education, flexibly shaped to individual interest and need; (c) they are as often financed by foundation or general education as by vocational education funds; (d) they seek to broaden the range of occupations for which an individual is prepared; and (e) they assume change and the need for adaptability and continuous refurbishing of skills.

Each of these characteristics reflects a major contemporary issue in vocational education. Enrollments in postsecondary education are rising rapidly. High-school students have little experience upon which to base vocational choices. School hours are limited, and time spent in one form of education and training is inevitably at the expense of some alternative. As pointed out, vocational education is expensive and losses are considerable if no use is made of the training received. The skills that can be provided in high-school courses are limited, and many of the more rapidly growing technical occupations are almost precluded. For all of these reasons, preparation for specific occupations is often increasingly delayed until after high school.

However, about three out of five youth still receive no formal postsecondary training, and one out of four fail to complete high school. Despite the high dropout rate for vocational students who, as previously shown, tend to be drawn from dropout-prone populations, occupationally oriented education at its best could presumably raise the school retention rate significantly. Experimental programs have attempted simultaneous solutions to these interrelated problems. They seek to acquaint elementary and junior-high-school students with the nature of the world of work, motivating them to absorb general education at the high-school level by molding it around a core of occupational skills with training for broad job clusters rather than specific occupations. The latter tend to be the responsibility of postsecondary schools and employing institutions. Experimentation in skill upgrading and remedial education and training has been sponsored largely under the Manpower Development and Training Act (MDTA) and other federal manpower programs rather than vocational education, though vocational educators have been deeply involved.

Understanding the World of Work

Among the many impacts of technological change on society has been the growing gap between the home, the school, and the world of work. In an agrarian society, the home and the workplace were one. The industrial worker's child at least new where his father and the men of his neighborhood worked and had some idea of what they did there. For increasing numbers of today's advantaged youth, work is somewhere the father goes each morning with a full briefcase and from which he returns with an equally full one at night. The youth has little idea of the job content, and neither home nor school can fill the void. The disadvantaged child may have no father in the home; the family may be supported by a welfare check and wage-earning role models may be lacking.

A few central-city school districts—sometimes with foundation funds, sometimes with Elementary and Secondary Education Act (ESEA) funds, and less often out of their own budgets—have begun programs of early childhood or elementary-school orientation to the world of work. Through field visits, role playing, and other methods, elementary-school children are exposed to some of the vast variety of occupations. Such courses are often designed to include a general understanding of the workings of the economy as well as the nature of the jobs within it. At its best, this process continues with a broadening exposure through the elementary and secondary stages.

Melding Academic and Vocational Education

A basic premise underlying the Smith-Hughes Act of 1917 was the academic orientation of the U.S. education system. Unless separate funds were made available through a separate administrative structure, it was thought, educators would concentrate on general education and college entrance to the exclusion of preparation for work. Academic educators were just as willing to tolerate a separate, subordinate type of education which they considered of lesser value. They conceived of education as preparation for professions, and hence the verbal skills important to those pursuits, not manipulative skills and problem-solving attitudes, have been fostered and rewarded. Lecture and discussion have been emphasized, not learning by doing. And, not surprisingly, vocational courses have had a bad name among most teachers and students.

Increasingly, with the changing occupational mix, the separation of academic and vocational education is becoming less tenable. The fusion of general and vocational education would not automatically create instructional content that is more palatable to the student. But when the student perceives the information as meaningful in helping him to achieve sought-after goals, instructional content may become more attractive. Molding an academic package around a core of practical skills capped with work experience provided by cooperative employers could be expected to increase the relevance of the educational experience, particularly for those from deprived backgrounds with limited verbal skills and short time horizons. There are more examples of efforts both to offer a broad academic education and to increase motivation and provide salable skills by structuring the academic content around a core of manual or technical occupational skills than there are of world of work orientation projects, though the basic objective is the same.

For specific occupational training, the cluster concept is now widely accepted and practiced. Rather than prepare students for a narrow specialty and risk technological obsolescence or economic displacement, they are trained in a broad area encompassing a number of specific jobs. For instance, office occupations might encompass typing, filing, shorthand, bookkeeping, and several office machines. Machine shop practice has always involved training on a variety of machines. Electricity and electronics, business machine repair and maintenance, and graphic arts are other examples.

Manpower programs for the disadvantaged have contributed new approaches to skill training. Remedial basic education, which many need, has proved more effective if the subject matter is related to the vocational skill. Its availability, in turn, allows a promise of open entry, regardless of past education or experience. The unemployed could not wait for training until the beginning of a quarter, semester, or academic year, so training modules were developed to allow entry at more frequent intervals. Thus, a new trainee can enter a class in session and pick up previous modules later. Individualized instruction permits every enrollee to progress at his own speed. The cluster concept was adapted into an open-ended ladder approach, with each occupational area segmented into specialties. If the enrollee lacks the capability, motivation, or financial support to continue he can leave at any point with a salable skill. For example, a full course in automobile mechanics could progress through service station attendant, engine tune-up, brake and front end, radiator and transmission specialties, engine overhaul and rebuilding, and so forth. Prevocational orientation to aid the inexperienced make occupational choices and to emphasize work attitudes, continuous counseling, and on-site placement services also have proven useful. These and the other approaches are only beginning to influence vocational education in general.

Postsecondary Training

Perhaps the most significant development in vocational education has been the rapid expansion of postsecondary occupational training. Technical, health, and office occupations—which are experiencing the greatest growth among occupations not requiring college training—all involve job content difficult to cover in the time available in high school. The needs in those occupations coincide with the development of the community college concept. The latter, which contrasts with both the college transfer priorities of the junior colleges, and the ambitions of many postsecondary technical schools to turn out carefully selected and narrowly but highly trained technicians and craftsmen, lends itself particularly well to preparation for these occupations. A growing number of community colleges are committing themselves to serving the total education needs of the areas from which their students are drawn. They were among the first to adopt the lessons from manpower programs. Students are offered open entry without educational prerequisite, constant recruitment and no-wait admission, remedial education modular training components, numerous and open-ended occupational offerings of varying lengths, and close employer relations in addition to community service activities and college transfer possibilities.

A SYSTEM OF EDUCATION
FOR EMPLOYMENT

These piecemeal developments at the elementary, secondary, and postsecondary levels are sufficiently far advanced to permit a description of the system that might emerge. Among the attributes that make a worker employable, job skill ranks behind such factors as (a) mental and physical health, (b) a conviction that work is inherently good and is the most appropriate source of income, (c) good work habits and the acceptance of discipline, (d) mastery of the basic skills of communication and computation, (e) knowledge of the fundamentals of science and technology, and (f) possession of the information needed to make a wise vocational choice. Only the last three have traditionally been considered to be responsibilities of the educational system, and the last is rarely provided.

Educators have been reluctant to give primary emphasis to preparation for employment, fearing that it would thwart the more general goals of education for "life"—usually meaning citizenship, culture, social skills, and pursuit of learning for learning's sake. The dichotomy between employability and academic goals has arisen from the tendency to think only of specific job skills as the necessary employment requirement. Listing the other and more critical requirements of employability should make it clear that no such dichotomy exists in fact. The goals of education are difficult to define, but they would certainly include knowledge and understanding of one's society and of one's self in relation to that society, the ability to accumulate and process information and make rational decisions based upon it, identification and development of one's talents as a productive member of society, and a positive start in developing one's own life values. Nothing about preparing oneself for effective labor market participation need conflict with these broader goals, though conflict certainly can occur if preparation for employment is not pursued within an appropriate framework.

We have stressed earlier, however, that in our present stage of economic life human resources are the critical resources and that the individual's formal education and training are the primary determinants of his income and status. A school system that once offered a modicum of the three Rs to the general population and then selected out the relative few needed to fill the demands for skilled workers and the even smaller number needed for professional positions, now must put first emphasis on the individual's employment needs and then relate them to the demands of the labor market. Because most members of society find their highest achievement in their vocational activity (including homemaking), preparation for employment is critical not only to income and living standards but also to prestige, status, and self-image. In fact, occupational preparation as the core of the total curriculum might, for many students, provide greater motivation and more academic achievement than might be possible in its absence.

Students' vocational goals, to the extent they have any, may be a product of parental pressure and/or supposed "glamour," a factor which may account for the high dropout rate in some vocational courses and the low proportions seeking employment in the occupations for which they have been trained. A considerable emphasis is now being given to programs directed at helping students to establish realistic goals. This essential pragmatism is the motivation for earlier introduction and orientation to the world of work, improved counseling and guidance techniques, and exploratory programs. That same sense of relevance is easily recognized, but equally important, in the growing need to upgrade skills in an atmosphere of change and in the increasing emphasis on remedial help for the underprepared and victims of displacement. Vocational educators, it often is alleged, resist change by training for obsolete skills. However, it should be remembered that it was federal legislation, relevant in its day but unchanged over time, that locked the system into the occupational structure of 1917. It is not surprising that those with a vested interest in that structure did not urge change.

That innovative programs recognize the interrelatedness of career development with personal and social development, of academic with vocational education, of all levels of the educational process with the need for adaptability throughout a working life are promising harbingers of improvement. Vocational educators are, for the most part, competent people pursuing their jobs as they see them. However, the existing system is not well designed to make needed changes attractive. Discontent and, therefore, experimentation and innovation too often must come from outside the system. There is need for a system of accountability in which public funds become available only as the best of known techniques are embraced, adapted to the needs of particular communities, population groups, and individuals.

NOTES

1. Report of the Panel of Consultants on Vocational Education, *Education for a Changing World of Work* (Washington, D.C.: U.S. Government Printing Office, 1963), pp. 206–214.

2. Public Law 88-210, 88th Cong., 1st Sess., 1963.

3. A. Harvey Belitsky, *Private Vocational Schools and Their Students* (Cambridge, Mass.: Schenkman, 1969).

Chapter 10
The Role of Higher Education

Higher education, defined in this chapter as all postsecondary education in colleges and universities, plays an important role in labor markets and human resource development. Postsecondary education also is an important industry, providing employment to over 500,000 faculty members in more than 2,400 educational institutions. This system had total expenditures in excess of $20 billion during the 1968–1969 academic year. About 7 million degree-credit students were enrolled in these schools in 1971. This represented a dramatic increase in college enrollments from the previous two decades. The number of degree-credit students increased from 2.3 million in 1947 to 6.8 million in 1968, and is expected to increase to 9.7 million in 1976.

Postsecondary schools are important sources of technicians, managers, and professional workers. These institutions also advance knowledge, preserve cultural heritages, and facilitate upward social and economic mobility. The efficiency of the postsecondary education system and the access to it by all sectors of the population are thus very important for human resource development and for political, economic, and social stability.

The importance of higher education is not vitiated by doubts about either the precise relationships between education and productivity, discussed in Chapter 7, or the fact that the higher-education system is necessary to provide the manpower to operate a society that becomes increasingly complex as it develops. It is clearly possible to exaggerate the importance of the scientific and technical requirements of an industrial economy. Although the number of scientists and technicians increased during the 1960s, this increase resulted mainly from government action and the demand for teachers rather than from a demand for highly educated manpower by the private industrial sector. Moreover, studies of output per worker and occupational-skill mix between 1950 and 1960 do not indicate that those industries with the fastest rates of growth of output per worker increased their employment of skilled or white-collar workers faster than those whose productivity did not increase as fast.[1] Similarly, in studies of postwar developments in European countries, Denison found no significant relationship between productivity and educational changes.[2] The experiences of countries such as Japan demonstrate the possibility of operating a sophisticated industrial economy with average educational levels much lower than those prevailing in the United States.

There nevertheless can be little question that postsecondary education serves to increase the incomes of individuals, whether or not there is a causal relationship between this kind of education and GNP. The evidence shows workers with college degrees to have a number of employment and income advantages, such as higher beginning salaries, lower unemployment rates, higher labor-force participation rates, and higher lifetime earnings.

COSTS AND RETURNS ON INVESTMENT
IN HIGHER EDUCATION

Insofar as individual workers are concerned, the net rate of return on education can be determined by calculating the discounted values of projected salaries (lifetime earnings) and deducting the costs (or investment) incurred in obtaining an education.

Cartter estimates the following cost figures of obtaining a four-year college degree and a doctoral degree at a representative private university in 1968:

Cost of four years of college, beyond high-school education	
Direct personal costs (tuition and fees)	$ 8,000
Personal income foregone	20,000
Subsidized direct costs	4,000
	$32,000

Cost of doctoral degree over and above college education	
Direct personal costs (tuition and fees)	$ 6,000
Personal income foregone	30,000
Subsidized direct costs	12,000
	$38,000 [3]

These figures thus show foregone personal earnings to be the largest cost factor for college students, although other expenses can be very significant, especially to low-income groups.

However, the expenses of going to college vary considerably according to the type of institution. Of the total expenses incurred by colleges and universities, about 55 percent are for instructional services and 45 percent for housing and food services, organized research, extension and other public services, student aid, and other student services. In 1965–1966, the cost per standard undergraduate student in American postsecondary schools ranged from $652 in public junior colleges to $1,305 in private universities and $1,085 in public universities.

Because tuition and fees cover only part of the costs of higher education, postsecondary students are subsidized by their institutions. This subsidy declined during the 1960s as greater reliance was placed on tuition and fees to cover costs. In 1961–1962, the subsidy was $909 per standard undergraduate student; the subsidy declined to $859 in 1965–1966. However, there was considerable variation in the amount of the subsidy, ranging from $1,099 in private universities to $549 in public junior colleges.

Costs of higher education influence the labor market in a variety of ways, but principally as they redistribute income between income groups and influence access to higher education. Because a much larger proportion of students from wealthy families attend college, as will be shown later in this chapter, the wealthy are subsidized more heavily by higher education expenditure than the poor. However, once students are admitted to colleges and universities, there is very little variation in subsidy between income classes. In 1966, for example, the mean subsidy of college students was $612; students from the lowest quartile of income recipients received $660, and those from the highest received $586.

Costs seem to be barriers to higher education in the United States mainly at the undergraduate level, because the majority of students who qualify for graduate schools apparently find the means to go. The U.S. Office of Education estimated that in 1965 about 40 percent of the cost of financing graduate students came from government or institutional sources; another 40 percent came from earnings of students or their spouses; 3 percent came from loans; and the rest came from parents and other sources.

Bureau of the Census lifetime income estimates show that a college graduate earns an average of approximately $363,000 more in a lifetime than a worker who has less than eight years of formal education. According to these figures, a college education is worth $212,000 more than a high school education—a substantial return on a $32,000 investment (Table 10–1).

As pointed out in Chapter 7, however, these calculations of return on investments in higher education do not imply causation or that educated workers are more "productive" than those with less education. The questions of productivity and cause are very complex. We do not know the extent to which college merely separates people with superior ability, intelligence, socioeconomic status, and motivation from the less well-endowed. As Chapter 7 reveals, some writers have attempted to assess these factors

TABLE 10–1   *Lifetime Income by Levels of Education, 1967*

EDUCATION	LIFETIME INCOME (THOUSANDS OF DOLLARS)
Less than 8 years	$177–183
8 years	240–246
1–3 years high school	275–283
4 years high school	325–338
1–3 years college	383–401
4 years college or more	529–558

SOURCE: U.S. Bureau of the Census, *Statistical Abstract of the United States* (Washington, D.C.: U.S. Government Printing Office, 1970), p. 111.

and to attribute the largest part of the differential to educational experience rather than environmental factors, but there is considerable doubt about this conclusion.

In the United States, higher education has been perceived by persons from low-income backgrounds as an important means of upward social mobility. To some extent, this belief stems from the observation that college-educated persons have had higher incomes and less unemployment, especially during depressions such as that of the 1930s, when many of those who suffered from unemployment and loss of income acquired strong motivations to educate their children in order to make them "depression proof." [4]

There seems to have been a similar rise in aspirations to go to college by low-income groups during the 1960s, undoubtedly because these groups suffered high unemployment rates during that period and because civil rights developments raised the aspirations of many blacks and other minorities. Before the 1960s, the aspirations of high-school graduates from all income groups increased gradually, but during the 1960s a new trend apparently set in, and the gap between the aspirations of the poor and those of the rich began to close. Indeed, the proportion of high-school graduates in the lowest income quartile who aspired to college between 1959 and 1966 increased from 23 to 46 percent. In the second income quartile, the proportion desiring to go to college increased from 40 to 52 percent, and the aspirations of those in the highest two quartiles rose from 52 to 65 percent and 68 to 74 percent, respectively. Nevertheless, although there was a dramatic closing of the gap, high-school graduates from the lowest income quartile aspired to college much less than those in the highest quartile. Whether our system of higher education is a force for social stability clearly will depend upon the extent to which the rising expectations are matched by opportunities to acquire higher education.

Although it has clear economic significance, higher education cannot be evaluated in monetary terms alone. The higher-education system does much to preserve those cultural and intellectual traditions that influence the quality of life. In this role, institutions of higher education provide such benefits as extending the general base of technology, contributing to the advancement of knowledge and the arts, and providing support for public leadership. These benefits accrue to society as well as to individuals and therefore cannot be measured in benefit-cost or market terms alone.

The American emphasis on formal education undoubtedly was strengthened by a number of developments during and after World War II, which strengthened the conviction that education was important for national security. The emphasis on technology during the war gave considerable impetus to higher education, an impetus accelerated by the development of the atomic bomb and the space race in the postwar period. Clearly, much of the increased demand for college graduates following World War II was stimulated by the federal government. This stimulation resulted, in part, from the Cold War, which gave considerable emphasis to national prestige derived from scientific and technical achievements and the rate of economic development. Federal support for education initially concentrated mainly on the physical sciences and engineering, but it was extended to other areas as the federal government sought to strengthen educational institutions during the 1960s. In addition, the federal government stimulated college enrollments after World War II through the GI Bill of Rights and to some extent by granting draft deferments or exemptions to college students during the 1960s.

Postwar population developments also influenced the demand for college graduates. The college-age population declined during the 1950s because of the low birth rates during the depression of the 1930s and World War II. Indeed, there were actually fewer 15–24-year-olds in 1950 than there had been in 1930, even though the total population increased 45 percent during those years. As a consequence of these developments, there was only a slight increase in college enrollments in the 1950s, resulting mainly from a rising trend in the proportion of college-age people going to college rather than from an increase in the numbers of people in the college-age group. During the 1960s, the number of college graduates increased greatly because of the coming of age of those born during the postwar baby boom. The number of bachelor's or equivalent degrees increased from 187,000 in the 1940s to 287,000 in 1956 and 505,000 in 1965. The graduation of the postwar baby boom generation and the lower rate of population growth during the 1960s are expected to cause the demand for teachers to be lower during the 1970s and 1980s relative to the supply than was the case during the 1950s and 1960s.

ENROLLMENT IN HIGHER EDUCATION INSTITUTIONS

There is great diversity in the American system of higher education. There are over 7 million students at the postsecondary level in a great variety of institutions. About 60 percent of the class-hours offered to these

TABLE 10–2   *Actual and Projected Earned Degrees, 1940–1980*

ACADEMIC YEAR ENDING JUNE 30	BACHELOR'S AND FIRST PROFESSIONAL DEGREES	MASTER'S DEGREES	PH.D.'S
1940	186,500	26,731	3,290
1948	271,000	42,000	4,200
1958	363,000	65,000	8,900
1968	667,000	177,000	23,100
1969	755,000	189,000	26,100
1970	772,000	211,000	29,000
1975 [a]	928,000	302,000	45,600
1980 [a]	1,074,000	382,000	59,600

[a] Projected.

SOURCE: 1940 figure from U.S. Bureau of the Census, *Statistical Abstract of the United States* (Washington, D.C.: U.S. Government Printing Office, 1969). Other figures taken from U.S. Department of Labor, *Manpower Report of the President* (Washington, D.C.: U.S. Government Printing Office, 1970), p. 164.

students are in the social sciences, humanities, liberal arts, and law; 17 percent are in the physical sciences; 10 percent are in fine arts and applied arts; the remainder are in computer sciences and other fields.[5] Almost two-fifths of the class-hours offered by American postsecondary institutions are at the freshman and sophomore levels; 29 percent are in upper division courses, and about 8 percent are graduate courses.

The number of college graduates at all degree levels has sharply accelerated since World War II and is expected to continue to increase, although at not so fast a percentage rate (Table 10–2).

From 1940 to 1968, the number of bachelor's degrees earned increased 258 percent, the number of master's degrees increased 562 percent, and the annual number of doctorates increased by 602 percent. Correspondingly, the number of college graduates is expected to increase 61 percent from 1968 to 1980, while master's degrees are projected to increase by 115 percent and doctorates by 156 percent.[6]

The Commission on Human Resources and Advanced Education has estimated the total number of educational degrees for the 1966–1975 decade and compared those projections with the previous ten years. Except for medical degrees, it is anticipated that significant increases on the supply side will continue to occur (Table 10–3).

These enrollment increases reflect a much larger proportion of the population completing high school and a much larger proportion of those who complete college going to graduate school. In 1950, for example, 59 percent of the population 17 and older had graduated from high school. By 1969, this proportion had risen to 80 percent. The proportion of high-school graduates who go to college has not fluctuated as much and was about 50 percent during the 1960s; however, the proportion of college graduates who

TABLE 10–3   *Total Number of Degrees Granted by Level, 1956–1965, with Projections for 1966–1975 (figures in thousands)*

	TOTAL NUMBER FOR DECADE 1956–1965	PROJECTED DECADE TOTAL, 1966–1975		PERCENTAGE INCREASE 1966–1975 [a]
		Low	High	
Bachelor's degrees	3,795	6,970	7,710	84–103
Master's degrees	797	1,620	1,790	103–125
Advanced professional degrees [b]	365	583	643	60–76
M.D. degrees	76	89	92	17–21
Doctoral degrees	111	231	290	108–161

[a] Over 1956–1965 decade.
[b] Includes degrees in medicine, law, theology, library science, social work, business, and a few smaller fields.
SOURCE: John Folger, Helen Astin, and Alan Bayer, *Human Resources and Higher Education,* Staff Report of the Commission on Human Resources and Advanced Education (New York: Russell Sage Foundation, 1970), p. 28.

went to graduate school increased dramatically from one-sixth in 1961 to one-half in 1965. The heaviest increase in demand for persons with graduate degrees during the 1960s was in teaching; Ph.D.s have taught mainly in colleges and universities and M.A.s mainly in secondary schools and junior colleges. Because of rising enrollment, the demand for college teachers increased from 161,000 in 1960 to 247,000 in 1966, and will be about 200,000 in 1972.

OUTLOOK FOR COLLEGE GRADUATES

We should enter a word of caution about projections of the demand for and supply of college graduates. Although some aspects of these demand and supply conditions are fairly predictable, especially those that depend heavily on population projections, other are not as predictable, particularly those related to demand or to distant future events. In the long run, even population growth patterns change, as they did during the late 1960s and immediately following World War II. Projections also are complicated by biases in judgment, especially when those making the projections have vested interests in the outcome of those projections. For example, Allan Cartter, a leading authority of the economics of higher education, warns that federal agencies, such as the U.S. Office of Education, "cannot always be expected to be the frankest analysts of the needs in their own areas of concern" because "they must go to Congress each year for budget appropriations." [7] Despite these uncertainties, however, projections of probable developments in the demand for and supply of college graduates provide better individual and public planning than would be possible without these projections.

The Supply of College Graduates

The most important factors influencing the future supplies of college graduates are the proportions of college-age people in the population and the proportion of these who complete college. On the demographic side, college enrollments can be predicted with a fair degree of accuracy by looking at the proportion of 18-year-old high-school graduates who go to college. In 1970, the tendency was for about 61 percent of 18-year-olds who graduated from high school to go to college and 12 percent to other postsecondary schools. Of those who enter college about one-half graduate.

A major factor affecting college enrollments during the 1970s and 1980s will be the low fertility rates of the late 1960s; there actually will be fewer high-school graduates in 1986 (3,158,000) than in 1975 (3,459,000), even assuming that the proportion of 18-year-olds who graduate from high school will continue increasing at about 1 percent a year so that about 90 percent of them graduate by 1982. The number of 18-year-olds will peak at 4,344,000 in 1979 (as compared with 3,614,000 in 1969), decline to 3,509.000 in 1986, and rise gradually thereafter. The 16–21-year-old college-age population will peak in 1980 at 17,033,000, decline to 14,273,000 in 1988, and increase gradually thereafter. As a consequence of these developments, college enrollments in full-time equivalents will increase from 5,810,000 in 1968 to 9,834,000 in 1982 and decline thereafter to 8,541,000 in 1988.

The supply of college graduates increased sharply during the 1958–1968 period and is likely to continue rising during the 1970s, but it will decline in line with the above enrollment trends during the 1980s. Bachelor's and first professional degrees increased between 1958 and 1968 by over 80 percent—from 363,000 to 667,000. According to projections by the U.S. Office of Education, the number of bachelor's and first professional degrees probably will increase from 667,000 in 1968 to about 1.1 million in 1980, or by approximately 60 percent. These projections assume: (a) the trends in the college-age population discussed above and (b) the continuance of recent upward trends in college enrollment and graduation rates.

An even greater increase in graduate than in baccalaureate degrees is projected by the U.S. Department of Labor, based on the assumptions that past trends of those graduates obtaining higher degrees will continue and that there will be greatly expanded support of higher education. The growth in the number of M.A.'s awarded is projected at well over 100 percent between 1968 and 1980 (from 177,000 to 382,000), in Ph.D.'s at more than 150 percent (from 23,100 to 59,600). In absolute numbers, 13.3 million degrees are expected to be awarded during the period 1968–1980—10.2 million B.A.'s, 2.7 million M.A.'s, and 400,000 Ph.D.'s.

Of those receiving degrees, the BLS estimates that about 9.3 million college-educated persons will enter the civilian labor force—8.4 million

B.A.'s, 900,000 M.A.'s, and 18,000 Ph.D.'s. In addition, approximately 1.2 million reentrants and delayed entrants will enter the civilian labor force, making a total of approximately 10.5 million college-educated persons.

Demand for College Graduates

Looking on the demand side of the picture, employment requirements for college graduates and skilled manpower are expected to increase considerably as a result of employment growth, replacement needs, and rising job-entry requirements. It is estimated that 10.4 million new college graduates will be needed between 1968 and 1980 (6.1 million to meet needs of occupational growth and 4.3 million for replacement purposes).

These projections are contingent upon the following assumptions: (a) that a state of full employment will exist, (b) that the 1980 unemployment rate will be 3 percent, (c) that the size of the armed forces and the pattern of defense expenditures in 1980 will reflect a "cold war" rather than a "hot war" situation, (d) that scientific and technological advances will continue at about the same rapid rate as in the past, and (e) that expenditures for research and development (R&D) will continue to increase, although at a slower rate than in the late 1950s and early 1960s.

SUPPLY AND DEMAND RELATIONSHIPS

On the basis of Department of Labor projections, it appears that there will be a rough overall balance between the supply of college-educated workers and the requirements for them in professional and other fields. Demand and supply will each total somewhat more than 10 million over the 1968–1980 period. There will still be imbalances between supply and demand, however, in some individual occupations and specialties as well as in some areas such as small cities and rural communities.

Teachers

The outlook for teachers is important for higher education because about three-fourths of all jobs defined as requiring college education are in teaching. On the elementary and secondary levels, the aggregate supply is expected to exceed the demand significantly if recent entry patterns in the occupation continue. The number of new college graduates seeking to enter elementary-school teaching during the 1968–1980 period could be nearly double the projected demand, and the number seeking secondary-school positions could be nearly 75 percent above requirements. As noted below, it is predicted that the supply of potential teachers holding advanced degrees will grow more rapidly than the college population. The Commission on Human Resources and Advanced Education predicts that after 1970, the demand for college teachers with less than a Ph.D. degree will decline sharply. There might be some additional opportunities for teachers without a Ph.D. in expanding nondegree programs in four-year institutions, junior and community colleges, predominantly black colleges, and in extension, mail, and TV teaching.

In spite of the projected excess supply of teachers, it still appears that shortages will remain in rural and city ghetto schools and in the fields of remedial education, specialized education for handicapped children, preschool and kindergarten teaching, and vocational education.

Health Manpower

There are and probably will still be critical shortages in health occupations in the United States in 1980. The U.S. Public Health Service estimates that the shortage of physicians is probably as high as 50,000, a shortage rate of approximately 15 percent. It would be even higher were it not for immigrant doctors who comprise approximately 14 percent of all physicians in the country. The limited capacity of medical schools is a major cause of the shortage of doctors, but supply imbalances also result from the tendency of doctors to concentrate in larger cities and to avoid small towns and rural areas, many of which have grossly inadequate medical facilities. The outlook for the dentistry profession is much the same, and there is already severe shortage of nurses and paraprofessionals in virtually all segments of the health services industry—hospitals, nursing homes, offices of medical practitioners, and medical laboratories.

Natural Scientists and Engineers

Regardless of short-term fluctuations in employment opportunities, which result mainly from cutbacks of federal research and development funds, the long-term employment outlook for scientists and engineers appears to be one of strong growth. The increase in demand for engineers is projected by the Department of Labor at about 40 percent between 1968 and 1980; for natural scientists, the projected growth is about 50 percent. To meet projected requirements, approximately 45,000 engineering graduates and slightly under 45,000 new scientists will be needed annually. For natural scientists, this would include an average of over 20,000 openings per year for physical scientists, over 15,000 for biological scientists, and close to 8,000 for mathematicians. Recent enrollment trends indicate that this need for natural scientists can be met on an overall basis. For engineers, however, U.S. Office of Education projections indicate that the supply will fall slightly short of the demand.

On the whole, the United States should be experiencing the end of a general shortage of trained scientific manpower. Naturally, supply deficits in specialties will still occur, such as in new programs in marine science and environmental control. It also appears that there will be shortages of chemists, geologists, and geophysicists. Other areas for which potential shortages of professionals are in prospect include counseling, social work, urban planning, and a variety of jobs related to the planning and administration of local government.

Technicians

Bureau of Labor Statistics projections indicate that about 1.4 million engineering and scientific technicians will be employed in 1980. This represents an increase of over 50 percent above the 1966 total of 885,000. Physics and mathematics technicians are expected to have the fastest rates of growth. Engineering technicians are expected to grow more than 50 percent, from 300,000 total in 1966 to 450,000 in 1980. The balance between supply and demand will be improved if there is a continuation of the current trend toward expansion of enrollment in technical training programs offered in junior colleges, technical institutes, and area vocational schools.

Women

The number of women seeking a college education is rapidly rising. In the fall of 1968, the total number of women college students was 2.8 million, about two and a half times the number of ten years before. There has also been a steady rise in the number of women pursuing graduate studies. Between 1957 and 1968, the proportion of women receiving M.A.s rose from 33 to 36 percent, and that of those receiving doctorates rose from 11 to 13 percent.

Due to the changing supply-and-demand situation in teaching, college-educated women will have to shift their pattern of employment if they are to hold jobs matching their abilities. It is expected that more women will enter nursing, social work, nutrition, library science, and other traditional "women's professions," but that the demand requirements of these fields will not be sufficient to meet the increasing supply of female college graduates.

Some limited inroads have been made by women college graduates in the traditional male fields of social sciences, psychology, health technology, physical and occupational therapy, editing and reporting, accounting, mathematics, and statistics. However, in law, medicine, dentistry, engineering, and architecture—all shortage occupations—the proportion of women remains very small. For example, in 1968 women represented only 7 percent of the nation's physicians, 2 percent of all dentists, less than 1 percent of the engineers, and only 3 percent of the craftsmen.

Changing employer attitudes, emphasis on equality of opportunity, pressure by women's groups, and better preparation of women indicate that the employment of women will adjust to manpower requirements of the 1970s better than in the past.

TABLE 10–4   *Students with Federally Supported Predoctoral Fellowships and Traineeships, 1961–1970*

ACADEMIC YEAR ENDING JUNE 30	NUMBER OF STUDENTS AIDED (IN THOUSANDS)	PERCENT OF ALL FULL-TIME GRADUATE ENROLLMENTS
1961	9.4	7.5
1965	22.3	11.3
1966	28.3	12.3
1967	41.7	16.1
1968	53.6	17.8
1969	53.7	16.9
1970	45.1 [a]	n.a.

[a] *Preliminary.*
SOURCE: U.S. Department of Labor, *Manpower Report of the President* (Washington, D.C.: U.S. Government Printing Office, 1970), p. 165.

Workers with Postgraduate Degrees

There are likely to be considerable adjustments in the market for people with postgraduate degrees during the 1970s and early 1980s because graduate schools are expected to turn out 30–50 percent more degree holders than can be used in the jobs traditionally available to them. The most significant demand adjustment will be for college teachers. This relationship can be projected from college enrollments, because for each 100,000 new students, about 5,000 new teachers are required. Therefore, because of the enrollment trends discussed earlier, the demand for college teachers will decline absolutely between 1984 and 1989. The ratio of the output of Ph.D.'s to the demand for college teachers will increase from 2.5 percent in 1965–1969 to 9.5 percent in 1980–1984. Of course, all Ph.D.'s do not go into teaching. There is, however, considerable variation by fields in the extent to which Ph.D.'s enter teaching: about 90 percent for English and anthropology and about 33 percent for chemistry and physics.

Those fields that have had a low percentage of Ph.D.'s in teaching are expected to experience the greatest oversupply of Ph.D.'s during the 1980s. This is largely because the fluctuations in nonacademic demand have hit this group hardest. The decline in federal aid has been particularly important (Table 10–4).

During 1956–1966, nonfederal (R & D) expenditures increased at a rate of about 7.5 percent a year in real terms (adjusted for price changes). During this period, federal R & D support to universities increased about 14 percent a year in real terms, and federal R & D support to nonacademic agencies increased by 10 percent a year. However, between 1963 and 1970, total federal R & D support declined about 2 percent a year in real terms, amounting to a decline of about $0.5 billion. Because the reductions hit the physical sciences hardest, the demand-supply imbalances in these fields are likely to be particularly large during the 1980s (Table 10–5).

TABLE 10–5   *Ratio of New Ph.D.'s to Faculty Needs, 1970 and 1980*

FIELD	1970			1980		
	NRC [a]	OE [b]	AMC [c]	NRC	OE	AMC
Chemistry	4.1	3.9	4.1	9.0	6.6	6.1
Physics	4.7	4.6	4.7	11.2	7.9	8.1
Biology	3.1	2.7	3.1	10.0	4.5	5.4
Mathematics	3.3	3.6	3.2	6.6	8.4	5.5

[a] National Research Council.
[b] U.S. Office of Education.
[c] Allan M. Cartter.
SOURCE: Allan M. Cartter, "Scientific Manpower for 1970–1985," *Science,* Volume 172 (April 9, 1971), p. 136.

However, not all Ph.D.'s are employed in universities, and these projections of oversupply for traditional jobs are not expected to be very serious until during the 1980s and perhaps not even then, as we shall argue later. Charles Falk's study of the total supply and utilization of science and engineering doctorates projected no large "oversupply" during the 1968–1980 period.

The approximately 147,000 Ph.D. scientists in 1968 were utilized as follows: [8]

Activity

Research and development	48 percent
Teaching	38 percent
Other	14 percent

Sector Analysis

Universities and colleges	59 percent
Private industry	26 percent
Government	10 percent
Other	5 percent

Falk notes that the labor market for this sector had moved from a situation of widespread shortages to a rough equilibrium by 1968. Although the job market had tightened considerably for science and engineering doctorates, as shown by a decline in the number of placement offers and an increase in the use of more formal placement procedures, it was estimated that less than 1 percent were unemployed and that less than 1 percent were engaged in occupations outside their area of training.

By projecting future enrollments in the science areas (at both the graduate and undergraduate levels) and by taking into account projected retirements, deaths, emigrations, and so forth out of the sector, Falk projected a future supply of expected doctorates of 320,000 to 350,000. These figures are likely to be maximum estimates because there is some evidence of shifts of student interest away from the sciences. A 10 percent decrease in doctorate production in the last half of the 1970s would decrease the supply to 335,000; a 20 percent decrease during those years would lower the supply to 320,000.

Also assumed was a growth rate of 14 to 20 percent in the ratio of doctorates engaged in the so-called "other" activities (such as management, industrial operations, etc.). This basic utilization method indicated a 1980 utilization level of 277,000 to 301,000—slightly below the minimum supply projections. However, the basic utilization estimate does not provide any improvements in the utilization of scientists. An alternative projection provided for the following changes (based on the ratio of doctorates to non-doctorates): (a) graduate faculty from 85 to 95 percent; (b) other four-year faculty from 50 to 75 percent; and (c) two-year faculty from 8 to 16 percent. Other changes were that R & D spending would return to the growth rate exhibited during 1953–1966—about 10 percent per annum for federal R & D spending and about 7 percent per annum for private spending. It also was assumed that the ratio of doctorates engaged in "other" activities would increase to 25 percent.

Given these modifications, Falk derived the following projections:

Type of Modification	1980 Utilization (in thousands)
(1) Basic projection	277–301
(2) Return to previously experienced R & D funding growth rates	337–342
(3) Increase in doctorates (total faculty in postsecondary educational institutions)	300–334
(4) Increase in doctorates in "other" activities/total doctorates from 20 percent to 25 percent	296–310
(5) (2) plus (3)	365–370
(6) (2) plus (4)	349–365
(7) (3) plus (4)	320–343
(8) (2) plus (3) plus (4)	383–389

NOTE: The variance in utilization estimates derives from different estimating procedures —depending upon whether employment of scientists is broken down by sector or by activity.

With respect to the implications of his study, Falk concluded that significant numbers of Ph.D.'s are likely to be engaged in activities that are markedly different from those of most present doctorate holders. It is therefore very important that new Ph.D.'s be offered a variety of options of graduate training programs, including some that are more suitable for these new activities. Furthermore, students must not be educated with "false" aspirations for solely research careers. At the same time, it is very important that society transmit to graduate students an awareness that careers other than in research play an important role in both national and scientific affairs.

Whether these projections are realized will depend on a number of factors, especially: (a) what happens to nonacademic demand for Ph.D.'s;

(b) the ease with which supplies can adjust to demand; and (c) the validity of enrollment projections. There is little question about the enrollment projections through the last part of the 1980s because all of those who will be of college age at that time already have been born. The nonacademic demand for Ph.D.'s is the most questionable variable, but it will probably increase at least slightly. There can be some adjustment of supply to demand, but, as we shall see, the labor market for college graduates is very imperfect, and supplies are not likely to adjust to reduced demand very rapidly. The more prestigious private universities undoubtedly will cut their Ph.D. output because they are in financial difficulties which are likely to deepen during the 1970s unless they get more government support. Because graduate education is very expensive, this is one area to save money. Balanced against this, however, are a number of factors that tend to sustain the Ph.D. supply: (a) establishment of new Ph.D. programs in state universities; (b) the time (five to seven years) that it takes the graduate pipelines to be cleared; (c) the fixed costs many universities have in graduate education require large outputs in order to reduce the cost per student; and (d) the rising aspirations of women and minority groups to participate in the occupations requiring graduate training.

It would, however, be a mistake to conclude from these demand-and-supply relationships that many people with graduate degrees are going to be unemployed. As both Falk and Cartter emphasize, those with these degrees undoubtedly will move into jobs previously held by those with lower degrees. Moreover, as noted earlier, there will be considerable variation in demand for graduates and undergraduates in individual occupations.

Conclusions on the Outlook
for College Graduates

The United States is thus entering a new era with respect to its highly educated manpower—an era in which the demand for and supply of people with posthigh-school schooling will tend toward equality in many areas. This is in sharp contrast to the constant shortages that have characterized this employment sector since World War II. Although it is no coincidence that teachers, physicists, and others faced difficulties in finding jobs in 1969–1970 when the economy was experiencing its first recession since 1961, there are other long-term factors at work which seem to indicate that shortages of college-educated manpower will be alleviated. The impact of ever-increasing numbers of college graduates and doctorates is now being felt in the labor market. While this "surplus" benefits educational institutions—because they can now hire sufficient personnel to meet their needs at salaries that are more favorable from their point of view—it also results in frustration and dissatisfaction among students who have invested a considerable amount of time and money in the hope of finding a challenging, well-paying job in their desired field. However, the frustration of college graduates is likely to represent a "crisis of expectations" rather than a problem of unemployment. An American Institute of Physics survey found that 57 percent of doctorate holders wanted to work in universities, where there were declining job opportunities, almost none wanted to work in junior colleges, and only 4 percent wanted to work in government agencies.[9]

In time, the market undoubtedly will cause highly educated workers to be more evenly dispersed throughout the work force, but the adjustment process is not very rapid, even though salary appears to be a major, although not exclusive, factor in occupational choice. Because of the long periods of training required for members of this labor market, however, such responses tend to be "lagged"—often by as much as five years. Thus, while long-run adjustments move toward the desired equilibrium and allocation, short-run fluctuations remain troublesome. The operation of the market for educated manpower is discussed in the following section.

THE CHARACTER OF THE MARKET
FOR EDUCATED MANPOWER

Perhaps the best characterization of the labor market for high-level manpower is Arnold Weber's statement that when the invisible hand moves in the labor market, it appears to be all thumbs. The market does function, but in areas where much education is required it takes considerable time for supply to adjust to demand. This is true not only because of the time taken for education but also because once young people do one or two semesters of work in their chosen fields in college, there apparently are very limited changes in direction. Moreover, the market for educated manpower is not one homogeneous market but many discrete markets with separate demand and supply characteristics. As a consequence of market imperfections, to be explored at greater length below, there is considerable waste of high-level manpower because of limited knowledge about the relationship between education and work requirements and overstaffing of high-level manpower during times of manpower shortage.

The primary adjustment and allocative mechanism of high-talent manpower is its labor market. The terms "shortage" and "surplus" are essentially market related, and it is natural for the economist to use the market as an indicator of either of those manpower conditions. Critical shortages in particular occupations should reveal themselves through relative salary gains; surpluses, through relative salary declines. During the mid-1950s, for example, when private and government voices were expressing deep concern about the critical shortage of engineers, an economic study revealed that engineers' salaries were actually lagging behind those of many professional groups—a kind of market behavior that would suggest the absence of acute scarcity. Thus, while the many different definitions of scarcity as applied to the labor market and other conceptual difficulties must be overcome, the market provides a frame of reference for verifying and quantifying conflicting statements concerning the value and utilization of high-talent manpower.

The market for educated manpower is complicated by a number of factors. First, demand and supply are interrelated to the extent that the amount supplied to the market (in the form of college graduates, etc.) determines, in part, the degree of utilization by those demanding the services of educated persons. Thus, it becomes very difficult to predict and quantify the demand. The supply of highly educated manpower also tends to be inelastic in the short run, causing the burden of short-run adjustment to be placed upon salary increases or substitution of less-qualified personnel.

The labor reserve of an occupation—defined as "those persons who are trained and qualified to work in an occupation and who last worked in that occupation but are not currently employed" [10]—also is a means of adjustment, especially in those occupations such as nursing, teaching, and social work that employ a high proportion of women. The labor reserve has the advantage of being a potentially rapid form of adjustment—as much as 5 to 10 percent in several years' time. Salary levels are probably not as important in influencing those in the labor reserve as opportunities for part-time work and work schedules that fit children's school schedules.

The short-run forces that operate through the labor market determine the current salary level, and this is undoubtedly related to entry on the supply side of the market for educated manpower. But the relationship between salary and long-run supply is ambiguous and hazy. There seems to be no real consensus of opinion about the factors that affect entry into a given profession, although employment does seem to expand most rapidly in those fields with the highest lifetime earnings, after allowances have been made for costs and nonpecuniary benefits.

Analysis of supply and demand conditions also is complicated by the fact that few labor markets are "closed." Because workers cross international boundaries, it is not possible to restrict market analysis to factors influencing domestic demand and supply conditions. In 1969, for example, approximately 10,300 scientists and engineers migrated to the United States, and, as noted earlier, about 14 percent of medical doctors were immigrants. Although it is not known how many of these people obtained employment in their professions, in view of the past shortage situation, it is likely that most of them were able to do so. There are few data on the number of college trained people who migrated from the United States. The number of immigrants in 1969 was 20 percent below the 1968 figures, primarily because of revisions in the immigration laws, and, in 1971, many highly trained foreigners were returning to their countries.

Rhine and Creamer estimate that 1800 scientists and 5100 engineers immigrated to the United States annually during the 1960s. This constituted about 9 percent of the net annual increase in scientists and 15 percent of the net annual increase in engineers.[11] If the net inmigration turns to net outmigration during the 1970s, the pressure on the supply side of the U.S. market for these workers will be relieved somewhat.

Career choices are also influenced to some degree by such volatile events as the current social issues facing the nation. This would help to explain the increase in beginning students' plans to major in social sciences during 1961–1965, when there was considerable ferment over race, manpower, and poverty problems. We might also expect the current environmental crisis to expand enrollments in biology and other ecologically related courses. However, using intentions of students entering college to predict future supply is usually not very successful because as many as 50 percent of all undergraduates change their plans between their freshman and senior years.

In the past, the response to short-run problems has been focused upon expanding the educational output, and this method of adjustment can do little to relieve manpower problems in the short run. This lack of adjustment results in large measure from the considerable time lags in adjustments of supply to demand for highly educated manpower. High current salaries seem to induce many people to enter a field, but when they graduate, the large supply tends to depress wages unless something happens to increase demand. The relatively low salaries then tend to reduce the supply of people entering the field.

Another reason for the rapid changes in this labor market is found in the accelerator concept. Such change is especially prevalent in higher education, where a relatively fixed ratio is maintained between faculty and enrollment. Marginal increases in enrollment can cause a large increase in the number of teachers required, just as decreases in the rate of increase in enrollment (as was expected in the 1970s) can cause the demand for new teachers to fall rapidly.

Although the terms "shortage" and "surplus" are used to describe the demand-supply relationship in the labor market, these terms can be defined in a number of ways. Also, serious problems of interpretation of relative salary trends result from a labor market disequilibrium. In one sense, "shortage" means that the actual number is less than the number dictated by some social goal. However, this is a difficult concept to use because no objective measure of it is possible. A second type of shortage is the so-called "wage-rise" shortage which occurs when demand increases faster than supply at the prevailing market wage, and, as a result, competitive forces increase wages. However, such an approach has its conceptual problems. If a shortage is never defined as anything other than a price rise and the analysis is always in terms of relative prices, the awkward situation is predicted in which there might be a shortage of engineers relative to teachers but not relative to medical doctors. For example, Blank and Stigler concluded that there was no shortage of engineers from 1929 to 1954 because the ratio of median engineering salaries to the average wage and salary of full-time employees had declined from 100 in 1929 to 67.9 in 1954.[12]

A third type of shortage is dynamic in nature and consists of job vacancies caused by salaries temporarily too low to clear the market. If, for example, employers do not raise salaries sufficiently fast in response to rising demand, dynamic shortages exist which ultimately would be eliminated by rising salaries. Arrow and Capron think that one of the causes of alleged shortages in various disciplines is caused by this reluctance (or inability to pay the necessary equilibrium rate). Using the postwar family-servant market as an example, they state:

> . . . at the price they had been paying for household help, many families found they could no longer find such people (household servants). Rather than admit that they could not pay the higher wages necessary to keep help, many individuals found it more felicitous to speak of a "shortage." There is reason to think that at least some of the complaints of shortage in the scientist-engineer market have the same cause.[13]

Such dynamic shortages could take place readily in view of the very high skill requirements in many of the markets for workers with higher educations. In a short-run situation, a drastic rise in going salary might entice only a few more entrants into the market. And the nature of the process of career selection, while definitely having some relationship to earnings, is sufficiently vague to warrant an opinion that a salary increase, even of a large magnitude, might not affect the supply of talent in the manner predicted by traditional economic theory—namely, a shift outward.

The final type of shortage involves what is called projected, or cumulative, supply shortfalls and excesses. In this instance, the supply of a particular occupation is projected, based upon certain arbitrary ratios such as enrollments and student populations, and then the supply projections are compared with utilization or demand projections. The difference between the two projections enables the forecaster to predict either a supply shortfall or a supply excess. Although this approach is useful, it presents two difficulties. First, past trends must necessarily be used to determine such ratios as employment and enrollment, and there may be no basis for assuming that such ratios will remain the same in the future. But this is a problem faced by all future predictions. Second, there is the problem of determining demand because the supply of manpower will influence the degree of utilization.

Because the demand for labor is a derived demand, some of the market imperfections for educated manpower are caused by the nature of the product market. For example, private and public benefits from research, which is a heavy user of educated manpower, are apt to diverge in a market society. First, many of the benefits of private research activity cannot be capitalized in the market. Firms, for example, have great difficulty in extracting the full economic value of knowledge that, once sold, can be resold in the market. This causes private benefits from research to be much less than the social benefits. As a consequence, the competitive market will cause inadequate basic research to be done.

Attempts to rectify this divergence by issuing patents or permitting royalties to be charged for private information do not solve the problem because such measures tend to impede widespread application of new and useful ideas. Moreover, R&D costs for a particular research project financed by private enterprise over a definite time period probably are subject to the law of diminishing returns, but because individual projects may complement each other, research expenditures as a whole may not be subject to that particular phenomenon. Thus, the wide variety of projects undertaken yields total benefits that are greater than the sum of the individual project benefits.

The risk, uncertainty, and the length of time between project conception and fruition also may make it difficult to finance research entirely through market mechanisms. It is not always possible to anticipate the results of research. Moreover, more research might be desirable for purposes of general education and the advancement of knowledge unrelated to the *profitability* of the investments. In a sense, of course, the market might allocate research personnel after policy makers decided to expend funds for this purpose.

Conclusions on the Market for Educated Manpower

As noted in Chapter 12, labor markets are basic economic institutions, although we need to know much more than we do about how they operate. There are many kinds of interrelated labor markets. For example, there are many differences between the markets for people with postgraduate and undergraduate degrees, and, within the professional labor market, the market for medical manpower is quite different from the market for economists or attorneys, although they have certain things in common and both fall into what we define as the professional labor market in Chapter 12. We have noted, however, that labor markets for educated manpower do operate in rough conformity with economic theory and undoubtedly could be improved considerably by reducing the barriers to market adjustments, including the barriers to entry to undergraduate and professional schools.

However, even if the labor market for educated manpower were perfected, we have noted that it would not perform such functions as basic research, preservation of cultural values, and the advancement of knowledge, all of which are essential to the quality of life, very effectively. These decisions, therefore, must continue to be made by public policy or private nonprofit groups.

THE SOCIOECONOMIC STATUS OF COLLEGE STUDENTS

There is considerable evidence that the opportunity to attend college depends very heavily on socioeconomic status as well as on race. Perhaps the most important evidence of this was produced by Project TALENT, sponsored by the U.S. Office of Education, which found a very high correlation between socioeconomic status and the probability of entering college. Socioeconomic status of families is based on income, father's educational attainment, and several other factors within ability quintiles. In the top-ability quintile, 95 percent of all high-socioeconomic-status high-school graduates, but only 50 percent of low-socioeconomic-status high-school graduates, attended college. In the bottom ability quintile, 40 percent of high-socioeconomic-status high-school graduates, but only 15 percent of low-socioeconomic-status high-school graduates, attended college. Moreover, in 1966, 46 percent of students' families, but only 14 percent of all families, had incomes of $10,000 or more per year. At the other end of the income scale, 14 percent of all families, but only 4 percent of students' families, had incomes of less than $3,000 per year. There also is considerable variation in the kinds of institutions of higher education that high- and low-income families are likely to attend. For example, students from high-income families are less likely to attend junior colleges and four-year public colleges but are more likely to attend larger institutions and schools where students make high grades on aptitude tests.[14]

Although the tests might have some bias in them, the general trend to use aptitude tests for admissions purposes probably has made it possible for many talented students from low-income families to attend college, especially when scholarships or fellowships are available to those with limited incomes and high abilities. According to John Gardner, formerly Secretary of the Department of Health, Education and Welfare,

> Before the rise of objective tests, American teachers were susceptible —at least to some degree—to some social distortion of judgment. Against this background, modern methods of measurement hit the educational system like a breeze. The tests couldn't see whether the youngster was in rags or in tweeds, and they couldn't hear the accents of the slums. The tests heard the intellectual gifts of every level of the population.
>
> This is not to say that the tests completely eliminate unfair advantages for the young of privileged social background. They do not. But they are much more fair than any method previously used.[15]

Moreover, the tests also made it possible for teachers to identify talented youngsters who were doing poorly in school and adopt remedial programs to make it possible for them to develop. If Gardner is right, the answer to greater educational opportunity is not to do away with tests but to perfect them and to make them more useful in predicting the performance of youngsters from different backgrounds in college.

Our comments about the correlation between socioeconomic status and college attendance are not meant to imply that those who attend college have lower ability levels than those who do not. Indeed, the evidence suggests that of those going to college the number with ability is far greater than the number without. Although higher-income groups clearly have an advantage in attending college, there is a clear tendency for middle- and lower-class groups to increase their college attendance. The relative increase in the proportions of college entrants from the lower-middle and lower classes were much higher than the proportionate increases of those from the upper-middle class.

The Higher Education of Black Americans

Although we do not know all of the reasons why some talented persons do not attend college, we do know that college education is not evenly distributed according to ability, social class, or race. The proportions of non-whites who have completed at least one year of college are far below the proportion for whites in each age group.

As contrasted with other races, black college students come from families with much lower incomes. Blacks are, therefore, undoubtedly handicapped more than whites by financial barriers to education. Fifty-six percent of black students' parents had in 1968 incomes of less than $6,000 per year, while only 14.2 percent of the parents of nonblack students were in this income class. Moreover, 70.4 percent of the nonblack students' families had incomes of $8,000 and above compared with only 27.5 percent for the families of black students. It is, therefore, not surprising that a survey by the American Council on Education indicated that financing education was a major concern for 20.6 percent of black freshmen compared with only 7.7 percent of nonblacks.[16]

Because black and white high-school graduates compete in the same labor market the relative quality of education of blacks is very important for manpower purposes. In this connection, there is some concern about the relative quality of black and white education, at least as measured by aptitude test scores. One study claims, for example, that "the typical freshman (at a black college) usually performs at about ninth grade level . . ." and that a "white student with the same aptitude as the typical Negro college entrant has only about one chance in ten of entering college and completing his freshman year in good academic standing." [17] There is considerable variation, however, in performance among predominantly black colleges and among black college students. Moreover, black colleges are not inferior because they are predominantly black but because of the cumulative effects of institutionalized discrimination.[18]

Although a number of studies, especially the Coleman Report,[19] have consistently discovered that black students fall farther behind the longer they stay in school, other authorities have questioned the validity of the aptitude tests upon which these conclusions are based as predictors of success for black students. Clark and Plotkin, for example, report that blacks who generally scored low on the College Board Scholastic Aptitude Test (SAT) performed better in college than white students in the same colleges.[20] However, Berls concludes from an examination of this issue that "there is extensive and very careful evidence accumulated . . . to show that the SAT and similar tests predict Negro students' grades in Negro and integrated colleges just as well as they predict for white students." [21] Moreover, according to Berls, racial isolation causes the educational aspirations of blacks to be unrealistically high.

Equalization of the quality and quantity of black education would require considerable improvement in elementary, secondary, and college education available to blacks. However, improvement is not likely to occur at a very rapid rate, although integration of black elementary, secondary, and college students can accomplish a great deal toward equalizing educational opportunities. Most observers feel that the black colleges have an important role to play in improving the quality of black education. For one thing, many of the students attending black colleges could not gain admission to white colleges and therefore would be denied educational improvement if the black colleges did not exist. The remedy, therefore, seems to be to improve the quality of black colleges and to attract white students to them rather than to seek admission of all black students to white colleges and universities. Moreover, it should be emphasized that improving the quality and amount of higher education alone is not likely to resolve the problem of unequal economic opportunities for blacks without improving the incomes of black families or making more scholarships available to blacks.

For those blacks who have earned college degrees, employment opportunities in both professional and managerial occupations increased greatly during the 1960s. Eighty percent of male black college graduates and 82 percent of female black college graduates were in professional and managerial occupations in 1969. These proportions were substantially higher than those for male and female whites. Effective change in industry and government hiring policy since the Civil Rights Act of 1964 have increased recruitment on predominantly black campuses, broadened curriculum offerings in traditionally black institutions, and widened opportunities for black graduates. The growing number of black enrollments in predominantly white colleges and universities, in addition to the factors listed above, has been the major contributing factor to the opening of doors in professional and managerial occupations for blacks.

CONCLUSION

This chapter has demonstrated the close association between higher education for personal occupational mobility. However, the reader is reminded of the difficulties involved in establishing *causal* relations between income and education discussed in Chapter 7. Regardless of the experts' reservations about the returns to education, there is no question that higher education plays and will continue to play an important role in determining occupations. Moreover, these choices are made for many reasons other than anticipated economic returns. Improving the effectiveness of higher education for labor market considerations will require not only the basic kinds of educational reforms suggested in Chapter 7 but also the means to make it possible to equalize educational opportunities between racial and socioeconomic groups more on the basis of ability to profit by higher education than on the ability to pay for it from private family income.

NOTES

1. Joseph Froomkin, *Aspirations, Enrollments, and Resources: The Challenge to Higher Education in the Seventies,* U.S. Department of Health, Education and Welfare, Office of Education (Washington, D.C.: U.S. Government Printing Office, 1969), p. 10.

2. Edward F. Denison, *Why Growth Rates Differ* (Washington, D.C.: Brookings Institution, 1967).

3. Allan M. Cartter, "The Economics of Higher Education," in Neil W. Chamberlain, ed., *Contemporary Economic Issues* (Homewood, Ill.: Richard D. Irwin, 1969), p. 150.

4. E. Wight Bakke, *The Unemployed Worker and Citizens Without Work* (New Haven, Conn.: Yale University Press, 1940).

5. Froomkin, *op. cit.*, Ch. 4.

6. U.S. Department of Labor, *Manpower Report of the President* (Washington, D.C.: U.S. Government Printing Office, 1970), p. 164.

7. Allan M. Cartter, "Scientific Manpower for 1970–1985," *Science* (April 9, 1971), p. 133.

8. Charles E. Falk, "Science and Engineering Doctorate Supply and Utilization, 1968–1980," *Mosaic* (Spring 1970), p. 15.

9. "The Changing Job Market," *Science* (May 15, 1970), p. 781.

10. John K. Folger, Helen S. Astin, and Alan E. Bayer, *Human Resources and Higher Education,* Staff Report of the Commission on Human Resources and Advance Education (New York: Russell Sage Foundation, 1970), p. 352.

11. Shirley H. Rhine and Daniel Creamer, *The Technical Manpower Shortage: How Acute?* (New York: National Industrial Conference Board, 1969).

12. David M. Blank and George J. Stigler, *The Demand and Supply of Scientific Personnel* (New York: National Bureau of Economic Research, 1957), p. 23.

13. Kenneth J. Arrow and William M. Capron, "Dynamic Shortages and Price Rise: The Engineer-Scientist Case," *Quarterly Journal of Economics* (May 1959), p. 307.

14. Roger E. Bolten, "The Economics and Financing of Higher Education: An Overview," in U.S. Congress, Joint Economic Committee, *The Economics and Financing of Higher Education in the United States,* 91st Cong., 1st Sess. (Washington, D.C.: U.S. Government Printing Office, 1969), Table 3–6, p. 64.

15. J. W. Gardner, *Excellence* (New York: Harper & Row, 1961), pp. 48–49.

16. Cited by Robert H. Berls, "Higher Education Opportunity and Achievement in the United States," in U.S. Congress, Joint Economic Committee, *The Economics and Financing of Higher Education in the United States,* 91st Cong., 1st Sess. (Washington, D.C.: U.S. Government Printing Office, 1969), p. 183.

17. Christopher Jencks and David Riesman, *The Academic Revolution* (Garden City, N.Y.: Doubleday, 1968), pp. 428–431.

18. Kenneth B. Clark, "Higher Education for Negroes: Challenges and Prospects," *Journal of Negro Education* (Summer 1967), p. 199.

19. James Coleman *et al.*, *Equality of Educational Opportunity* (Washington, D.C.: U.S. Government Printing Office, 1966).

20. Kenneth B. Clark and Lawrence Plotkin, *The Negro Student in Integrated Colleges* (New York: National Scholarship Service and Fund for Negro Students, 1963).

21. Robert H. Berls, *op. cit.*, p. 188.

Chapter 11
Apprenticeship and On-the-Job Training

The basic idea behind apprenticeship is to have the trainee work with master workmen on the job while he acquires the necessary academic, or "job-related," training in classroom situations. Ideally, apprenticeship produces well-rounded craftsmen who know the theory and practice of their trades and who, therefore, can adapt to a variety of work situations. Well-trained journeymen not only should be more productive than those with less training but also should be less vulnerable to the technological changes that might render obsolete the skills of narrow specialists.

This chapter outlines the nature of the apprenticeship system in the United States and discusses some of the issues raised by this form of training. Public policy on apprenticeship will be discussed first, followed by an outline of the dimensions, trends, and role of apprenticeships. It also treats some of the controversies concerning this training system. The last part of the chapter considers the extent and nature of on-the-job training whereby workers are trained in the course of production, which is the most common manner in which skills are acquired in the United States.

PUBLIC POLICY

The basic federal law establishing apprenticeship policy is the National Apprenticeship (Fitzgerald) Act of 1937, administered by the Bureau of Apprenticeship and Training (BAT) in the U.S. Department of Labor.

The BAT has a field staff and offices in every state, and its main function is to promote apprenticeship programs by giving technical assistance to unions and employers, who determine their own requirements and administer their own programs within the framework of broad standards laid down by the BAT or state apprenticeship agencies.

The administration of apprenticeship is complicated by the fact that 30 states have programs of their own, containing over three-fourths of the nation's registered apprenticeship programs. These state programs are administered by state apprenticeship councils (SACs). The SACs take major responsibility for the registration of apprentices and the administration of apprenticeship programs in SAC states. There is, however, no clear line of jurisdiction between the functions of the SACs and BAT's state and regional officials in SAC states.

The BAT approves state programs that meet certain minimum standards. To receive federal approval, a state apprenticeship program must be administered by a state's department of labor. Other federal standards for apprenticeship programs include:

1. A starting age of not less than 16 years.
2. A schedule of work processes in which the apprentice is to receive training and experience on the job.
3. Organized instruction designed to provide the apprentice with knowledge in technical subjects related to his trade. (A minimum of 144 hours a year is normally considered necessary.)
4. A progressively increasing schedule of wages. Wages for apprentices ordinarily start at a certain proportion of the journeyman rate and progress to the journeyman levels over the period of the apprenticeship. [Generally, the programs with relatively more applicants than openings (electrical, pipe trades, sheet metal workers) start apprentices at relatively lower proportions of the journeymen wages than those programs with fewer applicants relative to openings.]
5. Proper supervision of on-the-job training with adequate facilities to train apprentices.
6. Periodic evaluation of the apprentice's progress, both in job performance and related instructions, and the maintenance of appropriate records.
7. Employer-employee cooperation.
8. Recognition for successful completions.
9. Selection of men and women for apprenticeship, without regard to race, creed, color, national origin, or physical handicap.[1]

If apprenticeship programs meet the standards set up by the Federal Committee on Apprenticeship and the state apprenticeship agencies, they can be registered by the BAT or the SAC, and those who successfully complete those programs are given certificates of completion either by the state agency or by the BAT.

Although some programs rely on correspondence courses for related instruction (and for keeping journeymen up to date), academic or job-related training normally is given through the public school system and is financed through state, federal, and local funds. The Smith-Hughes (1917) and George-Barden (1946) Vocational Education Acts provided for partial reimbursement from federal funds for salaries of teachers and vocational administrators to states with approved vocational plans. Some joint apprenticeship programs supplement the salaries of apprentice instructors. Moreover, an increasing number of programs seem to have their own training facilities for related instruction.

The local supervision of apprenticeship programs registered with the BAT usually is by Joint Apprenticeship Committees (JACs) representing labor and management. There are approximately 9000 joint apprenticeship committees; these committees may be national, state, or local in scope. Depending upon the trades, they usually are plant- or company-wide in manufacturing and nationwide in the crafts. These national committees do not impose standards or supervise individual training programs, although their standards usually are followed by the local committees. Local JACs might comprise a group of employers (as in the construction industry), a single employer and union, or an employer without a union. JACs sometimes merely advise employee and employer representatives who actually carry out the programs, but in a few states JACs actually direct the programs.

Table 11–1 shows the trend in registered apprentices since 1947 in selected trades. The number of apprentices peaked in 1949 and 1950, partly as a result of the G.I. Bill of Rights which provided stipends and costs for veterans taking apprenticeship training.

Although the trend in numbers of apprentices has been upward since 1962, there is considerable cyclical variation. One study found that more new apprentices were hired when unemployment was low, which probably reflects lenient attitudes on the part of both the employers and the unions.[2]

Apprenticeship not only is concentrated in a few industries, but also varies considerably in importance within those industries. Overall, apprenticeship is not very important for some trades, viewed either in terms of the proportion of journeymen who acquire their training through apprenticeship or completion rates; but it did account for the proportions of training for the crafts indicated, according to a 1963 Labor Department survey, shown on page 176.

Moreover, within a given sector of an industry—usually the part that is most heavily unionized—apprenticeship is known to account for some-

	Total Number Taking Formal Training (in thousands)	Percent Taking Apprenticeship Training
Compositors and typesetters	171	30.6%
Construction craftsmen	2,708	43.9
Linemen and servicemen, Telegraph, telephone, and power	260	36.8
Machinists	732	34.9
Meat cutters	132	56.1

SOURCE: U.S. Department of Labor, *Manpower Report of the President* (Washington, D.C.: U.S. Government Printing Office, 1964), Table F-9, p. 256.

what larger proportions of journeymen than it will in the nonunion sectors.

The ratio of new registrations to completions varies considerably from trade to trade. The carpenters have by far the most new registrants but fewer completions than the electricians and the plumbers. The carpenters' programs have a high dropout rate partly because many apprentices are able to work at the trade without completing apprenticeships. The carpenters also have relatively low admissions standards as contrasted with the mechanical crafts.

Students of apprenticeship seem generally agreed that among the construction trades, the electricians, pipe trades, and sheetmetal workers have the most extensive programs and rely more heavily on apprenticeship as a source of journeymen. This opinion is supported by studies of apprentices per thousand journeymen, completion rates, and such indicators as attendance at related instruction classes and scores on the General Classification Test for those entering the armed services in World War II.[3]

The reasons for the size and quality of the mechanical crafts' apprenticeship programs seem to be (a) the craftsmen in these trades are employed by subcontractors and therefore have steadier employment than workers (carpenters, bricklayers, laborers) who work mainly for general contractors; (b) their trades require more intellectual training as contrasted with those learned primarily by on-the-job training; and (c) these are growth trades compared with the carpenters, plasterers, and painters, whose employment has been declining.

APPRENTICESHIP ISSUES

Limited Understanding of Apprenticeship

Apprenticeship became controversial during the 1950s and 1960s because of the emphasis during those decades on black employment, poverty, shortages of skilled workers, and inflation—each a problem touched by apprenticeship. Nevertheless, this training system was not very well

TABLE 11–1 *Registered Apprentices in Selected Trades, 1947–1970 (in thousands)*

YEAR	ALL TRADES[a]	METAL TRADES	TOOL AND DIE	PRINTING TRADES	BUILDING TRADES			
					All Building Trades	Carpentry	Electricians	Plumbers and Pipefitters
1947	131[b]	—	—	—	—	—	—	—
1950	231	54	5	17	108	34	18	22
1953	159	15	6	10	77	21	14	16
1957	190	22	9	14	114	27	19	22
1962	155	22	7	13	101	22	19	20
1966	184	34	13	12	114	24	22	23
1967	208	45	17	12	122	23	25	25
1969	238	56	21	13	133	26	27	27
1970	274	57	22	14	137	27	27	28

[a] Includes trades other than those listed.
[b] Further breakdown not available.
SOURCE: U.S. Department of Labor, Bureau of Apprenticeship and Training.

TABLE 11–2   *Apprentices in Selected Trades,*
January 1970 (in thousands)

TRADE	NUMBER OF APPRENTICES
All trades	274.0
Construction	137.0
Bricklayers	9.9
Carpenters	27.4
Cement masons	2.0
Electricians	27.4
Painters	5.7
Pipe trades	28.2
Sheet metal workers	13.8
Iron workers	6.8
Other construction	15.8
Metal trades	56.7
Machinists	17.7
Tool and diemakers	21.6
Other metal trades	17.4
Printing trades	13.8
Compositors	4.3
Lithographers	3.3
Pressmen	3.3
Other printing	2.9
Miscellaneous trades	39.3
Butchers, meat cutters	2.8
Draftsmen, designers	2.8
Linemen	2.6
Electrical workers	3.9
Maintenance mechanics	7.8
Millwrights	3.2
Other	16.2

SOURCE: U.S. Department of Labor, Bureau of
Apprenticeship and Training.

understood by either the public, government officials, or civil rights leaders.

Confusion results, in part, from considerable diversity in apprenticeship programs. Apprenticeship sometimes is a very informal system, with
little attention given to providing the trainee a variety of work experience
and academic instruction related to the requirements of the particular craft.
Other programs are better organized and provide all of these things. Some
of the better programs are registered with either the BAT or various state
apprenticeship councils, while others are not registered with any governmental agency. As noted earlier, registered programs vary considerably
from place to place with respect to such matters as ratio of applicants to

openings, completion rates, duration of training, proportion of journeymen who have served apprenticeships, employer participation in training, value and nature of related instruction, ratio of apprentice to journeyman wages. This diversity makes it difficult to generalize about apprenticeship.

Outsiders also are likely to confuse the ideal or expressed apprenticeship standards and requirements with the actual but less formal system. The formalized apprenticeship programs depicted in the BAT brochures are likely to conceal considerable flexibility and diversity, particularly in the construction industry where more registered apprentices are employed than in any other industry. The formalized system shows rather rigid apprenticeship requirements which have not changed very much through time, whereas in actuality there is considerable flexibility and diversity, with some apprentices, in fact, becoming journeymen before completing the formal apprenticeship period—depending upon such factors as the relevance of the standards and procedures to job requirements, labor market conditions, and the degree of control exercised over the program by unions and employers.

While a formal statement of the craft structure in the construction trades might suggest inflexible apprentice and journeyman classifications, there are, in fact, a wide variety of actual classifications, specializations, and statuses according to type and degree of skill. Moreover, there are regular flows of people between residential jobs (which are ordinarily the least desirable and require lower skills) and the better and more highly skilled commercial and industrial jobs. In this process, depending upon craft and industry, workers learn their trades by a variety of means, including (a) completing part of an apprenticeship; (b) picking the trade up on the job or in the armed forces; and (c) working in nonunion jobs and transferring into unionized programs during organizing campaigns or during periods of full employment of union craftsmen.

Adequacy of Apprenticeship

Some of the controversy relates to the adequacy of apprenticeship training to meet the nation's manpower needs. But because of technical difficulties in projecting manpower requirements, this is likely to remain an unresolved issue. Because they would like to see tight labor markets, the unions are suspicious of projection that would call forth demands for increasing the supplies of labor beyond what the unions consider adequate to maintain steady employment. Government officials, however, want to avoid labor shortages which put upward pressure on wages and prices and therefore want to increase labor supplies.

The nature of this problem was revealed in the dispute over the President's 1963 *Manpower Report* projection that by 1970 apprenticeship completions as a percent of the need for various construction trades would be:

Electricians	36%
Bricklayers	22
Sheetmetal workers	21
Pipe trades	17
Iron workers	15
Plasterers	15
Carpenters	6
Painters	3

The projections of manpower needs on which these estimates were based were denounced as unrealistically high by President C. J. Haggerty of the AFL-CIO Building and Construction Trades Department and have not been reprinted in subsequent manpower reports.

Controversy over apprenticeship also results from confusion as to the role this system plays in those trades where it is concentrated. While the construction industry, for example, considers apprentices to be well trained and affords the journeyman who has served an apprenticeship a special status, many men have not served apprenticeships. Not all workers in the construction industry need to be all-round craftsmen with a knowledge of the theory and practice of their trade, but each employer must have a cadre of key men who meet his manpower needs. These key men, who often have served apprenticeships, supervise those who are not as well trained.

Many people question whether in every instance apprenticeship provides better training than informal means. Many of these critics ask whether all workers need to serve apprenticeships of the same length, and some apprentices believe they have the necessary academic training and resent having to go back to school. Representatives of the apprenticeship establishment (unions, employers, and specialized government agencies dealing with apprenticeship) argue that workers who came into the trades through other means might be just as competent at particular tasks as apprentice-trained men, but they are less likely to have received systematic instruction. Moreover, the defenders of the system argue from the worker's point of view that apprenticeship makes it possible for trainees to become craftsmen and enter supervisory ranks faster than through other means.

Unfortunately, there is very little objective evidence to test the validity of the claims made for and against apprenticeship. However, available evidence does suggest a number of at least tentative conclusions about this system.

1. The time required for training differs among individuals—a factor recognized by some crafts which permit apprentice dropouts to become journeymen before completing the period of apprenticeship. Moreover, other individuals take longer to complete their training than the prescribed standards because they fail one or more periodic tests and are required to repeat this phase of their training.

2. Little logical difference would appear to exist between the methods of acquiring skills in terms of the competence of the craftsmen; the important thing for this point is that the skills and knowledge are acquired, not the method of acquisition. However, the limited evidence available supports the conclusion that systematic training such as that provided by the ideal apprenticeship program makes it possible to become an all-around craftsman faster than informal types of training.[4]

3. The limited evidence available suggests that men who serve apprenticeships are upgraded faster than those who do not.

There is no objective evidence concerning the relevance of admissions standards and procedures, and this question is not likely to be easily resolved. Highly specific tests would be required to clarify the issue because of the diversity of situations. Moreover, to a considerable extent this is a judgmental question not subject to precise determination. Industry representatives, who presumably have superior information, disagree among themselves. Resolution of this controversial question will, therefore, probably be more in terms of agreement on the mechanism for determining qualifications and standards than in terms of precise determination of the standards and qualifications themselves.

Racial Discrimination

The issue of racial discrimination has caused more controversy about apprenticeship than any other. Civil rights leaders attacked the apprenticeship system during the 1950s and 1960s, when demand for unskilled workers was declining, because these programs led to good jobs in skilled trades which had very few blacks in them. According to the 1960 census, only 2,191 apprentices, or 2.52 percent of the total, were nonwhite. The lack of black apprentices has been confirmed by many other studies.[5]

The reasons for the paucity of black apprentices also seem to be fairly clear, though the relative weights to be assigned the various factors are not precise. Most of the reasons directly or indirectly involve racial discrimination—through specific and overt refusal to accept black applicants, but even more through the more pervasive institutional segregation which discourages blacks from applying for apprenticeship programs and apprenticeship committees from including black sources in their recruitment patterns. Institutionalized discrimination also causes a lower percentage of blacks to meet the qualifications for admission to many of the apprenticeship programs.

As a result of agitation for change by civil rights groups, there have been many efforts to increase the number of black apprentices and journeymen, especially in the construction industry. In 1963, Secretary of Labor Willard Wirtz approved new federal standards requiring all registered apprenticeship programs to select participants on the basis of "qualifications alone," to use "objective standards," to keep "adequate records of the selection process," and to "provide full and fair opportunity for application." Programs established before January 17, 1964, did not have to select on the basis of qualifications alone so long as they "demonstrated equality of opportunity" in their selection procedures.[6]

These regulations had a limited impact for a variety of reasons. Basically, few blacks applied for or could meet the qualifications and testing procedures of the JACs. (Nor was this surprising because discrimination had become institutionalized, causing few blacks either to know about apprenticeship or to think they could gain admission. In addition, few blacks who meet the qualifications for apprenticeship aspire to manual trades.) Moreover, the BAT, which administers the program, has very limited enforcement powers. Deregistration, the BAT's main weapon, apparently would be more of an inconvenience than a serious deterrent to discrimination.

In addition to the federal regulations, apprenticeship programs are subject to Title VII of the Civil Rights Act of 1964, the National Labor Relations Act, government contract committees (which require observance of the BAT's apprenticeship regulations as a condition of compliance with the nondiscrimination clauses included in government contracts), and various state apprenticeship regulations and fair employment practices laws. Policies for increasing black participation in apprenticeship programs include the creation of apprenticeship information centers and the funding of specialized programs to recruit, train, and tutor blacks to get them into apprenticeship programs.

A number of organizations, especially the Workers Defense League (WDL) and the National Urban League, have undertaken specific outreach programs designed to get blacks into apprenticeship programs. The WDL's approach in New York City was successful in increasing the number of black apprentices, and it has been used as a model in many other cities. It was endorsed by the AFL-CIO at its 1967 convention and by the Building and Construction Trades Department in February 1968. By August 31, 1970, apprenticeship outreach programs had been installed in 74 cities. Of these, 25 were sponsored by the National Urban League (which had produced 2,659 indentured minority apprentices), 16 by the Workers Defense League (with 2,104 indentures), 24 by building trades councils (with 2,120 indentures), and 9 by miscellaneous groups (with 831 indentures), for a total of 7,714 indentures, distributed as follows:

Asbestos	60
Bricklayers	424
Carpenters	1,659
Cement masons	370
Electricians	820

Elevator constructors	155
Glaziers	118
Iron workers	461
Lathers	100
Machinists	161
Operating engineers	433
Painters	722
Pipe trades	716
Plasterers	130
Roofers	473
Sheet metal workers	543
Tile setters	43
Miscellaneous	328

SOURCE: U.S. Department of Labor, Bureau of Apprenticeship and Training.

Mainly because of the outreach programs, there have been relatively large percentage increases in minority apprentices since 1964. Former Secretary of Labor George Shultz announced in March 1969 that there were 7,260 registered black apprentices, or 4 percent of the total; there were 16,200 registered nonwhite apprentices. Blacks constituted 3.3 percent of registered apprentices in 1968, but were increasing at about twice the rate of all apprentices, reaching 4.9 percent of the total in June 1970.

Although apprenticeship outreach programs have been more successful than any other approach to this problem, it remains to be seen if they can cause the kinds of changes throughout the country that replace institutionalized discrimination with institutionalized equal opportunity. So far, however, they have demonstrated the importance of a comprehensive approach which recruits and prepares black youngsters for apprenticeship programs. Moreover, this approach also has demonstrated its effectiveness in getting blacks into jobs outside the apprenticeable trades more effectively and at lower costs.[7]

Quotas and Preferential Treatment

Various programs to increase black employment opportunities in construction and other industries have raised the highly controversial issues of quotas and preferential treatment. Policies proposed by some civil rights leaders and government agencies are based upon the belief that progress in eliminating patterns of inequality requires compensation for past discrimination against blacks. Others, especially some unions and employers, have resisted these efforts on the grounds that they discriminate against white workers and cause inefficiency. This issue is treated at greater length in Chapter 25.

Union and Employer Attitudes
Toward Apprenticeship

Although there are a few registered nonunion apprentice programs, the U.S. apprenticeship system is mainly a product of collective bargaining. A study of Wisconsin apprenticeship programs, for example, revealed that 96 percent of the employee members of joint apprenticeship programs in the building trades belonged to unions and 79 percent of the employer members belonged to contractors' associations.[9]

As an extension of collective bargaining, programs reflect the interests of the parties at the table. Most students and practitioners seem to agree that apprenticeship training in the United States is primarily supported by craft unions because this training system satisfies a number of their important objectives—most significantly the maintenance of wages by controlling craft competence and therefore productivity. Control of apprenticeship also provides job security by giving unions some control over the supply of labor. Apprenticeship programs exist mainly in casual occupations such as the building trades where job opportunities are characterized by seasonal and cyclical variations and periods of unemployment. A main union objective in these situations is to gain greater job security for members and protect the craftsman's investment in his skills. In the long run, it would be difficult for union craftsmen to maintain their wages unless their productivity made it possible for them to have unit labor costs at least as low as the alternatives available to an employer. Craft unions also see apprenticeship as a form of union security. In the absence of unions, employers have a tendency to fragment crafts in order to reduce training costs and increase profits. Craft unions resist such fragmentation because it makes their members less adaptable to change and threatens the power of unions.

Unions also support apprentice programs in order to prevent the excessive use of low-wage apprentices in competition with their journeyman members, as a means of controlling the supply of labor, and as a technique for providing job opportunities to friends and relatives.

The unions' interest in apprenticeship is such, according to one authority, that:

> ... although some people feel that apprenticeship is moribund, many in organized labor feel just the opposite and so strongly that if the federal government discontinued its modest programs, these unions would continue to develop apprenticeship training as they have over the years.[10]

Employers' views on apprenticeship vary considerable from industry to industry. Construction and graphic arts employers seem to share their unions' interests in apprenticeship though they are often willing to leave the administration of these programs to the unions. Employers in industrial plants are interested in apprenticeship training if they need craftsmen in identifiable and recognized classifications. Employers in the larger high-wage industries seem willing to support apprentice programs because they are less likely than lower-wage employers to lose their skilled workers once they are trained.

Unlike their counterparts in construction, printing, and some metal crafts, many industrial employers do not seem anxious to register their apprenticeship programs with the BAT or an SAC. Although registered programs do not have to be jointly administered by unions and employers, some employers consider the federal apprenticeship program to be too closely tied to unions. Others, including some government installations, are not interested in training well-rounded craftsmen with general skills which might be transferred to other employers or labor markets; rather, they seek primarily to train workers for the specialized tasks required in their particular operations. These employers are more interested in flexibility of manpower utilization across several craft lines and therefore are not interested in the in-depth training in a particular craft provided by the apprenticeship system. Some large employers also have no interest in registering their programs because they want to avoid government regulation and red tape.

The wage and certification advantages to be derived from registering an apprentice program, therefore, seem to be more attractive to the construction and printing industries than to others. Although little use apparently is made of these regulations because apprentice rates usually are above the minimums, federal and state minimum wage regulations often permit registered apprentices to be paid less than the minimum wage. The Davis-Bacon Act of 1931 provides for the establishment of prevailing wages on federal construction projects, allows apprentices to be paid less than journeymen, and requires the maintenance of journeymen–apprentice ratios. If a program loses its registration, apprentices must be paid the journeyman rates.

Another advantage to registered apprentices is the recognition which the certificate of completion bestows on the journeyman. The graduate of a registered apprentice program knows that his training is a passport to jobs in other geographic areas because of the standards to which his certificate of completion attests.

Standards, Qualifications, and Procedures

Qualifications, standards, and procedures used by apprenticeship sponsors vary considerably, though registered programs must meet the minimum federal standards listed above. The specific standards are fixed by the particular joint apprenticeship committee. The numbers of apprentices usually are controlled by prescribing eligibility standards, fixing ratios of the numbers between apprentices and journeymen for each employer, and prescribing the duration of the apprentice training period.

Characteristics of Apprenticeship Programs

While there is considerable diversity in apprenticeship training programs, we can make some generalizations about the usual procedures involved in becoming an apprentice. Many youngsters get information about apprenticeship programs from friends or relatives. However, the traditional father-son relationship in many skilled crafts apparently is weakening because it discriminated against minorities and because many craftsmen with higher incomes send their sons to college. Aspirants who do not have friends and relatives in a trade can now obtain information from employers, unions, the employment service, apprenticeship information centers, or other sources.

The numbers of apprenticeship openings varies from trade to trade and city to city. Some trades—for example, electricians, plumbers, sheet metal workers, and printers—typically have long waiting lists, while others —for example, roofers and carpenters—are more easily entered. The number of positions with any given employer depends upon how many journeymen he has; agreements between unions and employers typically specify a so-called journeymen–apprentice ratio. These ratios apparently have considerable influence in specific cases, but, in the aggregate, employers do not train as many apprentices as their ratios would allow. An applicant who otherwise meets the requirements for entry into an apprenticeship program usually must take an oral or written examination given by the employment service, a private testing agency, the employer, the union, or a JAC. The JACs traditionally have constructed and administered their own tests, but there appears to be a trend toward reliance on professionally developed written tests. The oral interview, usually administered by the JACs is designed to determine the applicant's interest in the trade and whether he is likely to complete it successfully.

Critics of apprenticeship procedures contend that the oral interview should be eliminated or given little weight in the selection process because it offers the JACs an opportunity to discriminate against blacks or others they wish to bar. But defenders of interviews counter that it is necessary to determine the applicants' likelihood of successfully completing the program because the JAC often allots scarce positions to apprentices and devotes considerable time and resources to their training. Unions also are fearful of "flooding the market" with partially trained journeymen. Moreover, the JACs are interested in getting the "right kind" of people in their training programs, which means persons who are socially acceptable as well as productive workers. There is a certain mystique and fraternal character about apprenticeship to which the JAC expects the new apprentice to conform. Part of the ritual in many trades takes the form of hazing and menial assignments designed to "initiate" the apprentice into the trade.

Once the apprentice is formally registered or "indentured," he is paid a progressively increasing proportion of the journeyman wage scale. He gains the journeyman's rate when he completes his apprenticeship—at least one year and typically four years after he enters a program.

In some cases, the apprentice can enter the program by passing a simple aptitude test but must find his own job. In other cases, the JACs seem to be able to assure employment to the apprentice and assume responsibility for finding him a job. Many in the apprenticeship establishment are fearful that the "hunting license" approach, whereby the apprentice finds his own job, will bring too many people into the trade.

Some apprenticeship sponsors supplement the salaries of apprentice instructors and provide apprentice coordinators to supervise the training, but overall policy and guidance is established by the JAC or other sponsors. The apprentices' wages often are paid by the employer while he attends classes during the day, but this practice varies considerably. In some cases, related training classes are held in the evening.

ON-THE-JOB TRAINING

On-the-job training (OJT) is the main way in which most workers acquire their skills. A 1963 Labor Department Survey found that only 30 percent of all workers sampled had learned their jobs through formal training programs.[11]

In spite of its importance, very little is known about the OJT process. There are many reasons for this lack of knowledge. OJT takes place during the production process, often is very informal, and occurs incrementally over a long period of time. Indeed, very often little identifiable instruction takes place, and the worker undergoing the training may not even be aware of the process. As a consequence, the process cannot be described by those who are undergoing it.

Nevertheless some generalizations can be made about OJT. Much of our knowledge derives from special studies conducted during the 1960s, when efforts to train the disadvantaged focused general attention on OJT procedures. Although we do not know much about the magnitude of this form of training—in the sense of being able to measure the changes in skills accruing to workers per unit of time—OJT probably accounts for an overwhelming proportion of the skill-gains in the work force. Indeed, some of the gains in income attributed to formal education probably are due to OJT.

To some extent, the use of seniority in promotion is tacit recognition by unions and employees of the importance of OJT. In many occupations, seniority districts defining lines of job progression serve training as well as production needs. It is assumed that workers who have been in closely related jobs are in the best position to learn the next higher job in terms of skill. Moreover, the fact that workers in the line of progression have some assurance that they will fill higher jobs provides a motivation for junior workers to learn the higher jobs. But OJT is not limited to jobs in the line of progression. Some workers familiarize themselves with jobs outside their immediate seniority lines by talking with workers on those jobs, observing their operations, and perhaps operating the equipment during lunch breaks or other free-time periods. Because of the importance of these informal learning procedures, incumbents sometimes have considerable influence over which outsiders learn their jobs.

OJT is apparently very popular with workers and employers. Workers prefer this form of training because they can see its relevance and are not as likely to consider it to be a "waste of time" as they are classroom training. Indeed, some kinds of training cannot be learned in classrooms because it is difficult to simulate the actual conditions of the work place. OJT also has very limited "wasted" training, because the worker uses the skills he acquires on the job. Moreover, he is paid a regular wage and not a "stipend" as under institutional training.

OJT is preferred by employers because there is little question of its effectiveness and because it is more flexible and less expensive for many jobs than other types of training. OJT's impact is readily apparent to supervisors, who can observe whether the worker is learning the job. This form of training is flexible because it can be adapted to a wide variety of work situations and can be combined with all other forms of training. In some cases, for example, workers can be given minimal instructions and left to learn the trade pretty much on their own or by observing other workers who perform the same job. But OJT also can be supplemented with (a) formal demonstrations by other workers, instructors, supervisors, or engineers; (b) basic classroom training in theoretical or academic concepts which cannot be taught on the job; (c) vestibule training for new workers to familiarize them with the job; or (d) correspondence courses.

OJT also is flexible because it is a means whereby employers can adjust to technological changes and shortages of skilled manpower. As Doeringer and Piore have demonstrated, minor innovations are adopted by casual learning of the new process on the job, while major changes might require more changes in the normal training patterns. Innovations that create new jobs might require a period of relatively formal instruction by engineers, factory representatives, or others who have learned to operate the new equipment. OJT also makes it possible for employers to adapt to a variety of labor market conditions. For example, if there are shortages of skilled workers, employers can, through OJT and work rearrangements, utilize less skilled workers.[12]

Employers like OJT because it is economical. The training is a by-product of production and therefore does not require the establishment of training staffs and procedures. The efficacy and importance of OJT undoubtedly account for the fact that very few companies have formal training programs.[13] Moreover, OJT training can be carried out with craftsmen who would not be very effective in teaching formal classes, but who might command considerable respect from trainees because of their demonstrated skills on the job. Similarly, OJT does not require the purchase of expensive additional training equipment.

In spite of its advantages, however, OJT is not suitable for all kinds of training, and, although less expensive than some other forms of training, it is not without its costs. Just as some skills are difficult to teach in classes, some kinds of knowledge cannot be taught very effectively on the job. For example, theoretical training is important to many kinds of jobs because it teaches the worker the basic causal relationships underlying his job. Workers who understand theoretical relationships undoubtedly are adaptable to a greater variety of work situations than those who only know "how" things happen but not "why." Indeed, it can be argued that those who do not understand the basic theoretical aspects of their jobs probably have imperfect understandings of "how." Theoretical training is difficult to teach on the job because the basic causal relationships—for example, the forces conditioning the flow of current through electrical wires or causing the strength or other properties of metals—usually are "invisible" and therefore must be demonstrated with abstract models. The noisy hustle and bustle of the job rarely is conducive to instruction in these abstractions. And supervisors and other regular production workers might not be the best instructors for such abstract "academic" subjects. But the effectiveness of classroom instruction is not limited to theoretical training. Although academic subjects such as reading and computation skills probably can be more effectively taught off the job, the knowledge that those skills are useful for job performance undoubtedly is a powerful motivating influence, and motivation is very important to learning.

Moreover, OJT has costs which employers must consider. Workers undergoing OJT might be unproductive for a period and waste material and productivity of supervisors and skilled craftsmen might be impaired if they spend much time teaching trainees. At the same time, craftsmen often make poor teachers because they resent having to train "greenhorns" or because they frequently have trouble explaining what they do or are reluctant to impart "trade secrets" which give them some job protection. And there might be economies of size and scale in a classroom where a number of workers must acquire the same kinds of training.

As a consequence of the advantages and disadvantages of OJT, some employers and JACs combine OJT with more formal training. Apprenticeship training is a clear example, but so are the "coupled" programs under the Manpower and Development Training Act (MDTA), to be discussed below. As noted earlier, moreover, there are many possible combinations of OJT with other forms of training. Indeed, academic subjects often can be taught very effectively when OJT makes it possible to provide concrete illustrations of the effects of abstract principles.

OJT and the Disadvantaged

Although little emphasis was given to it during the first few years of the Manpower Development and Training Act of 1962, OJT became more important after 1965. At first, the major emphasis under the MDTA was on institutional or classroom training (discussed in Chapter 17). Some MDTA-OJT programs were administered by so-called "national" contracts, while others were administered by individual firms. Under the national contracts, an organization such as a union or the National Urban League was the prime contractor and subcontracted with individual trainees. Althugh the Job Opportunities in the Business Sector (JOBS) program was started by the Johnson Administration, President Nixon revised the program and merged it with the individual OJT projects. According to the 1970 *Manpower Report of the President:*

> As the JOBS Program becomes nationwide during 1970 and as its parameters are enlarged to include upgrade training and training for skill shortages, the regular OJT program will be merged with JOBS. The JOBS '70 Program is designed to offer the same kinds of government-private industry collaboration in on-the-job training that has characterized MDTA projects, while maintaining JOBS' unique arrangements for business leadership in employing the disadvantaged. National OJT Contracts will be continued, however, because of their distinct advantages as a channel for developing projects in many geographic areas.[14]

The peak number of workers trained under MDTA-OJT was 101,000 in 1968; this declined to 91,000 in fiscal 1970.

OJT apparently has considerable support from political leaders. There are a number of reasons for this, including both its low federal cost per trainee compared with institutional training and the higher posttraining employment built into the system. Not only is institutional training more costly, but also there is no assurance that its graduates will be able to find jobs. Levitan and Mangum reported that in 1966 the cost was about $400 per OJT enrollee, approximately one-fourth of the cost per institutional enrollee.[15]

In addition to the limitations discussed above, OJT has a number of disadvantages for training the unemployed. For one thing, OJT requires the disadvantaged worker to find an employer willing to take him, which might be difficult to do because employers are extremely reluctant to train the disadvantaged, even when compensated by the federal government.[16] During times or rising unemployment, it is difficult to place people in OJT training slots because experienced workers are unemployed and there are likely to be very few job vacancies. Moreover, because employers select many of the workers to be trained under OJT, they tend to "cream" the available labor force, taking the best qualified applicants and making it difficult for the truly disadvantaged worker to get trained. As a consequence, blacks and other minorities have been much better represented in institutional than OJT programs. In 1963–1969, for example, blacks and minorities held 31 percent of OJT slots and 39 percent of the institutional slots funded under MDTA. In 1968, blacks and other minorities held 36 percent of the OJT and 48 percent of the institutional positions.

However, if a disadvantaged worker acquires on OJT position, it is likely to do more to help him become and remain employed. For example, in 1966, blacks had 50 percent as much chance getting an OJT as institutional slot, but once in OJT, they had a 34 percent greater chance of getting employed. There appeared to be no bias in institutional enrollments, but considerable in OJT, though the relative culpability of local administrators and employers was not readily apparent.

Because of the relative advantages of on-the-job and institutional training, "coupled" programs"—designed to provide the advantages of both —have been tried under MDTA. The results of coupled programs have not lived up to expectations, but this probably is due more to administrative difficulties than to any basic defect of the concept. In 1967, for example, provision was made for 72,500 "coupled" slots, but only 54,600 of these were filled by June 1967. Major administrative difficulties for these programs were created by conflicts between the federal agencies primarily responsible for them. OJT was administered by the BAT which was suspicious of institutional training, and the institutional training was administered by the vocational education establishment, which was suspicious of OJT. As noted earlier in this chapter, however, apprenticeship, which is a form of "coupled" training, has been a fairly successful, predominantly private training system.

CONCLUSION

While the apprenticeship system in the United States is ragarded by its supporters as a good training procedure which provides the academic and on-the-job training necessary to produce all-around craftsmen, it is criticized as obsolete, inadequate to meet the nation's manpower requirements, and characterized by racial and other forms of discrimination against outsiders. The objective evidence, although very limited, suggests the following conclusions:

1. Apprenticeship in the United States is primarily an extension of collective bargaining.
2. Apprenticeship programs, while very diverse, are significant primarily in those industries and crafts where employment is casual and where the union is likely to be the predominant and most stable labor market institution.
3. The number of apprentices fluctuates with the business cycle, but the post-1962 trend seems to be upward.

4. Although how specific craftsmen acquire their skills makes very little difference in terms of competence, workers who serve apprenticeships become well-rounded craftsmen in a shorter time and are upgraded faster than those trained informally (this, of course, does not mean that there are not ways to improve apprenticeship programs).

5. Although apprenticeship outreach programs have been more successful than other efforts to increase the number of minority apprentices, these outreach programs are too new to give a clear indication of their impact on those institutional arrangements that have barred blacks and other minorities from apprenticeships. Moreover, outreach programs have been assisted by a number of other measures to reduce discrimination. In addition to outreach programs, an important determinant of entry into apprenticeship programs by blacks (and others) and their employment as journeymen craftsmen will be the nature of the qualifications required to enter these training programs and work at these crafts. Because of their significance for economic and manpower policies as well as discrimination, apprenticeship qualifications, standards, and procedures undoubtedly will remain controversial issues for some time. But the range of controversy can be reduced by careful evaluations of the apprenticeship system, which remain to be undertaken.

On-the-job training, which is part of the apprenticeship system, is the main way most workers acquire their skills. It has many advantages over classroom instruction. However, both classroom and OJT are necessary for most crafts because mathematics, science, and other "academic" subjects cannot be learned very effectively at work sites.

NOTES

1. U.S. Department of Labor, *Apprenticeship* (booklet, no date), p. 24.
2. David J. Farber, "Apprenticeship in the United States: Labor Market Forces and Social Policy," *Journal of Human Resources* (Winter 1967), p. 70.
3. Includes trades other than those listed.
4. George Strauss, "Apprenticeship: An Evaluation of the Need," in Arthur M. Ross, ed., *Employment Policy and the Labor Market* (Berkeley, Calif.: University of California Press, 1965).
5. See, for example, Morris A. Horowitz and Irwin L. Hernstadt, *The Training of Tool and Die Makers* (Boston: Department of Economics, Northeastern University, 1969). This study found that only one method of training tool and die makers, vocational high school combined with apprenticeship, uniformly rated high on such measures of effectiveness as performance ratings by supervisors, duration of training, and amount of time it took to become a competent craftsman.
6. Ray Marshall and Vernon M. Briggs, Jr., *The Negro and Apprenticeship* (Baltimore: Johns Hopkins, 1967), and Ray Marshall and Vernon M. Briggs, Jr., *Equal Apprenticeship Opportunity* (Ann Arbor and De-

troit, Mich.: National Manpower Policy Task Force and Institute of Labor and Industrial Relations, University of Michigan–Wayne State University, 1968); George Strauss and Sidney Ingerman, "Public Policy and Discrimination in Apprenticeship," *Hastings Law Journal* (February 1965), p. 285.

7. 29 CFR 30, 1964.

8. See Marshall and Briggs, *Equal Apprenticeship Opportunity, op. cit.*

9. Alan C. Filley and Karl O. Magnusen, "A Study of Joint Apprenticeship Committees in Wisconsin Building Trades," in Center for Studies in Vocational and Technical Education, *Research in Apprenticeship Training* (Madison, Wisc.: University of Wisconsin Press, 1967), p. 84.

10. Felician F. Foltman, "Public Policy in Apprenticeship Training and Skill Development," in U.S. Congress, Senate, Subcommittee on Employment and Manpower, *The Role of Apprenticeship in Manpower Development: United States and Western Europe,* Vol. 3 of *Selected Readings in Manpower* (Washington, D.C.: U.S. Government Printing Office, 1964), p. 112.

11. U.S. Department of Labor, *Manpower Report of the President* (Washington, D.C.: U.S. Government Printing Office, 1964).

12. Peter Doeringer and Michael Piore, *Internal Labor Markets and Manpower Analysis* (Lexington, Mass.: D. C. Health, 1971).

13. John L. Iacobelli, "A Survey of Employer Attitudes Toward Training the Disadvantaged," *Monthly Labor Review* (June 1970), pp. 51–55.

14. U.S. Department of Labor, *Manpower Report of the President* (Washington, D.C.: U.S. Government Printing Office, 1970).

15. Sar A. Levitan and Garth L. Mangum, *Federal Training and Work Programs in the Sixties* (Ann Arbor, Mich.: Institute of Labor and Industrial Relations, University of Michigan–Wayne State University, 1969), p. 85.

16. Iacobelli, *op. cit.*

Part III
Labor
Market
Institutions

Chapter 12
The Structure
of Labor
Markets

In modern times, labor, as other factors of production, is allocated partly by labor markets and partly by institutionalized arrangements which may or may not reflect market tendencies. It is, therefore, extremely important to separate basic market forces from these institutional arrangements. A major objective of this chapter is to discuss the operation of labor markets, first in terms of basic theory, second in terms that relax some of the theoretical restrictions, and third in terms of some of the institutional arrangements that make it difficult for labor markets to operate along the lines prescribed by traditional economic theory. Before doing this, however, it will be useful to discuss the role that theory can play in illuminating the operation of labor markets and in prescribing remedies for market-related problems.

ROLE OF THEORY

Theory attempts to identify certain basic underlying causal relationships. As such, its usefulness derives from its ability to simplify otherwise complex phenomena. Theory, therefore, is not a mirror reflection of reality. Indeed, the factors discussed in some theories might not even be observable in the real world, where the basic factors may be obscured by others that are more apparent than real. For example, people tend to infer that unions "cause" inflation when wage increases are followed by rising prices. However, rising wages and prices may, in reality, be caused by other, more fundamental forces which are less obvious or measurable. It might even be difficult to measure the "results" of underlying causal forces because of the timing problems. When, for example, do we start measuring the impact of union wage pressures on prices? The wage pressures might actually be caused by price increases that occurred *before* we started our measurements.

The fundamental generalizations or principles about causal relationships are more important to our understanding of the basic factors at work than a detailed description of "real" situations. This is true because the "facts" change constantly. Indeed, excessive description can obscure our understanding of basic causal relationships.

Theory can also play an important role in policy formulation. Indeed, with inadequate theories, or conceptual frameworks, correct policies can be formulated only by chance. For example, combating inflation or unemployment requires an adequate theoretical underpinning. Wage and price guidelines, for instance, are designed to combat cost-push inflation. Therefore, they will not be effective if, as Milton Friedman argues,[1] inflation is basically a monetary phenomenon caused by increasing the supply of money relative to the output of goods and services and not increases in wages or other costs. Similarly, a theory of wages is necessary to an understanding of the probable impact of minimum wages on employment.

Different theories of labor markets prescribe different policies for the resolution of the problems of unemployment and unequal employment opportunities. In vogue recently has been emphasis on a dual labor market theory which assumes some "secondary" markets more or less separated from "primary" markets (traditional analysis treats the whole economy as essentially one big labor market). Those who believe in dual markets argue that the problems of disadvantaged workers, who are employed mainly in the secondary markets, cannot be solved with general monetary and fiscal measures which assume some national queue for jobs.

Although theories are very useful for simplifying basic causal relationships, they also pose certain dangers which must be guarded against. It is particularly important to remember that theories are *abstractions* and therefore only a starting point to understanding particular situations. Because a theory is based upon certain assumptions, the predictions that flow from it are *theoretical* predictions, which means that they will obtain only so long as the basic assumptions underlying the theory are valid in particular situations being examined. Policy makers, however, often are not interested in theoretical predictions but in *actual* predictions; that is, they are likely to be interested in more than the economic tendencies underlying a particular situation. Policy makers must, therefore, be concerned about the various noneconomic phenomena that influence the economic variable. In the case of racial discrimination, for example, the theorists can claim quite correctly that competitive markets would tend to erode racial discrimination, and this would be an accurate theoretical prediction. However, it might not be an accurate prediction of events in the real world because social events and institutions such as institutionalized racism make it very difficult for the tendencies to work themselves out in the real world. For the policy maker, therefore, economic tendencies that are counteracted by social forces are merely *theoretical,* but not *actual,* predictions of events. It is important for the policy maker to understand the theoretical economic tendencies in order to adopt proper policies, but he must know more than that. He also needs to know the institutional setting within which a particular problem must be solved.

We must also be careful, when using theoretical constructs, to avoid letting theories lead to rigid analysis. For example, the theories designed to explain labor markets at one time might be very useful because the theoretical construct reflected the basic underlying relationships at that time. However, there is a danger that the theory will be used long after the basic underlying relationships have changed and the theory is no longer useful in explaining the labor market. For example, a labor market theory adopted during the Middle Ages clearly would not be valid in the twentieth century, primarily because during the Middle Ages the labor market was relatively insignificant and tradition was a much more important determinant of wages. The development of the free labor market, therefore, requires modification of the theory of wage determination. As we shall see, theory also causes people to generalize and therefore to ignore basic differences between labor markets. And theory might cause rigidity by focusing on certain phenomena at the expense of others. Because the theories cannot always be validated in the real world and because they frequently are based on events that cannot be observed, it is very difficult to keep theories flexible enough to adapt to changing circumstances.

In conclusion, therefore, theories are very useful in helping to simplify very complex labor market phenomena, but we must be very careful to be sure that the theory has indeed focused on basic causal relationships and that it does not induce such inflexibility in thinking that important variables in a particular situation are ignored as we move from the theory to the policy level.

NATURE AND SIGNIFICANCE
OF LABOR MARKETS

"Labor market" means different things to different people. To some, it refers to a particular geographic place—as the New York labor market or that of some other area. However, we shall see that each locality contains many labor markets, and therefore it is very difficult to identify a labor market with a place.

For the economist, the labor market is an *abstraction* which defines an area in which exchanges take place. Some labor markets are national in scope while others are local. The market for economists, for example, tends to be national or international, but the market for electricians tends to be much more localized. In geographic terms, the scope of the labor market is likely to be the areas in which buyers and sellers are in sufficiently close communication that wages tend to be equalized throughout the labor market area. It is important to emphasize that people need not be in direct physical communication in order to be in a market with other people. The important condition is that the many individual exchanges that take place are closely interrelated by some common forces or principles. These common forces or principles relate to the nature of the labor being sold and the demand and supply conditions underlying its sale.

As a general rule, the labor market refers to a fairly homogeneous type of labor. For example, we speak of the building trades labor market or the plumbers labor market or the market for college graduates or engineers, economists, accountants, or other particular groups which can be distinguished from other kinds of labor. The appropriate physical areas to which these abstractions refer depend largely on the nature of the work and the mobility of the labor force. To some extent, the scope of the market is related to the number of people in it; if there are skills that are in great demand throughout wide areas, the labor market is likely to be more localized and to refer primarily to daily commuting patterns of the workers in the particular markets. But in markets with relatively few workers who are demanded over a wide geographic area, the daily commuting pattern no longer defines the labor market. For example, labor relations arbitrators probably have a national labor market whereas physicians restrict their activities primarily to a local labor market.

Let us next take a closer look at the basic underlying forces which tend to relate the many individual exchanges in a labor market. We shall first examine the traditional competitive labor market of economic theory, a market system characterized by unregulated market forces. The market system in a modern industrial economy has as its main functions the allocation and distribution of labor among alternative uses and the determination of the prices to be paid for that labor. These prices, in turn, are costs to employers and income to workers. This pricing system is based upon the assumption that free labor markets can perform the literally millions of allocation decisions necessary in an economy with efficiency and a maximum of individual freedom. However, it is important to emphasize again that the perfectly competitive labor market is a norm or ideal against which we can measure the operation of the actual labor market. Our approach, therefore, will be to outline the nature of this abstract labor market and then to relax some of the restrictive assumptions upon which the theory is based in order to get a closer approximation of how the labor market operates in the real world.

The Demand for Labor

The competitive labor market is based on the following assumptions:

1. Employers and workers have fairly accurate knowledge about wages and job opportunities throughout the market.
2. Employers and workers are "rational" in the economic sense— that is, employers act to maximize profits and workers act to maximize satisfaction from real wages.
3. Each employer and worker represent such a small part of the total demand or supply for labor that their individual decisions have no influence on wages.
4. There are no obstacles to mobility of labor and other factors of production.
5. Workers and employers act individually and not in concert with other workers (through unions) or employers (through associations) in making wage and employment decisions.
6. Labor within a particular market is homogeneous and interchangeable.

As we shall see, these assumptions clearly do not hold firm in the real world, but competitive labor markets provide a norm or ideal against which we can measure real world performance.

To anticipate the reader's objections to these assumptions, we should point out that the real world does not have to fit the assumptions completely for the theory to be useful for our purposes. For example, labor is not perfectly mobile, though it is mobile enough to produce a rough tendency for wages to be equalized throughout a market area. And the framework assumes relatively static situations, while the real world is dynamic. Nevertheless, the model world provides a benchmark against which we can measure the dynamism of the real world. Moreover, there is considerable evidence that in the real world, labor market information is very imperfect. Much research has shown that (a) manual workers, in particular, have very limited labor market information about companies other than the ones for which they work; (b) a high proportion of new entrants to the labor market accept the first job offered them; (c) most labor market information comes from friends and relatives, and much of that is inaccurate; (d) ignorance of labor markets makes workers extremely cautious in making changes; (e) many unemployed workers take the first job offered them rather than make more extensive searches; and (f) many of those who take jobs are not satisfied with their choices and quit within a short time for this reason. However, a comparison of these barriers to the operation of the market for labor with the competitive norm provides some insight into the kinds of policies which might make the labor market operate more effectively.

Labor markets are closely related to product markets and markets for other factors of production, especially capital. The demand for labor is, therefore, a *derived* demand, which means that it tends to reflect the demand for the product upon which labor is to be used. Moreover, capital and other factors of production can be substituted for labor, so there is no magic about the various factor mixes used to produce a particular product, at least in the long run. We have assumed, moreover, that employers are motivated only by profit considerations in making these decisions.

Other abstractions to facilitate our analysis, which will be dropped later, are the concepts of a "unit" of labor and "the wage rate." These concepts do not conform with real market conditions where there are many wage rates and where labor is not a homogeneous product. Nevertheless, for purposes of understanding the competitive model, it is useful to refer to units of labor and not mixes of workers. It is also useful to assume a uniform wage throughout the labor market. The use of the unit of labor concept makes it possible for us to ignore (for the moment) the differences in efficiency among various workers; we assume that the efficient worker embodies more units of labor in a product per unit of time than a less efficient worker.

Demand for Labor
by the Individual Employer

Given the assumptions underlying the theory of the competitive market, the demand for labor by the individual employer is based upon two fundamental concepts: (a) the *physical product* of those units of labor and (b) the *revenue* the employer can derive from the sale of those products. The physical product of labor of most interest to the employer in making his employment and wage decisions is the change in physical output associated with the use of an additional unit of labor, or $\Delta O/\Delta N$, where Δ signifies change, O is output, and N is a unit of labor. We call this the marginal physical product (MPP) of a unit of labor N. It may, therefore, be expressed as the total output (TO) at N minus the total output at $(N-1)$ or

$$TO_N - TO_{N-1} = \Delta O/\Delta N = MPP_n$$

where the subscript n refers to a particular level of employment of labor units.

The MPP concept is based on the principle of diminishing returns, which states that as units of a factor are added to other fixed factors, output per unit of variable factor (MPP) will at first increase and then decline. The increase is due to a more optimal relationship between the variable and fixed factors as other units of the variable factor are added; after some point, however, the output per unit of variable factor will decline.

Another useful concept in explaining the demand for labor is the average physical product (APP) per unit of labor, which is the total physical

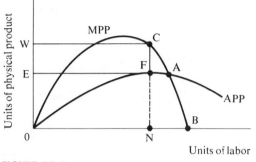

FIGURE 12–1.

product averaged over the units of labor, so $APP_N = TO_N/\Sigma N$. It is important to distinguish between *APP* and *MPP*. These relationships are shown graphically in Figure 12–1. The relevant portion of the MPP curve is below the APP curve but above the horizontal axis. An employer would not operate at negative MPP (below point *B* in Figure 12–1), which would be the case if MPP crossed the horizontal axis, and above point *A,* where the wage bill would be greater than the total product, so the company would be better off to close down the entire plant than to operate where *MPP* > *APP*. At point *C,* for example, with *N* units of labor, total output $(APP \times N) = OEFN$, and, if wages were equal to *W*, the total wage bill $(W \times N) = OWCN$. The company therefore would save *EWCF* by closing down entirely. Point *A* can, therefore, be regarded as a break-even point, and the relevant stage of the MPP curve is between *A* and *B*.

Because employers and workers are interested in income, we need to convert our MPP to money in order to find out what contribution units of labor make to total revenue and therefore profits. In order to do this, we need to introduce the demand schedule for the firm's product, which under competition would be as depicted in Figure 12–2.

Under competitive conditions, where the firm can sell its entire output without affecting prices, the contribution the sale of each additional unit makes to total revenue $(MR = TR_0 - TR_{0-1})$ is the same as average revenue where $AR = TR_0/O$, where *O* now stands for output. Note that in the *product market* we have *output* on the horizontal axis, whereas in the *labor market* units of labor are on that axis. Thus, in our illustration, if \$2

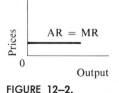

FIGURE 12–2.

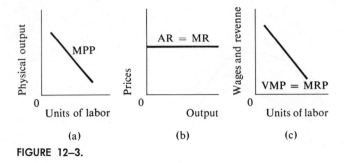

FIGURE 12–3.

is the market price per unit of output, MR at an output of 50 would be $100. If we sell another unit of output for $2, total revenue becomes $102 at an output of 51, and MR is $2 ($TR_0 - TR_{0-1}$, or $102 - 100 = 2$). Now, if we combine the labor and factor markets, the value of the marginal product ($VMP_N = AR_N \times O_N$) at an output of 50 units is $2, and the marginal revenue product ($MPP_N \times MR_N$) also is $2. (As we shall see later, when we relax the assumption of competition in product markets, the VMP [$AR \times MPP$] will not equal MRP [$MR \times MPP$].) Figures 12–3(a), (b), and (c) show the derivation of the MRP curve, which is the demand curve for labor. We derive the MRP curve by multiplying MPP at various *units of labor* (Figure 12–3[a]) by MR for the *output* associated with those levels of employment (Figure 12–3[b]), giving us the contribution to revenue of the units of labor (Figure 12–3[c]).

In order to demonstrate the equilibrium wage and employment conditions for firms under competition, we need to introduce the supply schedule, which shows the wage rates at which various quantities of labor will be sold. It is possible to talk about the market supply schedule, which is generally assumed to have a positive slope as indicated in Figure 12–4, as well as the individual supply schedule for workers or individual plants, to be discussed later. The market supply curve is based on the assumption that workers are willing to supply more units of labor at higher wages. The market demand schedule (Figure 12–5), however, is negative, indicating that more units of labor will be demanded at lower wages.

Figure 12–6 shows the equilibrium wage in the market when 5 million units are sold at $2 per unit. The supply schedule to the firm is depicted

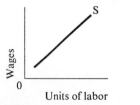

Units of labor

FIGURE 12–4.   *Market Supply*

FIGURE 12–5. *Market Demand*

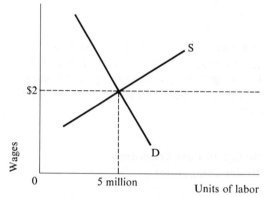

FIGURE 12–6. *Market Demand and Supply*

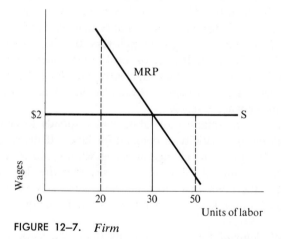

FIGURE 12–7. *Firm*

in Figure 12–7. To the firm, the supply schedule is horizontal or perfectly elastic because the firm employs so few units of labor that it could easily satisfy its entire demand without influencing the wage rate at all.

A moment's reflection will show that the firm's equilibrium position is where the demand schedule for labor (*MRP*) equals the supply. At any quantity of labor less than 30 units in Figure 12–7, the firm could increase its profits by adding units of labor because $MRP > W$, meaning that units of

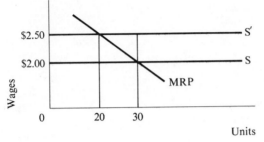

FIGURE 12–8.

labor would add more to revenue than to cost. But it would not pay the employer to hire more than 30 units of labor (where $MRP = W$) because beyond that point $MRP < W$, and the added units of labor contribute more to costs than to revenue. The maximum profit for the firm would, therefore, be at the point where $MRP = W$.

Observations About Equilibrium Conditions in Labor Markets Under Competition

A number of important properties of the individual firm's demand and supply schedules for labor should be emphasized. The first is the distinction between a change or a shift in the demand for labor and moving along the demand schedule. Figure 12–8, for example, assumes that the market wage rate increased to $2.50 per unit, causing the employers to reduce the quantity demanded from 30 to 20 units. It is erroneously said under such conditions that the demand for labor has dropped; clearly, the demand schedule has remained unchanged, and the *quantity demanded* has gone down because of the increase in the wage rate.

The extent to which the quantity of labor sold responds to changes in wages is determined by the elasticity of demand for labor. If the demand schedule is relatively flat so that the change in wages would lead to a relatively great change in the units of labor sold, we say that the demand is relatively elastic. But if the labor demand schedule is relatively steep, the change in the wage rate will not lead to very large changes in the quantity of labor demanded.

The elasticity of demand for labor depends upon the slope of the MPP curve, which depends on the physical relationships between units of labor and units of fixed factors of production. If the MPP declines rapidly with increases in units of labor, the MPP schedule will be relatively steep, as will the demand schedule for labor. But because the MRP schedule (the demand schedule for labor) is a *derived demand schedule,* it also depends upon the elasticity of demand for the product. If the elasticity of demand for the product is relatively great, so will be the elasticity of demand for labor. Conversely, a relatively inelastic demand schedule for the product causes the demand schedule for labor to be relatively inelastic.

The demand schedule for labor also will be relatively inelastic if labor forms a small part of total costs. This is true because a change in wages will not lead to a very great change in employment if labor is a relatively small part of the total cost. Moreover, the demand for labor will be relatively inelastic if it is difficult to substitute other factors for labor in the production process. In this case, if wages rise, employment will not fall by very much because the employer has few alternatives to the use of labor. But if it is relatively easy to substitute other factors for labor, an increase in wages might lead to a relatively great decline in employment. Finally, the demand for labor will be relatively inelastic if the supply of one or more nonlabor factors of production is inelastic. In this case, an increase in the supply of one of the nonlabor factors would reduce its price and would lead to a greater quantity demanded of labor to go with that factor, but the decline in the prices of other factors would offset the increased price of labor.

Figure 12–9 depicts a change in the quantity sold as a result of an increase in demand. It will be observed that because of elasticity of the individual firm's supply schedule, demand can increase with no increase in wages. Increases in demand for labor might come about because of new production techniques which lead to increased productivity for each worker, or it might result from increases in the quality of the labor force. The main difference between the situations depicted in Figures 12–8 and 12–9 is that in Figure 12–8 the change in the quantity sold came about because of the change in wages, whereas in Figure 12–9 wages remained constant, and demand changed.

Individual Labor Supply Schedules

Relatively little is known about the individual supply schedules of different kinds of labor. We do know, however, that a variety of possible supply schedules is possible. A supply schedule is defined as the individual worker's willingness to offer units of labor for sale at different wage rates. There is some evidence that many individuals have a labor supply schedule similar to the one depicted in Figure 12–10(a). This is a so-called backward-bending supply schedule of labor. The underlying assumption is that as wages increase, the worker is willing to offer more labor; but as wages continue to rise, the amount of labor he will offer declines. In other words, the assumption is that once the worker acquires enough income to meet certain basic needs, his demand for leisure increases relative to his demand for income, and therefore he substitutes leisure for income as wages continue to rise.

The supply schedule depicted in Figure 12–10(b) assumes that the worker is willing to offer more units of labor as wages increase throughout the range of the supply schedule. This supply schedule assumes that work-

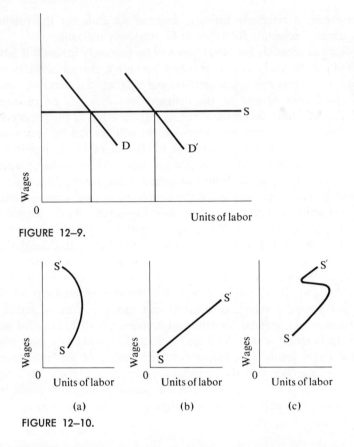

FIGURE 12–9.

FIGURE 12–10.

ers are willing to offer more labor at higher wages because of the increasing disutility of labor.

Another alternative is depicted in Figure 12–10(c). This curve assumes that workers are willing to offer more units of labor at low levels of wages, but then at some intermediate range their demand for leisure overrides the demand for added income as wages rise and the worker offers fewer units of labor. At some high-level range of wages, it becomes attractive for the worker to offer more units of labor as wages rise. Clearly, therefore, the shape of the individual supply schedule depends upon the worker's relative preference for income and leisure.

Equilibrium Under Conditions of Imperfect Competition

So far we have assumed that the product and labor markets in which labor is sold are perfectly competitive. Few markets in the real world are so constructed. Thus, it is useful to see what effect the relaxation of these assumptions would have on the equilibrium conditions for the sale of labor.

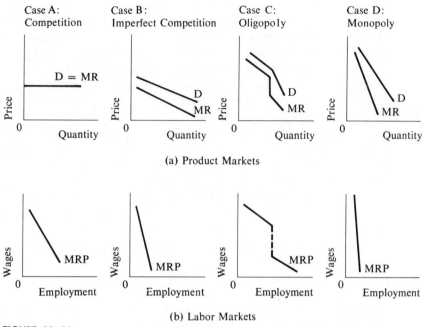

(a) Product Markets

(b) Labor Markets

FIGURE 12-11.

Let us first relax the assumption of competition in product markets. The effect of this change is depicted in Figure 12–11, which contrasts various degrees of product market competition. It will be observed that the competitive case which we have discussed is Case A, in which the demand and marginal revenue schedules are identical and the demand for the product is perfectly elastic. In this case, the marginal revenue product schedule has a negative slope only because of the downward sloping marginal physical product schedule.

In Case B, where there is imperfect competition and the firm has some elements of competition and some of monopoly (such as product differentiation), the demand schedule no longer equals the marginal revenue schedule because the firm can now raise its price for the product and not lose all of its sales. Therefore, the marginal revenue schedule slopes downward and to the right and more steeply than the demand schedule; and the marginal revenue product now has two factors causing it to have a negative slope— namely, the downward-sloping marginal physical product schedule as well as the downward-sloping marginal revenue schedule. It will also be observed in this case that if we calculated the value of the marginal product and the marginal revenue product, these terms would no longer be equal, as they were in the competitive case. The reason for the equality in the competitive case, of course, is that the value of the marginal product is equal to the price (= average revenue = demand) times the marginal physical product, whereas the marginal revenue product is marginal revenue times the marginal physical product. Because the demand in the marginal revenue curves diverges under imperfect competition, the value of the marginal product would be greater than the marginal revenue product.

The product market situation depicted in Case C of Figure 12–11 is the oligopoly case drawn on the assumption that the demand schedule is kinked at the prevailing price. It is assumed that the firm's competitors will not follow a price increase, so the firm would tend to lose business above the prevailing price; the curve, therefore, is relatively inelastic at prices above the market price. However, it is assumed that the firm's rivals will follow price cuts because the curve is inelastic below the prevailing market price, indicating that it will take considerable price reductions in order to gain a relatively small increase in quantities sold. The marginal revenue product schedule derived from this marginal revenue schedule and marginal physical product will, therefore, have a discontinuity at the prevailing price. The significance of this case, of course, is that the labor supply schedule can shift within the range of the discontinuity of the marginal revenue product schedule with no change in employment.

The curve in Case D assumes a monopoly, or one seller. The curve is very similar to the one depicted in Case B except that the curves are steeper, which reflects the assumption that the monopolist has greater control over the market and can, therefore, raise the price more without losing as much quantity sold as would be the case in imperfect competition. The marginal revenue product schedule derived from the monopolist's marginal revenue schedule is, therefore, relatively inelastic.

If we relax the assumption that the firm is a competitor in the labor market, the resulting situation is predicted in Figure 12–12. This curve assumes that buyers have sufficient impact on the market that they will have

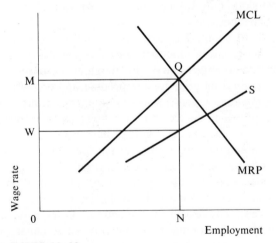

FIGURE 12–12.

to raise the wage rate in order to attract a larger supply. However, because the firm is interested in the effect of higher wages on its total wage bill, it must be concerned about the marginal cost of labor schedule, which shows the increase in the cost of labor as a result of raising wages along the supply schedule. The marginal cost of labor schedule is greater than the supply schedule because the firm probably would have to raise the wages of *all* of its employees, not just the marginal units of labor hired; therefore, total labor costs would go up more than the average wage rate, which is depicted on the supply schedule. The equilibrium level of employment in Figure 12–12 would be at N, and the equilibrium position would be indicated by point Q, where the marginal revenue product crosses the marginal cost of labor schedule. However, because the supply schedule shows the wage rates to be paid for N units of labor, employment in the wage rate would be at W.

It will be observed that the wage rate in this case is not equal to the marginal revenue product, but that the concept of the marginal revenue product and marginal cost of labor still makes it possible to determine the equilibrium wage rate. In the situation depicted in Figure 12–12, the employer is assumed to be a monopsonist, or a single buyer, and the workers are assumed to sell their labor under competitive conditions. The wage rate could be increased within the area between Q and W with no change in employment in the short run. However, in the long run, employment might change if it is assumed that the firm only earns normal profits at a wage of W. Normal profits are defined as the amount necessary to keep the employers in this industry, so that a profit below the normal amount will cause the firm to go bankrupt in the long run. However, if the difference between wages and marginal revenue product is above normal profits and captured by the employers, it would be possible for wages to be raised to M with no change in employment.

We have assumed that the workers in the labor market are selling under competitive conditions and that the employer is operating under monopsonistic conditions. However, if we assume that the workers organize and attempt to fix wages, we might have the situation depicted in Figure 12–13. Under this condition, it is assumed that the workers have organized their side of the market but that the employers still buy under competitive conditions. In this case, it is assumed that the union is a monopolistic seller of labor and operates in the same fashion as any other monopolist. Because the demand curve has a negative slope, the monopolistic union would have to lower wages in order to sell more labor. In this case, the union, therefore, becomes concerned not just with the wage rates or average revenue (depicted for it in the demand schedule) but also with the effect of having to lower wages on the total income of its membership. Because the wage would have to be lowered for all members, the marginal demand schedule would fall faster than the demand schedule, and equilibrium would no longer be at the point where demand equalled supply. In this case, the

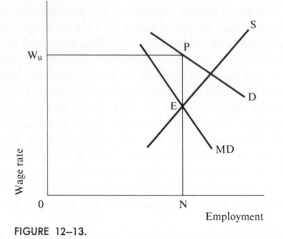

FIGURE 12–13.

equilibrium point would be located at *E,* and the equilibrium wage would be located at the point *P* on the demand schedule corresponding to W_u.

If the employer is a monopsonist and the union is a monopolist, we have the situation depicted in Figure 12–14. In this case, the monopolistic union attempts to locate the point that would maximize its advantage at point *d* at a wage corresponding to point *b* on the demand schedule, or W_u. This is true, of course, because the supply schedule is the marginal cost schedule to the seller, and therefore point *d* corresponds to the point where marginal cost equals marginal revenue and therefore would maximize the union's profit position. But the employer, who is now a monopsonist, attempts to maximize his profit by locating the point where his marginal cost equals marginal revenue, or at point *a,* and would attempt to establish a wage W_e corresponding to *c* on the supply schedule. It should be observed that under this condition the employer would like to buy N^1 units of labor at a wage of $W_e,$ and the union would like to sell *N* units of labor at a wage

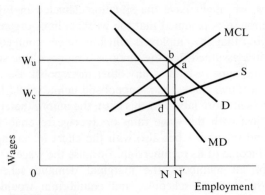

FIGURE 12–14.

W_u. The wage and employment relationships are therefore indeterminate and would be established by bargaining between W_u and W_e.

The situations depicted in Figure 12–13 and Figure 12–14 are based upon business firm analogies which are not very realistic. When we consider union and employer bargaining over wages, the union's cost curve, for example, is very difficult to define because unions do not sell labor but merely fix the terms. Although the bilateral monopoly model might, therefore, be useful for illustrating the kinds of situations that might obtain if unions did sell labor, it is not very realistic for depicting realistic bargaining situations.

To portray more realistic situations, various bargaining theories have been developed. In these models, A's bargaining power is ordinarily defined as his ability to induce his opponent, B, to agree on A's terms. The important question in these models, therefore, becomes the parties' will to resist a particular situation or position. The bargaining power of any particular party depends on the extent to which that party's objectives differ from those of his opponent. In other words, if the union adopts a wage objective that is too far removed from the employer's wage objective, the union's bargaining power might be very weak. In this situation, if the union makes a concession to move its objectives closer to those of the employer, it actually strengthens its position with respect to the employer, because now the employer would be more willing to agree on the union's terms.

The basic ingredient of a bargaining model is defined as the bargaining attitude of either party, which is the ratio of the cost of disagreeing with one's opponent divided by the cost of agreeing on the opponent's terms ($BA_u = CD/CA$ and $BA_e = CD/CA$, where BA_u is the union's bargaining attitude and BA_e is the employer's bargaining attitude). The cost of disagreeing in a union bargaining situation is the cost of a strike. The cost of agreeing is determined by the difference between the wage rate under consideration and the wage rate each party would consider to be its optimal position. For example, if the employer's object were $4 an hour, and he finally agreed on a new contract for $4.25 per hour, the cost of agreeing with the union is the extra 25 cents per manhour. Therefore, for any particular objective for which a union is striving, the greater the gap between its wage goal and the employer's wage goal, the larger the employer's cost of agreeing on the union's terms.

Because we have expressed bargaining attitudes as the ratio of the cost of disagreeing to the cost of agreeing, bargaining attitudes are clearly favorable to settlement whenever they reach 1 and are unfavorable to settlement whenever they are below 1. In other words, if the cost of disagreeing is greater than the cost of agreeing, the ratio will be greater than 1, and that party would tend to cave in and agree on the wage under consideration. But if the cost of agreeing is greater than the cost of disagreeing, the bargaining attitude ratio will be less than 1, and there will be a tendency for that party to hold out.

Of course, these models can become much more complicated because determining the cost of agreeing and the cost of disagreeing requires analyses of many variables.[2]

These collective bargaining models have some advantages over the inconclusive bilateral monopoly explanation depicted in Figure 12–14. First, bargaining models ordinarily reflect the actual bargaining situation in which one of the parties has the power to inflict some damage on another. Traditional economic theory usually assumes that sellers make take-it-or-leave-it offers, whereas the usual situation is more akin to the bargaining situation. Second, bargaining models are more realistic in demonstrating that the art of compromise is a positive bargaining weapon. It is sometimes assumed, for example, that a concession by one party to another is a sign of weakness, but the bargaining models make it clear that one's bargaining position can be strengthened by a concession. Finally, the bargaining models also come closer to a determinate conclusion than bilateral monopoly models. This is true because, at least conceptually, the outcome of the bargaining situation can be known in advance. However, we must emphasize that these models are determinate only in the conceptual sense. They have not yet been developed to the point where the outcome of the bargaining can be predicted in advance; the models contain too many unknown and unmeasurable variables.

Conclusions on the Competitive Model

Perhaps a good way to set the stage for comparing the competitive model with the real world is to state the implications of the competitive model for the operation of labor markets. If the competitive model prevails, wages would tend to be equalized for the same quality of labor throughout a labor market area; the employer would face a perfectly elastic supply schedule of labor, indicating that he could get all of the labor of a given quality he wanted without raising the wage; and he could get no labor if the wage paid were lower than the prevailing market rate. Moreover, there is an assumption that the only differences between wages would be those that tended to equalize the differences between jobs. That is to say, wages in some occupations would be higher than those in others because those occupations had offsetting costs or disadvantages which required that high wages be paid. The competitive model also assumes that wages are fairly volatile and fluctuate freely with changing demand and supply conditions. In this model, moreover, labor would be allocated between firms and labor markets on the basis of the net advantages to workers and employers. Workers would move from low- to high-wage jobs, and employers would tend to replace high-wage workers with those who were willing to work for lower wages.

In a general way, the labor market tends to operate according to these propositions; but none of the implications are realized in the real world.

Wages probably are not as equal for the same quality of labor as the competitive model implies. Moreover, differences between wage rates persist which probably cannot be explained by offsetting costs or disadvantages of the higher-wage jobs. Indeed, the higher-wage jobs seem to have advantages which cause the gap between these and lower-paying jobs to have wider differentials than the money wage rates would imply. Finally, we shall see that labor probably does not always move in such a way as to equalize differences between wage rates. We keep saying "probably" because the competitive model contains assumptions which make it very difficult to test in the real world. We are, therefore, forced to rely much more heavily on suppositions and probabilities than we would like.

External and Internal Labor Markets

One of the first qualifications that must be made in the economists' traditional conception of a labor market is to distinguish the internal and the external labor markets. While the competitive model concerns itself mainly with the so-called external labor market (that outside the firm or craft), the internal labor market concerns itself with the rules that are made within the firm or craft to fix wages and allocate labor among alternative uses. The internal labor market is controlled more by institutional rules which are not always compatible with the assumptions of the competitive labor market. For example, workers' wage rates and occupational positions within a manufacturing firm are much more likely to be determined by seniority than by relative productivity. These rules might be highly formalized if there is a union present, and they might be more informal if there is no union and the work group sets its own rules. In a very real sense, of course, there is no such thing as an unorganized work group because each group tends to be informally organized and to establish its own code of conduct and ethics, whether or not unions are present.

Because of these internal rules which govern the relationship between workers and employers, the employer does not necessarily act (in the internal labor market) as the competitive model assumes he will. For example, the employer is not very likely to cut wages in order to reduce costs as the labor supply schedule shifts to the right because he fully realizes that a wage cut could seriously damage the morale of his workers. Nor are employers always likely to increase wages when the demand for labor increases. To some extent, then, the internal labor market is isolated, at least in the short run, from the market forces of the external labor market. The main areas where internal labor markets are connected with external labor markets are what Dunlop calls the "ports of entry" into the company.[3] These are defined as the points within the company at which the firm hires from the outside. Because labor market adjustments are not as volatile as the traditional theory assumes they will be, if employers equate wages with productivity, as competitive theory assumes, average wages must be equated to productivity for groups of workers over time because constant adjustments clearly are not made at the margin where marginal revenue equals marginal cost at any given time.

Kerr has referred to the process of establishing institutional rules which structure labor markets as "balkanization." [4] In Kerr's analysis, institutional rules (among other things) cause labor markets to be structured. He cites Lloyd Fisher's description of the harvest labor market in California as a good illustration of a structureless market. Fisher defines a structureless market as possessing five conditions:

(1) There are no unions with seniority or other rules, (2) the relation between the employee and the employer is a transitory impersonal one, (3) the workers are unskilled, (4) payment is by unit of product, and (5) little capital or machinery is employed.

In contrast to this, Kerr conceives of other markets as possessing various degrees of structure which can be caused by other things as well as the institutional rules. For example, many workers have skills that restrict their employment to particular occupations in which they seek work. Similarly, workers and employers form attachments for each other which are not lightly broken. Therefore, these customs and attachments tend to isolate the internal labor market from the operation of external forces.

The degree of isolation, or balkanization, to use Kerr's term, is increased with the establishment of internal rules that limit entry into the market and determine the movement of workers within those markets as well as their exit from them. In Kerr's words, once these institutional rules are established, "market forces seemingly impersonal in the aggregate, but exceedingly personal in individual situations, give way to personal rules which may seem exceedingly impersonal when applied to specific workers." [5] The main purpose of these rules, of course, is to establish control over the job territory for the people who are already in the market.

Kerr distinguishes two general systems of institutional rules, each with important subtypes. The first is "communal ownership." This is the type of institutionalization typical of the building, printing, trucking, and similar trades. In this kind of labor market, the workers assert control over all jobs in the labor market. The workers are likely to enter the market through unions rather than through employers because unions. are likely to be the most stable elements in this labor market, partly because workers change jobs frequently in these casual markets. Moreover, the unions assert control over some traditional managerial functions such as training. The unions will, therefore, establish fairly strict rules for admission into the market as well as the conditions under which people are allowed to work within the labor market. In this labor market, the worker's loose tie to his employer is compensated for by a very tight tie to his occupation, and movement is, therefore, within the market and primarily horizontal rather than vertical. That is to say, workers can move about quite freely within the labor market once they gain entry into it. They have a strong identification with their craft, but they do not form strong attachments to particular employers. The significance of the union in the craft-type labor market is demonstrated by the fact that although the employer can remove the worker from the job by discharging him, only the union can remove him from the market because the discharged worker can move freely to another job.

In the industrial situation, the second of Kerr's general systems, each worker tends to occupy his own job; when he vacates it, only one person is eligible to fill it. The group ordinarily establishes the rules, usually giving heavy weight to seniority to determine which workers will fill the job, although the workers' preference for seniority is often compromised by the employer's need to get the most productive people in particular jobs. In the industrial internal labor markets, therefore, seniority becomes much more important, and movement is largely vertical within families of jobs. The main contact of the internal and external labor markets is through the so-called "ports of entry." Except for these ports of entry, competition between workers inside a labor market and those outside it tends to be very restricted.

> Competition among workers is reduced, the internal and external labor markets are joined only at restricted points, and within the internal market, craft jobs are likely to be fairly standardized and industrial jobs filled in accordance with seniority, so that workers are not actively contesting with each other for preference. Beyond this, the distribution of work opportunities by the craft union and the rehiring rights of the industrial contract tend to hold unemployed workers in a pool attached to the craft or plant and thus keep them from competing for jobs so actively elsewhere. . . .[6]

Reduced mobility is one of the main ways in which institutional rules isolate workers in the internal labor markets from external competition. The potential mobility of workers is the main sanction that makes wage rates interrelated. Once a worker builds up a certain amount of seniority in a plant, his mobility is undoubtedly restricted, and the penalty for his withdrawal from the internal labor market becomes greater and greater. It might, therefore, be very difficult for a worker to find another job with comparable pay and status if he withdraws from a particular labor market.

Doeringer and Piore [7] discuss in considerable detail the forces generating the internal labor market as well as some of the economic and manpower implications of the operation of such markets. In their view, internal labor markets appear to be generated by skill specificity, on-the-job training, and customary law. Skill specificity means that the skills possessed by particular workers are useful mainly for the specific jobs in a particular labor market. On-the-job training is the way most workers acquire their job skills; customary law is important because the work place is a social institution where various customary rules and procedures tend to attach workers to particular internal labor markets. Although external labor market forces might tend to be very important in the long run, many customs persevere in the short run in the face of contrary economic pressures, thus nullifying the validity of traditional labor market concepts.

Although traditional economic theory ordinarily regards the institutionalized rules of the internal labor market as inimical to efficiency, some aspects of this internal labor market promote efficiency. Custom, for example, helps employers minimize costs because workers place a high value on custom, and custom tends to reduce turnover, which could be expensive for employers. Moreover, the internal mechanism for recruiting, training, and screening labor might be very efficient because workers have greater knowledge of the internal labor market situation than outsiders do. Likewise, employers would incur certain costs in replacing and terminating workers discharged from the internal labor market and replaced by those outside it. Similarly, the internal promotion process causes a certain amount of efficiency in training because people are familiar with the jobs in their lines of progression and because the internal promotion gives workers more incentive to learn the next higher job. Doeringer and Piore explain the processes by which internal labor markets emerge and reinforce each other in the following terms:

> When one internal labor market emerges in a previously competitive labor market, some workers and some jobs are gone from market competition, thereby encouraging other workers and managers to institute internal labor markets within their enterprises. Managers will do so in order to retain their competitive position in both product and labor market. Incumbent workers would do so in order to protect or enhance their employment security. Once these markets are prevalent, workers and managers will seek to stabilize the work relationship and to reinforce further the internal labor market.[8]

During periods of labor shortage, substandard skills and abilities are adjusted to job requirements through such internal labor market instruments as recruitment procedures, training, and compensation.

> These instruments . . . exist because a number of functions conventionally identified with the competitive labor market have been internalized in the enterprise. These instruments individually and collectively constitute a series of labor market adjustment processes by which the internal labor market adapts to change in both production techniques and labor market conditions.[9]

Multiple Labor Markets

The traditional economic theory outlined earlier in this chapter also must be modified to account for broad differences among external labor markets. Within each broad classification, moreover, various submarkets could be analyzed, although we do not do so here. Public policy requires an adequate understanding of how these labor markets operate in order to avoid the mistakes that are likely to be made by assuming that the whole economy is a giant queue from which workers are hired on the basis of their productivity. If this were so, perhaps it would be possible to solve problems of unemployment and low incomes with aggregate economic policies alone. However, increasing aggregate demand by increasing the supply of money and spending through monetary-fiscal policies clearly has a differential impact on various types of labor markets. These aggregate measures might cause hyperinflation in some markets with no change in employment while leaving pockets of unemployment virtually undisturbed in other labor markets. The queue theory is, therefore, of some value *within* labor markets, but it has limited utility when applied to the whole economy.

Similarly, a "dual labor market" theory is deficient if it assumes that the economy can be neatly divided into two types of labor markets; one of which workers have experienced considerable progress while those in the other lag behind. Similarly, it is not very useful to divide labor markets into such simple aggregate categories as "agricultural" and "nonagricultural." We are persuaded that there are many labor markets, but that several broad classifications might be described as ideal types for purposes of illustration. Much more work needs to be done in order to identify and define types of labor markets and their interrelationships.

The Professional Labor Market

The first of these broad labor markets can be termed the "professional" labor market. It comprises the various professions and is characterized by no tangible product and usually a high income elasticity of demand, which means that the demand for this kind of labor increases disproportionately with increases in incomes. Moreover, professional labor markets are characterized by very imperfect competition. Professionals often discriminate between clients according to their ability to pay, and often consider it unethical to compete either through advertising or price competition. The professional market also requires considerable formal education for entry. This market is imperfect compared with the competitive norm, not only because of the absence of competition but also because of the time lags for demand to adjust to supply and because professionals tend to control the supplies of labor in their professions through licensing and various forms of "self-regulation."

The implications of this kind of labor market are clear. As national income increases, the income of professionals will increase, but there is no assurance that their productivity will go up, individually or in the aggregate. Indeed, there are very limited objective ways in which the performance of professionals can be measured by outsiders. Because of the imperfections in this market, professionals can raise their prices in accordance with their customers' ability to pay, need not be evenly distributed geographically, and are very difficult to regulate by indirect means. For example, how would a "guidelines" policy gearing salaries and wages to productivity operate in an industry where there is no product?

The second market, which we shall call the "mainstream," is characterized by extensive political and economic power, control of markets through product diversification and differentiation, considerable integration of production processes, the power to distribute products throughout a wide market, and ready or preferential access to credit and financial resources. Mainstream labor markets probably also have relatively high product-market concentration ratios, which means that a few firms account for large shares of total sales. The workers in this labor market usually require extensive training (either formal or on the job), have high skill requirements, are relatively well unionized, have considerable upgrading opportunities within the internal labor markets, and receive high wages. The firms in the mainstream also tend to be growth industries, with high ratios of capital to labor costs. Because of their political and economic power, the firms in the mainstream labor market are likely to have close interlocking relationships with various government agencies, particularly at the federal level but also at the state level, and account for a disproportionate amount of funds expended on government contracts. In short, the firms in the mainstream labor market are characterized by considerable power and prestige, and the workers in that labor market are likely to share that power and prestige through unions, which tend to be stronger in this labor market than in any other.

The Marginal Labor Market

A third labor market may be characterized as "marginal." Firms in this labor market lack most of the advantages of those in the mainstream, are highly competitive, have low profit margins, and are characterized by a very high ratio of labor cost to total cost. Unions are weak or nonexistent, and both the unions and employers in this labor market have very limited power and prestige.

The working poor are heavily concentrated in the marginal labor market. Examples of the kinds of industries in this sector (which have average hourly earnings below the minimum wage of $1.60 per hour and in which over half of the workers earn less than $1.60 per hour): southern sawmills and planing mills; nursing homes and related facilities; work clothing; children's hosiery mills; men's and boys' shirts; laundries and cleaning services; men's hosiery mills; synthetic textiles; cotton textiles; wood and household furniture; limited-price variety stores; eating and drinking places; hotels and motels; drug and proprietary stores; gasoline service stations; apparel and accessory stores; department stores; and miscellaneous retail stores.

If we assume that a worker works 40 hours a week and 50 weeks a year, the minimum wage of $1.60 per hour will yield him exactly $3,200 a year; so what we are saying is that in all of these industries either the average hourly earnings were less than $1.60 an hour in 1968 or that a majority of the workers in the industry earned less than $1.60 per hour in 1968. Therefore, a worker could have worked full time in these industries and made less than a poverty wage if he were head of a family. Indeed, in 1968, of all families who had incomes of less than $3,500 a year, 50.2 percent had heads who worked at least some time. Moreover, 41 percent of the heads of families who made less than $3,500 a year worked full time. There were approximately 11 million families with incomes of less than $5,000 year in 1968, and 30 percent of these were headed by persons who worked full time.

Looking at this question from another angle, there were approximately 10 million people in jobs paying less than $1.60 an hour in 1968, which amounted to about one-fifth of the private nonsupervisory work force. Workers in these marginal industries, therefore, have low wages and very limited upgrading possibilities. They also have relatively low levels of education and limited skills and training. Because the jobs they hold are relatively unskilled, they likewise have very limited opportunities for acquiring higher skills on the job.[10]

The Submarginal Labor Market

A fourth type of labor market can be called "submarginal." This is a much more difficult market to define: Many of the people who work in it do not show up in the income tax or social security accounts because often they do not pay income tax or social security. Moreover, this labor market may be further subdivided into those engaged in legal and those engaged in illicit activities. This market contains a very large number of teenagers, adults with poor work histories, other adults with various obstacles to employment, and those who do not participate in the work force but are involved in various illicit activities or are on welfare. Many of the jobs in this labor market are characterized by very low entry requirements, low wages, high rates of turnover, informal work patterns, and work skills and competencies specific to ghetto life, which were acquired mainly through on-the-job training rather than through formal channels.

Many of the jobs in this sector have high turnover partly because they are very low-wage, dead-end jobs. Therefore, the employment disadvantages of this sector are due more to limited high-wage opportunities than to barriers to such job opportunities as exist in this labor market. Indeed, there apparently are many low-wage jobs in the ghetto which are readily available to ghetto dwellers. The clear determinant of the character of the jobs in the submarginal labor market is that the jobs there do not provide adequate

security or wages to make it possible to stabilize employment. As a consequence, both employers and workers in the market have adjusted to this
unstable routine. Many of the younger people in the ghetto are underemployed for long periods and spend their time hanging around on the street.
This time is punctuated occasionally by exciting events, which the people
of the street tend to recall with considerable relish. Indeed, one of the
attractions for the submarginal labor market in its casual and sometimes
exciting character. Employers adjust to this labor market because they
expect to have workers who will be absent or late, and therefore they do
not enforce discipline. Because the jobs are not very attractive anyway, it
is no great tragedy for the worker to lose one, and it is very difficult to maintain high levels of work discipline and motivation. Of course, tragedies often
occur when workers are forced to rely on submarginal labor markets to
support their families. The main tragedy of submarginal ghetto markets
is that they tend to be associated with factors—such as racism, poverty,
low levels of education—which tend to be self-reinforcing and from which
it is therefore difficult to escape. Not all jobs in the submarginal labor market are necessarily characterized by low wages, and many of them have
high wages per unit of time. However, these tend to be mainly the illicit
and dangerous activities, such as prostitution or the sale of narcotics, which
have a high risk attached to them. It probably is closer to the truth to say
that most of the lawful jobs in the submarginal labor market are low-wage
jobs but that many illicit activities carry very high returns per unit of time
worked.

These four types of labor markets have important implications for
theories of labor markets. For example, the equilibrating processes of
traditional labor market theory are rendered inoperative by impediments to
the movement of people among these markets. The first of these impediments might be *personal,* insofar as the worker might have inadequate
education, training, work history, and motivation to move from the submarginal to the marginal labor market. But because workers in the submarginal
labor market frequently have higher incomes than those in the marginal labor
market, they have little incentive to aspire to the jobs in the latter category.
Moreover, in order to reach even some jobs in the marginal labor market, it
would be necessary for the workers to overcome the disutility of geographic
and occupational mobility. This is true to some extent because the jobs in
marginal labor markets are located outside the central cities where many of
those who work in the submarginal market are likely to reside. Residents
of the submarginal labor market who want to reach marginal jobs must
expend time and money to move from the central cities to the outer ring of
metropolitan areas, sometimes a distance of many miles. It is, therefore,
understandable that workers who have low-wage jobs readily available to
them in their immediate areas will not be too interested in traveling long
distances to get jobs at the minimum wage. Clearly, however, transportation

costs would be more readily borne by these workers if they could acquire jobs in the mainstream. Ironically enough, many professional and mainstream jobs are located in the central cities not too far from the places where workers attached to the submarginal labor market are likely to live.

Certain *industrial* barriers may also impede movement of people among labor markets. Employers, for example, may discriminate against people from the submarginal labor market in general and racial minorities in particular. Moreover, some workers from the submarginal labor market or the marginal labor market may be barred from the mainstream by union discrimination. Unions, like employers, can discriminate against people with the values (e.g., dress, language, or life-styles) held by those who work in the submarginal labor markets; they also have a history of discrimination against blacks regardless of the areas from which they come. Moreover, during periods when the mainstream labor market is relatively loose, employers are able to recruit adequate labor supplies without dipping into marginal and submarginal labor pools. Many workers in the latter two markets might have superior qualifications for the work that actually needs to be done but still be barred from mainstream jobs because employers have unrealistically high educational requirements.

Finally, there are various *social* barriers to the movement of people between labor markets. One of these is the cost of relocating from familiar to unfamiliar areas. Workers might therefore incur considerable personal risk in moving from familiar areas which provide some security of income (however low) and personal relationships to other areas where there is some promise of higher wages but where a worker is required to enter at the bottom of a seniority line, have limited opportunities for advancement, and where he might be discriminated against because of race or culture. Moreover, the lack of market information about distant places makes many workers reluctant to incur the risk of moving. In addition, the income-earning alternative of workers in the submarginal labor market might be superior to those in the marginal labor market. Indeed, the low wages in marginal and submarginal industries probably offer very limited incentives for people to even enter the labor market if they have welfare or other income alternatives.

We know much less than we should about the movement of people among these markets. The extent to which one can see movement among labor markets depends to a significant degree on his overall theory of the labor market. Traditional economic theory has been based on a queue theory which assumes that people are lined up by employers on the basis of their productivity in relation to their wage rates. In this theory, workers in the submarginal labor market have lower productivities than those in the mainstream, and therefore it is assumed that the personal characteristics of the workers themselves account for this limited employment and income-earning opportunities. Moreover, the queue theory would recommend general economic policies to reduce the level of unemployment and give employers the incentive to move down the queue in order to hire disadvantaged workers.

The foregoing is meant to imply not that no mobility takes place among various types of labor markets, but rather that barriers among the labor markets are much more significant than those within each general labor market category. As labor markets tighten, of course, it is quite possible for firms in the mainstream to dip into the marginal and submarginal labor markets in order to meet their manpower requirements. When the labor market is slack, employers in the mainstream can use relatively inexpensive recruiting procedures and recruit internally or through referrals of outsiders by its own employees at the ports of entry into the internal labor markets. In the mainstream, employers can impose general restrictions which yield the results desired, primarily by recruiting people who are overqualified for available jobs. This can be done by imposing unrealistically high education and other requirements. But when the labor market tightens, employers achieve limited results from the traditional and less expensive recruiting and screening procedures and therefore have to adopt new techniques which require them to recruit first from the marginal labor market and then from the submarginal labor market. They must also adopt more refined screening procedures and hiring criteria, and, as a consequence, the formal qualifications of the people hired probably tend to decline during these times. However, companies are able to continue to meet their manpower demands primarily through on-the-job training programs, supplemented by hiring new workers at the ports of entry.

Many people feel that the queue theory is inadequate to explain the operation of the labor market, particularly the movement of people among the professional, mainstream, marginal, and submarginal jobs. According to these critics, the labor market must be conceived of as coming in two, three, or maybe more noncompeting segments; therefore the queue theory would apply mainly within the particular segment and not among noncompeting labor pools. The implication of this multiple labor market theory is that expansion of aggregate demand will not necessarily solve the problems of those in the submarginal labor market because it will simply exhaust the people in the professional or mainstream markets, bid up their wages and prices, and have relatively less effect on the incomes and earnings of people in the submarginal or marginal labor markets. Those who reject the queue theory therefore argue for remedial labor market policies directed at the specific characteristics of each kind of labor market.

Other Labor Market "Imperfections"

Many observers have also questioned the assumptions of the competitive theory that businessmen maximize their profits, particularly with respect to wage payments. One difficulty in testing such a theory, however, is that the observed differential wage rates within a labor market are not necessarily incompatible with the assumptions of traditional economic theory because the workers might really have different levels of efficiency, which would account for some of these differentials. A company that appears to pay more than a competitor in order to attract more efficient workers might, in reality, be paying no more for efficiency units than a competitive market would justify. A company might believe that this wage improves its public image or helps it avoid union attempts to organize its employees. Nevertheless, there is evidence that some employers pay wages that are much more than they would have to pay in a competitive labor market. There is, for example, a very high correlation between sales margins and average hourly earnings, which Sumner Slichter argued "reinforces the view that wages, within a considerable range, reflect managerial discretion, that where managment can easily pay higher wages they tend to do so, and that where managements are barely breaking even they tend to keep wages down." [11]

Ulman has found additional evidence that the labor market does not behave in conformity with the assumptions of traditional theory. Those assumptions are that in a full-employment economy, firms in expanding industries will have to raise their relative wage rates in order to attract additional supplies of labor. However, firms not already operating on their supply schedule (which means they are paying wages above the market) can expand employment and not necessarily reduce their wage rates. Ulman has called this the vacancy model of a labor market. He notes that there is little correlation between *percentage changes in wage rates* and *percentage changes in employment* for 57 industries he studied between 1948 and 1960. Indeed, firms that already had high wages in 1948 increased their relative wages between 1948 and 1960. Ulman concludes that the wage practices of these firm during the 1948–1960 period were contrary to the assumptions of competitive theory that ". . . since the relatively high wage industries did not tend to increase employment more rapidly than the others, they did not on the average have to raise wages more rapidly, as in fact they did in order to attract additional labor." [12] However, Ulman also found some evidence that sizable changes in demand and supply relationships are associated with changes in relative wages, even though the more moderate demand and supply changes do not appear to be so related. In Ulman's study, for example, wage and employment changes were closely associated in the 10 percent of industries in which wages rose most and the 10 percent in which they rose least.

Another assumption of the competitive theory that does not appear to conform with the realities of labor markets is that the demand and supply curves are independent. In the real market, there are close relationships between these curves. For example, sudden, dramatic increases in wages might tend to increase the demand schedule as well, either through the influence of wages on the demand for products or through the so-called "shock effect," in which wage increases cause employers to be more efficient than they might have been in the absence of the increase.[13] The shock might come about because of an increase in minimum wages or because of an increase in union wage pressures. However, the number of times the "shock effect" can be used in a given situation might be limited as successive "shocks" reduce the efficiency slack that can be taken up.

SUMMARY AND CONCLUSIONS

This chapter has emphasized the significance of theory for policy matters and has examined the traditional economic theory of labor markets. However, we have pointed out that even though the competitive model has some usefulness, its validity for understanding the operation of real markets is limited by a number of factors. Some of these factors—for example, the theoretical assumptions upon which the competitive model is based—can be dealt with by refining the theory and relaxing the assumptions, which we have done.

However, some of the other problems—for example, institutional rigidities which make it difficult for the market to operate, cannot be assumed away. Therefore, any realistic analysis of operational labor markets requires some understanding of these institutional forces. It is particularly important to understand the relationship between the internal and external labor markets and to know more than we presently know about the inter-relationships betweeen such broad labor market types as the professional, mainstream, marginal, and submarginal labor markets discussed in this chapter. Moreover, there is an obvious necessity to have a better theoretical explanation of the interactions of the various kinds of labor markets and the adjustment of firms and labor markets to changing general demand and supply conditions. Without an adequate theory, we will be hard pressed to come up with policies that overcome the imperfections and problems discussed in this chapter. It is particularly important to try to distinguish between the so-called queue theory and those that view the labor market as being compartmentalized. It is our feeling that the truth probably lies somewhere inbetween these positions: That is to say, the queue theory operates, albeit imperfectly, within each labor market and with less speed and precision between the labor markets, but there is a great deal to be learned from studying the characteristics of different kinds of labor markets. Unfortunately, however, we know too little theoretically and empirically about labor market operations.

NOTES

1. Milton Friedman, "What Price Guideposts?" in George Shultz and Robert Aliber, eds., *Guidelines* (Chicago: University of Chicago Press, 1966), p. 17.

2. For further discussion of bargaining models, see N. W. Chamberlain, *A General Theory of Economic Process* (New York: Harper and Row,

1955), chapters 6 and 7; J. Pen, *The Wage Rate Under Collective Bargaining* (Cambridge, Mass.: Harvard University Press, 1959); *idem.*, "A General Theory of Bargaining," *American Economic Review* (March 1952); and G. L. S. Schackle, "The Nature of the Bargaining Process," in John T. Dunlop, ed., *The Theory of Wage Determination* (London: Macmillan and Company, 1967).

3. John T. Dunlop, "Job Vacancies Measures and Economic Analysis," in National Bureau of Economic Research, *The Measurement and Interpretation of Job Vacancies* (New York: The Bureau, 1966), pp. 27–38.

4. Clark Kerr, "Balkanization of Labor Markets," in E. Wight Bakke *et al.*, *Labor Mobility and Economic Opportunity* (Cambridge and New York: M.I.T. Press and John Wiley, 1954), pp. 93–109.

5. *Ibid.*, p. 96.

6. *Ibid.*

7. Peter Doeringer and Michael Piore, *Internal Labor Markets and Manpower Analysis* (Lexington, Mass.: D. C. Health, 1971).

8. *Ibid.*, p. 40.

9. *Ibid.*, pp. 189–190.

10. Barry Bluestone, "The Tripartite Economy: Labor Markets and the Working Poor," *Poverty and Human Resources* (July–August 1970), pp. 15–37.

11. Sumner Slichter, "Notes on the Structure of Wages," *Review of Economics and Statistics* (February 1950), quoted by Lloyd G. Reynolds, *Labor Economics and Labor Relations* (Englewood Cliffs, N.J.: Prentice-Hall, 1970), 5th ed., p. 115.

12. Lloyd Ulman, "Labor Mobility in the Industrial Wage Structure in the Postwar United States," *Quarterly Journal of Economics* (February 1965), pp. 73–97.

13. See Lloyd G. Reynolds and Peter Gregory, *Wages, Productivity and Industrialization in Puerto Rico* (Homewood, Ill.: Richard D. Irwin, 1965).

Chapter 13
Manpower Planning in the Business Firm

To the extent that the availability and quality of labor have risen relative to capital and natural resources as economic considerations, one would expect to see manpower looming larger among the planning efforts of the rational business firm. Just as a firm is led by its pursuit of profit to plan ahead to obtain adequate supplies of raw materials and to invest in productive capital equipment, it should now be motivated to plan for an adequate labor supply. The growing number of firms engaged in such activities is evidence of the increasing importance of manpower. That the firms are still few in number and their planning is rudimentary, illustrate how far there is to go. In this chapter, we review the extent of manpower planning in business firms, the pressures for such planning, the techniques employed, the pitfalls, the future prospects, and the relationships between private and public manpower planning and between manpower planning and personnel administration.

THE EXTENT OF MANPOWER PLANNING

Manpower planning has been defined as "the process (including forecasting, developing, implementing, and controlling) by which a firm insures that it has the right number of people and the right kind of people, at the right places at the right time, doing the things for which they are economically most useful." [1] A Labor Department-sponsored review of the literature describes the concerns of "micro manpower planning as proposed designs and methods of action or procedure in using manpower resources to attain organizational objectives." [2]

Given the inclusiveness of these definitions, it is difficult to select from among management functions those that should be described as manpower planning. None of the definitions differentiate between manpower planning and the management of manpower. Overlap with what has been traditionally known as personal administration is obvious. In our review of literature and practice, we attempt to differentiate between planning to assure adequate future supplies of qualified manpower, and implementation to make effective use of existing manpower.

The Bureau of National Affairs polled a sample of personnel officials representing 300 large companies in mid-1968 to ascertain the extent of manpower utilization and planning.[3] Five of every six companies had some formal procedure for meeting future manpower needs. Three out of four firms conducted manpower audits for managerial personnel, two-thirds for professionals, 70 percent for clerical employees, and 56 percent for blue-collar workers. Nearly one-half of those conducting manpower audits used projections ranging from six months to five years. Over one-half conducted formal periodic audits or reviews of manpower supplies and needs. Instruction in manpower analysis or planning was given to first-line supervisors in 44 percent of the firms. More than half had some plan for coordinating staffing requirements so that surplus manpower in one subdivision could be loaned to others experiencing shortages. Somewhat parallel findings emerged from a 1968 survey of 592 firms. Three-fourths of the firms engaged in some form of job analysis, from 50 to 90 percent identifying one of the following among practices related to manpower planning:

1. Determining qualifications required of jobholders of the firms.
2. Providing guidance in recruitment and selection.
3. Evaluating current employees for transfer or promotion.
4. Establishing requirements for training programs.
5. Establishing responsibility, accountability, and authority.[4]

Much of the interest in manpower forecasting seems to be caused by labor shortages in the firm's external labor supply. Thus, when it becomes difficult to recruit from the outside, other internal, existing supplies of labor must be developed and used. This occurred during the relatively low unemployment of the late 1960s. If the labor market became loose again, the authors of a 1967 Minnesota study predicted, the costs of manpower development and planning programs might be greater than the potential benefits (i.e., it would be cheaper to recruit from the outside). Their findings expressed doubt that the involvement of firms in such manpower programs represented a lasting commitment.[5]

It is impossible from the fragmentary data available to estimate the total amount of formal manpower planning. One can only say with assurance that it is growing and that there are significant pressures toward continued expansion.

MOTIVATION FOR MANPOWER PLANNING

What are the reasons for the increased interest in and commitment to manpower planning? In a profit system, the basic motivation for manpower planning, as for most activities of the firm, would be its contribution to profitability. But added are the public's expectations that business firms will pursue social welfare goals directly as well as serve the public at its customers. In addition, the reasons underlying manpower planning include the nature of the human resources and the tendency toward recurrent shortages of critical manpower supplies.

The Nature of Manpower Resources

Manpower resources exhibit four critical characteristics. First, particularly for the higher skills, an extraordinarily long time is required for workers to achieve full productivity. Second, rather than depreciate with use, a person generally achieves higher productivity the longer he is on the job. Third, investments in manpower, whether made by the employer, the public, or the worker, belong to the individual who may take his skills where he will. Finally, in contrast to other factors of production, a person's satisfaction with his lot can affect his productivity.

United States employers, public and private, can take advantage of high levels of educational attainment. Only when their manpower requirements are unique need employers themselves invest in long months or years of training. Certain industrial training processes that consume years of time such as apprenticeship involve more production than they do training. Yet many years of education, training, and experience enter into the preparation of a professional, an engineer, a scientist, a technician, or a skilled craftsman. Whether or not he supplies the training, the employer contributes through his wage bill and his taxes to the public and private costs of that extended preparation. And because relatively fewer potential workers are willing to undertake such training, the employer faces a relative shortage of supply.

Whereas machines depreciate and buildings deteriorate with use, worker skills tend to increase with experience. Of course, to the extent that a job requires only physical strength, the worker's productivity may decline with age. But such jobs are in relative decline, as they are increasingly absorbed by machine production. Manipulative skills tend to be maintained as long as the employee is alert and challenged. Yet with accelerating technological change, obsolescence threatens both the specialist and his employer, requiring foresight and planning for maintenance of skills and upgrading.

When a firm invests in a machine, that machine becomes its property to do with as its will. But (barring slavery) human beings enjoy relatively unimpeded mobility. No matter how great the employer's investment in him, there is little to keep the worker from moving on when other employment appears more attractive.

Given this mobility and the fact that the worker's productivity is largely in his own and not management's control, the employer has a stake in the worker's job satisfaction. No one need be concerned whether a machine is happy and contented. An employee's well-being off the job may be as important to the employer as the employee's satisfaction with the work environment.

The Supply of Talented Manpower

Because employees are all different and seldom of equal value, talented and productive individuals are always in short supply. Even during the depression of the 1930s, trade association journals lamented the shortage of skilled manpower. Now as the most rapidly growing manpower requirements encompass those occupations with the longest training time, the employers' concern for the quality of employees is increased. The projected 50 percent growth during the 1970s in the employment of professional and technical workers, compared to a one-fifth increase in the total labor force, is indication enough. These are the occupations in which workers are least likely to be trained on the job.

Business's demands for high-talent manpower increased concomitantly with those of the public sector and the expanding private not-for-profit sector—just at the time that the low birth rates of the 1930s took their toll by restricting the 30–45 age group, which included the bulk of those with sufficient training and experience to be most useful. The mid-1950s–mid-1960s decade-long slack in demand for labor caused many companies to neglect or abandon training programs, which contributed to an even greater shortage during the rapid growth years of the late 1960s. This constriction should ease during the 1970s as the swollen youth cohorts of the late 1940s and 1950s complete their educations. Nevertheless, the 35–45-year-old managerial group will not reach 1960s level until 1978. Demographic factors, the reinauguration of industrial training, and persistently rising educational attainment should ease pressures in the future, but the trend toward longer periods of training is probably irreversible.

Costs of Recruitment and Hiring

The more important the new employees's preexisting skills and knowledge, the greater is the incentive to careful recruiting. The more careful the recruiting, the stiffer the competition. Each of these factors adds to the likelihood that the individual participates in a national labor market. As firms have become larger, they have found they need manpower inventories to insure that individual employee needs are being met and that the best qualified employees are selected for the many job openings. The higher costs of nationwide recruiting encourage upgrading from within. As a general experience, net employee costs—that is, the time during which an employee's net contributions are less than his net costs of employment—are likely to be lower for the employee promoted from within than for a new employee recruited from outside. One student, for instance, has estimated that some firms invest as much of $20,000 in a new engineer before he starts contributing to net profits.[6]

The proliferation of employment costs encourage planned recruitment and internal employee development. Pensions, health insurance and other fringe benefits as well as recruitment and training costs raise the cost for hiring a new worker. Seniority privileges, other job rights and benefits, and union employee protection reduce mobility and turnover, while the employment costs encourage planned retention.

Response to Social Pressure

A prominent industrial personnel director's statement indicates the pressure of changing social expectations upon the manpower planning requirement:

> The public will expect more from business with respect to the "quality of life" in business organizations and the quality of business contributions to society. . . . companies are going to have to live with the fact that both the public and government will be more inclined to recognize their performance in such areas as:
> —establishing long-range goals that are in harmony with national manpower policies;
> —running the business with prime consideration for the human factor in the equation;
> —locating plants in urban or rural underdeveloped areas;
> —hiring, training, and testing practices that represent a real "outreach" into the community;
> —providing opportunities for employee's continuing education.[7]

From a long-term perspective, one of the startling changes in our traditionally private enterprise society is the degree to which we now expect businessmen to undertake unprofitable and even costly social activities. The assumption underlying the private enterprise system was that profit (barring monopoly power) was the best evidence that the businessman was contributing to the social welfare. That society expects business firms to run Job Corps centers, employ the disadvantaged, contribute to and even run schools, and a myriad of similar activities may suggest spreading doubt that the original assumption is still valid. That the businessman is willing to engage in these social activities suggests an equal change in philosophy.

Firms have even established whole divisions and subsidiaries to do nothing else but perform public service, sometimes at a profit but never a high one. Other firms have emerged to make the social welfare their primary business.

In part, these developments are a consequence of the growing importance of human resources. Unlike capital investment, human resources are developed largely at public expense, and society expects a direct return from their use. Professional business managers, compensated more by salaries than profits and educated to social needs, often welcome the opportunity for broader involvement. Whatever the reason, business firms have invested essential resources in battling social problems. Their role, as long as it does not interfere with the necessity of profit, is an additional motivator for internal manpower planning.

Involvement in public manpower programs requires more formal examination of job content, wage structures, seniority systems, and recruitment and hiring practices. Efforts of business firms on behalf of the disadvantaged frequently have led management to improve their practices vis-à-vis their total work force. Not the least important motivator is the willingness of government to subsidize the costs of those services.

Profitability

One reason for manpower planning is the growth of corporate planning as a whole. High capital-labor ratios, vulnerability to technological change, the commitment to management by objectives, and, by no means least, the presence of managers and technicians trained in planning techniques are all important in stimulating corporate planning.

But the fundamental reason for growing interest in manpower planning in the business firm is the familiar one: the conviction that it pays. Wages, salaries, and associated employee costs are the single largest outlay for most firms—as much as 40 percent of the expenses of many corporations. The recognition that employee productivity is a major factor in profitability has long fired interest in rationalization of work and incentive systems to motivate the worker. Training has, typically, received less emphasis. Only emerging is a recognition of the need to plan ahead to insure the availability of critical skills and to treat manpower as an investment at least equal in importance to capital equipment.

TECHNIQUES OF MANPOWER PLANNING

A complete manpower plan would entail projecting requirements, comparing them to expected internal supplies, and planning all of the necessary steps to assure enough workers of adequate quality when and where needed.

As in any form of planning, the essential problem of manpower planning is foreseeing the future accurately enough to take sensible actions related to it. Manpower planning also has special difficulties, in that the supply of the productive factor consists of people with minds of their own, but the demand for labor is derived from the demand for the employer's product. The employer's manpower needs will depend upon what product mix in what amounts he can sell, the technology he will use, and the price he receives and the profitability it implies. What is available to him depends upon the population, the labor force participation rate, the quality and retention-power of the schools, and the demands and wages offered by other employers.

In addition, the relationships between outside labor market conditions and internal practices will determine turnover and influence productivity. Projections of manpower needs, therefore, entail projection of economic conditions, product demand, market share, wage rates, other costs and prices. Based upon these projections, manpower planning entails job descriptions and specifications, inventories of the present work force, recruitment, selection, training, and reduction of turnover as well as orderly layoff and separation. Few manpower planning efforts go much beyond forecasting. Nevertheless, there are enough examples to examine the components of current practice.

Projecting Manpower Requirements

There are as many approaches to projecting the manpower needs of the firm as there are firms and projectors. A logical beginning is projections of output for the firms various project lines. Decisions must be made concerning future product innovations and the overall diversification of the firm. Underlying these forecasts are the firm's goals of market share. Projects may vary in sophistication from simple time-series projections of sales to detailed analyses of present and potential markets. The choice of method necessitates another forecast—whether trends are reasonably stable and predictable or subject to drastic change.

Occasionally, correlation analysis can substitute for both time-series projections and more detailed analyses. If a firm can find a variable that correlates with sales, it may be able to predict output by determining the value of the other variable—for instance, estimated GNP. A drug firm, for example, found a correlation between disposable personal income and industry sales of pharmaceuticals. For every 10 percent change in national disposable income a corresponding change of 5 percent occurred in industry sales.[8] Knowing this correlation, and assuming it will hold in the future, the company can make more accurate forecasts by projecting disposable income, calculating the result for industry sales, and then forecasting its own sales by estimating its future market share. However, unless at least a theoretical cause-and-effect relationship is assumed between the two variables, the same objections hold for correlation analysis as for simple time-series projections—the relationship may change at any time, yielding invalid predictions.

Because there is no really infallible method for predicting the future, errors of prediction continue to plague manpower planners. An alternative method involves constructing a decision tree to assign a measure of probability to projected sales and employment figures. Estimates of a market demand, in particular, should be constructed on a probabilistic basis to account for projection error and random factors.

Once an estimate of future output has been made, decisions concerning anticipated personnel needs must be faced. Anticipated changes in the firm's organizational structure must be integrated with predicted manpower requirements. Thus, a future organizational chart must be available. Technological changes may also have a drastic effect on the level and structure of requirements for some types of manpower. But forecasting technological change requires awareness not only of new technologies becoming available, but also of such issues as the timing of the introduction into the patricular firm, the speed with which the new technology replaces the old, and the impact on manning and productivity. Firms that are always at the forefront of available technologies make life difficult for their manpower planners; those that are dependably slow to change require adoption of new technologies rather than their invention and make projecting simpler.

Though limited by the assumption that traditional manpower-output relationships will continue to hold, correlation analysis can again be used to predict manpower requirements on the basis of predicted output. As an example, correlation analysis was found to work quite effectively for manpower forecasting at one large diversified company.[9] It was determined that the average amount of sales per manager was quite consistent each year, even in the various classifications. After this relationship was determined, the company's sales forecast was used to estimate the total number of managers in the future, taking retirements and estimated turnover into account, an estimate was made of the number of managers that would have to be developed. A good correlation was also found to exist between sales and the number of technical employees, but sales showed little correlation with laboratory personnel. However, a risk remained for planning future actions. Without a theoretical model explaining the sales-personnel ratio, there was no way of foreseeing a change in the sales-personnel relationship.

This example also reflected the limitation of projections to executives and various high-level personnel. There is little interest in planning for personnel that seems to be in plentiful supply. Most firms prefer simple techniques—projecting from internal data and estimates of outlook. There is no evidence that these produce less valid results than more sophisticated techniques. Yet the pressures are in the latter direction.

Inventory of Current Personnel

Any projection of future manpower requirements must begin with an inventory of current personnel. In gross numbers, recruiting and hiring needs will depend upon the turnover rate of current employees through quits, retirements, transfers, and promotions. In occupational detail, the present positions, promotability, and the talents, interests, trainability, and unused present skills of current employees must be considered. Thus, such inventories must be combined with appraisals or performance reviews so that employee capability and potential can be ascertained.

A good manpower inventory usually includes:

1. personal history data—age, sex, marital status, number of dependents, draft status, etc.
2. basic skills information—education, training, work experience, hobbies, languages, etc.
3. special qualifications—foreign travel and residence, patents, publications, honors, membership in professional organizations, special assignments completed, etc.
4. occupational and salary progression
5. company personnel data—service and seniority dates, retirement information, benefit plan data
6. measures and judgments of capacity
7. employee interests—job and locational preferences, etc.

The widespread use of computers has greatly facilitated manpower inventories. Not only have computers eliminated much of the clerical work, but they have also decreased the time necessary to obtain information about a specific employee. Printouts can be made to isolate employees with certain skills and interests. For instance, a research and development firm with a high-talent work force and sophisticated equipment and procedures would be able to identify, say, a Ph.D. engineer of the right age who had a certain specialty and the required language skills, and had expressed willingness to travel on short notice for an urgent assignment anyplace in the world.

Performance appraisals are the next step in determining the adequacy of the present work force and its potential for jobs of increasing importance and responsibility. Such appraisals may concentrate on objective standards of performance or emphasize personality traits. Setting up performance standards requires determination of the key results expected on the job, development of the terms in which these may be measured, and agreement on the actual quantitative standards that are expected to be maintained. The personality-trait approach tackles the more difficult task of identifying traits that characterize the promotable manager. Both types of appraisal are vital to forecasting future performance.

The firm must also decide what is to be done with those people whose evaluations indicate no further promotions or even inadequacy at their present job (according to the Peter Principle, many executives ultimately end up in a job with which they are unable to cope, having been promoted one level past their optimal ability).[10]

Implementing the Plan

The steps to implementation of a manpower plan have been summarized as follows:

1. Examine historical data to determine the relationships between the size and composition of the work force and sales, production and inventories.
2. Examine historical data to determine retirements, deaths, quits, and dismissal rates, promotions and transfers, and retraining periods and retrainability rates.
3. Determine the relationship of staff functions to line employees, sales volume and production.
4. Examine the rate of product development and its impact on the workforce.
5. Determine the rate of productivity increase in terms of the ratios of manhours to output, capital equipment to output and of the manhour productivity index to the capital productivity index.[11]

Then taking forecasts of sales, capital outlays, and product development as givens, the following steps would be taken:

1. Make forecasts of turnover, promotion, and transfer, retrainability and productivity increases, both from on-going methods of improvement, work simplification, etc. and from major installations of automation, electronic data processer equipment, plant layout revisions, etc.
2. Construct a model to forecast future needs based on forecasted variables.
3. Use the model to make two-year, five-year, and ten-year projections.[12]

With these projections, the company can compare its projected manpower supply with its projected needs and make plans to meet its potential deficit or surplus.

Once its requirements for the future have been determined, the firm must decide whether its needs can and should be met from its current employees and to what extent outside recruiting may be necessary or desirable. The answer may come from such pertinent questions as:

1. Can the voluntary separation rate be reduced, particularly among the most promising younger employees, and can the replacement problem be met by opening up positions in middle management for

younger men? What changes would this mean in present promotion and retirement policies?

2. Do all management positions require the equivalent of a college education? Are there men among the hourly and clerical work force with managerial potential? Can women be used for some of the supervisory jobs?

3. Are there any departments with problems of greater or lesser severity than the overall firm? Can capable men be obtained by transfer from other units of the firm?

4. Can incentive factors (salaries, fringe benefits, promotions, job status, etc.) be revised so as to achieve greatest effort from available manpower? [13]

5. Should the firm begin to hire outsiders who will provide the talent and age requirements needed?

A foresighted firm will have established criteria for choice between internal development and promotion and outside recruiting. Though internal development is usually preferred, there are times and jobs for which the firm has no available talent or lacks time to develop the skills, knowledge, and judgments of existing personnel. Even then the firm may prefer to develop and promote an employee whose faults are known to the manager than hire a new and unknown, though possibly better trained, person.

Present employees have the obvious advantage of familiarity with the organization, policies, procedures, and overall operations—a fact that reduces the amount of training they need. However, moving a present employee into another position may affect the power structure within the organization. Personal relationships and prejudices which have developed over an extended period of time may hamper the individual's performance on the new job. The infusion of a new personality with new ideas and new philosophies into an organizational structure may break up undesirable organizational patterns.

The blue-collar work force traditionally has not been considered a source of managerial talent. However, as the number of white-collar workers continues to increase and the ratio of blue-collar workers to the total labor force continues to decline, this potential source of supply is being increasingly utilized. In examining the extent of blue-collar to white-collar mobility in the Milwaukee area, Johnson and Stern [14] found that 22 percent of all white-collar male employees hired over a two-year period had blue-collar backgrounds.

WHO DOES MANPOWER PLANNING?

There seems to be little agreement about where the manpower planning function should be placed in the organization. One survey found that approximately 26 percent of the companies had no centralized manpower function, while approximately 10 percent had placed the responsibility directly under the president or chairman of the board. The researcher concluded that the optimal organization would place the planning function with those having responsibilities for generating and evaluating performance of the operating plan.[15] Others argue that manpower planning, like budgeting, should begin at the lowest organizational level and be reviewed at successively higher levels because, they maintain, the organization can profit from the thinking of persons who are familiar with both day-to-day problems and the broad perspective of overall company policy.

There does appear to be some agreement that manpower planning is separate and different from personnel administration and requires involvement at a higher policy level. For one thing, it is considered inappropriate for personnel departments to develop the plans against which their effectiveness will be measured. For another, manpower planning is as integral to the firm's future structure and progress as capital investment, marketing, and budgeting.

PITFALLS IN MANPOWER PLANNING

Experience with manpower planning in the business firm is now sufficient to identify some of the inherent pitfalls. Because the total process rests upon the initial step—estimating future manpower requirements—prospects for effective planning are limited by the shortcomings in projection techniques noted in Chapter 6. Considering the uncertainties of a future over which management has little control, it is not surprising to find errors in either direction in two-year projections. The Minnesota study previously quoted found 5 percent to be the median error, but 7 of 11 firms had errors above the median.

If the skills required by a firm's departments differ substantially, there can be no tendency for errors to cancel each other out. The key to successful forecasting is to identify the significant and known dependent variables which determine the manpower needs and assign appropriate weight to them. Firms attempting manpower projections frequently find that manpower requirements do not correlate well with output, sales, profits, or any other readily projected variable. Simple linear projections of manpower upon sales estimates are rarely adequate. Inflation and rising production costs distort familiar relationships between sales and manpower requirements. Manpower forecasts based simply on production estimates do better. Time regressions require the unlikely assumption that causal forces will continue to act upon specified variables in a consistent way.

Skills inventories have other problems. Some organizational structures and philosophies are not conducive to acceptance of the skills-register concept. For example, functionally structured organizations often have no need for such an inventory, and permissive management policies tend to oppose any systematic inventory of skills. Some managements take the philosophical position that the threat of impersonalized staffing—with the careers of employees dependent upon "randomly" placed holes in IBM cards—more than offsets any beneficial effects from a central register of employees. A massive register of thousands of employees, each with a number of skills, is a major administrative problem; and new specialities are being created daily.

Determining the "quality" of job skills is an especially difficult problem because no test can reliably measure such personality traits as dedication, energy, loyalty, drive, and creativity. After all of the expense of a complex search for an unusual combination of skills from a completed registry, the employee may be unwilling to transfer or the supervisor to let him go.

Personnel appraisals confront their share of problems as well. For instance, one study found that, through a "halo-effect," supervisors tend to give an employee the same rating for every factor being analyzed.[16] Company standards often mean different things to different supervisors, with advancement accelerated or hindered depending upon the particular supervisor. Fear of adverse employee reaction or concern that low ratings of employees will reflect upon his own ability may account for the excessive leniency or strictness noted among supervisors. Finally, some supervisors tend to be less interested in developing subordinates than in enhancing their own standing in the organization. Developing subordinates has no personal payoff in most organizations; developmental efforts cannot be gauged and are often regarded as paternalistic.

Though manpower planning in the business firm is something different from personnel administration, there are major areas of overlap—so much so that personnel administration problems can pose problems for manpower planning. Equitable salary compensation is one of these. For instance, the salary levels of new college graduates and new employees, which are determined by the external labor market, are often out of line with a company's current salary schedule. As many as 36 percent of the firms surveyed in the previously mentioned study had problems adjusting salaries and maintaining appropriate salary differentials between new college graduates and older, less-skilled employees.

Significant among general problems of employee development are corporate practices that often make it possible for managers to hoard good people to the detriment of the total organization. One study cites a case in which a manager's good record was achieved by not recommending any of his assistants for promotions.[17] Managers tend to promote from within their own departments or from among personal acquaintances without considering others in the organization. Thus, an individual's opportunity to be considered for other jobs in the organization is largely controlled by his present supervisor's opinions and knowledge. When a promotion is announced, those not chosen seldom learn why they did not get the job or even whether they were considered. As a consequence, individuals doubt their future in the organization and may leave for other opportunities.

These problems directly reflect upon the adequacy of personnel appraisals and employee-supervisor feedback. While operating within an external labor market with a certain competitive structure, the firm itself operates an internal labor market. These markets meet at certain "ports of entry" where new hiring occurs and present employees compete with potential employees. But at all other points the two systems are largely insulated from each other. The internal labor market tends to function less effectively than the more open external labor market because of the breakdown of information flows which is one of the characteristics of a closed system. An interview with a company official is an example:

> When I came to the company, it was grossly overstaffed. This occurred because each division manager could refuse to permit his men to be considered for jobs elsewhere in the company if so desired. So, when a division had to expand, it could not do so by taking up the slack from another division. It had to hire from the outside. The result was that we ended up carrying too many "essential" men.[18]

Supervisors who are paternalistic toward some of their highly regarded subordinates tend to advance their pay and responsibilities more rapidly than their performance and potential justify. To counteract these defects, the same study recommends an open internal labor market in which all available jobs are advertised throughout the company and where any employee can apply for the job of his choice. Such a system would eliminate organizational impediments to applicants, and preference would be given to internal manpower by withholding advertising until the job has been on the internal market for several days.

THE FUTURE OF MANPOWER PLANNING

Manpower planning is a new function among the formal planning efforts of business firms. Its practitioners are few, its techniques rudimentary, and its utility challengeable. Yet changes in the structure and functioning of labor markets and the pressures of the social environment dictate its expansion. To understand the future of manpower planning, it is necessary to review its current status, areas for research, and potential social contributions.

The Status of Manpower Planning

In 1965, the American Society for Personnel Administration published a report entitled *Managerial Manpower Forecasting and Planning.* Their tentative conclusions, though limited to top-level executive manpower, still provide a good summary of the status of manpower planning in the business firm.

1. Many firms develop managers for the future but only to staff present positions. Little attention is paid to what the positions of the future might be.
2. Overrecruiting is sometimes used as a hedge against future shortages even though the high costs involved are readily acknowledged.
3. Manpower forecasting and planning are more formalized and more extensive in rapidly growing companies in expanding industries.
4. Attempts have been made to forecast managerial manpower as much as ten years ahead but time spans have been reduced when initial results prove disappointing.
5. Approaches range from simple guesses to sophisticated statistical methods involving regression analysis techniques. Simple linear relationships between manpower needs and such factors as products, sales, volume, number of employees, and additional units have not proven reliable. Where statistical techniques are employed, the practical judgment of seasoned executives is necessary to temper the forecasts before planning can be attempted.
6. The feasibility of long-range forecasting and planning for managerial manpower is a function of the nature of the industry. For example, the pharmaceutical industry's growth is directly determined by new product development—the rate of which is hard to forecast. No one can guarantee what, if anything, research will produce during any time period. In contrast, growth patterns in the automobile and other consumer desirables industries are largely determined by such stable variables as family formation, population growth, and income trends.
7. A gap exists in most companies between the objectives of the organizational planner and the end result of the management development program. Careful manpower forecasts and plans help fill this gap.
8. The need for managerial manpower forecasting and planning is not apparent to all top managements. Even where personnel men perceive the need, top management approval for initiation of action is not automatic. Nevertheless, wherever managerial manpower forecasting and planning is being done, the responsibility is at least shared with top management by professional manpower managers.[19]

RESEARCH ISSUES

Current manpower planning efforts are scattered and sporadic, in part because the objectives are not clear. At times planning occurs because it is a hobby for a firm's influential officers or staff. But, in general, an activity is undertaken only if it meets some specific objective such as increasing profit, cutting costs, encouraging growth, relieving administrative pressures, or making a social contribution the firm is under pressure to make. A critical question for research is, therefore, what are reasonable objectives for manpower planning? What can and does it accomplish? What does it cost? How do the costs and benefits compare? Does manpower planning increase profitability? Are the benefits greater than the costs of the planning?

How can the results be measured? Manpower planning probably yields more benefits to the firm when the labor market is tight than when workers are plentiful. Expenditures on long-range manpower planning are part of the firm's total manpower investment. As with other long-term economic investments, the payoff, if any, occurs over a considerable period of time. The costs of the planning unit are easily observed, but the payoffs are not. The returns—which should be a more capable and better utilized work force and elimination of waste in hiring, training, and development activities—are exceedingly difficult to measure. Some managers have indicated that the most important benefit of any manpower plan is the required awareness of the future and the emphasis upon planning and anticipation of future events.

Having committed itself to manpower planning, the firm's projections of future manpower requirements are the basis of all that follows. Yet it is precisely at this point that techniques are most rudimentary. What is the most dependable basis for projection? What forces influence future requirements? What are the relative roles and specific impacts of national and local economic activity? Of the firm's competitive position? Of changing product mix? Of productivity? Years of effort have gone into development of techniques for national, total-economy projections of manpower requirements by industry and occupation; techniques for regional, state, and local projections are in a development stage. But techniques for business firms have received little or no academic attention.

What is the interface between public and private planning? How do national, regional, and local projections relate to those of the firm? What is the relation between efficient allocation and utilization of manpower in the economy and in the firm? What policies and what information from the public sector are relevant to managerial decisions?

What are the realistic requirements of a job within a firm? In Chapter 7, we speculated on tendencies toward overqualification, at least in educational requirements. Is the planner to project the prejudices and misconceptions of present selection practices or should he limit himself to objective technical requirements?

The qualifications of present employees as well as the demographic structure of present employment are critical to estimations of supply. How can performance appraisals be improved and how can they contribute? We do not know.

At this time, there is no reliable measure of individual performance. Predictive instruments must be developed to identify potential talent, to predict employment turnover among employees, and to predict employee performance. The overlap between manpower planning and personnel administration is important because the number of people needed depends in part upon their motivation. What motivates human performance? How do these factors relate to demand and supply projections? What practices work and do not work? The literature on manpower planning in the firm is relatively sparse, compared to the voluminous material on personnel administration. The area should be a fruitful one for research.

PUBLIC AND PRIVATE
MANPOWER PLANNING

As noted above, the pressures for social contribution by industry and the examples of public planners are major factors in the growth of private manpower planning. Each merits brief review.

The Social Consequences
of Private Planning

Manpower planning by private enterprise is gaining increasing acceptance among business managers. But manpower problems facing firms are intimately related to the nation's manpower problems. The private sector is where most of the jobs are, and public employment is not very different from private employment. The consequences of manpower planning and personnel administration in the firm are of national importance. But, often, private employment practices and public manpower programs prove to be incompatible with one another. In times of manpower shortage, for example, hoarding manpower may be wise for the firm but harmful to the economy.

One quite evident trend is the increased level of hiring standards for many jobs. Firms argue that the higher standards are used to insure that a new employee has sufficient flexibility and knowledge for later jobs of increased responsibility. Rather than concentrating upon employee development within the firm, many firms apparently prefer to hire overqualified people under the rationalization that unneeded talents will be utilized as the employee is promoted. A primary reason for employee discontent is overqualification; and yet one of the major reasons that minorities are not hired is excessive entry-level job requirements. These may be simply a convenient screening device for lazy personnel staff or reflect a deliberate intent to discriminate against minorities with low average education. This trend in employment practices frustrates any public program whose goal is to encourage the employment of disadvantaged workers.

The reluctance of many employers to train employees on the job is also costly to the public. Employers see no need to train while the labor market is slack, and they have little or no training capability and few available people to train when labor shortages occur. Yet one can understand employer reluctance when the cost of an employee's training may be expropriated by a competing firm. Despite this, many firms are finding that manpower planning and a commitment to internal employee development and training is consistent with good management practice and profit maximization.

Full and stable employment is a major economic and social goal in the United States. To the extent that manpower planning facilitates retention and retraining of employees whose skills have become outdated, it furthers that goal. Judicious selection of employees during the employment process can also reduce layoffs because of the employer's ability to reassign workers to new jobs. Employers' anticipation of the future skill mix of their work forces also would enable those responsible for public manpower programs to offer training in jobs with good future prospects. And educators could use such planning to design curricula around future job and employment prospects.

THE CHANGING WORK FORCE AND MANPOWER PLANNING

We began this chapter by listing the motivations for manpower planning in the business firm—the nature of manpower resources, the demand of and supply for talented manpower, the increased costs of recruitment and hiring, response to social pressure, and profitability. We conclude by taking note of a new phenomenon with possible profound implications for manpower management and personnel administration among all employers, private and public. Notable changes, only beginning to be recognized, are occurring in the work ethos of the society in all advanced countries. Their causes and impacts are uncertain, but their importance is beyond doubt.

ABSENTEEISM   In the United States and around the world, employers complain of rising absenteeism.[20] Ordinarily, jobs become more valuable and absenteeism falls with rising unemployment. In 1970, it was not so. In 1954, when the layoff rate per 100 employees increased from 1.3 to 1.9, the quit rate dropped from 2.3 percent to 1.1 percent and productivity rose. In 1958 and 1960, the quit rates were at a low base of 1.4 percent and did not drop with increasing layoff rates, but productivity did rise. Preliminary data for 1970 showed the layoff rate rising from 1.2 percent to 2.0 percent while the quit rate remained inflexible at 2.5 percent and productivity did not appear to be responsive.[21] A Labor Department study found that average job tenure had fallen from 4.6 years in 1963 to 4.2 years in 1966 and 3.8 years in 1969. For those 16–24 years of age, the average was only 8½ months.[22] A standard Detroit joke was the need for some identifying mark on new automobiles so that purchasers could avoid those built on Monday and Friday when absenteeism was at its worst.

EARLIER RETIREMENT   Though longevity continues to climb, the retirement age continues to fall, under particular pressure from collective bargaining. The problems of youth dominated the 1960s, but the postwar baby boom was a temporary phenomenon and birth rates are now at unprecedented lows. For the long run, the aged are more likely to be dominant politically. The costs of Medicare are a harbinger. If work is not attractive to older workers, those still in the working years can expect to carry an increasing burden of retirement costs.

PART-TIME EMPLOYMENT   Part-time employment has doubled as a proportion of all employment in a decade. Employers of women and youth are increasingly willing (or under pressure) to adapt work schedules to the workers' preferences. The four-day week has arrived in a few areas of employment, and demands for longer weekends will grow. A few employers are responding to demands by removing distinctions between white-collar and blue-collar workers—salaries rather than hourly pay, no more time clocks, equal privileges in parking, dining, and other amenities are illustrations of these demands.

The business firm has passed through the age of job simplification into an emphasis on job enrichment during the same period when it is being pressured to employ the less prepared for social reasons despite the availability of better prepared people. A new mood is apparent in the work place; there is a new worker, new rules, and a new employer. The discontents of blue-collar and lower-level white-collar workers have been well advertised and politically recognized. Though these are merely emerging symptoms with unclear directions and magnitudes, the corporate manpower planner appears to have a growing role. He must not only assure that there are enough people of the requisite skills but that the work place (and work pace) fits them as well as they do the work.

NOTES

1. Edwin B. Geisler, "Manpower Planning: An Emerging Staff Function," *Management Bulletin No. 101* (Chicago: American Management Association, 1967).

2. U.S. Department of Labor, Manpower Administration, *Employer Manpower Planning and Forecasting,* Manpower Research Monograph No. 19 (Washington, D.C.: U.S. Government Printing Office, 1970). This source is excellent for its extensive bibliography.

3. Bureau of National Affairs, "Effective Utilization of Manpower," *Personal Policies Forum,* Survey No. 83, August 1968.

4. Dale Yoder, *Personnel Management and Industrial Relations* (6th ed.; Englewood Cliffs, N.J.: Prentice-Hall, 1970), pp. 211–212.

5. *Manpower Planning and Forecasting in the Firm: An Exploratory Probe* (Minneapolis, Minn.: Industrial Relations Center, University of Minnesota, March 1968).

6. Eric W. Vetter, "Company Long Range Manpower Forecasting and Planning—A Methodological Approach," unpublished Ph.D. dissertation, University of Michigan, 1963, p. 3.

7. Virgil B. Day, "Managing Human Resources in the Seventies," *Personal Administration* (January–February 1970), p. 26.

8. George A. Steiner, *Top Management Planning* (New York: Macmillan, 1969), p. 223.

9. Wendell W. Burton, "Forecasting Manpower Needs—A Tested Formula," in David Ewing, ed., *Long-Range Planning for Management* (New York: Harper & Row, 1958), p. 533.

10. Laurence J. Peter and Raymond Hull, *The Peter Principle* (New York: Bantam, 1969).

11. Vetter, *op. cit.*, p. 218.

12. Vetter, *op. cit.*, pp. 218–219.

13. Vetter, *op. cit.*, pp. 144–145.

14. David B. Johnson and James L. Stern, "Blue Collar Workers: A Recruitment Source for White-Collar Openings," *Personnel Journal* (June 1970), p. 472.

15. E. B. Geiser, *Management of Personnel Quarterly* (Spring 1968), pp. 30–33.

16. Bureau of National Affairs, "Effective Utilization of Manpower," Personal Policies Forum, Survey No. 83, August 1968.

17. Theodore M. Alfred, "Checkers or Choice in Manpower Management," *Harvard Business Review* (January–February 1967), p. 158.

18. *Ibid.*, p. 162.

19. *Managerial Manpower Forecasting and Planning* (Cleveland, Ohio: Indiana University Graduate School of Business and American Society for Personnel Administration, 1965).

20. Peter Taylor, "Absenteeism," *Science Journal* (April 1970); also *Wall Street Journal* (June 30, 1970), p. 8.

21. U.S. Department of Labor, Statistical Supplement, *Monthly Labor Review* (October 1970).

22. Robert Janson, "Job Enrichment, The Challenge of the 1970s," *Training and Development Journal* (June 1970).

Chapter 14
The Role
of Unions and
Collective Bargaining

Labor organizations have become important labor market institutions in all industrialized economies. It is, therefore, important to understand their role in labor markets. In order to do this, however, it is necessary first to outline the origin, development, and structure of unions. This will be followed by a discussion of the role of collective bargaining in labor markets. We conclude with an assessment of the impact of unions on manpower and training programs.

THE NATURE OF LABOR MOVEMENTS

The term "labor movement" means different things in different countries. In most, it refers to trade unions, political parties, and other cultural or educational organizations which represent workers. However, in the United States, "labor movement" refers almost exclusively to trade unions.

The differences between the labor movements in the United States and other countries are rooted in political, social, and economic institutions. The main reason American unions have not formed a labor party relates to our political and economic conditions, which combined to create less class consciousness than in European countries. In Europe, workers had to form political parties in order to gain the right to vote. The franchise became particularly important with industrialization and the growing importance of government in the lives of individuals. In the United States, however, workers were "born free" in the sense that they had the right to vote at an early

date. It was, therefore, not necessary for the working class to organize itself in order to gain the right to vote. Moreover, unlike European workers,
Americans did not conceive of themselves as a permanent working class.
In part, this was because no political stigma attached to them by denial of
the right to vote. Moreover, the United States did not have feudal traditions as did European countries. Feudalism was a class system whose impact on social relations remained long after the system itself ceased to be
important. No titles or other formal class distinctions existed in the New
World.

Although American workers had serious problems—which they
sought to alleviate through collective bargaining and the political process—
they were comparatively better off than their European counterparts. Their
economic well being was due, in large part, to relative labor shortages as
the United States was being developed. Economic mobility made it difficult
for socialists, who were active in the United States at a very early date, to
organize workers on a class basis. As the twentieth-century American
socialist leader Norman Thomas put it, socialists had difficulty gaining labor
support in the United States because American workers found it easier to
rise out of their class than to rise with it.

The American political system also has worked against the formation
of a labor party. Because of the vast power of the Presidency, a political
party must have some chance to elect a President in order to become significant nationally. However, the manner in which the American President is
elected gives great advantage to major national poltical parties and makes it
very difficult for third parties to become established. The President is
elected by electoral college in which states get votes according to their congressional (senators and representatives) representation. This system gives
inordinate power to sparcely populated and rural states, since each state has
the same number of senators. Even in the House of Representatives a non-
urban voter has much greater representation than an urban voter. Since
union members are minorities even within urban areas, where they have
been concentrated, they have not had the political power by themselves to
challenge the Democrats and Republicans in electing a President. In European parliamentary systems, the chief executive is elected by parliament
and not from geographic areas. Moreover, those systems sometimes have
proportional representation, which gives urban workers more equal representation. As a consequence, minority labor parties can exercise political
influence in selecting prime ministers by participating in coalitions within
the parliament and gradually building their political strength to become majority parties.

Another aspect of the two-party tradition in the United States which
makes it difficult for third parties to get started is the ability of the major
parties to incorporate popular features of third party platforms, thus denying the latter popular issues with workers and other voters. As a consequence of their lack of class consciousness, their relative economic mobility,

and the American political system, American workers have organized mainly around the job.

Although American workers were relatively better off economically than their European counterparts, they had serious problems which they sought to redress within the political system and through collective bargaining. Moreover, American unions had to overcome stiff opposition from employers and governments in order to achieve their status as generally accepted institutions. Before the 1930s employers generally were free to oppose unions by a variety of tactics, including discharging workers for union activity; requiring employees to sign "yellow dog" contracts (agreeing, as a condition of employment, not to join unions); planting company spies in union ranks; blacklisting union members, which made it difficult for those discharged for union activity to find new jobs in their localities, crafts, or industries; and intimidating union members and organizers with armed guards and physical violence.

Governments not only permitted use of these anti-union tactics, but actively opposed unions by a variety of tactics of their own. The courts interpreted many union tactics as being illegal and often nullified legislative attempts to outlaw yellow-dog contracts and other anti-union tactics. The Sherman Anti-Trust Act of 1890 was used against union activities and courts issued injunctions against strikes, picketing, and boycotts. Injunctions were particularly onerous to unions because they could be issued by pro-employer judges without a hearing and be sweeping in their prohibition. Union leaders and members were subject to fines and imprisonment for defying these injunctions, however unfair their restrictions. Labor leaders therefore had to spend considerable amounts of money and time defending themselves from hostile judges.

Also at the state and local level, courts were hostile to unions as were legislatures and governors. Union organizing, strikes, picketing, and boycotts therefore were actively counteracted by state officials, who used state and local police to curtail union activity.

Unions also suffered from periodic recessions and depressions before the 1930s. Even without government opposition rising unemployment made it very difficult for workers to win strikes. Recessions and the hostile legal environment made it hard for any other than the strong craft unions in the transportation, printing, and construction trades to become very well established before the 1930s.

The social ferment of the 1930s created an environment much more favorable to union growth, though workers with limited skill—like those in agriculture, Southern textiles, food processing, sawmills, and other low wage industries—continued to have great difficulty getting organized. The main factors facilitating union growth in the 1930s were:

1. The depression, which was blamed in part on the private enterprise system. Sentiment grew that it was good social policy to pro-

mote collective bargaining in order to make it possible for workers to protect themselves from arbitrary employer decision and to combat future depressions by sustaining wages and therefore purchasing power.

2. As a consequence of growing acceptance of collective bargaining, new legislation curtailed some traditional anti-union tactics of governments and employers. Courts, which had been particularly hostile to such union tactics as strikes, boycotts, and pickets, became much less hostile. The main favorable laws were the Norris-La Guardia Act of 1932, which limited the use of court injunctions against unions and outlawed the "yellow-dog contract" and the National Labor Relations Act of 1935 which curtailed employer's anti-union activity, created the National Labor Relations Board (NLRB) as an enforcement agency, and provided for representative elections supervised by the NLRB.

3. Active organizing caused by intense rivalry between the American Federation of Labor, organized in 1886, and the Congress of Industrial Organizations formed in 1935. The CIO challenged the AFL for leadership mainly around the question of organizing workers along industrial lines (e.g., steelworkers, rubber workers, auto workers, etc.) instead of around particular crafts (electricians, plumbers, sheetmetal workers, etc.). In general, the CIO adopted broader social objectives than the more conservative AFL. The CIO was actively supported by many intellectuals who saw the new federation as a vehicle to reform society. There can be little question that the CIO spurred the AFL to action, but both organizations agreed that rivalry ultimately caused more harm than good. They merged to form the AFL-CIO in 1956.

4. World War II greatly encouraged the growth of union organization, particularly among semiskilled workers. Organization was facilitated by tight labor markets, which made it easy for unions to exhibit gains for the members; a favorable government attitude because the government wanted union cooperation in the war effort; and the activities of the War Labor Board, which had the power to compel employers—under threat of seizure by the armed forces—to sign government contracts.

Despite changes in the political, social, and economic environment within which they operate, the basic character of the American labor movement—its emphasis on collective bargaining and disinclination to form a labor party—remains.

The Origin of Labor Movements

The role of unions and collective bargaining in American labor markets will be illuminated if we look at some of the major forces causing labor movements to start and to develop. Although they disagree over the roles and objectives of labor organizations, most authorities agree that labor movements originated with industrialism. Industrialism invariably creates a number of problems for workers. Chief among these is the fact that the workers depend on employers for jobs in a market often characterized by unemployment. It might be argued that demand and supply will protect workers, but these impersonal forces have little regard for workers' welfare. Industrial societies are characterized by economic instability because of difficulties in maintaining a balance between the production and the sale of goods. Because industrialization causes workers to be dependent on wages, workers have considerable insecurity unless they acquire some means to protect themselves from competitive market pressures.

Producing units in industrial societies also tend to be larger and more impersonal than under preindustrial conditions. Impersonalization makes it necessary for workers to create machinery through which they can express their grievances to management.

Workers in industrial societies may also be deprived of income by such factors as industrial accidents, early superannuation, and illness. Social security was much less of a problem in preindustrial societies because the family was the basic producing unit. The family took care of its own in time of distress, and in any event was much less dependent on the market than the industrial society family. Industrialization created needs for new social security procedures as the family ceased to be the basic producing unit.

The industrial society, therefore, creates a need for workers to have some means of protecting themselves from market forces and of participating in the formulation of rules governing wages, hours, and working conditions. Every industrial society, therefore, has produced a labor movement. However, not every industrial society has produced the same kind of labor movement. In some cases, the movement is dominated by revolutionaries who believe that the workers' problems are inextricably bound up with the capitalist system, and that that system must be eliminated if the workers' problems are to be solved. Other labor movements are socialist-dominated and hold that destruction of the system by revolution might not be necessary, but that solutions to the workers' problems will require considerable modification of capitalist institutions. Specifically, the socialists advocate the public ownership and/or control of all large-scale man-made and nature-made means of production. Socialists believe that control of the socially necessary industries and considerable economic planning will be required to eliminate economic insecurity while maintaining individual freedom and initiative.

American unions have believed they can solve the workers' problems through collective bargaining and political action within the framework of the existing economic system. Although the movement's ideology is not necessarily immutably fixed, the forces that shaped it for the most part remain—the standard of living, the rate of economic growth, the absence of class consciousness, the nature of the American political system, and the relative success of collective bargaining.

However, it should be noted that the American and Western European labor movements have drawn closer together ideologically since World War II. European socialist labor movements have deemphasized radicalism and given greater emphasis to collective bargaining, while the American labor movement has become much more active politically since the Depression of the 1930s. Indeed, American unions have actively backed much of the social legislation adopted in the United States since the 1930s and have participated in every national campaign.

Labor Movements in the Developing Countries

The labor movements of the developing countries are quite different from those of the United States and Europe. Indeed, when examined from Latin America or Africa, the European and American movements appear to resemble each other closely. In Western industrial countries, trade unions are likely to be more independent of political leaders and place more emphasis on collective bargaining and economic gains for their members. The labor movements of the developing countries, however, face unique pressures. They have greater difficulty establishing collective bargaining relations with employers, partly because their leaders are likely to be intellectuals whose talents and interests incline them toward political activities rather than collective bargaining. In some countries—for example, India, Indonesia, Ghana, and Israel—the labor movements were used to establish political independence. Collective bargaining also is impeded by the workers' weak bargaining power, caused by labor surpluses and limited skills. A major obstacle in the developing countries is opposition from political leaders who consider collective bargaining to be incompatible with industrialization. The basic argument is that unions increase consumption at the expense of production, promote economic instability, and divert resources from capital formation. Political leaders in these countries, therefore, are likely to insist that unions play a productionist role until the economy is developed, when they can become more consumptionist.

The insistence on a productionist role for trade unions has been advanced by leaders with a wide variety of political persuasions. Countries led by dictatorships have greater power to hold down consumption through centralized planning and the military power of the state. Countries that try to follow democratic procedures have greater difficulty, but their industrializing elites also ordinarily insist on a productionist role for unions. We might note in passing that where labor movements have been used to help countries achieve independence, political leaders have encouraged consumptionist roles for the labor movement before independence and productionist roles after independence.[1]

FACTORS SHAPING THE AMERICAN LABOR MOVEMENT

An examination of some of the factors shaping the growth of unions in this country will help to explain their current role in the labor market. One of the most important influences has been the spread of markets. Although some labor unions existed in preindustrial times, there was nothing that could really be called a labor movement because these local unions were isolated and rarely came in contact with each other. However, with industrialization and the widening of product markets, workers in formerly isolated labor markets came in direct competition with each other and therefore organized in order to protect their wages and working conditions. The spread of the market influenced wages by causing workers as well as goods to compete directly over wider areas. For example, before industrialization, shoemakers in Philadelphia could operate on the basis of the demand and supply conditions within the Philadelphia labor market; but with the spread of the market, they had to be concerned with competition from shoemakers throughout the United States. Transportation and communications improvements made it possible for merchants to buy in the cheapest market and undermine the wages and working conditions of workers throughout wide geographic areas. In order to prevent wage competition indirectly through the flow of goods or directly through the flow of workers, local unions in various parts of the country formed national unions and federations. The national unions were concerned mainly with the activities of a particular trade or industry, whereas the federations organized different local unions at the city or state level and different national unions (made up of affiliated locals) into national federations. The federations were concerned more with political and interunion matters than with collective bargaining directly. In other words, the spread of the market gave workers all over the United States common interests which they organized to protect and promote.

Another factor influencing the growth of unions in the United States has been the size of firms. In the manufacturing sector particularly, unionism is directly related to the size of the firms. There are a number of reasons for this. For one thing, large firms are more easily organized by unions because the cost of organizing is less than it would be to organize the same number of workers in many smaller firms. But, more important, employers and employees in large firms rarely have close working relationships. Consequently, rules must be adopted to govern wages, hours, and working conditions. Workers, therefore, are likely to organize either into informal groups or formal trade unions in order to have some influence on the formulation of working rules and some means of redressing their grievances. Grievance adjustment is particularly important in a large firm because of the difficulties involved in communicating directly with management.

Skill levels are also important in determining union growth. The earliest unions to be organized usually were among the skilled workers in the printing and building trades or on the railroads. In such industries, the workers' investment in their skills gives them a common interest to protect. Moreover, a union of skilled workers has more bargaining power than one of unskilled workers because the skilled workers are much more difficult to replace in the event of strike. The ability to inflict damage on an employer during a strike is an extremely important aid to the growth of unions which emphasize collective bargaining. Unions of skilled workers perpetuated their power by controlling the supplies of workers in particular crafts through control of entry into their unions and crafts.

Not all of the unions which have been able to acquire strength in American labor markets have had great skill. Unions of workers located at strategic points in the production or distribution process hold a strategic advantage. For example, teamsters and longshoremen have had very strong unions, mainly because of their strategic location rather than the amount of skill they possess. Their ability to win strikes has been due to the damage they could cause by refusing either to move goods or to load or unload ships.

Business cycles have played an important role in the fluctuation of union strength in the United States. As a general rule, unions have gained membership and power during period of prosperity and lost ground during periods of recession or depression. The reason for this is not hard to find. During prosperity, the unions' power to win a strike is considerably enhanced because there are likely to be labor shortages and employers are likely to offer less resistance because they can usually pass wage increases to consumers in the form of higher prices. Moreover, employers are likely to lose sales if strikes occur when there are backlogs of unfilled orders. Conversely, during recessions and depressions, employers are under much less pressure to give in to union demands and therefore likely to offer more resistance. Moreover, employers might be able to win strikes when rising unemployment gives them a plentiful supply of strike-breakers. It should be observed, however, that unions sometimes have gained considerable membership during recoveries immediately following prolonged depressions. At such times, workers have accumulated dissatisfactions stemming from the depression period but which could not be translated into union organizing because of their inability to win strikes. When recovery starts, the workers' power increases relative to employers, and union membership therefore grows very rapidly.

Wars also have played an important role in the growth of union membership. Indeed, many of the same forces influencing the growth of unions during periods of prosperity are present during war—particularly tight labor markets. Moreover, during wars the government is likely to adopt a more favorable attitude toward unions in order to gain cooperation with war production. Governments, therefore, are likely to enhance the prestige of union leaders by appointing them to important positions in the war effort, and to assent to other measures that will encourage union growth. Thus, a combination of the government's favorable attitude and tight labor markets often causes union membership to increase considerably during and immediately after wars.

These great spurts in union membership are, however, ordinarily followed in the postwar period by counterattacks from anti-union forces which make it difficult for the unions to hold their wartime gains. For example, in the aftermath of World War I came the so-called "open shop" movement of the 1920s in which employers all over the United States joined in a concerted effort to reduce union strength. The movement was so successful that this was one of the few prosperity periods when union membership actually declined after reaching a peak in 1920. By the 1930s, only the strongest unions had survived.

Public opinion also has an important influence on the growth of unions. Public opinion influences legislation and government attitudes toward unions, as well as the workers' willingness to associate with them as organizations. Ironically, there seems to be some inverse relationship between the unions' public image and their economic power. During the Great Depression of the 1930s, when the unions' economic power declined, their public image benefited from public sympathy for the underdog. Other factors were at work then, too, of course. Similarly, during World War II and the immediate postwar period, when unions grew greatly and increased their economic power, public support apparently declined because they were no longer considered to be the underdog.

Laws and court action also have influenced union growth. As noted earlier, before the 1930s governments—especially the judiciary—were generally hostile to unions and collective bargaining. The legislation and court decisions of the 1930s and 1940s created a more favorable legal environment. But the tide turned again after World War II. Congress passed the Taft-Hartley Act of 1947 and the Landrum-Griffin Act of 1959 (both of which restricted union activity and made organizing more difficult); many states, particularly in the South, passed anti-union "right-to-work" laws which sought to prevent unions and employers from entering into contracts making union membership a condition of employment. Although courts restricted union activities more than during the late 1930s and early 1940s, neither they nor other branches of government have returned to the anti-union stances they took before the 1930s.

It is very difficult to gauge the importance of these laws and court decisions for the growth of unions. There seems to be little question that early court hostility hurt unions, particularly those of semiskilled and unskilled workers who were not strong enough to withstand the employers' anti-union tactics. Discharging and blacklisting workers for union activity made it difficult for unions to organize. Moreover, the need to defend themselves in time-consuming and expensive litigation often sapped the strength of unions.

The more favorable legal environment of the 1930s made most of the employers' anti-union activities illegal and greatly reduced the use of injunctions against unions, but did not necessarily make it easy for unions to organize. The Norris-La Guardia and National Labor Relations Acts reduced union-management relations more to a purely economic (instead of physical, economic, and legal) struggle, but did not necessarily allow unions to win those economic struggles by striking or boycotting employers. As a consequence, unions in many industries—textiles, food processing, and work clothes, for example—have not been able to organize. Moreover, in spite of numerous organizing campaigns, unions remain relatively weak in the South. On balance, therefore, the evidence suggests that legislation is only a marginal factor in union growth and that the basic determinants are the economic, strategic, and skill factors influencing a union's ability to induce employers to bargain.

Of course, to argue that labor laws have had limited impact on union growth does not mean that governments *could not* influence union growth. The activities of the War Labor Board clearly stimulated membership in the weaker unions. Moreover, Presidents Kennedy and Johnson stimulated union membership among federal employees by encouraging collective bargaining between federal agencies and unions. The federal government *could* encourage union membership in countless other ways, especially by giving preference in contracts to employers who engage in collective bargaining.

Another factor influencing the growth of unions has been product market concentrations. Since the 1930s concentration of product markets controlled by a few firms has been directly correlated with union strength, as measured by contract coverage. To a very large extent, this relationship obtains because the larger firms tend to have the highest concentration ratios and, as noted earlier, are more likely to be unionized. However, the concentration ratio is a measure of market control as well as size, and those firms that have the greatest ability to control their destinies in the market can tolerate unions more successfully than highly competitive firms such as those in the textile industry which resist unions for fear that collective bargaining will undermine their competitive positions. We should also note, moreover, that the change in public opinion during the 1930s apparently influenced the organizability of large firms with high concentration ratios. Before that time, large and powerful firms were able to use their political, economic, and physical power to prevent unions from unionizing. With the change in public opinion during the 1930s, however, it became much more difficult for these companies to employ anti-union tactics. Under these conditions, it was much easier for the unions to organize large companies.

Public Support of Collective Bargaining

Another force influencing the growth of unions in the United States has been the emergence of general public support for the concept of collective bargaining. When their employees were first organized many companies dealt with unions as necessary evils, but as these relationships became established, a rationale for collective bargaining emerged which has become widely accepted among unions, employers, and the general public. Some of the main ideas supporting collective bargaining were embodied in the National Labor Relations Act of 1935 (Wagner Act) and reaffirmed in the Taft-Hartley Act of 1947. One of the reasons for passage of the Wagner Act was the belief that collective bargaining was a good anticyclical measure. The depression of the 1930s, it was argued, was caused in part by the workers' inability to organize and bargain collectively and thus maintain their wage levels.

Another rationale for collective bargaining is the assumption that rules governing wages, hours, and working conditions are best made jointly by workers and employers. Indeed, collective bargaining has been considered an extension of democracy to the work place. Rules based on participation, it is argued, are much better than those unilaterally imposed by employers on unions or by unions on employers. Moreover, this form of rule making is considered superior to government-imposed rules because it can be more flexible. The argument continues that the people who experience the problems are in a better position than anyone else to make the rules governing those problems. Collective bargaining, therefore, permits greater flexibility because the rules can be made to fit the circumstances. And collectively bargained rules can be changed more rapidly to fit changing circumstances than would be possible with government regulations.

The idea of participatory democracy, therefore, has been accepted by many employers as a force for social stability. This concept is based on the belief that by participating in the formulation of working rules and joining political organizations workers gain a stake in the system. For this reason, many employers support efforts to extend the so-called "free" labor movements to the developing countries. They feel that collective bargaining will buffer the spread of revolutionary unionism in those countries. Supporters of this idea are impressed by the fact that revolutionaries never seem to make much progress in countries with advanced collective bargaining systems.

Another rationale for collective bargaining is equity. The National Labor Relations Act declared that governments had helped employers gain power by permitting them to form corporate and other forms of business activities, but that the power of the state had been used to impede union growth before the 1930s. Thus, it was only equitable to protect workers in their right to organize and bargain collectively. This reflected the belief that individual workers had unequal bargaining power when dealing with individual employers and that it was therefore unjust to enforce the freedom of contract between parties who were not of substantially equal bargaining power.

Problems of Collective Bargaining

Collective bargaining generates many problems. First, there is the problem of strikes which become increasingly important as the economy becomes more interdependent. The strike creates a dilemma for those who have accepted the institution of collective bargaining because it would be very difficult to have collective bargaining without the right to strike. At the same time, strikes can inflict considerable inconvenience, if not damage, on the public. Much attention has, therefore, been given to the problem of how to maintain collective bargaining while preventing the damage that might be inflicted by strikes. To date, no effective solution has been found.

Another drawback of collective bargaining is that because it is based on power and conflict it does the most for the people who need it least. The stronger workers in the labor market such as skilled electricians could protect their incomes because of their skills; the weakest workers in the work force, those in marginal and submarginal labor markets, have very limited ability to form unions because they have great difficulty winning strikes. However, there is some evidence that unions might be adopting different strategies to organize submarginal and marginal workers. Weapons other than strikes—including consumer boycotts— are being used to bring pressure on employers.

A third problem is the ability of an entrenched labor organization to exclude outsiders. Moreover, the public interest might be ignored by collusion between strong unions and employers to fix prices. This is a particularly important problem with respect to discrimination against blacks and other minorities. If a union effectively controls the labor market, it can exclude blacks from operating in that market by refusing them admission to the union.

UNION STRUCTURE

Union structure tends to define the power relationships between different levels of a labor organization. In the United States, the basic labor organization is the local union which is typically restricted to workers in a particular craft in a local area or a particular industry or group of related industries in a local area. For example, the carpenters in a local construction labor market might be members of a local carpenters union, whereas the workers in an automobile assembly plant might be members of the United Automobile Workers union, regardless of their particular craft or occupation.

Craft and industrial locals differ in several fundamental ways. Craft unions are ordinarily made up of workers who have very limited attachments to particular employers. In the building trades, for example, the craftsmen change employers quite frequently and therefore rely on unions for jobs, which gives the union considerable power in the labor market. If the union can control the supply of skilled craftsmen, employers must hire workers through the union. Moreover, labor organizations may have considerable control over training through their control, jointly with employers, of the apprenticeship system. Finally, some craft unions enhance their power in a labor market by influencing licensing arrangements.

The industrial union, however, has very limited control over hiring. Most of its power comes from control over the internal labor market in a particular firm. Its main impact ordinarily is to formalize arrangements that were already in existence. For example, the lines of progression, which determine promotion priorities within the internal labor market, are determined to a significant degree by the logical relationships between jobs, which reflect the technology of a particular process. The industrial union can formalize this relationship, help establish seniority as the main factor determining progression, establish grievance procedures, and exert some influence on wage rates, but these unions ordinarily have much less control of the labor market than craft unions.

Local unions are affiliated with national unions or, if they have locals outside the United States, with international unions. The internationals are combinations of locals within an industry or group of related industries or crafts or groups of related crafts. To follow up our early example with the locals, the local auto workers' union would be affiliated with the United Auto Workers (UAW) nationally, and the local carpenters union would be affiliated with the United Brotherhood of Carpenters and Joiners of America (UBCJ). The UBCJ is an "international" based mainly on the craft principle and the UAW is an international composed mainly of local industrial officials. A union is an international if it has affiliates outside the United States—in Canada for instance—but the terms "national" and "international" are used interchangeably.

Power relationships between local and national unions depend largely on the scope of the market. If the market is mainly local, as in the building trades, the local union has more influence vis-à-vis international unions than would be true if the market were national in scope, as with the automobile industry. But relationships between the local and national unions also are influenced by such factors as the national union constitutions, the political power of the particular local leaders, the power and personality of the national leaders, and the collective bargaining alternatives available to the local if it secedes from the national union. If, for example, the local union can secede and affiliate with another national union, its power in dealing with a particular national union is enhanced. However, the local's ability to continue its collective bargaining relationships depends upon whether the scope of bargaining is national or local. It might be very difficult for a local to pull out and affiliate with another union if all other local unions in the same company in other areas are affiliated with another national union and if all deal with the same company.

The next level in the union structure is the federation. Federations might be city, state, or national. These organizations are comprised of groups of local unions at the city or state levels and groups of national unions and nonaffiliated local unions at the national level. Although their power is probably increasing somewhat, the federations are the weakest link in the American union structure. A city or state federation has very limited power over local unions because locals can continue to operate independently of the federation. Similarly, national unions can and have withdrawn from the AFL-CIO, which has been the main national federation in the United States since 1956, without seriously impairing their collective bargaining position. The United Mine Workers never joined the AFL-CIO, the United Auto Workers (UAW) withdrew in 1967, and the International Brotherhood of Teamsters (IBT) were expelled from the AFL before that organization merged with the CIO in 1956. The federations' main functions are political and mediatory; that is to say, it represents the labor movement in dealing with public agencies and helps settle disputes between unions affiliated with it. Because the federations are the keepers of the labor movement's conscience, they ordinarily take broader positions on public issues than the national and local unions, which are mainly economic collective bargaining organizations. If the federation were a bargaining agency, as it is in many countries where federations deal on a more centralized basis with employers, its power over the local unions would be strengthened considerably, because expulsion from the federation would cause the national or local to lose bargaining rights.

THE IMPACT OF UNIONS ON WAGES

Economists have differed sharply over the extent of the union's power to influence wages. Not surprisingly, this topic has received considerable public attention: The impact of unions on wages has significant implications for economic growth and stability as well as for the distribution of income between union and nonunion workers and between labor and other factors of production.

The layman may be surprised to learn that economists have questioned whether unions have much impact on wages. The role of unions generally has been exaggerated by employers, newspaper editors, and even unions leaders, who take credit for wage increases which might have been caused by increasing productivity and rising general price levels. Because wages rise when unions negotiate contracts, many assume that unions cause the wages to rise; actually, some wage increase might have occurred in the absence of unions.

Economists, and particularly economic theorists, tend to minimize policy decision, especially in the long run, and to emphasize market forces as determinants of wages and employment.[2] The classical view has it that market forces are the only determinants of wages in the long run; but after the depression of the 1930s revealed such obvious imperfections in the market mechanism and spurred the growth of unionism and government regulation of wages and employment, few economists could deny the importance of nonmarket forces in wage determination. Nevertheless, most economists continue to give major emphasis to markets in wage determination, even if laymen give greater emphasis to bargaining and policy.

If we compare wages under union and nonunion conditions, economic theory would lead us to expect that the elasticity of demand for union labor would be an important determinant of the unions' impact on wages. If the demand is relatively inelastic, unions will be able to raise wages without greatly increasing unemployment. Elasticity of demand, however, is determined by derived demand, which means that the demand for labor is derived from the demand for the final product and the demand for other factors of production. Economic theory would also lead us to expect that the demand for labor would be more inelastic (a) the more essential union labor is to the production of the final product, (b) the more inelastic the demand for the final product, (c) the smaller the ratio of the cost of union labor to the cost of the product, and (d) the more inelastic the supply of other factors of production.

Although this economic analysis is fairly straightforward, measuring the impact of unions on wages is much more difficult because it is hard to isolate the unions' influence as we are dealing here with a problem of multiple causation. For example, unions are influenced by such factors as the ratio of labor cost to total cost and economic conditions, which also influence wage levels. There is consequently a strong positive correlation between the percentage of workers organized in a given industry and wage rates in that industry. However, it is difficult to determine whether unions are strong because of the factors that make wages high, or whether wages are high because of the unions. An empirical investigation also might find very little difference between union and nonunion wages because employers in nonunion sectors raise wages in order to avoid unions. If a union established a pattern that was followed by the nonunion sector, measurement of the differences between union and nonunion wages would fail to detect the impact of the union.

In spite of the measurement difficulties, a large number of empirical investigations have produced some consensus among economists concerning the relative extent of union influence. These investigations have been primarily of two types: (1) cross-section analyses at a given time to determine the difference between union and nonunion wages and (2) time-series analyses, which attempt to study union and nonunion conditions through time.

These studies indicate that the unions' relative impact is strongly influenced by business conditions. Unions seem to exert their greatest influence relative to nonunion control groups during the early stages of a recession or depression, in part by producing a downward rigidity in wage movements. If the depression is prolonged, however, the union influence tends to disappear because not even the strongest unions can withstand the adverse effects of a severe depression. Unions also seem to have an advantage during periods of high employment and stable prices, but the extent of the advantage depends upon the strength of the union. Strong unions raise wages by as much as 15 to 25 percent above what they would have been in the absence of unions. The strongest union influence seems to have come from unions of skilled craftsmen and organizations such as the United Mine Workers, which have been able to organize large sections of their labor markets. Strong industrial unions such as the United Steelworkers probably have an impact in the range of 10 to 15 percent when employment is high and prices are stable. But even during periods of high employment and stable prices, some unions have very limited impact on relative wages because of adverse economic conditions which make it very difficult for nonunion sectors to organize or for unions to raise wages without generating substantial unemployment.

Albert Rees, a careful student of the impact of unions on wages, concluded in the early 1960s that "my own best guess of the average effect of all American unions on wages of their members in recent years would lie somewhere between 10 and 15 percent." [3] Rees also concludes that because unions enter into contracts for fixed time periods, their relative impact on wages is least during periods of rapid and unexpected inflation because union wages lag behind those in nonunion sectors and because employers, knowing that unions will resist wage cuts when labor markets slacken, resist union wage pressures during inflated periods.

In a detailed review of 20 empirical studies of the impact of unions on relative wages, Lewis found some uniformity in the evidence concerning the union's advantage. The ratio of union to nonunion wages seems to have been greatest during the bottom of the Great Depression of the 1930s, when the union advantage might have reached 25 percent. With recovery from the depression, the union advantage decline to between 10 and 20 percent by the end of the 1930s and almost disappeared during the 1940s. Lewis concluded: "I estimate that in recent years the average union/nonunion relative wage was approximately 10 percent to 15 percent higher than it would have in the absence of unions." [4] Lewis thus agrees with Rees' estimate of the unions' relative impact.

As for the unions' impact on labor's share of the national income, empirical studies are highly inconclusive, although (as with relative wages) there are a number of measurement difficulties. It is not inconsistent to argue that unions influence relative wages but not labor's share, because it is possible for unions to redistribute income from the nonunion to the union sector.

With respect to the size distribution of income, the evidence suggests that unions have raised incomes of more highly paid blue-collar workers, narrowed the income gap between the best-paid manual workers and more highly paid white-collar workers, and widened the gap between the best-paid blue-collar workers and the very poor. This is largely due to the fact that unions have had their greatest influence in mainstream labor markets and have done very little in marginal and submarginal markets.

One reason for the unions' concentration in the mainstream is that they are likely to have greater success in raising wages in the less competitive firms which predominate in that labor market. The unions' success in mainstream markets is due, in part, either to the fact that they have helped employers control their product markets or to the fact that they occupy strategic positions in the labor and product markets, as is the case with the Teamsters. In assessing the significance of product market structure, it also is important to emphasize the multiplicity of causes influencing the determination of both wages and union structures. Of course, to say that there is a strong correlation between market structures and wages is not to deny that other factors are at work.

The prevailing institutional arrangements must also be considered in assessing the importance of market structures on union strength. For example, as noted earlier, before the 1930s, unions undoubtedly had much less influence on wage determination in oligopolistic industries than they did after that time. In the institutional setting of the 1920s, large employers were freely able to use their economic and political (and in some cases, physical) power to prevent unions from organizing their employees, but this changed during the social ferment of the 1930s.

This is not to argue that in dealing with unions, oligopolistic employers conceded larger wage increases than if workers had not been organized, even though a number of factors might have caused higher wage increases in unionized oligopolistic firms. Because many of these companies had considerable monopsonistic power in the labor markets, traditional economic theory would hold that wages might be raised without reducing employment. However, if the monopsonists are making only normal profits (sufficient to keep firms in this industry) before unionization, raising wages might reduce employment in the long run because the firms could not continue to operate. The sudden reduction of monopsony power in the short run may explain the phenomenon commonly found in empirical studies: Unions have a sizable wage advantage over nonunion firms during the early stages of unionization, but the discrepancy disappears through time. Obviously, a continuing advantage to firms operating under oligopolistic conditions would require changes in the extent of the monopoly powers through time, which is hardly realistic.

Similarly, in oligopolistic firms whose product and labor demand curves are kinked at prevailing prices, increasing costs will not necessarily reduce employment. In such cases, unions might be able to raise wages within the limits of the discontinuity of the marginal revenue product curve without creating unemployment. Indeed, oligopolistic employers might offer less resistance to wage increases that they could shift to consumers in the form of higher prices. It is even conceivable that oligopolies that raise prices by some percentage amounts as they increase wages could actually profit from wage increases, depending on the ratio of labor cost to total cost and the elasticity of the demand for the final product.

Other conditions exist where wage increases will not necessarily lead to unemployment. One of these is the so-called "shock effect," in which rising wage pressures cause employers to become more efficient and therefore able to absorb the wage increases without reducing employment.

The argument that union wage policies distort resource allocation does not necessarily assume that the labor market would be perfect without union influence; there are many market imperfections besides the operation of unions. Moreover, some unions perform functions—such as providing better job information and training—that improve the operation of some labor markets. Furthermore, the judgment that unions make for a worse allocation of labor implies that a higher GNP is "better" than such things as greater worker participation in the formulation of work rules. Finally, a large GNP is not necessarily "better" for all groups in the economy.

Other authorities doubt that the impact of unions on wages can be ascertained through the uses of traditional economic theory. Lloyd Reynolds, for example, has advanced the proposition that "the effects of trade unionism cannot be deduced from first principles and that on the contrary, simple economic models of union behavior are likely to be quite misleading." Reynolds' survey led him to the following hypotheses:

(1) Collective bargaining has reduced occupational differences within particular industries and has probably brought them closer to what they would have been under perfect competition.

(2) Collective bargaining has reduced interplant differentials, on a national scale in industries characterized by regional or national competition and on a local basis in local industries. In this respect, also, collective bargaining has probably produced a closer approximation to the competitive wage structure.

(3) Collective bargaining has probably widened interindustry differentials and in an anticompetitive fashion. Unionism has penetrated most effectively into the relatively high-wage industries and has tended to make the rich richer.

(4) Collective bargaining has probably reduced geographical differentials, but this effect has been weaker than the first three effects and largely incidental to the reduction of interplant differentials. The reductions of

geographical differentials have probably brought the wage structure closer to competitive standards than unions in a few industries that have overshot the mark.[5]

Conclusion of Unions' Impact on Wages

In conclusion, therefore, there is a consensus among those who have studied the problem that unions have had considerable influence on relative wages in the labor markets where they have gained strength. But their relative impact varies with business conditions, being greatest during recessions and least during inflation. The unions also tend to have a relative advantage immediately after becoming organized that declines with time. In general, the unions' ability to raise wages depends upon the elasticity of demand for labor, which is, in turn, influenced by the nature of competition in the product market. Unions have had their greatest impact in mainstream labor markets and therefore probably have narrowed the income gap between the higher-paid blue-collar workers and white-collar workers, but probably have widened the income gap between the well-organized blue-collar workers and those working in marginal and submarginal labor markets, who tend to be less well off.

UNIONS, EDUCATION, AND MANPOWER

Trade unions vary widely in the interest they show in education and training. Craft unions such as those in the construction trades are interested in apprenticeship and other training programs as a means of maintaining wages (by limiting the supply of labor as well as improving its quality) and craft identity (by instilling pride in a particular craft). (See Chapter 11.)

Industrial or noncraft unions, however, have a different stake in education and training, which reflects their collective bargaining concern over maintaining wage rates, protecting wage rates from being undercut by trainees, gaining educational and training benefits for their members through collective bargaining, and using training programs to protect such vital collective bargaining interests as seniority. This last objective may be achieved by giving senior employees the right to be trained for jobs for which their seniority makes them eligible. Industrial unions might also use training as a means of protecting their members' jobs from technological changes or merging or relocating of plants.[6]

Because of their special interests and functions, state, local, and national federations are likely to take a broader view of education and training. For example, they are apt to favor general education which enables workers to participate in the political process. They have also been major supporters of free education for workers and programs to help the disadvantaged. Federations also are interested in education and training as a part of manpower programs and other policies designed to reduce unemployment. The federations' broader interests derive in some measure from their political role, which requires them to work actively with civil rights and other groups to achieve common economic, social, and political objectives. Still, federations are likely to see social objectives in terms of their effect on the institution of collective bargaining. They tend, therefore, to insist that education, manpower, and training programs be compatible with such established collective bargaining procedures as union wage scales, the apprenticeship system, job referral procedures, and seniority. But more often than most national or local unions, federations attempt to promote the interests of blacks and other minorities who sometimes are barred from union benefits by racial discrimination.[7]

American unions played an important role in establishing universal free education in the United States in the nineteenth century. The labor movement realized that workers were not likely to make very much progress in an industrial society without education, which in the early 1800s was too costly for workers' children. Workers' demands for free public education were met with vigorous opposition from the conservative classes who feared that educated workers would turn to radical politics and who simply balked at paying taxes to educate the children of the working class. Selig Perlman explains the situation in the following terms:

> That the education situation was deplorable much proof is unnecessary. Pennsylvania had some public schools, but parents had to declare themselves too poor to send their children to a private school before they were allowed the privilege of sending them there. In fact, so much odium was attached to these schools that they were practically useless, and the state became distinguished for the number of children not attending school. . . .
>
> To meet these conditions, the working men outlined a comprehensive educational program. It was not merely a literary education that the working men desired. The idea of industrial education, or training for a vocation, which is even now young in this country, was undoubtedly first introduced by the leaders of this early labor movement. They demanded a system of public education which would "combine the knowledge of the practical arts with that of the useful sciences." [8]

Although the labor movement supported academic training in order to prepare workers for citizenship, they were more interested in vocational training. But their attitude toward vocational education was somewhat ambivalent. Unions were strongly committed to the apprenticeship system as a means of preparing workers for the skilled trades, in part because apprenticeship systems usually were products of collective bargaining and therefore controlled to a significant degree by unions, and also because apprenticeship training combined academic with on-the-job training—which workers always seem to have favored. Hence, even though unions endorsed vocational education very early—Samuel Gompers supported both the Smith-Hughes and George-Dean Acts which established the vocational educational system in the United States—they have rarely deviated from a traditional belief that most trades cannot be learned in classrooms and that vocational education by itself does not provide adequate preparation for the skilled trades. Unions have, therefore, favored vocational schools that provide instruction in academic subjects and otherwise prepare students for the apprenticeship programs.[9]

Union Concerns: Manpower and Education

The unions' attitudes toward education and manpower programs can be understood by considering their fundamental concerns. First, the American labor movement has always given top priority to collective bargaining as an institution. Unions, therefore, have strongly favored those forms of education and training that were most directly related to the collective bargaining system.

Second, the skilled trades derive their power in large measure from their control of labor supplies. They have, therefore, been very much interested in controlling the means of training skilled nonunion workers who might compete with them and have always taken a dim view of skill training outside the collective bargaining system.

Third, unions are very much concerned with the productivity of union members. Union leaders realize that they will not be able to maintain high wages unless unionized workers are more productive than the alternatives available to their employers—unproductive union workers give employers an incentive to substitute machinery for labor or to operate under nonunion conditions. In order to police their jurisdictions, therefore, unions have found it necessary to have an adequate supply of well-trained labor. Thus, craft unions strongly favor the apprenticeship system not only because it is controlled by collective bargaining but also because they are convinced that it gives the worker practical on-the-job experience as well as some understanding of the theory of his trade. The unions believe that workers trained in both the theory and the practice of their trades will be much more flexible and able to perform a greater variety of jobs than would be the case if training were narrow and specialized. General training, they feel, makes workers less vulnerable to unemployment than specialized training, which employers are more likely to favor. Employers tend to retain the best-trained workers when demand for labor declines.

Although unions prefer training through apprenticeship, they admit members who are trained by other means. Indeed, a majority of craftsmen have not served apprenticeships. Unions are likely to admit such workers in order to maintain control of the labor market: They would clearly weaken their position if there were many workers the employers considered to be craftsmen who were outside union jurisdiction.

Unions have recently become interested in education, manpower, and training programs because of the pressures to admit more blacks and other minorities to the skilled trades. Historically, craft unions on the railroads and in the printing and construction trades barred blacks from membership. In part, this practice stemmed from a monopoly instinct which caused local unions to exclude all except certain favored groups from their unions and therefore from union-controlled crafts. But the civil rights movements of the 1950s and 1960s generated considerable pressure on unions to admit minorities to membership. The unions responded by insisting that blacks and other minorities come into the crafts primarily through the apprenticeship system. They realized that not many blacks could get into their crafts this way because apprenticeship programs graduate very few workers each year. But they argued that blacks who entered unions through apprenticeship would be well trained and therefore the markets would not be flooded with unqualified craftsmen.

Union Training Programs

A number of unions participate in joint union-management programs for training apprentices and journeymen. Journeyman-training programs are necessitated in some crafts by rapid changes in technology and work procedures. For example, the International Typographical Union (ITU), which has long had an interest in education, has established a training center in Colorado Springs which specializes in short courses to teach journeymen new techniques in the printing and publishing trades. The ITU has attempted to insure that members whose jobs are destroyed by technological changes are given first claim to jobs utilizing the new techniques.

The International Brotherhood of Electrical Workers (IBEW) and the United Association of Journeymen and Apprentices of the Plumbing and Pipefitting Trades (UA) also have maintained strong apprenticeship and journeyman-upgrading programs. As early as 1944, the IBEW established an electronics school at Marquette University to train instructors who in turn trained journeymen at the local level. The IBEW and the National Electrical Contractors Association established a national Joint Apprenticeship Committee in 1941; in 1947, when other training became more important, the name was changed to the National Joint Apprenticeship and Training Committee for the Electrical Industry. The National Committee has adopted national standards for training programs administered by local joint committees. Programs are jointly financed, but a percentage of payroll contributions by employers was becoming the most widely used plan for financing during the late 1960s.

In 1956, the UA and the National Contractors Association established a national retraining program for steamfitters and plumbers. In order to finance this program, the union and employers established a national training fund to which the contractors contribute on the basis of the number of hours worked. The program is administered by a joint union-management committee which assists local joint training committees and provides equipment and national guidelines for journeyman-upgrading training. The UA

has a staff of training coordinators and a program for training superinten-
dents and instructors at Purdue University. The plumbing industry feels that
training is necessary in order to keep journeymen abreast of new materials
and methods. In 1956, the plumbers had 32 training programs for about
1,000 journeymen; by 1967, there were 397 training programs which
trained 18,000 journeymen. Between 1956 and 1967, the plumbers' program trained over 80,000 journeymen. Grants from the national fund for
training average about $1.2 million a year and are supplemented by much
larger funds from local unions and contractors.[10]

　　Union interest in education and training has not been restricted to the
crafts; many industrial organizations also have established programs to
educate and upgrade their members. The industrial unions are mainly
interested in preparing their members to advance in the internal labor
market. Some interest in education and training programs has been stimulated by federal manpower training programs which seek to help the
disadvantaged and civil rights movement insistence that lines of progression
be desegregated. Many older workers, already on the job but unable to get
upgraded because of limited education, are apt to resent these efforts to help
blacks and other minorities. Moreover, many black workers lack the necessary qualifications to be upgraded. Finally, industrial workers face the
threat of technological displacement and have attempted to use retraining
programs to help them adjust to new jobs.

　　One of the most widely known cases of an effort to retrain workers
who have lost their jobs because of tchnological change is the Armour and
Company experience. In 1959, Armour permanently closed six plants, thus
losing about 20 percent of its total capacity and displacing 5,000 production
employees. In order to soften the shock of unemployment, Armour and
United Packinghouse Workers and the Amalgamated Meat Cutters agreed
to establish an automation committee which had a $500,000 fund to carry
out its program. The program screened workers on the basis of aptitude
tests, but its placement rate was not very satisfactory, and many of those
who were retrained were offered jobs that paid lower wages than they had
earned at Armour. As a result of this experience, the committee concluded
that retraining on a crash basis would be of little help to displaced workers
who were middle-aged and had limited education. Moreover, the retraining
program clearly required jobs that many of the workers could not find.[11]

UNIONS AND THE MANPOWER PROGRAMS
OF THE 1960s

　　It is difficult to generalize about the labor movement's attitude toward
remedial manpower: Reactions have varied widely according to the multiplicity of motives and interests within the movement. The federations, which
are mainly public relations and political organizations, viewed the new

training activities more favorably than did national unions, which, in turn, viewed them more favorably than did their local affiliates. Many local craft unions feared that the manpower programs would flood the labor market with partially trained craftsmen who would depress wages and generally undermine working conditions. They also saw the new training programs competing with the established apprenticeship activities. Union fears were aggravated by those who oversold the manpower programs as a solution to the social and economic problems of the disadvantaged. It was understandable, for example, that a construction union in a labor market that ordinarily admitted no more than 100 new craftsmen a year would be alarmed by claims that 2,000 or 3,000 disadvantaged people were to be trained in these crafts. Fears were intensified by the civil rights advocates' attack on the all-white policies of many local unions. These unions, therefore, were persuaded that manpower programs would be used to channel blacks into union training programs from which they had been excluded.

THE STEEL PROGRAM   Labor opposition to the new programs was not restricted to the craft unions. Many members of industrial unions feared that the new programs would give preferential treatment to the disadvantaged and advance them ahead of workers already in factory jobs. A frequent complaint of union members was that the disadvantaged were being given opportunities that older workers had never enjoyed, even though these older workers also had limited qualifications for advancement. In the steel industry—as in many other basic industries—a large number of workers with very limited education were recruited during World War II, (many workers with very low levels of education had been hired even before that time). At the Inland Steel Company, for example, more than 1,000 Mexican-Americans who could not speak English were hired during the war.

In response to the problems of old as well as new workers some unions simply adopted programs that would help all of the workers similarly situated and not just the disadvantaged. For example, in 1965, the United Steelworkers and ten major steel companies agreed to establish an education and training program to increase workers' educational levels and make them eligible for promotion. The program was to be administered by a nonprofit organization called the Board of Fundamental Education. The contract negotiated that year by union and management included the following clause:

> In order to serve the basic educational need of the employees and thereby enhance their qualifications for job opportunities on new and improved facilities and enable employees, including those on layoff, to improve their capacities for advancement or re-employment with the Company, the Company and the Union, together with various agencies of the United States government, have been and will continue to actively explore the development of certain training programs under the Manpower Development and Training Act of 1962 (MDTA) and other applicable laws.

At the same time, the Departments of Labor and Health, Education, and Welfare were concerned about the limited educational levels of many American workers and were planning a pilot program for in-plant remedial education. Representatives from the federal government and the steel industry adapted the Cooperative Steel Industry Education Plan. The curriculum included two levels of instruction:

I. A basic level for individuals performing below the 4.5 grade level.

II. An advanced level designed for individuals performing between the 4.5 and 8.0 grade levels in both work meaning and arithmetic computation.[12]

Labor-management participation was stressed at every step in the program. Special efforts were made to brief supervisors, workers, and union leaders. The classes were conducted in a very informal manner, and every effort was made to have the students encourage each other. To the maximum extent possible, the program's administrators sought to avoid the schoolroom atmosphere.

The steel industry program is considered to be a success by unions, employers, and government representatives. McCauley reported that 4100 steel workers have attended classes in basic elementary education; of the 2762 workers who attended at least one class the first year, 1726 (62 percent) graduated. Union-management satisfaction with the program was reflected in the 1968 collective-bargaining agreement which stated that "these efforts have been sufficiently beneficial to warrant the continuation of this type of program for further exploratory development under MDTA, other applicable laws, and through other mutually agreed-upon means."

EXTENT OF UNION PARTICIPATION   The AFL-CIO and its affiliates also have supported the new manpower programs and have actively participated in a number of them. In August 1969, for example, it was reported that there were 13 national contracts with 7 unions, providing for 15,000 training slots under the MDTA-OJT program. The largest contract with any union was with the United Brotherhood of Carpenters (UBC), which was training almost 5,000 persons. The International Brotherhood of Electrical workers, the Laborers International Union, the International Union of Operating Engineers (IUOE), and the AFL-CIO Appalachian Council also held OJT contracts. Indeed, the Operating Engineers have been particularly active in the manpower field. It was reported in 1966, for example, that the IUOE had received over half of all OJT money going to building trades unions. A number of regional labor councils and state federations and local unions had an additional 3,300 training slots for MDTA-OJT programs in August 1969.

JOB CORPS   Organized labor also has supported the Job Corps concept of residential training for hard-core disadvantaged youths. The first union to become involved with this program was the IUOE, which ran training programs for heavy equipment maintenance workers at the Jacobs Creek Center in Tennessee. The instructors were journeymen IUOE members; the union agreed to place the trainees who completed the training course. Trainees were allowed to enter the IUOE apprenticeship program and ultimately to become regular journeymen. The IUOE subsequently entered into an agreement for two Job Corps conservation centers to train 130 disadvantaged workers in equipment repair, maintenance, and operation. The UBC also trained several hundred Job Corpsmen to be slotted into the union's regular apprenticeship program.

THE APPALACHIAN COUNCIL   Some of the OJT programs provide greater insight into the nature of the labor movement's involvement with this kind of training. One of the largest of these programs is Operation Manpower, which is sponsored by the AFL-CIO Appalachian Council in cooperation with the Departments of Labor and Health, Education, and Welfare. The Appalachian Council, which was formed in 1964, works closely with the Institute for Labor Studies at West Virginia University and covers an 11-state area (Alabama, Kentucky, North Carolina, Virginia, Georgia, Maryland, Ohio, Pennsylvania, Tennessee, West Virginia, and South Carolina). Operation Manpower began in June 1967 with the award of two federal job development contracts. The Appalachian Council was awarded a number of additional job training contracts in subsequent years. The Council's basic approach is to work through affiliated local unions or their employers. It has emphasized OJT as well as coupled programs which combine OJT with vocational and basic education. Although it has worked with such large employers as Kaiser Aluminum, Goodyear, and Hayes International, most of the jobs developed by the Council have been with small firms, many of which are located in rural areas. By November 1970, Operation Manpower had developed 13,361 jobs and placed 7,817 trainees, at an average actual cost of $445.08 for each trainee placed.

PROJECT BUILD   Unions also have been involved in a number of programs to draw minority workers into the building trades by preparing disadvantaged youngsters for participation in apprenticeship programs. One of the most important of these efforts is Project Build, started in 1968 by the Greater Washington (D.C.) Central Labor Council in cooperation with the local Building Trades Council. Project Build recruited and selected youths and young adults for apprenticeship programs in the building and construction trades. The training provided for individual remediation and counseling and training in eight participating crafts through workshop and on-site activities. The youths trained were between 17.5 and 24 years of age. During its first year, which covered two training cycles, 143 trainees completed the program, and 72 dropped out. Of the 143 who completed, 124 went into apprenticeship, and 79 were still in apprenticeship one year later. The preapprenticeship program completers increased their average hourly earnings about 60 percent compared with 20 percent for the control group. Completers raised their weekly earnings by about 55 percent compared with about 25 percent for the control group. Employment of the control group increased by only 0.75 weeks a year, or 2.26 percent, while completers increased their employment by 3.63 weeks, or 10.41 percent. Roberts estimated that the cost of the investment to the economy would be paid off in increased output, assuming constant net benefits and no workers displacement, in three years. For the government, the training costs would be paid back in 13 years by increased tax payments. The gross cost per enrolled trainee, including completers and dropouts, was $2260, but the cost increased to $6090 per trainee remaining in apprenticeship after one year. Roberts concluded:

> The evidence suggests that disadvantaged youth who get preapprenticeship training enter apprenticeship on approximately equal terms with nondisadvantaged youths, particularly in terms of remaining in apprenticeship for one year.
>
> Furthermore, there is a relatively high, fast economic payoff from the investment in preapprenticeship training. The present value of the training far exceeds the costs of such training.[13]

TOP   The Transportation Opportunity Program, Inc. (TOP) is an experimental and demonstration program sponsored by the Teamsters Joint Council No. 42 of Southern California. In August 1967, TOP began to train the hard-core unemployed as professional heavy-duty truck drivers, automotive specialists, or brake repair, front-end alignment, and tune-up workers. This program also seeks to upgrade the skills of men already employed in the transportation field. TOP's basic approach is to provide remedial and basic education, counseling and training, and job placement. The basic target populations are the inhabitants of the economically depressed areas of Watts and East Los Angeles. TOP makes a special effort to recruit in penal institutions; as evidenced by the fact that 30 percent of the first truck-driving trainees were prison parolees.

Between August 1967 and February 1969, TOP graduated 331 men from its truck-driving program, and 252 from its automotive program. Of 209 truck driver graduates in a follow-up survey in the fall of 1969, 189 were employed—167 in jobs related to trucking. Wages earned by graduates averaged $4.87 per hour. Of the 583 graduates of both programs, 378 were surveyed in the fall of 1969, average wages were $2.83 per hour. Their overall employment rate was 82 percent, and 73 percent were employed in training-related jobs.

THE HUMAN RESOURCE DEVELOPMENT INSTITUTE   As a result of the apprenticeship outreach programs, Operation Build, and other programs in which unions participated, it became apparent that a joint effort between the U.S. Department of Labor and the whole labor movement could produce beneficial results for manpower programs. Such a cooperative arrangement, it was felt, not only would take advantage of the labor movement's network of affiliated organizations, but also would overcome worker resistance to helping the disadvantaged. It was also considered to be important for the labor movement to (a) convince field-level government officials and employers that unions could participate effectively in manpower programs, and (b) establish its credibility with the hard-core unemployed—especially minority groups, which were assuming an increasingly anti-union stance because of publicity given to discrimination against blacks and other minorities by various unions.

In order to accomplish these objectives, the AFL-CIO Executive Council created the Human Resource Development Institute (HRDI) in September 1968. HRDI received some $4.2 million from the U.S. Department of Labor for a "nationwide program to recruit, train, employ, and upgrade the unemployed and underemployed." [14] HRDI's staff of 50 people from 27 different unions also seek to promote better coordination of manpower programs. Staffers come from a wide range of backgrounds and involvements in civic and community organizations. HRDI is particularly active in apprenticeship outreach programs—which it encourages and provides with local liaison and followup—and in preapprenticeship training programs.

One of HRDI's major activities has been to develop, in cooperation with the National Alliance of Businessmen (NAB) on the Job Opportunities in the Business Sector (JOBS) program, a "buddy system" to ease the transition of the disadvantaged into plants where unions have contracts. By December 1970, more than 200 companies in 50 cities had developed systems in which 1000 members of 47 national unions had served as "buddies" to give assistance on and off the job to the newly hired during their probationary periods.

CONCLUSIONS ON UNIONS
AND LABOR MARKETS

Although unions represent only about 28 percent of all nonagricultural employees in the United States, their influence extends far and wide in American labor markets because collective bargaining covers most of the blue-collar workers in the mainstream transportation, construction, high-wage manufacturing, printing and publishing, and other industries. The unions' overall impact on wages might be debated, but it is generally agreed that they have influenced wage structures and have a significant impact on wages of their members—although the specific impact varies with the particular labor market and general economic conditions.

We also noted that unions and collective bargaining have played an important role in education and manpower programs. Historically, the labor movement was a major influence for universal free public education. Unions have been particularly interested in vocational education, although union leaders generally consider it inferior to apprenticeship training. Reflecting the workers' preference for "practical" on-the-job training, unions feel that few crafts can be learned in the classroom. They also prefer job training that is established under collective bargaining to that provided unilaterally by employers. Labor leaders point out that collective bargaining makes it possible for training to reflect the interests and needs of employers and workers and also ties the costs of training to those who are to benefit most from it. They argue, for example, that employers by themselves would not provide broad, general training to make employees more "unemployment-proof" and adaptable to diverse job situations. Rather, they argue, employers are more interested in minimizing training costs and maximizing profits, which often dictates narrow, specialized job assignments. Moreover, employers tend to desire excessive supplies of workers in order to meet peak labor requirements and minimize upward pressures on wages. In contrast, the unions attempt to see that workers are well trained and that supplies of labor are no greater than necessary to meet the demand for workers at negotiated wage rates. Unions have used training programs not only to provide general training but also to train members for the new jobs generated by technological changes which render older skills obsolete. Moreover, some unions—especially those in casual occupations in the transportation and construction industries—maintain job information and referral systems for their members.

The labor movement's manpower functions create problems for those who advocate comprehensive national manpower programs. For one thing, unions use their control of training and referral systems to monopolize job opportunities for their members. They are, therefore, very suspicious of government or other training programs that are not at least partly controlled by unions or that compete with union programs. Where unions are strong enough to impose closed-shop conditions (whereby workers must join unions *before* they come to work), they can prevent the employment of the workers trained in public programs by refusing to accept the trainees as union members. Although the closed shop is outlawed by the National Labor Relations Act, strong unions have been able to enforce *de facto* closed-shop conditions because of their control of labor supplies.

The AFL-CIO generally gave strong support to the manpower legislation of the 1960s, even when some of its affiliates and their members were unenthusiastic. With few exceptions, unions participated only in manpower programs that were compatible with collective bargaining. Unions can be expected to resist programs that are incompatible with that system—if they threaten to undermine union control of training or referral systems.

In view of the growing importance of public and private manpower programs, education and training will undoubtedly become an increasingly important subject of collective bargaining in the future. Moreover, it can be expected that agencies such as the AFL-CIO's HRDI will be strengthened to link manpower programs to collective bargaining, and that machinery will be established to resolve conflicts between union-controlled programs and public policy. Conflicts are particularly likely because of continued pressure to enlarge the employment opportunities of blacks and other minorities who have not had adequate access to many training, upgrading, and referral programs controlled by unions. Government agencies probably will become increasingly concerned about the implications of control of labor supplies for price stability. To whatever extent these pressures threaten the "sanctity" of collective bargaining, they undoubtedly will elicit continuing and increasing resistance from labor unions.

NOTES

1. Good discussions of labor in the developing countries can be found in Walter Galenson, ed., *Labor in Developing Countries* (Berkeley, Calif.: University of California Press, 1962), and *idem., Labor and Economic Development* (New York: John Wiley, 1959). See also Everett M. Kassalow, *Trade Unions and Industrialization: An International Comparison* (New York: Random House, 1969), Part II.

2. For example, the statements of eight leading economic theorists in David McCord Wright, ed., *The Impact of the Union* (New York: Harcourt Brace Jovanovich, 1951).

3. Albert Rees, *The Economics of Trade Unions* (Chicago: University of Chicago Press, 1962), p. 79.

4. H. G. Lewis, *Unionism and Relative Wages in the United States* (Chicago: University of Chicago Press, 1963), p. 5.

5. Lloyd G. Reynolds, "The Impact of Collective Bargaining on the Wage Structure of the United States," in John T. Dunlop, ed., *The Theory of Wage Determination* (New York: St. Martin's Press, 1957), p. 220.

6. Jack Barbash, "Union Interests in Apprenticeship and Other Training Forms," *Journal of Human Resources* (Winter 1968), pp. 63–83.

7. Ray Marshall, *The Negro and Organized Labor* (New York: John Wiley, 1965).

8. Selig Perlman, *History of Trade Unionism* (New York: Augustus M. Kelly, 1950; reprint of the original 1922 edition), pp. 14–15.

9. Sumner H. Slichter, James J. Healy, and E. Robert Livernash, *The Impact of Collective Bargaining on Management* (Washington, D.C.: Brookings Institution, 1960), p. 70.

10. Derek C. Bok and John T. Dunlop, *Labor and the American Community* (New York: Simon & Schuster, 1970), p. 347.

11. *Ibid.* See also Arnold Weber, "Experiment in Retraining," in Gerald G. Somers, ed., *Retraining the Unemployed* (Madison, Wisc.: University of Wisconsin Press, 1968), p. 257, and George P. Shultz and Arnold L. Weber, *Strategies for the Displaced Worker* (New York: Harper & Row, 1966).

12. John S. McCauley, "A Cooperative Steel Industry Education Program," in Peter B. Doeringer, ed., *Programs to Employ the Disadvantaged* (Englewood Cliffs, N.J.: Prentice-Hall, 1969), p. 134.

13. Markley Roberts, "Labor-Sponsored Preapprenticeship Training: What Is the Payoff?" *Labor Law Journal* (October 1970), pp. 663–667.

14. Richard Fiester, "Putting Labor in Work Training," *Manpower* (December 1970), p. 24.

Chapter 15
The Military as a Manpower Institution

The armed forces is one of the largest single industries in the United States. In recent years, it has accounted for about 4 percent of the total labor force, a proportion comparable in size to the entire work force of the construction industry. Only six states have a greater number of working people than the armed forces.

An institution of such scope has a significant effect on the nation both economically and socially. The size of the armed forces has fluctuated widely since the first peacetime conscription was adopted in 1940. Its ranks swelled from 334,000 on active duty in 1939 to 12,123,000, or 18.6 percent of the total labor force, in 1945.[1] Since the end of World War II, the size of the armed forces has ranged from 2.5 to 3.6 million persons; its strength was about 3 million in 1970. At that time, about one-third were in the Army, with the Navy and Air Force claiming 700,000 and 800,000, respectively, and the Marine Corps enlisting another 300,000. The source of armed forces manpower also has fluctuated; the balance between enlisted and inducted personnel is constantly shifting (Table 15–1). The distribution of manpower among the services has changed significantly, accompanied by a shift in skill requirements. The most obvious trend is toward more technical skills and more sophisticated training (Table 15–2). There is an indisputable trend away from the combat specialties (at least until the Vietnam War), with concurrent increases in the technical and mechanical occupations.

TABLE 15–1   *Enlisted Versus Inducted Military Personnel*

YEAR	ENLISTED	INDUCTED
1950	100.0%	—
1955	69.1	30.9%
1960	79.5	20.5
1965	77.3	22.7
1970	65.6	34.4

SOURCE: 1950–1965 data from Harold Wool, *The Military Specialist: Skilled Manpower for the Armed Forces* (Baltimore: Johns Hopkins, 1968). 1970 data from the Office of the Secretary of Defense.

TABLE 15–2   *Occupational Distribution of Enlisted Men, Selected Years, 1945–1974 (Percent)*

OCCUPATIONAL GROUP	1945	1953	1957	1963	1969	(PROJECTED) 1974
TOTAL	100%	100%	100%	100%	100%	100%
Ground combat	23	18	14	14	15	10
Electronics	6	10	13	15	10	11
Other technicians	7	7	8	8	14	17
Administrative and clerical	15	20	18	19	18	18
Mechanics	22	23	26	25	24	24
Craftsmen	11	7	8	7	7	7
Services	16	15	13	12	12	13

SOURCE: *The Report of the President's Commission on an All-Volunteer Armed Force* (Washington, D.C.: U.S. Government Printing Office, February 1970), Table 4–VII, p. 44.

THE MILITARY AS A CLAIMANT OF MANPOWER

Of a total of 592,000 men who entered the armed service in fiscal 1970, two of every three were voluntary enlistments (Table 15–3). Why did almost 400,000 young men and women enlist in the armed services in one year? Harold Wool concludes that three underlying factors affect the supply of voluntary military manpower. First, the pressure of the draft suggests that many of those enlisting are only technically volunteers. Second, a certain percentage of the population is always anxious to serve, and the large number of youths in their late teens insures a supply of volunteers. Third, the high youth unemployment rate encourages young people to enlist in the armed forces.

The evidence produced by Altman and Fechter points to a relatively stable supply of volunteers.[2] The most important consideration appears to

TABLE 15–3   *Draftee and Nondraftee Recruits by Service, Fiscal Year 1970 (thousands)*

	ENLISTEES	INDUCTED
TOTAL	388.2	203.7
Army	156.2	195.6
Navy	96.2	0.0
Air Force	68.5	0.0
Marine Corps	67.3	8.1

SOURCE: Office of the Secretary of Defense.

be the pressure from the draft. Nearly two of every five enlisted men indicated that they entered the service to avoid the draft. As in any labor market, the wage rate must also be considered a key variable, but the complexity of the military pay system makes any analysis difficult. Basic pay is only part of the total compensation; it is overshadowed by numerous allowances, special pay scales, allotments, and benefits. But one clear fact is that military pay lags behind civilian pay, especially for low-ranking enlisted men and officers. The total annual compensation of a first-term enlistee in 1970 was $3,251 compared with $5,200 he would have earned in civilian life.[3] Moreover, military compensation is highly compressed and allows only minimal differentials. According to one study,

> . . . a three-star general earns an income only slightly over three times that of a sergeant major. One would be hard pressed to name large-scale industrial enterprises where the salary differences between line employees and top management approach such a low ratio.[4]

Despite initially low pay, the opportunities offered by military services are attractive to some. There is much evidence that enlistment rates are closely related to changes in compensation.

Opinion surveys are another source of information about reasons for enlistments. A 1964 survey conducted by the National Opinion Research Center (NORC) of the University of Chicago focused on two populations: active-duty military personnel and civilian males between ages 16 and 34. The major conclusion was that the most highly educated men felt that the draft was their major reason for enlisting while those with the least education viewed the military as a chance for educational and occupational advancement (Table 15–4).

"Middle America" is overrepresented among volunteers. Enlistment rates, which are highest in the South, apparently are related to economic factors. Low earnings and limited job opportunities make the military more attractive to southern youth than to those in other regions. The services are most heavily represented by high-school graduates: 62 percent of enlisted personnel have a high-school diploma but no college experience. The least educated are unable to qualify for service; the most highly educated

TABLE 15–4 *Service Entry Reasons of Enlisted Volunteers by Educational Level, 1964*

EDUCATIONAL LEVEL	PERSONAL	PATRIOTIC	DRAFT MOTIVATED	SELF-ADVANCEMENT
TOTAL	28.8%	11.2%	36.9%	23.1%
Less than high school	32.5	14.0	25.7	27.8
High-school graduate	27.9	10.5	38.0	23.6
Some college	27.8	10.5	46.1	15.6

SOURCE: National Opinion Research Center Survey, 1964, adapted from Charles C. Moskos, Jr., *The American Enlisted Man: The Rank and File in Today's Military* (New York: Russell Sage Foundation, 1970), p. 199.

are able to avoid serving in the armed forces. A clear majority of volunteers come from working-class backgrounds, as indicated by data on fathers' occupations (Table 15–5).

The characteristics of inductees differ significantly from those of enlistees, and distributions of inductees by education and mental ability vary widely from those for volunteers. The mental capability distribution of draftees is heavily skewed toward the least capable. Supporting data indicate that almost half of all college graduates see no military service at all and that only 12.7 percent of all male college graduates are drafted. In contrast, over two-thirds of those men with less than a high-school education see military service and almost 20 percent are drafted. The inductee population is weighted toward the least able and the least educated. This reflects a system that allows the more educated to avoid service and that has lower standards of acceptance for inductees than for enlistees.

THE SELECTIVE SERVICE SYSTEM

The present draft system dates back to 1917 when Congress passed the Selective Service Act. It was essentially a wartime draft and completely precluded any enlistments. The law expired shortly after World War I and

TABLE 15–5 *Fathers' Occupations of Army Enlistees*

White collar	17.0%
Blue collar	52.8
Farmer	14.8
Military	1.8
Father absent	13.6

SOURCE: National Opinion Research Center Survey, 1964, adapted from Charles C. Moskos, Jr., *The American Enlisted Man: The Rank and File in Today's Military* (New York: Russell Sage Foundation, 1970), p. 195.

the draft was not renewed until shortly before the United States was embroiled in World War II. The Selective Training and Service Act was passed on September 14, 1940, and its system supplied two-thirds of the armed forces personnel in that war. The entire system of deferments, exemptions, and orders of call so familiar to young men today was established at that time.

The Act expired in 1947 only to be reinstated in 1948 as the Selective Service Act in response to Cold War pressures. After some experimentation with the size of calls and periods of service, Congress in 1951 passed the Universal Military Training and Service Act, which remained substantially unchanged until 1969 when opposition to the draft was engendered by the unpopular Vietnam War.

During its first two decades, the selective service system evolved into a complex and vast organization. Its basic component is the 4,100 local draft boards. The system is administered by a national headquarters and state directors who represent the governors of their respective states. There are also 96 appeal boards to hear complaints against actions taken by the local draft boards, where the fundamental functions of military manpower procurement are performed.[5]

Every young man is required to register with his board at age 18 and, on the basis of the information he provides or is gathered by the board, he is given a draft classification. Other than the 1–A (available for service), the most common classifications are II–A (occupational deferment), II–S (student deferment), and IV–F (not qualified for any military service because of physical defects).

The local board system was designed to maximize personal contact with and knowledge about service-age men, but with the increasing urbanization of the nation this premise is more theory than fact. The local boards long exercised a great deal of individual discretion, a practice that led to the acute lack of uniformity among board operations.

Among the many abuses prevalent in the system were the ability of many young men to pyramid student deferments into virtual exemptions and the easy access to occupational deferments, especially among the better educated. Inductions made on the basis of "oldest first" led to the maximization of hardships, career disruptions, and efforts to avoid the draft.

The basic problem, however, involved the selection of men for conscription. The growth of the number of men eligible for service coincided with a decrease in the manpower needed for national security. It has been estimated that in the future the armed forces will only need one-half to one-third of the nearly 2 million men annually reaching draft age.[6]

To overcome many of the inequities and to make the system more rational, Congress in 1969 amended the existing draft laws to allow modifications of the selection process.[7] These amendments represented the most significant reforms of the selective service since its inception in 1940. The order of call was changed to "youngest first"; the period of greatest vulncrability was reduced from seven years to one; and a random selection process was instituted to distribute equally the risk of call. Graduate deferments were eliminated to prevent the pyramiding of student deferments.

The first lottery was held on December 1, 1969. Critics, however, claimed procedures for selecting a cutoff number for inductions were inadequate and that uniformity of undergraduate student deferments was not achieved among local boards. During the second year of the lottery, improvements were made in specifying a uniform cutoff number and rules on student deferments were standardized. Legislation pending in 1971 would suspend the state and local draft board quota system. A new uniform call system would lead to the same lottery number ceiling throughout the country.

One of the most controversial portions of the selective service law deals with student deferments. Before passage of the 1969 amendments there was no uniform policy on college student deferments despite their authorization under law. Several factors were considered in efforts to establish an equitable policy. It was no longer clear that the nation suffered from a chronic shortage of college-trained manpower, the original justification for college deferments, and there was strong evidence that young men could attend college after their service. Perhaps more importantly, it was argued that deferment of college attendance allowed many young men to avoid serving in the Vietnam War.[8]

Despite these arguments, the 1969 reforms continued undergraduate student deferments (with the understanding that the year of maximum draft vulnerability would come whenever the deferment expired). Several safeguards have been suggested to prevent future abuse. One would extend student deferments to postsecondary schools other than four-year academic colleges. Others would preclude further deferments for students granted a college deferment and terminate student deferments during any period of substantial military casualties. President Nixon indicated his intention to end all undergraduate deferments.

THE MILITARY AS A TRAINER OF MANPOWER

Military training and occupations have changed considerably over the years. The type and quality of training this manpower receives has fundamental ramifications for the economy at large. Accordingly, military training has ranged from basic education to courses required for a Ph.D. degree.[9] However, the quality of instruction is very difficult to assess because the military must cope with conditions and restrictions not confronted by nonmilitary training institutions.

One such condition is the very high rate of personnel turnover, which complicates followup and evaluation of training effectiveness. Over 60 percent of total military personnel are rotated during every two years. One authoritative estimate placed the potential "return" on training investment as much as ten times greater in the civilian economy than in the military.[10]

Another problem peculiar to military training institutions is the heterogeneity of the entering work force. The wide variation in mental abilities and educational backgrounds poses a serious challenge to the military in devising training curricula.

Many of the military's objectives are peculiar to its special needs and therefore are not shared by nonmilitary trainers. A private company is, for the most part, interested in training the most capable work force available in order to maximize its profits; a school is concerned with the educational process itself. The military, however, must concern itself with a wider variety of considerations and constantly changing strategic situations. Training men of low intelligence or limited educational attainment is not necessarily consistent with the objective of optimal labor-force effectiveness—at reasonable cost.

Approximately 400,000 servicemen attend service schools each year. The formal service schools are a rather recent development: The bulk of schooling was either on-the-job or apprenticeship training until the late 1940s. These schools tend, however, to focus on training for a relatively low level of skill, while the more advanced training is learned on the job or in civilian institutions. Furthermore, both the proportion of enlisted personnel trained in service schools and the average length of the training courses usually vary directly with the technicality of the skill.

All recruits must go through 8 to 11 weeks of basic training, about one-third of which is spent in the classroom. After this, recruits go to a technical school or on-the-job training. The choice of skill or occupation still lies basically with the service, but some element of personal choice exists, depending upon the branch, demand factors, and type of enlistment.

Because of the short duration of service, course length is kept to a minimum. Classes last five full days a week for a few months. Theoretical aspects are reduced to a minimum with major attention focused on the more practical and immediate facets of a job specialty. Nonetheless, the armed forces can claim credit for many innovative training techniques. They have pioneered in the use of synthetic training devices, or simulators, closed circuit television, and teaching machines. These methods, and the highly successful language schools, have emerged as significant military educational achievements.

The adaptability of the training techniques to changing skill requirements have been proven. The utility of military manpower training in civilian life, however, is unproven. Furthermore, the high turnover of military personnel in recent years has severely taxed training capability.

The analysis of military training is replete with difficulties because there are basic differences in training philosophies and practices among the services. While the Navy trains its men first as generalists and then as specialists—congruent with its self-concept as a diverse technical and logistical fighting force—the Army trains its men to be specialists on narrowly defined jobs. Although all Air Force enlisted personnel are volunteers, its training program is similar to that of the Army.[11] Perhaps even more confusing are the occupational classification systems. Efforts to devise a single uniform classification code have failed because of differences in training and occupational philosophy. Definitions of occupations and skill-level classification methods are rarely the same among services, and men in the different services with similar occupations would not be functionally interchangeable because they have been trained on different equipment and have skills of varying degrees of specificity.

Military occupations have changed in response to several factors, particularly advances in military technology and weapons systems. The trend toward more complicated technology, automated systems, and nuclear power was slowed down, however, by the need for more combat troops in Vietnam. The continued deployment of extensive overseas forces has led to an increased percentage of support service and administrative personnel. Shifts in the relative strengths of the four armed services have led to greater number of personnel involved in occupations closely associated with air power. Finally, competition from expanding civilian labor markets has compelled the military to improve opportunities within the service. Plans for career development and more attractive job choices have had to be developed.

The military seems to place low priority on combat occupations: In the mid-1960s, about 28 percent of draftees were assigned to ground combat occupations, compared with 21 percent of career regulars. Also, those with the least education served in this capacity—41 percent of those with less than a high-school education, compared with only 16 percent of those with some college. And men serving only one term are most likely to perform traditional military duties such as combat and manual labor.

ARMED FORCES AS A SOCIAL INSTITUTION

The armed forces have had to develop special programs for servicemen who could not meet regular service requirements. In the late 1950s, enlistment and induction standards were stiffened, the minimum score on the Armed Forces Qualification Test was raised, and consequently the number of disqualifications rose. The incidence of disqualifications for all reasons rose from 23.6 percent during the Korean War to 31.7 percent within five years, an increase attributable largely to the higher mental standards.

A report released in 1963 by the President's Task Force on Manpower Conservation, *One-Third of a Nation*, focused on the armed forces' high rejection rate. The report indicated that more than one of every three youths, an average of 600,000 a year, failed to meet mental and physical requirements. Rejections were concentrated among the low-income and minority groups, and were highest for southern blacks.

In response to public concern, the Secretary of Defense announced the creation of Project 100,000 in August 1966. Its purpose was to bring into the armed forces each year up to 100,000 young men who could not meet mental, physical, and educational standards. The thinking was that the armed forces—the largest and most experienced vocational educational system in the nation, with disciplinary power and vast technical capabilities for large-scale training—would provide remedial training, individual counseling, and medical care for correctable physical defects for the "new standards" trainees (as Project 100,000 recruits were called).

During the program's first three years, 246,000 men were admitted. About 95 percent completed basic training and 90 percent finished formal skill training. The success rate was much higher in fields stressing practical work than in those requiring reading and mathematical abilities. Occupational assignments were primarily in the less technical areas, including 37 percent in combat-type skills—compared with 23 percent for all other men. The experience with Project 100,000 suggested that the armed forces, like any other employer, had tried to obtain the best qualified personnel, but when faced with labor shortages, it found that those once considered ineligible could be made fit through proper training. This has crucial implications for such civilian training institutions as federal manpower programs and public schools.

In addition to upgrading the less qualified, the military must also contend with the hostility of many highly educated men to military service and consequent disruption of their lives. But men at both ends of the spectrum share the desire to obtain the most suitable and attractive military occupation possible.

While 37 percent of the new standards men received their training in combat fields, 27 percent of enlisted college graduates were similarly assigned in 1969.[12] This has led to the oft-voiced complaint that the military underutilizes educated men. In fact, 27 percent of college graduates were in administration and 11 percent were medical and dental specialists. The relatively high percentage of college-trained combat personnel reflects a desire by the military to "spread the risk." However, available data indicate that the armed services are currently making an attempt (within given constraints) to match capabilities and interests with military training both for the least and the most educated.

THE MILITARY AS A SOURCE OF MANPOWER

At the end of 1970, nearly 28 million Americans had served in the armed forces, including about one-third of all men between the ages of 20 and 29. In the same year, over a million persons were released from the service to return to civilian life. Certainly the large number of veterans has important implications for the nation's economy.

Military service is worthy of analysis as a form of investment in human capital. Economists have applied similar techniques to examine returns from investments in education. To appraise the value of military service, it is necessary to focus on the experience of veterans with respect to the specific questions of military "spillover," or "crossover." The armed forces and others have long promoted the notion that the skills, knowledge, and attitudes acquired while in the service prepare veterans for a more productive and rewarding civilian life. The military has used the skill-transferability argument in its recruitment literature, and almost half of the enlisted men in the Air Force have entered the service expecting to learn a usable occupational skill.[13] This question of transferability is especially relevant to the 60,000 to 100,000 men who annually retire from the military.[14]

Much of the belief held by servicemen concerning the easy crossover and transferability of skills into civilian life is rooted in the so-called "convergence" of military and civilian occupational structure. The most obvious indication of this convergence is the rapid growth in technology and the concurrent growth of technical specialties in both military and civilian sectors. Less obvious is the similar decline in the relative numbers of persons working in uniquely military and uniquely civilian occupations—for example, ground combat and agriculture.

The simplistic conclusion is that military training is increasingly applicable to civilian occupations. Broad trends, however, do not adequately describe the actual job structures in the two sectors. Comparative frequencies of occupations indicate that 13 percent of the enlisted positions account for less than 2 percent of the male civilian labor force. Alternatively, occupational groups with high civilian frequencies account for about 8 percent of enlisted positions. And this analysis does not even account for the differences between military and civilian jobs with similar titles. A 1964 Bureau of the Census survey indicated that only 10 percent of the veterans under age 35 said they had made considerable use of military training and work experience in their civilian lives. Another factor accounting for the low transferability of military skills is the growing trend toward the replacement of servicemen with civilians in support categories. The number of civilians working for the Department of Defense has risen considerably in recent years; in 1970 there were almost 1.4 million civilians, or four for every ten active-duty personnel. Most of the civilians were in administrative, clerical, and service occupations, which decreased the number of military personnel in the high-convergence occupations.

The transition from military to civilian occupations has proven difficult. Retired military personnel experience high rates of unemployment, and retirees with the least amount of formal education are most likely to be unemployed or to hold low-paying jobs. Retirees not only find little relationship between their military jobs and civilian employment, but those in military occupational groups with high civilian unemployment also experience the least crossover of military to civilian skills.[15]

It has been suggested that preservice occupations have a significant effect on postservice employment and income. Individuals apparently utilizing their military training are often actually benefiting from preservice jobs related to their military training rather than from the military experience itself. Returning to any preservice job has a significant positive income effect regardless of military training, and those who pursue a postservice job related to their military training are most likely to have held a similar position prior to entrance into the military.[16]

Several reasons have been offered for the lack of crossover between military and civilian skills. It seems that the military tends to offer training in skills that are not financially rewarded in the civilian labor market, and ex-servicemen either fail to look for a related job or fail to accept one that has been offered. Similarly, training in the military is either inadequate or unrelated to civilian operations. Even military occupations that would seem transferable to civilian employment such as police and telephone personnel are not comparable with the requirements of similar jobs in the civilian world. And civilian employers often refuse to recognize military training as a qualification for similar civilian positions.

TRANSITION TO CIVILIAN LIFE

The federal government has taken an active role in helping veterans in the transition to civilian life. The single most important source of such aid is the Veterans Administration (VA). Until the late 1960s, the VA limited its operations to the delivery of services and assistance—including financial education assistance; training assistance allowances for veterans pursuing on-the-job or apprenticeship training; loan benefits, particularly for homes and farms; disability benefits; and insurance. Veterans themselves were expected to seek out the agency and apply for help. This "come to us when you need help" approach proved inadequate and the VA became more active in seeking out Vietnam veterans.

The Vietnam veteran differs in several crucial ways from a World War II and Korean War veteran. He is younger, less likely to be academically oriented than the nonveteran, and has less work experience. When he returns to civilian life, the veteran may be a victim of widespread opposition to the Vietnam War and hence be denied special consideration for his service to the country. Moreover, pre-Vietnam veterans were discharged in large groups and could more easily receive necessary information about assistance programs.

The lack of special recognition and the lack of knowledge of available help seriously affects the Vietnam veterans. By mid-1970, there were nearly

4 million Vietnam verterans, most in their twenties, and they were subject to a heavier incidence of unemployment than nonveterans in the same age brackets.[17]

To better serve the Vietnam veterans, the VA initiated Operation Outreach in 1968. Efforts were made to contact servicemen before they were discharged in Vietnam—at separation points, in military hospitals, and back in the community. Perhaps the most important step, however, was the establishment of 71 U.S. Veterans Assistance Centers (USVAC) across the country. These centers offer counseling to all returning veterans and information on the total range of VA programs. All federal, state, and local agencies providing services for veterans were centralized to make it easier for the individual to obtain the kind of assistance he needs. Special efforts were made to assist economically and educationally disadvantaged veterans, and job development and referral quickly became the most important USVAC function. The number of veterans participating in VA programs increased sharply, in part because of the economic downturn in 1970.

The government also has given veterans preference in federal employment, and the Civil Service Commission assists veterans. For those with less than 13 years of schooling, there are Transitional Appointments in lower grade levels provided that the veteran agrees to continue his training or his education under the GI Bill (Veterans Readjustment Appointments). More important are the five-point and ten-point disabled veteran preferences on civil service examinations. Time spent in the armed services is also credited to job experience, and veterans have preference during layoffs.

The Department of Labor, through the U.S. Training and Employment Service, provides job counseling and placement services for veterans —who are also eligible to collect unemployment insurance upon discharge from the service. The GI Bill also guarantees reemployment rights to returning veterans without loss of status or seniority. Because of the lack of work experience of recent veterans, this right is not exercised as much as it was by earlier veterans.

The need for additional training to qualify for civilian jobs is obvious. Forty-eight percent of the officers and 36 percent of the enlistees who held jobs after retirement and 48 percent of the officers and 46 percent of the enlisted men who were seeking jobs after retirement definitely felt there was a need for additional training before they could qualify for civilian work.

Project Transition, a major effort to facilitate the adjustment process, is administered by the Department of Defense. The armed forces make an implicit admission in their operation of this program that occupational crossover is limited and that new veterans are often unprepared to make a living in the civilian world.

First announced by President Lyndon Johnson in April 1967, Project Transition is a voluntary program involving counseling, skill training, education, and placement within the last six months of service. While all interested personnel are eligible for the program, priority is given to those who are disabled, ineligible to reenlist, or did not acquire a civilian-related skill while on active duty.

Project Transition education is oriented toward meeting requirements for a specific occupation or toward completing minimum educational standards for adequate employment. Skill training is provided by the military through regular schools and through on-the-job training by federal, state, and local agencies; on-the-job and institutional training under the Manpower Development and Training Act; and by private industry through on-the-job training. Efforts are made to find for each individual the training best suited to his interests and capabilities and the demand of the particular labor market to which he will return. Participants are allowed time during duty hours to attend training sessions on or off base, and nonfederal assistance is actively sought by the Defense Department to place the soon-to-be-discharged servicemen.

The program has received generally high ratings, except for its lack of success with veterans living in city ghettos and depressed rural areas. The Bureau of the Budget (now the Office of Management and Budget) reported that only 9 percent of a sample of disadvantaged men had participated in Project Transition; 4 percent of the sample had received skill training and less than 1 percent were employed in the skill for which they were trained.[18] Overall, the percentage of servicemen participating in Project Transition has been low; but of the 719,000 servicemen surveyed between January 1968 and March 1970, 91 percent had received counseling. Approximately 20 percent of those counseled began training, and 82 percent of the trainees completed the program.

AN ALL-VOLUNTEER MILITARY FORCE

As the level of armed forces has declined and the population eligible for service has risen, proposals to abolish the draft and return to an all-volunteer military have received increasing attention. Serious analysis of the question began in the early 1960s within the Department of Defense. The public and congressional debate over Vietnam led to the eventual appointment of three separate public study commissions. The first was the President's National Advisory Commission on Selective Service (1966). Although the Commission recommended many changes in the selective service system, which ultimately were adopted, it concluded that the draft must continue,[19] a position seconded by the Civilian Advisory Panel on Military Manpower Procurement appointed in 1968 by the Committee on Armed Service of the House of Representatives.[20] However, the President's Commission on An All-Volunteer Armed Force, under the chairmanship of former Secretary of Defense Thomas S. Gates, Jr., recommended the institution of an all-volunteer force supplemented by a standby draft system. This Commission opposed conscription as "costly, inequitable, and divisive" and denounced the procedure as intolerable when the alternative of an all-volunteer force would be more consistent with the country's basic values.[21]

The economic feasibility of conversion to an all-volunteer military is based upon the response (or elasticity) of the supply of enlistees to increased military pay. All estimates of the budgetary cost of a conversion depend on the extent of this elasticity. The Department of Defense study indicated an elasticity ranging from 0.70 to 1.26 percent—that is, a 1 percent increase in military pay would mean voluntary enlistments would rise by 0.70 and 1.26 percent.[22] The Gates Commission estimates ranged from 1 to 2.2 percent, and other elasticity estimates are of the same general magnitude.

Harold Wool is one of the few investigators to present evidence of a zero or insignificantly positive elasticity of supply. The other estimates were based on cross-sectional studies; Wool's analysis related enlistment rates to the ratio of civilian to military wages over time. He also cited attitudinal surveys to indicate that pay is a relatively unimportant factor in enlistment decisions.

The various estimates of supply elasticity account for the broad range of estimates of the budgetary cost of an all-volunteer armed force. Department of Defense estimates ranged from $4 to $17 billion for a force of 2.65 million. The Gates Commission estimated the added budgetary cost for a 2.5 million force to be $2.7 billion. These figures include only rises in federal budgetary outlays and do not consider the actual or real costs of the armed force.

The major difference between federal budget outlays and the real cost of the military is the burden imposed on those serving. Those who serve bear an implicit tax representing the economic loss of being drafted or coerced into service by threat of conscription and the monetary difference between military conscription wages and wages necessary to persuade them to volunteer for enlistment.[23] While these taxes in-kind are unbudgeted, they are still very real costs. Military wage increases to close the gap between the actual wage and that necessary to induce draftees or draft-induced enlistees to volunteer freely are reflected in budget increases.

The institution of an all-volunteer armed force would involve no increase in real cost. Milton Friedman has argued that

> . . . a shift to a volunteer armed force . . . does not, in fact, involve an increase in total government expenditures properly measured. It involves a reduction in total government expenditures properly measured. . . . But it does involve shifting from a tax in kind, shifting from acquiring services through a forced levy, to buying it on the market. And as a result, the recorded bookkeeping expenditures of the government will run higher.[24]

The real savings would come from several sources. First, it costs about $6,000 to train a soldier; this amounts to a yearly expenditure of over $3 billion for draftee training. These expenditures would be sharply reduced with the institution of a volunteer force.[25] Second, the additional outputs of the reluctant draftees now spared from military service would add to the national income and hence to tax revenues. Finally, and perhaps most important, it is assumed that the efficiency of the military would improve because of the servicemen's better attitude, greater pride, and increased professionalism. The military establishment would be induced to use more efficient methods because "the draft undoubtedly contributes to a greater use of manpower than would be the case if the services had to pay market prices for labor." [26]

An important point made in the Gates Commission report and in congressional debate is the relatively small number of additional volunteers actually needed. Assuming a total armed force of 2.0 to 2.5 million, 440,000 new enlistees will be needed each year if the draft is continued. The Gates Commission estimated that without a draft, which would lead to a lower turnover rate, 325,000 enlistees a year would be required. But, the Commission noted, because there is currently a minimum of 250,000 true volunteers a year only an additional 75,000 men would have to be persuaded to volunteer annually.

Three basic arguments have been raised against the concept of an all-volunteer force. Opponents allege that the flexibility inherent in the draft system would be sacrificed.[27] All-volunteer advocates question whether this flexibility actually exists. They emphasize that training draftees takes many months and that flexibility can be found only in the maintenance of reserve forces. The Gates Commission recommended the continuation of large reserves on an all-volunteer basis. Most plans for an all-volunteer armed force also include a standby draft for national emergencies. Friedman has argued that pay and conditions of service in the voluntary armed forces could be made sufficiently attractive to induce an excess of volunteers permitting as much flexibility as is available under the selective service system.[28]

The second argument relates to the political and social ramifications of an all-volunteer force. It is feared that the armed forces would attract professional mercenaries who would threaten our democratic institutions and that the military would become an independent force isolated from civilian control and criticism. Abuses within the service and questionable adventurism by its leaders would come under less scrutiny. Additionally, an end to the draft would mean the absence of the civilians in uniform who are so often the agents of change within the military.[29] However, the correlation between volunteerism vs. conscription and military control remains to be established. The source of political instability is often the officer corps, which in peacetime has always been composed of volunteers, and the beneficial safeguards of lowest-rank conscripts are questionable. Furthermore, the vast majority of servicemen and officers are career personnel who control the internal operation of the military even in the presence of a draft system.

Probably the most effective argument against an all-volunteer armed force centers around the characteristics of those who will serve. Basically, it is thought that the higher wages and improved working conditions will attract lower-class, primarily black, recruits. And the moral injustice of a heavily black armed force is especially obvious during wartime. Supporters of an all-volunteer force counter this argument by saying that if the military offered the best opportunities for poor blacks, then this would maximize satisfaction; the workings of the market should be followed. Other proponents believe that the concept of an all-volunteer military should not suffer because the relative position of blacks is a problem for society as a whole. The military offers the poor and the black a chance and should not be condemned for the opportunity it provides. Moreover, the draft system discriminates against the poor and the black because of the availability of educational and occupational deferments to middle- and upper-class youth. Finally, if the inducements are substantial, there might be a sufficiently large supply of volunteers to enable the military to be more selective of their personnel. If necessary, quotas could be set for particular groups.

The Gates Commission estimated that blacks comprise 11.6 percent of true first-term volunteers and 12.7 percent of all volunteers. It projected that blacks would constitute 15.0 percent of a completely voluntary armed force, compared with 14.1 percent if the draft continues.

The possibility of an all-volunteer armed force raises significant issues for the entire society. Certainly, the decision whether to retain the present system or to introduce a new one should depend on its equity and efficiency. The occupational and educational abilities and desires of young men should be considered as well as the effectiveness of the method of selecting them for military service.

Any future major changes in the structure of the armed forces depend upon the end of hostilities in southeast Asia and the withdrawal of American troops from that area. Military manpower policies are being devised under that assumption with most emphasis directed toward the establishment of an all-volunteer armed force. In recognition of the fact that pay raises alone might not be an adequate inducement to raise an all-volunteer force, the armed forces have moved to take the "Mickey Mouse"—defined as "demeaning or abrasive regulations"—out of service life in order to make military life more attractive. Reveille is being phased out; uniform and personal appearance regulations are being eased; more liberal liquor and entertainment rules are being established; and many inspections and housekeeping chores are being eliminated. Personal rights, including limited rights of dissent, are to be given greater recognition. In short, the trend is toward treating servicemen as professionals, an obviously necessary step in the formation of a professional military. By increasing the dignity of service life through the elimination of traditional but unnecessary duties and regulations, the appeal of service life will presumably increase and the need for draftees decrease.

But the major roadblock to an all-volunteer armed force remains the low pay. A Defense Department survey found that 12,589 military families were receiving public assistance in 1970. The bulk of these cases came in the low-pay grades with pay and allowances averaging about $4,200 for a serviceman with three dependents.

It still remains doubtful whether enough youths would apply for a military career. Recent figures on voluntary enlistments have been somewhat discouraging for the supporters of the all-volunteer concept. Cuts in draft calls and the institution of the lottery system have coincided with a drastic decrease in volunteers. The sharpest drop occurred soon after the implementation of the lottery system. Even the downturn of the economy has not had its usual positive effect on enlistments. The figures for 1970 indicate some reversal of this trend for first-term enlistments, but the 30.5 percent reenlistment rate in fiscal 1970 was the lowest since 1955.[30] Whether the effects of recent and planned future reforms in the military will attract and retain enough volunteers remains to be tested.

NOTES

1. Harold Wool, *The Military Specialist: Skilled Manpower for the Armed Forces* (Baltimore: Johns Hopkins, 1968), p. 2.

2. Stuart H. Altman and Alan E. Fechter, "The Supply of Military Personnel in the Absence of a Draft," *American Economic Review* (May 1967), pp. 19–31.

3. *Congressional Record* (daily edition), August 19, 1970, p. S13715.

4. Charles C. Moskos, Jr., *The American Enlisted Man: The Rank and File in Today's Military* (New York: Russell Sage Foundation, 1970), pp. 44–45.

5. U.S. Selective Service System, *Semi-Annual Report of the Director of Selective Service for the Period July 1 to December 31, 1969 to the Congress of the United States* (Washington, D.C.: U.S. Government Printing Office, 1970), p. 1.

6. National Advisory Commission on Selective Service, *In Pursuit of Equity: Who Serves When Not All Serve?* (Washington, D.C.: U.S. Government Printing Office, 1967), p. 3.

7. U.S. Congress, House Committee on Armed Services, *Authorizing Modifications of the System of Selecting Persons for Induction into the Armed Forces,* Report No. 91-577, 91st Cong., 1st Sess. (Washington, D.C.: U.S. Government Printing Office, 1969), p. 1.

8. National Advisory Commission on Selective Service, *op. cit.*, p. 41.

9. Harold F. Clark and Harold S. Sloan, *Classrooms in the Military: An Account of Education in the Armed Forces of the United States* (New York: Bureau of Publications, Teachers College, Columbia University, 1964), p. 6.

10. Harold Wool, "The Armed Services As A Training Institution," in Ginzberg, Eli, ed., *The Nation's Children: Development and Education,* vol. 2 (New York: Columbia University Press, 1960).

11. Paul A. Weinstein, *Labor Market Activity of Veterans: Some Aspects of Military Spillover* (College Park, Md.: University of Maryland, 1969), pp. 25–27.

12. Office of the Assistant Secretary of Defense for Manpower and Reserve Affairs, *Statistics on the Utilization of Enlisted College Graduates in the Department of Defense* (Washington, D.C.: U.S. Government Printing Office, June 1970), Table III.

13. U.S. Department of Labor, Manpower Administration, *Transferring Military Experience to Civilian Jobs: A Study of Selected Air Force Veterans* (Washington, D.C.: U.S. Government Printing Office, October 1968).

14. Laure M. Sharp and Albert D. Biderman, *The Employment of Retired Military Personnel* (Washington, D.C.: Bureau of Social Science Research, 1966), p. 86.

15. Albert D. Biderman and Laure M. Sharp, "The Convergence of Military and Civilian Occupational Structures: Evidence from Studies of Military Retired Employment," *The American Journal of Sociology* (January 1968), pp. 381–399.

16. Eugene L. Jurkowitz, "An Estimation of the Military Contribution to Human Capital," unpublished Ph.D. dissertation, Columbia University, 1968.

17. Elizabeth Waldman, "Viet Nam War Veterans—Transition to Civilian Life," *Monthly Labor Review* (November 1970), p. 23.

18. U.S. Bureau of the Budget, *A Survey of Socially and Economically Disadvantaged Vietnam Era Veterans* (Washington, D.C.: U.S. Government Printing Office, November 1969), pp. 24–25.

19. National Advisory Commission on Selective Service, *op. cit.*, p. 12.

20. U.S. Congress, House Committee on Armed Services, *Civilian Advisory Panel on Military Manpower Procurement,* House Document No. 374, 90th Cong., 2d Sess. (Washington, D.C.: U.S. Government Printing Office, 1968), p. 24.

21. *Report of the President's Commission on an All-Volunteer Armed Force,* (Washington, D.C.: U.S. Government Printing Office, 1970), pp. 9–10.

22. Walter Y. Oi, "The Economic Cost of the Draft," *American Economic Review* (May 1967), pp. 39–62; and Harry Gilman, "The Supply of Labor to the Military: A Cross Sectional Analysis of First Term Reenlistment Rates in the Navy in Fiscal Year 1964," cited in Wool, *op. cit.,* p. 159.

23. James G. Miller III et al., *Why the Draft: The Case for a Volunteer Army* (Baltimore: Penguin, 1968), pp. 53–54.

24. Milton Friedman, "Symposium on the Volunteer Military," *Congressional Record* (daily edition), August 19, 1970, p. S13758.

25. Senator Mark Hatfield, *Congressional Record* (daily edition), August 20, 1970, p. S13795.

26. Harry J. Gilman, "Military Manpower Utilization," in Stephen Enke, ed., *Defense Management* (Englewood Cliffs, N.J.: Prentice-Hall, 1967), p. 264.

27. Civilian Advisory Panel on Military Manpower Procurement, *op. cit.,* p. 18.

28. Milton Friedman, "The Case for a Voluntary Army," *New Guard* (May 1967), pp. 12–17.

29. Peter Barnes, "All Volunteer Army? No—But Not the Present System Either," *The New Republic* (May 9, 1970), pp. 19–23.

30. Associated Press, "Armed Forces Lag on Retaining Men," *New York Times,* December 11, 1970.

Part IV
Remedial Manpower Programs

Chapter 16
The Emergence of Manpower Programs

Development and use of manpower resources has always been essential to economic production, but the term "manpower policy" came into use only in the 1960s. Its context was the emergence of programs designed to improve the employability and enhance the employment and earnings prospects of persons and groups suffering various disadvantages in competition for jobs.

Though the manpower policies of the 1960s contrasted sharply with the emphases of the previous two decades, they emerged in part as a reaction to the earlier policies. An exploration of the economic and social context from which the manpower programs of the 1960s evolved is essential to identifying their objectives and assessing their achievements.

HISTORICAL MANPOWER POLICIES

The dual issues toward which manpower policies have been addressed —the use of people as an economic resource and employment as a source of income for workers and their families—are far from new. However, most of the manpower effort prior to the last three decades was at the private, state, and local levels, and it is, therefore, difficult to trace. The national manifestations indicate the nature of the concerns. Manpower as an economic resource was a paramount consideration of slavery, immigration, the 1862 Morrill Act establishing land grant colleges and the 1917 Smith-Hughes Act which initiated federal funding of vocational education. Concern for the welfare of workers motivated, in part, the abolition of slavery and child labor and was—and is—the raison d'etre of wage-and-hour, safety, and income-maintenance legislation. Both concerns have been present throughout this century, fluctuating and alternating in priority, but in recent years the social-welfare orientation has been dominant.

Impact of the Great Depression

Of all the issues that might call forth policy action, the overwhelming influence on manpower policy has been unemployment. The depression of the 1930s was a traumatic experience, fomenting a sharp break with the past economic policies of most Western democracies, including the United States. Most of the U.S. innovations were short-run, such as the New Deal work relief programs, but some, like banking regulation and the Social Security Program were permanent reforms. The most lasting contribution of the depression was recognition that the insecurities of an industrial society imposed new public responsibilities, and that the economically insecure, when numerous enough, could bring about public action.

The impact of the Great Depression was similar in Western Europe and the United States, but their post-World War II manpower policies differed. In Europe as in the United States, maintaining full employment was accepted as a public responsibility. Western European nations attempted to achieve this goal through aggressive fiscal actions. When these proved inadequate, manpower policies designed to ease adjustment and increase labor-market efficiency were developed. Labor as an economic resource began to receive attention in Western Europe only as more advanced technology and labor shortages increased the demand for more highly trained manpower.

U.S. Employment Policy, 1946–1960

In contrast to the activist European manpower policies, the immediate postwar U.S. policies appeared to be a detour. The war required that attention be focused on the allocation of scarce manpower, but fear of a recurrence of serious unemployment was a constant policy goad. That fear was manifested in the Full Employment Bill of 1945, which in diluted form became the Employment Act of 1946. Through it, the federal government accepted the responsibility of maintaining "maximum employment, production and purchasing power," not "full employment." However, nearly two decades were to pass before there was any intensive effort to fulfill even that vague commitment. The postwar boom quieted fears of unemployment, while the frustration of the Korean conflict, following hard upon global war, brought demands for a recess from public exertion. There followed seven years during which other national concerns took priority over economic growth, and inflation, mild though it was, appeared to be a greater threat than unemployment.

In the massive unemployment of the 1930s, job creation had been almost the total concern. Little interest was shown in training people for jobs which did not exist. Historically, education had been considered important to democracy but not a federal responsibility. The federal role gradually changed in the postwar years, but at first this was for demographic rather than economic reasons as the schools were overwhelmed by a rising flood of children.

The GI Bill, passed in 1944, was one of the most far-reaching social decisions ever made in the United States. A quiet revolution was purchased as men whose backgrounds made higher education improbable were lifted into totally unexpected positions in life. However, manpower development was not a primary goal of the bill, and the education and training provisions must probably be listed as accidental by-products of a desire to repay veterans for their lost years—and to slow their return to the labor market.

While the main theme of postwar foreign policy became competition with communism, antiinflation dominated domestic policy. Russian development of nuclear weapons and her launching of the first satellite plunged us into a race to produce scientific and technical manpower, which was signaled by the National Defense Education Act of 1958. Emphasis did not return to welfare-oriented manpower policies until the early 1960s.

The Rebuilding of Consensus

The limited emphasis on employment and manpower policies between 1946 and 1960, indicates less a loss of interest than a loss of consensus. With each recession, rising concern over unemployment became apparent, but the periods were short-lived and affected few people. Legislation introduced to implement the Employment Act during the 1949 recession was forgotten when the downturn proved brief. The 1954 recession was marked by proposals for tax reduction, public works, and "depressed areas" legislation and by criticism of public inaction on unemployment. The proposals and criticisms were heard again in 1958; the results of that year's congressional elections indicated increasing support for government action.

UNEMPLOYMENT AS A POLICY ISSUE

One month after a new Administration took office in January 1961, unemployment climbed to 8.1 million persons, the highest number since before the war. Yet consensus that unemployment was a priority policy problem was just beginning to develop, and agreement was still lacking on the appropriate weapons to use. Each success in reducing unemployment only peeled away one layer to reveal a more intransigent employment problem beneath, leaving the search for solutions no less intense at the end of the 1960s than at the beginning—despite reduction of overall unemployment to the lowest point ever recorded by any substantial period of time in the absence of wages and price controls. But at least the feeling that ours were less adequate than European employment and manpower policies was gone. By the decade's end, it was doubtful that the United States had anything significant to learn from any other nation about manpower policy. How to reduce unemployment at will, it also knew, but not how to do so without inflation, the dilemma which led to deliberate re-creation of unemployment in 1970.

It later become evident that the paramount need in 1961 had been to increase the rate of economic growth. But that simple conclusion required a degree of economic and political sophistication not available in the Administration, Congress, or the country at large. The new President, no less than Congress, viewed unemployment as a local problem and shared the national fear of unbalanced federal budgets. The threat of a balance of payments deficit held monetary policy captive. The concept of "fiscal drag" as an explanation for the sluggishness which kept the economy from rebounding in the historically cyclical manner was available but not yet popularized. A tax structure introduced in wartime and appropriate during postwar adjustments was restraining economic growth by absorbing purchasing power in a period of rapid increases in the size of the labor force and in output per man hour.

The full implications of this "fiscal drag" were not to strike policy makers until the cyclical recovery failed to make substantial inroads on unemployment. The first official Kennedy Economic Report in 1962 defined full employment as a 4 percent unemployment rate and prophesied a 5 percent unemployment rate by the year's end.[1] The actual rate was 5.5 percent. The failure of a 17 percent increase in federal expenditures accompanied by a $2.5-billion investment tax credit to substantially decrease unemployment finally brought a presidential proposal for a major tax reduction in August 1962.

Because there had been no effective leadership from the Administration throughout 1961; the initiative for action against unemployment rested with Congress. Given the legislator's characteristic view of the national problem, the first weapons considered were a series of proposals already familiar from past debates and hearings—all directed at aiding particular constituents in particular communities.

THE AREA REDEVELOPMENT ACT (ARA)   First priority in 1961 went to Senator Paul Douglas' twice-vetoed depressed areas bill which sought to attract new industry to such areas by providing low-interest loans and grants for community facilities. Politics "dictated" that some of the largesse be funneled into each congressional district; thus funds were spread too thinly for them to have a significant effect, especially during a period of generally slack economic conditions. There was little motivation for business to move to depressed areas or for those businesses already there to expand. As a result, the mild federal incentives had no noticeable impact on general levels of employment in the nation or in target regions.

Accompanying the ARA was the Accelerated Public Works Act, essentially a localized reincarnation of the Public Works Administration of the 1930s. It financed the construction of community facilities in pockets of high unemployment. However, the jobs, which were filled largely by skilled workers, "disappeared" as soon as the federal funds were exhausted.

THE MANPOWER DEVELOPMENT AND TRAINING ACT (MDTA)   An important adjunct of the ARA was a modest ($14.5 million per year) program to retrain the unemployed into a ready-made labor force, which, it was hoped, would attract new employers to depressed areas. The retraining proposal had been aired during the ARA debates, and the Senate Special Committee on Unemployment Problems had recommended a national program unrestricted to depressed areas. The initial objective of the final legislation, the Manpower Development and Training Act (1962), was to retrain mature, experienced family heads who had been displaced by technological and economic change, while providing them with income to make the training possible.

The extensive bipartisan support MDTA enjoyed was based upon its ability to encompass the conflicting analyses and varied interests of a wide variety of adherents. Title I instructed the Secretary of Labor to "improve the adequacy of the Nation's manpower development efforts to meet foreseeable manpower needs and recommended needed adjustments . . ." and required an annual Manpower Report of the President analagous to his annual Economic Report.

Title II authorized a small-scale, federally financed, state-operated training program, primarily for unemployed but experienced adult workers. Local offices of the employment service could identify occupations with "reasonable expectations of employment" and unemployed workers in need of retraining. The local public schools could be reimbursed for use of their facilities to provide the necessary training, while the employment service paid subsistence allowances equivalent to the average unemployment compensation benefit in the state.

To Joseph S. Clark, the chief Senate sponsor of MDTA, the training title was primarily a national extension of a successful pre-ARA Pennsylvania program for training depressed-area residents for prospective employers. To Representative Elmer Holland, the chief House sponsor, it was a defense against automation, which he feared was making obsolete the skills of his Pennsylvania steelworker constituents. Representative Thomas B. Curtis, William McChesney Martin, chairman of the Federal Reserve Board, and ex-chairman of the Council of Economic Advisers (CEA) Arthur F. Burns, Martin's successor at the FRB, among others, looked upon

MDTA as a means of giving the unemployed skills to match what they believed to be widespread job vacancies. Some in the Labor Department had a longer-term interest in a program for the development of manpower resources. General economists, led by the CEA, viewed training as a helpful medium which would also generate increased spending.

YOUTH UNEMPLOYMENT—1963   The focus of congressional concern in 1961 had been depressed areas and the emphasis in 1962 had been on experienced workers; 1963 was the year for attacking youth unemployment. Unemployment among teenagers had also fallen slightly between 1961 and 1962, but it was still nearly 15 percent, and it was to rise again to over 17 percent during 1963. More important legislatively than the actual rate of unemployment was the publicity concerning the "social dynamite" of its concentration in the slums and the imminent flood of post-World War II babies, which would bring 40 percent more youth into the labor force in the 1960s than had entered during the 1950s.[2]

In 1959, Senator Hubert H. Humphrey had introduced and guided through the Senate by a narrow 47–45 vote a bill to establish a youth conservation corps modeled after the popular Civilian Conservation Corps (CCC) of the 1930s. Opposed by the Administration, the bill was killed by House inaction. With the advent of the Kennedy Administration in 1961, new versions of the Youth Employment Bill were submitted. A "home town youth corps," which also had a New Deal ancestor, the National Youth Administration (NYA), was proposed. Anticipating objections from the House Rules Committee, the Senate leadership awaited House action on the lower chamber's Education and Labor Committee version. The House Rules Committee killed the bill for the 87th Congress, but the Youth Employment Act become S.1 (H. R. 5131) in the 88th Congress. Because of widespread concern for youth employment and the enthusiastic support of conservation groups, S.1 passed the Senate early in 1963 by a 54–30 vote. However, the House Rules Committee, which was opposed to "welfare legislation" and integrated conservation camps, provide a graveyard for H. R. 5131.

In 1963, however, the "cause" triumphed with passage of MDTA amendments and of a new Vocational Education Act. MDTA became law in March 1962, but funds were not appropriated until August and the first training contracts were signed in September. Even with the limited number of training completions, many problems had become apparent. Only 5 percent of MDTA training allowances could be allocated to youth— who accounted for 28 percent of the nation's unemployed and nearly 25 percent of the first MDTA "class." In part because they were anxious to make a good initial showing, administrators focused on recruiting experienced workers and, hence, the undereducated were underrepresented among the first year's trainees. Representation by race and age, however, more closely corresponded to their proportion in the population.

Other factors contributed to the disproportionately small number of undereducated MDTA trainees. The Labor Department's Office of Manpower, Automation, and Training had interpreted the Act as a mandate to establish experimental and demonstration programs (E&D), which bypassed the whole multiagency, federal-state initiation and review process. Concentrating on youth and the "hard core" unemployed, these programs had turned up difficulties not yet uncovered by administrators of the regular program—notably that traditional training methods assumed a literacy level that substantial numbers of the unemployed lacked, and that training allowances were inadequate for many enrollees with family responsibilities.

MDTA was amended, again with widespread bipartisan support: Twenty-five percent of the trainees receiving allowances could be youth; the authorized training period was extended; the program was expanded to include basic education; and training allowances were liberalized. In addition, the House Special Subcommittee on Labor slipped in an authorization for $4 million to demonstrate the effectiveness of relocation allowances in reducing unemployment. The traditional reluctance of politicians to vote for the relocation of their constituents appeared to be breaking down under the weight of persistent unemployment.

The Vocational Education Act of 1963, like the depressed areas and retraining legislation, had both long- and short-run goals. Vocational education had been criticized for its alleged failure to change as old occupations declined and new ones emerged, for the quality of its teaching and the currency of its equipment, and for its neglect of disadvantaged members of society. The Smith-Hughes Act of 1917 had established fixed categories for federal assistance; subsequent legislation had merely added other categories. Partly as a result, vocational agriculture and home economics accounted for 54 percent of the expenditures and 63 percent of the students in federally supported vocational education in 1962. Mounting criticism during the 1950s and a growing emphasis on "liberal arts" education, were articulated by a committee on intergovernmental relations, which recommended cessation of all federal support to vocational education. The criticism remained intense, but by 1963 youth unemployment had swung a substantial body of opinion to the view that it was the obligation of the schools to supply each person leaving school with a salable skill.

ECONOMIC GROWTH AND JOB CREATION

These legislative efforts could be expected to have no effect on unemployment levels. After falling from 6.7 percent in 1961 to 5.5 percent in 1962, unemployment persisted at that rate during the following year. Failure to fall to 5 percent, as prophesied by the 1962 Economic Report, was a particularly bitter but educational pill for the Administration. The pressure to reduce unemployment was great but so was the commitment to "fiscal responsibility," and the relationship between the two was yet to be learned by policy makers.

A generation of economists had sought to convince the nation and its policy makers that federal budget deficits could be used to supplement the total demand for goods and services whenever private consumption, investment, and tax-financed public expenditures were inadequate to maintain the desired level of employment. However, a deliberate deficit had never been fostered to stabilize or expand the economy. In retrospect, the August 1962 decision to seek, for expansionary purposes, a tax cut designed to enlarge a deficit did not reflect any unusual degree of economic sophistication; but the success of the proposal was a high point in political persuasion.

The Administration, and particularly the Council of Economic Advisors (CEA), could rely on the argument that a deliberately fostered deficit would probably be smaller than the unintended deficit that would result from the decreased tax revenues and enlarged expenditure needs of a slack economy. It had the support of major business associations, traditionally conservative but now infiltrated by business school graduates. To convince voters that it was their economic duty to accept and spend the proceeds of a tax cut should not have been difficult. Yet defeat of fiscal orthodoxy came only after 18 months of persuasion, the persistence of unemployment, the death of one President and ascendancy of another with unusual knowledge of the legislative arts.

The effort to sell the new tax program was the occasion for an intense debate within the economics profession, which now appears to have borne unforeseen fruit. Labor market experts had argued since at least 1960 that "this unemployment was different." Unlike the "mass unemployment" of the 1930s, it was "class unemployment," concentrated by locality, race, age, education, industry, and occupation.[3] Accelerating technological change, primarily, was "twisting the demand for labor," destroying industries and occupations, isolating areas, and leaving little if any useful role for the underskilled and undereducated. Economists generally—and the CEA especially—anxious to allay any doubts of the efficacy of their tax cut nostrum, argued that the situation was not basically different from any past period of excessive unemployment. Unemployment always had a structure that concentrated it within certain areas and groups, but the structure was made of ice and would melt under the heat of increased demand.[4]

Despite the emotion that often accompanied the academic debate, the difference was not so much one of substance as one of judgment concerning the point at which structural rigidities would cease to yield to aggregate pressures within the limits imposed by the public's low tolerance for inflation. The structuralists expected the tax cut to generate demands for unavailable skilled and technical workers, thus preventing expansion of employment opportunities for the predominantly unskilled unemployed, and felt it would not lower unemployment below 5 percent. The CEA set 4 percent as the interim goal of aggregative approaches; to reduce unemployment below this level, structural tools would become necessary. Subsequent developments supported the CEA position, but debate on the issue accomplished two things: It focused public attention on the problems of competitively disadvantaged groups, and it helped foster the development of supplemental tools to continue the attack on structural problems at whatever point fiscal and monetary tools were thwarted by inflation.

The tax cut was designed to reduce 1964 income tax liabilities by $8.4 billion and those of 1965 by $14 billion. Its advertised goal was to reduce unemployment to 4 percent. The actual results demonstrated both the technical economic competence of its designers and the growing economic sophistication of Congress. Following the income tax cut in February 1964, the unemployment rate declined steadily to 5 percent in July, then fluctuated around that point for the remainder of the year. An accelerating rate of labor-force growth accompanied by continued high rates of productivity increase had caught up with the impetus of the tax cut and a new stimulus was required. By mid-1965, war expenditure, not tax reduction, had become the source of impetus.

The failure to achieve the 4 percent goal is attributable primarily to a change in one of the parameters upon which the technical judgments were based. As part of the political price of the tax cut, President Johnson restrained the administrative budget, and cut the budgetary increase for national income accounts to $1.4 billion for fiscal 1965, thus reducing the total anticipated spending impact.

Of both political and economic significance was the fact that tax reduction rather than expenditure increase was chosen as the economic stimulant. An increase in total spending, public and private, accelerates the rate of job creation. Tax reduction expands spending for private goods and services, whereas increased government spending creates more jobs in public employment. Both increase total employment, but affect different occupations and industries.

THE WAR ON POVERTY

Coincidence as much as any other factor explains why the initiative in manpower policy shifted to the Executive branch at the beginning of the Johnson Administration. (Of course, Congress retained—and in subsequent years exercised—its right to initiate policy.) The Labor Department had gained enough vested interest to begin requesting modification of existing programs, though advocacy of new ones was to come later. And the CEA had discovered a problem—income distribution—that could be attacked by manpower measures. Planning began in the CEA and the Bureau of the Budget in 1963, and an antipoverty program was endorsed by President Kennedy and by President Johnson upon assuming office. The resulting Economic Opportunity Act created a new agency, the Office of Economic Opportunity.

It was coincidence that unemployment was declining when the Johnson Administration launched the antipoverty campaign. Yet falling unemployment and concern for the poor were not unrelated. As employment problems first of experienced workers and then of youth were reduced by economic recovery, it became apparent that unemployment and povery were concentrated for reasons not necessarily directly connected to the labor market. At the same time, rising black militancy, which had begun with a quest for equal access to public facilities was swinging to demands for equal economic opportunity and equal results. As President Kennedy had said in his Civil Rights Message in 1963, "Employment opportunities play a major role in determining whether civil rights are meaningful. There is little value in a Negro's obtaining the right to be admitted to hotels and restaurants if he has no cash in his pocket and no job."

The mood of the country was illustrated by passage of the 1964 Civil Rights Act, an accomplishment unparalleled in the history of U.S. race relations. Concern for equality of economic opportunity was reflected in Title VII, which forbids discrimination in employment by all private employers with more than a minimal number of employees. Recognition that more than racial prejudice stood in the way of satisfactory employment and income was indicated by the emphasis of the Economic Opportunity Act of 1964 on remedial education, training, and work experience.

Recollections of the New Deal explains in part, opposition to proposals that the government directly provide jobs for the unemployed. The Senate Subcommittee on Employment and Manpower, after extensive hearings, submitted a comprehensive series of recommendations, including a proposal that the Employment Act of 1946 be amended to fix 3 percent unemployment as the national employment goal and that the federal government adopt a fiscal model calling for, in addition to the pending 14 billion tax cut, increases of $5 billion per year in federal expenditures to achieve the employment goal by January 1968. Yet despite what was considerable political audacity for 1964, the subcommittee's liberal chairman only reluctantly risked the politically damaging criticism he was sure would greet the proposal that jobs be created for the hard-core unemployed in depressed areas and poverty-stricken communities.

The same distorted image of the shovel-leaning WPA worker also plagued the designers of the antipoverty program, which probably is more deserving of the accolade "legislative landmark of 1964" than the tax cut. True to the experimental spirit of the times, a decision was made that an antipoverty program was both objectively and politically desirable before thought was given to the techniques to be employed. The interagency task force assigned to design the new program had two guidelines: The program was to provide "rehabilitation instead of relief" and it must not cost much money. The challenge was to eliminate poverty with an expenditure of less than $1 billion in a year when the President was promising to hold the budget line as the political price of the tax cut.

Essentially, the antipoverty program was a combination of manpower programs aimed at employing or preparing for employment the employable poor, particularly youth. It offered nothing for the aged and no direct help for dependent children or their mothers—by far the majority of the poor. Head Start, added later by administrative decision, was the only preventive program. The others were all remedial in nature, designed for those already facing difficulties in the labor market. The local agency carrying the administrative burden of the proposed program—was to be the "community action" agency (CAA), a concept drawn from the experience of the Ford Foundation "gray areas" program and the President's Committee on Juvenile Delinquency, which had attempted to marshal community agencies in a concerted attack on youth problems. Substantively, the bulk of the antipoverty program was an enlarged and modified version of the Youth Employment Act, which advocated, in effect, a reinauguration of the National Youth Administration (NYA) and Civilian Conservation Corps (CCC) of the 1930s. The local youth employment title became the Neighborhood Youth Corps—largely at the insistence of the Labor Department, which was already tooled up to administer it—and the Youth Conservation Corps became the Job Corps Conservation Centers.

Defense Department representatives were involved in antipoverty planning because of the high proportions of youth rejected by the armed forces. A "civilianized" role was found for the Department: Surplus military facilities were to be used as Job Corps urban centers—in reality residential vocational schools. The interagency task force favored the urban centers; but the conservation lobby, its appetite whetted by the Youth Conservation Corps proposal of 1963, was not to be deprived of its share of the antipoverty action. The administrators of the new program concluded that the conservation centers could serve as a preparatory stage for those youth too limited educationally to absorb skill training.

Among the new departures unsuccessfully proposed by Labor Department members of the interagency task force was a major adult work relief program. The concept was still controversial, and the Labor Department participants had to be satisfied with assurance that Title V of the Economic Opportunity Act would be written permissively enough to encompass their proposal. Title V followed the orientation of the Title I youth programs in supplying an employment program for adults, but also like Title I it stressed the training value of experience and good work habits rather than the simpler virtue of earned income.

Title V had its origins in the Social Security Act amendments of 1962, which were the first products of the "rehabilitation, not relief" philosophy. The amendments authorized federal matching funds for aid to dependent children in families having an employable but unemployed family head. This innovation was made more palatable by a small-scale authorization for matching grants to employ those family heads in Community Work and Training programs. This program was enlarged, opened up to needy persons in addition to public assistance recipients, and added to the antipoverty package as the Work Experience and Training program. Also related to the employment orientation was an Adult Basic Education program, a pending college work-study program, and proposals for small business loans and loans to subsistence farmers.

Notable in the whole design of the antipoverty program was a reluctance to involve the two established agencies with the most related experience, the employment service and vocational education. Constantly striving to "improve their image" by reaching upward to serve more attractive groups, they lacked a reputation for willingness to serve the poor. Rather than reorienting the established institutions, the designers of the Economic Opportunity Act favored creating new ones. Thus, instead of amending MDTA, the Vocational Education Act, or other existing legislation, new programs designed especially to serve the poor were developed.

Education and Job Creation—1965

The amount of federal aid to higher education had been growing for two decades and was increased by the Higher Education Act of 1965. However, even more significant to manpower policy was the Elementary and Secondary Education Act of 1965, which provided special federal assistance for schools in poverty-stricken areas. A subterfuge had been found more than a decade earlier to justify general aid to elementary and secondary education—ostensibly to compensate for the impact of federal installations on local schools. Beyond that, proposals had always foundered on the issues of segregation and parochial schools. Yet by 1965, concern for the compensatory education needs of those bearing the triple burdens of deprived homes, neighborhood environments, and slum schools was sufficient to break those barriers, and in fiscal 1966 $2.4 billion was authorized.

The 1965 session also saw the lessons of the Area Redevelopment Act applied in the Public Works and Economic Development Act and the Appalachian Regional Development Act. Believing that the ARA's fatal mistake was spreading its efforts too thin in a politically inspired attempt to place at least one redevelopment project in every congressional district, the new depressed-areas program adopted a "growth center" philosophy, hoping to spark new growth and provide employment opportunities through more concentrated support.

While new programs were being introduced, old ones had been expanding. The Vocational Rehabilitation Administration had been established in 1920 to qualify the physically and mentally handicapped for productive employment. New legislation in 1965 authorized the tripling of federal support, and the definition of handicapped was broadened administratively to include impairment due to "vocational, educational, cultural, social, environmental, or other factors."

New responsibilities in the manpower programs were assigned to the United States Employment Service and its budget was expanded, though perhaps not commensurately with the added workload. As a result of their participation in most of the new programs and competition from community action and other agencies, the public employment services began to extend beyond traditional concern into outreach, training, job development, and supportive services for the disadvantaged. As a former director of the agency put it, the mission had changed from "screening out" to "screening in." [5]

But the only specific addition to manpower legislation in 1965 was a new program of minor size but greater potential significance. Gaylord Nelson (D–Wis.), a new member of the Senate Subcommittee on Employment and Manpower and previously a "conservation governor" in Wisconsin, took the Subcommittee's 1964 job-creation proposal and adapted it to provide jobs for adults in conservation and beautification. With the enthusiastic support of conservation groups, it was added to the Economic Opportunity Act, although the $10 million authorization was only a fraction of Nelson's initial proposal.

THE DECLINE OF CONSENSUS

In mid-1965, a rift appeared in the painfully rebuilt consensus against unemployment and poverty. Programs had been launched on a small scale but with promised expansion as administrative capability was developed. Congress was amenable to new ideas and was showing a willingness to modify legislation to adapt programs to experience. The 1964 tax cut had demonstrated the efficacy of the "new economics," so much so that advocates of expenditure increases resented the "reactionary Keynesianism" that seemed biased toward further tax reduction. The concept of "fiscal drag," had become well understood; an estimated $5–6 billion of surplus federal revenues would have to be returned to the spending stream to keep employment rising. Everyone had his pet proposal for getting rid of the embarrassing surplus, which, with a progressive tax structure, would prevent unemployment from falling to the long-pursued 4 percent goal.

Though the voters clearly preferred tax reduction to expenditure increase, advocates of the latter hoped that further tax cuts could be offered as a sop to the affluent, leaving the surplus for public needs and the poor. Some proposed a $5 billion federal tax rebate to the states. Others argued that because taxes for business had been cut in 1962 and for middle- and high-income taxpayers in 1964 and a $5 billion excise tax cut for well-to-do consumers had been proposed, methods should be found that would, in effect, give a tax cut to the poor who paid few taxes. The negative income tax was receiving serious discussion in the inner circles of government, when escalation in Vietnam dissipated the opportunities offered by the fiscal drag threat.

By February 1966, acceleration of economic growth had brought unemployment to the lowest point in 13 years. Inflationary pressures were threatening, demands to "cool off" the economy were widespread, and the financial pressures of war provided arguments for domestic frugality. The manpower programs were being challenged to show results; too often they could demonstrate little more than administrative chaos. All historical precedent would have suggested withdrawal from concern with unemployment. However, the awareness of structural problems, growing black unrest, and an inchoate constituency with a vested interest in the manpower and poverty programs were sufficient to prevent retreat. The issues of the subsequent years were thus a confusing kaleidoscope of criticism, frustration, and compassion.

The Impact of Economic Growth

The 1964 tax cut can be viewed as either a major triumph of the "new economics" in stimulating a sluggish economy or as a much belated removal of the hobbles of a wartime tax structure, which freed the economy's inherent buoyancy. Either way, the consequence was an impressive demonstration of the ability of a rapidly growing economy to create an environment of opportunity, even for the disadvantaged. The 1962 growth rate was adequate to offset the year's labor-force growth and productivity increases and still reduce unemployment to 5.5 percent. A slower growth rate during the next two years could no more than hold the ground gained in 1962. Without the tax cut, 1964's growth probably would have been closer to 3 percent, not the actual 4.5 percent, and unemployment would have risen back above the 6 percent level rather than falling to 5 percent by the end of the year. By December 1964, the outlook was less than sanguine. The economy was still growing faster than would have been the case without the tax cut, but even with that stimulation the growth rate was once again no higher than that required to offset labor-force growth and productivity increase. The new reality was that an economy with a historical growth rate of 3 percent a year, confronted with the effects of higher birth rates, more advanced technology, and improved education, would have to attain a growth rate in excess of 4 percent in most years just to keep the unemployment rate at a standstill. That it also meant the economy now had the capacity to grow faster was often overlooked in the pressures of the moment.

The CEA contented itself with saying that unemployment would be reduced no further during 1965 without greater stimulation, but others were less optimistic. The Administration's estimate of political realities dictated continued restraint on expenditure, thwarting the hopes of those who saw vast opportunities in the necessity to declare continuing "fiscal dividends" to offset the growth-inhibiting effects of the progressive tax structure. A $5 billion excise cut was proposed, but international developments supplied an alternative outlet. However, in view of subsequent claims, it is important to remember that, under deliberate fiscal stimulus, unemployment had worked its way steadily down to well below 4.5 percent before rising military expenditures took over as the major source of new job creation.

While the new manpower programs were still too small in scope to have a significant effect on the total problem of unemployment, rising demand was helping many who faced disadvantages in the competition for jobs. When economic growth lagged, employers absorbed the most attractive workers, leaving behind the unskilled, the undereducated, the inexperienced, and those who ran afoul of biases concerning race, national origin, or age. As growth accelerated, those groups who had been disproportionately burdened by unemployment obtained a greater than proportionate share of the new jobs. After all, the others were already employed, though they could move to the better of the new jobs, leaving the disadvantaged to compete for the less attractive ones.

Manpower Programs and the Price Level

After March 1964, when the tax cut became effective, unemployment fell 0.5 percent in three months, but there was no further reduction during the last half of 1964. Then with the excise tax cut followed by the escalation in South Vietnam, the level of unemployment declined another 0.5 percent during the first seven months of 1965, then plunged 0.8 percent during the next six months. The rapid growth, which treated so favorably those who had suffered most from stagnation, also accelerated the slow upward drift of prices. In doing so, it brought into stark conflict the interests of those whose welfare depended upon the final increments of job creation and those, both rich and poor, to whom price stability carried a higher priority.

It was, on logical grounds, difficult to defend training and other manpower programs as weapons against unemployment in the short run. The programs could not create jobs, though they might speed the filling of existing ones. Individuals could be helped by improving their competitive position, but it had been feared that they obtained jobs at the expense of those who otherwise would have obtained them. A more defensible argument was that only increases in total expenditures, public and private, could create new jobs. However, the expenditure route could be followed only so far before tight product and labor markets would encourage price and wage increases beyond those the public would accept. The rational role for manpower programs in that case was to reduce the tradeoffs between high employment and price stability by providing needed skills, bridging geographical and information gaps, and matching men and jobs with a minimum of lost motion.

The results of 1965–1966 were disappointing. The magic 4 percent unemployment level had been last breached briefly in 1957, when the inflationary cost of relatively low unemployment had been a two-year jump of 4.7 percent in the consumer price index and 5.8 percent in wholesale prices. The inflationary impact of falling unemployment was even higher in 1967–70, despite the availability of manpower programs. It can be argued that the manpower programs were not ineffective as price-level restraints, but were merely too small in size for their accomplishments to be measurable against the aggregates of the economy and labor force. After all, total full-time enrollments in all manpower programs averaged less than 250,000 at any point in time out of a labor force of 75 million. The speed with which unemployment plunged between August 1965 and February 1966 might have produced even greater inflationary pressures in the absence of the manpower programs. A wartime decline in unemployment—when goods are produced for destruction rather than sale—may be inherently more inflationary than a peacetime decline. Yet food and services rather than industrial commodities provided the greatest initial impetus to the price level. Whatever the explanation, it was clear that no solution yet tried had contributed substantially to changing the tradeoff rates between price stability and employment.

EMPLOYING THE DISADVANTAGED

By 1966, the manpower programs had come full circle. Proven wrong were those who, in the early 1960s, had argued that enough jobs existed to absorb the unemployed if only they had or would acquire the requisite skills, were willing to work, or lived near the jobs. Others had blamed technological change for unemployment, saying that major portions of the labor force had been condemned to unemployability. Return to rapid growth had demonstrated the labor market's remarkable versatility at employing those previously "unemployable." But it also showed that providing jobs for all those "able, willing, and seeking to work" in the absence of wage and price controls was blocked by structural and institutional obstacles.

Prices were rising, federal budgets were under wartime pressures, and further reductions in general levels of unemployment were not politically feasible. Unemployment for married men was below 2 percent. Yet unemployment remained high for minority groups, particularly those in central-city slums and rural depressed areas. A special Labor Department survey conducted in 13 slum areas in the fall of 1966 found that unemployment averaged 3 times the national rate. Adding those holding part-time jobs but looking for full-time work, those working at very low wages, and the "discouraged workers"—those of working age not working and, for no apparent reason, failing to seek work—a "subemployment" rate averaging 34 percent was developed.

Until 1966, only the aggregate demand measures had been successful in reducing unemployment and poverty. Because that route was now politically exhausted, further reductions could be produced only by directly attacking the problems of those who were left out of the general prosperity. Training programs were attempting to enable those left behind to compete more effectively for existing jobs, though reluctance to raise program budgets was preventing a meaningful test of that approach. Relocation assistance was restricted to pilot projects.

Those still unable to find jobs, particularly blacks in the large city ghettos, were becoming more and more restive. Perhaps because blacks were becoming more politically conscious, perhaps out of frustration with the constant failure of highly touted "answers" to make any significant difference in their living conditions, perhaps from the temptations of prosperity just out of reach, civil disorders accelerated in the summers of 1965, 1966, and 1967. With intransigent problems and only limited budgets, it appeared necessary to concentrate efforts on those who were most disadvantaged in competing for jobs.

In the doing, a new hypothesis explaining unemployment and underemployment began to emerge. The initial assumption had been that, given an adequate supply of jobs, unemployment must signify shortcomings in the unemployed and could be remedied by training, basic education, and work experience programs. Title VII of the Civil Rights Act was an initial indication that perhaps the hiring system rather than the unemployed worker was actually at fault. As the concentration of unemployment and underemployment among minority groups, the undereducated, and other competitively disadvantaged workers persisted, though at lower rates, intervention in the hiring process began to rise to equal respectability with making the worker employable as a cure for manpower ills.

Public Service Employment

The Nelson Amendment to EOA, the Neighborhood Youth Corps, the Work Experience and Training program, and the Community Action Programs had already given some reality to the 1964 Clark subcommittee proposal for the creation of public jobs. During 1966, two more programs to provide public service jobs for the competitively disadvantaged were added to EOA. The next two years saw a shift to an even more "unthinkable" approach—public subsidies for private employers to encourage hiring the disadvantaged. Throughout these developments, the clash continued between the war-engendered pressures to withdraw from aggressive social programs and compassion for the poor and fear of rioting, which dictated continuation of antipoverty efforts.

The National Commission on Technology, Automation, and Economic Progress, appointed by the President to assess the impact on the economy of automation and technological change, had been in session throughout 1965. The Commission's educational task of assuring the country that inadequate economic growth, not technological change, was the basic cause of the persistent unemployment was eased by the rapid decline of the unemployment rate in the latter stage of the Commission's deliberations. At the same time, the Commission was disturbed, not so much by the rising pressures on the price level, as by the public reaction, which appeared to place a higher priority on restraining inflation than on further reducing unemployment.

The Commission endorsed efforts to reduce unemployment by increasing aggregate demand and ameliorating structural defects. But neither of these offered the promise of useful employment opportunities for all those able, willing, and seeking work—which the Commission took to be the obligation accepted by the federal government in the Employment Act of 1946. To approach fulfillment of that promise, the Commission thought it would be necessary to create jobs tailored to the abilities of those still left behind after the public's low tolerance for inflation had thwarted further progress through aggregate measures. In its February 1966 report, the Commission recommended that the federal government constitute itself as "employer of last resort, providing work for the 'hard-core unemployed' in useful community enterprises." [6]

Simultaneously, OEO staffers were developing a proposal for a public service employment program patterned after the Community Action Program (CAP) experience in employing the "indigenous" poor as subprofessional aides in the antipoverty program. A $60 million version of the proposal was subsequently submitted to Congress in March 1966 as part of the OEO proposals for amending the Economic Opportunity Act. Meanwhile, the Full Employment Steering Committee of the Democratic Study Group offered a combination of the two proposals. The chairman of the Steering Committee, James H. Scheuer (D–N.Y.) then introduced legislation based upon the proposal, which became the "New Careers" amendment to the Economic Opportunity Act. The money was to be used primarily to fund subprofessional jobs for the poor in public and nonprofit private institutions offering an upward ladder into "New Careers for the Poor." [7]

Simultaneously, New York Senators Robert Kennedy and Jacob Javits advocated a program to create private sector jobs in poverty-stricken urban areas. Senator Kennedy initially sought authority to use the indigenous poor in rebuilding central cities. Senator Javits had in mind a quasigovernmental corporation to involve private employers in hiring the poor. The result was neither, but a broadly written authorization for almost any activity that would develop employment opportunities in areas "specially impacted" with concentrations of poverty.

In 1965, almost anything had seemed possible, but in 1966, the rising demands of the Vietnamese war had put a damper on manpower and antipoverty legislation. Most economists were recommending tax increases to restrain an increasingly war-strained economy. The Administration was reluctant, perhaps because of the obscurity of the economic situation, perhaps because of the uncertainty of the potential impact on the 1966 congressional election. The key to the economic consequences was the prospective levels of defense expenditures. As the Defense Department budget was forecast, the case for a tax rise was not proven, but had the much larger actual expenditures been known, the case would have been clear to most professional economists. The antipoverty program became one of many victims sacrificed in attempts to restrain expenditures as a substitute for higher taxes.

However, despite widespread general criticism of the administration of the Economic Opportunity Act in general and the Job Corps and Community Action Programs in particular, no politician wanted to be against the antipoverty effort and therefore "for poverty." It was safer to be "for economy" but avoid substantive issues. As it developed, congressional battlelines formed entirely over the issue of authorizing a total of $1.75 billion or $2.5 billion for EOA in fiscal 1967. In the end, Congress authorized essentially the smaller amount, which the President had requested. With the debate focused on poverty and economy, the new program elements emerged without substantive discussion.

Subsidizing Private Employment

Rising military expenditures continued to dominate political priorities in 1967. The Administration had come to favor a tax increase, while a slight slackening of economic activity had created ambivalence among the economists. Significant increases in the manpower and antipoverty efforts were unlikely within the foreseeable future. Yet, dampening riots and cutting the remaining unemployment and poverty appeared to require increased concentration of effort.

Garnering nearly $100 million in unspent funds from existing fiscal 1967 budgets, the Secretary of Labor early in 1967 announced a Concentrated Employment Program (CEP). Nineteen cities and two rural areas (a twentieth city was added later) were asked in March to design proposals fundable by June 30 to focus an average of $5 million on selected target areas. JOBS NOW, a Chicago experimental and demonstration project, had achieved some success in recruiting members of youth gangs, putting them through a two-week orientation, and placing them with private employers with the continuing assistance of "job coaches." This was to be the focus of the CEP program, with placements divided equally between private jobs and public programs.

The antipoverty program appeared to be in real trouble in 1967. There had been no evidence of a significant impact on poverty. The Job Corps residential training program had proven very expensive. More important, the CAAs had become a focal point in many cities for organized opposition to the local political establishment. Domestic frugality to counter rising military budgets was even more popular. The fact that the EOA was renewed, without expansion but also without any reduction in the previous year's expenditures, was further evidence that the program was creating its own vested interests and was likely to endure.

A most significant part of the 1967 EOA was the support developed for a multibillion dollar proposal by Senator Joseph S. Clark of Pennsylvania and Representative James O'Hara of Michigan to make the federal government the employer of last resort. The Newark and Detroit riots of 1967 were still fresh in congressional minds. The notion that government had a responsibility to create jobs in the public sector for those the private sector failed to absorb seemed to have growing support in the country and in Congress. Had it not been for the adamant opposition of the Administration, some version of the supposedly radical proposal might have become law. The Johnson Administration found the notion of emergency public employment distasteful and expensive, however, and continued to emphasize involving private employers in training and employing the unemployed. In the spring of 1966, the Labor Department had announced its intention to focus 65 percent of the MDTA effort on training the disadvantaged. At the same time, the goal for on-the-job training was raised from a little over 25 to 50 percent of MDTA enrollments—in order to train more enrollees with the limited budget while at the same time making a direct connection between training and jobs. It was hoped that by reimbursing employers for the costs of on-the-job training they could be encouraged to hire disadvantaged workers. The emphasis of the Concentrated Employment Program on involvement of the private employer was a further move toward the same objectives.

In January 1968, the President announced in the State of the Union message his intention to reallocate funds from existing programs to subsidize jobs in private industry for 500,000 hard-core unemployed by mid-1971. A new program, Jobs Opportunities in the Business Sector (JOBS) to be promoted by a National Alliance of Businessmen (NAB), was to use the subsidy approach to persuade employers to hire and train the disadvantaged. Money would be obtained by deemphasizing preschool education, classroom skill training, and other programs. In appearances before the 1968 Democratic Platform Committee and in fiscal 1970 budget proposals, the Secretary of Labor reversed his previous stand and advocated a public service employment program. Nevertheless, the practice of the outgoing Democratic Administration and the rhetoric of the incoming Republican continued to emphasize government subsidies for the private employment of the disadvantaged.

A Revolt of the Industrial and Service Worker?

The Johnson Administration closed in a climate of ambivalence toward the manpower and antipoverty policies which had been the hallmark of its innovative years. Expenditures on programs to promote the employment and employability of persons with less than a college education increased tenfold between 1961 and 1969, and a thirteen-fold increase was projected for fiscal 1971 (Table 16–1). The new work and training programs introduced specifically to remedy the employment handicaps of those ill-prepared for successful job competition had expanded from nothing to approximately $2 billion per year; and with the expanded funding of vocational education, vocational rehabilitation, and the employment service, the total was above $3 billion a year in the early 1970s.

While widespread unrest underscored the urgency of employment problems in the slums, it also called the effectiveness of work and training programs into question. Despite rapid economic growth and years of effort and billions of dollars for programs to employ the disadvantaged, there were, the Labor Department estimated, some "11 million chronically poor people for whom employment could offer an escape route from poverty." [8] In many large cities, low-wage, low-prestige jobs were without takers and the quality of jobs was becoming more of an issue than the quantity.

Yet at the same time that minorities and the poor pressed for greater attention, resentment against rioting slum residents encouraged a "we've done too much for them already" backlash. Sympathy for the politically potent "over 65" population led to Social Security Act amendments in 1967, which substantially increased old age and survivors' insurance benefits. But proposed legislation to help public assistance recipients was stymied in Congress.

The number of recipients of federally aided public assistance rose from 6.1 million in 1961 to 11.3 million in 1970. Cash payments increased from $1.9 million to $7.6 million over the same period. Of this amount, the federal share in 1970 was 52 percent, with state and local governments contributing 37 percent and 11 percent, respectively. In addition, 930,000 persons received completely state-funded general assistance, a slight decline from 1961; however, money payments climbed from $351 million to $422 million. Of the recipients of federally aided public assistance in 1970, 16 percent were elderly poor, 8 percent blind or disabled, 50 percent dependent children, and 18 percent dependent children's mothers or disabled fathers. In only 26 states could the family of an unemployed but employable family head receive assistance. Only 105,000 families headed by an able-bodied employable male were receiving public assistance. Nevertheless, the conviction was widespread that most welfare recipients were chiselers who should and could be earning their own way.

Congress lashed out at the "malingerers" in the 1967 Social Security amendments by creating the Work Incentive program (WIN). Determined to reduce the burden upon working taxpayers, Congress dictated that all those over 16 years of age in families receiving public assistance who were not specifically excused for one reason or another were to be placed in jobs, trained for employment, or employed by public agencies. Day care centers and other supportive services were to be established so that mothers of small children could be trained. The appropriations committees were reluctant to fund the new amendments, because of the costs. They appropriated only $100 million to implement the new WIN program in fiscal

TABLE 16–1 *Federal Outlays for Manpower Programs, Fiscal 1961, 1964, 1966–1971 [a] (millions of dollars)*

PROGRAM	1961	1964	1966	1967	1968	1969	1970	(est.) 1971
TOTAL	$239	$537	$1,579	$1,889	$2,208	$2,289	$2,502	$3,187
Institutional Training								
MDTA Institutional	—	93	249	221	250	248	260	292
Job Corps	—	—	229	321	299	236	144	158
Concentrated Employment (CEP)	—	—	—	1	25	52	59	61
Work Incentive (WIN)	—	—	—	—	—	25	71	112
Social Services and Education	—	—	12	17	24	34	50	62
On-the-Job Training								
Jobs in the Business Sector	—	—	—	—	5	42	86	167
Jobs Optional	—	5	27	53	69	65	50	52
Public Service Careers	—	—	—	—	—	—	—	30
New Careers (PSC & CEP)	—	—	—	—	13	17	17	18
WIN and CEP-OJT	—	—	—	—	3	7	6	7
Work Experience and Work Support								
Neighborhood Youth Corps	—	—	241	253	341	287	306	345
In-School and Summer	—	—	178	126	198	182	208	236
Out-of-School	—	—	63	127	143	106	98	109
Concentrated Employment	—	—	—	—	27	56	70	73

Operation Mainstream	—	—	10	9	31	37	42	50
Work Experience and Training	—	—	76	120	98	26	1	—
Foster Grandparents	—	—	5	6	8	8	8	9
Work Incentive	—	—	—	—	—	1	2	4
PSC-STEP	—	—	—	—	—	—	—	49
Job Placement and Support								
Employment Service Operations	126	181	249	276	294	293	325	344
CAA Outreach	—	—	12	13	16	22	21	22
Child Care and Social Services	—	—	3	3	24	59	108	214
Computerized Job Placement	—	—	—	—	—	5	6	26
Administration, Research, and Support								
Administration	4	8	47	56	63	73	72	82
Research	—	2	3	4	5	5	7	6
Experimental and Demonstration	—	7	6	32	26	23	19	22
Technical Assis. & State & Local Planning	—	—	1	1	2	10	11	22
Labor Market Information	—	—	21	22	26	30	32	38
Evaluation	—	—	—	—	1	4	2	6
Vocational Education	55	157	234	266	265	260	286	383
Vocational Rehabilitation	54	84	154	215	293	363	441	533

[a] Includes only outlays by the Departments of Labor and Health, Education, and Welfare and the OEO.
NOTE: Details may not add to totals because of rounding.
SOURCE: U.S. Office of Management and Budget.

1969; even so, outlays for WIN amounted to only $27 million in fiscal 1969, $75 million in fiscal 1970, and about $123 million in fiscal 1971. Spending priorities within these limited funds softened the impact of the harsh Congressional strictures. However, the 1967 Social Security amendments provided the foundation for the Nixon Administration's startlingly innovative antipoverty proposal, the 1969 Family Assistance Plan (FAP), which would guarantee minimum incomes to both the working and nonworking poor.

Employing the disadvantaged was not the sum and substance of manpower policy, however. The same 90th Congress that agonized over continuing antipoverty efforts found no difficulty in legislating threefold increases in the authorizations for vocational education and vocational rehabilitation, established programs with predominately lower-middle and middle-class constituencies. Not whether the nation should continue policies to develop and employ manpower resources but who should have priority seemed to be the question.

NIXON ADMINISTRATION PROPOSALS

In the final years of the Johnson Administration, Secretary of Labor Willard Wirtz and his Assistant Secretary for Manpower, Stanley H. Ruttenberg, had sought to win jurisdiction over more of the manpower programs and improve the functioning of their own Manpower Administration. Bringing their own empire under control seemed to require elimination of the Bureau of Employment Security, which, though a constituent part of the Labor Department, had its own independent power base in the Interstate Conference of Employment Security Agencies and its own direct access to congressional appropriations committees. After several years of maneuvering, they set out to accomplish the desired reorganization, but were undercut by the President, who was irked by Wirtz's public criticism of Vietnam policies.[9] President Nixon's first Secretary, George P. Shultz, and his Assistant Secretary of Manpower, Arnold Weber, consulting all relevant parties, took advantage of the limbo in which the reorganization was left and promulgated the long-sought reforms.

Explorations in 1968 on behalf of the National Conference of Governors expressed concern that all communities were treated alike by national policies and that enrollees had to adapt to programs rather than the program adopting to the enrollee. Consequent suggestions included decentralization of the manpower programs, giving more authority to governors and mayors, replacing categorical programs with a functional approach, and allowing adaptation of manpower services to community conditions and individual need. As chairman of a preelection and preinauguration advisory task force, Shultz had endorsed the concept. Representatives William Steiger of Wisconsin and James O'Hara of Michigan introduced legislation for decategorization and decentralization, and the Administration soon followed with its Manpower Training Act.

The campaign promise to eliminate the Job Corps was opposed by a solid front of private firms who had a vested interest in operating the centers. Transfer to the Labor Department, closing off enough centers to save $100 million in the proposed 1970 budget, and opening of some nonresidential "mini" Job Corps centers was the extent to which the commitment was filled. The Neighborhood Youth Corps program was later cut back, restricted to 16 and 17 year olds, and refocused from work experience to training. The 1968 congressional authorization for expansion of vocational rehabilitation and vocational education clashed with the need for federal restraint to check inflationary pressures—the consumer price level rose 4.7 percent in 1968, 6.1 percent in 1969, and 5.5 percent in 1970. In addition, Bureau of the Budget (now Office of Management and Budget) aides were doubtful of vocational education's ability to use the proposed funds effectively, and the search was on for dollars to be added to the NAB-JOBS program which the new Administration had endorsed. Congress defied the President by appropriating over $1 billion more for education than requested, more than a quarter of the increase being for vocational education, but was unable to override a veto. However, a replay of the scenario in 1970 did include an overridden veto. Despite the attempt to constrain the budget and some debate over where the money should go, the Nixon Administration proposed spending no less than the Johnson Administration had advocated for manpower programs.

The great surprise of President Nixon's domestic policy came in the public welfare area. For several years there had been agitation to replace the public assistance system—particularly its Aid to Families with Dependent Children component—with some form of guaranteed income. The program, it was charged, was unwieldy, niggardly, and capricious. Enforcing the means tests and assuring eligibility left caseworkers no time to act as professional social workers. In 1970, AFDC payments per person varied among the states from $12 to $82 per month, with an average payment of approximately $49. It was alleged that reluctance to allow families with an unemployed but employable family head to draw benefits contributed to family breakup. There was a new awareness that unemployment was not the major factor in poverty. In 1969, an estimated 1.4 million persons, including 1.1 million family heads with 4.2 million dependents, worked full time, full year, but remained poor.

Couching his proposal in conservative language promising "workfare rather than welfare," the President advocated a guaranteed minimum income for all families with children. Incentives to work would be included along with a WIN-like proposal for training and employment. Philosophically, the inauguration of a guaranteed income would be an event of major significance, perhaps equal to that of the original Social Security Act. Actually, however, the minimum welfare payment in most states already exceeded that proposed by the President. The immediately meaningful innovation was the recommendation that income supplements be granted the working poor. This new eligibility promised that the immediate result of the Family Assistance Plan (FAP) proposal would be rising rather than falling welfare rolls.

Even more surprising than the proposal, however, was its passage in the House by an overwhelming margin and the likelihood of Senate passage had the bill not been bottled up by the Senate Finance Committee, primarily because of opposition from the President's own party.

The President's proposals for administrative reform of manpower problems had little political sex appeal and came up for floor action only after, in an atmosphere of rising unemployment, substantial public service employment amendments were added. President Nixon vetoed the measure because Congress had failed to guarantee that the new public service job opportunities would not become a permanent work relief program. A new year and a new Congress saw (a) the legislators lose all interest in administrative reform and concentrate upon public service employment legislation; (b) the President both threaten to veto any public service employment bill emerging from the Democratic Congress and propose a considerable public service component for his reintroduced FAP bill; (c) the Administration suddenly reverse itself and accept a $1 billion public service employment bill as unemployment persisted at a high level and rose for veterans; and (d) the Administration carry the decentralization concept to its extreme by proposing a "no strings attached" special revenue sharing approach to manpower funds. Manpower moneys would be allocated to the cities and states by formula (described more thoroughly in Chapter 20) to be used at their discretion without federal direction or supervision, a proposal unlikely to win much congressional support.

Exciting ideas were being proposed, but political and philosophical differences between the Republican President and the Democratic Congress impeded action. The President was threatening to veto congressional recommendations; the Democrats were unwilling to endorse the Administration's proposals. There was to be neither retreat from manpower programs nor new initiatives either in the divided political environment.

One can only conclude that, like Social Security and compensatory fiscal policies, manpower programs designed to assist the disadvantaged are permanent aspects of the public policy scene. Certainly, the programs should be evaluated to ensure more effective performance.

NOTES

1. *Economic Report of the President, January 1962* (Washington, D.C.: U.S. Government Printing Office, 1962), p. 66.
2. National Committee for Children and Youth, *Social Dynamite*, Report of the Conference on Unemployed Out-of-School Youth in Urban Areas (Washington, D.C.: The Committee, 1961), p. 26.

3. John T. Dunlop, "Public Policy and Unemployment," in Special Committee on Unemployment Problems, U.S. Senate, 86th Cong., 2nd Sess., *Studies in Unemployment* (Washington, D.C.: U.S. Government Printing Office, 1960).

4. The opposing views are presented by Walter Heller and Charles Killingsworth in Garth L. Mangum, ed., *The Manpower Revolution* (New York: Doubleday, 1965), pp. 97–146.

5. Frank H. Cassell, *The Public Employment Service: Organization in Change* (Ann Arbor, Mich.: Academic Publications, 1968), p. 122.

6. *Technology and the American Economy,* Report of the National Commission on Technology, Automation, and Economic Progress (Washington, D.C.: U.S. Government Printing Office, 1966), pp. 35–37, 110.

7. Arthur Pearl and Frank Riessman, *New Careers for the Poor* (New York: Free Press, 1965).

8. U.S. Department of Labor, *Manpower Report of the President* (Washington, D.C.: U.S. Government Printing Office, January 1969), pp. 141–142.

9. Stanley H. Ruttenberg, assisted by Jocelyn Gutchess, *Manpower Challenge of the 1970s: Institutions and Social Change,* Policy Studies in Employment and Welfare No. 2 (Baltimore: Johns Hopkins, 1970), pp. 96–97.

Chapter 17
Skills
for the
Disadvantaged

The role of training in the manpower programs was shaped by three successive debates, each going to the causes as well as the cures of unemployment. Between 1961 and 1963, the dispute centered on the issue of structural unemployment vs. deficient aggregate demand with the MDTA and the 1964 tax cut as conflicting policy alternatives. Considering the haphazard way in which manpower programs pieced together, it is not surprising that the MDTA program to retain the unemployed emerged before fiscal and monetary policies were developed to create jobs for trainees. Although passed in early 1962, MDTA was just getting underway as economic growth accelerated in the spring of 1964. Skill training was the initial emphasis of MDTA, but it could easily have encompassed, with minor amendments, every manpower service function subsequently endorsed or legislated. The Job Corps, created in 1964 as part of the Economic Opportunity Act, shared the basic assumption of MDTA: If people had skills they could get jobs.

A second issue pitted remedial efforts in behalf of labor force members already in trouble against preventive training for the potentially disadvantaged not yet in the labor market. In 1962, MDTA represented the former approach and the Vocational Education Act of 1963 the latter. Then the manpower pendulum swung clearly to the remedial side with passage of the EOA in 1964.

The third debate hinged on whether institutional obstacles or individual deficiencies were the major blocks to employment. Congress and the

Administration tended to move in divergent directions on this question. For instance, the Concentrated Employment Program (CEP) drew funds away from MDTA institutional training. The NAB-JOBS program launched in 1968 assumed that the hiring system, not the unemployed was responsible for joblessness. Additional funds were reallocated from skill training to subsidized employment to reduce employer reluctance to hire the disadvantaged.

Congress, however, elected to express continued support of MDTA in 1968, and directed that MDTA skills centers be used in any skill-training activities undertaken. Congress also demonstrated major concern for preventive efforts by authorizing unprecedented appropriations for vocational education, a declaration of faith in that institution neither the Johnson nor the Nixon Administrations were willing to endorse.

In this chapter, we shall first review the changing emphases of MDTA and discuss the results of its two major components, institutional and on-the-job training. We then discuss the early administration of the other major remedial training program, the Job Corps, and the response made to the intense criticisms of it. The chapter briefly treats the Adult Basic Education program, and concludes with an assessment of the current state of training policy.

THE MANPOWER DEVELOPMENT
AND TRAINING PROGRAM

Appropriate to the employment problems of greatest concern in 1961 and 1962, the Manpower Development and Training program was originally designed to supply experienced family heads with skills to replace those made obsolete by economic and technological change. As a slowly expanding economy provided new jobs for these workers, however, attention shifted to the rising unemployment rates among youth. The addition of basic education to MDTA's remedial tools in 1963 indicated a growing concern with those who would encounter difficulty in finding satisfactory jobs even at relatively high rates of economic activity. By 1966, the primary emphasis was clearly entry-level skills for those experiencing serious disadvantages in competing for jobs. Diversion of MTDA funds to CEP in 1967 and to the NAB-JOBS program in 1968 marked the decline of skill training as a tool of manpower programs.

The original skill-training objective posed a conceptual problem which nagged the program from the beginning. Though a better trained labor force might encourage economic development and growth in the long run, training people would not create jobs. In the tight labor markets which prevailed between 1966 and 1969, the labor shortages were of two types: (a) jobs requiring substantial training or skill and (b) unattractive, high-turnover, low-wage, unskilled jobs. After 1965, MDTA training could be extended up to 104 weeks, bringing the first category within reach; but limited budgets dictated courses with entry-level jobs for larger numbers as the objective.

One could argue from the beginning that, regardless of the availability of jobs, everyone deserved a reasonable chance to compete. The dilemma was resolved as attention shifted to the competitively disadvantaged—those who were still unemployed despite high levels of economic activity. It became the declared policy to lift them to competitive levels, even, by implication, if the effort were detrimental to the employment prospects of the better prepared. But while emphasis on the disadvantaged justified MDTA training, it also raised doubts about its effectiveness. The disadvantaged trainee, restricted by such barriers as racial discrimination or poor transportation, might only be supplied with a skill that was a "hunting license" to seek a nonexisting job.

Employing the Unemployed

Once emphasis was placed on the disadvantaged, MDTA could be evaluated by its ability to bring about the employment of those who otherwise would have remained unemployed, rather than its effect in reducing the overall rate of unemployment. The first test of the program's accomplishments is the extent to which its participants found themselves more adequately employed than they would have been in the absence of the program. Closely related is the need to assure that those enrolled are significantly more in need of rehabilitative efforts than those who otherwise would have obtained the jobs. In effect, MDTA has been two programs in one. Between 1962 and 1970, two-thirds of the enrollees were trained in vocational training institutions; the remainder were trained on the job by employers who were reimbursed for their training costs. Because the characteristics of the trainees and their posttraining experience differ markedly for the two components, it is useful to consider them seperately.

Nearly a million persons enrolled in institutional training projects during the first eight years of MDTA, and about 70 percent completed training. When contacted during the first year after training, three of four were employed (data available only for 1967 showed that nine of ten had been employed at some time during the posttraining year).

The relevant question is not the extent to which MDTA completers were employed following training but the extent to which their posttraining experience was more favorable than it would have been in the absence of training. A dependable approach for determining the employment contribution of the MDTA program would be to compare the posttraining employment experience of those who completed the program with the experience of comparable control groups. Unfortunately, such studies have been few, fragmentary, and limited to the early years of the program. However, all found that MDTA completers suffered a disturbing amount of posttraining unemployment yet had substantially more stable employment and higher earnings than the control groups of nonenrollees and dropouts.

In the first years, when the act was aimed at experienced, unemployed adults, the program was deliberately "creaming." As labor markets tightened, institutional enrollments moved steadily in favor of most groups still burdened by high unemployment—the nonwhite, poorly educated, and underemployed. The nonwhite and those with 9 to 11 years of education have been more than proportionately represented in institutional training when compared to their numbers among the unemployed; those with 8 years of education or less and those aged 45 and over have been underrepresented.

Even with these trends, recruitment procedures tend to favor the most experienced and motivated among the disadvantaged. It is the responsibility of the employment service to identify unemployed or underemployed workers who need training and occupations in which there is a "reasonable expectation of employment," then contact state vocational education authorities to request establishment of a training course. Those who seek out the employment service for help are likely to be less disadvantaged than applicants at CAAs, which have played no role in MDTA, and applicants at CEPs, which have few MDTA slots available. Because applicants for any program usually exceed authorizations, outreach for MDTA has been a rarity. Even after the passage of the 1963 MDTA amendments authorizing basic education, verbally oriented tests and local employment service practices and policies continued to impede enrollment of persons with limited education. Basic education could be included, but it adds to the costs and reduces the number who could be enrolled. Hence it has been made available only to about 25 percent of the enrollees.

As might be expected, posttraining employment and unemployment rates vary widely by trainee characteristics. The percentage of nonwhites employed after completing training has been significantly lower than that of whites, even when controlled for age, education, occupation, and duration of pretraining unemployment. Similarly, trainees with 8 years or less of education experienced significantly higher unemployment than those with 12 years or more. Nonetheless, the most extensive follow-up study to date found employment gains by age, race, sex, and education, with females and whites benefiting more than males and nonwhites—but with gains roughly equal for all education groups and most age groups. Thus, as bad as the posttraining employment experience of some of the disadvantaged groups has been, their situation clearly would have been worse had they not been enrolled in MDTA.[1]

Nearly 500,000 persons had been enrolled in on-the-job training (OJT) through the end of fiscal 1970 and 81 percent had completed training. The lower dropout rate for OJT than for institutional training is understandable because to drop out of OJT involves either quitting or losing a job rather than simply withdrawing from training. When last contacted, 80 percent of those who had completed OJT under MDTA had either been retained by the contracting employers or had other jobs.

No controlled study has ever been made to assess the extent to which those employed through MDTA-OJT would have been employed in the absence of that program. The major analytical difficulty arises because MDTA support is available for OJT of current employees as well as for the unemployed. About one-third of OJT trainees have been underemployed rather than unemployed before training, and presumably most were already employed by the training employer. A second difficulty arises in determining whether in tightening labor markets MDTA-OJT results in a net increase in training and employment. There has been no administrative control over selection of those to be trained, or of those to receive the entry-level jobs assumed to be opened up by the upgrading effect of MDTA.

The OJT portion of MDTA was, until December 1967, administered by the Bureau of Apprenticeship and Training (BAT). In addition to making its own contacts with employers, the BAT used trade associations and community groups as prime contractors, who in turn subcontracted for OJT with employers. The difficulty of controlling enrollments under this administrative structure is indicated by the wide variation in the proportion of trainees drawn from the unemployed during 1965: 79 percent for contracts directly administered by BAT or state apprenticeship agencies, 43 percent for contracts with CAAs, and 25 percent under contracts supervised by trade association. Because an OJT trainee could be enrolled only if an employer was willing to hire and train him and because employers tended to be interested in obtaining the best help available, the enrollment of disadvantaged persons in OJT was inherently difficult.

Employment success in OJT means something quite different from success in the institutional programs. The institutional completer still has his greatest hurdle ahead: He must find a job. Once accepted, the OJT enrollee has surmounted that obstacle and retention is his goal. The nonwhite, the undereducated, and those at the age extremes have had a difficult time achieving OJT enrollment, but their retention rate has not been notably less than that of other groups. Because no comparison has been made of disadvantaged institutional and OJT enrollees, it is unclear which has been the most cost-effective approach to employment for this group. The presumption has been that neither has reached deeply into the disadvantaged but that institutional training has the best record. Suspicion that many of those in OJT would have been trained at the employer's expense in the absence of the program was partially responsible for replacing OJT with NAB-JOBS as the preferred way to use MDTA money on behalf of the disadvantaged.

Contributions to the Antipoverty Effort

MDTA's original target was the unemployed; later emphasis was on those who are *both* unemployed *and* poor. Because of the Act's original goals, family income was not considered a relevant statistic for the MDTA reporting system. According to earnings data from Old Age, Survivors, Disability, and Health Insurance (OASDHI) records of the family heads trained in 1966, 81 percent of institutional trainees and 50 percent of on-the-job trainees had reported earnings of less than $3,000 for the last full year before entering training. Other studies confirmed the tendency for MDTA enrollees to be drawn from groups with higher family incomes than most EOA programs', yet still below the poverty line.

A major difficulty of evaluating manpower programs is the unavailability of control groups to identify what might have happened to the enrollees in the absence of training. The MDTA success might be evaluated, in part, by its ability to raise low incomes. The majority of trainees had substantially higher earnings after training than would be expected on the basis of the mere passage of time. However, those with lower pretraining earnings have generally made the greatest gains. Individuals with higher pretraining earnings, who had substantial skills and seniority but had to start over in entry-level jobs after training, were still ahead after training, but the others had gained relatively more.

Available pre- and posttraining wage data indicate that the average participant has experienced wage gains in excess of those to have been expected from prevailing wage trends. Interestingly, whites and nonwhites, male and female have tended to make about the same average percentage gains even though there were substantial differences in their wage levels both before and after training. Yet even after experiencing substantial wage increases between the last pretraining and first posttraining job, few family heads would have escaped poverty. The median posttraining wage, though substantially above the pretraining one, was still insufficient even under full-time, full-year employment to bring any but a small family above the poverty line. Too many have been trained for low-paying jobs. Yet with limited budgets, the alternative would have been a longer and more costly training period for fewer trainees.

An important contribution of the Manpower Development and Training Act was the development of a new type of training institution. As the MDTA program began, few institutions had the competence or commitment to train disadvantaged people. Supportive services were needed which were not normally available in training institutions. Prevocational schools were filled with regular students during the day and were available for MDTA training only at night. The need for a separate institution dedicated to and having the facilities for providing skill training along with basic education and supportive services, was answered by the MDTA skills centers. Rather than focusing on a single occupation, multioccupation projects were developed offering a number of alternatives. Counselors were available to help with occupational choice and personal problems. A prevocational orientation period acquainted the trainee with the world of work and allowed him to try out various occupations before choosing one. Thus he was not obliged to make decisions on the basis of his limited experience and he was not shunted into one or another field on the basis of his performance on a culturally biased aptitude test.

Freed from many institutional constraints and focusing on an adult but predominately disadvantaged clientele, the skills centers have brought about a number of innovations. Enrollees learn job-hunting techniques, grooming, and other aspects of employability as well as skills. The relevance of basic education can be demonstrated because it is integrated into skill training. Training modules, occupational clusters, and training "ladders" are combined, providing a number of broad skill areas in which trainees can find the specific occupation that best suits them. Flexibility is also attained through open-entry/exit operation—students enter at frequent intervals and leave when they reach their training goal.

The typical skills centers have served a consistently more disadvantaged population than other representative MDTA projects in the same communities, as well as most other manpower programs. Skills centers have been successful in dealing with disadvantaged people largely because they provide counseling assistance and related services. It was found that matters often unrelated to training retard the trainee's progress. Counselors help the trainee identify problems and find solutions, often drawing upon such supportive services as medical, legal, day care, and financial aid. Techniques developed in these skills centers have often had a noticeable effect on practices on behalf of disadvantaged students in the public schools of the same areas.

However, these institutions are not without their problems. Skills centers and other MDTA projects tend, because the training is cheaper, to emphasize high-turnover occupations rather than those characterized by actual skill shortages. And because the tendency has been to locate in whatever building is available, the surroundings are often shabby compared with postsecondary schools in the same communities. Equipment that was adequate in the beginning has not been replaced and often suffers from depreciation or obsolescence.

Most serious of all, the separate centers originally established to serve the disadvantaged become marked over time as another form of segregated institution just for the disadvantaged. A new move, just getting underway, is to integrate MDTA skills centers into community colleges. The combination allows greater prestige, a mingling of manpower and regular students, and a broader selection of occupations; occasionally, motivating trainees to continue into regular enrollment.

The Future of MDTA

As nearly as can be determined, between 1962 and June 1970, the federal government invested $2 billion in the 1.5 million MDTA enrollees. MDTA has enjoyed bipartisan congressional support for its continuance but not for substantial increases in funding. Enrichment of the program's services has been authorized from time to time but without commensurate additions to its budget. In order to serve a larger number of trainees, basic education has been reduced and emphasis has shifted to limited skills requiring briefer training.

A debate continues between the Labor Department, which tends to champion OJT, and the Department of Health, Education, and Welfare and its public school allies, who prefer institutional training. Employment services also tend to prefer individual referral of MDTA enrollees to ongoing vocational programs while vocational educators seek the more permanent financial support typical of skills centers.

Unemployed persons (e.g., suburbanites) who lived where jobs existed and who lacked only skills profited quickly from MDTA enrollment. But those in central-city ghettos and rural depressed areas too often become only more skilled and still unemployed. OJT seemed unable to reach the disadvantaged. As a result, funds were diverted from institutional training to the CEP and JOBS program. MDTA skills-center enrollments fell far below their capacity because of lack of funds. Slackening labor markets in 1970 dissuaded employers from hiring the disadvantaged; hence, funds assigned to NAB-JOBS were not spent, and the pendulum swung back toward institutional training—which could not prepare the unemployed for jobs that did not exist, but could offer stipends while they used otherwise idle hours to prepare for a resurgence of job opportunities.

Philosophically, a disparity exists between the commitment of educational institutions to long-range preparation for a working career and the demands of the disadvantaged for an immediate job. The skills centers have demonstrated that most disadvantaged persons can be trained in the right environmental circumstances and, in terms of the benefits, at costs that are not excessive. However, because restrictions on per-capita expenditures limit preparation primarily to entry-level, semiskilled occupations, which the nondisadvantaged could obtain without training, they may also underutilize the potential of the disadvantaged. Though placement records are generally impressive compared with pretraining experience, the result has been to mix the "instant jobs" and long-range employment-preparation concepts to the advantage of neither. Attempts to couple institutional and on-the-job training—providing enough rudimentary training to make the individual attractive to an employer, then subsidizing his employment—foundered upon the distrust between the agencies and staffs involved.

Where jobs were plentiful, MDTA institutional projects were quite successful; but training by itself was not enough in the central city where most jobs were at two extremes—low-pay, dead-end jobs and white-collar and technical jobs requiring education and skills that could not be acquired in the 30 to 40 weeks of the typical MDTA courses. The alternative was to use up the full 104 weeks allowed under the law but to serve fewer people. Contracts with private employers encouraged recruitment of the disadvantaged, but employers offered only entry-level jobs with little training and these only when new hires were necessary. Because MDTA institutional projects provide training, while contracts witih private employers stress a direct job tie-in, the two programs are locked at two extremes, neither by itself meeting adequately the needs of the ghetto.

A number of fragmentary studies of particular MDTA projects in particular locations, along with calculations based on total program data, leave little doubt that the program has been a good economic investment. No other manpower program has a better substantiated claim to public support. The MDTA experience has also been valuable in demonstrating the need for better basic education and skill training as insurance against labor-market difficulties and a remedy for abortive school-to-work transitions.

Though MDTA has more to offer the "silent majority" among the lower middle class than have other manpower programs, funds were diverted from MDTA to programs that emphasized the disadvantaged. In the long run, the ghetto disadvantaged must be prepared for more than entry-level, semiskilled jobs. MDTA's future depends upon demonstrating its ability to assist all those needing remedial help and upgrading from where they are to where they have the potential ability to go.

THE JOB CORPS

The MDTA concept is appealingly simple—find open jobs and trainable people and match them. Vocational education's primary task is to train those still in school in occupations of their choice that are demanded by the labor market, thus preventing employment difficulties rather than remedying them. The Job Corps justification is more complex. Poor youth needing remedial education and skills could enroll in MDTA (as many have done) or in vocational education. However, vocational education has little provision for school dropouts, and postsecondary courses presuppose high-school graduation. The antipoverty planners—doubting the willingness and ability of either vocational education or the public employment services to serve their clients and wary of MDTA because of its involvement in both institutions—insisted on a training program of their own.

Origin and Objectives

The Job Corps was based on the premise that some young people were burdened by a home and community environment so negative that they could not be rehabilitated unless they were removed to a controlled situation. When first proposed the Job Corps was limited to men on the theory that they would be the future family heads; but Congresswoman Edith

Green of Oregon argued successfully that high unemployment rates, particularly for nonwhite teenage girls, justified inclusion of females. When female enrollments failed to come up to her expectations, she won a legislated requirement that they rise to half of total enrollments as soon as possible after 1967.

The Job Corps has been afflicted with many criticisms, but "creaming" has not been one of them; recruiters have generally been successful in finding the most disadvantaged trainees. In fiscal 1970, for example, only 7 percent had completed high school and 37 percent had not gone beyond the eighth grade. Mathematics and reading achievement averages below the sixth-grade level. Despite all-out efforts to avoid the eventuality, three out of five enrollees were black, with 16 and 17 year olds predominating. With some interviewees being rejected and a substantial portion of enrollees not showing up at the assigned training center, there was difficulty in filling quotas in the first two years, though increased efforts and restricted budgets kept enrollment and capacity in line thereafter. Altogether, one of every seven youths interviewed by the screening agencies ended up in the Job Corps, the vast majority either showed no interest in enrolling, were referred to other programs, or received no help at all.

The Job Corps originally chose to ignore the vocational education establishment, believing itself capable of innovative breakthroughs. But these were not achieved, and the instructors and methods were not appreciably different from those found in MDTA and vocational education. The use of business firms as contractors was thought to be a great innovation. While they did prove themselves more flexible and adept at getting facilities equipped and centers underway, they showed no greater ability or success at motivating and training youth. In fact, the center generally recognized as the most successful, the Gary Job Corps Center in Texas, is operated by an independent nonprofit corporation established by the state's educators. The private firms, by and large, have hired personnel from public education or industrial training divisions.

Costs and Benefits

In addition to complaints by local residents who lived near the urban centers, the Job Corps was continually criticized for high costs. The total annual cost per enrollee was more than $8,000 in fiscal 1967. Congress imposed statutory ceilings of $7,500 for 1967 and $6,900 for 1968, not including costs for national and regional overhead, recruitment and selection, or capital investment. The administrators had already taken steps to eliminate some of the more expensive training programs before the legislative ceilings were imposed, perhaps to the detriment of the quality and success of training. However, the increased emphasis on the more expensive women's centers offset downward cost trends.

Criticisms of Job Corps costs would likely have been temporary had it been shown that a one-time expenditure put a seriously disadvantaged youth on the road to successful employment and adequate earnings. Unfortunately, there was no clear demonstration of success. The Job Corps curriculum was designed to allow a youth to complete his course of training in nine months or less. However, dropouts were high and completers few. At the beginning, half the enrollees departed in less than two months. Retention rates improved over time, but the median stay never rose above six months. The length of stay was crucial because the measures of performance showed a clear relationship between it and success.

The accomplishments of the Job Corps can be measured in part by the enrollees' education and training achievements. Evidence on educational gains is conflicting. It appears that the Job Corps has not achieved any more rapid educational advancement than public school norms, but the enrollees' amount of gain has probably been more than they would have maintained in the public schools. The limited abilities of the trainees and the short enrollment period restricted training to the most basic of jobs. For these reasons, emphasis shifted from training for specific skills to programs oriented to developing work habits, improved attitudes, and entry-level preparation for a cluster of related skills.

Ultimately, the Job Corps, like any other skill training program, must defend itself on the basis of its trainees' subsequent employment experience. Surveys of employers have found them generally pleased with the training their Job-Corps-graduate employees had received. Studies in 1967 and 1969 of those who had left the centers 6 and 12 months earlier found around one-half to be working, one-tenth to one-eighth in school, 6 to 15 percent in the military, and one-third unemployed. However, the high unemployment was still from one-fifth to one-third lower than the pre-enrollment experience of the same corpsmen. Although aging may have had some influence, the fact that trainees who stayed in the program longer were more likely to use their training suggested a positive contribution from the enrollment.

Similar results were found for earning potential. Eighteen months after termination from the Corps, graduates' average hourly wages increased from the pre-Corps average of $1.24 to $2.12; for those who left in less than three months the gain was from $1.19 to $1.84. Whether the difference was accounted for by the training or by greater innate employability on the part of the more stable corpsmen was left to speculation. Whites did better than blacks and men did better than women. Differences between urban and conservation center corpsmen were minor.[2]

Conclusions from the Job Corps Experience

That the Job Corps enrolled a disadvantaged clientele was never in doubt. However, the premise that all trainees came from environments so negative that removal to a residential center was necessary was not proven;

nor was a method devised to identify the youth who could be trained only in a new environment. Foregoing the residential facilities, the youth probably could have been served under MDTA at a fraction the cost. Because experiences in the armed forces tend to support the validity of Job Corps operating costs, the question is not whether they were excessive but whether they were really worthwhile. A few youth have no homes at all. Beyond that, the only demonstrated need for residential facilities is for youth from areas of such scattered population that no meaningful nonresidential program can be mounted. The value of training youth at facilities averaging nearly 1,000 miles from their home communities, to which they will supposedly return, is questionable.

A good portion of the trainees left the Job Corps before completing the nine-month program. Those who stayed longer tended to profit from the experience. The administrators made it into an increasingly viable program, and the better centers developed new training materials and techniques for remedying the educational handicaps of a clearly disadvantaged population. Inability to show that these gains could not have been duplicated at lower costs was the Job Corps' critical weakness.

Administration Response

In response to widespread criticism and high costs, candidate Richard Nixon singled out for elimination only the Job Corps among manpower programs. Business firms functioning as Job Corps contractors had developed divisions and corporate officers with a vested interest in social programs and mounted a politically potent defense. Communities that had objected initially to Job Corps locations were anxious to retain Job Corps payrolls. The program was continued, but some change had to be made to satisfy campaign promises and to improve many questionable Job Corps practices.[3]

Job Corps operation was shifted in 1969 from the OEO to the Labor Department which acknowledged most of the criticisms leveled at the program. It closed about half of the 123 centers then in operation, reducing the enrollment which had stabilized at 34,000 by nearly half. However, the choice of how many and which to close seemed largely budgetary and political. An objective formula was developed to evaluate center performance, but data were insufficient and faulty, and the resulting rankings were ignored in several instances.

Considering the intense criticism of the program, the decision to continue it was more interesting than the fact than some centers were closed. The Labor Department's reorganization plan called for five separate types of Job Corps centers which would continue the bulk of the program. The first would be 4 men's and 12 women's "comprehensive regional residential skill training centers," primarily for youth from rural areas where equivalent training was unavailable. Second, 32 rural conservation centers would serve youths needing the most elementary education and skill training. Third, 10 near-city centers were planned which would provide only work-week residential services. Fourth, 12 small residences with no training facilities were planned for youth participating in other manpower programs who needed away-from-home residences with supportive services. The final type was an innovation, the urban "mini center"; 8 of these inner-city residential training centers were to be created to serve both residents and non-residents. One inner-city skills center was also retained under OEO. In all, 66 centers serving 24,500 Corpsmen were closed; 48 centers serving 18,081 remained open; and 30 new residential manpower centers, created to serve 5,000 Corpsmen, were to be opened. By the end of 1970, nine of the new centers had been opened and sites had been selected and contractors identified for 13 additional centers.

The residential needs of those from scattered rural areas and a limited number of urban youth are well documented. Residential vocational schools had been authorized by the 1963 and 1968 vocational education legislation but never funded. The Job Corps centers could partially meet this need. The addition of the new urban centers was more surprising in view of the widespread availability of underutilized MDTA skill centers to which residential facilities might have been added. Using several types of centers simultaneously, as provided for in the reorganization, should add to lessons learned from past operations. However, if enrollments in the Job Corps centers continue to be made on the basis of available openings rather than enrollee characteristics and need, the new structure will have little advantage over the old.

ADULT BASIC EDUCATION

With the increasing complexity of today's labor markets, workers without basic literacy skills bear a disproportionate share of unemployment and poverty. Though those with eight years or less of education comprise only one-fifth of the labor force, they account for three out of ten of the unemployed. In an attempt to improve this situation, the Adult Basic Education (ABE) program was developed, mainly for adults 18 and over who have had less than eight years of formal schooling.

The program originated in Title II-B of the Economic Opportunity Act, but it was subsequently transferred from OEO to the Office of Education and included as part of the 1966 Adult Education Act. Ninety percent of the financing of ABE projects comes from federal funds, with the other 10 percent originating from state and local jurisdictions. During 1970, approximately 544,000 persons received instruction through ABE programs administered largely through state departments of education at a federal cost of about $66 million.

Despite the fact that the legislation authorizing ABE gives employability as its intent, in practice there appears to be surprisingly little labor-market orientation. Only three in ten enrollees reported they enrolled in ABE to improve their vocational situation; 63 percent wanted "general self improvement." It is estimated that only 10,000 of the over 400,000 who completed ABE classes enrolled in manpower training courses. Though several other programs, particularly in MDTA, contain adult education components, there has been no meaningful coordination between them and ABE.

More reliable data are needed on the characteristics of and requirements for those who might benefit from basis education. No data are available on the content of ABE courses, the success of the courses in reaching individual students, and ABE graduates' utilization of their experiences. A portion of the budget has been spent on teacher training and experimentation and demonstration projects, both worthwhile activities. Remedial basic education is good in itself, but both congressional intent and potential economic benefits are being ignored because of the failure to tie it directly to preparation for employment.

A TRAINING POLICY?

Despite the experience of the programs discussed in this chapter, the country has not evolved an identifiable training policy. MDTA slipped from center stage as the emphasis shifted to the disadvantaged, for whom placement rates remained low. The MDTA institutional program lacked the direct linkage to employers often needed to give the underprivileged realistic access to a decent job. Never resolved was the choice between short-term training for entry-level jobs, available to most without any training, and the long-range technical level training contemplated by MDTA's unused 104-week training authorization. The Labor Department started with a bias against institutional training and HEW had reciprocal attitudes toward OJT. The funds diverted for CEP and NAB-JOBS prevented experimentation with more useful training directions and durations.

The Job Corps was unable to defend its higher residential costs against the example of appropriately located MDTA skills centers, retention being its critical weakness. It also demonstrated the inability of even determined policymakers to wipe out a program once in existence.

Vocational education may have filled the need in a simpler day when only a few needed formal job preparation. It provides far more skill training than any other source. However, as Chapter 9 has shown, vocational education has been slow to shift to the target populations of greatest concern during the 1970s. It has proven resistant to congressional directives for change. It equips many with skills, but the basic question of how best, below the college level, to prepare for employment has not been satisfactorily answered.

Most pick up their skills haphazardly and perhaps that is the least-cost way. It does not suffice to remedy the obstacles preventing the employment of the disadvantaged. But are they to be trained institutionally or on the job? Can they be placed in existing jobs, perhaps with a subsidy to the employer, or should public service jobs be created for them? Despite considerable training experience, there is no indication that a coherent training policy, remedial or preventive, is near.

NOTES

1. Earl D. Main, *A Nationwide Evaluation of MDTA Institutional Job Training Programs,* Report No. 118, National Opinion Research Center (Chicago: University of Chicago Press, October 1966).

2. Louis Harris and Associates, *A Survey of Ex-Job Corpsmen,* Sample Surveys 1968–1969 (mimeographed).

3. U.S. General Accounting Office, *Review of Economic Opportunity Programs,* a report to the Congress of the United States, prepared for the Senate Committee on Labor and Public Welfare and House Committee on Education and Labor, 91st Cong., 1st Sess. (Washington, D.C.: U.S. Government Printing Office, March 1969), pp. 50–67.

Chapter 18
Job
Creation
Programs

Throughout the 1960s the need for a general program of public service employment (or work relief) to create jobs for those not absorbed by the private sector was frequently, often heatedly, debated. No such general program was legislated, though several programs offered a limited amount of "work experience" in public agencies for selected age groups among the poor. It is not surprising that public service employment was advocated prior to 1965 or after mid-1970, when unemployment was either persistently high or rising. But the fact that it remained an issue between 1965 and early 1970—when, the unemployment rate was the lowest ever persistently recorded in the absence of wage and price controls—was one of the most significant manpower policy developments during the decade. An important shift in policy objectives had clearly occurred. The goal of the Employment Act of 1946 was a low (though undefined) general level of unemployment. During the 1960s, a new objective was adopted: the provision of acceptable employment opportunities for various disadvantaged groups. There are signs that the next search among escalating public policy objectives will be a satisfactory working career for each individual.

There were four phases in the expression of concern over job opportunities during the 1960s. Depressed areas legislation, the first foray into the New Frontier, was passed in 1961 but had actually been proposed six years earlier. With the economy just beginning to recover from the 1960 recession and unemployment the highest since the Great Depression, there was little hope of attracting companies already experiencing overcapacity to build new plants in depressed areas. Ultimately more than one-third of the nation's population, 1,061 areas, was made eligible for area development assistance, and thus funds were spread too thin for them to have a lasting effect. In fact, none of the depressed areas projects had a measurable impact on job creation, but they did contribute lessons for later programs.

From job creation in depressed areas, attention shifted to the general level of unemployment. The aggregate demand-structural rigidity arguments resulted in the use of both types of measures—notably the 1964 tax cut and the MDTA retraining programs for displaced but experienced workers. Economic growth following the tax cut demonstrated the overriding importance of aggregate demand. But it also revealed (a) groups of persons too undereducated and untrained to compete successfully for the growing number of jobs, (b) locations relatively untouched by improvements in the general economic environment, and (c) institutional obstacles between the new jobs and people who could have held them. Various work and training programs to aid these disadvantaged persons emerged as the third phase of concern for employment opportunity.

When consistently rising unemployment brought the problem of joblessness back into focus at the beginning of the 1960s, the federal government's most extensive experience lay in the emergency creation of public sector jobs. However, the unjustifiably bad reputation of the New Deal public works and work relief programs made the subject politically taboo throughout most of the decade. Nevertheless, the appeal of combining idle people and unmet public needs was so obvious that programs modeled on the earlier experiences began to creep in under the semantic guise of "work experience and training." Programs were introduced to provide direct public employment for the most disadvantaged, but they applied only to special groups and areas and only small sums of money were involved.

Use of the classification "work experience and training" rather than "job creation programs" reflected the view inherent in training programs that the critical obstacle was the individual's lack of the prerequisites of employability. However, the persistence of unemployment pockets and growing central-city unrest in 1967 and 1968 shifted attention to factors in the employment system that blocked access of the disadvantaged to available jobs. One answer was to subsidize private employers and thus reduce their reluctance to hire the disadvantaged by decreasing the costs or increasing the rewards for doing so. This approach was responsible, in part, for a negative reaction of employed blue-collar workers who resented increased competition for their jobs. Another step, development of business opportunities and entrepreneurship in the ghettos largely dissipated into political rhetoric by the second year of the Nixon Administration.

With unemployment rising again in 1970, the Nixon Administration inaugurated a small-scale public service careers program as a public sector equivalent of the subsidization of private employment under the JOBS program. The program sought to aid the disadvantaged to obtain merit system jobs by reallocating existing jobs rather than creating new ones. The Democratic Congress passed a substantial public sector job-creation proposal in 1970 which the President vetoed. Then, in 1970, with unemployment persisting at 6 percent and digging into the ranks of veterans and other politically potent groups, a $1 billion public service employment program became law. The President was at the same time pursuing his welfare reform bill, FAP, to which had been added a job-creation proposal which would undoubtedly prove to be at least of equal size.

WORK EXPERIENCE PROGRAMS
DURING THE 1960s AND 1970s

Despite the prevailing antipathy toward work relief programs, the combined enrollments in work experience and job-creation programs exceeded by a substantial margin the number of skill-training slots available in MDTA and the Job Corps. These programs suffered in comparison with those of the 1930s, however, in that little attention was given to the output of the enrollees. The programs of the 1960s were primarily concerned with income and employment. Thus, no one kept track of the work performed, and claims of useful work experience are unsubstantiated. This chapter reviews the experience of the Neighborhood Youth Corps, New Careers, Operation Mainstream, Special Impact, and the NAB-JOBS program. The Work Experience and Training program, now defunct, was the forerunner of the Work Incentive Program (WIN); it is discussed in Chapter 21.

The Neighborhood Youth Corps (NYC)

NYC was for some time one of the most popular of the EOA programs because it offered almost free labor to public and private nonprofit agencies for in-school, summer, and out-of-school projects. As employment and wages rose, however, fewer youths were interested in an unchallenging $1.25 to $1.40 an hour "slot" in a manpower project. Evaluators raised doubts about its efficacy, but its popularity with local sponsors was undiminished as long as they attracted enrollees. Project sponsors matched federal funds with 10 percent "in kind" facilities and services. The participants averaged about 12 hours a week for in-school programs, 28 hours for out-of-school programs, and 24 hours in summer programs. Age limits were 14–21 years for in-school and over 16 for out-of-school enrollees; all participants were to come from poor families.

NYC has suffered from an ambivalence of objectives. The in-school program is designed to help schools retain poor youth by providing them income and work experience. However, no overall data on retention are available and the results of fragmentary studies in individual schools are mixed. The out-of-school program has provided income and employment for poor youth, but it appears to have done nothing more for their employability than the passage of time would have accomplished. Extending employment opportunities to the greatest number dictated a "lean" program with a minimum of supportive services such as counseling, remedial education, and skill training. The summer program has been essentially riot insurance, though for this there need be no apology as long as society turns school-age children and teachers loose each summer to compete for an inadequate supply of jobs.

The quality of the NYC work experience apparently has been of little interest to federal legislators and administrators. Limited evidence suggests that it is easier to provide meaningful work for girls, who can be interspersed with other employees in clerical activities. Attractive jobs are more difficult to find for boys, who are more likely to be assigned in work gangs to maintenance, custodial, and cleanup activities. Federal administrators have developed no way of determining what is and what is not a valid margin for overhead costs of local sponsors.

As a result of high rate of turnover, a large number of youth have been served by NYC projects, perhaps as many as 500,000 per year. However, length of stay in NYC appears to have made little difference in whether "graduates" are employed, in school, in training, in the armed forces, unemployed, or out of the labor force. They are more employable after than before participation, but no more so than others of the same ages who did not enroll—giving rise to the view that NYC has served primarily as an "aging vat" during the difficult teenage years. The program offers income and activity to people who are unemployed and poor, but the significance of the experience is limited because some sponsors do not appear to use the "free labor" as efficiently as they might. Work experience and the opportunity to gain a few years in age and maturity may be worthwhile. However, it is reasonable to assume that basic remedial education and skill training, reinforced by the motivating influence of training allowances, are a better use of trainees' time and taxpayers' money. Basic education and even some skill training had been part of the original plan, but a commitment to enroll the maximum number possible precluded such "frills."

The shortcomings of NYC were well documented by 1969, when the incoming Nixon Administration had to decide whether to overhaul the program or scrap it. The budget was reduced severely, the age population served was narrowed, focus was shifted to the in-school program. Out-of-school enrollments were reduced and limited to 16- and 17-year-olds. New project standards placed greater emphasis on, first, return to school and, second, skill training. NYC was no longer to be a wage subsidy program—its stated goal now was to return dropouts to the classroom. The size of the NYC out-of-school enrollment would be tied not to community need but "to the number of jobs or opportunities for continued training in the community."

The interim program standards placed stringent limitations on the types of work experience allowable in an NYC program. For instance, the work experience component of out-of-school programs could fill no more than one-third of an enrollee's time. Trainees would receive not only a $1.60 hourly wage for work experience but also a "stipend for time spent in training and other supportive service activity." However, in no case could the gross training allowance exceed $25.60 a week, far lower than the existing payments which ranged up to $40 a week.

The decisions affecting the out-of-school component were criticized on several counts. If out-of-school NYC was inappropriate for 18–21-year-olds, why was it good for those 16 and 17? Why not enroll the 16- and 17-year-olds in other training programs rather than dilute what was originally a work experience program in order to maintain NYC as an entity? Returning dropouts to the classroom is a worthy ambition, but no effective blueprint currently exists for convincing them. Furthermore, the decision to assign the 18–21-year-olds to other manpower programs assumed that such programs existed in all the communities with NYC programs, an invalid assumption.

Equally critical is the question of supportive services. Do young people need treatment significantly different from that provided adults? Which is easier, to add youth services to an adult training or work program or to add training and subsidized employment to a youth program?

Pressures from enrollees and sponsors transformed the $26 a week stipend for the out-of-school and summer programs into a floor, with most trainees getting $30–$40 a week. The experience has demonstrated again that, although program changes and decreased budgets may debilitate them, manpower programs rarely are phased out once they develop a vested interest. Many local sponsors are concerned that changes in NYC may be a prelude to its demise and perhaps that of all youth-oriented federal manpower programs. By the early 1970s, out-of-school NYC budgets, which had peaked at $143 million for fiscal 1968, were holding at a little over $100 million a year. Even while consultants were trying to turn NYC into a comprehensive manpower program for youth, including basic education, skill training, on-the-job training, and subsidized public and private employment, the decentralization and special revenue-sharing proposals were threatening its continuance.

Operation Mainstream

Operation Mainstream, Senator Gaylord Nelson's 1965 amendment to the EOA, was at first a token rural work-relief program for older workers but was later brought partially into the urban setting as a holding station and outlet for the near-unemployable in the Concentrated Employment Program (CEP). After a little over a year of operations in OEO, most of the program was delegated to the Labor Department. Most Operation Mainstream projects became components of rural CEPs and many of the remainder are sponsored by CAAs as part of the urban CEPs. Little training or basic education is provided by these projects; and the work is primarily manual and unskilled cleanup-type activities on public property.

Nelson Amendment funds also financed two special programs—Green Thumb—for retired farmers, and Foster Grandparents, for elderly persons willing to spend time helping institutionalized children. Green Thumb is administered in 14 states under contract with the National Farmers' Union and in cooperation with state and county highway departments, city park departments, and similar local agencies. Services performed include community and highway beautification and park maintenance. The federal funds are used for wages and supervision, with 84 percent going for enrollee wages; states and localities provide equipment, shrubbery, and the like. The goal was to provide $1,500 per year to supplement the $700 average family income the Green Thumbers were receiving before entering the program.

For most CEPs, Operation Mainstream has functioned as an adult NYC, providing (a) income for needy people in all cases, (b) useful but low-level public services in most cases, and (c) some helpful work experience for a few enrollees. Community acceptance of Mainstream projects has been generally favorable because most of the work activities are highly visible and take place in rural areas where they can be easily identified. Turnover tends to be high, with Mainstream projects often used as a "parking place" for enrollees until a better training slot or a job is available. Because the adults are more accustomed to work discipline they are less likely than young people to profit from the limited work experience. Mainstream projects have been imaginatively used to "dry out" drunks and start a few drug users on the road to rehabilitation.

Operation Mainstream enrollees have been predominately male, with a median age of 45 years; the median family income has been less than $1,800; 63 percent have been family heads; 60 percent have been white; 25 percent black, and 15 percent Indians and other nonwhites. Over four-fifths of all Mainstream moneys have gone directly into enrollee wages. Nearly 90 percent of the enrollees have engaged in improvement or maintenance of community physical property.

The rhetoric of Operation Mainstream established two apparently contradictory goals: hiring chronically unemployed workers in community service jobs, and providing for upward mobility. It is not likely that the latter can be achieved because (a) Mainstream participants are older, (b) many of the projects are located in rural areas with few alternative employment opportunities, and (c) none of the projects provides work experiences particularly different from those the enrollees have had in the past. Mainstream projects have served as employers of last resort, generally paying minimum hourly rates to people with few if any viable alternatives.

Rhetoric aside, the direct-employment concept is a useful and straightforward one. The program has the unambiguous goal of expanding the total number of income-producing jobs available to those in need. But it must be noted that "Operation Mainstream" is a misleading label. Even in those few areas where it is currently operating, the program can assist less than 5 percent of those eligible for its services. Though funds are scarce and evidence is limited, the program does appear to be achieving modest objectives.

New Careers

In concept, New Careers is perhaps midway between pr grams that create new jobs for the disadvantaged and those that reallocate existing employment in their favor. Both types of program seek to cause new services to be provided and to relieve scarce and overworked professionals from tasks that less-skilled persons can accomplish—and in the process begin stepping up the ladder to semiprofessional careers.

The practice of using subprofessional aides began even before the passage in 1966 of the New Careers Amendment to the EOA. Interpreting EOA's directive for "maximum feasible participation" of the poor to pertain to staffing as well as planning, low-income persons have, from the start, been employed full or part time as so-called "nonprofessionals" in various community aspects of the poverty program—for example, as teachers aides in education and day-care activities; clerical aides; neighborhood aides who visit homes, bars, and other places to recruit persons eligible for available services; counseling aides; and employment aides who assist professionals in counseling, job development, and placement.

In response to both professional shortages and a desire to create better opportunities for the poor, the use of subprofessional aides has spread to other social service activities—for example, such aides work in programs funded by Title I of the Elementary and Secondary Education Act and Head Start. Generally, nonprofessionals have performed well, but the goal of devising career ladders has not been fulfilled. In many cases, those employed in education and the health services, the two large areas of subprofessional activity, are performing very low-level duties. The jobs of those employed by CAPs are, with few exceptions, dependent on the vagaries of community action budgets, and there rarely are analogous private or public jobs, which would allow lateral movement.

The New Careers amendment sought to build upon and institutionalize the indigenous-aide approach by offering subsidies and incentives to public employers—depending upon their willingness and ability to develop career ladders. In theory the new program was viewed by its designers as capable of solving two separate problems simultaneously: (a) a severe shortage of subprofessional support personnel in a variety of human service occupations; and (b) the employment needs of the poor. It was believed that the entry requirements for many professional and paraprofessional occupations were artificial—calculated more to protect the incumbents than to determine the qualifications actually required by new entrants. Hence, the new legislation was seen as a vehicle for basic labor market reform. It would eliminate "credentials traps" and, as noted previously, provide career ladders.

Nearly half of all New Careers projects under the EOA Act were established as part of the CEP. The rest were operated independently, mostly by CAAs (as were most CEP projects), which, in turn, delegated their operation to the actual "user" or employing agencies in the human services.

The Labor Department assumes responsibility for full support of New Careers trainees during their first year and supposedly funds only 50 percent of the support in the second year. At the end of two years' subsidized training, the "user" agency presumably hires the trainee on a permanent basis and pays his entire salary. This has not yet occurred because very few New Careerists have reached their third year, and in a few programs the Labor Department has continued to pay at least half the costs into the third year after the agencies claimed they were unable to afford the additional expense.

New Careers is, at its best, a training program for the "elite" of the poor. New Careerists are better educated when they enter the program than the enrollees of other manpower training programs; 40–50 percent of them had completed high school compared with less than 20 percent in Mainstream and less than 30 percent in the JOBS program. An estimated 70 percent are females, and at least one-third are divorced and separated. Some observers believe that the high proportion of women, divorcees, and high-school graduates indicates that many women enrollees are on a temporary downswing into poverty. These women, who do not lack innate ability, need only a "lift" out of poverty, not a long, complex, "dragged out" process.

The goal of providing better human services appears to have been abandoned, and employment with dignity is left as the sole objective. Health and education appeared to be the fields offering the largest job potential, but these have proven the most disappointing in terms of quality of employment. For instance, little progress has been made in establishing career ladders that enable nurses' aides or licensed practical nurses to become registered nurses without leaving the system for formal training.

Corrections and police departments have produced some, albeit few, of the most impressive successes. A California prison project is an example. Eighteen men, most without high school and from impoverished backgrounds and incarcerated for a variety of offenses, were carefully selected for their intelligence and their ability to speak and produce ideas. They were trained in group dynamics, interviewing skills, organizational strategies, and research procedures. After correctional agencies balked at employing them, they all became employed in career development and community organization activities spawned by OEO from Washington, D.C. to Los Angeles. The average salary of these men rose to more than $13,000 per year.

New Careers law enforcement projects were begun in Oakland, Richmond, and Los Angeles, California, drawing to a considerable degree on the experience of the original project. Low-income male enrollees work with youth in poor communities. The new start in life that these programs have given ex-convicts is, in nearly every case, the break they have needed. Whether there is a career ladder for them to pursue in the police department is not entirely relevant, for they can probably move to other jobs, gaining whatever self-confidence and education they need on the way.

Most New Careers projects share a number of common problems. Because the subprofessional concept is new, the process of developing such jobs is unfamiliar. It is the line of least resistance to assign menial tasks to the new employees rather than invest the imagination needed to carve out tasks not requiring professional training and combine them into challenging jobs. Even though the New Careerists are initially paid entirely from federal funds, their positions must be slotted into existing and notoriously low wage structures. Permanent jobs and career ladders are often hindered by merit systems and budgetary restraints. The training necessary to perform subprofessional jobs and advance has not been determined. The "failure syndromes" from the disadvantaged workers' past experiences are even greater obstacles in subprofessional than in manual and service work.

Professional protectionism and concern for the quality of public services are likely to limit the number of professional careers for the noncredentialed. There are obvious artificialities in professional requirements, but the fact that even the New Careers program tends to select only the best prepared among the poor suggests that many of them have elements of reality. Whether competence can be achieved through experience rather than formal education is not being tested. The same can be said for the feasibility of carving out new subprofessional tasks. What is being tested to a small degree is whether some disadvantaged people have sufficient ability and ambition to pursue formal educational degrees while employed on public service jobs. Credentialing requirements have not been reduced. Rather, enrollees are encouraged to seek the credentials or avoid them by taking lower-level assignments.

Despite initial difficulties, there have been real achievements, and many of the disadvantaged have shown latent talents. Some professionals have been freed for more challenging tasks; new services not previously available have been provided; barriers have been broken down between professionals and clients; and a few organizations have been motivated to rethink their selection requirements, hiring practices, job structures, personnel utilization, and client relationships. A formal New Careers "movement" has emerged. In fields not yet professionalized such as housing inspection, youth work, and community action components, New Careerists have quickly gained full status. As long as the federal government is willing to supply most of the supporting funds, it is likely that meaningful subprofessional positions can be made available to disadvantaged persons. However, a New Careers program meeting its designers' criteria depends upon professional acceptance, and institutionalization is probably years away. Certainly the concept is important and worth pursuing, and though plagued with obstacles thus far, it can come up to the exalted expectations which have made it a new religion with some.

SUBSIDIZING PRIVATE EMPLOYMENT

In the anxiety to provide jobs for those still unemployed or unsatisfactorily employed even in times of relatively low unemployment, an elemental economic fact of life was often overlooked: Jobs are created only by the spending of money for goods and services. Increasing the number of jobs requires increasing demand. Each of the programs described thus far in this chapter provided money to hire people to perform tasks that would otherwise have remained undone. Thus, unless sponsoring state and local agencies reduced other expenditures, the result was a net increase in the total number of jobs.

An alternative approach is to attempt to bring economic development to the ghettos and rural depressed areas and thus spark the growth of private sector jobs. The Area Redevelopment and Economic Development Acts were aimed at general rejuvenation of the nation's depressed regions and the Special Impact program focused on specific ghetto situations, but aid to minority capitalism proved to be more talk than action.

Another group of programs and policies, advertised as solutions to unemployment, were concerned only with supplying job opportunities to particular groups, not with increasing the total number of available jobs. Whether recognized by legislators and administrators or not, the justification had to be that those who would obtain the jobs were entitled to preferential treatment over those who would have held the jobs in the program's absence.

The failure of training programs to lead ghetto dwellers to acceptable jobs and the seeming inability of work-experience programs to change their employability, built up pressure for more general government intervention in the job market. One tool was to be federal subsidies for locating plants in ghettos; another, subsidies for direct hiring of disadvantaged persons. Commitment to direct hiring involved a large-scale program for private employment and a low-key effort to encourage hiring the disadvantaged as civil servants. Each of these offers more job opportunities to target locations and groups, but they do not create new jobs because they do not add to the total demand for goods and services.

When large and stable business firms were willing to establish plants in ghetto areas and give them a guaranteed market as suppliers to the parent firm, good and dependable jobs became available. Attempts to launch new businesses generally foundered on the lack of economic viability that had been impeding private entrepreneurship in the ghettos. Of course, large and permanent subsidies could have carried the firms, but often this would have required subsidization of opportunism and mismanagement. There have been heartening exceptions, and it can be argued that minorities and the poor also have the right to succeed or fail in self-employment. As a manpower solution to concentrated unemployment and under-employment, however, the "plants in the ghetto" approach has contributed little.

NAB-JOBS

The JOBS program emerged in the winter of 1967–1968 in response to growing concern that completion of job-training programs often offered ghetto residents only the shells with which to seek jobs that did not exist and to the fact that MDTA-OJT programs did not reach the disadvantaged. Perhaps the disadvantaged could be motivated by "instant jobs" after employers had been convinced to "hire first and train later," at government expense if necessary. Early in December 1967, the Labor Department announced the new concept, and in his January 1968 Manpower Message, President Johnson announced the Jobs in the Business Sector (JOBS) program which was to be promoted by the National Alliance of Businessmen (NAB). Prodded by the national NAB office, which was actively directed by a Ford Motor Company executive on leave, 50 local NAB offices, each staffed with business executives, sought signed pledges from private employers to hire the disadvantaged. The original goal was 500,000 jobs by June 1971, but in the blush of initial success this was raised to 614,000. The business response was a surprise to all but the most optimistic. There had been hope but no certain faith that, for a large enough subsidy, private employers would put the disadvantaged on their payrolls and provide needed training afterward. To the astonishment of many observers, two-thirds of the initial pledges were so called "freebies" (pledges to hire the disadvantaged without application for government reimbursement).

It soon became apparent that getting pledges was one thing, and that turning them into job orders and then into placements was another. Pledging employers had not been asked to specify the date of the intended hiring or the rates of pay and qualification of applicants. Employment service representatives discovered that some intended to fill the positions through their own recruiting efforts, or promised to do so at some time in the future. Others claimed they had already made good on their pledges but offered no evidence. Also disappointing was the fact that some public employment service agencies and CEP administrators were unable to fill NAB job orders because their outreach efforts were inadequate or because they were not trusted by members of the poverty community. Furthermore, many of the jobs offered had already been listed at employment services.

By the fall of 1968, job openings equaled less than one-third of the pledges, and placements were less than one-half of the openings. As soon as the deficiencies became obvious, the business executives assigned by their companies to run the national and local NAB offices began pressuring their employer constituents. The Labor Department sought better relations between the employment services and NAB. Establishing good relations with target groups was even more difficult; employers were reluctant to work through CEPs, and NAB metro directors had difficulty determining the appropriate contacts among the many self-proclaimed ghetto leaders. One of the most important lessons of this initial period was to count success in terms of people placed rather than jobs pledged. The realization that retention and upgrading were even more important soon followed from additional experience.

To qualify for government reimbursement, NAB-JOBS employers must hire workers who meet the standard Labor Department definitions of disadvantaged. The program's focus on minorities was minimized in public statements: Hired employees were described as being "subject to special obstacles to employment." Most workers hired were black. Employers who did not apply for federal subsidies were not subject to certification requirements; many of them apparently considered black and disadvantaged to be synonymous.

Enrollees under Labor Department contracts to reimburse the employers were somewhat more likely than nonsubsidized enrollees to be drawn from minority groups, to be poor, to have limited education, and to have suffered long-term unemployment. The requirement that a state employment service or CEP certify that subsidized employees conform to the criteria of disadvantaged makes those figures more dependable than those for noncontract employees which have no such certification. There has been no check of the validity of the claims of noncontract employers, and the sample reported is too small to be statistically dependable. Considering the tight labor markets that prevailed in the first two years of the program as well as the locations of many of the firms involved, it is difficult to know whether the proportion of disadvantaged among noncontract hires exceeded that which would have occurred without the program.

Contracting costs were based on employers' estimates, as restrained by the Labor Department's notions of an appropriate per-capita ceiling. Employers were to be reimbursed in equal monthly (usually twelve) installments, which were to cease if the employee quit or was fired and was not replaced by another disadvantaged worker. High starting costs would have to be recouped by the company during later months, creating "front-end loading" with a built-in incentive for retaining workers for the full contract period.

It is extremely difficult to determine what training is provided workers by the contracting employers, and it is impossible to do so for more than a scattering of noncontracting employers. A study of 178 firms involved in the NAB program (only 50 of them with more than six months' experience) found all to have altered their normal screening procedures and standards to favor NAB recruits.[1] Most had dropped aptitude testing or lowered qualifying scores. High-school diplomas were no longer a fixed prerequisite for blue-collar employment, but white-collar firms seemed reluctant to lower education and literacy requirements. Four of every five firms had altered previous standards regarding criminal records, though most firms continued to disqualify applicants for convictions involving arson and sexual or narcotics offenses. Most companies also bent their rules against hiring employees with garnishment and indebtedness records. Physical disability was the largest single cause of rejection, and few companies attempted to help remedy such defects.

One-third of the companies treated their NAB-JOBS employees no differently from any others. Six of every ten reported that they gave no special consideration to them once the training period was completed. Yet the 38 firms able to compare turnover of new employees with that of regular employees produced surprising results. In industries that had long hired large numbers of low-skilled minority workers, the application of the "hardcore" definition to recruits had no significant effect on turnover. The higher retention rate of the more formalized government-funded programs was impressive. However, only 4 percent of all the firms, contract and noncontract, reported any special efforts to upgrade the disadvantaged into better jobs. The most frequent reasons given for not doing so were seniority problems and the hostility of regular employees.

An Appraisal of NAB-JOBS

As with any public program, the key to evaluating the NAB-JOBS effort is to distinguish between the sponsors' rhetoric and reality. Once the wide margin between employer pledges and actual placements became apparent, both NAB and Labor Department officials, to their credit, shifted the emphasis to placement. The Labor Department claimed 620,300 job placements through December 31, 1970—430,000 noncontract and 190,300 covered by contracts. NAB reported that 43 percent of these 620,300 placements were still on the job at that date. Data on the number enrolled at a point in time who are still employed several months later have not been compiled or supplied. But in evaluating the NAB-JOBS retention rate, the typically high turnover in low-skilled entry-level jobs must be kept in mind. Only 55 percent of the total labor force is employed full time all year, and many of these workers undoubtedly change jobs in the process.

The experience of employers varied greatly according to their expectations. Those offering unskilled and semiskilled jobs and accustomed to hiring poorly educated and minority persons found little difference between the new employees and their traditional work forces. Those accustomed to hiring from a less disadvantaged population, particularly in white-collar work, found themselves plagued by absenteeism and tardiness and shocked by dress and language. Competence in performing duties and retention were less of a problem.

In many cases, the training of supervisors and fellow employees turned out to be more important than training the new recruits. "Sensitivity" training often was provided to help supervisors understand their new responsibilities. Working with the AFL-CIO, NAB developed a "buddy system" to involve the rank-and-file in aiding the new workers. However, the attitude of most national and local unions has been one of neutral but watchful waiting, in full awareness of the explosive internal political repercussions of any apparent favoritism to minority groups.

The speed with which national NAB officials, all on temporary loan from their jobs in industry, sold the program to the business community and got it under way was impressive. Their evangelistic fervor gained solid support from Labor Department officials and staff who carried the actual burden of administration, negotiation, and support at the national, regional, and local levels. As with most new voluntary organizations, local NAB efforts varied in effectiveness according to the ability, interest, and resources of the chairman and metro-director. In some cities, the programs never came to life because of an inactive chairman; in other places, the level of activity changed with the turnover of on-loan personnel. Cities experiencing the most success tended to those which one firm accepted major responsibility for promoting and underwriting the program. Occasionally, a consortium of firms provided a training facility that served all participants.

Proportionately few firms participated. In one city, even though the Chamber of Commerce assumed special responsibility for promoting the program, only 125 employers out of 7,000 (including 3,000 Chamber of Commerce members) made pledges. Perhaps predictably, the cooperating employers tended to be either the largest or most visible—public utilities and banks, for instance—or those with large demands for unskilled and semiskilled help. Automobile companies have been especially visible because they have so many relatively well-paid, semiskilled service jobs. Forty-five firms accounted for one-third of the money obligated under the 1,050 contracts during the first 18 months of the JOBS program. One automobile manufacturer accounted for one-fifth of the first year's placements.

A three-way controversy over minimum wage scales raged for some time among employers, the Labor Department, and ghetto leaders. The Department understandably refused to negotiate contracts for jobs paying less than the federal minimum, employers complained that any prevailing wage was legitimate, and ghetto spokesmen argued that a job without status and upward mobility is little better than no job at all. In fact, there was a definite pattern of minimum acceptable hourly wages ranging, in 1969, from $1.60 in Dallas to $2.50 in Seattle.

Only careful evaluation—including longitudinal follow-up studies and cross-program comparisons—can determine which route, skill training or subsidized employment, provides the better long-run employment and earnings record. Skill training could prepare workers for better initial jobs, whereas, subsidized employment offers primarily entry-level positions. In practice, however, few training programs have prepared the disadvantaged for other than entry-level jobs.

On the clearly positive side, JOBS has stimulated participating firms to reexamine their personnel policies. Though labor shortages undoubtedly lowered educational barriers, the NAB-JOBS experience has underscored the questionable relevance of educational credentials to job performance. Police records, once an absolute block to employment in many if not most firms, are increasingly applied selectively according to the nature of the crime and the job. Companies without training programs or with fragmented ones have been moved to establish coherent and centralized policies.

The apparent initial success of NAB-JOBS can be attributed to a combination of riot-born fears, presidential publicity, evangelism on the part of prestigious business leaders, growing sensitivity to human distress, and labor shortages. However, the program's "Achilles heel" was exposed as unemployment rose during 1970 and 1971. Memories of riots soon faded and President Nixon could not be as enthusiastic as President Johnson, who considered the program his "own." Employers who were obliged to lay off some workers could not hire the disadvantaged. Only one-third of the funds allocated to the program for fiscal 1970 could be spent because of the reluctance or inability of employers to become involved. Expenditures rose again the following year, not because there were more placements but because a higher proportion of the employer participants chose to accept reimbursement from the Labor Department. The program cannot create jobs; it only seeks to reallocate them in favor of the disadvantaged. That the effort continues when the times are so unfavorable to the approach is heartening evidence of business communities' increasing social commitment. That the impact has been no larger indicates that corporate considerations still have priority.

The program's emphasis will continue to shift with experience. Upgrading was added to the initial activities of "hire, train, and retain." The intense political criticism of the program in 1970 was perhaps to be expected with a Congress and a President of different political parties. However, it did uncover significant abuses, indicating that administrators under pressure to make a record had not always been selective enough about the nature of the jobs pledged or the approximate amount of reimbursement. In some places, NAB executives, impatient with the procedures and capabilities of local public agencies, argued for taking over outreach, recruiting, screening, and other public functions. In others, companies grew weary of the costs, individuals tired of the sidetracking of their careers, and the constant turnover of loaned personnel was unsettling. Some were tempted to seek government funding for permanent NAB staff. Instead, the tendency has been for more and more of the routine employer contacts to become the responsibility of the employment service. The ultimate resolutions of the issue will have a major impact on the nature of the program. The individual accepting a permanent public service post with little opportunity for advancement, even though on a private payroll, is very different from the ambitious business executive on the way up. Thus far, in general, NAB executives have been the salesmen, and civil servants the technicians; there is little evidence that either would be good at the other's role, yet there is evidence that the enthusiasm of loaned executives cannot be maintained.

Despite these adaptations and the Administration's continuing commitment to JOBS, the number of firms signing contracts on a case-by-case basis is bound to remain small. Separate negotiations and contracts with individual employers or employer associations do not lend themselves to massive enrollments, especially if monitoring is taken seriously. Winning by persuasion or requiring a commitment to reserve a definite proportion of jobs for the disadvantaged is probably the only route to large numbers. Smaller firms must become involved—and can through consortiums or partnerships of public agencies and businesses, the businesses offering the jobs and the agencies the training and other services small firms cannot provide. Small employers will want their employees "processed" before rather than after they come on the job, but this will not preclude tying a job guarantee to a training program.

Subsidized private employment is one more tool in the kit available for helping the competitively disadvantaged find their way into sustained labor market participation. It is no substitute for adequate preparation, nor is it a way to open the door to jobs requiring substantial skills. In the long run, the emphasis should be on improvements in education that would prepare ghetto youth for the good white-collar jobs that abound in central cities but that currently remain in the domain of qualified suburbanites. If the promise of education or training is to be believed by those made cynical by the failure of past commitments, a direct and observable tie to a job guarantee must be involved.

GUARANTEEING JOB OPPORTUNITIES?

The implication of the various efforts either to create or redistribute jobs for those not absorbed by the competitive job market brings a new meaning to the 1946 Employment Act: a guarantee of some type of job opportunity for all individuals able, willing, and seeking to work, in contrast to merely maintaining high general levels of employment. The critical handicap of every manpower program is the lack of available jobs at the end of every effort to increase employability. The quality of the job offered may be controlling for two groups: the young with limited financial commitments who put a high premium on prestige, and the welfare recipient with only a choice of accepting welfare or receiving a similar income from low-paid work. But for manpower programs, the choice is either to enroll all the persons the budget will support or to limit enrollment to the number of job opportunities that can be developed. Because the trainers are not responsible for placement, MDTA institutional projects and the Job Corps choose the former; CEPs rarely having training to offer, leaving work-experience programs and placement as the limited alternatives. WIN and the proposed Family Assistance Plan also confront this issue.

Absence of the right job at the right place at the right time for the disadvantaged job seeker has been the impetus for repeated congressional proposals for a major program of public-sector job creation. The concept is attractive: Public service needs are certainly going unfulfilled, often because the potential clients are poor and cannot pay for the services while taxpayers have chosen to do without them rather than pay their full costs. But if the taxpayers' alternative is to support dependent people in idleness, why not hire them to meet the public need? These programs have provided employment and incomes for the otherwise deprived but have suffered from a confusion in emphasis between providing jobs and providing public services.

Experience with current job-creation programs suggests caution. There is no satisfying evidence that the NYC in-school program has reduced the dropout rates of its participants significantly. The out-of-school and summer NYC programs have provided income and activity for poor and idle youth but nothing more lasting. Current plans to turn NYC into a comprehensive manpower program for youth may change its image, but that must be attested to by future evaluations. Operation Mainstream activities appear to have a favorable record, primarily because its objectives have been modest: income and useful activity for disadvantaged adults lacking better alternatives. New Careers is a difficult concept, and its payoff will be slow and limited, though positive. Special Impact moneys were used initially for other than job-creation purposes and its later efforts at ghetto economic development do not appear promising. MDTA-OJT has never been able to prove conclusively that its trainees were any different in characteristics and needs from those the employer would have hired in the absence of any subsidy. The NAB-JOBS experience has established that its objective of hiring the disadvantaged now and training later is desirable but that the appropriate mechanism for private employment of the disadvantaged has not yet been developed.

Job-creation programs have suffered three major shortcomings. First, they have concentrated primarily on youth, who need to be prepared for regular employment. NYC goals—of providing part-time employment to support school attendance, summer employment, and even emergency employment while awaiting training or a job—make sense for youth. But activities such as the NYC out-of-school program are preferable only to idleness. The Summer Youth Employment Campaigns have registered some success along the two lines open to them: (a) using federal dollars to purchase jobs for youth by putting them on the payrolls of public agencies or enrolling them in manpower programs, and (b) influencing employers to hire youth from disadvantaged backgrounds rather than those they otherwise would have hired. Beyond providing temporary work for needed immediate income, youth programs should concentrate on both institutional and on-the-job training efforts to increase long-time employability, and job-creation programs should concentrate on adult workers, especially on those living in areas where few alternatives exist.

The second major shortcoming is the consistent failure of the work-experience concept. Because most people have always learned their jobs on the job and then moved on to better ones, why so little improvement in employability? In an effort to maximize enrollment within budget limits, programs have lacked basic education and other employability measures. Work-experience projects consistently fail to impart a sense of the importance of production. Actually, the lack of useful work experience is probably best explained by the observation that neither administrators nor enrollees appear to consider the work stations as "real" jobs. As long as enrollment is regarded as an end itself, any possibility of useful work experience is thwarted.

The subsidized employment programs face two challenges: (a) insuring that those employed are more deserving of support than those who would have filled the same jobs in their absence, and (b) insuring that the jobs lead to a permanent gain in employability and employment. As is often the case, the administrative machinery for meeting these challenges has always been more in doubt than the validity of the concept.

The Public Service Careers (PSC) program to apply the NAB-JOBS concept to public sector jobs has received little emphasis. There has been a tendency to view public and private employment programs as sharply different with the latter obviously the more desirable. This is being recognized as a false dichotomy. The issue is not whether the employers are in the economy's private profit-making sector, private not-for-profit sector, or public sector. All are equally legitimate, all provide useful goods or services demanded by consumers, and all offer job opportunities which are expanding at varying rates. The realistic dichotomy is between orthodox competitive jobs, which exist for production's sake, and those specially created for employment's sake. The first set are those for which the consumers of the production are willing to pay the full cost. A private employer may be reimbursed for low productivity or training costs or perhaps only a payment to overcome his prejudices. Programs for hiring the disadvantaged in these jobs do not result in more than a marginal increase in total employment opportunities.

The PSC concept is to provide funds for training or other supportive services thus enabling agencies to hire disadvantaged persons without disturbing existing merit system arrangements. The effort deserves much more emphasis because many more artificial barriers exist in public than in private employment. Private employers are urged to "hire, train, and retain" the disadvantaged by federal government units that have not put their own houses in order. State and local governments are even more derelict. Merit systems designed to protect the public payroll against the political "spoils" system have also served to insure that those jobs go to those most capable of achieving high scores on formal examinations. Even if the tests are valid, this practice often leads to hiring overqualified employees, while denying opportunities in public service to those who have the potential ability but who rarely come to the top of a civil service exam roster.

Continued Congressional advocacy has finally achieved a program to create new jobs in the public sector, and not simply reallocate current ones as in JOBS or PSC. This Emergency Employment Act (EEA) contemplates funding only temporary state and local government hirings during periods of high unemployment, quite different from programs for those still left without jobs in high employment periods. Experience has shown that in the areas and for the people to which manpower programs are addressed the shortage of attractive jobs at rates above welfare benefits persists even in better times. It probably is impossible to avoid a make-work atmosphere in temporary emergency job creation. Experience would suggest expanding the number of "real" jobs in public agencies and reserving a certain percentage of them for the disadvantaged, rather than creating special programs with the job as the objective and none but the disadvantaged employed.

The experience with job-creation programs during the 1960s, added to that of the 1930s, has demonstrated that subsidized private jobs, economic development efforts, new careers-type jobs, and "last resort" public jobs are all legitimate tools for employing the disadvantaged under varying circumstances. The true economic justification for job-creation programs is that unmet needs are joined with idle but willing labor. Any productive use made of otherwise idle resources is a clear gain for the economy. If the programs have not satisfactorily answered the key question, "Is it possible and desirable to guarantee jobs so that no one able, willing, and seeking to work need be denied employment opportunities?" they have provided insights into some of the practical consequences of attempting to provide job opportunities for all persons.

NOTE

1. E. F. Shelley & Company, Inc., *Private Industry and the Disadvantaged,* prepared for the Urban Coalition (New York: The Company, 1969).

Chapter 19
The Role
of the Public
Employment Service

Lack of skills is not the only obstacle faced by individuals in competing for available jobs. Some lack knowledge about jobs or how to make contact with potential employers. Many live in depressed rural areas or inner-city slums and thus do not have access to the jobs available in the burgeoning suburbs. For others, the obstacle is prejudice against race or ethnic origin, age, or sex. As often as not, the handicaps are compounded one upon the other. And for a significant number, the problem is not lack of access to jobs or lack of skill but the absence of any jobs they can fill that would be more attractive to them than the various alternatives to work.

Scattered and diffused attacks have been made on each of these problems. The various manpower programs have broadened the measures available to the public employment service in pursuing its assignment of matching men and jobs. Relocation assistance has been a subject for experimentation, but it has not won legislative endorsement. Legislative proscriptions against job discrimination based on race, sex, and age have been imposed. The vocational rehabilitation program has demonstrated the value of a comprehensive effort centered around a one-to-one relationship between a handicapped client and a trained counselor. None of these devices has made major changes in the way labor markets work, but all are worth reviewing for the lessons they supply and the foundations they have provided for more intensive effort. Assuring equal employment opportunity is, in part, the subject of Chapter 25, and Chapter 27 reviews the experience with relocation of surplus workers. This chapter reviews the changing role of the public employment service.

THE ROLE AND GOALS OF THE PUBLIC EMPLOYMENT SERVICE

At the beginning of the 1960s, only two public institutions existed at the local level for administration of manpower programs: the public schools and the federally funded, state-operated employment services. Schools were involved only in the basic education and skill-training aspects of the manpower effort. The federal-state employment service was the only nationally available local manpower agency and offered the widest range of services.

Changing Objectives and Functions

Few institutions have been asked to change so much in so brief a period as the employment service system during the past decade. New functions have been assigned, new and often inconsistent goals have been set, and major shifts have occurred in the distribution of power within the system. Often these new assignments have not been related to existing employment service responsibilities, competence, or objectives. With its policies and practices rooted in legislation and fixed by tradition, its leaders' willingness to adjust to new goals and perform new tasks would be a major determinant of the system's success or failure.

The employment service's primary goal has been defined successively, as, first, to administer the work test for unemployment insurance claimants; then to act as a labor exchange providing employers with qualified workers; subsequently, to serve the entire community as a manpower center providing diverse information and services for present and prospective employers and employees; and, more recently, to give special priority to the employability and employment problems of the disadvantaged. In shifting gears to accomplish each new objective while meeting current demands, some parts of the system invariably have lagged several stages behind. Inevitably, these attempts to bring rapid changes in such a large institution have engendered frustration and ambiguity as to goals and functions.

A nationwide public employment service created during World War I all but died out during the 1920s. It was reestablished at the low point of the Great Depression with the Wagner-Peyser Act of 1933, whose broad charter provided "for the establishment of a national employment system and for cooperation with the states in promotion of such system." However, the permissive language of the legislation has been less influential in shaping the agency than has its sources of funding. The Wagner-Peyser Act provided federal matching funds for states as an incentive to establish employment services. The federal funds were drawn from general revenues. Twenty-four states picked up this option during the first two years. Whether more would have done so is not known because Title III of the Social Security Act of 1935 created a trust fund for the payment of unemployment compensation financed by a payroll tax. Because it was considered essential to insure that a claimant was "ready, willing, and able" to work, the employment service was assigned this "work test" responsibility, and funds were made available for its support from the proceeds of the payroll tax. The states could either establish and administer an employment service with 100 percent federal financing or lose the proceeds of the tax to other states.

During the 1930s, with few jobs available in private industry, the employment service was mainly an instrument for screening applicants for welfare and work relief projects. The system was barely operative when it was challenged by the manpower problems of the imminent war. Shortly after our entry into World War II, the state employment services were federalized and placed under the direction of the War Manpower Commission where they became a mechanism for allocation of scarce manpower. The prewar status was restored with the termination of hostilities, and the employment service became intimately involved in demobilization. To ease the adjustment of returning veterans, the employment service developed a six-point program—an effective placement service, employment counseling, special services to veterans, personnel management services, labor market analysis and information, and cooperation with community organizations and government agencies in community employment planning—which provided the goals that prevailed through the 1950s. It was also involved in the Korean War mobilization and adjustments.

Following those years of intensive activity, the employment service subsided into the "doldrums" that, in spite of the 1946 Employment Act commitment to full employment, characterized domestic manpower policy during the 1950s. Periodic recessions kept unemployment insurance claims loads high and resulted in the diversion of employment service staff and attention to the administration of unemployment insurance (UI). With no other specific assignment, it was not surprising that many local offices were content to process UI claims and passively match a limited number of employer job orders with available workers. Because unemployment insurance overshadowed other employment service activities, the growth of an "unemployment" office image was also to be expected. Economy drives were so successful that the 1960 budget was smaller than that for 1948. As budgets declined and staffing was cut back, a minimum staff was maintained in small town offices, imposing relatively greater cuts on metropolitan offices and amplifying an already existing small-town and rural bias.

This moribund state was noted in 1958 by Secretary of Labor James P. Mitchell in a speech to the Interstate Conference of Employment Security Agencies, an organization of state administrators. In a strong statement, he accused the employment service of failing adequately to maintain its role as a placement agency. He pointed out that not only had the employment service's volume of placements not kept pace with the nation's expanding labor force, but also that its regular nonagricultural placements had actually declined. His feeling that "the employment service stands or falls upon its main purpose, placement, and that all subsidiary activities fail when placement fails," led him to conclude that there had been "a steady decline in the activities of the employment service." Mitchell, and those providing the staff work upon which his criticisms were based, were disturbed not only by the limited extent of employment service involvement in the labor market but by its nature as well. They wanted to move from concentration on lower-level skills to involvement in the technical and professional fields which were also being emphasized by the schools.

The Mitchell speech was followed by plans for a resurgence of employment service activity but not by additional budgets to implement them. In addition to greater emphasis on white-collar and professional manpower, plans included enlarged staffs and better facilities, an improved public image, and a sharper separation between unemployment insurance and employment functions to remove the "unemployment office" stigma. However, new funds came only with a new Administration—and after policy emphasis had shifted. Thus, funds were provided to serve employers by finding them highly educated manpower and avoiding labor shortages for them at a time when public concern was shifting to the unemployed.

Presidential candidate Senator John F. Kennedy promised in a West Virginia campaign speech to improve the employment service. In his first economic message as President in February 1961, he directed "the Secretary of Labor to take the necessary steps to provide better service for unemployment insurance claimants and other job applicants registered with the United States Employment Service." The report of the Special Committee on Unemployment Problems and the discussions surrounding passage of the MDTA both appeared to assume that unemployed were mostly recipients of unemployment compensation. Subsequent experience was to identify target groups needing employment assistance for whom the unemployment assistance system was totally irrelevant.

The efforts to implement the President's declaration had broader implications, however, because they were developed as the result of planning in the Labor Department after the Mitchell speech and of work by several of President Kennedy's task forces. Funds were provided in fiscal 1962 for a substantial addition to employment service staff positions, which were allocated primarily to the major metropolitan areas. Previously, a workload and performance budget had encouraged minimizing the time spent with each client. The new procedure made funds available to the large cities at the expense of rural areas. In that sense, it put the money where it was needed; but having no performance measures, it allowed, but did not require, either volume or quality of service. Nevertheless, the response to this infusion of funds and the recovery from the 1961 recession was immediate—nonagricultural placements jumped more than 800,000 between 1961 and 1962 to a 6.7 million level which has not been duplicated.

Outside of its wartime activities, the employment service had, until 1962, been completely at the mercy of employers who listed job openings and demanded the "best qualified" applicants. Lacking any substantial leverage, the employment service catered to the employers and administered the work test. Practices varied by state and local office; but, in general, UI claims were processed and UI recipients and other applicants were referred to fill whatever employer job orders were listed. Only limited attempts were made to attract job applicants.

The 1962 reorganization included a promise to cease operating "merely as a system of labor exchanges but to take on expanded responsibilities as a manpower agency concerned with all aspects of manpower." It stipulated further that "Each local office must serve as the local community manpower center and beyond that, must also function in a strongly-linked nationwide network of offices operating to meet national manpower purposes and goals." The goal was more efficient labor market operations and, to achieve it, the employment service had to be deeply involved with employers, schools, unions, community development efforts, and almost every aspect of the local economy.

The philosophy was compatible with the placement focus in emphasizing employer contacts and in establishing separate white-collar and professional placement offices to move the employment service into the most rapidly growing occupational fields, but it went further in encouraging the outstationing of employment service personnel on college campuses to offer counseling and placement services and in revitalizing the Cooperative School Program which sends employment service personnel into high schools for the testing and counseling of noncollege bound seniors. Considering that criticisms of its apathy had goaded the employment service into a more activist stance, it is ironic that its moderate responses created for the first time some bitter political opposition. Private, fee-charging employment agencies resented the competition in the more lucrative professional and white-collar field and the College Placement Council was disturbed at campus activities.

New Tools for the Employment Service

The most notable change in the public employment service during the 1960s was the addition of a number of new services for those who found it difficult to compete successfully for jobs. At the beginning of the 1960s, services were limited to counseling, testing, referral in response to employer job orders, and, for those eligible, payment of unemployment compensation. The first fundamental change occurred when MDTA added the goal of improving the qualifications of those not meeting employers' standards. The employment service was to identify occupations with "reasonable expectation of employment," recruit and screen eligible unemployed and underemployed as trainees, work with vocational educators in setting up training courses, and place graduate trainees.

The 1963 MDTA amendments provided for annual expenditures of up to $5 million to test the potential of relocation assistance as a solution to unemployment. These labor mobility demonstration projects, though of little current importance, represent another development of long-term significance. Funds were made available for grants or loans to pay the transportation, moving, and "settling in" costs of unemployed workers relocated from labor surplus areas to those where a specific job offer could be identified.

Relocation assistance was a new tool of limited availability but considerable promise. In pilot projects it helped to effect more rational moves. Most of those who accepted help in relocating were people who had moved before and would probably have moved again. However, the pattern of unassisted moves was heavily dependent upon kinship ties. Workers moved near relatives and friends, often adding to an excessive supply of people with certain characteristics. With planned relocation, people went where the jobs were. The cost per move turned out to be less than $300 because few relocatees had any household effects worth moving. The living allowances provided to support the family until the first paycheck were more important in whether they remained in the new location than the moving costs. Relocatees were more likely to remain if they had assistance with moving arrangements, housing, and family problems, and were helped to find new jobs. Coupling relocation assistance with education and training increased retention substantially.

Only 14,000 persons were located in fiscal years 1965–1969, enough for a meaningful demonstration to the possibilities and problems although not significant in terms of the number of unemployed. Unfortunately, the follow-up period was limited to two months; two-thirds had remained that long. More relevant for present purposes is that most of the state agencies have now had some experience with relocation.

The state employment services have proven their ability to identify persons who are both interested in moving and attractive to employers. Because relocatees have been recruited from among regular employment service applicants and a job offer was required in advance of the move, it is doubtful that many have been drawn from "hard core" groups. The interarea placement system has been tested and found to be too slow and cumbersome; direct telephone contact between supply and demand areas is required. Employment service offices proved to be very poor collection agencies, and the default rate on loans was high, dictating a shift to grants. Employment service offices in supply areas also encountered political problems when they encouraged seasonal farm workers and laid-off industrial workers to migrate. The whole experience suggests the necessity of a total services approach to the problem of the disadvantaged and the importance of the employment service's having a variety of measures with which to assist them.

In 1964, a national network of Youth Opportunity Centers (YOCs) —to be located near but not in central-city ghettos—was established within the employment service. Shortages of personnel for the YOCs led to crash training programs for 3300 new youth counselors, two-thirds of whom were offered and accepted jobs within the state agencies. The development of the YOCs led to employment service involvement in other training and referral activities: referrals to and limited job-creation activities for the Neighborhood Youth Corps, referrals to the Job Corps, and assistance to certain Selective Service rejectees through referral to jobs or training programs. These are only a few of the new experiences which have made significant changes in employment service attitude and capabilities.

New Objectives

In addition to the new responsibilities, the EOA brought a competitive challenge to the employment service in the form of the new community action agencies whose funds come directly from Washington, by-passing the states. Initially, some CAAs viewed their role as one of making existing services available and responsive to their clientele, the poor. Not infrequently they took belligerent positions vis-à-vis established institutions such as welfare departments, schools, and the employment service. Other CAAs felt the best route was to organize one-stop neighborhood centers within target areas where all services could be offered, eliminating the need to shuffle the poor from one place to another. In some cases, the CAAs attempted to establish competing institutions, particularly for employment-related functions—for example, outreach to locate the out-of-work poor and job development to sell employers on "hiring now" and training later.

The makeshift outreach services drew many slum residents who would have been reluctant to approach the more formidable employment service offices, although their inability to provide jobs often created disappointment. In some cases, the CAAs successfully sought to have employment service personnel outstationed in their neighborhood centers. Administrative control over the personnel generally remained with the employment service, but the funding agreement varied from city to city.

The poverty emphasis proved to have great staying power. The original target of MDTA had been the displaced family head of long labor force attachment. Rising employment levels helped many of the unemployed, but it soon became clear that regardless of the level of economic activity some people would require special assistance in order to find a satisfactory place in the world of work. Increased sensitivity to human distress and long, hot summers of ghetto riots kept their problems from being ignored. Thus, just as the notion of a community manpower service center had begun to supplant that of a labor exchange at the state and local levels, the Labor

Department sharply shifted emphasis toward serving the poor and disadvantaged—and sent another shock wave through the employment system.

In 1965, Secretary of Labor W. Willard Wirtz announced a Human Resources Development program (HRD) which would combine the resources of a number of agencies in an intensive effort to solve the employment problems of ghetto residents. A new U.S. Employment Service (USES) director, Frank Cassell, brought in to direct the reorientation, stated the new priority:

> To serve the disadvantaged in whatever ways were deemed necessary, in cooperation with other agencies, so that the greatest needs are met first, and that those who were last in everything else would receive the services of USES first.[1]

The national office moved to have the HRD concept adopted as operating policy at all levels of the employment service. The goal was "to screen in rather than screen out" the disadvantaged; it was to be implemented through outreach into urban slums and rural pockets of poverty, referral to supportive services to improve the employability of those not ready for training or a job, counseling and interviewing, training, job development, and placement geared to the special needs of the disadvantaged. The new policy was fostered by shifts in funding, by the push for local "plans of service," and by adoption of a new budget system designed to abandon the "transaction orientation" of the past and concentrate on achievement of the new objectives. Not all personnel were convinced of the desirability of these moves. Many feared the new emphasis would hamper their ability to service other groups and damage their image in the eyes of employers and communities. Nevertheless, the national leadership was determined to redirect the federal-state system.

In 1968, the employment service was awarded responsibility as "presumptive provider of manpower services" in the CEP, after it protested assignment to the CAAs of the role of "presumptive sponsor." Later that year, the new WIN Program made the employment service responsible for the training and placement of welfare recipients, and soon thereafter it was directed to recruit disadvantaged applicants for JOBS.

In the same 12-month period CEP, WIN, JOBS, and the Cooperative Area Manpower Planning System (CAMPS), were introduced. New budgets and reporting systems were undertaken as were experiments in computerized recordkeeping and placement. All of these changes occurred before the HRD concept had been clarified and relations with the CAAs defined. In 1969, computerized "job banks," a more dominant role in CEP, and an excursion into the realms of vocational rehabilitation with experimentation in work evaluation and work adjustment followed closely upon a major reorganization of the federal-state structure. Thus, new tools had accompanied new objectives and responsibilities in such rapid succession as to give the system an acute case of administrative indigestion.

The impact of these successive reverberations kept the internal politics of the employment security system in turmoil. Following World War II, the Bureau of Employment Security (BES), with its U.S. Employment Service (USES) and Unemployment Insurance Service, was transferred from the Social Security Agency to the Labor Department, where it became the only significant operating agency. Distrust of the autonomy that BES enjoyed dissuaded administrators from simply assigning all the new manpower programs to it. When, instead, a Manpower Administration with authority over BES and other operating bureaus was created within the Labor Department the USES and the state agencies found themselves torn between competing interests and loyalties.

These resulted in a division within the traditionally conservative and unemployment-insurance oriented Interstate Conference of Employment Security Agencies; an Urban Affairs Committee was created within the Conference. The final result was abolishment of BES, along with all the other separate bureaus within the Manpower Administration, a downgrading of unemployment insurance into minor status, and the metamorphosis of the USES in the U.S. Training and Employment Service (USTES) as the major operating arm of the Manpower Administration. The state employment services were still the major operating arm for manpower policy at the state and local levels, but their relations to the federal government were primarily in a straight line to the Manpower Administration through the Regional Manpower Administrators.

AN EMPLOYMENT SERVICE
FOR THE 1970s?

As the employment service confronted the new decade, it was clearly a quite different institution than it had been at the beginning of the 1960s. How much, if any, better was difficult to ascertain objectively. If the changes represented progress, many throughout both the federal and state components had been "dragged kicking and howling" into the new era. The measure of success had changed from number of total transactions to serving those in greatest need, but the reward system remained the same.

Measures of Performance

A major handicap to employment service operations throughout the 1960s was ambiguity of objectives and lack of agreement on priorities. It was all things to all people, serving everyone from the professional to the unskilled, inexperienced poor. All assignments, new and old, were top priority. The Johnson Administration's insistence on serving the disadvantaged was not accompanied by any clear signals to downgrade attention to others. Those who had hoped and assumed the new emphasis would prove transitory were disillusioned when what was expected to be a more conservative Administration pushed the same trends. Thus, the advent of the Nixon Administration, accompanied by reorganization of the Labor Department, helped clarify priorities.

The establishment of the USTES marked more than a juggling of bureaucratic acronyms; it provided an opportunity for implementation as well as clarification of objectives. The hardest to serve were the most in need and were to get priority. Plans were laid for a system in which those in demand in the job market and capable of seeking employment on their own would be provided information on job location and quality and encouraged to pursue those jobs under their own initiative. Staff help would be directed at those less capable of independent action. What remains to be achieved is a readjustment of the agency's reward system that will measure performance on behalf of these objectives and distribute budgets and staff accordingly.

The emphasis between 1958 and 1965 on placement encouraged concentration on those who were easiest to place or could be placed most frequently. Recognition of this effect brought the elimination of placement as measure of performance and determinant of budget; but no standard has been developed to take its place. Goals expressed in terms of "meeting community manpower needs" or "serving the disadvantaged," while adequate for indicating direction and emphasis, provide no standards of performance or means of evaluation. Unless some measures are developed for answering such important questions as "How can one tell if the presence of the employment service makes any significant difference in the labor markets?" or "Does the employment service effectively serve the disadvantaged?" the employment service can only operate on hunches.

Reporting procedures before 1969 produced masses of data on the number of transactions but provided no information on who was served and how well, and no measure of the quality of performance. Hence, the service lacked a firm understanding of what things worked or why, or even if new programs were superior to old ones. For example, significant funds had been channeled into YOCs, but it could not be determined whether disadvantaged youth were being better served. When a methodological study raised doubts about the value of counseling and testing in the placement process, the employment service had no way of marshaling the facts to evaluate the procedures' worth. After a quarter of a century of counseling and testing, and with increasing reliance on them under HRD, the effectiveness of these procedures was simply accepted on faith.

This basic problem—how to measure employment service performance—is yet to be resolved. With the disadvantaged meriting priority, service to them is a useful indicator of who is being helped. In 1969, for the first time, the Labor Department initiated regular reports on the extent to which target groups were being served. The reporting was made possible by the definition, in 1968, of "disadvantaged" for programs funded by the

Labor Department: those who were both poor and without satisfactory employment and, in addition fit into at least one of the following categories: (1) under 22 years of age, (2) over 45, (3) less than high-school education, (4) member of a minority group, or (5) handicapped.

Seventeen percent of all fiscal 1969 employment service applicants, a total of 1.7 million persons, met the "disadvantaged" criteria. Of these, 74 percent had less than a high-school education. There were 1.2 million placements of disadvantaged persons and 286,900 enrollments in manpower programs, though many individuals were probably placed more than once and there may have been a few multiple enrollments. Disadvantaged applicants accounted for 48 percent of counseling interviews, 58 percent of MDTA enrollments, 89 percent of referrals to Job Corps, and 77 percent of referrals to NYC (why the two latter figures were not 100 percent is mystifying).

Twenty-five percent of 1969 employment service applicants were nonwhite, a figure in excess of their proportion in the over-16 population and among the unemployed. Compared with all employment service applicants, nonwhites accounted disproportionately for regular as well as short-term placements and an equal proportion of professional placements—a hopeful sign of effective service.

Disadvantaged and minority applicants and placements have become a key measure of appropriateness of employment service activity. Thus, the employment service has initiated the reporting of numbers of disadvantaged processed as well as total transactions. The development of a refined evaluation system now rests on the perfection of a more sophisticated measure based on the difficulty and the quality of each placement. However, response to such evaluation will require a further step. The current budgeting system still distributes funds and staff according to the number of *total* transactions, often rewarding states that have experienced population and employment growth but that serve the disadvantaged poorly.

Employment Service Activities

The employment service might have been more reluctant to give up placements as the appropriate measure of its performance had not the number of nonagricultural placements declined steadily since its 1962 peak (Table 19–1), despite an increase of 12 million in the size of the national labor force and rising employment. The employment service attributes the drop to the amount of time invested administering the manpower programs. The fact that between 1962 and 1970 there was also a considerable drop in the total number of applications suggests that more was involved; whether it is because employment is shifting in the direction of occupations and industries not accustomed to using the employment service or because the service is becoming less attractive to the nondisadvantaged is not clear.

TABLE 19–1   *Total Employment Service Placements, Selected Years, 1958–1970 (millions)*

CALENDAR YEAR	NEW APPLICATIONS FILED FOR EMPLOYMENT SERVICES	TOTAL NONFARM PLACEMENTS
1958	10,414	5,126
1960	10,117	5,818
1962	10,792	6,725
1964	10,754	6,281
1966	10,532	6,493
1968	10,693	5,760
1969	9,963	5,524
1970	9,957	4,604

NEW DIRECTIONS

A special 1965 Employment Task Force—appointed by the Secretary of Labor and chaired, as it turned out, by his successor—recommended that the institution be reoriented to become a Comprehensive Manpower Services Center in each community. Emphasis was given in the report to specialized efforts on behalf of those with special needs, including: (a) identifying these persons and providing special counseling services in order to determine their rehabilitative needs; (b) developing plans commensurate with individual needs, such as referral to another agency for remedial education, institutional training, or on-the-job training; (c) seeking employment opportunities of a special kind to accommodate the capabilities of persons in this group; and (d) providing supportive follow-up services while they are on the job until they develop self-confidence in the employment relationship.

In pursuit of new approaches, the federal-state system is rife with experimental programs. Efforts are underway to automate every aspect of the employment service that lends itself to computerization. The most important examples are the job bank system, the computerized job-matching system, and the Employment Security Automated Reporting System (ESARS).

In essence, the job bank is a system of rapid accumulation and dissemination of current job-order information. The job orders submitted to the employment service in a particular city or metropolitan area are accumulated in a job bank book, on microfiche, or on film and are distributed daily to public agencies that can effectively utilize this information in the placement process. This system has been very effective in providing current job-order information for all applicants, but especially those in areas outside the operational scope of a particular local office. Now, for the first time, welfare agencies, CEPs, CAAs, high schools, and other public agencies that provide services to the disadvantaged have current, complete, and systematic access to all job orders in employment service files. The system does not include applications for jobs and does not match applicants and job orders. Its advantage is widespread circulation of knowledge concerning the availability of jobs. The information is readily available not to job seekers but to those who have reason to represent job seekers, particularly the disadvantaged. There are currently 55 banks in the largest cities, and it is anticipated that eventually more than 80 will serve our major metropolitan areas.

Federal planners intend that a computer-assisted placement system should evolve from a network of job banks into a computerized job-matching system. The key word is "matching," and its importance cannot be overemphasized. The job bank is a relatively simple, inexpensive, easily installed mechanism. Computerized job-matching is precisely the opposite.

There are currently four systems in the United States that can be classified as computerized job-matching systems. The first, which was developed in California, is known as LINCS (Labor Inventory Communications System). It is operational in two local offices and serves only professional, managerial, and technical workers. The second, the Utah Job-Matching System, is the only operational system that is occupationally and geographically comprehensive. In operation since 1968, it has seven automated and five nonautomated offices and currently serves about 93 percent of the state's population.

The third system is being developed in Wisconsin. Officially designated as ESOPS (Employment Service On-Line Placement System), it is capable of comprehensive occupational coverage and is presently operating in two local offices in Madison. A unique feature is the use of an "open-ended" vocabulary in the descriptor system. Briefly, this method of description utilizes *all* words commonly included in both job and applicant descriptions (the traditional method assigns a DOT code to each job or applicant).

The fourth system, which is located in New York City, is designated AMDS (Area Manpower Data System). It utilizes the DOT descriptor system, but is planning an extended system using the DOT *and* qualitative applicant and job characteristics—for example, interest, appearance, and the like. Originally designed to serve primarily disadvantaged applicants, AMDS has extended its coverage to all groups except professional, casual, and short-time workers. AMDS operates now in four local New York City offices; it is anticipated that coverage will be extended to about twenty offices.

Use of these four systems is spreading to other states. All are in an experimental stage, and it is not yet clear whether the additional benefits will justify the additional costs.

Computerized placement systems strive to accomplish the same objective: to facilitate or improve the placement process. However, each attempts to improve the placement process by using different methods of describing men and jobs; by utilizing different "search strategies" which, in effect, direct the internal file search for a job or an applicant; by focusing their development efforts on particular groups that require more assistance; and by utilizing various hardware configurations, specialized forms, and local office operating procedures.

No single computer-assisted placement system has attained universal acceptance. Each has characteristics that may ultimately be utilized in a national system, but, as the four systems now stand, they reflect the political, social, and economic factors unique to a particular city or state. One of the most difficult challenges facing designers and administrators in USTES will be the selection and integration of job-matching systems and the job bank system into a functional national network.

The employment service has traditionally accumulated statistics on activities performed—that is, placements, referrals, counseling interviews, and the like. But the individual applicant could not be identified, and, hence, there was no way of determining what applicant was receiving what services. With the new emphasis on serving all applicants, but primarily the less fortunate, a method of identifying the applicant was required. ESARS was developed to fill this need; it is being extended throughout the states, to supplement not replace other statistical series. In effect, each applicant is identified in the system and the services provided him are recorded as they occur. No longer is one referral or placement the same sort of datum as any other. For instance, if three counseling interviews are necessary to prepare an applicant for work, all three are directly attributed to his case.

Several cities have been designated as experimental "model offices" in which, all disadvantaged clients will receive the services of "employability development" teams. A job bank will disseminate job orders and coordinate job development. Information will be provided job-ready clients who will be encouraged to seek their own employment insofar as possible.

While automation of employment service functions is destined to have a significant impact on its overall operation, other activities seek to increase its role and effectiveness. For example, new guidelines for the CEP are enlarging the employment service role. Training sessions are underway for employment service staff who will provide technical assistance to JOBS contractors. As enthusiasm of volunteer executives wanes, the employment service will undoubtedly take over the total function of seeking and servicing employer pledges to hire the disadvantaged. Though only 14 percent of employment service staff in the nation are members of minority groups, they represent nearly 80 percent of those hired by state agencies between 1968 and 1969.

CONCLUSION

The employment service of the 1970s is a changed institution because of its involvement in the manpower programs of the 1960s. What previously appeared to be intractable political and personnel obstacles seem to be giving way, and the direction of change is clearly toward serving those most in need of service at the expense of those who can best get along by themselves. Despite the change in intentions, it is still not possible for the employment service to prove either that labor markets work any differently or that the disadvantaged (or others) have better employment and earnings because it exists.

Some academic observers as well as agency personnel object to the emphasis on the disadvantaged, arguing that the appropriate stance is to provide the resources needed to all who seek them. At best, the employment service has always tended to have in its files the people hardest-to-place and jobs hardest-to-fill, because the other job-man matches tend to work out informally. Attracting employers to use a service with a reputation for emphasis on disadvantaged may be difficult, and an employment service without jobs is of limited value. Yet the employment service is much more likely to be able to prove that its existence makes a difference if it is serving those who need help, not those who could have found jobs on their own. In fact, placement may not be the most important function. Focusing manpower services to improve the basic employability of a worker may have a greater effect by enabling the individual to compete successfully in his own job search. Indeed, teaching the techniques of job search and providing clues as to where to search may facilitate the informal placement process. A commitment to serve everyone ordinarily implies a tendency to emphasize the easiest task—to place those who seek help and have skills to sell. After the metamorphosis of the past decade, it is probable that the same inertial tendencies that made reorientation difficult will tend to make it permanent.

NOTE

1. Frank H. Cassell, *The Public Employment Service: Organization in Change* (Ann Arbor, Mich.: Academic Publications, 1968), p. 184.

Chapter 20
Delivering Manpower Services

Among the lessons learned from the manpower programs of the 1960s, not the least important was the vast distance between a congressional enactment and a presidential signature, on the one hand, and a viable program on the other. It is one thing to authorize services and even to appropriate money to pay for them. It is quite another to deliver those services efficiently to eligible clients in such a way as to help them overcome their handicaps.

The legislative development of manpower programs to aid the competitively disadvantaged was complete (with the exception of WIN) by the close of 1966. The emphasis then shifted to implementing programs already authorized. In the process of legislating without experience, the tendency had been to specify the authorized services in vague terms, leaving the administration considerable discretion. Confrontation with unexpected obstacles led to further broadening of the legislative authority. Whether to use existing agencies or create new ones, how to handle relationships among federal, state, and local governments and private institutions—these questions were subject to dispute. Programs such as CEP and JOBS were introduced administratively by bending somewhat the boundaries of congressional intent.

Because problems were identified one by one in a crisis atmosphere and because ambitious political leaders wanted individual credit for specific legislation, the political system produced a new act and a distinct program for each newly recognized need. Thus, many separate federal programs offered support for closely related, overlapping clientele, and each program had its own funding sources, eligibility rules, application procedures, and administrative guidelines. Yet none of these programs, nor all of them together, had sufficient appropriations to serve more than a fraction of those eligible. The need for federal leadership produced "uniform" programs not easily adaptable to local needs. The program-by-program structure and project-by-project federal approval necessary to control the quality of services prevented an approach aimed at proficient service to the individual. Persons in need of help had to adapt to the services available rather than receiving services indicated by their need.

With the concentration on launching programs and delivering services, monitoring and evaluation were neglected, leaving federal agencies unprepared when Congress began asking them to defend their stewardship. Absorbed with defending the next appropriation request, or looking good for the next election, the administering agencies lacked the time, energy, and interest to develop long-range strategies or even identify long-range objectives.

Beginning with 1966, after most of the manpower legislation was on the books, continuous experimentation sought to improve the delivery of the contemplated services, but never with impressive success. Trends within and between the Kennedy, Johnson, and Nixon Administrations shifted emphasis from coordination of manpower programs and agencies through improved and centralized administration, to a proposed consolidation in a comprehensive manpower program, and finally to a "no strings attached" shift of responsibility to state and local government through revenue sharing. Throughout, the issues were which agencies should control funds and deliver services, which clients should receive priority, how the various services should be packaged, and what the federal, state, and local roles should be.

COORDINATION OR CONSOLIDATION
IN MANPOWER PROGRAMS?

One of the first serious administrative problems to surface was that of coordinating the complex array of programs and agencies, all seeking ultimately to serve essentially the same clientele. Its federal symptoms were interagency conflict and competition. At the local level, it was manifested in the difficulty of drawing from the multiple funding sources a viable package of projects and services adapted to the needs of the community and its people.

Coordinating Federal Activities

The administrative complications started in 1961 with the creation of the first manpower program under the Area Redevelopment Act (ARA). When the training component was included in the Act, established federal divisions within OEO and the Bureau of Employment Security (BES) lobbied for jurisdiction. As a result, the Secretary of Labor was made responsible for the selection and placement of applicants, while the Secretary of Health, Education, and Welfare was assigned responsibility for the development and administration of the training courses. When MDTA followed, and later absorbed the minuscule ARA training program, two additional claimants for a piece of the action appeared. To help allay labor union fears that the on-the-job training aspects of MDTA would compete with apprenticeable occupations, they were placed under the auspices of the Labor Department's Bureau of Apprenticeship and Training (BAT), where the unions had considerable influence. Then, as a result of doubts about the capability of BAT and BES and their state-affiliated agencies to administer the new training program, an Office of Manpower, Automation, and Training (OMAT) was created within the Labor Department.

Though representatives of the established agencies participated in the design of the federal antipoverty strategy, most of the poverty fighters believed that existing agencies had not served the poor and could not be made to care. As a result, EOA manpower programs were to be administered mainly through new agencies. The youth employment and training programs were divided between OEO and the Labor Department, and a new agency was established in each to administer the Job Corps and the Neighborhood Youth Corps, respectively. The Community Action Program with its manpower components became another separate OEO bureau. Only the Work Experience and Training program was made part of an existing agency, the Welfare Administration in HEW, which had little experience in administering manpower programs.

The new programs were accompanied by a maze of regulations controlling eligibility, duration, and conditions of training or work, and pay received by participants—some imposed by Congress and others by administrative guidelines. The need for developing interagency coordination conflicted with the ambitions of agency heads, some of whom were already beginning to think in terms of absorbing other programs.

Local Coordination

It is at the local levels that people are served or not served and programs succeed or fail, and the effects of program proliferation showed their most painful symptoms there. Except for most Job Corps conservation centers, manpower programs were administered and manpower services delivered by state and local agencies. The MDTA institutional training program, vocational education, and vocational rehabilitation were administered through long-established state agencies and, though the new legislation required coordination and strained available capability, they did not add to the total number of state or local agencies. MDTA-OJT and JOBS involved private employers in consort with familiar public agencies. MDTA experimental and demonstration projects and EOA programs by-passed the states and even local political jurisdictions, showing a preference for ad hoc community action groups and both profit-seeking and nonprofit private organizations. A Cooperative Area Manpower Planning System (CAMPS) sought to achieve orderly joint planning, but having no authority to reallocate funds, it had little effect on outcomes. The Concentrated Employment Program (CEP), though ostensibly a "delivery system" for existing programs rather than a new program itself, added a new administrative structure in the community, as did the National Alliance of Businessmen (NAB).

Funds from the older programs were distributed by federal agencies to the states on the basis of fixed formulas, but the budget of EOA programs was disseminated largely at administrative discretion. Even with a fixed formula, MDTA provided that funds not used within a prescribed length of time could be redistributed to other states at the discretion of the Secretary of Labor. Local officials were confused by the variety of programs; and when the less aggressive among them (often in the areas of greatest need) failed to develop proposals, funds went elsewhere. As a result, some communities received more than their share of funds on the basis of their population and need, while others, which had not acquired the technical expertise to file applicants, were slow in getting their share of manpower funds. Yet fixed formulas suffered two drawbacks: Using such indices as population or industrial employment was not satisfactory for all localities, and nonreallocable funds assigned to unaggressive states went unspent. Even communities that mastered the art of grantsmanship found it difficult to piece together effective and comprehensive programs.

Each federal funding source tended to generate its own local constituency, which encouraged further proliferation at that level. The different sources of funds posed serious if not unsurmountable obstacles to development of integrated local manpower programs. For example, prevocational training and skill training could be funded from ten program sources, on-the-job training could be subsidized from five, and supportive services funded from nine. Income maintenance was also available to participants under nine programs. The eligibility rules, application procedures, allocation formulas, expiration dates, and contracting arrangements varied as widely as the funding sources.

Just as there were numerous federal sources for funding each manpower service, no state or community had a unified manpower planning or operating organization. Various combinations of federal, state, and local agencies often competed to serve the same clientele. The development of state and local projects depended upon the initiative of a diverse group of agencies. Skill training, for example, could be initiated by various agencies including local public employment offices, public or private welfare organizations, community action agencies, vocational rehabilitation agencies, public schools, private educational institutions, employers, trade associations, or unions. The trade associations and community organizations to whom BAT delegated OJT contracting authority subcontracted, in turn, with employers, usually without in any way communicating with other local manpower agencies. Other services emanated from a similar multiplicity of sponsors. A wide variety of pay and allowances structures biased the choices of eligible clients in ways not necessarily to their long-run benefit. Delays occasioned by the project-by-project approval often discouraged clients and caused dissipation of well-conceived projects because of the loss of state personnel.

THE SEARCH FOR SOLUTIONS— FEDERAL LEVEL

Faced by the practical necessities of day-to-day operation administrators at federal, state, and local levels first set out to develop machinery, both formal and informal, to coordinate the efforts of the numerous agencies and institutions involved in manpower programs. For a time coordinating mechanisms proliferated—for example, the President's Committee on Manpower, the Inter-Agency Committee on Education, the Economic Opportunity Council for federal antipoverty efforts, and ad hoc task forces convened by Housing and Urban Development to deal with specific urban problems. All they proved was that equals cannot coordinate equals and, lacking aggressive interest at the White House level, each, in turn, drifted into oblivion.

Obstacles to effective coordination stemmed not only from the natural tendency of officials to guard their respective jurisdictions, but also from the influence of outside groups, public and private, that had an interest in the activities of the various departments and bureaus. The internal structure of the Labor Department is an example, though it is not unique in that respect. Because of reluctance to assign all new manpower programs to BES, the one significant operating bureau, it appeared necessary in 1964 to appoint a Manpower Administrator to coordinate the manpower activities of BES, BAT, and OMAT. A management consulting firm had recommended that the separate bureaus be replaced by an integrated functional organization. The recommendation was never implemented because it was opposed by outside groups that supported BES and BAT and had friends in Congress. Yet time and logic were on the side of a consolidated manpower administration. A gradual erosion of the autonomy of Labor Department bureaus followed.

Agencies had incentives to cooperate as well as to compete, and on the pragmatic level of day-to-day operation, ad hoc interdepartmental agreements and joint funding arrangements were negotiated. Though subject to revocation by either party, they provided for joint operation of programs, transfer of funds, and the purchase and exchange of services. These ad hoc devices remained in use, but rising congressional criticism of OEO, combined with ambitions of the Labor Department, served to bring about consolidation of the manpower programs. Its bargaining position weakened by the antiestablishment activities of the CAAs, OEO acquiesced, during 1967, to delegating the Special Impact, New Careers, and Operation Mainstream programs to the Labor Department. Later, when Congress was legislating the new training and employment program for welfare recipients (WIN), the Labor Department was able to win jurisdiction of its components except for the original screening and referring of clients by HEW welfare departments. HEW retained vocational education and vocational rehabilitation, but, with the exception of its relatively small MDTA role, eventually lost its hold on the remedial manpower programs.

After considerable political maneuvering within the Labor Department in both the Johnson and Nixon Administrations, the semiindependent bureaus were cut away from their independent power bases in the state and in Congress. A new United States Training and Employment Service (USTES) assumed program authority within the Manpower Administration, an Office of Policy, Planning, Evaluation, and Research, and an Office of Financial and Management Services completed the Manpower Administration organization chart. The Regional Manpower Administrators (RMAs) became the direct line of communication between Washington and the state and cities. With these developments, the Labor Department had become the administrator, legislatively or by delegation, of programs accounting for 80 percent of the budget for manpower services to the competitively disadvantaged. The Manpower Administration was in almost unchallenged control of the remedial manpower programs—if it could exercise its authority.

However, there was no management system to feed to the RMA the information he needed to monitor each project within his jurisdiction, let alone evaluate performance. EOA-delegated projects relied on contractual rather than grant-in-aid authority, and the Labor Department found itself dealing with 10,000 separate project sponsors with 30,000 contracts in force. With late appropriations and continuing resolutions delaying full-year funding, many of these had to be extended month by month. Simply negotiating all the contracts necessary was beyond the RMA's staff capability, without his fulfilling further responsibilities for monitoring and evaluating the contracts once in operation. With modern communication and transportation facilities, personnel within regions would have been able to relate to Washington as well as to regional headquarters. However, having an office responsible for a particular piece of geography was one way of dividing up and delegating assignments.

Responsibility for vocational rehabilitation, vocational education, and MDTA institutional training remained with HEW, along with its legislated authority for such EOA education programs as Adult Basic Education and Head Start. OEO was being removed from the field as a manpower service agency, keeping for itself such functions as community action programs, neighborhood legal and health services, and experimental and demonstration projects on behalf of the poor. Consolidation of authority within the Labor Department, the agency having the bulk of control of remedial manpower programs, had been accomplished. Attention in early 1970 shifted to consolidating programs rather than agencies.

THE SEARCH FOR SOLUTIONS— LOCAL LEVEL

The actual delivery of manpower services depended not upon Washington agencies but the instrumentalities of state and local governments, the EOA-sponsored CAAs, other private nonprofit institutions, and private employers. Therefore, the viability of the manpower effort was limited by the fragmentation typical of local political structures as well as by the proliferation of federal programs, agencies, and funding sources. The major credit for initiating improvements in local coordination and for experimentation with new systems for the delivery of manpower services must go to federal agencies. At first, they were more interested in developing their own direct relationships with particular local agencies than in improving the coordination among them. By the spring of 1966, however, congressional, state, and local concern had led to the creation of three-man teams representing the Labor Department, OEO, and HEW, which were to coordinate manpower programs in 30 major metropolitan areas.

Because these teams possessed no real "clout," their success was dependent upon the personal resources and effectiveness of team members. Working under the auspices of the President's Committee on Manpower, the teams mediated interagency disputes, unclogged lines of communication, negotiated proposals for coupled and jointly funded projects, and prodded local officials to submit new proposals. The effort proved to be short-lived, but it contributed to the development of two new instruments for coordination among programs at the state and local level, CAMPS and CEP. The shortcomings of these were among the factors leading to comprehensive manpower legislation proposals at the beginning of the 1970s.

The Cooperative Area Manpower Planning System (CAMPS)

The CAMPS system grew out of Labor Department efforts to introduce more consistent planning into the MDTA program. A controversy had arisen over the appropriate state vs. federal role in the program. Originally, each training project required federal approval even though MDTA funds were allocated among the states according to an established formula. As a result of complaints about delays and difficulties of continuing institutional programs, Congress amended the Act, giving the states the right to undertake small projects within their allocations without federal approval. To minimize the impact of the new amendments on the existing system, the Labor Department introduced a state-planning concept for these small projects. The Labor Department would provide guidelines and each state would require federal approval but, once approved, the states could initiate the individual small projects throughout the year without further federal involvement.

The state-planning proposal for these small contracts appealed to the Manpower Administrator so much that he directed its use for the total MDTA program. Continuing the emphasis, the Manpower Administration won approval from HEW, OEO, the Department of Commerce, and the Department of Housing and Urban Development for a Cooperative Area Manpower Planning System to consist of area, state, and regional coordinating committees. The CAMPS agreement was reached in March 1967, and guidelines were developed and sent to the states soon thereafter. The states, in turn, were to require local area CAMPS committees to formulate joint programs to be consolidated into state plans in time for regional approval. Final approval of the state and regional plans as well as individual projects would remain the prerogative of the individual federal agencies.

Initial state and local reaction to the CAMPS concept was highly favorable, but disillusionment soon set in. The planning process was impaired by the fact that no one knew how much and when Congress would appropriate for manpower programs. Appropriations were rarely forthcoming until at least three months of the fiscal year had gone by, and nine months of fiscal 1970 passed before some programs were funded for that year. With each program constrained by its own budget and procedures, the area and state plans were better described as individual agency plans stapled together than as comprehensive planning documents. Complaints of the costs and administrative burdens of the CAMPS operation grew until it was necessary to request funds for staff support.

However, it was not these understandable and seemingly inevitable problems that disturbed local participants, but what they viewed as bad faith on the part of the federal sponsors and a lack of discretion in giving meaning to their planning efforts. The state and local committees complained that the Labor Department itself violated the spirit of CAMPS by superimposing the CEP and later JOBS. The Labor Department promised to include the new programs in the next planning cycle. However, the basic conflict between decentralized planning and national innovation was made clear.

The other federal agencies were giving no more than lip service support. The Departments of Agriculture and Defense and the Civil Service Commission were added as signatories but had no meaningful involvement. The Labor Department secured an Executive Order stating its primacy and requiring interagency commitment, but it was considerably weakened in the interagency clearance process. In years of budgetary frugality and with the siphoning off of available funds to JOBS, CEP, and other federally dominated uses, the CAMPS committees felt they were given no meaningful decisions to make. The Labor Department's CAMPS guidelines were so specific in program mix and enrollee characteristics that little discretion remained. A particular complaint in 1968, for instance, stemmed from federal specification of the mix between institutional and on-the-job training in each state, unrelated to the differing balances among such factors as the nature and size of industry and migration patterns. The end product, the state and local participants maintained, was interagency communicating not planning.

The regional offices appeared not to know what to do with the CAMPS plans when they arrived. However, in a few states, governors appointed their own representatives as CAMPS chairmen with orders to bring the usually autonomous state agencies into subjection. Under pressure from their states, a number of senators and representatives pressed for an enlarged state role and expansion of the areas of discretion and appeared to view CAMPS as a potential instrument for achieving it. The concept of federal guidelines, local and state planning, federal approval, and state and local administration was an attractive one. A few states and cities moved to establish effective planning and administering mechanisms, and federal legislation contemplated a system that would give clout to state plans—the power to affect the flow of funds.

The Concentrated Employment Program

The Concentrated Employment Program differed from and was in some ways inconsistent with CAMPS in origin, concept, and objective. While CAMPS followed the MDTA model, relying heavily on state agencies, CEP was constructed on the OEO model, by-passing the states and to a lesser degree the cities in preference for CAAs. CAMPS was strictly an interagency planning mechanism; CEP was conceived as a "delivery system" for manpower services.

The CEP concept was almost entirely the personal contribution of Secretary of Labor W. Willard Wirtz. Special surveys to test the relationship between unemployment rates in slum neighborhoods and the more traditional measures for standard metropolitan areas had highlighted the concentration of job needs and promoted the subemployment concept. Revelation of the numerous fragmented programs in various cities had stimulated him to testify before congressional committees of the need for a "rifle rather than shotgun" approach to urban problems.[1] In a 1965 speech he had launched the Employment Service Human Resources Development program, promising to knock on every door in the ghetto if necessary to identify the disadvantaged and their needs and bring them in for services. He had also been impressed with the JOBS NOW program funded by the Labor Department and run by the YMCA in Chicago. This program recruited members of youth gangs, ran them through a two-week orientation stressing grooming, conduct, and use of the transportation system, then placed them with cooperating employers under the tutelage of "job coaches" who counseled them on individual problems and worked to establish appropriate relationships with supervisors and fellow employees. That one-fourth to one-third seemed to make the grade was considered a mark of success, considering the behavior patterns of the clientele.

During December 1966, the Secretary of Labor sent to the President a memo proposing an urban slum employment program. A request for $135 million was to be added to the fiscal 1968 budget, while $95 million of unobligated and deobligated funds would be found from existing programs to launch the new concentrated effort—and marshal evidence of success before the appropriations committees completed their work. Nearly half the money came from MDTA, with the rest from NYC and the not-yet-implemented Special Impact and New Careers programs. Twenty cities of diverse size and wide geographical distribution were selected from among those with the most serious concentrations of unemployment. Two rural areas were later added.

At its launching in early 1967, CEP marked the transition from an emphasis on coordination to concentration of effort within a single institution and upon limited target areas. Its initial objectives were to (a) concentrate limited funds on a few target areas in pursuit of a measurable impact, (b) involve private employers in hiring the disadvantaged, and (c) create a centralized administration to interrelate the variety of separate programs operating in those target areas. The second goal proved unrealistic in the absence of financial incentives to break down employer reluctance. CEP, operating without legislative authorization, could provide no new services and was actually a delivery system for existing services. It brought under one roof and into one administrative structure all the funds and slots available among the various programs for a restricted target area, inevitably limiting the amount available outside that area.

The delegation of EOA manpower programs to the Labor Department had not been completed, and CEP planning provided that, except under rare circumstances, the CAA would be the program sponsor in each city. Then when the state employment services protested that they had previously been designated as the local arm of the Manpower Administration, they were promised the role of "presumptive provider of manpower services." Nevertheless, major portions of the funds in each CEP were subcontracted to other public agencies and various private nonprofit organizations. The multiple institutional involvement not only slowed inauguration of the program but also insured divisiveness and administrative conflict.

The CAAs, few of which had mounted significant manpower programs up to that time, were to prepare proposals to fit local circumstances and submit them for Labor Department approval and funding. Then they had to organize the CEP, hire a director for it, find staff and facilities, work out relationships with the employment service and potential subcontractors, and begin the process of recruitment, training, and placement. The mayors were involved to the degree that they participated in the CAAs; governors had no other role than to waive the veto rights given them by EOA. Of particular significance was to be a business advisory council, which, it was hoped, would be a source of jobs in private industry.

Because JOBS NOW had two weeks of prejob orientation, it was assumed that all CEPs would have the same beginning phase under CAA direction. The employment service would provide outreach, intake, counseling, testing, referral to jobs, job development, job coaching, and follow up, but the training programs themselves would be subcontracted. The orientation phase was paid for with MDTA money and included weekly stipends, but the regular MDTA programs were never adequately integrated with CEP.

The CEP experience was chaotic from the start. It was launched too hurriedly and was pressured for results too soon without adequate capable leadership and staff and without time to plan and prepare. Initial goals were highly unrealistic. Various cities launched into the outreach and orientation phases without considering whether enough jobs or training slots would be available after the first two weeks. People completing one phase were often recycled through orientation or placed "on furlough" after having been promised a job or training leading to a job.

During the first year, half of those who completed training reverted to a standby basis awaiting job placement. Content and method of the standard two-week orientation program were often dependent more upon what the designers and instructor knew than what the recipient needed. Outreach was thwarted by a flood of female applicants (over 90 percent in some cities and averaging 75 percent overall in the first few months) amidst prevailing concern for the status of the male in the Negro family. No one had any valid criteria to determine which program fit which enrollee, and there were far too few slots to go around anyway. Job coaching was an attractive concept, but no one had any experience at doing it.

Many of these shortcomings were the result of inadequate planning, but others reflected basic structural weaknesses. The central staff of each CEP served only as a "holding company" for a variety of separate and competing programs and subcontractors. The CEP director might be able to ask "Which program?" for a particular client, rather than forcing him to fit the one available, but he still could not ask "What service does he need?" And he had no criteria for choosing among programs. Subcontractors (who might otherwise have received the same funds directly) as well as the employment service tended to view the CEP as a temporary competitor.

As the creatures of the CAAs, the CEPs inherited the internal struggles of the former. The community action program had provided the patronage base for new forms of political action and was consequently buffeted by rivalry for that source of power. Various increasingly militant groups struggled for access to such attractive jobs as CEP director. While those with the most administrative experience were white, nationalistic racial and ethnic groups were struggling to capture the entire antipoverty effort at the local level. No leadership training was available. CEP directors had no adequate control over their subcontractors and their limited authority was often undercut by CAA staff.

Few CEPs enjoyed significant cooperation and support from employers, either public or private, and without jobs there was no payoff. With the inauguration of NAB-JOBS, the CEPs could provide incentives to employers, but NAB representatives often preferred to ignore the CEPs in their efforts to fill employer pledges. The CAAs had been initiated, in part, to bypass such established agencies as the employment service, and the two were ill-prepared to work in concert. The employment service offices often refused to exchange job information with the CEPs arguing, "We have spent years developing employer relations and we are not going to risk them by referrals from CEPs." Yet duplicative job development efforts continued among the numerous agencies.

A Manpower Administrator's representative was placed in each CEP city to exert a federal presence. Some performed skillfully and were largely responsible for the limited success. Others were less energetic or were drawn from mistrusted established agencies and lacked rapport with the CEP staff and clientele. Regional Manpower Administrators were too new and too harried to exercise effective control.

Success in both recruitment and placement was determined more by the nature of the individual programs than by the quality of the delivery system. MDTA institutional slots were popular, but the employment service–vocational education administered program was difficult to integrate into the CEP structure. OJT programs for CEP enrollees were difficult to sell to employers, and the orientation courses were inadequate to make them "job ready." Too little use was made of basic education. NYC slots were usually filled but had little relevance to eventual job placement. New Careers programs were hard to mount, and most CEPs had difficulty spending that share of their funds. Operation Mainstream was used mainly as a "waiting room" while seeking better alternatives. Special Impact was used initially as administrative "glue" to hold the package together, then removed entirely from the CEP relationship.

The first year's experience might have caused the basic concept to be challenged, but the commitment had been made at a level too high for reversal. Rather than pull back or delay expansion, administrators proceeded to expand the number of CEPs in succeeding years. Expansion within the limits of available funds required some reduction in the budgets of the original CEPs. In addition, most had started so slowly that their rate of spending at the end of fiscal 1968 was considerably greater and sometimes several times their total funds. Thus, the cutback in programs and layoff of staff was painful. The number of new CEPs to be funded also meant that on the second round the CEPs received only an average of $2 million compared to $5 million the first round, further limiting the potential of concentrated effort.

Guided by the previous year's experience, planning grants and technical assistance contracts were provided to improve the quality of local planning. The RMAs were by now more on top of their jobs and their authority had been augmented and clarified. Nevertheless, with higher turnover, the staffs of the older CEPs were not always experienced, and the CAA staffs in the newly added cities were no more experienced than their counterparts the previous year. Proposals were slow coming in and often of disappointing quality. Staff training was still grossly inadequate. The technical assistance contractors had multicity responsibilities and tended to be available only on their own scheduled visits rather than being on call as needed. Then, under time pressures, they tended to perform the task in question rather than teach the staffs to do so.

The Nixon Administration, in its pattern of modest restructuring rather than major redirection of manpower efforts, retained the CEP concept, attempting to weaken only the role of the CAAs. Just as earlier with the Job Corps and later with NYC, the announced change reverberated loudly in Congress, indicating the growing strength of the antipoverty establishment at the local level.

The Nixon Administration's manpower policies tended to enhance the role of the employment service, possibly because incoming leadership at top levels in the Labor Department had strong employment service connections. In the summer of 1969, without advance consultations, the Labor Department issued new CEP guidelines which, if followed literally, would have left the CAAs in a figurehead position as CEP sponsors, but would have assigned all service functions and all staff direction to the employment service. Included was adoption of the WIN pattern of an employability team which was to work out an individual plan leading ultimately to a job for each applicant. The realities of city-by-city contract renegotiation, however, appear to have enlarged the employment service role largely where it was capable of more and better services, but to have increased its role no more than a token amount where it had demonstrated little ability or commitment on behalf of the central-city target populations.

In theory, the CEP concept of concentrated delivery of manpower service made sense. In practice, however, existing conditions made achievement of the goals impossible. Even with concentration on restricted target areas, the problems were almost overwhelmingly complex and the resources too limited. Enrollees got around the target area restrictions by giving false home addresses. The proliferated programs caused by an involved federal legislative structure were too complex to be administered effectively, given the limited leadership and staff capability available. There was still no adequate system for delivering the needed services. Enrollee expectations often were raised only to be dashed by the lack of meaningful program slots but more particularly by the lack of acceptable jobs.

State and Local Coordination Efforts

The new federal manpower programs would have required some change in priority and practice in such traditional state agencies as employment services, vocational education, and vocational rehabilitation. However, the most unsettling factor for these agencies was the competitive challenge from the CAAs and their impact on city politics. CAAs were originally conceived as comprehensive planning, coordinating, and service delivering units for all services to the poor, including manpower. In practice, they were, except for a handful of cases, just one more limited competitor for fragmented pieces of the action.

Though their activities cut across jurisdictions of long-established institutions—schools, welfare agencies, employment services, health departments, and many others—the CAAs were as noted for fomenting controversy as for mobilizing resources in aid of the poor and coordinating local antipoverty efforts. The by-passing of state and local governments had been the deliberate intent of the CAA designers. However, in a few cities, strong city administrators had gained control of them and used them either as vehicles to improve services to the poor or as devices to control and quell opposition, depending upon their predilections. The 1967 EOA amendments gave to local governments their choice of taking over CAAs or leaving them independent, but only 29 cities out of some 800 chose to exercise the option. A major factor limiting takeover was undoubtedly the reluctance of mayors to accept responsibility and, therefore, blame for programs of uncertain success.

Ad hoc arrangements were worked out among many local manpower agencies, particularly the CAAs and state employment services, despite their inherent hostilities. Many of the CAAs established neighborhood centers to minister to the various needs of the poor in their areas, and placing the unemployed poor was a basic function of many. The state employment services resented the competition but complained that their limited budgets did not permit them to assign their employment counselors to the centers. A few CAAs succeeded in obtaining funds from OEO to purchase such services from the state employment agencies. In other cases, either in response to the competition or because of growing interest, state employment services themselves footed the bill for employment service personnel outstationed in neighborhood centers.

The state agencies through which MDTA, vocational education, vocational rehabilitation, and other grant-in-aid programs were administered tended to be self-perpetuating organizations largely independent of gubernatorial or direct political control. EOA gave the governors only an overridable veto over antipoverty activities within the state. After largely ignoring the antipoverty programs during the first few years, a few governors began to demand a stronger direct role in manpower activities toward the end of the 1960s. Several states organized manpower development councils of various kinds for planning and coordination, but most of these organizations refrained from involvement in the politically sensitive problems of operating programs and attempting to deliver services. A few governors attempted to gain control over all federally funded manpower activities within their states by appointing their own chairmen for state manpower committees which consisted of the heads of state operating agencies. CAMPS then gave them an opportunity through appointment of the state chairman to have some influence on the total planning process.

The probable future direction of state manpower coordination was indicated by California in 1968. An alliance between a liberal Democratic state legislature and a conservative Republican governor produced a Department of Human Resources Development. It subsumes under one head all the state agencies involved in administering federal manpower and antipoverty programs as well as all related state activities. As written, the legislation would allow comingling of all federal allocations and state moneys in a single Manpower Development Fund to be used by the director of the new department according to his own priorities, regardless of federal appropriations purposes. The comingling is forbidden by federal law, but it makes sense from a state viewpoint. One of the most interesting concepts in the California design is a job agent—modeled on the activities of the vocational rehabilitation counselor—who is to identify the barriers to employment for each disadvantaged person, develop strategies to aid each individual in overcoming those barriers, and become his advocate in procuring the needed services and in getting and keeping a job.

Utah was the next state to move forcefully toward an "umbrella" manpower agency. Its choice was a State Manpower Planning Council, but with more than planning authority. Its members were the heads of all manpower-related agencies, including education, vocational rehabilitation, and public welfare as well as representatives of management, labor, the public, minority groups, and the state legislature. The chairman and the executive director were gubernatorial appointees. The Council has independent staff and budget and the authority to review and evaluate all agency programs. Agencies were forbidden by the Council's enabling law to submit proposals to the federal government without Council approval.

Even though New York City had launched a consolidated Human Resources Administration in the mid-1960s and despite the greater direct impact of manpower and antipoverty programs on city politics, mayors, in general, followed the few pioneering governors in setting up manpower administrations. However, with the help of Labor Department funding for city CAMPS secretariats, the city manpower administrations soon outnumbered those of the states. After all, a governor's awareness of manpower problems depends upon his alertness; a mayor of a city any size has no choice but recognize the issues. These efforts set the pattern for federal legislation advocating consolidation of manpower programs and decentralization of their administration.

THE VOCATIONAL
REHABILITATION MODEL

The vocational rehabilitation program, which served as a model for the job agents in the California system and the employability teams in WIN, came to be reflected in a number of other manpower programs. Officials of the Rehabilitation Services Administration in HEW object to the classification of their vocational rehabilitation program as a manpower program. However, its tools are those of employability and its objective is employment. While it offers both skill development and job creation, its special significance for other federal manpower programs is the process by which employability and employment services are delivered.

The clientele, their handicaps, and the services provided them vary too greatly for comparison, but the vocational rehabilitation program each year places in competitive employment more disadvantaged persons than MDTA or any of the EOA programs and at lower average costs. The high success rate is built in because the process begins with careful evaluation of the potential employability of the client. When that is determined positively, the Rehabilitation Services Administration has within a single program the authority to fund nearly any activity related to employment for any eligible client. Essentially any service that contributes to achieving the individual's employment objective is acceptable including: (a) comprehensive evaluation, both psychological and medical; (b) medical, surgical, and hospital care, and related therapy to remove or reduce disability; (c) prosthetic devices; (d) counseling and guidance for vocational adjustment; (e) training; (f) service in comprehensive or specialized rehabilitation facilities; (g) maintenance and transportation; (i) tools, equipment, and licenses needed for work or in establishing a small business; and (j) placement and follow-up. Eligibility has been expanded from the physically handicapped to the mentally handicapped and more recently to "behavioral disorders characterized by deviant social behavior or impaired ability to carry out normal relationships with family and community which may result from vocational, educational, cultural, social, environmental, or other factors."

The key element of the program is a personal relationship between a handicapped client and a trained counselor equipped, as it were, with a blank checkbook to purchase whatever medical, educational, or other services are needed to successfully place the client in satisfactory employment. After evaluation to ascertain potential employability and to determine handicaps and strengths, the counselor and client jointly work out an employment plan merging the client's interests and realistic possibilities.

The program encompasses not only the client's service needs but also the agencies staffing and research needs. The rehabilitation services themselves are provided by state agencies financed by 75–25 federal matching grants. In addition to providing leadership and financial support for state and private rehabilitation agencies, the federal agency has funds for research, design and construction of facilities, and allowances for both pre-service and in-service training of counselors and other personnel.

With an estimated 5 million to 6 million pool of eligible physically and mentally handicapped persons, it is doubtful that vocational rehabilitation will become a major competitor in the general manpower field. The program's success has been largely based on selectivity, and there is no evidence that the rehabilitation rates could be sustained when dealing with more complex social, cultural, and economic handicaps. The significant lesson for manpower programs is the value of one-to-one personal counseling, the development of individual employability plans, and the flexible authority to provide or purchase whatever services are needed to achieve satisfactory employment. The impact of this concept is increasingly evident in the restructuring of the delivery services in other state and local agencies.

LESSONS FROM EXPERIENCE

Few solutions emerged from the trial-and-error process of program design and implementation during the first decade of manpower programs. But the major issues involved—the day-to-day management of programs, federal-state-local relations, and the problem of adapting the mix of services to individual and community need—were clarified.

Managing Manpower Programs

Some of the most difficult current problems in the administration of manpower programs—yet ones that involve no basic conflicts and are amenable to well-known solutions—are those growing out of day-to-day program management. The difficulties are primarily those of policies, personnel, and information. Among the important lessons of the past few years has been the demonstration of the gap between legislation and efficient delivery of intended services. Some federal agencies have chosen the easy escape by parceling out money to state and local governments, leaving the practical management problems to them. Others have played more active roles in providing guidance and leadership in matters of program detail, despite the political consequences.

Management problems begin with the budgetary process. Funding is one year at a time at best, which does not encourage thorough analysis of problems and long-range planning. The incentives for short-range, "crash" thinking are strengthened by the increasingly laggard appropriations process. Staffs are constantly demoralized by uncertainty. Project proposals are hastily drawn and funded without adequate analysis and begin operations without sufficient preparation. Communities that fail to meet nearly impossible deadlines lose out in the competition for funds.

Next, because time is always short and staff inadequate, too little attention is devoted to develop clear policies and procedures for the conduct of programs. The quest is always for "instant success" and the result is administration by crisis. If the federal agencies handing out the money do not concern themselves with policy manuals, program guides, and administrative details—and they usually do not on a continuing basis—the state and local and private recipients of the funding cannot be expected to do so. Determining whether money is efficiently spent should command no less than the considerable attention now invested in auditing procedures.

Lack of adequate staffing is a chronic complaint; even more frequently criticized is the lack of competency and the absence of coherent staff training. Business experience has shown that administrators are made, not born; yet training for public administrators, particularly on an in-service level, is rarely attempted. Without adequate policies, procedures, and trained staff of their own, federal manpower and antipoverty agencies are ill-equipped to provide the technical assistance required by new and inexperienced state and local organizations. The latter need help at the most rudimentary levels, with the managerial tasks of developing staffing patterns and recordkeeping systems, choosing and renovating facilities, and acquiring property, and managing the more substantive techniques of outreach and job development, the development of curriculum materials, and teaching methods. Just circulating among all local sponsors throughout the country the bitter lessons learned and the best practices developed by others would be a major contribution. If the decentralization of administrative responsibility contemplated in the comprehensive manpower proposals is to be more meaningful than the vocational education–state planning process has been in the past, technical assistance and staff training will be as important as federal monitoring and evaluation.

Finally, agencies at all levels lack the day-to-day information flow needed for efficient program management and the pre- and postenrollment comparative data required to evaluate results and identify program strengths and weaknesses. It is not surprising that in the crisis atmosphere that prevailed at the beginning of each program and under the built-in pressures for short-term thinking few gave thought to data needs. The data-reporting systems of the various programs reflect their origins and orientations and show little evidence of adjusting to new objectives. For instance, state employment services formerly counted only the numbers of transactions, have only recently concerned themselves with the characteristics of those served, and have devised no measures of the contributions of the services. MDTA, staffed in part by former Bureau of Labor Statistics employees, had an adequate reporting system which gathered such data as trainee characteristics and posttraining follow-up. Unfortunately, there was neither the top-level interest nor the staff resources to assure accurate and complete reporting and analysis of the accumulated data. EOA programs, being more publicity conscious, reported numbers enrolled and enrollee characteristics but paid little attention to measuring results.

Evaluation is still in a rudimentary stage. Evidence is just becoming available that manpower programs have produced results worth the cost. Evaluations have concentrated on how well programs are managed, but few have investigated whether the employment and earnings experience of appreciable numbers of the persons completing the programs has been significantly affected. Both the Labor Department and HEW decentralized contracting and monitoring authority to regional offices, then left those offices without information systems to provide data on the conduct and results of programs within their jurisdiction. Prospects for improvement in managerial ability are favorable, but the goal is distant.

Federal-State-Local Relations
in Program Administration

The CEP and CAMPS efforts illustrate a key issue in the administration of manpower programs: the appropriate responsibilities and relationships of federal, state, and local governments. With the emergence of MDTA and EOA manpower programs, the trend has been toward a federal role greatly expanded from its previous emphasis on funding. This is to be expected—because the federal government has the most lucrative revenue source, interdependence is increasing within the economy, and there is national concern for social objectives which sometimes clash with local perspectives. However, a state and local counterattack may lead to a readjustment of the balance. The important question is that of efficiency: "What can federal, state, and local governments each do best?"

A variety of federal-state-local relationships currently exist among the various manpower programs, with the newer models involving an increasingly direct federal role. They are (a) the vocational education–vocational rehabilitation, grant-in-aid model which provides federal funds for discretionary state use within legislatively proscribed limits but with little federal guidance or control, modest reporting requirements, and no evaluation; (b) the employment service trust fund model with full federal funding but state operation, though with more stringent federal guidelines for allocation of funds; (c) the MDTA model which involves federal determination of objectives and guidelines but state initiative in planning projects for federal approval (funds are allocated by formula with a portion reserved for federal discretion, within a prescribed length of time can be recovered and reallocated); and (d) the OEO model which by-passes the states and often local governments to make grants and contracts with ad hoc community organizations.

A number of dilemmas are involved when a federal agency deals with state and subordinate jurisdictions. Disbursement of funds through state governments reduces the number of federal contact points and the need to become involved in local problems. But many states are notable for their unresponsiveness to community, particularly urban, problems. Allocation of funds by formula reduces federal decisions, but formulas do not always allocate according to need and often hand funds to apathetic groups who do not use them. Funding on a project basis often excludes communities with the greatest need but the least energetic leadership. The power to make or withhold contracts creates uncertainties and sometimes gives federal agencies life-or-death power over local institutions, but it also provides leverage to force appropriate action. A contractual relationship allows the federal agency to determine objectives and require local adherence to them without awaiting the slow process of conversion and commitment. However, there are too many cities, counties, and other jurisdictions for federal agencies to negotiate and monitor contracts effectively with each one. Delegation of administrative decisions to regional offices can widen the span of effective control, but that, in turn, raises the question of discretion, flexibility, and relative responsiveness to national policy vs. local control.

Communities differ, and programs must be adapted to local needs. The program mix should differ between cities with concentrations of industrial and white-collar employment, adequate and abysmal schools, tenement-style ghettos and more diverse and open housing, compact and far-flung geography, and vigorous and apathetic leadership as well as between rural, small-city, and metropolitan areas. But there is no assurance that such local decisions would be in accord with national goals. The new clients of the federal manpower programs tend to be socially and politically as well as economically handicapped. In the absence of federal pressure, local agencies are apt to expend their limited resources on the persons easiest to serve. Yet the mere existence of federal guidelines is no guarantee that they will be followed, and experience has shown that detailed federal regulations are frequently observed only in the breach. Federal legislators who initiate programs represent states and communities, and the persons who run community programs are local residents. As a result, the potential gains for federal operation appear to be limited.

The basic issue is one inherent in the nature of the American federal system—and one for which there is no ideal solution. Employment problems are more concentrated in large cities than in other parts of the state, and often the state does not understand the problems. Pressure from other cities may prevent the largest one from getting its share of funds that pass through state hands. Under such circumstances, direct contact between city and federal agencies is certain to emerge. If the federal government chose to concentrate its manpower and antipoverty efforts on the 30 Standard Metropolitan Statistical Areas (SMSAs) of over 1 million population, the federal-city relationship typified by CEP would be feasible. Maintaining separate direct relationships with every community and with rural areas becomes increasingly complex.

Lack of close working relationships between federal and state units is attributable to faults at both levels. Unfortunately, federal manpower and antipoverty objectives are clear to none—and endorsed by few—of the states. Federal manpower officials have tended to be distrustful of the states and impatient with the necessity of converting another level of bureaucracy to new objectives. Federal officials often have not clarified their objectives, even to themselves, and are unable to communicate them to the states. Legitimate state objectives also are often ignored by the "feds," who have tended to overestimate what they can accomplish by direct intervention at the local level. Yet state officials frequently are further removed from critical problems than either federal or community representatives and more inclined to continue business as usual. Educational establishments, welfare departments, and vocational rehabilitation agencies tend to be self-perpetuating and independent. State employment services play the governors and federal agencies against each other by quoting federal regulations to the former and flaunting states rights before the latter.

After a decade of experimentation, it was clear by the beginning of the 1970s that some redress in the federal-state-local relationship was necessary in manpower and other social welfare programs. The federal agencies appeared to have no other realistic choice but to use the states and cities as policy and program instruments. Yet to do so included the difficult task of winning their commitment to national objectives. Those federal agencies accustomed simply to passing out money to the states by formulas without monitoring programs had been ignoring their responsibility to see that national objectives were achieved with federal dollars. The Labor Department had been overly arbitrary at times, but this was preferable to the permissive stance often adopted by other agencies.

Federal agencies should clearly articulate objectives and establish guidelines for their achievement. States and local governments should pursue those goals by the means most appropriate to the community environment. It is a currently neglected federal responsibility to see that guidelines are followed and that programs are evaluated to identify strengths and weaknesses, failures and accomplishments. Some states and communities will inevitably be out of harmony with national objectives. The current MDTA reservation of 20 percent of total funds for national approval outside of state apportionments provides federal administrators discretion to contract directly with public or private schools in a state that refuses to follow federal guidelines—an example of what might be done throughout the federal manpower system. With that exception—and the additional one of research, experiment, and demonstration—distribution of funds according to formulas related to need is preferable to the vagaries of federal prejudice or political pressures. Even the grant-in-aid approach poses no insurmountable difficulties if matching formulas are rationally related to priorities and if the federal agencies have the will and the political leverage to impose and enforce guidelines for reasonable performance.

The state-city issue is more difficult to resolve. State governments have tended to ignore city needs, causing mayors to appeal to Washington for assistance. But city boundaries are not contiguous with labor markets, and no real model of a metropolitan government exists. Mayors tend to have within their jurisdictions the people needing jobs but not the jobs they need. Thirty-three SMSAs transcend state boundaries. The experienced manpower agencies are also instruments of state government, and the cities have at hand no other delivery system for manpower programs. Cities large enough to have their own congressional representation will probably always find the federal government more responsive to their needs than the state, or at least will choose to play the two superior levels of government against each other. The mayors had been much more aggressive than the governors in lobbying with the federal government for manpower and social welfare assistance. As a result, legislative proposals tend to favor the local government even in relatively small cities. Allocation of funds to states with a "pass through" provision determining the amounts that must go to cities of various sizes is a possible compromise, but it is likely to be satisfactory to neither level. The ultimate solution must team the mayors' closeness to urban problems and the governors' broader political and economic jurisdiction.

A related issue is the conflicting roles of long-established agencies, most of them instrumentalities of state governments, and the ad hoc private and quasipublic institutions emerging outside the traditional political structure to serve previously neglected populations. The community-action organizations, which invite the policy participation of their poor clientele, have served an important role as a focal point for opposition to apathetic establishment institutions but have shown little ability as deliverers of services. The established agencies have the professional capability to provide services but tend toward inflexibility in objectives, methods, and choice of clients. The major reason for the consensus that now appears to have been reached —that either the mayor or the governor as elected officials, rather than anonymous agency heads, should have responsibility for the delivery of manpower services—is the expected greater responsiveness to the target groups. From present clashes between "participatory democracy" and "the establishment" may emerge a set of institutions through which the clients can develop the political wherewithal to demand services, yet leave delivery to professionals.

Delivering Manpower Services

A trial-and-error legislative process characterized by federal initiative could do little but produce fragmented programs. After a decade of development, it was difficult to think of any manpower service that could not be provided somewhere within the complex structure of existing laws and practices. Yet those in need of manpower services were still being required to fit themselves to program requirements, rather than available services being tailored to their needs. Offering the needed flexibility to the individual client would require something like the vocational rehabilitation approach of joint counselor-client evaluation and planning of a series of services adapted to the client's needs and ambitions. All the services would not need to come from the same source, but there would be a single advocate for the client who could represent him and purchase or otherwise obtain the needed services. Achieving such flexibility would require dissolving all manpower programs into a single program encompassing all budgets without earmarking for particular services. In 1967, Congress authorized "collapsing" into a single Community Work Training Program all of the manpower programs authorized by Title Ib of EOA: Neighborhood Youth Corps, New Careers, and Operation Mainstream. By 1971, the provision had yet to be implemented, suggesting the difficulty of changing administrative patterns once they are set.

If services are to be available to clients according to need, it should follow that national decisions cannot fix the combinations of services available in states and communities. Small nonindustrial states often have little use for OJT and great use for institutional training. Cities with much heavy industry and high demands for unskilled and semiskilled workers have different needs than those where employment is primarily white collar. Housing patterns and transportation systems vary widely from city to city. National objectives, guidelines, monitoring, technical assistance, and evaluation seem to be the appropriate federal roles with local objectives, detailed planning, and delivery of services occurring where the people are. Many if not most of the administrative problems which persist at all levels appear to be the direct result of the fragmented structure of the federal manpower legislation. Efforts such as CAMPS and CEP at the state and local levels were primarily devices to compensate for proliferation of programs and lack of coordination at the federal level.

Given these pressures, a serious search began in the last year of the Johnson Administration for some means of resolving the issues. The growing awareness of a few governors and mayors that they were being by-passed by programs using their agencies, serving their citizens, and funneling money into their states and cities was the immediate impetus for a series of legislative proposals for both decategorization and decentralization of manpower programs. One of the task forces appointed by President-elect Nixon to recommend policies for the new Administration endorsed such a measure. The various proposals discussed differed in detail but shared a common intent. All called for a single comprehensive manpower law, structured along functional rather than program lines and lending itself to tailoring according to community and individual need. The law was to list the services to be made available but not fix the amount of money to be allocated to each service or function. The budget was to include everything to be spent for remedial purposes, and appropriations committees were to allow distribution of funds without fixing in advance the proportions to be spent for various services. The bulk of manpower funds was to be allocated to state and city governments by a formula encompassing population, labor force, unemployment, and poverty criteria. Some proportion of the total appropriation was to be left in the hands of the federal agency for research, experimentation, and demonstration, for technical assistance and staff training, for interstate programs, and for serving populations neglected by recalcitrant states.

Planning was to be the responsibility of the elected officials—governors and mayors—with incentives for the various jurisdictions within major metropolitan areas to plan jointly. Contrary to the long-term trends to take education and similar functions "out of politics," funds were to be spent only by or through units of government directly responsible and responsive to the electorate. Private organizations, profit or nonprofit, could be used, but only if answerable to elected officials. Each state and city involved was to prepare and update annually a multiyear plan for using its share of the funds. City plans formulated by the mayors were to be included in a state plan encompassing the governor's plan for the rest of the state.

Development and operation of the planning organizations at the state and local levels were to be left to the discretion of governors and mayors. The planning and operating functions were to be separate, with evaluation a function of the former. All relevant interests, public and private, were to have access to the planners. The city and state plans were to relate manpower needs and functions to education, economic development, housing, and other problems and activities in the communities and state. The relevant federal agencies were to prepare and disseminate planning guidelines, review and approve plans enforcing the guidelines, and furnish technical assistance. Continuous monitoring and evaluation, either in-house or by contract, would enable the federal agency to assess state and local performance. Allocation formulas were to include sufficient flexibility to reward or punish performance in the following year's appropriation.

Though centralized planning at each of the three levels—federal, state, and local—was held to be necessary, consolidation of state and local agencies delivering manpower services was not. A single "project sponsor" —either the governor or the mayor, an agency of their choosing, or in the absence of their choice, a community action agency or other claimant— was recommended. This prime sponsor would be the recipient of the state or city share of the manpower budget. Choice of the agency or agencies responsible for actual delivery of services to individuals was to be made by the prime sponsor. It was usually assumed that the employment service would receive the major share of this assignment, though no agency would be given any residual rights as a provider of services. But governors and mayors would be free to designate any agency they chose, with the most committed and able agency expected to emerge from the competition. It was recommended that the function of OEO would be to organize and represent the poor vis-à-vis the service agencies whose professional staffs would be better able to provide services. But if a CAA could demonstrate competence and win the approval of a mayor or governor, it could receive the assignment to deliver services.

All the bills introduced to implement the proposals agreed upon the decategorization of the manpower programs, which would make available in one program the services currently available from all. Each required federal guidelines, monitoring, and evaluation, and each retained substantial funds for the Secretary of Labor to use at his own discretion for national programs and for projects in states that did not accept and meet their responsibilities. They disagreed upon the extent of decentralization. For instance, one would have made the governor responsible for all manpower programs within a state. Another would have provided incentives for the mayors in an SMSA to combine and choose one among them as prime sponsor. Another would simply have authorized any city or county of 100,000 inhabitants or more to become a prime sponsor. These latter two would have left the rest of the state to the governor. A fourth would have authorized the Secretary of Labor to choose the appropriate prime sponsor for each state or city.

The 91st Congress provided the final legislative test of the proposals—and with interesting results. Public education organizations were fearful that the bills presaged a Labor Department "power grab" designed to create a "dual education system." The Conference of Mayors and League of Cities went all out in their lobbying efforts for the bill while the National Governors' Conference largely ignored it, thus assuring an emphasis on the role of the cities vis-à-vis the states. The House of Representatives hewed staunchly to the decategorization line. The Senate gave it lip service, and thought of innumerable reasons why existing programs or agencies deserved special recognition and funding. Sitting on the Senate committee developing the legislation were several senators whose pride of authorship and reputation were involved with specific programs. Program staff throughout the country, who had a vested interest in the existing structure, applied considerable pressure. The result was a "Christmas tree bill" with something for everyone and exceptions outnumbering the existing programs.

The proposals for administrative reform foundered upon bipartisan politics and confusion over a related but more controversial issue. With rising unemployment stemming from Administration efforts to cool the economy, Congress added and passed as part of its manpower bill a substantial public service employment program. The President's veto message identified that program and the failure to decategorize as justification for rejection.

The Administration's commitment to decentralization of not only manpower programs but also much of the traditional responsibility of the federal government was evidenced by a decision in 1971 to shift from controlled grants in aid to a "no strings attached" revenue-sharing approach to federal funding. For manpower, this meant putting all programs funds in a single package—decategorization—and passing the funds to the cities and states, requiring only that a plan be prepared and that the money be spent for manpower purposes. All federal responsibilities for guideline preparation and enforcement, plan approval, monitoring, and evaluation would be eschewed. But lacking experienced staff and means for formal staff training, few cities and states had the capability to plan and administer their own programs.

The challenge in the administration of manpower programs is to create an adequate system for the delivery of manpower services. It is assumed that business administrators, social workers, guidance counselors, and others must be trained; yet there is no recognized and accepted training for manpower administration. Cities and states may receive responsibilities for which they are ill-prepared. But the span of federal control is insufficient to reach to the individual recipient of manpower services. Yet a few years is a short time in the creation or the reorientation of institutions. Amid all of the administrative chaos, it must be remembered that legislation has been passed, procedures have been developed, staffs have been assembled, funds have been expended, and people have been served. Pressures for efficient management are being recognized and improvements are being made. But designing, legislating, and funding programs is only the beginning. The payoff is improvement in the employment and earnings experiences of the target populations. In between is a difficult and challenging administrative task.

NOTE

1. U.S. Congress, Senate Subcommittee on Intergovernmental Relations of the Committee on Government Operation, *Hearings on Creative Federalism, Part I, The Federal Level,* 89th Cong., 2nd Sess. (Washington, D.C.: U.S. Government Printing Office, 1967), pp. 245–249.

Chapter 21
Work and
Welfare

Three major considerations have traditionally controlled the design and implementation of programs to aid of the poor: First, those who can find employment or be trained for jobs should work; second, those who are employable but cannot find jobs should be temporarily assisted; and, finally, those who are not employable should be supported by society. More recently, a new principle has become increasingly prominent—that the working poor are also deserving of help and that they should earn a "decent" income. As long as eligibility for aid was harshly circumscribed and assistance levels were low, there was little difficulty in applying these principles. But as the welfare floor was raised and as the number of welfare recipients increased drastically, the sharp distinction has blurred—between those who should work and persons for whom society should provide. It has become ever more difficult to define and identify employability and employable persons, or, for that matter, productive employment. And the prevailing rhetoric notwithstanding, the boundaries between work and welfare have become increasingly vague.

THE GROWTH OF WELFARE

The Social Security Act of 1935, passed in the depths of the Great Depression, was the federal government's first general attempt at income maintenance on a sustained basis. The Act established two groups of programs: (a) social insurance programs—including old age, survivors, disability, and unemployment insurance—which distribute income payments on the basis of prior earnings and tax contributions; and (b) public assistance programs—for the elderly, the blind, the disabled, and families with dependent children—which provide income support on the basis of need alone.

Because benefits under the social insurance programs depend on earnings history and labor-force attachment, only those with income in the past qualify for future payments. Thus, those most in need may be excluded. Public assistance payments, however, depend on need alone and were initially designed to help the unemployable. The welfare system was originally based on a presumed dichotomy between those who could work and had to fend for themselves and those who could not be expected to work and were therefore eligible for public assistance.

When the Social Security Act was passed, female household heads with small children were usually considered to be unemployable. The prevailing assumption was that they should remain in the home to strengthen family life instead of entering the labor force. Because unemployment averaged over 15 percent during the depression, jobs were not available and few women had the choice between gainful employment and support at home. But even when jobs became more plentiful, the structure of the law discouraged work by some who might have been able to earn at least partial support. Benefits were often subtracted dollar for dollar from any earnings, and this "100 percent tax" discouraged any work effort. Moreover, because the only jobs most welfare recipients could find offered little stability, income from employment was uncertain. A mother on relief who succeeded in achieving economic independence was likely to experience difficulty in returning to the welfare rolls if her income fell. Thus, there was often no financial gain in working, and frequently the efforts to achieve self-support could be undertaken only at a risk of losing even the meager sustenance provided by public assistance. Not until 1969—more than three decades after the beginning of federal public assistance—were some incentives offered generally to recipients who sought partial or complete self-support.

The problem of persons preferring welfare to work was necessarily small in the first years of the Act because relatively few individuals were involved and the majority on public assistance rolls were disabled or too old to work. In the quarter-century since 1945, however, profound changes have occurred in the size and composition of public assistance Aid to Families with Dependent Children (AFDC). Increasingly the dominant public assistance program, AFDC has been criticized for supporting employable adults (Table 21–1).

The rise of AFDC during the 1960s seems not at all congruent with other trends of that decade. Between 1960 and 1969, the number of Americans below the poverty level dropped steadily from 40 million (or 22 percent of the population) to 24 million (or 12 percent); the unemployment

TABLE 21–1   *Number of AFDC Recipients, Selected Years, 1936–1970*

DECEMBER OF YEAR	NUMBER OF RECIPIENTS
1936	546,000
1946	1,190,000
1956	2,270,000
1966	4,666,000
1968	6,086,000
1970	9,657,000

SOURCE: Department of Health, Education, and Welfare, National Center for Social Statistics, *Program Facts on Federally Aided Public Assistance Income Maintenance Programs, 1970* (Washington, D.C.: U.S. Government Printing Office, 1971), p. 4.

rate, after a spurt up to 6.7 percent in 1961, fell to 3.5 percent in 1969. But AFDC payments more than tripled during the decade, rising from $1.0 billion to $3.2 billion.

Originally expected to be a "transitional" program which would wither away as the contributory insurance components were broadened, AFDC grew for many reasons. First, population growth could be expected to expand the welfare rolls over time, other things being equal. Between 1940 and 1970, total population increased by over 50 percent, and the population 14 years and under grew by more than 80 percent.

Second, federal legislation extended coverage to groups not previously eligible. In 1961, children who were dependent because of the unemployment of an employable parent were included (AFDC-Unemployed Parent). In mid-1969, a foster care component was added, and most states have also adopted a provision that permits children to receive assistance after age 18 if attending school. These extensions of coverage added some 800,000 persons to AFDC rolls by 1970.

Third, the Supreme Court has struck down two typical state provisions that prevented many persons from receiving AFDC. In 1968, the Court ruled unconstitutional the "man in the house" rule which made a man living in an AFDC home responsible for the children's support; the decision precluded cutting off aid because the mother cohabited with a man not obligated by law to support the children. The following year, the Court invalidated the residency requirement for public assistance. Because more than 40 states had this second restriction, the decision had a wide impact; HEW estimated that, as a result, up to 200,000 persons were added to welfare rolls.

Fourth, at least as important as the foregoing have been alterations in family structure. Divorces, desertion, and illegitimacy have risen sharply since the mid-1930s. All such changes, which leave a mother as head of household, increase the number of potential AFDC clients. While the rate of marriage per 1,000 population has been virtually unchanged since 1935, the divorce rate has doubled. Moreover, the average number of children involved per divorce decree has been rising steadily. Illegitimacy has increased even faster. Between 1940 and 1968, the illegitimacy rate more than tripled, from 7 to 24 illegitimate births per 1,000 women aged 15 to 44, and the proportion of all illegitimate births rose from 1 in 25 to 1 in 10.

The structure of AFDC itself has been criticized for encouraging female-headed families. For example, an able-bodied man who cannot earn enough to support his family may not qualify for AFDC-UP. To provide income for them he may desert and thus enable them to qualify for assistance. Similarly, the father of an unborn child may not marry the mother so that she may qualify for AFDC.

A fundamental basis of the increase in AFDC has been the broader availability and attractiveness of AFDC relative to other sources of income. As the federal government assumed a larger share of the burden, states became less reluctant to qualify individuals for aid; and, as the level of aid also grew, participation in the program became increasingly preferable for those eligible. Between 1962 and 1970, for example, the average AFDC payment increased by 60 percent; the average spendable earnings of all private employees, by only 37 percent. Significant increases in food stamps and medical care benefits for AFDC clients—not reflected in the cash payments—have tilted the balance even more in the favor of welfare. Far from necessarily resulting in penury, AFDC can be beneficent, especially in relation to earnings capacity. A full accounting of the benefits to recipients of AFDC must include also the potential income in kind from public housing, food stamps, and Medicaid. In Chicago, for example, a female family head with three children and no earnings can receive annually $480 worth of food stamps, full payments for her medical needs (worth an average of $790), her cash public assistance payment, and perhaps public housing. If she is among the three AFDC recipients in ten who live in public housing in Chicago, her payments of $3,160 will be reduced by almost $200, but she will be far more than compensated by a public housing bonus of $840. Thus, a family of four that lives in public housing receives cash and benefits totaling nearly $5,100. Without public housing, the family would receive about 4,400.[1]

Chicago is not atypical. A dozen states have higher standards of assistance. The same female-headed, four-person family with no earnings could receive—in cash payments, food stamp bonus or value of surplus commodities, and average Medicaid benefit—about $5,400 in New York City, $2,900 in Wilmington, Delaware, and $2,650 in Phoenix, Arizona. A few families also receive a public housing bonus of several hundred dollars.

Even for those who want to be self-supporting, a considerable work effort is required to equal available public assistance. In most big cities,

TABLE 21-2   *Comparison of Wages and Welfare, 1969*

	MAXIMUM AFDC PAYMENT FOR MOTHER WITH ONE CHILD	MEDIAN HOURLY WAGE FOR 16-19-YEAR-OLD FEMALES IN SLUM AREAS	HOURS OF WORK TO EARN EQUIVALENT OF AFDC MONTHLY PAYMENTS
Atlanta	$ 71	$1.53	46
Chicago	218	1.68	130
Detroit	181	1.68	108
Houston	81	1.38	59
New York City	208	2.00	104
Los Angeles	148	1.75	85

SOURCE: U.S. Department of Health, Education, and Welfare, *OAA and AFDC: Cost Standards for Basic Needs and Percent of Such Standards Met for Specified Types of Cases, July 1969* (Washington, D.C.: The Department, 1970), Table 3 and U.S. Department of Labor, *Youth Unemployment and Minimum Wages,* Bulletin 1657 (Washington, D.C.: U.S. Government Printing Office, 1970), p. 103.

more than two full weeks' work would be necessary to match cash payments alone (without regard to the income in kind add-ons) for a young mother with one child (Table 21-2). When the food stamps, health care, and perhaps public housing benefits are added, the necessary work effort also increases, as it does again when child care and other work-related expenses are considered. And for older women, the additional responsibilities and costs of large families are unlikely to be balanced by a proportionate rise in earnings capacity.

To determine who qualifies for AFDC, on the basis of income, states specify "standards of need" for various family sizes. However, states are not required to pay in full what they designate as the full standard. In July 1970, for example, only 14 states paid 100 percent of needs and 6 states paid less than 50 percent. As the standard is increased, more families fall short of it and hence are eligible for assistance. In 1967, the federal government required states to make cost-of-living adjustments in the standards by July 1969.

The amount of income disregarded in calculating assistance payments has become increasingly important. By 1968, 28 states had adopted a provision that permitted monthly earnings of up to $50 per child or $150 for the children in any family to be disregarded in determining eligibility. Since mid-1969, states have been required to exempt, in determining an AFDC family's needs, earnings of $30 plus work expenses each month, plus one-third of all additional income. They are also required to exempt full earning of a child who is a full-time student or a part-time student not working at a full-time job. Because the disregards now in effect apply only to families already receiving AFDC, they are not likely to add more persons to the rolls; however, they allow many recipients to remain who otherwise would have been disqualified.

THE INTERDEPENDENCE
OF WORK AND WELFARE

There is little public complaint about paying public assistance to the disabled, blind, and aged. Few of these people could work even if jobs were available. By contrast, most heads of AFDC households are of working age and without physical handicaps. Women whose children are in school all day or are able to take care of themselves may be receiving aid; unemployed males, eligible under provisions offering assistance to families with an unemployed parent, are even more often able to work if they can find jobs. As the number of AFDC recipients has increased, so has the proportion of those on welfare who could be supplementing their income through employment or could leave relief rolls altogether.

Recognizing that there were a growing number of welfare recipients who could work, the government mounted efforts to foster "rehabilitation rather than relief." During the 1960s, these efforts grew in scale and intensity as the number of AFDC recipients spiraled and public criticism of the program mounted against supporting those who can work.

The distinction made by the Social Security Act between those who can support themselves and those who cannot has proved unworkable. Instead, the worlds of work and welfare are closely intertwined. AFDC family heads need not make an "all or nothing" choice, but may select the best combination of the two.

Contrary to common misconceptions, welfare recipients are not unable or unwilling to work, nor do they languish on the rolls forever. Steady growth of the rolls masks a tremendous turnover. Of some 700,000 families who entered AFDC rolls in 1967, only one-third remained on the rolls continuously through mid-1969. Some of the families who left the rolls later returned, but there is, nevertheless, great dynamism in the caseload. During 1969, more than 40 percent of the 1.5 million cases on the rolls at the beginning of the year were closed during the year.

Changes in the income of AFDC family members figure prominently in the reasons for opening and closing AFDC cases. Of the cases where payments were discontinued in 1969, over one-quarter were due to an increase in the earnings of the AFDC father or mother. The loss of or reduction in earnings of the AFDC caretaker resulted in over 35 percent of the openings.

It is probably not an overstatement to suggest that for certain socioeconomic groups receipt of public assistance at some time is a normal occurrence for many families.

Nor is it true that AFDC recipients avoid work. During the 1960s, about one welfare mother in five was consistently in the labor force; moreover the proportion in full-time work increased.

	1961	*1969*
Total in Labor Force	19%	20%
Employed full time	5	8
Employed part time	9	6
Unemployed	5	6

A closer examination of these data reveals wide variation between states. In 1967, when the national labor-force participation rate of AFDC mothers was 20 percent, state rates ranged from 6 percent in the District of Columbia to 51 percent in Florida. Only somewhat more than 25 percent of welfare mothers have never been employed.

Although AFDC recipients are not far removed from the world of work, impediments to economic independence have increased over time. That the household head is a female immediately sets off AFDC families. Of all families in 1970, only one in nine was female-headed. As the percentage of unwed mothers has grown, so have the number and proportion of illegitimate children. During the 1960s, illegitimate children increased from 24 percent to 32 percent of all AFDC children. The racial composition of AFDC has also changed markedly. In 1942, nearly four of every five recipient children were white; blacks and other racial minorities accounted for only about one in five. By 1969, whites and nonwhites each constituted about half of all AFDC families (Table 21–3).

AFDC recipients are increasingly concentrated in a few states. The top five states contained 34 percent of all AFDC families in 1948 and 44 percent in 1970. AFDC recipients, who increasingly live in central cities of SMSAs, comprise a substantial proportion of the total population in many of the largest central cities (6.2 percent in the 20 largest).

However, assertions that people move in order to qualify for welfare (from the South to large northern cities) are not well supported. A study for the House Ways and Means Committee concluded that rising AFDC caseloads could not be attributed to recipients who migrate to receive public assistance.[2]

TABLE 21–3   *Percentage Distribution of AFDC Families, by Race, Selected Years*

	1942	1958	1969
TOTAL	100.0%	100.0%	100.0%
White	78.6	57.8	50.5
Nonwhite	21.4	42.2	49.6
Black	20.1	40.0	47.5
Indian	1.3	1.6	1.4
Other	a	0.6	0.7

a Less than 0.05.
SOURCE: Department of Health, Education, and Welfare surveys of AFDC recipients.

Not until the 1960s was there any significant change in the AFDC program. But, as the burden of the rolls became financially onerous, as the welfare population became less "deserving," and as the AFDC-UP component allowed relief for the first time for employable men, public assistance for dependent children came under increasing criticism. Moreover, few married women, and especially mothers, were in the labor force when the Social Security Act was passed. But in the succeeding three decades, not only was the burden of AFDC becoming increasingly onerous, but also a growing proportion of wives and mothers in all income levels among the general populace were entering the labor force as discussed in Chapter 4. The work-force participation rate for mothers jumped from 9 percent in 1940 to 40 percent in 1970, including 30 percent of mothers with children under 6. Exempting welfare mothers from employment when two-fifths of all married women were working no longer seemed justified.

THE EMPLOYABILITY
OF WELFARE MOTHERS

The public debate dealing with AFDC frequently has been concerned more with rhetoric than reality. The issue of whether welfare mothers *can* work has been confused with the issue of whether they *should* work. And because of failure to recognize that work and welfare are not mutually exclusive, the ability of welfare mothers to enter the labor market and earn some money has been confused with their ability to achieve economic self-support.

Employability is a complex balance of economic, social, and psychological factors. The presence of young children is the most obvious barrier to the employment of most welfare mothers and one that normally figures prominently in surveys of barriers to their employment. Even though it is increasingly acceptable for mothers to leave their children in another's care while they work, the limited supply of day-care facilities is a severe constraint.

Three of every five welfare mothers in 1967 had a child under 6; another 28 percent had no child under 6 but one under 13; only 12 percent had no child under 13. This means that 60 percent of the mothers probably need full-time, year-round day care; another 28 percent need care in the afternoon during the school year and all day during the summer; only the last 12 percent do not need child care facilities.

According to recent estimates by HEW, the total capacity of licensed day-care centers and family day-care homes in 1971 was about 780,000. In the same year, there were 1.6 million AFDC children under 6 (who presumably would need full-time care if their mothers worked) and another 2.1 million between 6 and 12 (who presumably would need part-time care). Licensed facilities fall far short of being able to accommodate the children of welfare mothers. And, of course, nearly 10 million working mothers are competing for existing facilities.

Largely because the potential demand is far greater than the available supply, child care has been hailed as the panacea for the employment problems of welfare mothers. Emphasizing the scarcity of child-care facilities, however, may divert attention from the ability of these mothers to locate such services on their own. A woman's willingness to bear the costs of leaving her child(ren) depends largely on the expected benefits of doing so, especially on the potential earnings. A survey for HEW of AFDC in ten cities found that of all the welfare mothers sampled, seven in ten "said they could make 'arrangements' to work if a good job were available." [3]

Thus, the problem of dependency is less one of the lack of jobs or of child-care services than the lack of *good* jobs. Even if welfare mothers were not limited in their labor-force activity by child care, health, and other problems, their earnings ability would be quite limited. Those who have worked or are now working are concentrated in the most unfavorable occupations, and 27 percent of welfare mothers have never been employed. They are also more likely to be members of a minority race and, therefore, face economic discrimination. Finally, the structure of AFDC puts severe limitations on their incentives to work and earn.

By virtually every available criterion, welfare mothers are concentrated in the most unfavorable occupations and their job status is likely to deteriorate in the future. According to projections by the Labor Department, welfare mothers' usual occupations are those that will expand least during the current decade.

The unfavorable occupational mix is due in large part to deficient education. The median educational attainment of welfare mothers in 1969 was 10.1 years compared with 12.1 years for all female adults.

In addition to the difficulties of child care, health, unfavorable occupations, and lack of education, nearly half of the welfare mothers must contend also with economic discrimination because of race. If the proportion who are black continues to increase, this problem will worsen.

A final consideration is the structure of work incentives. The treatment of income earned by AFDC recipients is a crucial variable in the choice between, or combination of, work and welfare. Factors reviewed above provide an indication of the extent to which welfare recipients *can* compete for employment and earnings in the labor market. But in the absence of a work requirement, their decision to enter the labor force—whether they *will* compete—hinges on the incentives offered for work effort. Thus, work incentives are at the heart of any consideration of the employability of AFDC recipients.

Until recently, the majority of AFDC recipients lived in states that provided for each family all or nearly all of the amount designated by the state as the full standard of need. Earnings were treated as income available toward this standard and assistance payments were reduced by the full amount of the earnings. This "100 percent tax" on earnings inevitably fore-stalled many attempts to achieve financial independence.

Other states, however, were less generous and paid only a proportion of the full standard. In 1968 for example, Indiana specified the full standard for a mother and three children as $287 but paid only $150, or 52 percent. Accordingly, the family could earn the difference of $88 without penalty, but any income above that was taxed at the rate of 100 percent.

The 1967 Social Security amendments, which also established WIN, provided the first general incentives for all states. Beginning in mid-1969 earnings of $30 per month plus work-connected expenses, plus one-third of the remainder, were to be disregarded in computing the family's as-sistance payment. Although this exemption cannot help but increase the labor-force participants of welfare mothers, it is still too soon to determine its effects.

WORK AND TRAINING
FOR AFDC RECIPIENTS

The presumption that AFDC recipients were "unemployable" and outside the work force became untenable in 1961, when the federal govern-ment extended coverage to families headed by an unemployed male parent (AFDC-UP). The need for the new law was clear: Because the original Social Security Act denied assistance to families headed by an able-bodied male, the whole family was penalized if the father could not find employ-ment. The presence of "employable" parents on relief prompted Congress, in 1962, to amend the Social Security Act to subsidize employment pro-grams for relief recipients; until 1962, all AFDC recipients were presumed to be outside the work force and public assistance funds could not be used to provide work. States were encouraged to adopt Community Work and Training (CWT) programs designed to offer work relief rather than hand-outs, and hopefully also to help AFDC-UP recipients achieve economic independence.

"Working-off" Public Assistance

The purpose of this amendment was twofold: to allay public criticism of relief payments to persons able to work and to create work relief projects that would train and "rehabilitate" recipients. "Working off" relief was justi-fied as being better for the recipients' morale and providing useful public services under safeguards to prevent exploitation or the displacement of regular workers. CWT's formal emphasis on training and rehabilitation re-flected the nascent movement in the early 1960s toward more organized manpower and training programs for the disadvantaged.

Although the 1962 amendments were hailed as a vehicle for encourag-ing work and training for persons on relief, the provisions of the law tended to reinforce the more traditional "social services" associated with public assistance. Only 50–50 federal matching funds were provided for the administration of CWT projects, compared with the 3–1 ratio (75 percent federal–25 percent state) to cover the costs of social services. Project sponsors also had to contribute all of the costs of supervision, materials, and training on CWT projects, in addition to their regular matching share of public assistance. It was, therefore, not surprising that, in order to obtain the maximum federal contribution, most states and localities chose to expand "social services" rather than set up CWT projects.

CWT projects provided little training that would improve the employability of participants. According to estimates by Bureau of the Budget (now the Office of Management and Budget), about 90 percent of the funds were disbursed for work payments, leaving very little for rehabilitative services. Nor did recipients have any monetary incentive for participating in CWT. A consistent feature of all projects, which varied considerably otherwise, was a prohibition on additional income for participants in return for work performed (other than work-connected expenses). Instead, participants were required to "work off" the amount of assistance they received, usually at the prevailing wage for comparable work performed in the community.

Antipoverty Work and Training

The Economic Opportunity Act of 1964 expanded the CWT program. Under Title V of the Act, grants were to be given to state and local welfare agencies to pay the full costs of "demonstration" projects so that the states could establish Work Experience and Training (WET) programs and provide for the expansion of CWT projects. In addition to unemployed parents on relief, "other needy persons," including single adults, were declared eligible. A 1965 amendment to the Act qualified farm families with less than $1,200 net annual income to participate in the program. But 70 percent of Title V clients were recipients of federally supported public assistance. The program reached its peak enrollment of 71,000 in 1967. Roughly half of these were male, and two-fifths black. Only two-thirds had ever had six months of continual work experience, and most were poorly educated.

The additional funds allocated to this effort, $112 million during WET's first year of operations, and the broadening of eligibility reflected an increasing realization that low national unemployment rates might not be sufficient to assure a job for everyone who wants work. Even though unemployment dropped throughout the 1960s, certain groups continued to experience considerable joblessness. A basic tenet of the antipoverty effort was an attempt to reach out, even beyond the welfare rolls, to help persons who cannot compete in the labor market—to remove the "structural" barriers to their unemployment.

The challenge to the sponsors of Title V projects, as under CWT, was to provide useful training and work for participants. This proved to be a formidable task; most enrollees had multiple handicaps and little attachment to regular work. While the enrollees' work assignments featured a certain amount of informal vocational instruction, the bulk of these assignments was limited to low-paying, unskilled occupations. This phenomenon was understandable in light of the trainees' limited skills and educational attainment. WET project administrators, however, advanced little evidence that occupational training has led to the upgrading of trainees over their former occupational levels. Nor is there evidence that Title V training led to more advanced vocational education.

Furthermore, Title V administrators insisted that their work-experience assignments be limited almost exclusively to government agencies and nonprofit organizations, and few trainees were assigned to private employers. This reluctance to become involved with the private sector hindered efforts to promote economic independence through employment for a significant number of persons.

There is little evidence that Title V administrators made adequate use of the flexibility they had in utilizing funds. While the basic combination of vocational training, work experience, education, and day care as part of the "individual employability plan" was certainly needed, the flexibility existed more in the rhetoric of WET officials than in project implementation. For instance, the most pressing need of some potential Title V clients may have been a second-hand car to get to an available job rather than complex "rehabilitative" services or work experience. Similarly, "transitional" supportive services—for example, helping individuals during the early stages of regular employment—might have been provided with Title V funds. Such services might have included subsidizing day care for mothers with young children once they secured employment, extending financial aid to cover work-connected expenses, or simply "hand holding." Only in isolated instances were these traditional services offered. The welfare agencies responsible for the administration of Title V projects found it difficult to expand their activities beyond traditional income-support efforts. With little or no prior experience with training or placement, or awareness of labor market operations, the state and local welfare agencies were hard put to design work-experience projects that would enhance the employability and earning potential of enrollees.

Despite laudable goals of rehabilitation and uplift, WET remained primarily a work relief and income-maintenance program. Expenditure patterns show this clearly: In fiscal 1968, for example, well over one-half of the funds were spent for income maintenance, but only one-sixth each for work-experience activities and vocational education. Table 21–4 shows estimated average costs per trainee in fiscal 1968.

The overall success of WET in reducing dependency through rehabilitation was modest. According to one survey, three of every four trainees departed without completing their assignments; only one-fifth left to take a

TABLE 21–4   *Work Experience and Training, Estimated Average Cost Per Trainee, Fiscal 1968*

EXPENDITURE ITEM	AMOUNT
TOTAL	$1,368
Agency administration and services	83
Cash payments	
Maintenance	
Group I [a]	332
Group II [b]	1,451
Work-connected expenses	110
Services	
Adult basic education	87
Vocational instruction	212
Child care	70
Medical	14
Work experience	180

[a] Trainees in this group received the difference between total basic needs, as defined by state, and amount of public assistance paid by state.
[b] Trainees in this group received full needs assistance, if not on state public assistance.
SOURCE: Based on Department of Health, Education, and Welfare data. Sar A. Levitan, *Antipoverty Work and Training Efforts: Goals and Reality,* Policy Papers in Human Resources and Industrial Relations No. 3 (Ann Arbor, Mich.: The Institute of Labor and Industrial Relations and the National Manpower Policy Task Force, 1967), p. 93.

job. Fifty percent of the trainees who left Title V (whether by "graduation" or drop out) continued on public assistance rolls; of these, 17 percent were employed and 83 percent unemployed.

Nor did the high dropout rate presage success for "graduates." Through June 1967, some 42,000 trainees had completed all training prescribed for them. While one-half obtained employment immediately and another one-eighth went on to advanced training under other programs, fully three-eighths were unable to find employment immediately following completion of their Title V training, even in the tight labor markets that prevailed at the time.

Thus, as a rehabilitation program, WET did not rate highly. This is especially true because the average family with an employable parent remains on relief for only nine months and thus most would have found employment even without the program.

The Work Incentive Program

The major failing of WET was that few participants moved on to become self-supporting through private sector employment. The limitations of the program's training and rehabilitative services were partly to blame, but perhaps of greater importance was the lack of incentives and the failure of participants to find jobs that paid above poverty income. There were some rewards for participation because enrollees could receive the full amount of the state's minimum standard welfare payment and allowances for work-related expenses; however, neither of these was available for former participants with private jobs. Without any "sticks" or "carrots," few chose to leave welfare rolls when they were not filling WET slots.

In an attempt to induce public assistance recipients to seek employment, to make work "worthwhile," Congress enacted the Work Incentive program as part of the 1967 amendments to the Social Security Act. By providing work and training incentives, Congress affirmed again the interdependence of work and public assistance, even though the incentives left much to be desired.

Rather than including persons not on AFDC as had WET, WIN consolidated its target population by aiming only at public assistance recipients in order to stem the burgeoning welfare rolls. This strategy also assisted WIN administrators. Because clients already received income maintenance, there was less pressure to place them quickly; instead, more thorough training could be provided. Moreover, funds did not have to be siphoned off for maintenance payments but could be concentrated to increase employability.

During training, participants received $30 per month along with continued welfare payments and the social services needed for successful completion of training. Along with the inducements for participation to entice welfare recipients to enter training or to find work, WIN also featured a work requirement. Most adults in AFDC families were required to register with a local welfare agency for referral. But because registrations far exceeded available positions, a list of priorities was used to ration the flow, in decreasing order of job-readiness. Included, in order of preference, were (a) unemployed fathers; (b) dependent youths aged 16 and over who were not in school, at work, or in training, and for whom there were no educational plans to be implemented within three months; and (c) volunteer mothers from AFDC rolls.

To make these persons employable, WIN offered a wide range of services, presumably adapted to each individual's needs. These could include orientation, job tryouts, basic education and other prevocational training, institutional training, OJT, referral to other manpower programs and follow-up, and day care for children. In theory, an "employability development plan" was to be developed for each participant, detailing the package of services appropriate to his needs. The intent of WIN was that participants would receive more intensive and more individualized services than they had under WET.

Despite its larger goals in replacing WET, WIN did not expand at its projected rate, nor were its rehabilitative services a marked improvement over what WET offered. Because instructions to the states on the establishment of projects were inadequate and limiting statutes in some states had

TABLE 21–5   *WIN Enrollment by Major Program Component as of December 31, 1970*

COMPONENT	ENROLLMENT
TOTAL	109,142
Orientation and assessment	7,206
Basic education	22,877
Vocational training	23,545
Other (prevocational) training	2,019
On-the-job training (including enrollees suspended to NAB-JOBS)	1,721
Suspended to other manpower training programs (excluding enrollees suspended to NAB-JOBS)	4,924
Work experience	2,274
Special work projects	1,057
Other job experience	866
At work and receiving follow-up services (job entry period)	12,304
In holding status awaiting an opening in first program component (initial component holding)	6,930
In holding between components (program-related holding)	9,263
Job-ready but not yet placed (job entry holding)	6,358
In holding due to problems such as health, day care, legal aid, etc. (nonprogram related holding)	7,790

SOURCE: U.S. Department of Labor, unpublished data.

to be repealed, WIN started slowly. Although officials had hoped to fill 150,000 slots by the end of fiscal 1970, only 109,000 were enrolled (Table 21–5).

WIN was a more ambitious program than its predecessors (Table 21–6). It emphasized institutional training, including basic education and day care. But at an average annual cost of $1,250 per slot (exclusive of work incentives once jobs are found), WIN could not offer much more extensive services than WET. Enrollees required an average of nine months of training, at an average cost per enrollee of almost $1,000.

Most WIN enrollees received either nominal instruction or no instruction at all, and many were provided orientation and placement counseling and little more. The training offered under WIN was probably little better than that under WET, and its permanent effect cannot be expected to be larger. Therefore WIN's manpower services are likely to have few long-run benefits, in contrast with its work incentives.

Day care is a necessary ingredient in increasing the employability of most AFDC heads. In many ways, it was the most critical component of WIN. In the past, meager day-care expenditures limited program performance. Indeed, former Secretary of HEW Robert Finch suggested that "the failure of day care in great part has contributed to the failure of the WIN

TABLE 21–6   *Work Incentive Program Costs, by Activity, 1969–1972*

FUNDING BY ACTIVITY	1969 ACTUAL	1970 ACTUAL	1971 ESTIMATE	1972 ESTIMATE
Total programs costs funded (in millions)	$37.4	$101.4	$166.8	$276.9
Distribution by component	100%	100%	100%	100%
Training and incentives	89	82	76	72
On-the-job training	2	1	1	4
Institutional training	58	59	55	46
Work experience and orientation	13	8	7	11
Work projects	a	a	1	1
Employability planning, job development, and follow-up	9	9	7	7
Program direction and evaluation	6	5	4	3
Child care	11	18	24	28

a Less than 0.5 percent.
SOURCE: Computed from U.S. Office of Management and Budget data published in annual federal budgets.

program. . . ." [4] Because of WIN's slow start and the large number of male enrollees in its early stages, only 85,000 children were receiving day care under the program as of mid-1970, and only one-fifth of these in regular day-care facilities.

These levels are not adequate for the expected child-care workload. One estimate for fiscal 1972, for example, projected that 55 percent of the average enrollment (160,000) would be mothers requiring day care. On the assumption that the average mother has 2.5 children in need of care, a workload of 220,000 results. If all AFDC households are considered as the universe of need, it became clear that day-care facilities will have to be vastly expanded if the goal of WIN to reduce sharply the AFDC rolls is to materialize. A study of AFDC households in 1969 revealed that about 90 percent had some combination of preschool and school age (under 16) children for whom care would probably be required.

Providing this child care is costly. HEW currently estimates that "acceptable" group day care for 3–5-year-olds costs $1,860 on a year-round basis. After school and summer care, for children from 6 to 13, costs an estimated $650 per year. These standards of acceptability and estimates of cost may be high—certainly, in many cases, cheaper arrangements can be made with relatives or friends—but the price tag will still be substantial.[5]

Even if day care were adequate and training intensive, the effectiveness of WIN would depend on the availability of jobs. Its basic assumption is that welfare recipients can be trained for and placed in private employment. Whatever the cost of its services, they are of little use if work is not available. And, so far, the performance of WIN has left doubts about the employability of participants and their prospects for self-support.

Of the 167,000 who had been enrolled in WIN through April 30, 1970, only 25,000 had moved into jobs, with only 10,000 receiving pay adequate to leave relief altogether. These, however, were probably the easiest to place among the clientele because the early enrollees were very definitely "creamed." Although AFDC-UP cases make up only 5 percent of the AFDC population, they constituted 4 percent of the WIN participants in fiscal 1969; and many of these would have found jobs on their own without assistance. After this more employable group was processed, placements became more difficult. There were 53,000 dropouts through fiscal 1970, many of whom were simply dismayed by the lack of prospects and left.

Placement difficulties intensified with increasing unemployment in 1970. Few employers were willing to hire welfare recipients when they were laying off more qualified workers or were being subsidized in hiring less disadvantaged ones under JOBS. Recognizing this problem, an expanded public employment program was proposed, along with employer subsidies for hiring WIN enrollees. It was claimed that such measures were necessary to put welfare recipients to work. However, these would add substantially to the cost of WIN. Private employer subsidies under the JOBS program cost around $3,000 per slot, and the price could be slightly higher for the more disadvantaged WIN enrollees. Despite these subsidies, wages are likely to be low. For instance, half of contract JOBS hires earned less than $2.00 per hour, and four-fifths less than $2.50. Because full-year employment is the exception, this is hardly enough to support the average-sized welfare family. Given the high probable cost of subsidies and low return in wages, it is pertinent to ask whether the effort is justified.

The argument that training is a one-shot proposition and that AFDC mothers will continue to work long after their children no longer need attention carries little weight. Most studies reveal that women work anyway when their children are old enough, that AFDC would be cut off at any rate when the youngest child reached 18, that the jobs for which they are trained are hardly lifetime positions, and that future child-bearing is very likely to interrupt work experience.

This is not to deny that many can be helped by WIN, and that for them it will be a cost-effective measure. The problem lies in determining how many, and who in particular, can benefit from participation in WIN to such a degree that it will justify costs. A variety of techniques have been used to calculate the universe of need and the prospects of success.

Probably only a minority of welfare recipients will ever be able to get off relief through employment. For a four-person, female-headed family, hourly earnings of $2.25 or more on a full-time basis would be needed to remove recipients from relief rolls in 30 states. In only nine states could the family head earn less than $2.00 per hour and become completely self-supporting. Leonard Hausman, for example, has estimated that no more than one-third of AFDC mothers and two-thirds of AFDC-UP fathers could, in the mid-1960s, have earned as much as they received from welfare.[6] Our review here of the employability of welfare mothers suggests that few families could earn as much as their AFDC payment.

Most of the evidence thus far accumulated suggests that, even without the advent of unfavorable economic conditions, WIN's success in helping welfare recipients to find and keep jobs will be limited. Earnings during 1969 of a sample of early (and the most employable) WIN graduates averaged only $2.30 per hour, even though many were in clerical and blue-collar occupations. One-fifth of the males earned less than $2.00 per hour and one-half earned $2.50 or more, while one-half of the females earned less than $2.00 and only one-sixth earned $2.50 or more.

Whether inducements and training will prove effective depends on how easily the obstacles impeding those with higher employment potential can be overcome. Given the limited earnings potential of most AFDC mothers, the obvious strategy is to concentrate on those who are most employable and face the fewest obstacles to work. This means that the ones who are served first should be mostly male family heads receiving AFDC-UP, female heads with access to free or low-cost child-care facilities, or those whose children no longer need day care.

This has been the strategy of WIN. But even in serving such a select clientele, performance has been meager. It is doubtful that, if a cost-benefit study were done of WIN experience, the investment would be shown to have a positive return.

Some would argue that this is beside the point, and that substituting "workfare for welfare" is worth whatever price may be involved. These arguments are based on the assumption that jobs are available for everyone who wants to work and that depending upon welfare robs children of self-esteem and breeds future generations of welfare recipients. Few would deny that a working family head sets a better example than one who lives on the dole, and it is probable that welfare begets welfare, but there is much debate about the degree of such effect. It has been demonstrated however, that lack of education, poor diet, and crowded housing also generate dependency. There is a need, therefore, to balance the impact of WIN with income-maintenance expenditures. The money used to create work, if a positive cost is involved, could be applied to other ends which might reduce future welfare rolls to a greater or lesser extent. Little is known about inter-generational effects of receiving welfare, or the impact of putting the family head to work and the children in day care. Without evidence, those arguing for jobs at any cost cannot be proven wrong, and the price to be paid in substituting welfare for workfare must be resolved politically.

ALTERNATIVES FOR THE FUTURE

The CWT, WET, and WIN programs tried with scant success to "solve" the welfare problem by rehabilitating AFDC recipients. Despite these efforts, relief rolls—and criticism of the public assistance system—continued to grow.

By the end of the 1960s, several schemes for reforming the welfare system had been proposed. Three broad criteria can be used to compare the wide variety of proposals: the extent of coverage and the levels of assistance; provisions made to enhance the employability of recipients (including work incentives and work requirements, provisions for training, and supportive services); and the costs involved. And the proposals can be grouped into three basic categories: guaranteed income, or negative income tax; family allowances; and employment guarantees including wage subsidies.

Income-Maintenance Strategies

The simplest and yet most comprehensive welfare proposal was the guaranteed income, or negative income tax. This would maintain an income floor for all persons by granting cash subsidies to those whose earnings fall below that level. To encourage low-income workers not to drop out of the labor force, a percentage of earnings would not be considered in calculating subsidies. Out of each dollar earned, the low-income family could keep some fixed amount without an equal reduction in its subsidy.

Proposals varied widely as to the minimum floor and the percentage of income that could be retained. The lower the floor and the proportion of income retained as a work incentive, the lower the cost of the program. If the guaranteed income were higher and incentives lower, costs would multiply and more people would be likely to drop out of the labor force and live off the dole. However, a lower floor would be injurious to those families whose head could not work and for whom incentives are meaningless. The basic problem of the guaranteed income is that it leaves such families at a minimum level of subsistence because their subsidy could be raised without increasing payments to all those who work and supplement their subsidies.

Another method of providing cash assistance for the poor would be to pay all families with children a regular allowance to supplement their own income and meet some portion of the costs of child rearing. This proposal recognizes that the wage system distributes income inadequately because wages are based on productivity or on tradition rather than on need. While the principle of equal pay for equal work is desirable as a protection against discrimination based on color or sex, it ignores the differing needs of families and tends to deprive children in large families of basic necessities. The underlying justification for family allowances is that a child's well-being should concern society at large.

Family allowances are now paid in one form or another in over 60 countries, including most industrial nations. But despite this wide acceptance elsewhere and its frequent proposal here, the idea has never received active consideration in the United States.

Family allowance programs are not a complete alternative to a guaranteed income because many poor do not have children; but because family size is so closely correlated with poverty such allowances would lift many adults out of poverty along with their children. As with the guaranteed income, family allowances make no distinction based on labor-force status. But the family allowance has several advantages. Because an income (or means) test is not needed the plan would greatly reduce administrative costs and would interfere relatively little with work incentives. Because the program gives benefits to all children it would probably find broader political support than any alternative.

Less heralded than the guaranteed income were proposals to guarantee employment and to subsidize wages. Immediate drawbacks were that only employable persons would benefit and that the government's role in the economy would be much increased. If the federal government became "employer of last resort," for example, it would expand greatly both as an employer and as a provider of goods and services. Furthermore, unless wage levels in the public sector jobs were low, workers might be induced to leave private employment for them. But low wages would not lift many, especially large, families from poverty. Similarly, wage subsidies would assist only the employed and might result in serious distortions of the market mechanism.

Combining Workfare and Welfare

The President's Commission on Income Maintenance Programs (the Heineman Commission) was appointed by President Johnson in 1968 to study the income needs of the poor and existing government programs designed to meet these needs. The Commission recommended a federally-financed and -administered universal income supplement program. Cash payments would vary with family size, providing a minimum of $750 per adult and $450 per child, and be available to any needy family or individual. A family of four, for example, would be guaranteed $2,400. To provide work incentives, the basic payment would be reduced 50 cents for each dollar of income from other sources. The family of four could receive some supplement up to $4,800. Such a program would have added about $6 billion of net income for 10 million families in 1970. Of this, $5 billion would go directly to the poor, making it a relatively efficient program, and the rest to those slightly above the poverty line. By this single effort, half of the income needs of the poor would be met.[7]

In August 1969, President Nixon proposed a Family Assistance Plan (FAP) which would establish a uniform floor for all families with children throughout the nation, increase work incentives, provide a work requirement, and expand training slots and supportive services. In addition to the traditional clients of public assistance, FAP would include almost 1.3 million families whose head worked full-time, year-round and another 650,000 families whose head worked substantially during 1969 but remained in poverty.

FAP would provide a uniform income guarantee of $500 per adult and $300 per child so that a family of two adults and two children with no other income would receive $1,600. An additional $840 worth of food stamps and medical services valued at $500 would bring total annual income to at least $2,940. Benefits would not be reduced until annual earnings exceeded $720, and thereafter by only 50 cents for each dollar earned. For the family of four, cash benefits would cease when earnings reached $3,920. Because many poor persons now receive more substantial benefits than this minimum federal guarantee, states would be required to supplement federal payments where necessary to maintain existing benefits levels for dependent families. However, states would not be required to supplement incomes of the working poor.

FAP would more than double the number of persons eligible to receive assistance and income supplements—at an estimated annual price tag of $8 billion. These added initial costs were intended to help avoid greater outlays in the future. The purpose of boosting work incentives, expanding training, and providing day care is to replace welfare with workfare, to move all those able to work off welfare rolls and onto payrolls, and to stop the growth of relief.

Persons would have a financial incentive for entering training, as under WIN. A family would receive either $30 per month or the difference between the allowance under the regular training program and their family assistance payment (plus state supplements), whichever is greater. In many cases, the increment would be larger than $30. Training is intended to enhance the employability and earnings potential of recipients, and the incentive is designed to make training immediately attractive.

Work incentives would also be increased over WIN levels to insure that individuals presently working would not stop once eligible for relief. The income disregard would be increased to $60 a month (or $720 annually). This is equal, according to the Labor Department, to the average level of work-related expenses. It should be noted, however, that WIN allowed exclusion of $30 plus work-connected expenses whereas FAP would allow a flat $60. The tax rate on earnings above the disregard would be reduced from the two-thirds under WIN to one-half. Marginal tax rates above one-half are thought to seriously discourage work effort because the individual is then "earning" more for the government than for himself.

If the "carrot" failed under FAP, there would still remain the "stick" —the work requirement. Any adult in a family eligible for FAP would be required to register with a public employment office, with the following exceptions: the ill, incapacitated, or elderly; a mother or other relative caring for a child under 6; a dependent youth between 16 and 21 if attending school; a person needed in the home to care for an ill member of the household; and persons working 30 or more hours weekly. Should a person not excluded from mandatory referral refuse to register, his portion of the family assistance payment would be withheld. Persons not required to register would, of course, be allowed to do so.

The requirement, however, has been criticized on one hand for being coercive and on the other for penalizing too lightly those who refuse to register. Moreover, concern has been voiced about the nature of jobs recipients might be obliged to take. Recipients deemed employable could be required to take "suitable" jobs paying either the applicable minimum wage or the prevailing wage for similar work in the community. Especially for those occupations where minimum wage provisions do not apply, the prevailing wage may be quite low.

FAP includes several improvements over AFDC. Extension of coverage to the working poor would eliminate the anomaly of welfare recipients receiving higher incomes than those who work regularly at low wages or intermittently. Because of the income disregard, the limit on marginal tax rates, and the coverage of the working poor, an individual would always gain by increasing his earnings. FAP would also reach far more of the poor and disburse larger amounts of money to them. While AFDC covers only 35 percent of poor children, for example, FAP would cover all. It is estimated that FAP payments by themselves would move nearly 2 million persons across the poverty line.

The pressures against family stability under AFDC would be reduced by FAP. The "man in the house" rule, failure of one-half of the states to adopt AFDC-UP, and stringent requirements in the 25 states that do have AFDC-UP all eroded family stability because a poor father could often increase his family's income by deserting them. FAP would diminish this incentive for family breakup—perhaps one of its most important features.

By establishing minimum standards on a nationwide basis, FAP would significantly decrease the fragmented provision of public assistance. Similarly, by reducing interstate differentials, it would diminish incentives to move to areas offering higher levels of assistance. But in failing to make adjustment for urban-rural cost of living variations, FAP would create some inconsistency.

Perhaps the major improvement of FAP over WIN is that day care would be expanded. Lack of child care, which limited the effectiveness of WIN, was to be counteracted by new administrative measures. Full federal funding, possible authorization of private agencies to provide child care, and expected revision of unreasonable licensing requirements are viewed as sufficient to remove the child-care bottleneck.

Despite these many potential improvements, the FAP approach has drawbacks. In attempting to put more welfare recipients to work, the issues raised under WIN become more critical. Are private sector jobs available? If not, is it worthwhile to subsidize employment? Are the high costs of day care, training, and subsidies justified? The answers to these questions are not at all clear cut.

Many people feel that jobs are available for those who really want to work. They point, for instance, to the unfilled needs for domestic workers in most upper-class neighborhoods or to openings for dishwashers. In fact, however, such jobs are limited in number, pay, and accessibility. WIN graduates who find jobs are not getting much above the minimum wage, and too frequently these jobs offer little opportunity for upward mobility. But even dead-end jobs are in limited supply, and if those welfare recipients who are not now seeking work were to do so, the job shortage would become even more acute. If unemployment rates level off at about 4.5 percent, as many have predicted, there is little likelihood that the projected welfare clientele of FAP can find private sector employment.

Congress did not adopt President Nixon's FAP, and alternative approaches were proposed. Most prominent was the plan of Congressman Wilbur Mills, Chairman of the House Ways and Means Committee. The changes he proposed included an increase of the income floor for a family of four from $1,600 to $2,400 and the elimination of about $840 worth of food stamps; full federal funding of the basic benefits, leaving to those states that paid higher amounts the discretion to maintain existing levels of benefits; giving added responsibility to federal authorities for handling job training and placement activities; and a greater emphasis on public sector employment.

Other alternatives include the Rehabilitation and Employment Assistance and Child Care Act (REACH) and the Adequate Income Act (AIA). In the former, Representative Al Ullman of Oregon attempted to distinguish between those who can work and those who receive public assistance. To assist the employable persons, child-care services and public service jobs would be substantially increased. However, the distinction upon which REACH rests has thus far proved unworkable and is not likely to become more useful in the future. AIA, introduced by the 11 House members of the Black Caucus, is modeled after the goals of the National Welfare Rights Organization. It would provide a family of four an annual income of $6,500 based solely on need; benefits would be available until total family income reached nearly $10,000.

Whether the FAP package of training, more liberal work incentives, and increased day care or some alternative plan is a wise investment to achieve greater employability of relief recipients is not known. Experience with WET and WIN does not justify great optimism in, or rapid expansion of, "rehabilitation" efforts.

CONTINUING ISSUES

The proposals pose the additional problem of determining the minimum income floor and appropriate incentive formulas. These are critical because all low-income families, not just those on welfare, would be eligible. If the floor were raised or the ratio increased, the cost of the program would be significantly magnified as those with a higher income became eligible for assistance. Payments to those who cannot or do not work could be raised only by increasing the subsidies to those who do work. Thus, the welfare of those at the bottom would probably suffer because they could not be helped without vast increases in welfare costs. But if the income floor were raised, it is likely that work incentives would be diminished, and persons able to work would be willing to remain in dependency.

Resolution of this dilemma will remain a basic social problem in an affluent society that strives to provide for the needy, but without damaging incentives to work, which help create affluence.

NOTES

1. U.S. Congress, Senate Committee on Finance, *H.R. 16311, The Family Assistance Act of 1970, Revised and Resubmitted to the Committee on Finance by the Administration,* 91st Cong., 2nd Sess. (Washington, D.C.: U.S. Government Printing Office, 1970), pp. 55–58.

2. U.S. Congress, House Committee on Ways and Means, *Report of Findings of Special Review of Aid to Families with Dependent Children in New York City,* 91st Cong., 1st Sess. (Washington, D.C.: U.S. Government Printing Office, 1969), pp. 33–40.

3. Andrew K. Solarz, "Effects of Earnings Exemption Provision on AFDC Recipients," *Welfare in Review* (January-February 1971), p. 19.

4. U.S. Congress, House Committee on Ways and Means, *Hearings on the Subject of Social Security and Welfare Proposals,* 91st Cong., 1st Sess. (Washington, D.C.: U.S. Government Printing Office, 1969), p. 367.

5. Ibid., pp. 283–286.

6. Leonard J. Hausman, *The Potential for Work among Welfare Parents,* U.S. Department of Labor, Manpower Administration, Manpower Research Monograph No. 12 (Washington, D.C.: U.S. Government Printing Office, 1969).

7. *Poverty Amid Plenty,* The Report of the President's Commission on Income Maintenance Programs (Washington, D.C.: U.S. Government Printing Office, 1969), Chap. 5.

Part V
Minority Income and Employment

Chapter 22
Black Income and Employment

Low income and inadequate employment opportunity were among the most important human resource development problems for blacks and other minorities in the 1960s. Underutilization and underdevelopment not only deprive blacks of opportunities to improve their material welfare but also cost the nation the economic contribution they could make if they had better employment and income-earning opportunities, to say nothing of the costs of social instability.

Minority groups, particularly blacks, did much to stimulate human resource development programs during the 1960s. The civil rights movement's concentration on political rights during the 1950s gave way to greater demands for economic equality during the 1960s, when it became abundantly clear that abstract rights without economic opportunity had little meaning. Moreover, the real nature of racial discrimination came into sharper focus as the adoption of programs to overcome specific overt acts of discrimination produced limited results. It became increasingly apparent that institutionalized racism was more deeply rooted and pervasive than more overt forms of discrimination and therefore that vigorous and comprehensive education, manpower, and welfare measures would be required to combat it. Institutionalized racism affects all aspects of life—education, housing, jobs, social affairs—and causes the persons discriminated against not to aspire to or prepare for the kinds of jobs from which they are barred.

BLACK POPULATION AND
EMPLOYMENT SHIFTS

Some of the nation's most significant race problems have come about in large measure because of the migration of blacks out of the rural South. Until roughly the time of World War I, almost all blacks were in the South and most of them were concentrated in the so-called "black belt," a crescent of counties extending from Washington, D.C., through east Texas, each of which had a majority black population until the 1940s. Indeed, as late as 1940, over three-fourths of the nation's black population resided in the South. Because of the great outmigration since around the time of World War I, today only about one-half of the nation's blacks remain in the South. Until the 1960s, black outmigration appears to have been largely in response to job opportunities, which opened up initially because of the cessation of immigration from Europe into northern labor markets with the outbreak of World War I.

In the South most blacks had been employed in agriculture or in certain "Negro" nonfarm jobs. In agriculture, the sharecropping system predominated; it provided little incentive for blacks or whites to improve either themselves or the soil. The sharecropping system required very little education or training. Indeed, even managerial experience which many farmers acquire on the job was denied the sharecropper because landlords made most of the major decisions.

Nonagricultural jobs available to blacks were, for the most part, hot, dirty, or otherwise disagreeable, except for jobs in the black community, where segregation protected black craftsmen and technical and professional workers from white encroachment. Outside their own communities, blacks were concentrated in labor and service jobs with very few exceptions, and these mainly in cases where blacks were too numerous to be excluded from an occupation or trade. For example, many blacks were trained as bricklayers and carpenters before the Civil War. After emancipation, whites had considerable difficulty excluding blacks from these jobs because there were sufficient numbers of Negro craftsmen to protect their share of the market. As a consequence, black bricklayers were admitted to white unions or were organized into segregated locals; on the whole, black bricklayers have suffered relatively little discrimination in employment.

Crafts (for example, electrical workers and plumbers) that flourished mainly after the Civil War had very few blacks in them. Thus, whites were able to freeze blacks out of these occupations except for limited work in the black community or in residential construction. Whites refused to permit blacks to work in commercial and industrial construction. If it had not been for the black colleges, which trained black craftsmen, there would have been very little opportunity for blacks to learn crafts that required considerable technical and on-the-job training. Blacks were uniformly barred from apprenticeship programs which supplied many skilled workers and could not work in the higher paying sectors of many industries except as laborers; hence, they had very limited opportunity to acquire skills on the job.

In manufacturing industries, blacks usually were restricted to laborers jobs regardless of their qualifications. Whites, of course, were hired into lines of progression that made it possible for them to move up into a wide range of jobs from which blacks were barred. Moreover, this pattern did not change significantly until the 1960s in the South.

As will be noted at greater length when we look at the statistics on racial employment patterns, very few blacks have held white-collar jobs and these have been restricted almost exclusively to southern black communities. Racial segregation is partly a caste system, so the prevailing sentiment in the South made it unthinkable before the 1960s that blacks would seek better white-collar jobs, especially those jobs whose occupants had supervisory authority over whites.

The ample supply of black labor and the workers' lack of permanent attachment to employers made it difficult for some jobs to be structured in such a way as to exclude blacks. In these cases racial quota systems were adopted. General longshoreman's work, for example, has been divided along racial lines in many southern ports since the Civil War. It should be observed, however, that the quota system usually gave blacks inferior job opportunities. In New Orleans, for instance, the general longshoreman's work was divided, although blacks greatly outnumbered whites in this labor market. This meant that each black received less employment than each white worker attached to the market. In addition, whites reserved the better clerical jobs for themselves.

Black migration out of the South, which was accelerated by World War I, continued during the 1920s, slowed down some during the depression of the 1930s, speeded up again during World War II, and has continued since then. In 1940, 77 percent of the nation's blacks were in the South, compared with 60 percent in 1960 and about 50 percent in 1970. This black outmigration from the rural South has been one of the most significant developments of the last half century. In a relatively short time the black population has been transformed from predominantly rural and southern to predominantly urban and equally divided between the North and the South. Although segregation was not as institutionalized outside the South, racism was a problem for blacks in the North as well as in the South. Moreover, because they were not very well prepared by training or experience for nonfarm jobs, blacks held mainly menial jobs in northern as well as southern cities. Indeed, in some ways the black's lot was worse outside the South. Blacks did not even hold the better jobs in black neighborhoods and were concentrated in central cities outside the South. In addition, those blacks who moved North during and after World War II found declining job opportunities in many of the industries that traditionally had absorbed large numbers of semiskilled and unskilled workers. Moreover, ghetto labor markets had characteristics that made it difficult for many young blacks to move into the mainstream even when discriminatory barriers were lowered. (See Chapter 12.) The ghetto labor market syndrome probably explains why blacks recently arrived from the South have better income and employment experience than blacks with similar characteristics who were born in northern cities. The submarginal or marginal labor markets, which predominate in ghettos, have many job openings that ghetto dwellers find unattractive or occupy only for short periods. Blacks fresh from the South probably find these submarginal or marginal jobs more attractive than the opportunities that had been available to them.

Other problems confronted blacks outside the South. Indeed, although greater political power was available to them than had been the case in the South, and they confronted less formal segregation imposed by law, blacks nevertheless encountered discrimination and hostility from whites in other areas. The influx of blacks from the South with different values and limited education or job training caused many northern whites to move out of central cities, leaving behind areas with larger black majorities, especially in the schools, and working-class or retired whites who had unsufficient income to move out or who had such large investments in their homes that they were reluctant to move. These developments created racial tensions between black and white workers. Indeed, some observers believe that these tensions will upset the New Deal coalition, which included blacks and white ethnics, who had been concentrated in many of the neighborhoods into which blacks have moved.

Migration created problems for the South as well as the North. Those southerners who thought they could export their black welfare problems to the North were very short-sighted indeed. By not taking measures to retain blacks, the South aggravated its human resource development problem because the most productive part of its black population moved out, leaving behind the older, less well-educated blacks who have limited productive potential and therefore are not attractive even to the marginal industries which predominate in the region's economy. These industries have moved out of the non-South into the South in search of workers with higher qualifications who will work at lower wages. Because of the rapid displacement of southerners from agriculture (discussed later) and the lower level of industrialization, labor markets have been more attractive to marginal enterprises in the South than they have been in the North. In addition, lower welfare payments in the South have forced more secondary workers in a family to work than is true in those areas where welfare payments are higher.

BLACK INCOME AND
EMPLOYMENT IN THE SOUTH

Some statistics will indicate the general dimensions of this problem:

1. Over 11 million of the nation's 24 million poor people, as classi-fied by the Social Security Administration in 1969, were in the South, and these were heavily concentrated in rural areas and among nonwhites.

2. The income disparity between nonwhites in the South and non-whites elsewhere is much greater than the disparity between whites in the South and the non-South. The South accounted for only about one-seventh of the nation's poor whites, but for two-thirds of its poor nonwhites. The average income of southern white families was about five-sixths that of white families outside the South, while the average income of south-ern nonwhites was only about three-fifths that of nonwhites in other regions.

3. A relatively large proportion of southern nonwhites are poor not because they are unemployed but because they are employed at low wages. In 1966, for example, one-third of nonwhite men, but only 7 percent of white men, who worked full-time in the South were poor.

4. Of course, because of differences in the cost of living the real in-come differentials between the South and the non-South are not as great as the money income differentials. In 1966, according to the Bureau of Labor Statistics, the cost of a moderate standard of living for a family of four was 13 percent lower in the South than in the non-South.

5. Incomes are particularly low in farming. Department of Agricul-ture data indicate that $10,000 worth of farm products are needed to provide the $2,500 net income regarded as the poverty line for farm oper-ators. In 1964, only 1.3 percent of southern blacks and 14.1 percent of white farm operators met this standard.

6. Not only are nonwhite farm incomes low relative to whites in the South, but also the racial income differential apparently widened during the 1960s. Social Security data that relate to the same individuals through time reveal that although the incomes of black male farm operators in the South averaged only about half those of nonblacks in 1960, the average increased by 39.7 percent for nonblacks but only 6.5 percent for ˙lacks between 1960 and 1965. According to these data, black farm opei ιtors gained only $76 in income on the average ($1,371 to $1,447) between 1960 and 1965, compared with a gain of $1,025 for nonblacks ($2,734 to $3,759). Because of his limited income, education, farm size, and access to credit, the black farmer faces special problems; his ability to adjust to technological and market changes is markedly different from that of whites; but, of course, many small white farmers face many of the same problems. The average size of farms operated by blacks is about one-fourth

that of farms operated by whites. Blacks also have less livestock and machinery and lower crop yields per acre and are much more dependent on cotton and tobacco, which are hardest hit by technological changes and federal agricultural policies. Indeed, about one-half of all black commercial farmers produce cotton, and one-fourth of them produce tobacco. Moreover, in spite of considerable displacement during the 1960s, agriculture remains the most important source of income for southern blacks; it provides four times as much employment for blacks as textiles, the largest manufacturing employer in the South.

Displacement of the Agricultural Population

Because of disadvantages that made it difficult for them to adopt to the changes of the 1950s and 1960s, blacks were displaced at a very rapid rate from southern agriculture, and this created serious problems for the South and the nation because it eliminated jobs for people who were not prepared by education, training, or experience for nonagricultural work. Consequently, these displaced people became unemployed or remained even more underemployed, and their increasing concentration in the rural nonfarm category or in urban slums has had serious social and economic consequences.

It is difficult to determine the extent to which the displacement of the agricultural labor force in the South has run its course. The technological revolution in cotton production is nearly complete, as indicated by the fact that aggregate production man-hours in 1966 were only 14 percent of what they had been in 1940. Future labor use in tobacco is uncertain because of potential technological changes and uncertain demand. Moreover, the demand for agricultural labor clearly depends on the future of public policies with respect to agriculture and rural development.

A fuller understanding of the agricultural displacement problem can be gained by comparing full-time jobs with the available work force, which gives a rough measure of underemployment. In 1950, there were about seven full-time jobs for every ten black or white workers. By 1969, there were about five full-time jobs for every ten white workers and 4.6 full-time jobs for every ten black workers. Moreover, the number of hired farm workers and farm operators declined in the South from 1,043,000 in 1950 to 513,000 in 1969. The amount of full-time agricultural employment in 1969—438,000 jobs—in the region apparently was split about equally between the races.

Combining the full-time job loss of 1,838,000 for family workers and 453,000 for hired farm workers gives a total loss of 2,291,000 agricultural jobs, which put considerable pressure on the South's economy. The magnitude of the pressure is shown by the fact that the agricultural job loss amounted to 14 percent of total nonagricultural employment in 1967.

Nonagricultural Employment

Some of the pressure was taken off the southern labor force by out-migration, which is not an unmixed blessing. For example, there is some evidence that migration caused racial income gaps in southern labor markets to widen because more productive blacks tended to migrate to other regions while more productive whites tended to come in. Welfare problems and economic conditions in the areas that productive people are abandoning are aggravated because they leave behind a less productive residual population. At the same time, however, the outmigrants create problems in the receiving areas because few who leave the rural South are prepared by education, training, or experience for nonagricultural jobs that pay much above the minimum wage. Blacks are disadvantaged not only by relatively few years of schooling but also by schooling of inferior quality. Adjusting for differences in quality, it is possible to conclude that more than 80 percent of black males who left southern agriculture had less than an effective seventh-grade education, and well over 50 percent had less than four years.

Black workers have special problems outside agriculture. Not only are they concentrated in low-wage jobs but also they apparently are increasing their proportions in declining industries. Employment statistics from the reports employers are required to file with the Equal Employment Opportunity Commission show that blacks make up over 25 percent of employment in seven industries with the poorest growth characteristics and only about 10 percent of employment in the seven leading growth industries. Of course, much, but not all, of the occupational differences between blacks and whites can be accounted for by differences in education and training because growth industries tend to have higher skill and education requirements than declining or stationary industries. In explaining employment patterns it is necessary to consider supply as well as demand conditions. Since blacks have lower education levels and less skill training and experience in the growth industries, it would be surprising to find racial equality in employment patterns even in the absence of discrimination.

THE RELATIVE INCOME OF BLACKS

Income probably is the best measure of economic welfare. It is, therefore, constructive to look at the long-run trends in black income relative to white income. However, because general comparisons are likely to conceal important differences, understanding is enhanced by examining various subgroups of blacks and whites. It is particularly important to examine the occupational and income differences between men and women, because the incomes of these groups clearly behave quite differently.

One major problem in measuring the long-run changes in the black's economic position is the construction of an appropriate index for this purpose. It is important to distinguish between relative and absolute gains. Blacks have made fairly steady absolute gains in income and occupational position, but the progress has not been as steady when the black's position is compared with that of whites. Becker, for example, found no noticeable change in black relative occupational status between 1910 and 1950.[1] This was true even though the blacks' average occupational level rose steadily throughout this period. The percentage of blacks in the skilled and semi-skilled occupations rose while the percentage in unskilled jobs fell, but the white work force went through the same upgrading process. To find a relative racial occupational index by region, Becker therefore constructed an index of occupational position by weighting average white wage levels for each occupation and found negligible regional changes over time in the blacks' position relative to whites. Becker's relative index of occupational position (black index divided by white index) for the North went from 0.73 in 1910 to 0.74 in 1940 and 0.77 in 1950 (reflecting slight wartime gains); the indexes for the South were 0.67 in 1910, 0.63 in 1940, and 0.67 in 1950.

In constructing any index, the weights used create a problem. Rayack, using varying weights for each period for unskilled, semiskilled, and skilled workers, found the following relative positions: [2]

	Black Index/White Index	
	North	South
1940	0.74	0.68
1950	0.85	0.80

However, if varying weights are used, changes in income as well as in job status are measured; Becker's constant weights permitted him to measure job status changes alone. If the wages of blacks rise because of wage leveling (which increases unskilled wages relative to skilled wages) and blacks remain concentrated in unskilled jobs, discrimination has not necessarily declined.

Alan Batchelder attempted to avoid the index number problem by using relative incomes as his measure. He found that the ratio of black to white income increased for women but declined for males during the 1950s and early 1960s: "The nonwhite-to-white ratio of men averaged 0.50 for 1958–1960 and fell to 0.49 for 1962." For females, the ratio "averaged .61 for 1958–1960 and rose to .67 for 1962."[3] Rashi Fein extended Batchelder's analysis and found the ratios for men to have been 0.52 in 1963 and 0.58 in 1964.[4] The female ratios stayed at 0.67 in 1963 and rose to 0.71 in 1964. The upward trend in black incomes relative to that of whites continued during the last half of the 1960s.

Andrew Brimmer, a black member of the Board of Governors of the Federal Reserve System, reviewed the extent of economic progress blacks made in the 1960s and projected these trends into the future.[5] His main theme was that blacks benefited more than whites from economic expansion during the 1960s, although the greatest gains have been made by blacks with the highest levels of education, and the disadvantaged in the black community are lagging behind. Brimmer expected the black community to benefit more than whites in the 1970s, primarily because of expansion in the national economy but also because of improvements in education. But he was concerned that black separatist programs would impede the economic progress of blacks by diverting them from the achievement of technical competence.

Nevertheless, blacks still lag considerably behind whites in these indicators, and there are some disturbing trends. Although black men gained in income relative to white men during the 1959–1967 period, the income gap widened within the black community because the greatest black gains were at the higher educational and income levels. Moreover, even though blacks have increased their incomes *relative* to whites, the *absolute* difference in family incomes increased between 1965 and 1970; in 1965 whites earned $3,365 more than blacks, but this had increased to $3,957 in 1970 (Table 22–1).

TABLE 22–1   *Median Annual Family Income of Blacks and Whites: 1965–1970*

	MEDIAN FAMILY INCOME RATIO		
YEAR	*White*	*Black*	*Black to White*
1970	$10,236	$6,279	0.61
1969	9,794	5,999	0.61
1968	8,937	5,360	0.60
1967	8,274	4,919	0.59
1966	7,792	4,506	0.58
1965	7,251	3,886	0.54

SOURCE: U.S. Bureau of the Census and U.S. Bureau of Labor Statistics, *The Economic and Social Status of Negroes in the United States, 1970,* Current Population Reports, Series P-23, No. 38; BLS Report No. 394 (Washington, D.C.: U.S. Government Printing Office, 1971), p. 27.

BLACK EMPLOYMENT PATTERNS

Claire C. Hodge argues that there was a "marked improvement" in the kinds of jobs held by black Americans between 1957 and 1967, although the data she uses also show that "the Negro today still holds a disproportionate share of the jobs at the lower end of the occupational ladder and is underrepresented in the higher skilled, better paying jobs." [6]

Between 1962 and 1967, blacks made considerable progress in medical and health occupations; the construction trades; as mechanics and repairmen; and in the protective service occupations. However, very little progress was made in managerial and sales occupations. Unlike Becker, Hodge does not attempt to account for the net effect of race on black employment patterns.

Although still not equal to that of whites, the occupational distribution of blacks and other minorities improved relatively rapidly during the 1960s. Between 1960 and 1969 blacks and other races increased their total employment by 21 percent compared with 18.1 percent for whites (Table 22–2). Moreover, blacks and other minorities gained relative to whites in the craftsman and white-collar categories. The racial occupational distribution also was equalized by the fact that minorities declined in the traditional "nonfarm laborers" category while whites were increasing their proportion of these jobs, and blacks and other minorities declined

TABLE 22–2   *Employed Persons 16 Years and Over, by Occupation Group and Color, Annual Averages, 1960 and 1969*

COLOR AND YEAR		TOTAL EMPLOYMENT	PROFESSIONAL & TECHNICAL	MANAGERS, OFFICIALS, PROPRIETORS	CLERICAL WORKERS	SALES WORKERS
Number Employed (thousands) and Percent Change						
White	1960	58,850	7,138	6,889	9,259	4,123
	1969	69,518	10,074	7,733	12,314	4,527
	Change	18.1%	41.1%	12.2%	33.0%	9.8%
Black and	1960	6,927	331	178	503	101
other races	1969	8,384	695	254	1,083	166
	Change	21.0%	110.0%	42.7%	115.3%	64.4%
Percent Distribution						
White	1960	100.0%	12.1%	11.7%	15.7%	7.0%
	1969	100.0	14.5	11.1	17.7	6.5
Black and	1960	100.0	4.8	2.6	7.3	1.5
other races	1969	100.0	8.3	3.0	12.9	2.0
Percent Distribution of Total						
White	1960	89.5%	95.6%	97.5%	94.8%	97.6%
	1969	89.2	93.5	96.8	91.9	96.5
Black and	1960	10.5	4.4	2.5	5.2	2.4
other races	1969	10.8	6.5	3.2	8.1	3.5

SOURCE: U.S. Department of Labor, *Manpower Report of the President* (Washington, D.C.: U.S. Government Printing Office, 1970), Table A-10, p. 227.

much faster than whites in the farm laborers and foreman categories. Consequently, blacks and other races increased their proportions of every other occupational group and although blacks are still disproportionately concentrated in the laborers and services category—jobs they have traditionally held, their proportion declined.

If blacks continue to improve their occupational distribution at the rate they experienced during the 1960s, nonwhites will fill 12 percent of all jobs by 1985, distributed at follows: [7]

Professional and technical	10.6%
Clerical	8.4
Sales	6.0
Skilled craftsmen	8.8
Nonfarm laborers	24.0
Private household workers	38.4
Farm laborers	24.6

Thus, blacks and other minorities will have to change their occupational positions even faster during the 1970s than they did during the 1960s if they are to attain occupational parity with whites by 1985.

CRAFTSMEN & FOREMEN	OPERATIVES	NONFARM LABORERS	PRIVATE HOUSEHOLD WORKERS	OTHER SERVICE WORKERS	FARMERS, FARM MANAGERS	FARM LABORERS & FOREMEN
Number Employed (thousands) and Percent Change						
8,139	10,536	2,602	991	4,836	2,557	1,778
9,484	12,368	2,795	917	6,372	1,759	1,176
16.5%	17.4%	7.4%	−7.5%	31.8%	−31.2%	−33.9%
415	1,414	951	982	1,214	219	622
709	2,004	877	714	1,525	84	272
70.8%	41.7%	−7.8%	−27.3%	25.6%	−61.6%	−56.3%
Percent Distribution						
13.8%	17.9%	4.4%	1.7%	8.2%	4.3%	3.0%
13.6	17.8	4.0	1.3	9.2	2.5	1.7
6.0	20.4	13.7	14.2	17.5	3.2	9.0
8.5	23.9	10.5	8.5	18.2	1.0	3.2
Percent Distribution of Total						
95.2%	88.2%	73.2%	50.2%	79.9%	92.1%	74.1%
93.0	86.1	76.1	56.2	80.7	95.4	81.2
4.8	11.8	26.8	49.8	20.1	7.9	25.9
7.0	13.9	23.9	43.8	19.3	4.6	18.8

Unemployment and Participation Rates

Blacks not only have been concentrated disproportionately in the lower income categories, but they also have suffered unemployment rates that generally are double those of whites, as was seen in Chapter 3. This pattern in unemployment rates developed during the 1950s; before about 1954, nonwhite unemployment rates generally were lower relative to whites.

Black and white labor-force participation rates have shown similar tendencies to shift during the postwar period. In 1948, the participation rates for nonwhite males and females were higher (84.8 percent and 44.4 percent, respectively) than the rates for whites (84.2 percent and 30.6 percent). In 1969, the participation rate for nonwhite females (50 percent) was still greater than that for white females (42 percent), but the nonwhite male rate (77 percent) was below that of white males (80 percent). Moreover, the participation rate for black male teenagers is below that of white male teenagers.

Income and Family Structure

Because women have lower incomes than men, regardless of race, the income disadvantages of nonwhites can be accounted for, in part, by differences in family structure. For example, a larger proportion of non-white families are headed by females (29 percent of nonwhites and 9 percent of whites in 1971), and a lower proportion are husband-wife families (73 percent of nonwhites and 89 percent of whites in 1966). If we contrast family income changes by race for craftsmen and operatives only, controlling in a rough way for differences in occupation and family structure, the relative income picture improves considerably. In 1966, for example, census figures show that median nonwhite family incomes were 60 percent of those of whites in the United States, ranging from 51 percent in the South to 74 percent in the North Central region. However, if we compare craftsman and operative families with husband and wife present, the nonwhite–white ratio rises to 72 percent in 1966 and 75 percent in 1970 for the United States and 63 percent in the South and 82 percent in the non-South.

Between 1960 and 1970, nonwhite craftsmen and operative husbands clearly had greater income gains in the South than in the non-South (56 percent and 30 percent) and their incomes increased faster than whites' incomes in both the South (where whites gained 58 percent) and the non-South (where whites gained 27 percent). The relatively large gains for nonwhites might be explained, in part, by the lower base from which they started in 1960, but it will be observed that southern nonwhites gained more than whites in *absolute* as well as relative terms. And southern non-whites gained more absolutely than northern nonwhites. In the South, white husbands who were heads of families gained $1,524 in median family incomes compared with $1,704 for nonwhites. Outside the South, whites gained $1,786 and nonwhites $1,677.

Nonwhite husbands in craftsman and operative families made considerably more relative income progress in 1966–1970 than in 1960–1966. Indeed, median incomes of nonwhite husbands actually *declined* from 84 percent of whites' in the non-South in 1960 to 82 percent in 1966. The relative income decline was particularly noticeable in the metropolitan non-South, where it went from 81 percent of whites' in 1960 to 77 percent in 1966. In the South, however, the nonwhite median income of husbands in craftsman and operative families increased more between 1960 and 1966 (26 percent) than between 1966 and 1970 (24 percent), due in part to the relatively better position of nonwhites in the rural South in 1960–1966 than in 1966–1970. In the metropolitan South, nonwhites made more progress in 1966–1970 than in 1960–1966. These differences undoubtedly reflect the displacement of blacks from southern agriculture during the late 1960s at a time of relative prosperity in metropolitan areas.

The income gap between whites and nonwhites is attributable, in part, to educational differentials. Although the median educational attainment of blacks and other races rose from 8.6 years in 1959 to 11.3 years in 1969, it still lagged over a year behind that of whites', which rose from 12.1 years in 1959 to 12.4 years in 1969. The median educational levels of white males equaled those of white females in the work force in 1970, but black males lagged 1.1 years behind black females (11.9 to 10.8). Black males thus lagged 1.6 years behind white males, whereas black females lagged only half a year behind white females. Of course, allowances also must be made for the differences in the quality of education of whites and blacks.

1970 data from the Bureau of the Census show the relationship between the median earnings of craftsman and operative husbands by years of school completed by race for 1960, 1966, and 1970. Nonwhite husbands who had completed high school lost in the 1960–1966 period but gained relative to whites between 1966 and 1970. Relative to whites, nonwhites with elementary educations gained in both periods. For husbands who had completed elementary school, the nonwhite/white median income ratio was 0.63 in 1960, 0.72 in 1966 and 0.71 in 1970. For those who had completed high school, the ratios were 0.75, 0.73, and 0.79. However, in 1970, whites who had completed elementary school had higher median incomes ($7,064) than nonwhites with one to three years of college ($6,909). This differential can hardly be explained by differences in the quality of education.

Part of the white-nonwhite income differentials also might be due to the age composition of the work force because incomes ordinarily increase with age, reach a peak, and then decline. Although the median age of white and nonwhite husbands who were craftsmen and operatives in 1960 was 42, ten years later the nonwhite median was two years lower (40) than that of whites. A major age difference for nonwhite husbands was in the below 35 category, which contained 38 percent of nonwhites but only 33 percent of whites.

FACTORS RESPONSIBLE FOR
BLACK EMPLOYMENT
PATTERNS

How are we to explain the low income and employment status of blacks and the forces responsible for the relative progress that has been made? It is fairly easy to make a list of the factors other than those discussed above that help answer this question, but it is much more difficult to assign weights to them. It is easy to conclude that discrimination is an important cause of the black workers' disadvantage, but discrimination is not uniformly defined and its results are difficult to quantify. Definition is important because to some people discrimination means specific, overt discrimination, illustrated by the case where somebody applies for a job and does not get it because of his race. However, discrimination also means institutionalized racial segregation, which pervades social and economic institutions and causes blacks to have inferior preparation for work as well as inadequate information about jobs other than those traditionally regarded as "Negro" jobs. Institutional discrimination has deep roots and is much more difficult to combat than specific overt acts of discrimination.

Although discrimination is an important factor, there are many measurable causes of blacks' low occupational status and income.

Education

A major factor consistently found to explain a large part of the variation in the occupational positions of blacks relative to whites is education, especially when adjusted for quality in order to reflect the tendency for black educational attainment to decline relative to whites with higher levels of education. But it is not surprising that education is such a significant variable; educational attainment is conditioned by housing, income, health, and many other factors. In a sense, therefore, relative educational differentials become indexes of institutional discrimination. Moreover, because these other factors are important, programs to increase the amounts of education alone would not necessarily solve the problem of poverty and inadequate employment opportunities among minorities.

The differential relative educational attainments of whites and nonwhites has narrowed through time. In 1962, the median educational attainment of nonwhites lagged 2.6 years behind whites, compared with only 1.1 years in 1969. However, nonwhites still were much more likely than whites to have less than five years of education and were less than half as likely to be college graduates. Nonwhites had closed the gap most noticeable at high-school level.

Nature of Industry

There also is the close relationship between black employment positions and the nature of industry. In part, this is because different kinds of industries have different labor requirements. For example, there is a rather consistent finding that blacks constitute a larger percentage of employment in industries that are declining in terms of employment than in industries that are growing. However, the growth industries tend, for the most part, to be technologically advanced and have relatively high skill requirements. Because blacks' skills, at least as measured by education and work experience, lag behind whites', this factor alone would account for some of the inadequate black representation in growth industries. Incidentally, there appears to be no consistent relationship between black occupational positions and firm size. A high correlation has been found between measures of monopoly power such as, concentration ratios (which reveal the extent to which firms control sales in product markets) and black employment patterns, but the causal relations probably are due more to skill requirements than control of product markets. Some students of this problem have argued that competitive firms are less likely to discriminate than firms with more market control. The logic of this position is that competition will force employers to practice merit employment. But this argument assumes a much more perfect labor market than in fact exists. Because concentration ratios are highly correlated with skill requirements it is difficult to factor out the precise causal relations. In addition, when there are large numbers of unemployed and underemployed white and black workers, competitive firms can meet their labor requirements by hiring white workers alone. Moreover, as we shall argue in the next section, even in tight labor markets, the employer's desire to carry out rational nondiscriminatory hiring and promotion policies might be counteracted by social pressures based on the racial prejudices of his white employees or his customers.

Housing, Location of Industry, and Transportation

Housing segregation and the location of industry also are important factors in black employment patterns. The concentration of the black population in central cities and the decentralization of jobs to outer rings around large metropolitan areas create transportation problems for black workers. Moreover, blacks often are barred by racial discrimination and inadequate education or training for many of the white-collar jobs available in the central city. Transportation therefore becomes a factor inhibiting black employment opportunities. In some cities, the basic transportation flows are designed to bring people (mainly white-collar suburbanites) into the central city in the morning and back into the suburbs in the afternoon. Blacks who live in the central city need to move out to jobs in the outer ring in the morning and back in the afternoon and evening. Moreover, many of the jobs available to blacks in the outer rings offer low wages, which might not justify the expense in time and money required to reach them.

In some cases, job information and referral systems cause blacks to have inadequate job opportunities. Many employers fill vacancies by referrals from existing employees. If the company has had a history of discrimination against blacks, there clearly will be very limited referrals of blacks. Even employers who recruit through white newspapers and other media are likely to miss blacks, who might be more likely to read black newspapers. Of course, employers could use black newspapers and other efforts to reach blacks, but very few of them apparently have done so. And, because of racial segregation in schools, many blacks might be excluded because employers recruit from predominantly white schools. Employers who use the public employment service are perhaps more likely to reach black workers, who often rely more heavily on it than whites, but this has been an unsatisfactory source of jobs for blacks because many good jobs are filled through other means. Although the practice undoubtedly changed some during the 1960s, the employment service was widely regarded by blacks as a discriminatory agency.

As a consequence of all of these factors, blacks often have had inadequate information about jobs except for the narrow range of jobs traditionally available to them. Once this pattern of job information and referral became institutionalized, they could be broken only by conscious programs to recruit and refer blacks to jobs from which they previously had been excluded.

Economic Conditions

The statistics on employment patterns show that blacks make their greatest gains in income and occupational position during periods of very low unemployment—for example, World War II. The reason for this is clear: A tight labor market provides incentives for employers to hire and train blacks because fewer whites are available. At the same time, tight labor markets reduce the white workers' resistance to the hiring and upgrading of nonwhite workers. Nevertheless, during World War II there was considerable opposition to and even strikes against the hiring and upgrading of black workers into formerly all-white jobs in northern cities.[8]

But tight labor markets by themselves are not sufficient to change black employment patterns. As noted in Chapter 12, general economic conditions have differential effects in different kinds of labor markets. Tight labor markets will not necessarily move blacks out of marginal or submarginal labor markets into mainstream jobs. Nor will they move black construction workers out of residential construction, which is largely nonunion, into better-paying commercial and industrial jobs, which are heavily unionized. Similarly, as Vernon Briggs noted, there is very little tendency for the tight overall labor market in Houston to facilitate the upgrading of disadvantaged blacks in the Houston labor market.[9]

Brimmer's finding that income differentials widened within the black community during the 1960s undoubtedly reflects the concentration of blacks in marginal and submarginal labor markets; blacks in the mainstream and in professional and technical jobs apparently made considerable progress during the 1960s, as did black husbands who were heads of families.

In conclusion then, economic conditions facilitate improvements in black employment patterns, but we shall argue in Chapter 25 that substantial improvements require other programs to make it possible for jobs to be opened to blacks and for blacks to prepare for those jobs.

Antidiscrimination Programs

Antidiscrimination programs will be discussed at length in Chapter 25, but we should note here that these programs undoubtedly have made it possible for blacks to enter jobs from which they previously were excluded. Antidiscrimination laws and programs have been particularly important in shaping prevailing moral sentiment on race relations and have caused many unions and employers who wished to do so to admit, hire, or upgrade blacks. And the threat of prosecution has caused employers and unions to accept blacks at least on a token basis. Nevertheless, antidiscrimination measures by government agencies are limited in their ability to improve black employment patterns because they (a) operate only on the demand side of the employment equation and do very little to change supplies; (b) require legal procedures which are costly, time consuming, and uncertain; and (c) combat overt discrimination more than they do institutionalized patterns of discrimination. We also shall see that most antidiscrimination programs have limited *power* to change racial employment patterns.

THE SUPPLY OF LABOR   As noted earlier, the supply of black labor qualified to perform a particular occupation has been an important factor in breaking down racial barriers. However, where skills are acquired mainly on the job, it obviously is difficult for blacks to acquire those skills on jobs from which they are barred by discrimination.

Employer and Union Attitudes and Practices

Blacks also have been disadvantaged by employer prejudices concerning the kinds of work for which they are suited. There has been a prevailing employer prejudice that black workers are suited for only certain types of jobs. Employer hiring practices also are determined by fears of white worker or customer reaction to hiring blacks. Antidiscrimination laws have protected employers from these fears and made it possible for their practices to be determined more by their own prejudices and preferences. As noted earlier, employers have screened out many black workers by their recruiting sources, selection criteria, and testing. Moreover, education requirements and tests are such that it is less likely that a black worker will be accepted for employment than that a white worker will be accepted. Perhaps the 1971 Supreme Court ruling that employment tests must be relevant to the jobs for which the tests are given will reduce this barrier to black employment. Attitudes, whether employers' or union leaders', do not *determine* practices with respect to hiring blacks or accepting them for membership. As will be noted later, attitudes determine the extent to which union leaders operate within the framework of certain environmental constraints. These environmental constraints will be discussed after we examine union racial practices.

The ability of unions to influence black employment patterns varies considerably with type of union and its internal composition. Local craft organizations, which are able to control labor supplies, have the worst record. In the building trades, for example, the electricians, plumbers, sheetmetal workers, iron workers, and elevator constructors unions have had tighter controls over their labor supplies than those of cement masons, roofers, carpenters, and painters. Craft locals have a strong motive to restrict labor supplies: They want to maintain wages. Thus, they tend to discriminate against all outsiders, but especially against blacks. Local craft union discrimination is strengthened by prejudices against blacks as inferior craftsmen who would dilute the status of their trades. Furthermore many of these unions were formed as fraternal or social organizations at a time when it was considered improper to have social relations with blacks.

Discrimination against blacks in industrial unions is less intensive and takes different forms. Because they are used by employers as sources of trained manpower craft unions often control entry into trades or occupations as well as unions. Industrial unions rarely control labor supplies or training; they try to organize all workers in their jurisdictions who are hired by employers. Therefore, the industrial unions' racial practices are conditioned much more by employers than is the case with craft unions. The industrial unions also are newer, most of them having been formed during the 1930s. Because the trend in race relations has been away from discrimination, newer unions or firms are likely to have more equalitarian practices than older ones.

Craft and industrial unions likewise differ in their need to appeal to public opinion in order to achieve their objectives. The craft unions depend heavily on their own economic power and have had very limited social and political objectives. Indeed, before the 1930s, the AFL's main political objective was laissez faire: It sought primarily to get government not to intervene in collective bargaining on the side of the employer, which it had done through injunctions and the application of restrictive legislation such as the Sherman Anti-Trust Act. Inasmuch as industrial unions were weaker economically than employers, they had to rely more heavily on political power to strengthen collective bargaining and to supplement it with minimum wage and other protective labor legislation. In order to achieve these objectives, the CIO had to gather support among black workers, who were heavily concentrated in some of the key industries the CIO sought to organize, and the black community. The CIO and Negro organizations such as the National Association for the Advancement of Colored People (NAACP) thus fashioned a mutually beneficial relationship which was a fundamental part of the New Deal political coalition.

Discrimination by unions is largely a local phenomenon, reflecting the prejudices and motives of local members. The farther away from the membership we move in the union hierarchy, the less likely we are to find overt discriminatory practices; union leaders are apt to need the support of outsiders to carry out their objectives. Consequently, other things equal, national unions are likely to be less discriminatory than locals and federations less discriminatory than nationals. Moreover, centralized organizations such as the national industrial unions are likely to be less discriminatory than craft unions, whose localized labor and product markets are apt to permit greater local autonomy. Thus, labor organizations that are most democratic, in the sense of being controlled by their members, are likely to be the most discriminatory—at least until blacks become an important force in the internal labor market controlled by that union.

Leadership also is likely to play an important role in determining discrimination by unions or employers. Wherever top management and union leadership communicate a strong nondiscrimination position unequivocally to all levels of the hierarchy of their organization, they have been able to minimize discrimination.

Within limits, therefore, the racial practices of companies and unions tend to reflect the attitudes of top management and union leaders. Because the CIO's leaders had broader social and political interests and believed in racial equality as an ideal, their unions were more likely than the AFL's affiliates to adopt equalitarian racial stances.

We have noted that the structure of the industry plays an important role in determining black employment patterns. But this probably reflects supply more than demand conditions. Because blacks are more unskilled and have less education than whites, they are predictably concentrated more heavily in industries requiring limited skills. On the demand side, however, a number of factors besides management practices influence racial employment practices. If companies are concerned with their public images or identify with local communities and see their interests bound up with community welfare and development, they will respond to community pressures either for or against discrimination. In this respect, consumer-oriented industries seem to be more responsive to community pressures than basic industries such as steel, which is more concerned with raw materials and sells mainly to producers.

Union as well as employer racial practices reflect job structures. As noted earlier, blacks are likely to be more heavily concentrated in industries whose demand requirements reflect the characteristics of the black labor force. Where technology causes considerable skill differential between the lowest and highest jobs in an internal labor market, as it does in the steel industry, there will be less racial unity than in industries such as coal mining, where skill differentials and wage structures are relatively narrow. Within industrial union situations, the main race problem is not exclusion from the internal labor market, but segregated job clusters or lines of progression within it. The unions do not create these structures, because employers determine hiring practices, but they make these procedures more formal through collective bargaining. In most industrial situations, racial discrimination is mainly due to employer hiring practices and unions have had only a marginal influence either positively or negatively.[10]

Unions have had positive as well as negative effects on black employment patterns. Seniority and grievance machinery within plants protects blacks who are able to penetrate internal labor markets. Moreover, black workers have been able to exercise sufficient political power within unions to use the unions' power for civil rights objectives. This has been especially true of unions with large and politically active black memberships. In addition, the labor movement has been a major supporter of civil rights and other social legislation of interest to the black community. Indeed, it generally is acknowledged that Title VII of the Civil Rights Act of 1964 could not have been passed without the active support of the AFL-CIO. Most black leaders, especially those in long-established organizations such as the NAACP and the Urban League, and men like the late Dr. Martin Luther King, have stressed the identity of interests between unions and black workers. To some extent, the unity between black workers and unions has been strengthened by the decline in overt union discrimination. Some forms of discrimination prevalent in 1960, for example, are almost nonexistent today. These include formal racial bars in union constitutions, racially segregated local unions, and racially segregated lines of seniority in industrial plants. Finally, evidence from a careful investigation by Orley Ashenfelter confirms the conclusion that unions have been a positive, but not major, factor influencing black incomes.[11] Considerable discrimination remains, but it is mainly at the local level and reflects institutional more than overt discrimination. The difficulties involved in eliminating institutional discrimination will be discussed in Chapter 25, after we examine the employment problems of Chicanos and Indians.

NOTES

1. Gary Becker, *The Economics of Discrimination* (Chicago: University of Chicago Press, 1957), pp. 108–114.

2. Elton Rayack, "Discrimination and the Occupational Progress of Negroes," *Review of Economics and Statistics* (May 1961), p. 210.

3. Alan Batchelder, "Decline in the Relative Income of Negro Men," *Quarterly Journal of Economics* (November 1964), p. 547.

4. Rashi Fein, "Relative Income of Negro Men: Some Recent Data," *Quarterly Journal of Economics* (May 1966).

5. Andrew Brimmer, "The Black Revolution and the Economic Future of Negroes in the United States," an address at Tennessee A & I University (June 8, 1968).

6. Claire C. Hodge, "The Negro Job Situation: Has It Improved?" *Monthly Labor Review* (January 1969).

7. Otto Eckstein, *Education, Employment and Negro Equality,* U.S. Department of Labor, Manpower Administration, Seminar on manpower policy and program (July 1, 1968), pp. 6–7.

8. Ray Marshall, *The Negro and Organized Labor* (New York: John Wiley, 1965).

9. Vernon M. Briggs, Jr., *Negro Employment in the South, Volume I: The Houston Labor Market,* U.S. Department of Labor, Manpower Administration, Manpower Research Monograph No. 23 (Washington, D.C.: U.S. Government Printing Office, 1971).

10. Herbert R. Northrup et al., *The Negro in Basic Industry* (Philadelphia: University of Pennsylvania Press, 1970), pp. 736–737.

11. Orley Ashenfelter, "Negroes and Trade Unions," a paper presented to the Western Economic Association Annual Meeting, Vancouver, B.C., August 30, 1970.

Chapter 23
The Status of Chicanos in the Southwest[1]

Chapter 22 dealt with the problems of blacks, the largest racial minority in the United States. The problems generated by unequal treatment of blacks have either created or been closely related to many of the most serious domestic crises the United States has faced. Although other minorities have employment and income problems which in absolute terms are worse than those of blacks, the problems of these groups have not been as pervasive or intractable as those of blacks. But the problems of other minorities, especially Indians and the Spanish speaking, are nevertheless very serious and are likely to become even more important in the 1970s as these groups follow the black man's example and demand economic equality with whites. Although many of the same causal forces and remedial programs applicable to blacks also apply to other minorities, the problems of the latter have cultural rather than *racial* origins. Moreover, Mexican Americans and other minorities have problems peculiar to their geographic and industrial concentrations. For example, Mexican Americans reside primarily in the Southwest, where they are heavily concentrated in agricultural jobs. The problems of special importance to Mexican Americans do not derive as much from overt discrimination as from social and economic conditions caused by the unique characteristics of the Southwest's agricultural and labor supply conditions, which are strongly influenced by the Mexican border.

We do not wish to minimize the importance of overt discrimination against Mexican Americans, which has existed and continues to exist. However, overt discrimination apparently has declined in intensity, especially since World War II, and was never as rigidly institutionalized as discrimination against blacks. While all of the antidiscrimination programs discussed in Chapter 25 apply to Mexican Americans, relatively few cases have been filed alleging discrimination against Mexican Americans. This undoubtedly is due, in part, to the fact that Mexican Americans have not been as vocal as blacks in demanding equality of employment opportunities; but also they recognize that institutional factors other than overt discrimination probably are more important causes of their disadvantages.

In this chapter we shall first explore the various terms used to define the Mexican American population, as well as some characteristics of that population. Then we shall consider some special features of the Mexican-American labor market—especially the importance of the border, the nature of agricultural employment in the Southwest, and public policy considerations of particular importance to Mexican Americans (especially various measures which provide legal, illegal, and quasilegal immigration from Mexico and deny the protections of social legislation to migrants and other agricultural workers). Finally, the impact of manpower policies for Mexican Americans will be explained.

OVERVIEW

The definition, identification, and measurement of Chicanos has caused considerable debate. Many people speak Spanish who cannot be identified with the "Spanish-speaking" designation used by the U.S. census. In addition, many Mexican Americans are more Indian in origin than Spanish. Most other terms commonly used to describe them are equally misleading because many people in the United States from Puerto Rico, Cuba, the Philippines, South America, and Europe speak Spanish. According to Census figures, the Spanish-American population of the United States numbered 9.2 million in 1969. Those of Mexican descent total over 5.1 million people, or 55 percent of this group. In fact, those of Mexican descent exceed in number the combined total of *all* minority groups other than blacks (i.e., Puerto Ricans, Cubans, American Indians, Chinese Americans, and Japanese Americans).

"Chicano" is the term increasingly used to designate Mexican Americans. According to Commissioner Vicente T. Ximenes of the Equal Employment Opportunity Commission and a former president of the American G.I. Forum:

> The word "Chicano" is being used by Mexican Americans of the nation. The word is not new, and in fact we used it to identify the people of the small rural villages many years ago. It is derived from the word Mexicano. I favor its usage.[2]

TABLE 23–1   *Percent of Nonwhite, Chicano, and Anglo Populations by Residence in the Southwest, 1960*

RESIDENCE	TEXAS	NEW MEXICO	COLORADO	CALIFORNIA	ARIZONA
Nonwhite					
Urban	75.1	32.5	86.4	91.4	36.2
Rural nonfarm	19.8	55.7	10.6	7.0	50.9
Rural farm	5.0	11.7	3.0	1.6	12.9
Chicano					
Urban	78.6	57.6	68.7	85.4	74.9
Rural nonfarm	15.0	36.7	25.2	10.8	19.0
Rural farm	6.5	5.7	6.1	3.8	6.1
Anglo					
Urban	74.3	73.4	73.4	86.0	79.7
Rural nonfarm	17.9	20.9	18.6	12.0	18.2
Rural farm	7.8	5.6	7.5	2.0	2.1

SOURCE: Donald N. Barrett, "Demographic Characteristics," in Julian Samora, ed., *La Raza: Forgotten Americans* (South Bend, Ind.: University of Notre Dame Press, 1966), p. 164 (data are from U.S. Census, 1960).

We shall, therefore, use the terms "Chicano" and Mexican American interchangeably.

The Mexican-American population is both a racial and a cultural minority; 95 percent of the Chicano population is part Indian.[3] The Chicano concept of *la raza* (the race), however, does not refer to a set of racial characteristics, because Chicanos are a blending of Spanish colonists, American Indians, Anglos, and blacks. Moreover, the Mexican-American culture is significantly different from that of the majority Anglos in language, religion, music, food, and literature.[4]

Almost all Chicanos live in the five southwestern states (Table 23–1). Thus, they contribute to and are affected by the Southwest's unique features. The 1960 Census indicated that the southwestern population was more urbanized (80 percent) than the nation as a whole (70 percent) and that the region's urban percentage was approximately the same for Anglos (81 percent), nonwhites (80 percent), and Chicanos (79 percent).[5] The urbanization of all racial groups has resulted from water shortages over much of the region which causes people to group together in an "oasis society." [6] There are significant differences, however, in population patterns in the five states (Table 23–1). In Texas, Colorado, and New Mexico Chicanos are highly concentrated in the poorest and least developed areas. In California and Arizona, they are relatively more dispersed.

Although current and accurate statistics are not available, the Mexican-American population apparently is growing both relatively and absolutely. The factors responsible for this growth include continued immigration (unrestricted until 1968, at which time a maximum of 120,000 a year from the Western hemisphere was imposed), inordinately high fertility rates (fertility rates for Chicanos are 70 percent higher than those of Anglos in the Southwest), and uncounted numbers of illegal entrants across the 1,800-mile common border between Mexico and the United States. In 1960, 54.8 percent of the Chicano population were native born of native-born parentage, and an additional 29.8 percent were native born of foreign-born parentage. Only 15.4 percent of Mexican Americans were born in Mexico.

Poverty and low education are serious for Chicanos. In 1960, 32.8 percent of the Southwest's Chicanos (or 1,082,000 people) were "officially" classified as poor. They represented 22.9 percent of the region's poverty population. Seventy-two percent of poor Chicanos lived in urban areas; 21 percent lived in rural nonfarm communities, and 7 percent lived on farms.

The median level of years of school completed by persons 14 years and over in the Southwest was 12.0 for Anglos, 9.7 for nonwhites, and 8.1 for Chicanos in 1960. Chicanos in Texas have the lowest median of any state, with 4.8 years for those over 25 years of age; the highest was California, with 8.6 years. Only 6 percent of the Chicano population had any college training (compared with 12 percent for nonwhites and 25 percent for Anglos). The Chicanos' functional illiteracy rate (0–4 years of schooling) of 27.6 percent in 1960 was seven times that of Anglos and twice that of blacks. The 1966 Coleman report on the equality of educational opportunity revealed that Chicanos are further behind Anglos on standardized achievement test scores in the higher grades; by the twelfth grade, for example, Chicanos were 3.5 years behind their Anglo classmates in verbal ability, 3.3 years in reading comprehension, and 4.1 years in mathematical achievement.[7] Although these tests made no pretense of being "culturally fair," it was alleged that their content measured knowledge that is "increasingly important for success in our society."[8] Nonetheless, it is significant that *one of the most characteristic aspects of Chicano labor market experience is their higher earnings than other minority groups when earnings are adjusted for differences in educational attainment.*

CHICANO LABOR MARKETS

Although Chicanos have long been identified with the Southwest, numerically they have become a sizable population only in the twentieth century, and thus have had less time to be assimilated. Immigration came in two major spurts: the first in the mid-1920s and the second from 1955 to 1964. Since 1900, a total of 1.4 million people from Mexico have been legally admitted and many more have come in illegally.

Several statistical problems complicate analyses of Chicano employment patterns. Data on the urbanization of Chicanos are likely to be overstated because a large number of Chicanos have urban addresses but work in agriculture. This is particularly true of migrant workers, who often use cities as home bases. A more serious statistical problem arises because Mexican nationals employed in the United States at the time of the Census are *included* in the head count. The small size of the Chicano population causes this distortion to be very serious. At the time of the 1960 Census, for example, there were 70,000 Mexican contract farm workers in the United States (33,000 in California, 24,000 in Texas, and the remainder scattered throughout the nation). The termination of the bracero program in 1964 should reduce the importance of this distortion in succeeding censuses. It would follow, then, that an improvement in the socioeconomic statistics for Chicanos between 1960 and 1970 would, in part, be illusory because of the presence of this poverty-stricken group in the former and its absence in the latter tabulations.

The economic status of Chicanos also is affected by "the border." The present Mexican–American border was established by the Treaty of Guadalupe Hidalgo in 1848 (following the Mexican-American War of 1846–1848) and the Gadsden Purchase of 1853. However, as Fred Schmidt argues:

> The border itself is something of a fiction. It becomes real when some national policy of either of the nations wants to assert the fact of its existence, but most often it is a permeable thing, a membrane that joins rather than separates the nationally distinct communities.[9]

Control of the land has played a major part in ethnic relations in this Southwest. The early Spanish settlers fought the Indians; the Mexicans fought the Anglos; the Anglos fought the remaining Indians and each other. There also was violent conflict between farmers and ranchers, sheepherders and cattlemen, and management and labor in the mining industries. Many conflicts over the legal ownership of land remain unsettled. For example, the Alianza movement in New Mexico, led by Reies Lopez Tijerina, centers on the validity of Spanish land grants supposedly guaranteed under the 1848 Treaty of Guadalupe Hidalgo. At the same time, the Indians have filed counterclaims challenging the Spanish king's right to give title to this land to the Spanish settlers.

However, economics probably was as much a cause of conflict as greed or bigotry. Agriculture, ranching, and mining have dominated the region's economy. These industries initially were very labor intensive and relied heavily on migrant labor. They also required considerable capital and attracted eastern money and absentee ownership.[10] Moreover, the sheer scale of operations in the Southwest meant that few immigrants could have the opportunity to become farm or ranch owners themselves. The only exceptions were the settlements in northern New Mexico, which date back to the seventeenth century and which were largely isolated from regional development until the 1940s. For this group, a major cause of discontent has been the incorporation of their communal grazing lands into the National Forest system.[11] But, as Grebler and associates demonstrate: "Most of

Southwest agriculture was always the province of big business and vast financing that people with modest means could not enter or even influence." [12] The scope of agribusiness of the Southwest has been described as follows:

> It has been said that the strings of California's $3.6 billion-a-year agribusiness are pulled from the redwood-paneled offices on San Francisco's Montgomery Street, the Wall Street of the West. In addition to growers, packers, processors, middlemen, and distributors, agribusiness embraces allied enterprises such as banks (the Bank of America, the world's largest, is the prime financer of California farms), shipping and transportation companies, land companies (Kern County Land Company for all practical purposes *is* Kern County), and utilities, plus other large corporations which have a stake in the prosperity of the field-to-table process.
>
> The anatomy of this "giant octopus," as one packing company executive put it, can be seen by studying the interlocking directorships of the agribusiness corporations. Packing executives sit on the boards of directors of banks and land companies. Bankers who trade in farm loans proliferate on the boards of packing and land companies. Realty executives who deal in farm acreage sit on the boards of shipping and packing companies. The labyrinth goes on and on.
>
> As a group, agribusiness executives are hardheaded and dollar-oriented, which is by way of saying they are not much different from executives in other fields. The tremendous technological advances of agriculture are all to their credit, but where they differ from executives in other fields is in their archaic concept of their responsibility to human beings.[13]

For Chicanos, this means that it is "almost impossible to convert hard work into a stable base for gain." [14] Scant opportunities exist for advancement because most agricultural jobs are deadend and low paying. The 1960 Census disclosed that 52.2 percent of the Chicano families living in rural areas had an income below $3,000 a year; 14.2 percent had an annual family income of below $1,000.[15] As a result: "Chicanos work more days, earn less, and have higher rates of unemployment than any other farm workers." [16]

Labor Supply and Public Policy

George I. Sánchez, an authority on Chicano life, considers successive population movements from Mexico to be the most serious threat to effective acculturation of Mexican Americans. They reinforce Mexican cultural patterns in the United States, making it difficult for any group to become fully acculturated.[17]

Immigration from Mexico since the 1920s has centered on agriculture, and Chicanos have dominated the Southwest's agricultural employment (Table 23–2). According to a 1964 report from California, for example, 41.9 percent of farm laborers were Spanish-speaking.[18] The original impetus to immigration from rural Mexico was the push of the Mexican Revo-

TABLE 23–2   *Employment Patterns of the Spanish Surnamed in the Rural Southwest, 1960*

INDUSTRY	THOUSANDS OF PEOPLE	PERCENTAGE
TOTAL	201	100.0
Agriculture, forestry, and fisheries	101	50.2
Mining	5	2.5
Construction	11	5.5
Manufacturing	15	7.6
Transportation, communication, and utilities	9	4.3
Wholesale and retail trade	21	10.4
Finance, insurance, and real estate	1	0.6
Personal services	23	11.2
Government	5	2.7
Not reported	10	5.0

SOURCE: US. Census of 1960 as reported in U.S. Department of Agriculture, *Low-Income Families in the Spanish Surname Population of the Southwest* (Washington, D.C.: U.S. Government Printing Office, 1967), p. 17.

lution and the simultaneous pull of labor shortages in the United States during World War I. These shortages not only were caused by the diversion of American workers into the armed forces, but also because immigration from Europe was stopped. After the war the demand for "Mexicans" remained, and because they were not covered in the quotas imposed by the National Origins Act of 1924, the supply was forthcoming to meet the demand. When the depression hit and displaced "Okies" and "Arkies" became the cheap labor supply, many Chicanos were forceably repatriated to Mexico.

There was another influx of Mexican farm workers during World War II, when an agreement between the United States and Mexico provided guarantees on working conditions and employment for short periods of seasonal farm work. This Mexican labor program was better known as the "bracero program." It remained in effect until the end of 1964. The program was strengthened in 1951 with the passage of Public Law 78, which was strongly supported by growers as a means of meeting labor shortages induced by the Korean conflict. Table 23–3 indicates the magnitude of this program. Obviously, its peak usage was *after* the Korean War years. This controversial program displaced many active Chicanos from the rural labor market. The proportion of Chicanos living in urban areas increased from 66.4 percent in 1950 to 79.1 percent in 1960.[19]

The bracero program is a good example of how public policy affects rural labor markets. The wages of agricultural relative to manufacturing workers declined sharply during the bracero period, forcing native Chicanos

TABLE 23–3   *Seasonal Agricultural Worker Sources, 1948–1969*

	TOTAL MEXICAN BRACERO USE	ILLEGAL ENTRANTS (DEPORTED TO MEXICO)
1948	35,345	193,852
1949	107,000	289,400
1950	67,500	469,581
1951	192,000	510,355
1952	197,100	531,719
1953	201,380	839,149
1954	309,033	1,035,282
1955	398,650	165,186
1956	445,197	58,792
1957	436,049	45,640
1958	432,857	45,164
1959	437,643	42,732
1960	315,846	39,750
1961	291,420	39,860
1962	194,978	41,200
1963	186,865	51,230
1964	177,736	54,525
1965	20,286	70,270
1966	8,647	88,567
1967	7,703	101,068
1968	0	126,055
1969	0	167,642

SOURCE: U.S. Department of Labor, as presented by William E. Scholes, "The Migrant Worker," in Julian Samora, ed., *La Raza: Forgotten Americans* (South Bend, Ind.: University of Notre Dame Press, 1966), p. 67, as amended by (a) the bracero figures for 1965–1969 from U.S. Commission on Civil Rights, *Hearings* (Washington, D.C.: U.S. Government Printing Office, December 1968), p. 984, and (b) authors' adjustment of the "Illegal Entrants, deported to Mexico" figures for the years 1955–1969 from the annual reports of the U.S. Immigration and Naturalization Service.

to migrate in search of jobs which paid them enough to meet living costs in the United States. Although growers complained of shortages of domestic workers during the bracero period, increases in wages since the end of that program have clearly shown that domestic labor is available at competitive wages. The bracero program also exemplified the indifference of public policy to the welfare of the native Chicano population:

Imagine, if you will, Big Steel importing as the nucleus of its work force Polish steelworkers willing to work at little more than Iron Curtain wages. Imagine the electronics industry bringing in cadres of patient Japanese assembly line workers at subpar Oriental wages. Imagine the various manufacturing and construction industries importing in wholesale lots of unskilled and semiskilled workers from impoverished countries, eager to toil for a pittance. All of this with the stamp of approval—and helping hand—of the United States government.[20]

Although the bracero program no longer exists, the problem of illegal entrants (or "wetbacks") remains. As late as 1968, it was estimated that 300,000 illegal entrants came from Mexico to the United States (a figure that is two and a half times the official quota that year for the entire Western hemisphere).[21] As indicated in Table 23-3 (which shows *only* those apprehended and deported), the illegal entrants were not affected by the bracero program. Indeed, because braceros were protected by the agreement with Mexico, many employers found it cheaper to employ illegal entrants. Braceros and most illegal entrants are single men; the domestic migrants are often families, who are more costly to house.

Commuters

Commuters who live in Mexico and work in the United States also depress wages and working conditions for native Chicanos. Commuters may be Mexican nationals or United States citizens. If they are aliens, they are either "green carders" (i.e., those who have been legally admitted as immigrants and are free to live and work in the United States) or "white carders" (i.e., legal visitors who can supposedly stay in the United States for only 72 hours at a time). "White carders" are technically not supposed to be employed, but that law apparently is not very well enforced.[22] Similarly, it is an "amiable fiction" that many "green carders" reside in the United States, because many actually live in Mexico. The "green carder" must obtain labor certification specifying that a shortage of workers exists in his particular occupation in the United States and that his employment will not adversely affect wages and working conditions. The certification is made only once—at the time of the initial application as an immigrant. Once the green card is obtained, the holder is free to come and go as long as no absence from the United States exceeds one year or the holder becomes unemployed for longer than six months.

The exact number of green- or white-card commuters is unknown. A 1969 report claimed that "approximately 70,000 persons cross the Mexico border *daily* to work in the United States." [23] A 1968 report by the U.S. Commission on Civil Rights placed the *total* "green carders" at 650,000 and "white carders" at 1,250,000.[24]

A 1967 restriction bars "green carders" from employment as strikebreakers where the Secretary of Labor certifies that a labor dispute exists. However, the effect of this antistrikebreaker restriction apparently is nullified by the fact that employers usually have ample time to employ "green carders" before a dispute is officially certified.

After Congress permitted the bracero program to expire, the Secretary of Labor issued new regulations which made it clear that braceros would not be admitted under various subterfuges. These regulations specify wages and other conditions which employers must offer to domestic workers before foreign labor can be imported. These regulations apparently have reduced the flow of Mexican nationals who applied for green cards after January 1, 1965. However, opinion differs as to the extent to which these rules really are enforced. Chicano and labor spokesmen still think too many commuters are permitted to enter and advocate tighter restrictions on entry, while employers complain of labor shortages.

The commuter system rests on administrative interpretation rather than statute. In 1927, the status of commuters was changed from alien visitors to immigrants by the Immigration and Naturalization Service. The justification for the perpetuation of this system is derived from a Board of Immigration Appeals decision in 1958: "The commuter situation does not fit into any precise category found in the immigration statutes. The status is an artificial one, predicated upon good international relations maintained and cherished between friendly neighbors." [25] Consequently, the U.S. worker who competes with Mexican commuters pays a substantial part of what the Secretary of State regards as foreign aid.

Although many commuters work in low-wage garment industries and retail shops on the U.S. side of the border, according to one estimate 60 percent or more of all commuters entering California and Arizona are farm workers; in Texas, the figure is 18 percent. According to the U.S. Civil Rights Commission:

> The impact of the commuter is particularly acute in agriculture where mechanization is rapidly reducing job opportunities. Due to the high concentration of farms along the border and the fact that commuters often work in the lowest skilled, lowest paid jobs, farm workers, who are already underpaid, are the first to suffer competition from the commuter. Furthermore, the use of commuters as strikebreakers is especially damaging to this group's organizational struggles.[26]

Moreover, according to the Civil Rights Commission 88,700 South Texas farm workers were forced to migrate elsewhere in 1968 in search of employment, while commuters easily found jobs in the local economy. A VISTA worker summarized the relationship of the commuter problem to migratory workers as follows:

> These people see the problem of the commuter as a very major one. They see that the people from Mexico, which are our brothers, come over on this side to work because the living conditions in Mexico are far worse than ours, they are poor. It is not their fault that they come and take our jobs, it is the fault of the U.S. government which exploits our brother because they pay lower wages and at the same time the Mexican Americans on this side are left without jobs and they have to travel up North.[27]

Numerous proposals have been offered to terminate or to lessen the effects of the commuter system.[28] Among these are its immediate termination; regularization of the labor certification process to require periodic reviews rather than simply the initial determination of the impact of the "green carder"; establishment of a nonresident work permit with regular review decisions; installation of a commuter tax on employers; purchase of tickets by those who cross the border for employment; a drive to give preference in employment to U.S. residents; the imposition of sanctions against U.S. employers who knowingly employ "white carders"; and specific limitations on the time a "green carder" can be employed in the United States before making it mandatory that he become a U.S. citizen. Moreover, Fred Schmidt contends that the current border employment practices violate Title VII of the Civil Rights Act of 1964,[29] which bans discrimination on the basis of national origin, by favoring Mexican nationals.

Agricultural Employment and Public Policy

Regardless of race or national origin, many agricultural workers are disadvantaged. For although large farm owners are the most privileged group in American corporate society (with import quota protection; antitrust law exemptions; price supports; soil bank purchases; subsidized research, irrigation, land reclamation, and erosion projects; and special property tax rates), farm laborers have few legal protections and very limited economic or political power.

Farm workers receive very limited coverage under state labor laws. The protection provided southwestern farm workers by state legislation in 1967 with regard to workmen's compensation, minimum wages, unemployment insurance, and housing conditions is presented in Table 23–4. No state minimum-wage law would bring the worker up to the minimum poverty level even if it were possible to secure year-round employment. Only California provides workmen's compensation, despite the fact that agriculture is one of the nation's most hazardous industries. And the hazards of agricultural employment have become greater because of increasing use of herbicides and pesticides—with their yet-unknown effects on farm workers. No state provides unemployment protection. Furthermore, most states have residency requirements, so migrant workers and their families are usually denied eligibility for welfare assistance and food stamps.

Agricultural workers also have inadequate coverage under federal statutes. The only federal statute with provisions designed to ensure minimum benefits for agricultural workers is the Sugar Act of 1937. Under it subsidies are made available to domestic producers of beet sugar and cane sugar. To qualify for the subsidy, however, a grower must pay a wage no lower than that set annually by the U.S. Department of Agriculture. The wage rates are set geographically and by crop (i.e., sugar beets or sugar cane) in an open hearing. Although employers tend to be well represented by

TABLE 23–4 *Status of State Laws in the Southwest Pertaining to Farm Workers as of December 1, 1967 (unless otherwise noted)*

STATE	WORKMEN'S COMPENSATION	STATE HOURLY MINIMUM WAGE	UNEMPLOYMENT AND DISABILITY INSURANCE	HOUSING
California	Compulsory	$1.65 for women and $1.35 for minors (16 to 18 years)	Disability is provided for most workers	Mandatory standards
New Mexico	Voluntary, at discretion of employer	$1.30 (as of 1969)	None	Mandatory standards
Texas	None	$1.10 (as of 1970)	None	None
Colorado	Voluntary, at discretion of employer	None	None	Mandatory standards
Arizona	Compulsory for some workers	None	None	Mandatory standards

SOURCE: U.S. Commission on Civil Rights.

various associations, the largely unorganized workers seldom have adequate representation at these hearings. Accordingly, it has been reported:

> The result has been in a sense worse than if the gesture had not been made. The wage thus established has tended strongly to become the wage paid. Though declared as a minimum wage, it has commonly been the only wage, supported by the sanction of government action and presented often by the growers to the workers as a rate which had become mandatory by government decree.[30]

For the Southwest, the applicable wage is that set for sugar beets in California and Colorado. Effective April 1969 the minimum wage was $1.65 an hour with exceptions for various hand-labor operations in which fixed wages per acre prevail. Deductions for meals and transportation costs provided by employers are permitted.

Several special enactments during the 1960s have affected rural Chicanos. Among these are the Bilingual Education Act (passed as Title VII of the Elementary and Secondary School Act Amendments in 1967) and amendments to Title I of the same act, which, for the first time, provided compensatory education funds for migratory workers. The earlier Migrant Children Educational Assistance Act of 1960 and the Migrant Health Act of 1962 represented the initial breakthroughs in federal legislation pertaining to the welfare of migratory workers. These programs, however, were based upon matching funds to state-initiated projects. In addition, the Farm

Labor Contractor Registration Act of 1963 was enacted in response to abuses by unscrupulous crew leaders. The Interstate Commerce Commission has imposed regulations affecting the transportation of 3 or more farm workers for a distance of 75 miles or more across state boundaries. The regulations pertain to equipment safety, required rest stops, seats for passengers, and regular driver changes. As for intrastate transportation of farm workers, only one southwestern state—California—has provided state regulations.

Rural Chicanos and Manpower Policy

The impact of the "manpower revolution" of the 1960s upon Chicanos has been negligible. The nationwide thrust of manpower policy has been upon improving the employment potential of urban workers. It is generally conceded by manpower officials that rural areas have not received a proportionate share of manpower funds.

· There are several reasons why rural workers tend to be ignored. First there is the political weakness of rural workers. Training slots for institutional MDTA (i.e., Manpower Development and Training Act) classes, MDTA on-the-job training, Neighborhood Youth Corps, New Careers, Special Impact, and Work Incentive programs represent dollars, and dollars represent patronage. Urban areas have had more power in securing these funds. The competition for supporting funds usually combines the vested interests of public schools, vocational schools, community action agencies, and junior colleges with the lobbying strength of city governments, organized community pressure groups, unions, and corporate interests. As one official of the Rural Manpower Service of the U.S. Department of Labor put it, "when the state politics divvy up the MDTA money, the rural areas don't get anything." Second, many rural areas fear that the formal training afforded under these programs is designed to prepare young people for jobs that can only be had if they migrate to the city. Hence, older people and employers tend to oppose them. The result, of course, is that the young leave anyway, suffering severely from inadequate academic and vocational preparation in anything other than agriculturally related subjects. Third, the rural poor have a severe "audibility gap." In urban areas, public officials have responded to civil disorder and collective action. Because population is diffused in rural areas, opportunities for organized protest are limited. Finally, there are few people in rural areas who have the expertise to formulate manpower plans, make application for funds, or administer programs. The lack of manpower expertise is particularly serious in those declining areas where local governments have been weakened by heavy outmigration.

Chicanos who live in rural poverty also suffer because their concentration in the Southwest leaves them virtually unknown to most Americans. Thus, they have been neglected in the formulation of program designs and in the staffing of program operations. Because the civil rights movement of the 1960s did not focus public attention on Chicanos, the impetus given by this movement to the development of manpower policies has included Chicanos only as an afterthought.

As indicated earlier, most of legislation affecting Chicanos has been designed for migratory workers—especially their health, transportation, treatment, and education. Little has pertained to occupational training. Only 2,343 people were participating in the Labor Department's CEP in rural southwestern states through 1969, and not all of these enrollees were Chicanos. Of course, individual manpower projects are also scattered throughout rural areas with heavy Chicano populations. No careful study of Mexican American participation in these programs is available, but our limited observations suggest that very little occupational training is being provided to Chicanos in these areas.

CONCLUDING REMARKS

This Chapter has explored the conditions of one of the most economically disadvantaged groups in the United States. Chicanos have worked primarily in agriculture and as migrants. Their concentration in the Southwest, where large-scale agricultural operations predominate, has limited the Chicanos' ability to become farm owners and operators. Moreover, large families, inadequate education, cultural isolation from the dominant Anglo groups, language barriers, discrimination, poor health conditions, and political powerlessness have caused the Chicanos' conditions to be self-perpetuating. Besides all of these disadvantages, Chicanos face the added problems of competition from Mexican nationals. Ironically, under the bracero program these Mexican nationals had even better working conditions, guaranteed by the federal government, than were available to many native Chicanos.

The Chicanos' conditions clearly will not be improved very much by the continuation of present policies. Improvement would require that human resource development measures be enlarged and intensified. One of the most urgent needs is job creation in areas where Chicanos are concentrated. However, many of these areas have few economic advantages other than a supply of cheap labor and therefore are not very attractive to private employers. Although some private employers might be attracted to these areas, there is little prospect that many unemployed or underemployed Chicanos will find private nonfarm employment in rural areas. Many of the employers who come into these areas are able to attract workers with higher levels of education and training, doing little for the more disadvantaged Chicanos. The obvious answers to these problems—training, public service employment, programs to move workers from labor surplus to labor shortage areas, education improvements, antidiscrimination measures, improved health care, and an income maintenance program for people who cannot or should not work—are easy to specify but difficult to implement in rural areas; it is even more difficult to muster sufficient political support to ensure that these programs are adequately funded. The rural poor in general, and Chicanos in particular, have been relatively powerless. However, a number of Chicano leaders are emerging who might change this situation. Significantly, all of the Chicano leaders who have attracted national attention—Cesar Chavez (whose "la cause" movement is based on organizing agricultural workers), Reies Lopez Tijerina (whose "la alianza" movement is built around land claims of rural families in Northern New Mexico), and Jose Angel Gutierrez (leader of the "la raza" movement) to secure educational and community reforms in rural areas of South Texas—are associated with rural life.

However, these human resource development measures are not likely to be very effective unless labor competition from Mexico is limited. Serious consideration should, therefore, be given to measures which further reduce the flow of Mexican nationals into United States labor markets. That this has not been done is a further reflection of the powerlessness of Chicanos, who have had little impact on public policies on these matters.

The exclusion of agricultural workers from workmen's compensation, unemployment compensation, minimum wages, and the right to collective bargaining cannot be justified on objective grounds. The only reasons for these exclusions is the powerlessness of agricultural workers relative to their employers. Hopefully, public policy will change as Chicanos become better organized and as public attention is drawn to their problem.

NOTES

1. This chapter relies heavily on a paper by Vernon Briggs, Jr., "Rural Poverty: The Economic Status of the Chicano Population and the Needs of Public Policy During the 1970s," prepared for the Center for the Study of Human Resources at the University of Texas, under a grant from the Office of Economic Opportunity. In this chapter, "Chicano" and "Mexican American" are used interchangeably.

2. Remarks by Vicente T. Ximenes, Commissioner, Press Conference (May 28, 1970), Washington, D.C., p. 1 (mimeographed).

3. Jack D. Forbes, *Mexican Americans: A Handbook for Educators* (Berkeley: Far West Laboratory for Educational Research and Development, 1970).

4. Leo Grebler, Joan Moore, Ralph Guzman et al., *The Mexican-American People* (New York: Free Press, 1970), Chapters 13–20.

5. *Ibid.*, p. 16. The "nonwhite" group in the Southwest is unique. It is only in Texas that "nonwhite" is predominantly black. In Arizona and New Mexico, American Indians dominate the group. Colorado has very few black citizens. In California, with its large Oriental population, 20 percent of the nonwhite population is nonblack.

6. Fred H. Schmidt, *Spanish-Surnamed American Employment in the Southwest,* prepared for the Colorado Civil Rights Commission, under

the auspices of the EEOC (Washington, D.C.: U.S. Government Printing Office, 1970), p. 50.

7. James S. Coleman et al., *Equality of Educational Opportunity,* U.S. Department of Health, Education, and Welfare, Office of Education (Washington, D.C.: U.S. Government Printing Office, 1966), pp. 274–275.

8. *Ibid.,* p. 273.

9. Schmidt, *op. cit.,* p. 61.

10. Steve Allen, *The Ground Is Our Table* (Garden City, N.Y.: Doubleday, 1966); see the discussion entitled "Agribusiness: The Corporate Sector," in Chapter 4.

11. Stan Steiner, *La Raza: The Mexican Americans* (New York: Harper & Row, 1968), Chapters 3–7.

12. Grebler et al., *op. cit.,* p. 90.

13. Allen, *op. cit.,* p. 46.

14. Grebler et al., *op. cit.,* p. 90.

15. U.S. Department of Agriculture, *Low-Income Families in the Spanish-Surname Population of the Southwest,* Economic Report No. 112 (Washington, D.C.: U.S. Department of Agriculture, 1967), p. 12.

16. Lawrence B. Glick, "The Right to Equal Opportunity," in Julian Samora, ed., *La Raza: Forgotten Americans* (South Bend, Ind.: University of Notre Dame, 1966), p. 100.

17. George I. Sánchez, "History, Culture, and Education," in Samora, ed., *op. cit.*

18. Rev. William E. Scholes, "The Migrant Workers" in Samora, ed., *op. cit.,* p. 74. The figure includes a small number of Filipinos.

19. Donald N. Barrett, "Demographic Characteristics," in Samora, ed., *op. cit.,* p. 163. The figures are from the U.S. Census for the respective years.

20. *Ibid.,* p. 51.

21. John H. Burma, ed., "Economics," in *Mexican Americans in the United States* (Cambridge, Mass.: Schenkman, 1970), p. 144.

22. "The Commuter on the United States-Mexico Border," staff paper presented in *Hearings* before the U.S. Commission on Civil Rights, San Antonio, Texas (December 9–14, 1968), p. 983.

23. Anna-Stina Ericson, "The Impact of Commuters on the Mexican-American Border Area," *Monthly Labor Review* (August 1970), p. 18. Emphasis supplied.

24. "The Commuter on the United States-Mexico Border," *op. cit.,* pp. 985, 1000.

25. *Ibid.,* p. 987 [the original citation is Matter of M.D.S., 7 Immigration and Naturalization, Dec. 209 (1958)].

26. *Ibid.,* p. 998.

27. *Ibid.,* p. 461.

28. *Ibid.,* p. 1001.

29. Schmidt, *op. cit.,* p. 46.

30. Lloyd Fisher, *The Harvest Labor Market in California* (Cambridge, Mass.: Harvard University Press, 1953), p. 107.

Chapter 24
The
Isolated
Indians

There is no universally accepted legal definition of an American Indian. Government agencies, depending upon their assigned functions, have used different measures of identification. The Bureau of the Census relies upon the individual respondent to decide his own race. Other government agencies cannot accept self-definition because eligibility to participate in their programs and services is normally determined by statutes or treaties. Eligibility under federal Indian law was made dependent upon being half-Indian or quarter-Indian or being listed on a tribal roll. These statutes are typically designed to fulfill obligations assumed by the United States when the Indians were forced to accept reservations of land in return for their "safety."

Most official definitions of an Indian are contrived at best. What is most significant—and the Bureau of the Census comes closest to recognizing this fact—is how an individual is perceived by both himself and his community. It is conceivable that a person with less than one-quarter Indian blood could be accepted by tribesmen and ostracized by whites in a given community, while a full-blood Indian could live in an eastern metropolis as a fully assimilated white. This consideration makes it easier to understand why estimates of the total American Indian population range from one-half million to more than twice that number.

POPULATION AND DEMOGRAPHY

It is important to stress that Indians are American citizens, free to move within the 50 states. Many have done so: Next to the Navajo reservation with a population of over 120,000 persons, the largest Indian "reservations" are found in Los Angeles, Chicago, and other large cities. Like other Americans living in central cities, Indians have their share of problems, and like other migrants, they face problems of adjustment. But the urban Indians have unique difficulties as well. In 1970, the Bureau of the Census counted a total of 792,000 Indians in the United States. By counting only reservation Indians living on or adjacent to reservations, the Bureau of Indian Affairs (BIA) estimated in 1970 the total Indian population entitled to its services to be 477,000; but this number included all Alaskan natives because the term "adjacent" in this case encompasses all of Alaska. The BIA also counts Oklahoma Indians who live on former reservations as its clients. Nearly nine of every ten Indians that the BIA considers in its jurisdiction live in nine states (Table 24–1).

According to one BIA official, there are 270 reservations, 24 other scattered land areas maintained in federal trusteeship for Indians, Eskimos, and Aleuts, and over 100 government-owned areas used by Indians and native people in Alaska.[1]

American Indians exhibit no single typical residential pattern: Some tribes group into small villages; other tribes scatter themselves with miles between neighbors; still others live in towns or familial groups or tribal

TABLE 24–1   *Estimates of Indian Population on or Adjacent to Federal Reservations, Total and Selected States, March 1970*

STATE	POPULATION
TOTAL	477,000
Arizona	115,000
Oklahoma [a]	81,000
New Mexico	77,000
Alaska [b]	57,000
South Dakota	30,000
Montana	23,000
Washington	16,000
North Dakota	14,000
Minnesota	11,000
All other states	54,000

[a] Includes former reservation areas in Oklahoma.
[b] Includes all Indians and Alaskan natives.
SOURCE: Bureau of Indian Affairs, *Indian Reservation Population, Labor Force, Unemployment, and Rate of Underemployment—March 1970* (Washington, D.C.: The Bureau, 1970), p. 2.

enclaves of greatly varying populations. By far the largest and most highly populated reservation is the Navajo, which spans part of Arizona, New Mexico, and Utah, and covers an area the size of West Virginia. Some 127,000 Navajos live on this reservation. At the other extreme are nearly 80 tribes with fewer than 100 persons each (Table 24–2). Some tribes are located near large cities, but more are located in isolated rural regions where there is no easily accessible transportation to urban areas. The 300 separate languages spoken by American Indians are evidence that these communities contain members whose traditions, values, and cultures vary as much among themselves as they do from other ethnic groups and the dominant white society.

TABLE 24–2   *Number of Indian Reservations by Size of Population, 1969*

POPULATION SIZE	TOTAL POPULATION	NUMBER OF RESERVATIONS
TOTAL	456,520	255
Less than 100	3,105	78
100–499	19,635	75
500–999	18,328	25
1,000–1,999	44,717	32
2,000–4,999	74,897	23
5,000–9,999	103,347	15
10,000–19,999	70,946	6
20,000–99,999	—	—
100,000 and over	121,545	1

NOTE: Over 100 Alaskan villages are administratively grouped into five agencies. These agencies are treated as reservations in this table.
SOURCE: U.S. Bureau of Indian Affairs, *Indian Reservation Labor Force and Unemployment—1969* (Washington, D.C.: The Bureau, 1970), pp. 1–9.

Indians are a comparatively young and growing population. Despite a mortality rate higher than the national average, an unusually high birth rate is causing the Indian population to increase by 3 percent annually— twice the national rate of natural increase. And it is a comparatively young population. The median age of Indians living on or adjacent to reservations is only 17 years, compared with a median age of about 29 for the rest of the nation.

From all indications, the Indian population will continue to increase substantially in the near future. If current preventive health and medical care programs reduce Indian death rates, especially in the younger age groups, the immediate effect will be to lower the death rate at all ages. While an increase in persons in the older age cohorts will tend to level the death rate and eventually decrease the birth rate, it will contribute to the rapid net growth in population.

TABLE 24-3   *Distribution of Per Capita Income by Reservations, 1968*

PER CAPITA INCOME	NUMBER OF RESERVATIONS	POPULATION
TOTAL	113	356,495
Less than $500	10	8,682
$500–$749	32	179,995
$750–$999	23	55,061
$1,000–$1,249	21	80,171
$1,250–$1,749	16	25,313
$1,750 or more	11	7,273

SOURCE: Bureau of Indian Affairs, *Summary of Reservation Development Studies and Analyses* (Washington, D.C.: The Bureau, 1969), pp. A–1 to A–3.

SOCIOECONOMIC CONDITIONS

The average per capita cash income for Indians on or near reservations was only $900 in 1968, less than one-third the national average. According to a BIA survey of 113 reservations containing three-fourths of its service population, two-thirds lived on reservations where the per capita income was less than $1,000. On only four reservations, with a combined population of less than 2,000, did per capita income equal or exceed the national average of $3,420 (Table 24–3). Among these were the 115 members of the Agua Caliente Reservation in California whose per capita income was $18,225, almost entirely earned as property income. In 1894, this tribe was allowed to establish title to some desert land which is now Palm Springs.

The median family income of Indians on the reservations surveyed by the Bureau was $3,600; nationwide, in contrast, whites and all nonwhite families earned $8,937 and $5,141, respectively, that same year. And nearly three-fifths of Indian households, but only 14 percent of white families and 36 percent of nonwhite families, had an income below $4,000. The lower income of reservation families must be shared with larger-than-average families, for it is estimated that Indian households are composed of between four and five persons compared with the national average of 3.2 members per household (Table 24–4).

Differences in the sources of personal income between reservation Indians and the national population further illustrate the Indians' economic deprivation (Table 24–5). Nearly one-third of the Indians' very low earned income came from antipoverty, welfare, and other government programs, compared with less than 15 percent from these sources for all Americans. And one-sixth, or twice the national proportion of 8.6 percent, of their income was derived from transfer payments.

Chronically depressed economic conditions and low wages, even where jobs are available, are major contributors to widespread Indian poverty. The average unemployment rate on Indian reservations is nor-

TABLE 24–4   *Distribution of Families by Income, 1968*

	MEDIAN	UNDER $3,000	$3,000–$3,999	$4,000 OR MORE
Whites	$8,937	9%	5%	85%
Nonwhites	5,360	24	12	64
Indians [a]	3,600	42	15	43

[a] Estimated from medians and distributions of households on 113 reservations.
SOURCE: For Indians, U.S. Bureau of Indian Affairs, *Summary of Reservation Development Studies and Analyses* (Washington, D.C.: The Bureau 1969). For others, U.S. Bureau of the Census, *Current Population Reports,* Series P-60, No. 66 (Washington, D.C.: U.S. Government Printing Office, 1969).

TABLE 24–5   *Sources of Personal Income for United States and 113 Indian Reservations, 1968*

	RESERVATIONS		U.S.
	In Millions	*Percent*	*Percent*
TOTAL PERSONAL INCOME	$319.5	100.0	100.0
Earned income	267.3	83.7	91.4
Wages, salaries, and other labor income [a]	223.1	69.8	67.8
Proprietors and other nonlabor income [b]	44.2	13.8	23.6
Transfer payments	52.2	16.3	8.6

[a] Less personal contributions for social insurance.
[b] Includes farm income, business and professional income, rental income of persons, dividends, and personal interest income.
NOTE: Details may not add to total because of rounding.
SOURCE: Same as Table 24–4.

mally higher than unemployment rates in even the most depressed city slum areas.

This job deficit and low income are further reflected in deplorable housing conditions. While nearly 80 percent of Indian families live in unsanitary, dilapidated housing, only 8 percent of all American families live in inadequate houses. Though federally funded public housing was initiated during the 1930s, a quarter-century elapsed before the federal government began to take steps to alleviate the poor housing on Indian reservations.

Moreover, poverty and substandard housing conditions are reflected in the serious health deficiencies suffered by American Indians. The average infant mortality rate among Indians is 50 percent higher than that for the rest of the population, and the life expectancy of those who do survive is much lower than that of either the white or black populations. The average lifespan for an Indian (44 years) is two decades shorter than for the average American (64 years). Poverty and its symptoms—poor diets and unsanitary living conditions—have contributed to a widespread incidence of disease caused by malnutrition.

EDUCATION

If Indians are to share in the high standard of living that surrounds their reservations, they will have to partake in the white man's education. Ever since the white man settled on this continent, he has made attempts at, or at least paid lip service to, "civilizing" the native "savages." Nearly three centuries ago, the Virginia House of Burgesses established a "college for the children of the infidels." Concern with educating Indian children has been sustained ever since and, some would add, with possibly too little change in attitude. Compulsory education applies equally to Indian as to all other American children.

In recent years, responsibility for the education of Indian children on reservations has tended to shift from the federal government to state and communities. But because Indians living on reservations are exempt from property taxes and contribute little to state or local taxes, the law provides for federal government reimbursement to states and localities enrolling Indian children in their schools. However, because of insufficient funds, late funding, confusing eligibility requirements, and the failure of some districts to use the funds for the education of Indian children, the majority of Indian children are denied help. Two-thirds of the 178,000 Indian children and youths attending school are registered in public schools. Mission schools, some dating to the colonial period, still enroll about 6 of every 100 children attending school. The balance, 27 percent, attend BIA schools. Enrollment in these schools ranges from a few children in an isolated Indian reservation to 2,100 in a modern boarding school. In 1970, the BIA operated 77 boarding schools attended by some 36,000 Indian children and 146 day schools for another 16,000 children.

Whether an Indian child attends an integrated public school or a federal school for Indians depends primarily upon locational access. BIA policy is to encourage the child to attend public schools whenever possible. If there is no public facility within a reachable distance of the child's home, the Bureau makes every attempt to allow him to attend a federal day school. In isolated areas where existing transportation is inadequate to allow school-age children to live at home, they are sent to federal boarding schools. A child may also be referred to a boarding school by the BIA Division of Social Services or the Public Health Service. Many students who are placed in boarding schools away from their homes are delinquent, overage for their grade achievement, orphans, or children of imprisoned, hospitalized, or separated parents. Students who have been unable or unwilling to adapt to a day school are transferred to boarding schools as a last resort with the mutual agreement of the youths and their parents.

Running the boarding schools for 36,000 Indian children is an expensive proposition—averaging more than $2,000 per child during the school year, or about three times as high as the cost per child in public schools. These schools have been subjected to a great deal of criticism, and the news media have played up frequently unverified incidents of cruel discipline and the meager achievements that the BIA can show for the high costs. In response to public criticisms and to avoid high costs, the BIA has attempted to place Indian children in regular public schools or reservation day schools. But completely viable alternatives to the BIA boarding schools have not been devised. Many substitutes have been offered, but none is a panacea or even a promising option. It is not economically feasible to deliver educational services to the thousands of Indian families that live in utter isolation; the boarding schools will remain the only means for providing these Indian children with any education.

The schools responsible for the education of the nation's Indians are plagued by all of the problems confronting American education in general, but compounding the situation are conditions unique to Indian education. Like other school systems, especially those located in areas inhabited by other minority groups, they are troubled by the lack of continuity between teacher training and the actual school setting, language barriers, the lack of empathy of teachers and administrators for the children with whom they are entrusted, a shortage of qualified personnel and instructional materials, and the absence of community involvement in scholastic affairs. Peculiar to schools serving Indian children are problems caused by the unique relationship of the tribes with the federal government and the distinct cultural heritage of the American Indian. Two-thirds of the students entering school have little or no skill in the English language and even more are totally unfamiliar with the ways of the white people that are perpetuated through the school system.

The effects of these problems can be seen in the statistics concerning Indian education. According to the 1960 Census, the average educational attainment for an American Indian under federal jurisdiction was only slightly more than eight years of schooling. The high-school dropout rate among reservation youths is nearly twice as high as for the rest of the nation. Few of those who drop out have a job waiting for them, and even those who graduate have at best an inferior education. According to the latest estimates, only one-eighth of Indian youths between the ages of 19 and 24 attend college, compared with one-third for the rest of the population. Moreover, relatively few Indians complete their college studies.

LABOR FORCE PARTICIPATION
AND EMPLOYMENT

Even though reservations are endowed with valuable mineral resources and Indians receive substantial transfer payments from the government and from their tribes, the bulk of their income is earned through employment, much of it related to natural resources. In the United States as a whole, about 70 percent of personal income is derived from wages and salaries, and the proportion of Indian income is very nearly the same. But because their earnings are meager, Indians usually live in poverty. They work inter-mittently if at all, and typically their jobs are low-paying, unskilled, and unattractive. There is a critical and chronic job shortage in and around most reservations, and Indians are usually ill-prepared for the few available jobs and are frequently discriminated against when they apply for work. The government accounts for a disproportionately large share of Indian employment, with private industrial and commercial enterprises providing jobs for less than 5 percent of the labor force on a man-year basis.

These severe employment problems can be measured in many ways. Perhaps most striking is the fact that less than one of three Indians aged 16 or over is employed, compared with six of ten for the country as a whole. Because far fewer adults have jobs and much more of the Indian population is under 16, on the average only 18 persons out of each 100 on reservations work to support themselves and their dependents, compared with 38 for each 100 throughout the United States.

Unemployment is extremely high on the reservations, though technical problems make it difficult to apply the normal unemployment measures. Because jobs are scarce on or near reservations, many Indians are not seek-ing work even if they would welcome employment and are, therefore, not counted as unemployed under conventional government practices. To secure more realistic estimates, the BIA began to compile its own statistics in 1963. Its measure of the labor force excludes only those who cannot work because of health problems, child-care responsibilities, or school at-tendance; those who can work but are not seeking jobs are included among the unemployed. According to this definition, 40 percent of reservation Indians were unemployed in 1970. This rate overstates the problem if it is compared with national rates, which averaged 4.9 percent in 1970 ac-cording to the Census definition. If the BIA measure were used, national unemployment would be severalfold higher than the reported rate. Even so, unemployment on Indian reservations still would be much higher than the national rate, and there is little doubt that it is critically high.

Underemployment and seasonal employment are also high. In a study prepared for the Joint Economic Committee, Alan Sorkin found that peak unemployment during the winter months is 70 percent higher than during the summer months when jobs are more plentiful because of agricultural work.[2] In a survey of five Indian reservations, Benjamin J. Taylor and Dennis J. O'Connor found that the proportion of Indians aged 16 and over who worked for more than ten months during the year ranged from a low of 12 percent on one reservation to a high of 36 percent on another reserva-tion.[3] Farming and related rural occupations, which involve a variety of chores, generally do not afford much opportunity for complete idleness even on small or marginal farming units. For example, while the Navajo sheepherder is not completely unemployed, neither can it be claimed that he is gainfully employed or that the income from his occupation is sufficient to support himself and his family.

Working Indians are also concentrated at the lower end of the employment totem, in part reflecting their rural residence. Over one-half of the male Indians employed in 1960 were farmers and laborers compared with three in 10 nationally. Few rural Indians held skilled positions: only about 4 percent of all males and 9 percent of females were professional, technical, and kindred workers, compared with 11 and 13 percent nationally. Similarly, few were in entrepreneurial and managerial jobs, with less than 2 percent of the male and female Indians being nonfarm managers, officials and proprietors; the national rates were 11 percent for males and 4 percent for females.

The federal government is the source of an inordinate proportion of full-time jobs held by Indians. The BIA employed an estimated 8,345 Indians full time as of November 30, 1969, the Indian Health Service, an additional 3,200, and OEO, EDA, and other federal agencies, hundreds more. This accounts for a huge share of total nonagricultural employment. Industrial and commercial enterprises located on or near reservations provided only an estimated 6,000 man-years of employment in fiscal 1969, compared with the 11,500 in the IHS and BIA alone.

Indians are concentrated in low-level jobs even when the government is their employer. Though Indians fill more than one-half of the jobs within BIA, they hold less than one-fifth of the executive jobs. In the Indian Health Service, only 18 percent of the Indians who are employed are paid more than $8,000, compared with two-thirds of all other workers.

The employment problems of Indians on reservations are severe. Though they cannot be attacked apart from the other Indian problems, two basic approaches must be taken. Efforts are obviously needed to increase the number of jobs available to Indians on or near reservations. More private firms must be attracted to the environs, and tribes and individuals should be assisted in initiating their own industrial and commercial enterprises. At the same time, efforts must also be expanded to improve the productivity of the Indian work force through manpower training, and to provide whatever other labor market services may be needed to put Indians to work. Manpower and economic development programs must work hand in hand to strengthen the economies and human resources of the reservations.

OBSTACLES TO ECONOMIC DEVELOPMENT

There are some very good reasons why more businesses are not located on reservations or near enough to hire substantial numbers of Indians. Most reservations are geographically inaccessible to product markets. With their low average income and typically widespread settlement, they provide only a limited market themselves for any products. The Indian labor force is generally unskilled; and because of their poor education, Indians may be expensive to train. Though many on a reservation may be unemployed, only a limited number are available for work at a single geographical point because of the dispersion of population. With differing cultural attitudes, Indians find it difficult to adapt to sustained employment and job discipline, and the result is higher labor costs due to absenteeism and seasonal turnover, at least in the early stages of operation.

Capital for public and private investment is also in short supply. Financial institutions are unfamiliar with reservations and unwilling to take the high risks often involved in lending to Indians—especially because lands, which are the Indians major asset, cannot be taken as collateral on loans. Public funds are equally limited, and the few tribes with substantial resources are reluctant to use them for commercial and industrial purposes.

Reservations generally lack the social overhead capital such as adequate transportation systems and sewerage and electrical facilities needed to attract businesses. Competing with many other localities for the limited number of new and relocating firms, they are usually at a disadvantage because they cannot offer the amenities available elsewhere.

To complicate matters, knowledge about conditions on reservations is scarce. Businessmen do not know what to expect because little information is usually available on labor forces, prevailing wage rates, skill levels, worker attitudes, and overhead capital. All of these factors can vitally affect the profitability of any operation. There is an equally severe shortage of trained personnel on the reservations to coordinate industrial development efforts; tribal leaders, who are often elderly, are sometimes unqualified or uninterested in planning and administering such programs. Faced with these uncertainties, businessmen understandably turn their attention to more predictable locations.

Improvement of reservation economies also depends on the health of the national economy. Even with special incentives, businessmen may not flock to out of the way reservations if labor is more readily available elsewhere. The Area Redevelopment Act of 1961 attempted to cope with the problem. Although chronic unemployment was more rampant on Indian reservations than in other areas in the country, Congress found it necessary to provide specifically for reservations to ensure that Indians would not be excluded. The program, however, was of little help to reservations while the labor market was slack generally. Tightening labor market conditions through the second half of the 1960s made reservations, with their abundant labor supply, increasingly attractive for expanding new companies, and carrots offered by the federally supported depressed-area programs added incentives to locate on reservations. Hardly any factories were located on reservations in 1960; a decade later there were more than a hundred factories employing over 4,000 Indians. The trend is likely to continue only if tight labor markets are sustained in the rest of the country and if adequate incentives continue to attract new industries to reservations. An overall increase in unemployment and a reduced demand for labor would no doubt reduce the attractiveness of reservations for the location of new or expanding plants.

FEDERAL MANPOWER
PROGRAMS

Unless more jobs are provided on or near the reservations, Indians will continue to have low employment rates; but Indians could hold many existing jobs if they were qualified. Without improvements in the labor force, it is unlikely that industrial and commercial development can proceed; hence, manpower programs must be coordinated with economic development efforts.

Many cultural factors can impair Indian labor-force participation. A major obstacle is that Indians often have a limited command of English and especially of the industrial lexicon. Another obstacle is that few Indians adjust their activities by the clock, which makes it difficult for them to adjust to factory discipline. Many Indians do not carefully plan for the future. For instance, they may abandon full-time, year-round jobs for attractive summer employment even though this means losing stable employment. Usually Indians value land holdings and open spaces, preferring to live in isolated units rather than in congested areas. As a result, they are often scattered around the countryside and, with the poor transportation system, are unable to get to a place of work.

Such cultural factors are significant and can add both to the costs of hiring Indians and to their difficulty in finding and holding jobs. Yet these obstacles are relatively easy to overcome. At the Fairchild Semiconductor plant in Shiprock, New Mexico, for instance, instructions, procedures, and expectations have been adjusted fairly successfully to these cultural differences. Industrial terms were added to the Indian language or approximate translations were used; "aluminum" was converted to the Navajo phrase for "shiny metal" and "oscillator" became "tunnel." Time schedules were adjusted, with the clocks in the plant being divided into ten sections, painted red and white alternately and numbered consecutively. Thus, a six-minute "section" was used as the basic unit of time rather than minutes and hours. Problems in attracting workers to the area and retaining them at their jobs were solved by offering adequate wages and opportunities for upgrading. The lesson has been that many Indians are willing to modify their own life styles to obtain jobs that are dependable and reasonably well paid and that offer opportunities for advancement.

What is much more basic and much more difficult to overcome is the fact that Indians generally lack the skills and the knowledge to be productive workers. Their educational attainment, as noted earlier, is substantially below national norms, and the education they receive is often inferior. Because they have lacked job opportunities in the past and because outside training opportunities are limited, they have acquired few skills. As education improves, so will the abilities of the labor force, but more direct steps need to be taken through remedial training and basic education, along with the other manpower services Indians may require to find employment and to improve their productivity and earnings. One such effort by BIA is a literacy program for 75,000 functionally illiterate adults.

BIA Manpower Programs

BIA has provided manpower services for Indians on reservations for almost two decades. Until recently, these were almost the only efforts made on behalf of Indians, and they still are of great significance despite the extension of Labor Department programs to the reservations. Nearly 9,600 entered BIA's employment assistance or manpower programs in fiscal 1970, and they received services costing more than $33 million, or over $3,000 per person. Though BIA's efforts may be less extensive than those of the Labor Department, they are much more intensive.

These programs are grouped administratively into two categories: direct employment and adult vocational training programs. Under the first (and older) program, Indians can be placed on jobs on or near the reservations or may be helped in finding urban jobs. Assistance is provided in the form of relocation allowances, temporary subsidies, medical services, placement, and counseling. Also using direct employment program funds, three "experimental" residential training centers are operated; they provide basic education and vocational training for entire Indian families who are so seriously disadvantaged that they cannot benefit from other training opportunities. The adult vocational training program, which accounts for the bulk of training, offers institutional courses both near reservations and at vocational centers in larger urban areas which serve a number of reservations. On-the-job training, also funded under this program, can provide placement, counseling, health, and other services for participants, but though usually it only pays wage subsidies to employers covering up to one-half of the minimum hourly wage for some training period. This subsidy has been used to attract employers to reservations and to induce them to hire Indians.

Under the direct employment program, the BIA attempts to assist each applicant, Indian origin and residence "on or near" a reservation being the only criteria for eligibility. Although there is no training component, some individuals who have received assistance may have participated in adult vocational training. Direct employment is designed to assist individuals who have a salable vocational skill for which there is no outlet in the Indian community. Based on individual needs, a wide variety of services—including interviewing, testing, counseling, and health care—are available. Perhaps most important are subsistence grants until placement. Rates depend on family size and whether the individual being assisted can commute to his job or must relocate. Arrangements can be made for an individual interested in being placed within commuting distance within two weeks, while relocation may take two months or perhaps more if the individual has some significant problem. However, more than 40 percent of the relocatees are placed in jobs within one week and nearly 30 percent more by the end of the second week. Total costs for individuals provided direct employment services in fiscal 1970 averaged $2,785 per person.

The critical issue underlying the direct employment program is whether assistance should be used to relocate Indians to urban areas where jobs are more readily available, or to help them find jobs on or near reservations. Fluctuations in the funding levels reflect a shift in national policy concerning the most appropriate method of serving reservation Indians. Direct employment—and termination—were obvious tactics of the dominant philosophy of the early 1950s, which favored integrating Indians into the economic mainstream. A change of emphasis, however, grew from such factors as disappointment with the effectiveness of such efforts, opposition from Indian groups lamenting the loss of their best human resources, increasing job opportunities resulting from industrial and commercial development, and greater awareness of the plight of urban Indians.

Almost all studies of the relocation effort have agreed that Indians working in urban areas earn substantially more than those placed on or near reservations, but that very few successfully adapt to urban life. For instance, a 1968 BIA follow-up of 1963 placements in urban areas found that almost three-fourths had moved back to or near the reservation. BIA records from 1953 to 1957 indicate that about one-half of the relocatees had returned within the first year. Others have estimated that between one-half and two-thirds of all relocatees eventually return to the reservation.[4]

Whatever success relocation may have in raising wage rates and income, the costs are not justified if clients return without gaining skills or saving money. However, those who want to leave the reservation should be helped because urban areas still offer greater opportunities. The BIA has, therefore, reversed its earlier preference for relocation and is trying to walk the tightrope of assisting without advocating relocation. Current policy, thus, seeks to make the reservations themselves viable economic units, and there is far more accent on locating jobs on or near reservations (Table 24–6).

Intensive services costing around $5,000 per trainee are provided in three residential centers funded under the direct employment program; they operate in Roswell, New Mexico, Madera, California, and Ft. Lincoln, North Dakota. To be eligible, a single individual or family head must lack a skill, have the equivalent of fewer than nine years of education, and be unqualified for institutional training. These centers care for the participant's

TABLE 24–6   *Direct Employment Placements, Selected Years, 1952–1970*

FISCAL YEAR	TOTAL	EMPLOY-MENT TRAINING CENTERS	PER-CENT	ON OR NEAR RESERVA-TIONS	PER-CENT	URBAN AREAS	PER-CENT
1952	442	—	—	—	—	442	100.0
1958	2,373	—	—	63	2.7	2,310	97.3
1964	1,985	—	—	254	12.8	1,731	87.2
1968	2,928	718	24.5	1,136	38.8	1,074	36.7
1969	2,975	612	20.6	1,614	54.2	749	25.2
1970	3,757	904	24.1	2,000	53.2	853	22.7

SOURCE: U.S. Bureau of Indian Affairs, *Annual Statistical Summary, 1970* (Washington, D.C.: The Bureau, 1970).

whole family and offer adults a wide range of assistance, including intensive and innovative basic education, skill training, and home economics instruction, as well as job placement. Day care is provided for younger children. Between the beginning of the program in 1967 and June 1969, 1,600 persons had entered the centers, with 700 completers and a relatively low 450 dropouts. Most of those connected with the program are enthusiastic, but effectiveness cannot yet be measured.

Institutional training is provided on a much larger scale under adult vocational training and is intended primarily for those 18 to 35 years of age. In fiscal 1969, 2,700 persons entered training, two-thirds at institutions in Chicago, Cleveland, Dallas, Denver, Los Angeles, Oakland, or San José, the remaining one-third received training on or near their reservations. Enrollees receive the same types of health and counseling services plus grants as those in the direct employment program, plus subsistence payments throughout the training period. In addition, however, they receive tuition and related expenses for vocational training, so that costs run over $5,000 per enrollee. Institutional courses typically last about ten months, but some trainees remain in school for two years. Some 1,800 courses in nearly 600 public and private schools have been accredited by BIA.

The BIA's institutional training program has demonstrated its effectiveness in increasing the employability and earnings of participants. The five-year follow-up of 1963 enrollees established that their earnings had increased several-fold over preenrollment levels. Those who went to urban training centers and then found jobs in these areas received much higher wages, but, as under the direct employment program, many gradually drifted back to the reservation. Here again, the question arises of whether it is wise to transport reservation Indians to urban training centers where they will be prepared for existing jobs within the area. And again the answer is uncertain, but there is little evidence that those who receive training are any more likely to remain in the cities than those who are simply relocated. Accordingly, training opportunities are being increased near the reservation, and the portion of participants who are sent off to urban institutes is being reduced.

In a minor component of the institutional program, about 40 families, primarily headed by widowed or unmarried women with children, are enrolled in the Solo Parent program in San Diego, California. In providing a residential setting, child care services, and home economics training, this program is similar to the education and training centers. However, enrollees receive instruction at accredited public or private schools, rather than basic education and training.

The OJT segment of adult vocational training is becoming increasingly important as industrial and commercial development efforts progress, and, as of 1970, nearly 6,000 Indians were participating. Employers receiving subsidies provide only nominal training in some cases; in others it is extensive. Although average cost per individual served in fiscal 1970 was $745, most contracts specified a training period longer than one year. Hence, average cost per placement is about $1,000. Whatever the manpower services provided, those enrolled benefit from jobs that might not otherwise be available, and almost all of which are close to or on the reservations. Given the demonstrated preference for such locations, OJT subsidies should be increased, which will, in turn, require that they be larger on a per enrollee basis. Few firms can be expected to locate near reservations to receive a $1,000 BIA subsidy when they can receive more than $3,000 per enrollee to locate near a ghetto and hire a usually better educated and trained group.

Recipients of employment assistance services in fiscal 1970 were generally young and well educated; males and single individuals predominated, and families were relatively small. However, nearly nine of every ten were unemployed when they applied for services. And the few who were employed held low-paying jobs.

An evaluation of BIA institutional and OJT programs in Oklahoma concluded that both programs resulted in significant increases in participants' annual earnings. Institutional trainees increased their pretraining earnings by slightly more than did on-the-job trainees; however, the significantly higher costs of institutional training suggest that on-the-job training may be a more effective method to upgrade the skills of American Indians.[5]

Labor Department Efforts

Public concern about this country's disadvantaged mounted during the 1960s and was enunciated in a series of antipoverty programs, most notably MDTA and EOA. A number of regular manpower programs operate on or near reservations, providing services to reservation Indians as well as those who have moved to urban areas. Nearly 24,000 Indians participated in fiscal 1970, though 13,000 were students receiving supplementary income with only nominal work and training under NYC.

Expenditures for Indians cannot be separated from the totals. However, extrapolations based on the percentage of Indians in the various Labor Department programs suggest that about $30 million is spent for Indians; of this, probably about two-thirds, or $20 million, is spent for reservation Indians. In addition, state employment security agencies placed a number of Indians in jobs.

The most important manpower program in terms of enrollments is NYC. In-school and summer projects sponsored by the Indian Tribal Councils are designed to provide students with some work experience and training, but mainly with a source of income during their school years. And the summer employment program has provided employment for 10,000 students. These NYC programs have enjoyed widespread support among Indians. The income provided, usually at the minimum wage, is large relative to the low average family income, and NYC tasks are not demanding. The problems are those that apply to the program nationally. Counseling and supervision are inadequate, and the jobs are often "make work." Little preparation for later employment is offered, but few challenge the value, on balance, of NYC programs.

Out-of-school NYC employs a much smaller number of Indian youth—on a year-round basis, only 630 in fiscal 1969. This program would have to be expanded drastically to serve the critical needs of young Indians who have dropped out of school and for whom jobs are almost nonexistent. But this segment of NYC is not popular among the tribes. For one thing, the minimum wage paid often exceeds what is available elsewhere, and older tribal members resent the fact that dropouts can earn more than they; the high wage could conceivably encourage dropouts. The program also has been plagued by alcoholism, absenteeism, and high dropout rates. Despite these shortcomings, some assistance is needed for Indians who have dropped out of school; they constitute perhaps the most serious problem group on the reservations.

Operation Mainstream is a highly popular program where it has been implemented, but through fiscal 1968 only 14 projects had been started because too little effort had been exerted by Labor Department field personnel. Mainstream is ideally suited to the needs of the reservations. It employs mostly older Indians, whose capabilities and prospects elsewhere are meager. They are put to work in road maintenance, planting, beautification, and conservation jobs which require little training and in which the older Indians usually have some experience. Little emphasis is placed on education and training, so the program has a low cost and high payoff in terms of useful work done. Mainstream has had problems with alcoholism among its older enrollees and high dropout rates among females who leave for family reasons. A major difficulty has been transporting participants from their homes to work sites, a matter that usually must be worked out before a project can get underway. Despite these problems, Mainstream is undoubtedly worthwhile and should be organized more actively on other reservations.

The other major manpower program operated on or near reservations includes projects initiated under MDTA. Though MDTA has substantial enrollments, most tribes prefer to work with similar BIA programs because they are more familiar with BIA activities. MDTA funds for reservations are not in short supply, but until recently activity was limited. In fiscal 1969, there were four regular MDTA institutional projects designed to serve 282 Indians; there was also a special facility in Montana, the Northwest Indian Manpower Training Center, intended to train 300 Indians from an 11-state area. There were 24 OJT projects also in operation in fiscal 1969; they offered subsidies of roughly $1,000 per person to private employers to hire and train disadvantaged workers.

Participants in OJT have jobs upon completion, but there is a serious question about the jobs for which institutional trainees should be prepared. Under MDTA, skill shortages must be demonstrated before training can be offered, but there are chronic job deficiencies for the most part in or around reservations. If MDTA is to be coordinated with economic development efforts, its policies must be made more flexible. The alternative of providing MDTA courses for job shortages in other areas is a debatable strategy. Where MDTA courses have been offered off reservations, participants have had serious financial and social problems leading to high dropout rates. If those trained on reservations are relocated to cities, these problems are likely to occur again. The Labor Department takes the stand that there is no purpose in training for relocation on a large scale because this will lead to more problems than it solves.

The employment service is playing an increasing role on the reservations, but much more needs to be done. In 1970, local public employment offices employed 200 persons, 119 of them Indians, to work directly with the tribes. In some states these personnel have played an active role; for instance, more than 14,000 Indians were placed in nontemporary jobs during fiscal 1969 in Arizona, New Mexico, and Wyoming alone. In most states, however, the employment services ignore the needs of Indians because they are not sure what they are supposed to be doing where job opportunities and training slots are few. Their active efforts are required as manpower programs for Indians grow and as economic development proceeds.

Increasing attention has been given to Indians under the manpower programs administered by the Labor Department; and based on the relative size of their population, Indians receive a disproportionate amount of funds. For instance, Indian enrollment in fiscal 1970 accounted for 2 percent of the CEP total, 1.3 percent of WIN program, 2.1 percent of MDTA, 2.8 percent of NYC, and 9.2 percent of Operation Mainstream. In all cases, these exceed the proportion of Indians in the population. But considering the concentration of need on the reservations, these shares still are inadequate; greater efforts must be directed toward making Indians employable, helping them to find work, and creating jobs.

In increasing the funds allocated for Indians, emphasis should be placed on upgrading, especially in public employment. A new Public Service Careers (PSC) program is being initiated, which, among other things, will subsidize the costs of preparing employees in government agencies for better positions. Because so many Indians are employed by federal agencies, efforts to raise the skills and responsibilities of these workers should be encouraged. This cannot be done without money, and PSC is one vehicle for subsidizing upgrading costs. There is no reason why Indians should continue to hold the lowest positions in government agencies such as BIA and IHS which are intended to serve them. There is justification for moving Indians upward in these agencies, even at the expense of non-Indian workers, if they are prepared for better positions.

In its manpower efforts, the BIA has cordial relationships with state employment services and administrators of the Labor Department's programs. Little conflict has occurred, probably because of the obvious need for all services that can be provided and because operations at the field level rarely overlap. Despite this cordiality, there has been little coordination, and the role of the various approaches has not been spelled out. Coordinated manpower services for Indians must become a reality if the original Americans are ever to become self-sufficient. Most of all, manpower programs must be expanded along with economic development efforts so that Indians can become self-sufficient and still maintain the reservation life that is so important to them.

TREATING CAUSES
RATHER THAN SYMPTOMS

To meet all the needs of reservation Indians, resources would have to be substantially increased. Some improvement can be accomplished through reallocation of resources, but this is difficult to engineer unless funds are increasing. The key, as in the solution of most social problems, is more money and more intelligent use of existing money.

The resources committed to solving Indian problems will probably increase as the public becomes more aware of their plight. But it is improbable that the forthcoming funds will be adequate to meet all demands. It will be necessary to make difficult choices between competing claimants and to determine priorities on the basis of rational analysis.

A significant proportion of disease and premature death among Indians is a direct result of poverty, dilapidated housing, unsanitary water, and inadequate diets. A sound economy would mean that the necessary resources would be available to both the tribal community and individual families to build adequate housing, purchase nutritional foods, and construct sanitation facilities. Schools and communities could offer health education programs and individuals would have the financial ability to follow their recommendations for better health care.

With economic development, the number of Indians dependent upon welfare would also decrease. For those not benefiting from increased economic opportunities, more intensive services and substantial assistance could be provided. Another potential benefit is that as Indians take on more responsibilities and are trained for meaningful jobs, they will become increasingly qualified for technical, managerial, and supervisory positions.

The primary goals of Indian programs are to increase Indian control over their own destinies and to improve their standard of living. The *sine qua non* to achieve both of these goals is the development of reservation economies. Past experience has indicated that a growing and productive economy is the single most important factor in the betterment of a population's social institutions. While this is not the only approach that can be taken to improve the conditions on Indian reservations, it does seem to be the most promising. And the right combination of Indian participation with federal assistance is the key to the development of Indian self-reliance and independence.

NOTES

1. Bill King, "Some Thoughts of Reservation Economic Development," in U.S. Congress, Joint Economic Committee, *Toward Economic Development for Native American Communities,* 91st Cong., 1st Sess. (Washington, D.C.: U.S. Government Printing Office, 1969), p. 68.

2. Alan Sorkin, "Trends in Employment and Earnings of American Indians," in U.S. Congress, Joint Economic Committee, *Toward Economic Development for Native American Communities,* op. cit., pp. 107–108.

3. Benjamin J. Taylor and Dennis J. O'Connor, *Indian Manpower Resources in the Southwest* (Tempe, Ariz.: Arizona State University, 1969).

4. Joan Ablon, "American Indian Relocation: Problems of Dependency and Management in the City," *Phylon* (Winter 1965).

5. Loren C. Scott and Paul R. Blume, "Some Evidence on the Economic Effectiveness of Institutional Versus On-the-Job-Training," paper presented to the Forty-fifth Annual Conference of the Western Economics Association, August 1970, University of California, Davis, California.

Chapter 25
Combating Discrimination in Employment

We have seen that black, Chicano, and Indian workers are situated in lower occupational positions and earn lower incomes than whites. They also incur higher unemployment rates and have lower labor-force participation rates than whites. Moreover, they suffer disproportionately from long periods of unemployment. The causes of minority economic disadvantages clearly are deeply rooted in social and economic institutions which cause them to be at the "end of the line" when it comes to obtaining jobs.[1]

Overcoming the complex constellation of forces causing blacks to be economically disadvantaged will require a variety of programs, the most obvious of which are measures to combat overt discrimination. This chapter will analyze the effectiveness of these measures.

LEGAL AND ADMINISTRATIVE REMEDIES

Since World War II, enforceable laws against discrimination have been passed in over half of the states and in many municipalities. These laws cover virtually the entire nonwhite population outside the South, where only Kentucky had adopted such a statute by 1971. Generally, these laws are administered by part-time commissioners who ordinarily have powers to (a) receive, investigate, and pass on complaints; (b) use conferences, conciliation, and persuasion in an effort to resolve complaints;

(c) conduct public hearings, subpoena witnesses, and compel their attendance under oath as well as requiring the production of records relating to matters before the hearings; (d) seek court orders enforcing subpoenas and cease-and-desist orders; and (e) undertake and publish studies of discrimination.

Before the Civil Rights Act of 1964, blacks also used the courts to overcome discrimination in employment, although most court cases dealt with unions because, in the absence of statutes or nondiscrimination clauses, employers had no legal obligation not to discriminate. However, unions acquired legal rights and duties as a result of the National Labor Relations and Railway Labor Acts. Specifically, the Supreme Court ruled that the Constitution imposed upon unions that acquired the privilege of exclusive bargaining rights the duty to represent all members of the bargaining unit fairly. Aggrieved minorities have, therefore, brought legal action for injunctions and damages against discriminating unions. Moreover, in the 1964 Hughes Tool case, the National Labor Relations Board (NLRB) held violation of the duty of fair representation to be an unfair labor practice, giving aggrieved minorities a measure of administrative relief because they can file charges with the NLRB instead of with the courts. But the most important of these antidiscrimination laws was Title VII of the Civil Rights Act of 1964, which proscibes discriminatory employment practices by employers, labor organizations, employment services, and registered apprenticeship programs which serve 25 or more persons. A five-member Equal Employment Opportunity Commission (EEOC) has the responsibility of assuring that hiring, promotion, and firing are on the basis of ability and qualification without regard to race, color, religious belief, sex, or national origin. The sex category was placed in the qualification primarily because of the desire of the bill's opponents to embarrass its backers. Next to race, sex has accounted for the largest proportion of charges filed and an even greater proportion of "recommended for investigation" action by the EEOC—24 percent and 30 percent, respectively, in 1967. However, the Commission's major emphasis has been on race matters, often to the consternation of women's organizations which have demanded equal treatment before the EEOC.

The Commission has limited responsibility and authority to exercise its functions. It may investigate complaints of discrimination on a case-by-case basis and encourage compliance through such informal procedures as conciliation. It has direct jurisdiction only in the 20 states that do not have Fair Employment Practices Commissions (FEPCs). In the 31 states with FEPCs, EEOC must defer action for 60 days until the state or local unit has shown an inability to resolve the complaint, whereupon the complainant may again reapply to the EEOC for direct action. EEOC has only limited powers to investigate, hold public hearings, and subpoena witnesses, although it has the right to hear voluntary witnesses and to pay fees on the same basis as a federal court.

Title VII also authorizes the Attorney General to bring suit against respondents referred by EEOC after it has been unable to obtain voluntary compliance—by direct intervention on his own volition if circumstances seem to justify it or by *amicus curiae* participation on behalf of private individuals who may bring suit in federal courts after notification of EEOC's failure to achieve compliance.

Within the Justice Department's Civil Rights Division, employment is but one of seven jurisdictional areas and prior to mid-1967, as division officials admit, the one with the lowest priority. After 18 months' experience, through the end of 1967, only 10 cases had been filed against Title VII violators, and some critics suggest that the lack of forceful legal action may be a partial explanation for the low (48 percent) success rate of EEOC conciliation efforts. Beginning in 1968, the Civil Rights Division was much more vigorous in prosecuting equal employment violators; 30 cases were initiated during that year alone. However, this case-by-case approach in ending job discrimination is inherently inefficient compared with industrywide and pattern discrimination investigatory procedures which are gaining increasing acceptance.

The other federal stick for enforcing equal access to job opportunities is Executive Order 11246, the sixth in a sequence of presidential directives since 1941 designed to prevent discriminatory employment practices. The order covers all employers who have federal contracts and includes companies with an estimated employment of 24 million persons, nearly one-third of the labor force. It not only forbids contractors to discriminate on the basis of race, creed, color, sex, or national origin, but also requires that they take "affirmative action" to guarantee equal access. Contractors are required to state in all job advertisements that they are equal opportunity employers; to notify their subcontractors, binding them to the order's provisions; to obtain union compliance to EEOC regulations; and to comply with information requests from the Secretary of Labor.

Although each federal agency is responsible for monitoring its own contract activities, an Office of Federal Contract Compliance (OFCC) within the Labor Department coordinates administration and policy formulation. The Executive Order, unlike Title VII, contains stiff sanction and penalty authority, including cancellation, termination, and suspension of contracts and "blacklisting" of companies for future contract participation if they fail to cooperate. However, no contract has been canceled or terminated under the order, and although delays in contract negotiation and infrequent "blacklisting" have occurred, there is a good deal of reluctance to enforce the order.

The final thrust of the federal government's activities to equalize employment opportunities for Americans is the variety of human resource development programs, discussed throughout this book, which are designed to equip the disadvantaged with the skills necessary to compete effectively in the labor market.

Implementing Federal Antidiscrimination Legislation

Title VII of the Civil Rights Act is concerned with processing individual complaints on a case-by-case basis. It generally operates passively, waiting for complainants to file charges against respondents. EEOC lacks effective "teeth" to put the bite on noncomplying institutions. Yet Congress has refused to legislate a "cease and desist" authority that could give the Commission a meaningful enforcement role or even to provide sufficient staff and budgets to allow the Commission to exploit its limited authority.

A major step in the more effective implementation of EEOC activities has been its recent self-initiated efforts to investigate industrywide and regional discrimination practices. Three of the most salient examples are the Carolinas' textile industry study, the New York City white-collar studies, and hearings on employment discrimination in Houston, Texas. After completion of the textile study in 1967, several affirmative action programs were initiated to resolve existing problems. The New York City reports on various industry and corporate groups illustrated the need for less rhetoric and more positive action on the part of groups that have professed a desire to achieve equal employment opportunities for everyone.

Preemployment testing has proved a major obstacle to hiring the disadvantaged, and, for this reason, EEOC has issued a handbook, *Guidelines on Employment Testing Procedures,* describing job techniques employers might use to assess a job applicant's future potential without discriminating against minority group members. Among the issues are those relating to job vs. ability requirements, retesting, and validating testing procedures for minority groups. It is the EEOC's position that tests are unlawful in the absence of evidence that they have been properly validated and are properly related to the specific jobs for which they are used. In 1971, the U.S. Supreme Court upheld the EEOC's position and ruled unanimously that an employer's use of broad ability tests or education standards that are unrelated to job performance and that operate to screen out minority groups is unlawful under Title VII.[2]

EEOC is responsible for coordinating federal data-collection activities relating to discrimination practices. EEOC staff members have utilized these data on their own account in preparing studies outlining specific geographical and industrial discrimination practices as well as contracting with outside groups in the preparation of these data reports. However, collection, analysis, and interpretation on these data are such that they have provided limited information on the nature of or possible cures for discriminatory practices.

Although Executive Order 11246 and its coordinating enforcement agency, the OFCC, offer conceptual advantages over Title VII, there is little evidence that they effectively combat discriminatory activities per se.

The enforcement provisions of the Executive Order, which include sanctions, are directed toward corporations rather than individuals. Although OFCC and agency contract reviewers may be more active than others in bringing discrimination charges against violators, there is little direct application of the enforcement mechanism.

Attempts to enforce contractor affirmative action programs have met considerable resistance. However, voluntary compliance such as that represented by the Plans for Progress Program also has shown little actual progress in improving minority employment patterns. (PFP originated in 1961 and included about 450 companies committed to "aggressively promote and implement equal employment opportunity"). Both EEOC and OFCC officials have publicly expressed doubts as to the effectiveness of voluntarism. In seven out of ten PFP companies studied, less than 3 percent of employees were from minority groups. One special study comparing New York City PFP companies and non-PFP companies found that, although neither group had done particularly well in minority group representation among their white-collar employees, the latter had a consistently better record than the former.[3] However, as explained in Chapter 22, the employment record of contractors and PFP companies may reflect selection criteria other than discrimination—for example, skill requirements—that relatively few black applicants can meet.

Current enforcement procedures are awkward. With EEOC case-by-case review, the necessity of deferring to states with FEPCs, and dependence upon negotiation for voluntary compliance, only limited success can be expected. Most who suffer from discrimination lack knowledge of both their rights under the system and the machinery for achieving their rights. Even among the knowledgeable, fear of retaliation and reluctance to face formidable legal machinery of the corporation, the lengthy review, the frequent rebuffs by EEOC because of the required deference to state FEPC's, and the low success rate of individual restoration or adjustment discourage initiation of charges. EEOC can only effectively implement an antidiscrimination program by showing greater innovation and aggressiveness in developing better procedures for using its limited resources. Individual complaint-handling procedures might well be deemphasized in preference to area- and industrywide hearings.[4] However, the most pressing individual need is that EEOC be given an enforcement as well as a conciliatory responsibility. Bills introduced in Congress have proposed giving cease-and-desist authority to the EEOC; the Nixon Administration has offered a counterproposal broadening EEOC's authority to file suits against discriminatory employers in federal courts.

If activities under Executive Order 11246 are to be made viable, the fragmentation of enforcement procedures requires adjustment. Only corporate institutions are now subject to the order's effectiveness. If labor organizations within affected companies are recalcitrant in accepting equal employment opportunity practices, then, in the words of one official, "that contractor has a very serious problem, and we expect him to solve that problem with the union."

Thus far, the federal government's record in improving minority employment opportunity consists largely of unfulfilled promises. EEOC still has not completely divorced itself from the view that it should educate rather than enforce. Of course, without an adequate cease-and-desist authority, EEOC is hobbled as an enforcer, which is partially illustrated by the fact that although successful conciliations increased from 52 to 88 between 1966 and 1967, unsuccessful conciliations increased even more, from 16 to 86.

Richard Nathan recommended transfering OFCC to EEOC in order to take advantage of Executive Order 11246's sanctioning power and EEOC's broader equal employment practices; this recommendation was incorporated in an Administration bill introduced to Congress in August 1969.[5] Undoubtedly, more aggressive enforcement of existing statutes as well as new authority is needed. Abolition of overt discrimination should be a minimum, assuring that attacks on more objective obstacles can be unimpeded by irrational ones.

Enforcement vs. Mediation

Perhaps the most significant contribution of the equal employment opportunity effort to date has been the informal impact of the considerable publicity and expanded public recognition of the problem. Many businessmen have been made keenly aware of the rising demands for equal jobs both by the efforts of federal officials and by the picket lines manned by civil rights activists. Most recognize the need to handle the black question with greater finesse than they handled the union demands of the 1930s. Efforts to be more responsive to the needs of minority groups have resulted in special programs to expand minority group recruitment and hiring and, to a lesser extent, advancement opportunities. Most apprenticeship and union spokesmen also now officially declare a policy favoring greater minority group participation. Previously all-white apprentice programs and union rolls are beginning to include minority group representatives.

Some of the problems involved in implementing nondiscrimination provisions in government contracts can be more clearly demonstrated by looking at the experiences in the construction industry and with the desegregation of seniority rosters, two very difficult areas for those who have attempted to improve minority employment opportunities.

THE CONSTRUCTION INDUSTRY

The civil rights movement's assault on racial employment practices in the construction industry increased in intensity during the 1950s and 1960s, when black employment opportunities were declining in major northern metropolitan areas. In a number of cities, coalitions of black organizations, formed especially for that purpose, closed construction projects through demonstrations in order to press their demands for more jobs for black workers.

The campaign also was pressed by the National Association for the Advancement of Colored People (NAACP). In announcing new legal attacks, Roy Wilkins, the NAACP's Executive Secretary, charged that the building trades were the "last bastion against employment of Negro workers as a policy" and said that blacks wanted their just share of the $80 billion budgeted for construction.[6] The NAACP filed suits to enjoin federal, state, and local officials from spending money and proceeding with construction until the job demands of black workers were met. NAACP Labor Secretary Herbert Hill said that the Association's new thrust would be to develop through law a public policy that would prevent the expenditure of public funds to subsidize racial discrimination.

Simultaneous programs were launched to increase the supply of black construction workers to fill jobs once they opened up. One of these efforts was a program to provide assistance for black contractors, who have traditionally been unable to acquire sufficient labor and capital resources and technical competence to perform large-scale commercial and industrial projects.[7] Organizations of black construction workers also were formed in a number of cities to challenge the building trades unions.

The Apprenticeship Problem

Civil rights leaders have concentrated on apprenticeship because these programs lead to good jobs in the skilled trades and because there have been very few blacks in them, in part because few black youngsters attempted to enter apprenticeship programs before the 1960s. Moreover, the craft unions' recruitment patterns excluded most black youngsters from any opportunity to enter the system. Blacks also have been disadvantaged in meeting the qualifications for entry into apprenticeship programs. Many programs require high school, and not only does the education level of nonwhites still lag behind that of whites, but many blacks have been handicapped by what Kenneth Clark calls "the massive inefficiency of the public schools where the masses of Negroes go." [8]

In 1963, Secretary of Labor Willard Wirtz approved new federal apprenticeship standards designed to "provide full and fair opportunity for application." These regulations had limited impact for a variety of reasons, but basically it was because few blacks applied for or could meet the qualifications and testing procedures.

The Bureau of Apprenticeship and Training (BAT), which administers the program, also has limited enforcement powers. Deregistration, BAT's main weapon, is more of an inconvenience than a serious deterrent to discrimination.[9]

In addition to the federal regulations, apprenticeship programs are subject to Title VII of the Civil Rights Act of 1964, the National Labor Relations Act, government contract clauses (which require observance of BAT's apprenticeship regulations as a condition of compliance with the executive orders), and various state apprenticeship regulations and EEO laws.[10]

Legal sanctions have not been especially successful, although they have perhaps had the effect of creating among apprenticeship sponsors a climate conducive to change; apprentice standards and programs have become more formalized; some apprentice sponsors have raised their qualifications. The possibility of sanctions also seems to have strengthened "voluntary" compliance programs. Although sanctions have been used very rarely (because relatively few formal written complaints have been lodged against discrimination in apprenticeship training and because discrimination is difficult to prove), antidiscrimination agencies have succeeded in making investigations that have clarified the extent of black participation in apprenticeship programs and have focused attention on some of the problems involved in increasing the number of black apprentices.

The limitations of legal sanctions led to the creation of apprenticeship information centers to give information about apprenticeship programs and outreach programs to recruit, tutor, and place apprentices. These programs were discussed in Chapter 11, so we need only note here that they were fairly successful in increasing the number and proportion of minority apprentices. The outreach approach used by the Workers Defense League (WDL) was so successful in getting blacks into apprenticeship programs that it has been used as a model in many other cities. By the end of 1969, there were approximately 20,000 minority apprentices in registered programs, 8,000 of whom were admitted in 1969. The outreach programs and apprenticeship information centers added 12,727 apprentices during 1969, 40 percent of whom were from minority groups. Four times as many minority group members were admitted to apprenticeship programs that year as the Census indicates were participating in 1960. From about 2.5 percent in 1960 and 4.4 percent in 1966, the proportion of minorities in apprenticeship programs rose to 8 percent by the end of 1969. About one-half of registered minority group apprentices in 1969 were black.

Although apprenticeship outreach programs have been more successful than any other approach to this problem, it remains to be seen if they can cause the kinds of changes throughout the country that will replace institutionalized discrimination with institutionalized equal opportunity. So far, however, they have demonstrated the importance of a comprehensive approach to recruiting and preparing black youngsters for apprenticeship programs. Moreover, this approach has demonstrated its effectiveness in getting blacks into other jobs more effectively and at lower costs.

Model Cities

The controversial Model Cities construction programs raised hopes for more jobs for black construction workers, but, by the summer of 1971, these programs were marked more by controversy than by their success in providing jobs for minorities. Much of the controversy centers on the provisions of the Model Cities Act that require maximum participation by residents of areas where housing is being constructed or rehabilitated. The AFL-CIO Building and Construction Trades Department (BCTD) agreed to the employment of residents of these areas in special residential construction classifications, but black militants insist that the programs be controlled by people from the areas. For example, a Model Cities agreement worked out in Boston and based upon the BCTD's guidelines was challenged as "tokenism" by militant blacks and the NAACP. The NAACP Labor Secretary called a plan (similar to the one proposed by the BCTD) worked out by the Construction Industry Joint Conference (CIJC) a "fraud" because it did not assure union membership or preferential treatment of ghetto residents in construction projects.[11] Moreover, according to the NAACP official, jobs would not be controlled by residents of the areas but by "discriminating building trades unions." The unions argue that membership will be available to all who are qualified and to trainees as they qualify. Of course, determination of qualifications is likely to be a continuing source of conflict, as is the question of who speaks for the residents of a Model Cities area.

Patterns of Discrimination

The Department of Justice's power under Title VII of the Civil Rights Act to move against patterns of discrimination has raised a number of difficult issues, especially that of the weight to be given to discriminatory procedures adopted before July 2, 1965, the effective date of Title VII. In a suit filed in February 1966, the Justice Department alleged that the St. Louis Building and Construction Trades Council and several of its affiliates had violated Title VII and were tortiously interfering with a nondiscrimination agreement between the United States and a contractor. Action was brought against the unions after their members walked off the job to protest the hiring of a black plumbing contractor and his employees who were represented by an integrated union not affiliated with the AFL-CIO. The unions offered to admit all who were qualified and argued that the strike had been called because substandard workers had been hired not because of race. Although the unions admitted discriminating against blacks before the Civil Rights Act became effective, they argued that they had discontinued their practices and were willing to take blacks who met their qualifications and paid initiation fees and dues required of all new members.

The U.S. Court of Appeals at St. Louis found that Local 36 of the Sheet Metal Workers and Local 1 of the International Brotherhood of Electrical Workers were not guilty of discrimination after the Civil Rights Act became effective but were guilty of a pattern or practice of discrimination in violation of Title VII. The Court of Appeals ordered modification in the unions' referral system to require them to place blacks who were "reasonably qualified" in the highest groups for which they were eligible. The court also required one union to modify its journeyman's examination so that tests were objective, relevant to the applicant's ability to do the work, and given and graded in such a way as to permit review.[12] The main impact of the St. Louis case was to uphold the Justice Department's contention that in pattern or practice cases the government does not have to prove specific practices of discrimination after the effective date of the Civil Rights Act. However, unions cannot be held guilty of discrimination committed before the effective date of the Act if they ceased their discrimination after that date, although the weight to be given past practices is far from settled. Another area of conflict involves the employment of building tradesmen on state government construction projects where unions have no black members. In a 1965 New York case,[13] plaintiffs brought suit to desegregate all state construction projects where labor was recruited by nine defendant unions accused of discrimination. The New York Court of Appeals decided the case for the unions, on the grounds that when they worked on public projects the labor organizations were not state agents and that their actions therefore were not "state action" under the equal protection clause of the Fourteenth Amendment to the Constitution.

The NAACP was more successful in a case decided in 1967.[14] A Federal district court in Ohio enjoined the State of Ohio from contracting to build a $12.8 million medical science building at Ohio State University until it was assured that the contractor obtained his labor supply from a nondiscriminatory source. The unions did not appeal this case, and the NAACP hailed it as a significant breakthrough in getting blacks into the building trades. The Association increased its legal staff from four to eight and planned a series of suits throughout the country relying on the Ohio ruling. The NAACP Labor Secretary said, "no Negroes, no work." The NAACP Executive Director said that his organization was calling for "absolute cancellation of building contracts if they do not observe Title VII or the Ohio ruling." [15]

QUOTAS AND
PREFERENTIAL TREATMENT

Various programs to increase black employment opportunities in the construction and other industries have raised the highly controversial legal and moral issue of quotas and preferential treatment. Policies proposed by some civil rights leaders and government agencies are based upon the belief that progress in eliminating patterns of inequality requires compensation for past discrimination against blacks. However, unions and employers have resisted these efforts on the grounds that they discriminate against white workers and cause inefficiency.

The Philadelphia Plan

One of the most important recent controversies over quotas in the building trades came in the summer of 1969, when Assistant Secretary of Labor Arthur Fletcher issued an affirmative action plan for government contractors in the Philadelphia construction industry. The order, designed to implement the provisions of Executive Order 11246, was a revision of a plan initially introduced by Secretary of Labor Willard Wirtz in November 1967, but withdrawn after the Comptroller General ruled that the plan violated the principle of competitive bidding.

However, subsequent investigations, later disputed by AFL-CIO President George Meany, revealed that the crafts in question had only about 1.6 percent minority group membership and adhered practices that resulted in few blacks being referred to jobs. As a result, the Labor Department issued the "revised" Philadelphia Plan. The revised plan required bidders on government contracts of over $500,000 to "commit themselves to specific goals of minority manpower utilization." Contractors and subcontractors were required to submit affirmative action plans that provided employment goals for six specified trades (ironworkers, plumbers and pipefitters, steamfitters, sheet metal workers, and elevator constructors) ranging between 4 percent and 9 percent the first year and 19 percent to 26 percent the fourth year. The criteria announced by OFCC in arriving at its standards included extent of minority participation in the trade, availability of minority tradesmen for employment, and need for training programs and impact of the program upon the existing labor force. The specific goals were "not intended and shall not be used to discriminate against any qualified applicant or employee." Moreover, in the absence of positive evidence of discrimination, if a postaward compliance review found that the successful bidders' goals were being met, the OFCC would assume that he was in compliance with the Executive Order. Even if the goals were not being met, "the contractor shall be given an opportunity to demonstrate that he made every good faith effort to meet his commitment." But "it is no excuse that the union with which the contractor has a collective bargaining agreement failed to refer minority employees."

The Philadelphia Plan produced strong opposition from some members of Congress, the construction industry, and Comptroller General Elmer B. Staats, who said that the plan imposed racial quotas in violation of Title VII. But the plan also gained some impressive support from influential newspapers, members of Congress, and the Nixon Administration and caused a rift in the civil rights and labor forces in December 1969, when the U.S. Senate added a rider to an appropriations bill that would have invalidated the plan. The AFL-CIO lined up in favor of the rider, while many civil rights leaders opposed it. After considerable pressure from the Administration, the rider was defeated.

A court challenge of the Philadelphia Plan was initiated by the Contractors Association of Eastern Pennsylvania, who charged that the plan violated the Constitution and laws of the United States and the laws of Pennsylvania. However, in 1970, a federal district court in Pennsylvania upheld the plan as valid under Title VII and the Constitution. The court pointed out that the concept of "affirmative action" had been upheld as a valid exercise of presidential powers in a number of cases and added:

> The heartbeat of "affirmative action" is the policy of developing programs which shall provide in detail for specific steps to guarantee equal employment opportunity keyed to the problems and needs of minority groups, including, when there are deficiencies, the development of specific goals and timetables for the prompt achievement of full and equal employment opportunity. The Philadelphia Plan is no more or less than a means for implementation of the affirmative action obligations of Executive Order 11246.[16]

Moreover, according to the court,

> The plan does not require the contractor to hire a definite percentage of a minority group. To the contrary, it merely requires that he make every good faith effort to meet his commitment to attain certain goals. If a contractor is unable to meet the goal, but has exhibited good faith, then the imposition of sanctions, in our opinion, would be subject to judicial review.[17]

Thus the court argued, in effect, that the establishment of goals is legal but that an attempt to force an employer to meet those goals might be illegal. Because much turns on the definition of "good faith" and the procedures to determine qualifications and standards, the issues involved in the Philadelphia Plan obviously have not been settled. In October 1971 the Supreme Court refused to review this case, letting the lower court ruling stand.

The Chicago Plan

In contrast with the Philadelphia Plan, which was imposed on the industry, the Chicago Plan—signed January 14, 1970, after months of conflict and negotiation—is very much in the collective bargaining tradition of attempting to negotiate a settlement between unions, employers, and minority communities.

The Chicago Plan was an agreement between the Coalition for United Community Action (comprised of ten civil rights organizations), the Chicago and Cook County Building Trades Council, and the Building Construction Employers Association of Chicago, Inc. It provided for recruiting or training of 4,000 black construction workers. Black leaders originally demanded training and admittance of 10,000 blacks to skilled positions in 90 days and the right to supervise the program, but they scaled down their demands in order to reach an agreement. At least 1,000 who could qualify for journeyman status were to be recruited by the Coalition and put to work immediately. A second thousand with two or more years' experience in particular crafts, after a 30-day probationary period, were to be slotted into apprenticeship programs at a level based upon their experience. Another thousand were to be recruited through an apprenticeship program of outreach and prepared for apprenticeship examinations. For those who failed apprenticeship tests or who did not wish to take them, the Chicago Plan provided for an on-the-job training program, with wages geared to apprenticeship rates, and supplementary schooling through evening classes. These recommendations applied to persons who had lived in Chicago for at least one year, and the plan established a goal of minority participation in the building trades equal to their percentage in the community at large. It was reported at the time of the agreement that there were 90,000 skilled construction workers in Chicago, 3 percent of whom were from minority groups.[18]

The Chicago Plan provided for an administrative committee representing Mayor Richard Daley, the Coalition, the building trades, and the employers association. Operations committees were established for each craft with four representatives from the Coalition and two each from the unions and employers "to formulate and determine particular plans for each craft and industry." However, in spite of high hopes of those who believed negotiated plans might succeed, the "Chicago Plan" was in trouble in 1971 because an administrator apparently misappropriated funds. Even before this was discovered, however, the Chicago Plan had encountered difficulties because the Building Trades Council could not bind its local union affiliate and the Coalition could not bind the black community. These negotiated plans cannot be effective unless the major parties to the agreement have the cooperation and support of their constituents.

Other Measures

While pushing the variations of the Philadelphia Plan, the Nixon Administration also attempted a new procedure to resolve these problems in the Seattle area. As indicated earlier, Executive Order 11246 did not give the OFCC authority to apply direct pressure on labor unions but insisted, rather, that the employers were responsible for implementing equal employment opportunity provisions. In 1969 the Justice Department filed a suit asking that labor unions in the Seattle area be enjoined from practicing racial discrimination. Several settlements with contractors and unions had been negotiated during the preceding months in the Seattle area, but whites walked off when blacks came onto the job. Simultaneously, efforts were made by the black workers, aided by the American Friends Service Committee, to get workers into the construction industry. The black workers' organization—the United Construction Workers—apparently played a major role in getting blacks admitted to construction unions in Seattle by bringing direct pressure to close construction sites and by recruiting applicants for the construction industry after a March 1970 federal court order required the hiring and training of blacks.

The Seattle court order restructured the membership and referral procedures of four construction unions—to make it possible for blacks more easily to enter these trades and unions. As a consequence of all of these measures—the law suit, organization of black construction workers, and outreach activities to recruit and place black workers—over 400 blacks got jobs in the Seattle construction industry between July 1970 and August 1971.

Finally in a separate development, the OFCC moved against 17 Chicago building contractors. In a letter to these contractors, the OFCC said that before any contracts would be released to these organizations in the future, it would be necessary for them to demonstrate that they were in accordance with equal employment opportunity provisions. Certainly, the contract officers had authority for preaward review. This was one of the first active demonstrations of a willingness to use that authority, and the result was a "voluntary" agreement considered highly attractive by the Labor Department.

Although the OFCC issued an order in February 1970 extending some features of the Philadelphia Plan to government contractors with 50 or more employees outside the construction industry, an October 1969 policy statement made clear the Labor Department preference for "hometown" solutions such as the Chicago Plan which differs from the Philadelphia Plan in several ways. For one thing, the Philadelphia Plan limits application to government contractors and the six stipulated crafts, whereas an areawide agreement can attach minorities to the entire labor market, which is much more significant in a casual industry such as construction. Moreover, a really effective plan probably requires the cooperation of unions and employers, and some means to increase the supply of qualified craftsmen must be realized. Programs are needed to upgrade journeymen as well as to produce them through apprenticeship and other training programs. The advantage for the Labor Department of "hometown" plans is that the latter reduce the strain on the OFCC's staff. Because of the Department's policy statement and the labor movement's aversion to the Philadelphia Plan, "hometown" plans have been negotiated in a number of other cities. However, the Labor Department's enthusiasm for these plans diminished after the trouble with the "Chicago Plan" and the failure of hometown plans in other areas to live up to expectations.

The Labor Department's preference for hometown solutions did not prevent it from imposing plans when the local parties failed to reach acceptable agreements. For example, the Department imposed such a plan in Washington, D.C. The Washington Plan covers 13 crafts on private as well as federal construction projects and also provides for a bipartite review committee.

Another noteworthy areawide agreement grew out of disputes over the Boston Model Cities program, especially the requirement for "maximum opportunities for employing residents of the area in all phases of the program." The local community groups wanted complete control but finally agreed to the HUD-BCTD model. A subcontract was signed for the WDL to recruit, train, and tutor potential journeymen and apprentices. However, this agreement was restricted to residential construction in the Model Cities area and did not assure union membership to the trainees.

The limitations of the Model Cities agreement, protest demonstrations, and the Labor Department's threat to impose a variant of the Philadelphia Plan led to the Boston areawide agreement, which resembles the Chicago Plan. As of September 1970, 285 minority workers were employed in the Boston construction industry—145 journeymen, 41 trainees, and 96 apprentices. It is not known, however, how many of these entered the industry before the Boston Plan was adopted.

Conclusions on Hometown Plans

Although they are generally regarded as better than the Philadelphia Plan, the voluntary areawide agreements are not without their problems. In Boston, for example, the pipefitters and sheet metal workers did not sign the agreement and some community leaders have denounced it as a fraud. An independent black union, the United Community Construction Workers, is attempting to place nonunion blacks on federal construction projects. Moreover, the administrative machinery does not work as efficiently as it might.

The main conclusion we draw about areawide agreements is that they show considerable promise where there are good faith efforts to make them work. However, they are not likely to be very effective where unions and employers continue to resist the employment of minorities. But, insistence by community leaders that they have complete control over the programs ordinarily will encounter opposition from unions, which fear a dilution of standards and increased competition for jobs, and employers, who are concerned about efficiency and costs. Industries with strong apprenticeship programs are particularly likely to encounter disagreement over taking workers into the skilled trades through means other than apprenticeship. Unions also are likely to continue to resist programs based on quota systems and preferential treatment. In the South, however, where there is a history of racial quotas on government contracts, some union leaders accept negotiated quota systems as a way to protect the interests of whites and blacks. In the South, quota systems have had the appeal of simplicity because they do not concern themselves with the mechanism whereby the quotas are met. If the quotas are compatible with labor supplies, they also ensure results in terms of minority employment. However, the quotas merely transfer racial conflict to negotiations rather than solving it altogether.

The debate over the Philadelphia Plan did not resolve the issues, in part because the protagonists addressed themselves to different questions. The defenders of the programs argued for the legality of the Executive Order and affirmative action, not whether "quotas" or "goals" could legally be imposed; opponents of the plan argued that it required quotas—which was not the case, at least in the sense that employees would lose the contracts for failing to hire a fixed number of black craftsmen.

Although the Philadelphia Plan may have stimulated areawide agreements such as the Chicago Plan, the latter have the advantages of goals without the emotional conflict accompanying the preferential treatment problem, even though at this writing, neither the Philadelphia Plan or the "hometown" solution have produced significant results. Nevertheless, the outreach concept has demonstrated its efficiency wherever its essential components are present. Administrators of outreach programs set their own achievement goals in consultation with the Labor Department or the appropriate funding agency or in negotiations with the parties involved. (It is significant that both Chicago and Philadelphia adopted goals.) Disadvantaged persons are given special help to meet entry requirements but are expected to meet the same performance criteria as anyone else. Unlike the Philadelphia Plan, which attaches goals to government contracts because of the limitations of the Executive Order, the outreach program can attach goals to a labor market and leave recruitment to the agency administering the plan. The agency also can render supporting services to help applicants meet objective industry criteria. Under the outreach concept the costs of helping the disadvantaged are borne directly by the government rather than by contractors, who are not likely to be as effective at recruiting the disadvantaged and rendering supportive services as a specialized agency can be. Of course, the outreach concept has the advantages and disadvantages of voluntarism, although the disadvantages are offset by other antidiscrimination pressures on unions and employers.

Although it is a key factor in minority participation in building trades, inadequate attention has been given to the "qualifications" question during conflicts with the construction industry over black employment. This question is important because, in the absence of some agreement over the definition of a particular craft, it is difficult to see how black workers in those crafts are to be identified and put to work. Although the technical difficulties involved probably account for the inadequate attention to this question, other factors undoubtedly are at work. For one thing, a prevailing assumption seems to be that there are many fully qualified black construction workers, who are ready to be put to work, who are unemployed or underemployed because of union discrimination. To some extent, this idea rests on the belief that the construction industry has exaggerated its qualifications for discriminatory reasons. There also seems to be a middle-class bias that qualifications and standards really are not too important for manual crafts— an assumption that *all* manual jobs are of low status and therefore do not really require mathematics or a four-year apprenticeship.

Public representation in determining qualifications is more important than attempting to agree on specific qualifications and standards for each craft. However, the standards and qualifications established for journeymen should be applied to whites who have worked in unionized sectors of the construction industry as well as to blacks who have been excluded from those sectors for racial reasons.

Of course, what many people fear is that quotas and preferential treatment will cause blacks with less than the minimum required qualifications to be hired ahead of more qualified whites, in order to compensate blacks for past discrimination. Regardless of its short-run consequences, this kind of "preferential treatment" has serious long-run implications. No better statement of this point can be made than the following comment by the noted psychologist Kenneth Clark:

> I cannot express vehemently enough my abhorrence of sentimentalistic, seemingly compassionate programs of employment of Negroes which employ them on Jim Crow double standards or special standards for the Negro which are lower than those for whites.
>
> This is a perpetuation of racism—it is interpreted by the Negro as condescension, and it will be exploited by them. Those who have been neglected and deprived must understand that they are being taken seriously as human beings. They must not be regarded as peculiar human beings who cannot meet the demands more privileged human beings can meet. . . . I suspect that the significant breakdown in the efficiency of American public education came not primarily from flagrant racial bigotry and the deliberate desire to create casualties but from the good intentions, namely, the sloppy sentimentalistic good intentions of educators to reduce standards of low-income and minority group youngsters. . . .[19]

SEGREGATED SENIORITY ROSTERS

Efforts to desegregate or integrate seniority rosters have involved many issues similar to those raised in the construction industry, as well as some that are unique. Indeed, in many ways the seniority question is more complex than the issues raised by minority participation in the construction industry. This is an important area because of the prevalence of job segregation, especially in the South where institutionalized discrimination confined blacks to agriculture and the most menial or undesirable nonagricultural jobs, and because desegregation is essential to significant improvements in black employment patterns. The main issues raised by this question relate to whether blacks are to be compensated for past discrimination when seniority rosters are merged; whether company or plant seniority will be used for blacks alone or for blacks and whites; and whether such impediments as wage reductions, time limitations, and loss of pay will be permitted to deter integration.

Considerable attention was devoted to the segregated seniority issue by various government contracting committees during and after World War II. However, the impact of the contracting committees was limited by their inherent weaknesses and the fact that they concentrated on industries where blue-collar employment was declining.

By the time of the Civil Rights Act, only token integration of blacks had taken place in major southern manufacturing plants. In addition to the factors mentioned above, seniority integration was impeded by the fact that many blacks hired as laborers lacked the education and experience to move up. Conversely, many senior blacks would have been forced to accept lower wages and lose job seniority in order to enter the bottom jobs in previously all-white lines of progression. Because seniority is a jealously guarded right and influences the profitability of industrial plants, it is not surprising that the terms under which seniority rosters are desegregated should be such a controversial and complex issue.

An important pre-Civil Rights Act decision came in the 1959 Whitfield case, where the Fifth Circuit Court of Appeals ruled that it was legal for unions to permit blacks to transfer to the bottom of the formerly all-white line of progression.[20] However, the Whitfield decision has not been followed in a series of post-Civil Rights Act cases.

In the 1968 Quarles case, departmental seniority at the Philip Morris plant in Richmond was held not to have been illegal per se. However, a system based on previous discriminatory practices was not legal, if employers "maintain differences in employee operations which were the result of discrimination before the Act went into effect." [21] In this case, "the restrictive departmental transfer and seniority provisions . . . are intentional, unlawful employment practices because they are imposed on a departmental structure that was organized on a racially segregated basis." The court also concluded that Title VII of the Civil Rights Act "does not require that Negroes be preferred over white employees who possess employment seniority. It is also apparent that the Congress did not intend to freeze an entire generation of Negro employees into discriminatory patterns that existed before the Act." The court required the company to permit permanent black employees who had been discriminated against to transfer into formerly all-white departments on the basis of company seniority. However, the Quarles decision, which has been relied on in other cases,[22] reduced the seniority rights of temporary black employees and did not disturb the departmental seniority system.[23]

Partly because the Supreme Court refused to review it, the Crown Zellerbach case has been regarded as a landmark decision by many civil rights leaders.[24] In this case, brought by the Justice Department under Title VII and Executive Order 11246, a U.S. District Court ruled that a departmental seniority arrangement at the company's plant in Bogalusa, Louisiana, violated the Civil Rights Act. As in Quarles, the court held that blacks who had been discriminated against could be promoted to jobs they were qualified to perform on the basis of company and not departmental seniority. Moreover, the court held that "institutional systems or procedures which deny to Negroes advancement to jobs held by whites with comparable mill seniority and ability consistent with [the] employer's interest in maintaining [the] skill and efficiency of [his] labor force . . . must be removed." These institutional arrangements included prohibitions on promotions of more than one job slot at a time where intermediate jobs did not afford training necessary for the next higher jobs or where employees had acquired the necessary training through temporary assignments; requiring black employees to enter the previously all-white lines of progressions at below those steps necessary to provide training for the next higher jobs; limiting time intervals for promotion to periods longer than necessary to learn the job before promotion; and "deterring Negro employees from transferring to formerly all-white lines of progression by requiring these employees to suffer a reduction in wages and a loss of promotional security as a condition of transfer."

In the 1970 Bethlehem Steel "pattern or practice" case, a U.S. District Court in New York found that a multiple-unit seniority system did not itself violate Title VII if that system "was not and is not designed or motivated by racial discrimination." However, because of the company's discriminatory hiring and assignment practices, the seniority system "operates in such a way as to tend to lock an employee into the department to which he is assigned." [25]

Although the courts' rulings on the question of the remedies for discrimination might appear confusing, and many of the issues remain to be resolved by the Supreme Court, some consistent threads seem to be emerging. With respect to imposition of "affirmative action" programs to correct pre-Civil Rights Act discrimination, the courts seem clearly to have held that no penalties can be imposed for preact discrimination, but that procedures adopted before the Act cannot be continued where the procedure was clearly adopted for discriminatory purposes, as was the case in Quarles and Crown Zellerbach. However, both of these cases, and Griggs [26] and Bethlehem, recognized that there might be legitimate business reasons for the practice (job seniority) if it is not designed to perpetuate discrimination.

These and other rulings in the building trades raise the question of the effectiveness of the "pattern or practice" suits. The Justice Department has been attempting to establish some general principles in this area in order to avoid a case-by-case approach, but a U.S. District Court observed in a leading case:

> ... while recognizing the desirability for enforcement purposes of having general propositions answered by the judiciary in categorical terms one way or the other, the court is convinced that both the proper administration of the statute and the goal of equality in employment opportunity will best be served by the essentially pragmatic approach of judging each case in the light of its own facts and the actual problems to be resolved.[27]

CONCLUSIONS ON
LEGAL REMEDIES

Obviously, the direct impact of state, federal, or local civil rights legislation and court decisions on black employment has been very limited. In part, the limitations of legal procedure are due to correctable defects such as inadequate funding and the EEOC's limited enforcement power. Moreover, the agencies themselves should be encouraged to coordinate their activities, although some differences between them are inevitable because of their different missions, constituencies, and powers. It is also possible to observe a trend toward strengthening legal remedies—from the relatively weak NLRB decisions before the Hughes Tool case in 1964 and the even weaker wartime FEPC and government contracting committees to the strong affirmative action requirements of OFCC and EEOC and the Justice Department under Title VII.

Even with all foreseeable improvements, however, legal procedures are incomplete tools in the fight for equality for a number of reasons. For one thing, under our system the evolution of the law and legal principles is a slow process. Experience to date suggests that there is little hope of avoiding a case-by-case approach, especially in the seniority cases where different racial histories, technologies, and skill requirements make it very difficult to generalize.

Legal sanctions, moreover, can do more to strike at overt forms of discrimination than they can to change the patterns that permeate social, political, and economic institutions. Hopefully, of course, measures that curtail overt discrimination also will initiate changes in the institutionalized patterns; but by generating conflict, legal approaches also cause a hardening of racial positions, therefore stiffening resistance to change.

Legal approaches also are limited because, in the economist's language, they operate only on the demand side of the problem and do little to change supply. Lowering the racial barriers does not ensure a supply of qualified people to take advantage of new opportunities. Positive approaches such as the outreach programs are required for this. Affirmative action programs, which are tacit recognition of this, can change supplies where they are established by consent decrees or by voluntary programs. However, under Title VII, employers and unions can be compelled to stop discriminating against blacks, but they apparently cannot be compelled to recruit actively and train them.

Experience with antidiscrimination programs seems to support the following conclusions:

1. Antidiscrimination measures are necessary but not sufficient to eliminate institutionalized discrimination in employment. These measures must be supplemented on the supply side by outreach programs.

2. While there is considerable apprehension by the collective bargaining establishment about the detrimental effects of the civil rights challenge, government agencies and courts seem, in general, to have strained to preserve traditional collective bargaining procedures. However, federal courts apparently are in no mood to permit subterfuges that perpetuate discrimination under the guise of legitimate business practices. In Seattle, Columbus (Ohio), Cincinnati, and other places, courts have ordered unions and employers to adopt measures to cure racial discrimination through reducing the unions' control of apprenticeship, referrals, and the determination of standards and qualifications.

3. The Chicago Plan, outreach programs, and the Model Cities agreements suggest that collective bargaining can yield, however reluctantly, to demands for greater participation by minorities in rule making. Indeed, the Chicago Plan was negotiated in the collective bargaining tradition of settling a dispute. However, the "hometown" plans still have not proved themselves and the impact of the civil rights challenge will depend upon the collective bargaining establishment's willingness and ability to take steps to ensure equal opportunities for employment. The parties will lose control of hiring, promotion, training, and referral systems that perpetuate discrimination. Just as federal controls were imposed on voter registration procedures when the states attempted to adopt seemingly "neutral" qualifications that nevertheless barred blacks, federal controls will be imposed on collective bargaining institutions that attempt to hide behind qualifications that, although seemingly fair and neutral, perpetrate discrimination.

4. The imposition of "affirmative action" requirements raises some difficult questions. The parties to collective bargaining should actively encourage programs such as Apprenticeship Outreach and plans to recruit and train minorities. Programs should help minorities meet entry and job performance standards, but they should not permit lower performance standards for minorities than for whites. Outreach programs should establish agreed-upon goals, but they should resist the establishment of rigid quotas. If Apprenticeship Outreach goals had been quotas, there would be fewer minority apprentices because the programs have almost uniformly exceeded their goals. Quotas, especially when imposed by the government, will generate unnecessary friction and ordinarily involve racial discrimination against either minorities or whites.

5. The establishment of fair and relevant qualifications and standards is essential to the resolution of many conflict areas in collective bargaining.

Fair procedures for establishing standards and qualifications, with outside participation, would go a long way toward closing the credibility gap between the collective bargaining establishment and minorities and others outside the system.

6. The segregated seniority question is complicated by considerable diversity in technology and local realities. However, it will be difficult to continue practices that were designed to discriminate because of race and that deter job integration. Federal courts have preserved employers' rights to demand that upgraded workers be qualified and have not eliminated job or departmental seniority per se.

7. In spite of differences in priorities and conflict over the speed of employment integration, which have strained black-union relations, the mutual benefits of collective bargaining and the civil rights–labor political coalition make it unlikely that most minority leaders will seek drastic changes in the collective bargaining system, especially if credible efforts are made to include minorities in the benefits of that system.

CONCLUSIONS ON MINORITY EMPLOYMENT

The causes of unequal employment opportunities and patterns are very complex and therefore will require that remedies be taken on many fronts. Antidiscrimination measures have an important role to play, but they are not sufficient to cause changes to take place. A tight labor market and adequate job vacancies also are important, but tight labor markets alone will not solve the problem if discrimination and unequal access to education and training bar blacks from meeting job requirements. In the final analysis, all of these conditions coupled with special remedial programs such as the apprenticeship outreach programs seem to offer some chance for success.

NOTES

1. Lester C. Thurow, *Poverty and Discrimination* (Washington, D.C.: Brookings Institution, 1969), Chap. 12.

2. *Griggs* v. *Duke Power Company*, 91 S. Ct. 849 (1971), 3 FEP 175.

3. Equal Employment Opportunity Commission, *White-Collar Employment in 100 Major New York City Corporations,* a report released by the Commission in January, 1968 (mimeographed). Plans for Progress merged with the National Alliance of Businessmen in July 1969.

4. Vernon M. Briggs, Jr., *They Have the Power, We Have the People,* Equal Employment Opportunity Commission (Washington, D.C.: U.S. Government Printing Office, 1970).

5. Richard P. Nathan, *Jobs and Civil Rights: The Role of the Federal Government in Promoting Equal Opportunity in Employment and Training* (Washington, D.C.: U.S. Government Printing Office, 1969).

6. *New York Times* (September 3, 1969).

7. G. Douglas Pugh, "Bonding Minority Contractors," in William F. Haddad and G. Douglas Pugh, eds., *Black Economic Development* (Englewood Cliffs, N.J.: Prentice-Hall, 1969).

8. *Social and Economic Implications of Integration in the Public Schools,* seminar on manpower policy and program, U.S. Department of Labor, Manpower Administration, Office of Manpower, Automation, and Training (Washington, D.C.: U.S. Government Printing Office, 1964), p. 6.

9. F. Ray Marshall and Vernon M. Briggs, Jr., "Remedies for Discrimination in Apprenticeship Programs," *Industrial Relations* (May 1967).

10. F. Ray Marshall and Vernon M. Briggs, Jr., *The Negro and Apprenticeship* (Baltimore: Johns Hopkins, 1967).

11. *Wall Street Journal* (March 29, 1968).

12. *U.S.* v. *Sheet Metal Workers, Local 36, and IBEW, Local 1,* 416 S 2d 123 (1969), 2 FEP 128. No. 68-C-58 (2), 1968. *U.S.* v. *SMW,* two FEP cases, 128.

13. *Gaynor* v. *Rockefeller,* 15 N.Y. 2d 120, 204 N.E. 2d 627, 256 N.Y.S. 2d 584 (1965).

14. *Ethridge* v. *Rhodes,* 268 F. Supp. 83.

15. *New York Times* (June 28, 1969).

16. *Contractors Association of Eastern Pennsylvania* v. *Shultz,* D.C.E. Pennsylvania (1970).

17. *Ibid.*

18. Seth S. King, "Chicago Negroes Win Accord on Construction Jobs," *New York Times* (January 13, 1970).

19. Kenneth B. Clark, "Efficiency as a Prod to Social Action," *Monthly Labor Review* (August 1969), pp. 55–56.

20. *Whitfield* v. *United Steelworkers,* 263 F. 2nd 546; cert. denied, 360 U.S. 902.

21. *Quarles* v. *Philip Morris, Inc.,* D.C.E. Va. (January 4, 1968).

22. *Irvin* v. *Mohawk Rubber Co.,* 380 S. SUPP. 152 (1970), two FEP cases (1970).

23. Herbert R. Northrup, *The Negro in the Tobacco Industry* (Philadelphia: University of Pennsylvania, 1970), pp. 78–80.

24. *U.S.* v. *United Paper Makers,* Local 189, 71 LRRM 3070 (1969); cf. *Hicks* v. *Crown Zellerbach, Corp.,* 69 LRRM 2005 (1968).

25. *Daily Labor Report* (April 24, 1970), p. A–1.

26. *U.S.* v. *Duke Power Company,* 91 S. Ct. 849 (1971), 3 FEP, 175.

27. *U.S.* v. *H. K. Porter,* 296 F. Supp. 40.

Part VI
Manpower and Economic Policy

Chapter 26
Manpower and Economic Policies

The goals of manpower programs fall into three general categories. First, the programs seek to help match up the supply of and demand for labor, increasing the efficiency of the labor market mechanism. Second, they are aimed at helping workers who suffer particular disadvantages in competing for available jobs. And finally, in the broadest sense, they are designed to provide every worker the vocational preparation needed for the occupation of his choice, while at the same time insuring that societal labor requirements will be met.[1]

Given currently limited public and private manpower resources, only marginal progress can be expected in the realization of these goals. Some "frictional unemployment" will always remain—when workers search and prepare for new jobs and are temporarily unemployed, or when employers relocate or close their businesses. Some "structural unemployment" will exist as long as technology continues to make some skills obsolete, as long as many entrants to the labor force are ill-prepared, and as long as the supply and demand for labor do not match perfectly. Workers will never have complete freedom of choice nor will industry's needs be exactly met when the future is uncertain, and particularly when industry's needs are not the same as workers' preferences.

Nonetheless, a persuasive case can be made that intensified efforts can minimize these labor market imperfections. Through improved labor market services—such as better reporting of job vacancies, testing, outreach, and counseling—the duration of unemployment and the number of unfilled jobs may be markedly reduced. Through special rehabilitation and training programs for disadvantaged workers, combined with increased efforts to break down discrimination and restructure jobs for those with few skills, workers with deep-seated and long-lasting employment problems can become more productive and self-sufficient. With increased education and training for work, with better vocational guidance, and with firmer projections of occupational demands, workers can increasingly be placed in occupations of their choice where their skills will be used productively.

Measures to increase the productivity, reward, satisfaction, and availability of employment are potentially far-reaching. Such improvements would affect all those who are in, can be drawn in, or will eventually enter the labor force, especially those who would encounter the most problems in their work life. Because of this potential impact, manpower programs must be recognized as an increasingly important economic factor. The relationship between manpower policy and the other economic policies of the government should be carefully examined and articulated.

MONETARY AND FISCAL POLICIES

The major objective of government economic policy is to regulate the aggregate demand for goods and services, which, in turn, affects the level of total output. Monetary and fiscal measures are the major tools. By changing the quantity of money in circulation (monetary policy), the government can stimulate or cool down business and consumer spending. As more money is made available, consumption increases, profits rise, interest rates fall, and investment is stimulated. Conversely, as the quantity of money is reduced, money incomes rise less quickly, so that consumers spend less and funds for investment are more difficult to acquire, decreasing aggregate investment. By changing its taxing and spending (fiscal policies), the government can change the amounts of cash in the hands of consumers and adjust its own demands for goods and services. Tax increases and reduced government spending will lead to a decline in aggregate demand, while tax cuts and increased government spending will add to demand.

One of the major reasons for regulating demand is to balance the economy's production of goods and services with consumption and, in turn, generate an economic climate in which the labor needed to produce these goods and services will be fully employed. In the aggregate, increasing the demand for final products will increase the demand for labor; thus, the level of unemployment can be altered through government fiscal and monetary measures. For instance, Arthur Okun, one-time chairman of the President's Council of Economic Advisors, estimated in 1962 that for every 1 percent increase in real GNP, unemployment is reduced by 0.3 percent. Though the exact figure has been modified by subsequent experience, "Okun's Law" suggests a rather straightforward relationship between monetary and fiscal measures regulating aggregate demand and the level of unemployment.[2]

Maintenance of full employment is, of course, not the only goal of monetary and fiscal policy. By affecting the domestic price level, these policies change the relative attractiveness of exports and imports, altering the balance of trade and the balance of payments. By regulating the pattern of business, consumer, and government spending and by changing aggregate economic conditions, these measures affect the level of investment in the short run and the rate of economic growth in the longer run. Most significantly, by regulating the money supply and the demand for goods and services relative to their supply, monetary and fiscal measures have an important effect on price levels. Because price increases, and especially changes in the rate of price increase, threaten those with fixed incomes and creditors generally, checking inflationary pressures is one of the major goals of monetary and fiscal policies. Unfortunately, this usually conflicts with the goal of reducing unemployment.

THE TRADEOFF BETWEEN INFLATION AND UNEMPLOYMENT

It is a fact of life that as unemployment is reduced and the pool of employable labor is diminished, firms must pay higher wages and salaries and accept workers of lower productivity. This increases the labor cost per unit of output, and in order to maintain their profit margins firms must increase their prices. The ultimate cost of goods and services to the consumer is raised, with the inflationary pressures intensifying as the supply of idle manpower decreases. The accepted strategy for achieving greater price stability is to reduce aggregate demand—which will lead to the termination of less productive workers, some reduction in wage and salary demands, and thus to falling labor costs per unit of output. Price stability, therefore, is facilitated by a higher level of unemployment.

In addition, price increases have some impact on the supply of labor and are, therefore, a cause as well as an effect of the level of unemployment. It has been postulated that when future price increases are expected, some workers may avoid taking jobs in the belief that their real wage will fall; others, who are unemployed, may wait for a better job offer because wages are rising. However, still others will actively seek work as they see better money offers or as a means of supplementing family income that is eroded by inflation.

Although the relationship between price changes and the level of unemployment is not exact—as the rising inflation and rising unemployment of 1970–1971 so bitterly demonstrated—it tends to be inverse, as shown by plotting the changes in cost of living and the level of unemployment (Figure 26–1). The curve fitted to these points slopes downward and to the right, meaning that lower rates of unemployment are correlated with

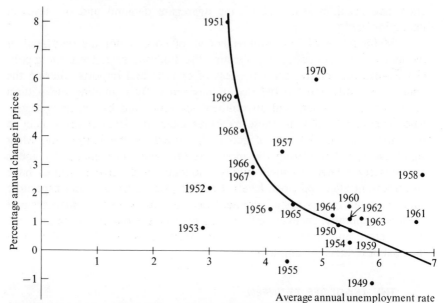

FIGURE 26–1.   *Annual Changes in CPI and Level of Unemployment, 1949–1970*
SOURCE: U.S. Department of Labor

increasingly higher rates of price change and vice versa. This graphical relationship is usually referred to as the "Phillips curve," after the British economist A. W. Phillips who first noted and measured the connection between unemployment levels and the rate of changes in wages. While wage and price changes are not synonymous, they are closely related, and the name "Phillips curve" has been applied loosely to both the price change-unemployment and the wage change-unemployment relationships. No harm is done in labeling both as Phillips curves as long as the distinction between wage and price changes is kept in mind.[3]

The Phillips curve postulates an inevitable tradeoff between price stability and reduced unemployment. Monetary and fiscal policies that affect the level of aggregate demand can shift the economy along the curve, but they cannot shift the curve itself. If the government pursues a policy of easy money and deficit spending, thereby increasing the demand for goods and services, production will be high and unemployment low; but, unfortunately, prices will increase at a faster rate. These expansionary monetary and fiscal policies will move the economy leftward and upward on the Phillips curve. However, tight money, increased taxes, and decreased government spending will cool off the economy and lead to more stable prices; but unemployment will increase as the economy moves to a new equilibrium downward and rightward on the curve. There is no way of moving off the curve through the manipulation of macroeconomic variables be-

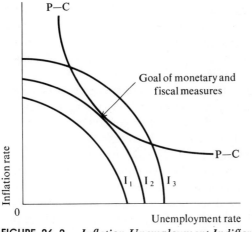

FIGURE 26–2.   *Inflation-Unemployment Indifference Curves*

cause reduced rates of unemployment must sooner or later be paid for with increased rates of inflation, and conversely.

In determining the thrust of its monetary and fiscal policies, the government must balance the harm caused by inflation with the bitter consequences of unemployment—though the latter may be reduced by unemployment insurance payments and other forms of income transfers. The tradeoff is not made explicitly, but pressures mount for anti-inflationary monetary and fiscal policies when unemployment grows. At any given time, there is some preferred point on the curve toward which monetary and fiscal policies are directed. This is suggested in Figure 26–2 by a series of indifference curves, I_1, I_2, and I_3. All combinations of unemployment and inflation rates represented by a single curve are equally acceptable to the formulators of public policy. The curves are concave because at lower rates of unemployment, policy makers will be more willing to trade off increased unemployment in order to reduce hyperinflation, and vice versa. They would prefer both a lower rate of unemployment and inflation—that is, any point on I_1, to any point on I_3, but they are indifferent to the combinations represented by any one curve.

The attainable combinations are represented by the Phillips curve, the P-C line drawn in the chart. In choosing the goal of monetary and fiscal measures, policy makers will try to move to the lowest possible indifference curve. This is the one that is tangent to the Phillips curve, or I_2 in the diagram.

The fluctuations in price change and unemployment rates in the post-World War II period resulted not only from exogeneous economic factors but also from misapplication of monetary and fiscal tools and changing notions about the proper tradeoff between inflation and unemployment.

Monetary and fiscal policies are inexact and often miss the mark. The 1964 tax cut, for instance, accompanied by expansionary expenditures resulting from the unforeseen escalation of war in Vietnam, precipitated too great an increase in aggregate demand. A surtax was implemented in 1968 to cool the economy and halt the rise in prices.

Equally important are shifts in the indifference curves of policy makers. During the Eisenhower years, more emphasis was given to fighting inflation than to lowering unemployment. The government's tight monetary and fiscal policies are usually blamed for the recession of 1958 and for the economic declines of 1954 and 1959. The Democratic victory in 1960 is frequently attributed to the high level of unemployment, which reached 6.8 percent in December 1960. Promising to "get this country moving again," President Kennedy emphasized the need for "full employment," proclaiming an "interim" goal of 4 percent unemployment. To this end, he proposed an income tax cut, which was not initiated until 1964, after President Johnson assumed office. During the Johnson Administration, increasing employment was still given priority over fighting inflation. Budget expenditures increased markedly without adequate monetary restraint or taxation, with the result that prices gradually crept upward. In 1968, the Republicans were inched into office pledging to stop the rise of prices. Tacitly, GOP economic advisors acknowledged that this would probably be accompanied by a rise in unemployment variously estimated at 4.3–5.0 percent; the rate actually rose to 6.2 percent, reviving charges of Republican insensitivity to unemployment. While these shifts in policy were not always explicit—because both parties gave lip service to the incompatible goals of low unemployment *and* price stability—it is safe to say that there have been some major swings in public preferences over the last two decades.

The fact remains, however, that monetary and fiscal policies can only move the economy toward a more preferred position on the Phillips curve, or at least in a preferred direction. Measures affecting aggregate demand can reduce unemployment only at the expense of accelerated price rises, though the tradeoff may not be exact.

Shifting the Phillips Curve

One hope for manpower policies is that they might alter the structure of the economy so that the terms of tradeoff between unemployment and price changes is improved, or, in technical terms, the Phillips curve is shifted leftward and any given level of unemployment can be achieved with less effect on prices—or, in terms of Figure 26-2, society can move to a preferred indifference curve. Rehabilitation and training programs, for instance, might reduce structural unemployment by preparing technologically displaced or educationally disadvantaged workers for useful work. Unemployment will be reduced and prices will be lowered to the degree that the social benefits of the training programs exceed their cost. Improved labor market services that increase the rate of placement reduce the waiting time between jobs and thus the level of unemployment. If the mobility of workers can be improved, jobs will be filled that would otherwise have remained vacant and would have raised prices in tight labor market areas. Thus, improved placement, counseling, outreach, and mobility-inducing measures could reduce frictional unemployment, resulting in a decline in both prices and unemployment. Finally, manpower efforts to improve vocational training and counseling for all workers and to insure a supply of skilled laborers where they are needed may increase productivity to the degree that preparation for employment is improved and to the degree that output is higher in more personally satisfying employment; and such efforts may reduce the pressure on prices from labor bottlenecks. Helping those with the most severe labor market problems and the highest rates of unemployment will reduce the disparity between the unemployment rates of various groups in the labor force, and, in turn, lower the pressure on wages so that there will be less price rise at any level of unemployment.[4]

The impact of past manpower programs on the tradeoff between unemployment and the rate of price change cannot be measured. Claims that manpower-training efforts have produced a noticeable shift in the Phillips curve are based on faith rather than empirical evidence. The effects of increasing manpower expenditures are undoubtedly dwarfed by other changes in the structure of the economy. Also, their impact will probably be felt only in the longer run because the payoff on manpower expenditures comes in increased earnings and productivity of assisted workers over many years. If increased manpower expenditures should result in a large positive effect, manpower policy should have an important role alongside the monetary and fiscal measures, making possible a more favorable tradeoff between inflation and unemployment.

Structural vs. Demand-Deficient Unemployment

The relationship of manpower policy to monetary and fiscal measures has been a source of controversy since the Kennedy Administration. Some economists claim that structural unemployment has increased markedly, as more and more workers have become obsolete because of technological change. According to this theory, there has occurred a twist in the demand for labor, so that educated and skilled workers are in short supply while large numbers of unskilled and poorly educated workers are no longer needed. If this is the case, an increased demand for goods and services will lead to wage increases in the occupations with a deficient supply of labor and to subsequent price rises. Though less skilled workers will be hired, a high level of inflation may also result, rendering impractical the necessary monetary and fiscal policies. Manpower programs, it is argued, are needed to train and retrain disadvantaged workers for available jobs and to employ those who cannot be trained.

There is continuing debate over the magnitude of such structural changes in the economy—and, consequently, over the policy implications. In 1964, argument raged openly between "structuralists" and those who urged a cut in taxes to increase aggregate demand and thereby reduce unemployment. Proponents of the tax cut claimed that it would reduce unemployment from the then current level of 5.5 percent to an interim 4 percent level, while "structuralists" predicted that reduction below 5 percent would be prevented by bottlenecks in the supply of professional and technical manpower.[5]

Following the tax cut in February 1964, the unemployment rate soon dropped to 5 percent, fluctuating around that point for the rest of the year. By June 1965, with excise tax reductions and other measures, the rate fell to 4.7 percent. War expenditures then began to increase markedly and the unemployment rate fell further. Whether the tax cut would have reduced the rate to 4 percent without drastic inflationary effects is conjectural; but, clearly, the combination of fiscal measures (i.e., tax cuts and increased government spending for defense and welfare) was able to accomplish what the structuralists claimed could not occur—reduction of unemployment to extremely low levels without significant increases in the rate of price rise. There is no way of knowing whether monetary and fiscal policies could have effectively prevented inflationary pressures in the absence of a war.

Low unemployment after 1965 silenced debate for some time, but with rising unemployment in 1970, the arguments resurfaced over proposals for an enlarged public employment program. Structuralists claimed that such a measure was needed to provide for an ever-increasing number of workers whose skills were no longer required by the industrial system. Reviewing past experience, they asserted that much of the decline in unemployment after 1964 was due to (a) the induction within three years of an additional 800,000 men into the armed forces, many of whom would have either been unemployed or would have filled jobs opened to disadvantaged workers; and (b) counting manpower program enrollees as employed. The decision so to treat enrollees reduced unemployment by about 0.5 percent and was justified by government officials as consonant with the practice of considering persons undergoing training as fully occupied. Critics charged that neither the level of stipends nor, in most cases, the quality of training justified the inclusion of enrollees among the employed.

Some evidence can be mustered to show that those with poor education or other disadvantages benefited only slightly from sustained prosperity in the 1960s.[6] Though unemployment rates declined among this group, their labor-force participation rates went down even more, and their relative earnings position deteriorated. This does not indicate what would have happened in the absence of sustained growth, and it does not disprove the necessity of monetary and fiscal policies to reduce unemployment. It does, however, highlight the fact that monetary and fiscal measures must work along the Phillips curve, and that they cannot counter the technological changes that may be shifting the curve rightward and making the terms of tradeoff between unemployment and price rises less favorable. According to this argument, as more and more workers are rendered obsolete while skilled workers are in short supply, increases in aggregate demand will produce more inflation with less effect on unemployment. Programs to train, retrain, and employ the structurally unemployed will actually shift the curve by reducing unemployment without putting as much pressure on the scarce supplies of more skilled workers.

MANPOWER PROGRAMS AS A COUNTERCYCLICAL TOOL

While manpower policy is an increasingly important adjunct to monetary and fiscal policies over the long haul, it has not been applied to the short-run goal of controlling "business cycle" fluctuations. Monetary and fiscal measures have been reasonably successful in limiting the more pronounced fluctuations in economic activity, which once seemed inevitable, and they have proved their ability to maintain sustained growth; nevertheless, minor business cycles still exist. During the 1960s, real growth rates varied from 1.9 percent in 1960–1961 and 2.4 percent in 1966–1967, to 6.6 percent in 1961–1962 and 6.4 percent in 1965–1966. In 1970, real GNP declined, suggesting that post-mortems for the business cycle may have been premature or at least that periodically engineered slowdowns may be necessary to reverse the upward creep of inflation.

Manpower policy has played little or no role in efforts to control economic fluctuations. Manpower expenditures and programs expanded continuously throughout the 1960s but were applied without any countercyclical intent. However, lessons have been learned about the effectiveness of various programs and approaches in different economic conditions. These lessons must be applied if manpower policies are to play a more active role in regulating or at least responding to economic fluctuations that occur despite monetary and fiscal efforts.

Lessons Learned from Manpower Programs

The first lesson is that programs oriented toward the private sector are most effective in tight labor market conditions. Subsidies to hire and train disadvantaged workers, to induce business to locate in depressed areas, or to eliminate discrimination will have their greatest impact when qualified workers are in short supply and when firms are expanding and opening new plants. Conversely, when firms are forced to lay off employees because of declining demand, when they have excess capacity and are trying to eliminate all but their most efficient plants, and when fears of unemployment lead to employee antipathy toward newly hired disadvantaged workers, OJT or locational subsidies will be less effective. This was clearly the experience under JOBS, where terminations increased markedly in the slack at the end of 1969 and the beginning of 1970, and the Administration was forced to reallocate funds originally earmarked for JOBS to other manpower programs because hiring under JOBS did not live up to anticipation.

The second lesson is that public sector training becomes more important and effective in slack times, if for no other reason than to fill the gap left by declining private sector participation. Institutional training provides at least income maintenance and perhaps useful training and basic education. Loose labor markets reduce trainees' chances of opting for jobs instead of training and diminish pressures by employers on training institutions to speed the delivery of trainees. Under these circumstances, trainees are more likely to complete manpower training courses. Since placements and employment rates are closely correlated with duration of training, institutional training programs probably become relatively more effective during slack times.

The third lesson is that the manpower programs serve a different clientele when unemployment is high than when jobs are plentiful. Increasingly during the 1960s, the more seriously disadvantaged workers were helped—to a large extent the result of expanding employment opportunities generally. The labor queue moved forward rapidly and the disadvantaged became next in line for employment and hence were most in need of manpower services. The fact that the manpower programs emphasized the needs of the unskilled, poorly educated, and members of minority groups subject to discrimination does not mean that the process is irreversible. In all programs, there is a tendency to "cream" the available and intended clientele for those most likely to benefit from assistance. When demand slackens, less disadvantaged workers seek out and are selected for manpower programs, so that those with more severe problems receive less attention. For instance, in the JOBS program, as unemployment increased in late 1969 and early 1970, the average family income of participants under contract increased steadily, indicating the selection of a less disadvantaged group.

The fourth lesson is that public employment can be expanded or contracted with little difficulty, if there is little regard for the productivity of hired workers. Many thousands of public service jobs apparently require little or no training and only a small capital investment, and people can be put to work on these jobs as a temporary measure with little prior notice. However, the productivity will be slight, and their personal benefits outside of wages only minimal. Temporary public sector jobs that will be more productive and beneficial are difficult to implement under a crash program.

The fifth lesson is that labor market services should be adjusted to changing economic conditions. When jobs are plentiful, the employment service can function as a labor exchange; but it can also reach out to disadvantaged persons to provide them with needed counseling and services and induce them to seek and find employment. However, when unemployment is high, fewer firms turn to the public employment service, and those that do can choose among recently employed and less disadvantaged workers. This is the time when job development and placement efforts should be increased, even though they will be less successful in terms of placements. While the recently unemployed should be aided in their return to the labor force, the hard-core unemployed should not be ignored. If private jobs cannot be found, they must be directed to manpower programs or to public employment. Unfortunately, the employment service becomes bogged down with the administration of an increasing unemployment insurance caseload during slack times, and its role as a labor exchange for the declining number of job offers is further impaired.

Countercyclical Strategy

These five lessons suggest that, if manpower programs are to be administered in a countercyclical way, there must be flexibility to shift between different programs and approaches as economic conditions change. This suggests the need to centralize the overall planning of manpower programs under a single agency which can develop priorities, allocate funds, and tie-in manpower with monetary and fiscal policy, though this may not be desirable to the extent that decentralized programs will be more effectively administered. At any rate, contingency funds should be available to finance the needed increases in manpower programs as well as shifts in program levels. One way to do this is to provide for an automatic increase in manpower funds when unemployment passes a certain level. This trigger mechanism might provide that manpower funds be expanded when unemployment reaches a predetermined level, say, 4.5 percent. Manpower and additional funds could be added if unemployment continues to climb. For example, for each 0.5 percent increase in unemployment above 4.5 percent, the law might provide for an additional 10 percent increase in manpower funds. Thus, if unemployment rose to 6 percent, manpower funds would rise by 40 percent. The formula might also be applied in determining allocations for each state and locality, to help depressed areas that are especially hard hit by rising aggregate unemployment.

In broadest terms, a countercyclical strategy might run as follows. When unemployment is low, with consequent inflationary pressures, the manpower programs should focus on the needs and opportunities in the private sector. On-the-job training should be increased to take advantage of employers' active search for additional manpower and to help meet existing shortages. Institutional training should be deemphasized but still be available for those with more serious problems or to train for occupations that can be more efficiently taught in an institutional setting. Incentives should be offered to firms for locating in depressed areas and for hiring disadvantaged residents. The employment service should streamline its placement services, while at the same time taking advantage of increased demand by reaching out to the disadvantaged and finding them jobs. Over-all, the manpower programs should concentrate on helping the more dis-advantaged workers and providing them the types of services that will improve their long-run employment experience. Public employment pro-grams should focus on the young or the aged who are unable to find private employment and should stress quality rather than quantity in opening meaningful career opportunities for family heads with inadequate earnings.

When unemployment rises, manpower expenditures should be in-creased, mostly in the areas of public work and training. Private employers will be less willing to hire and train disadvantaged workers, and many previously hired will be laid off because of slackening demand. Institu-tional training and public employment should be expanded to assist such workers. Enrollees are likely to remain longer in institutional programs, which should concentrate on basic education and the more serious prob-lems of marginal workers. Adequate income support should be provided along with this training. Private sector incentive programs should change their focus from increasing the number of disadvantaged who are hired and trained and the number of firms locating in depressed areas to reducing the number of workers who are dismissed or the number of depressed area plants that must be closed. In other words, they should emphasize a hold-ing action so that their accomplishments will not be undone. The employ-ment service, likewise, should increase job development and placement efforts for those recently unemployed, directing them to available man-power programs. Outreach efforts necessarily should be diminished, and a holding action should again be emphasized.

Underlying the suggested shifts in tactics is the heroic assumption that manpower programs can be adjusted to fit cyclical fluctuations. These shifts, however, will help at best only a small portion of the increasing number of unemployed. More jobs are needed, and the key is public em-ployment. Yet, although public employment is now provided for youths under the Neighborhood Youth Corps, for older workers under Operation Mainstream, and for primary workers under New Careers and Public Service Careers, sentiment is generally unfavorable toward the expansion of public jobs as a countercyclical measure. It is likely that higher levels of unemployment will quickly change such attitudes, which are based on many misconceptions in the first place. For instance, despite the popular image of idle leaf-raking under the New Deal public employment programs, vast amounts of useful work were accomplished: Between 1933 and 1940, otherwise idle and dependent workers produced 651,000 miles of roads and highways, 78,000 bridges, 35,000 public buildings, and a host of other improvements. Though technology has changed and many of the public works done by hand in the 1930s can now be accomplished by machines, there are numerous cases in the expanding public service area where needed jobs requiring few skills have been neglected. Because the test of a filled job comes in the hiring, estimates of job vacancies are necessarily speculative. Estimates of job vacancies in public employment are even more suspect and may frequently be blown up for political purposes to support claims of "unmet needs." Estimates of job potential in public employment have ranged from 5.3 million for the nation in 1966 [7] to 300,000 "needed" in 130 cities during 1968 in such areas as health, education, sanitation, welfare, and police work.[8] Whatever the precise magnitudes, it is apparent that large numbers, running into hundreds of thousands, could be absorbed in productive full-time public employment; many more could be put to use on a short-term basis during recessions when labor supply becomes abundant, though this type of effort has less payoff.

There are problems, however, in expanding and contracting public employment in a countercyclical fashion. Economic contractions since World War II have averaged less than a year in length, hardly enough time to initiate large-scale public employment efforts. The best that could occur in such periods is for existing programs to be expanded. Still, any reasonable expansion in manpower programs would absorb only a small proportion of recession victims. Enrollments in all the Labor Department-funded manpower programs in 1970 equaled less than one-fifth of the long-term unemployed and about one-twentieth of all those unemployed during the year. Manpower policy is hardly a substitute for monetary and fiscal measures in controlling economic fluctuations.

Nevertheless, manpower programs have a vital if limited role to play. While aggregate-demand management can change the level of unemployment, the effects must filter down through the economy. For instance, an increase in spending to reduce unemployment will lead to increased profits and increased earnings for those already employed as well as to the hiring of some additional workers. Manpower expenditures, however, are directed specifically to those who are most in need of help. For any dollar of expenditure, manpower programs probably have more impact on unemployment than other types of spending, and expansion of such programs may be the best way to help the unemployed when demand slackens.

WAGE-PRICE CONTROLS AND THE PHILLIPS CURVE

The relationship between price changes and unemployment, or as originally formulated by Phillips, between wage changes and unemployment, is neither exact nor inexorable. Econometric studies have suggested that many other factors—for example, the level of profits, variations in labor productivity over the business cycle, and, most significantly, the rate of change of unemployment—also affect the rate of price rises. The simple progression from increasing aggregate demand to a derived demand for more labor, an increase in wages, and a resulting rise in prices is far more complex in reality. As a result, monetary and fiscal measures to move the economy to a new equilibrium point, in order to reduce either unemployment or inflation, do not always have the predicted results. For instance, in 1958, restrictive monetary and fiscal policies were applied to brake the rise in prices. While wholesale prices took another year to stabilize, unemployment remained high, averaging 6.1 percent of the labor force for the 1958–1961 period. In 1970, this same phenomenon occurred, but at different levels. Consumer prices rose twice as fast as in 1958, despite restrictive monetary and fiscal policies; unemployment continued to climb, though not reaching the peaks of the earlier years.

The explanation for these "aberrations" is that our economy is not perfectly competitive. Most goods are produced by firms having some degree of control over prices, while labor unions and other associations of working people, such as professional associations, have some power to maintain or raise their wages or money income. There is a consequent rigidity in prices and wages because large firms are reluctant to lower prices and union bargainers will rarely accept wage reductions, even if sales and employment are slack. Perhaps even more serious, some firms with excess capacity and declining sales will raise their prices to bolster falling profit margins, labor unions will sometimes press for wage increases despite rising unemployment, and service industries will take advantage of shortages that may persist even in a recession. Concentrations of market power can thus lead to rising prices, wages, salaries, and fees despite reductions in aggregate demand.

The measured empirical relationship between unemployment and price changes reflects these structural characteristics of the economy. To the degree that corporations and labor unions have market power that they use to maintain or raise prices and wages where aggregate demand is falling, the tradeoff between unemployment and price rises will have worsened. And because market power implies discretionary behavior, the reaction of the economy to any monetary and fiscal measure has become less predictable.

One way to improve the tradeoffs and gain greater control over the economy is to enforce some type of regulation over wage and price changes, instituting what is called an "incomes policy." Through controls, power is shifted from the private to the public sector—that is, from firms, unions, and associations with a high degree of control over markets to the government. In this way, the Phillips curve might be shifted leftward and monetary and fiscal measures can be pursued more effectively.

Wage and Price Controls

Price and wage controls have been tried and abandoned several times over our history. In wartime they have been used to allocate goods to military needs and to insure that lower-income families get a fair share of scarce commodities, which otherwise would be available only to those able to pay inflated market prices. In 1971 wage and price controls were imposed for the first time during peacetime.

During World War II, the National War Labor Board, made up of business, labor, and other public representatives, was established to administer wages, while the Office of Price Administration was set up to stabilize prices and rents and to regulate the rationing of scarce goods. The mechanisms for controlling prices and wages were unequivocally successful. From 1914 to 1920, with only the very limited controls of World War I, average hourly earnings rose 142 percent and the cost of living 100 percent. From 1941 to 1945, when controls were in full effect, wages rose only 40 percent and prices 22 percent, despite more severe labor shortages and a much larger war.

Controls were also instituted during the Korean hostilities which lasted from June 1950 until February 1953. Despite relatively mild inflationary war pressures—federal purchases accounted for nearly one-half of GNP in the peak year of World War II, compared with one-seventh of total GNP in the Korean period—prices rose much more rapidly during the control period of the Korean War than during World War II. By the time wage and price controls were instituted, about eight months after the outbreak of hostilities, most of the inflationary pressures generated by the military action had run their course; and the wage and price controls administered by the Wage Stabilization Board and Office of Price Stabilization, respectively, remained a holding action, providing insurance and standby machinery in case the limited Korean action spread into a full-blown war.

Though experience with these wartime controls is not directly transferable to peacetime conditions, it highlights several issues that are relevant under any circumstances. Most obviously, the almost universal rejection of controls after both wars raises questions about their longer-run effectiveness. For instance, the pent-up postwar consumer demands and the expressions of serious labor unrest after World War II suggest that distortions had occurred in the allocative process and that resumption of market functions was necessary to relieve them. While World War II controls were effective, they raised many basic issues. The War Labor Board rejected arbitrary freezing of wages and permitted wages to catch up to the increases in cost of living prior to the imposition of controls in October 1942. After that period, the wage and price controls were maintained and no general wage increases were permitted until the war was won. Despite the inflationary pressures, President Roosevelt insisted that no increases in prices and wages could be tolerated. "The only way to hold the line," he declared, "is to stop trying to find justification for not holding it here and not holding [it] there." [9] This meant that wages could not be adjusted to increases in cost of living and that values in consumer products deteriorated. The President could make this order stick as long as the support of the war remained universal and as long as the nation was ready to allocate one-half of its production for war purposes. Such widespread support was lacking during the Korean period, and the inflationary pressures were milder; wage and price controls were therefore much less stringent than in World War II.

During the Korean War, an attempt was made to control real wages by stabilizing money wages. Not only did the Wage Stabilization Board approve wage increases based on overall rise in productivity, but also cost-of-living adjustments were sanctioned on the top of productivity increases. Under the circumstances, wage controls had little effect and prices had not stabilized prior to the imposition of controls.

Wage controls also raised problems concerning changes in hours of work, pensions, fringe benefits, shift premiums, vacations, upgrading, and merit or length of service increases. During both wars, these forms of remuneration increased markedly, frequently in lieu of general wage increases. Some of these resulted in deferred increases which were reflected in increased labor costs after controls were removed and others raised unit labor costs immediately but did not show up in average hourly wage or salary schedules and therefore could be glossed over by the officials who were presumably stabilizing wages and prices. Finally, there is the issue of raising the wages of workers receiving "substandard" earnings. Compassion dictates that such increases should be outside the pale of wage controls, and even the rigid controllers of World War II permitted such increases. But raising wages of low-paid workers reduces wage differentials and encourages more fortunate workers and their unions to press for upward wage increases in order to maintain historical advantages.

The Guideposts

Greater government control is more acceptable in war than in peace, and proposals to regulate wages and prices have received little support in peacetime. Even the brief listing of problems inherent in wage controls make a persuasive case for this opposition to controls. Though few goods are produced under perfectly competitive conditions, efforts at regulation usually meet with a stream of protest against distorting the allocative efficiency of the "free market." However, when inflation combines with high levels of unemployment, the public becomes amenable to some degree of control. This was the case in 1962 when President Kennedy, through his Council of Economic Advisers, announced a set of voluntary guidelines for price and wage changes. They carried no penalty for violation and were intended to show business and labor the limits of good behavior compatible with price stability. The guideposts were set forth by the CEA:

> The general guide for noninflationary wage behavior is that the rate of increase in wage rates (including fringe benefits) in each industry be equal to the trend rate of over-all productivity increase. General acceptance of this guide would maintain stability of labor cost per unit of out-

put for the economy as a whole—though not of course for individual industries.

The general guide for noninflationary price behavior calls for price reduction if the industry's rate of productivity increase exceeds the over-all rate—for this would mean declining unit labor costs; it calls for an appropriate increase in price if the opposite relationship prevails; and it calls for stable prices if the two rates of productivity increase are equal.[10]

Many complications concealed by these simple rules and some exceptions were recognized explicitly by the Council. Wage increases could exceed the guidepost rate in industries or areas that attracted insufficient numbers of workers, but they should be less in declining industries with an excess of workers. Prices could rise, or at least fall more slowly, in industries unable to attract capital to finance expansion, but they should rise at a lower rate where profits were being earned because of market power. Because almost every firm or industry could claim an exemption on one of these grounds, the guideposts were far from clear-cut. Nevertheless, the central idea was that wage and price changes would depend on productivity changes.

From 1962 to 1964, these guideposts were enforced with varying enthusiasm and success. Though there were no sanctions imposed on industries or unions violating the rules, the government applied a variety of pressures from "jawboning" to market retaliation. Three months after the initial declaration of the guideposts, the steel industry, led by U.S. Steel, announced a general increase for all products that exceeded the limits of approved behavior as spelled out by the CEA. The announcement came on the heels of a union agreement that was within the guideline limit, and the move was clearly a rejection of CEA policy. The reaction was immediate public censure by the Administration, plus threats of transferring government purchases to the other large companies which had delayed raising prices. As a result of government pressure and still slack economic conditions, the price increases were rescinded.

In other cases where the government used its leverage as a purchaser, subsidizer, or regulator, the guideposts were generally enforced. This occurred in confrontations with steel, copper, and aluminum producers in 1965 and maritime workers in 1966. However, there were cases where power existed and was not used—for example, in the inflationary settlement of the airline machinists strike in 1966. Where the government had little market power, the guideposts could not be enforced; and they were clearly a failure in trying to regulate wage increases sought and received by construction workers, as well as in limiting price increases by automobile producers.

These confrontations, whatever the balance of power, affected only a very small proportion of all settlements. Whether the guideposts had any impact outside the few cases of active intervention remains a subject of some debate among economists.

Empirical studies comparing wage and price changes during guide-post years with those of early years suggest that annual wholesale price changes were between 0.5 and 1.5 percent less than expected, and that annual consumer price increases were reduced, on the average, by 0.5 percent. These reductions were probably due to the guideposts, notwithstanding the other explanations that have been proposed. At the most, however, their impact was not large, and it could not check the price increases that resulted from increased war spending.[11]

CONSTRAINTS OF WAGE
AND PRICE REGULATIONS

Inflationary pressures in 1969 and 1970 revived interest in price-wage regulation. Among the suggestions were guideposts or some "stronger" medicine, including use of tougher tax or other penalties to punish offenders. The impact of jawboning is clearly slight and its effectiveness lost through frequent use. Only the government can check the market power of unions, large corporations, and professional groups; but this raises questions about the degree and technique of intervention and whether, in fact, intervention is justified. Whatever the answers to these questions, certain problems are inherent in any type of controls, as were discovered in the exercise of very minimal authority under the guideposts.

First, guideposts and limited controls must fall basically on the largest firms, the most concentrated industries, and workers in these firms and industries. If aggregate demand is high, more competitive sectors and less organized workers will benefit. This redistribution has positive and negative effects which must be given careful consideration.

Second, price and wage controls must be based on some implicit determination of the share of the output going to labor and capital. If wages rose by the increase in productivity and prices were changed as the guidelines suggest, labor and capital shares would remain constant. Understandably, unions might not be satisfied wtih the status quo and the lot of millions who are counted among the working poor would improve very slowly, if at all. Also, to the degree that prices continued to increase after controls were instituted, workers would suffer a decline in their real wage if there were no cost-of-living allowances. However, if automatic cost adjustments were allowed, the price-wage spiral would continue.

Third, any guidepost or control must face the problem of determining wage differentials between areas and plants and among workers within plants. If allowance were made for individual and interarea variation in productivity and cost, calculations would become extremely complex, almost requiring case-by-case determination.

Finally, any type of control encounters difficulty in allowing for changes in demand. Wages and prices based on productivity make no real allowance for changing consumer preferences, and these are extremely hard to measure. Allocative distortions are bound to result.

Such considerations become more critical as controls become more extensive, more strictly enforced, and more prolonged. Applied over several years in selective cases where wage and price actions are clearly out of line and enforced through jawboning and market measures, selective controls can be a useful weapon to fight inflation. However, these have only a limited aggregate effect because they regulate only those cases where the abuse of market power is the source of inflation. More widespread and strictly enforced controls, while they may temporarily check inflation, create many problems, and the cure is probably worse than the disease. A better strategy is to combine selective controls with expanding manpower expenditures to gradually improve the tradeoff between inflation and unemployment, but most of all to meet the needs of the disadvantaged who must bear the brunt of any adverse economic developments. In designing public policies to alter the tradeoff between inflation and unemployment, it is vital to protect the interests of workers at the end of the labor queue, who have little market power and little responsibility for the price-wage spiral.

NOTES

1. William G. Bowen, "What Are Our Manpower Goals," in R. A. Gordon, ed., *Toward a Manpower Policy* (New York: John Wiley, 1967), p. 59.

2. Arthur Okun, "Potential GNP: Its Measurement and Significance," *Proceedings of the Business and Economic Statistics Section of the American Statistical Association,* 1962, pp. 98–104.

3. Robert A. Gordon, *The Goal of Full Employment* (New York: John Wiley, 1967), pp. 162–191.

4. George L. Perry, *Inflation and Unemployment* (Washington, D.C.: Brookings Institution, 1970), p. 42.

5. The opposing views are presented by Walter Heller and Charles Killingsworth in Garth L. Mangum, ed., *The Manpower Revolution* (New York: Doubleday, 1965), pp. 97–146.

6. Charles C. Killingsworth, "Rising Unemployment: A 'Transitional' Problem?" in U.S. Congress, Senate Committee on Labor and Public Welfare, Subcommittee on Employment, Manpower, and Poverty, Hearings on *Manpower Development and Training Legislation,* 91st Cong., 2d Sess. (Washington, D.C.: U.S. Government Printing Office, 1970), Part 3, pp. 1254–1267.

7. National Commission on Technology, Automation, and Economic Progress, *Technology and the American Economy* (Washington, D.C.: U.S. Government Printing Office, 1966), p. 36.

8. Harold L. Sheppard, *The Nature of the Job Problem and the Role of New Public Service Employment* (Kalamazoo, Mich.: Upjohn Institute for Employment Research, January 1969), pp. 24–25.

9. Executive Order 9328, April 8, 1943.

10. *Economic Report of the President, 1962* (Washington, D.C.: U.S. Government Printing Office, 1962), p. 189.

11. John Sheahan, *The Wage-Price Guideposts* (Washington, D.C.: Brookings Institution, 1967), pp. 79–95.

Chapter 27
Industrialization and Human Resource Development

Economists have attempted to explain the causes of the wealth and income of individuals and nations since long before the time of Adam Smith. That economic productivity has been due to the joint efforts of capital, human and natural resources, and entrepreneurs is well established, but the weights to be given each factor of production and the precise causal relationships between them are not as clear.

In recent years, economists have devoted considerable attention to the economic development process. Some of this work has attempted to explain the role of human capital investments in economic development, especially in the developing countries. Others have been concerned with the differential rates of growth between regions, individuals, and sectors of the economy. Although we shall note in this chapter that the issues are far from settled, experience with the industrialization of either under-developed countries or lagging regions and sectors leaves little doubt that the development of human resources plays an important role in raising incomes.

AN OVERVIEW

Industrialization and human resource development (HRD) are closely linked because industrialization shapes people to its own requirements. Economic development, or the growth of income-earning opportunities, influences education and training by providing the resources to

528

support educational activities as well as means of acquiring on-the-job training experiences. The interaction between economic output and education and training is similar to the formation of nonhuman capital: Human resource development requires prior production to support education and training activities until those in whom these investments are being made can become productive.

However, the interactions between HRD and income-generating activities make it very difficult to establish with precision causal relationships between national incomes and investments in human resources. As noted in Chapter 7, such investments are unquestionably closely related to the growth of per capita income, but we do not know whether the HRD investments cause the incomes to grow or whether incomes cause HRD investments to grow. Moreover, there is some question over the extent to which joint returns to all factors of production can be attributed to human and nonhuman capital.

Similar linkages exist among manpower programs, economic development, and education. Manpower programs that match people and jobs increase individual and national productivity by helping people to be more productive. For example, mobility or training programs to move people from labor surplus to labor shortage areas increase national income if the costs of making these moves are less than the incomes gained. However, measures to influence the supplies of workers assume there are jobs available for them. Moreover, jobs are an important part of the training process because most of the skills and attitudes needed for modern industry are learned either on the job or by being exposed to economic activities.

However, our problem is complicated by the fact that HRD is not entirely economic. Education, for example, has consumption characteristics because it involves processes through which education improves noneconomic as well as economic aspects of life. Similarly, education and training might have social benefits in improving political processes and facilitating social order. Efforts to determine the economic returns to education and training therefore encounter the problem of how to factor out these consumption and social benefits, all of which undoubtedly facilitate economic development.

An HRD strategy must also concern itself with programs to eliminate barriers to personal improvement that are not related to productivity. The major factor here is discrimination because of race, sex, age, or national origin (discussed at length in Part V).

Similarly, while industrial societies must provide for the maintenance of those who cannot or should not work, many health and welfare activities have no direct measurable relationship to productivity, even though they play important roles in shaping economic development. The manner in which these health and welfare services are rendered also has important implications for economic development. Ill-fed children suffer psychophysical damage which permanently affects their ability to be educated and trained for productive work. Moreover, income maintenance clearly is necessary if workers are to support themselves and their families while they are being trained. The interaction of education, income, health, and jobs is nowhere more evident than in the well-known vicious cycle that makes it difficult for many poor nations and individuals to improve their positions.

INSTITUTIONS, HUMAN RESOURCE DEVELOPMENT, AND INDUSTRIALIZATION

Not only are there close causal interactions between the various components of HRD (jobs, education, manpower, antidiscrimination, and welfare) and industrialization, but industrialization itself interacts in a very significant way with political, social, and economic institutions. The nature of HRD programs is closely related to levels of economic development, national objectives, and the nature of the society in which industrialization takes place. Kerr, Dunlop, Harbison, and Myers, for example, demonstrate that human resource development programs are closely related to the logic of industrialization.

As these same authors show, industrialization requires increasing levels of technology, which have significant manpower implications. These levels of technology necessitate the development of a science and technology based upon a variety of research organizations, particularly in the advanced stages of industrialization. Moreover, industrial systems require wide ranges of skills and professional competence, which must be widely distributed throughout the working population. As a consequence, it is their view that the creation of a highly skilled professional and technical labor force is as important for industrializing societies as the accumulation of capital goods: "The professional, technical, and managerial component of the labor force, private and public, is particularly strategic since it largely carries the responsibility of developing and ordering the manual and clerical labor force." [1]

Because of the centrality of science and technology in the industrial society, technical competence tends to replace traditional ways of assigning people to jobs. Industrial societies tend to become meritocracies in which people are assigned to jobs primarily on the basis of their abilities, and not on the basis of caste, racial groups, sex, or family status. Moreover, the industrialization process has a profound impact on the family. In preindustrial societies, the family is likely to be the producing unit, whereas industrialism tends to disintegrate the family and to make the business firm the primary production unit.

A nation or a region adopting HRD strategies must decide (a) which people within the population are to be educated and trained, and (b) at what level of education. Moreover, decisions must be made about the kinds of education and training to be undertaken: Are resources to be devoted to scientific and technical training or to the arts and humanities? To some extent, these decisions might be made by the market because activities that are in greatest demand will provide for the largest rewards and therefore induce people to enter them. But choices about HRD cannot be left entirely to the market.

Harbison and Myers have shown that the HRD strategies adopted clearly depend on the level of economic development, among many other things.[2] These authors identify various levels of economic development with corresponding HRD strategies. In underdeveloped countries, for example, the main national objectives tend to be national sovereignty and independence, and the rapid development of primary industries is likely to be considered an important means for achieving these national objectives. Because educational levels tend to be quite low in the underdeveloped countries, the development of primary education is usually an important HRD goal.

As societies become partially developed, they concentrate upon building the base for industrialization while increasing productivity in agriculture. During this stage, there are likely to be shortages of skilled and technical manpower. As a consequence, these manpower needs are met by importing personnel from more advanced countries. The important HRD objective during this stage of economic development is likely to be extension of universal primary education, which becomes attainable because of the resources made available by economic development. Secondary education, especially in science and mathematics, must also be expanded in order to meet the need for subprofessionals and technicians. Because of the shortages of skilled and educated manpower, the extension of education and training requires improvements in educational technology in order to overcome critical shortages of teachers.

As the society reaches the third, or semiadvanced, stage, the national economic objective is likely to be rapid and massive industrialization. During this stage, large-scale unemployment of unskilled workers is likely to be coupled with continuing shortages of those with higher levels of education and skill. As a consequence of this imbalance, institutions of higher education, as well as those providing job training and adult education, are subjected to considerable pressures. It becomes particularly important that higher education emphasize science and technology and that vocational and adult education more closely meet the requirements of employers.

In advanced countries, HRD needs tend to emphasize innovations in order to maintain a rapid rate of economic development. Full employment will be elusive in advanced industrial societies because of the difficulty of distributing the output of a highly productive economy. As productivity rises and the same output can be produced with fewer people, it becomes necessary to adopt specific measures to prevent rising unemployment. During this stage—when science and technology play an important role in continuing innovation—higher education, particularly at the postgraduate level, is given priority. At the same time, however, advanced societies experience strong pressures for universal secondary education in order to place higher education within the easy reach of all people. Measures also are necessary in advanced economies, to eliminate inequalities between various segments of the population because these inequalities become increasingly apparent as incomes rise, and rising national incomes make it possible to reduce inequalities. Moreover, dynamic changes make skills obsolete and lead to knowledge explosions, all of which require perfection of education and training in order to prevent maladjustments and to promote equality of economic opportunity.

Attitudes of Political Leaders

Human resource development strategies are influenced not only by the stage of economic growth but also by the nature of the institutions and the attitudes of the political leaders in the areas undergoing industrialization. For example, revolutionary intellectuals tend to harbor quite different attitudes about the role of education and training than political leaders with middle-class values. The revolutionaries are likely to conceive of education as a primary means of achieving national objectives—as a means of developing man for the state and not for his own enjoyment. Moreover, the educational system is likely to be more specialized and functional with a high priority on science and technology. In Russia, for example, science and education have become important instruments for state power. Max Lerner has explained, "For the Russians, science has become mainly an instrument of state power, part of their Grand Design for world domination, indeed part of their political religion. This is something that we need to understand; for the Russians there is a political mystique of science. There is a belief that nothing is impossible for man once he has the weapons of science." [3]

Pluralistic societies such as the United States, however, are less likely to have unified educational objectives. Education, as other institutions, is apt to reflect the divergent interests and influences of different groups within the society. However, the society as a whole tends to emphasize widespread public education as a means of making political democracy more effective. Education in the United States also tends to stress human development not the establishment of functional relationships to the economic system. Scientific, technical, and vocational education are likely to become increasingly important in such a society, but not at the expense of training in law, art, and the humanities.

Regardless of the political persuasions of the national leaders, education is clearly regarded as "the key that unlocks the door to modernization." Not only does education have a direct impact upon development, but also it has an indirect effect through its influence on such factors as natural resources, markets, the ratio between people and human resources, political stability, social and cultural institutions, and leadership. Moreover, although education is likely to play an important role in the growth of national income, it is important to recognize that the particular type of education and training system is probably as important as the amount of education. In other words, at a given stage in economic development, some kinds of education and training are likely to be more important than other kinds. For example, increasing expenditures on art, humanities, and law when a country needs more scientists and technicians is not likely to promote economic development, and as countries develop the percentage of national income for HRD is likely to rise everywhere.

Building an Industrial Labor Force

Kerr and his colleagues identify four interrelated processes in building an industrial labor force. The first of these processes is *recruitment,* either through compulsory or voluntary means. Examples of compulsory recruitment are slavery and peonage. In modern times, however, only the Communist countries have relied extensively on compulsory recruitment of labor—partly because "compulsory methods generally have proved to be unreliable as a permanent means of building an industrial labor force." [4] Fortunately, as industrialization proceeds and the amenities of industrial jobs become clearer to workers, the recruitment process is relatively easy. This is not due entirely to the attractiveness of industrial jobs but to the fact that even the most unattractive industrial jobs are likely to provide benefits that are much greater than those available to the workers in agriculture. Because the recruitment process tends to be relatively easy, manpower shortages are likely to be mitigated fairly rapidly during the process of industrialization.

The second process, *commitment,* tends to be much more difficult. The "committed worker is one who stays on the job and who has severed all his major connections with the land." The process of commitment takes place in four stages—the uncommitted worker, the partially committed worker, the generally committed worker, and the specifically committed worker—the degree of commitment varying with the stage of economic development. The uncommitted worker takes an industrial job for a particular purpose with the intention of returning to the land when this limited purpose or objective is achieved. The partially committed worker takes an industrial job but maintains his rural connections. The generally committed worker has completely severed his rural connections and has become a permanent member of the industrial work force. The specifically committed worker has severed his rural connections and has become committed to employment with a particular firm. Specific commitment is particularly important in Japan, where workers have strong commitments to particular employers and where employers are likely to view some workers as lifetime employees. It is also significant in Italy, France, and England

and is becoming more important in the United States as a result of seniority systems and employers' heavy investment in the education and training of their employees.

Environmental factors, of course, may speed or retard the process of commitment. In large urban areas, commitment is more easily achieved than in more isolated communities. Cultural factors such as religious and ethical valuations, the family system, class, and race all have a bearing on commitment, but, in one way or another, workers are uprooted from the old order and relatively soon become generally or specifically committed to the new.

The third process is *advancement,* which means developing the skills and attitudes necessary for industrial production. This is a most critical process in building industrial work forces. Advancement may be carried out by workers themselves, by company training programs, or by governmental or community programs. However, in modern times, increasing education and skill requirements make it difficult for workers to train themselves. As a consequence, a very large part of industrial training must take place on the job. On-the-job training imparts to workers not only skills but also attitudes conducive to industrial efficiency.

Because skill acquisition requires formal education as well as on-the-job training, however, formal schools have an important role to play in the advancement process. As noted earlier, during the early stages of industrialization, schools are not likely to be particularly well suited to turning out efficient work forces. Hence, developing nations must draw their skilled manpower from other countries. But as the country develops, education becomes more closely related to economic institutions. In advanced industrial societies, workers are required to have considerable formal education; and because education is likely to have social as well as individual benefits, governments tend to expand their role in education and training.

The fourth process is *maintenance,* which involves providing for the general welfare and security of the population. Industrialization invariably gives rise to the need for unemployment insurance, compensation for accidents, maintenance of people during their old age, and other forms of social security. Public maintenance increases in importance because the family ceases to be the primary producing unit and workers become dependent on their work for a livelihood. Provisions must, therefore, be made for people who either cannot or should not work. However, maintenance systems frequently are closely related to the other steps in the development of an industrial work force—because the level of maintenance depends upon the productivity of the whole work force and because various incentive systems might be developed to facilitate the entry of people into productive work rather than relying on welfare for maintenance.

In commenting on the problems involved in developing an industrial work force, Walter Galenson admits that there is considerable evidence that difficulties are involved in commitment, but he warns that the difficulties appear to have been exaggerated. During the early stages of industrialization, there tend to be such problems as absenteeism, tardiness, high turnover, and high absentee or desertion rates during harvest times, but Galenson concludes that these problems appear to be more a function of poor management, which uses labor wastefully because it is cheap, than of any inherent characteristics of the labor force.[5] Galenson also concludes that, during early stages of industrialization, workers seem to be quite as responsive to monetary incentives as are their counterparts in the advanced societies. In some African countries, for example, employers have justified low wages on the grounds that the labor supply function is backward bending, so that as wages rise, workers are willing to offer less labor because they have a greater preference for leisure than for high incomes. But others have found that the absence of worker economic motivation does not appear anywhere as a serious consideration.

The lack of worker commitment during early stages of industrialization might have positive as well as negative effects. The tensions generated by the industrial routine probably are relieved by occasional visits to a worker's village. Low labor productivity is an important deterrent to economic development during the initial stages of industrialization, but it is not a very serious problem once industrialization gets under way. As Galenson emphasizes, the extent to which low productivity is overcome seems to be largely a function of the degree to which management assumes responsibility for training: ". . . the essential ingredient for rapid skill formation is the recognition by management that creating an efficient labor force may be every bit as demanding from a technical point of view as installing and operating machinery." Moreover, the developing countries often have shortages of high-level managerial talent.

THE RELATIONSHIP OF
EDUCATION AND TRAINING
TO ECONOMIC GROWTH

The relationship between the amount of educated manpower and economic growth has not been clearly established. For example, such countries as Great Britain and the United States have spent large sums on research, development, and scientific manpower yet have lagged behind Japan in economic growth—at least during the 1950s and early 1960s. We are not yet able to assert that a large pool of scientific manpower has a positive and direct impact on output and growth—even though theoretically such expenditures are considered as investment in educational capital and should raise productivity and output per person.

Harbison and Myers constructed an index of HRD consisting of (a) the number of teachers at the elementary and secondary level per 10,000 population, (b) the number of engineers and scientists per 10,000 population, (c) the number of pupils enrolled in elementary school as a percentage of total possible enrollment, and (d) several other measures of development in education. They finally arrived at a composite index—the total of "enrollment at second level of education (secondary equivalent) as a percentage of the age group 15–19, adjusted for length of schooling and enrollment at the third level of education (higher education) as a percentage of the age group, multiplied by a weight of 5 (reflecting a greater weight for the influence of higher education)." [6]

Using per capita GNP in United States dollars and percentage of population engaged in agriculture as indices of economic output, Harbison and Myers found a significant correlation (+.89) between their index and GNP per capita. There was negative correlation between the index and the percentage of population engaged in farming occupations (−.81). But these quantitative relationships, the authors caution, do not establish causal relationships. In some cases (such as Japan), however, a claim of causality between an educated labor force and economic growth seems to be supported by the evidence. Japan made an initial heavy investment in its educational system, which certainly contributed to later rapid economic growth.

Although Harbison and Myers are cautious about assigning causal relationships between education and economic growth (see Chapter 7), other economists have not been as reluctant. There is, however, increasing skepticism about the large role some economists have assigned education as a factor in economic growth. Clearly, these relationships are not linear and homogeneous. At early stages of development, general literacy is important in modernization. Moreover, the development of technicians and skilled workers also is important as the economy develops and becomes more technical. However, the relationship becomes more difficult to determine at later stages of economic development. Nevertheless, a relationship between education and individual incomes can be established because employers use education as a screening device.

MANPOWER PROGRAMS AND REGIONAL DEVELOPMENT

Economic development is significant for regions and smaller economic subdivisions as well as for nations. The development problem of regions derives from the fact that many areas are characterized by unemployment, underemployment, and incomes far below national averages. In the United States, government and private agencies have been anxious to develop these areas. A basic question is whether this approach is more sound, in the sense of improving per capita real income, than moving the people in those areas to jobs in places with greater economic potential.

The development of places is not necessarily incompatible with the development of people, but it can be. For example, creating marginal jobs might not be in the best interest of the younger, adaptable, better educated people for whom the jobs were created. Subsidizing industry to locate in a depressed area could be particularly disadvantageous because a town's costs for public services are likely to rise faster than its revenue, therefore depriving the town of funds to improve education, training, health, and other necessary investments in its people. Policies to improve mobility from such places into others might be in the people's best interest. (But marginal jobs might be in the best interest of *some* of the people in the depressed area.)

Even when successful, such efforts are likely to attract low-wage, labor-intensive enterprises with dead-end jobs which will make a very limited improvement of real incomes. High-wage firms are not as likely to be attracted by the blandishments of cheap labor and tax incentives as they are by skilled workers, markets, resources, or external economies found in growing cities and towns. Because industry adapts to the kinds of resources available, higher-paying extramarginal industries might be attracted if a region upgraded its resources through education and training.

Indeed, the need for HRD programs in lagging areas is suggested by the fact that many former residents, whose education and skills enabled them to migrate, often return when jobs open up—leaving those without education and training still unemployed. Lagging regions might, therefore, attract better industry by making investments in manpower than by giving direct subsidies to firms to locate there.

Regional Development Policy in the United States

The basic U.S. policy for assisting lagging areas was established by the Public Works and Economic Development Act of 1965. This Act is administered by the Economic Development Administration (EDA), which has attempted to aid development districts (defined largely in terms of high levels of unemployment and low income) by providing job opportunities in nearby growth centers to which migrants can be channeled through job information, resettlement assistance, and training.

Although this program has made some important contributions, it has several limitations. First, the EDA has not had adequate funds to produce significant economic development in many areas. Second, the cities selected were generally too small to provide significant growth prospects. While most regional economists consider places in the 200,000–750,000 population range to be the minimum for self-sustaining growth, as of March 1969, only 18 of EDA's 122 development centers had populations of 50,000 and over. Third, the development centers selected by the EDA also ignored cities outside the lagging areas, which might have had greater growth potential. According to Hansen,

. . . if a federal subsidy can accelerate growth in a center which is already rapidly growing, and if this subsidy is made conditional on providing employment opportunities for residents of lagging areas, then it might well be more efficient for EDA to tie into the growing environment than to attempt to create growth in a relatively stagnant area by putting in water or sewer lines.[7]

Finally, greater attention to investment in health, education, and training of the labor forces in lagging areas probably would be more effective than investing in sewer and water lines. Hansen argues:

. . . it is not clear that public works projects in which EDA is primarily involved, chiefly infrastructure in the narrow sense, will really lead to rational migration policy. If the unemployment and welfare difficulties of rural migrants in large metropolitan areas are largely a function of lack of job skills and education, as EDA correctly maintains, why should the migration of these people to smaller growth centers not pose similar problems? [8]

Marginal Economic Activities

While the long-run desirability of capital-intensive industry and manpower-upgrading programs for lagging regions is generally conceded, there are cogent reasons for arguing that HRD programs should also include a strategy for developing labor-intensive activities, at least in the short run. For one thing, labor-intensive jobs, especially in rural areas, are needed for people whose educations and experience have not prepared them for high-wage occupations. Many of these people are likely to work in marginal enterprises or receive welfare wherever they live. The limited welfare resources might be more effectively utilized in subsidizing marginal enterprises in the rural areas than in income maintenance alone. Measures are especially needed to improve the position of small farmers by making it possible for many of those who wish to remain in agriculture to do so. With adequate technical assistance and loan programs, many small farmers could switch from capital-intensive crops to such labor-intensive ones as vegetables and livestock production. It is possible that the ascendancy of large farms has resulted, in part, from federal agricultural policies, which favor large-scale activities, as well as from economies of size or comparative economic advantages that large farmers enjoy. The long overdue reform of American agricultural policies might slow down the displacement of small farmers.

Although cooperatives and other labor-intensive activities might be marginal economic enterprises, they could have significant noneconomic advantages which would have long-run beneficial implications for human resource development. For example, significant actions against discrimination, poor education, unwise agricultural policies, and inadequate health and welfare services are unlikely without political pressures. Marginal economic enterprises might, therefore, form bases to generate pressures for improving the productivity of the rural poor and their children as well as providing minimum income bases for those who wish to remain in rural areas. Marginal enterprises also make it possible to slow the deterioration of many rural communities. In addition to marginal enterprises, public service employment programs could be launched in lagging regions to give jobs to persons with limited education or nonagricultural work experience. As noted in Chapter 18, programs such as Operation Mainstream have been particularly valuable in rural areas.

PILOT MOBILITY PROJECTS

For younger, better educated, adaptable residents of lagging areas, mobility assistance programs would seem to have considerable promise as means of improving incomes. Between 1965 and 1968, MDTA funded demonstration projects which relocated some 14,000 unemployed and underemployed workers and their families, mainly from rural areas, at a cost of about $800 per family, including about $300 for moving and settling in. These projects were generally regarded as successful in moving the unemployed and underemployed to new jobs in labor shortage areas, where most of them stayed. Moreover, these programs made it possible to isolate some key factors facilitating mobility—for example, the need for a wide range of supportive services and the value of tying relocatees to specific jobs before they are relocated.

Rules of the Game

The legal restrictions imposed upon the mobility projects were deliberately confining. As defined by the Act, the workers had to be unemployed or underemployed persons, for whom there was no reasonable expectation of employment in their own communities. A bona fide job offer at the receiving end of the move was also required prior to relocation. Administrative guidelines added the requirement that the job be one that otherwise would not be filled by qualified local workers, by local workers who could be trained, or by relocation of more proximate workers. The only assistance authorized was grants or loans to cover relocation expenses. The pattern during the early period was to combine 50 percent grants with 50 percent loans, but experience led to almost complete reliance on grants.

Relocation projects were funded in three distinct phases. In the first phase, which was funded during fiscal 1965, emphasis was more on relocating people than on testing the results of relocation. Although no controlled studies were made, the circumstances differed sufficiently among the projects to offer numerous insights into the problems and apparent results of relocation.

The next series, which ended in 1967, was designed for more extensive follow-up and evaluation; it attempted to build in a more specific research orientation as well as to broaden the range of questions explored. Most projects in this phase built on the 1965 experiences, but a few new ones were added. For example, the Tuskegee Institute concentrated on MDTA graduates and used a job tryout system prior to full relocation. The Kentucky state agency conducted a project in cooperation with the state public assistance agency to relocate welfare recipients who had completed the Work Experience and Training program; social services were provided through public assistance resources. Montana enlarged program activities to cover the entire state and gave special attention to off-reservation Indians. Montana's state agency built into its project specific tests of the employment service's ability to provide social services from its own resources and the relative effectiveness of varied levels of relocation allowances. The Virginia and West Virginia projects involved the Travelers Aid Society. In Wisconsin and Iowa, the Smaller Communities teams of the public employment service were used as rural outreach agencies.

Whereas the 1965 projects emphasized rural-to-urban shifts, some of the later ones experimented with slum-to-suburb and rural-to-rural relocation. In Hartford, Connecticut, and in Chicago, efforts were made to relocate workers (welfare recipients in Hartford, young blacks in Chicago) from core-city slums to suburban or other areas where jobs were available. In Missouri, low-income, largely black tenant farmers were moved from the "boot heel" section to the more prosperous eastern part of the state, where farm jobs were more plentiful but where few, if any, blacks lived. Pennsylvania undertook two projects. One sought to measure the effectiveness of nonfinancial assistance for relocation with no allowances; the other was designed to test the significance of accumulated fringe benefit and seniority rights as barriers to mobility.

In the third phase, which ran through 1968, several new concepts were introduced. Perhaps the most significant was the development of a 12-state consortium of eastern states. This interregional project was designed to test interarea recruitment and data collection as well as to move the relocation concept from an experimental to a quasi-operational status.

With the experience gained from some 14,000 relocated workers, who with their families amounted to nearly 40,000 people in 29 states and nearly 40 different projects, the Labor Department recommended in 1968 that relocation assistance be made a permanent part of the federal manpower program arsenal.

As with all experimental operations, the relocation effort was blessed and cursed with examples of good and bad projects, competent and mediocre staffs, significant and meaningless project findings. There appears to have been a strong commitment to the need for a flexible, project-by-project approach in implementing relocation activities. Successful relocation of low-skill rural workers required services different from those needed by well-trained technical personnel displaced by mass layoffs in urban areas. Project results suggest that basic education and extensive skill training should precede any attempt at relocating the former, and that an extensive array of supportive services before and after the move is essential. However, assistance in locating jobs from a distance and/or financial aid apparently is all that is necessary for displaced skilled and professional people. The relocation of low-skill workers is obviously of higher priority, especially because many well-trained workers move without assistance.

Relocation Costs and Administration

Though some workers were willing to move without financial aid, nine out of ten received one or more of three types of general financial assistance. Basic financial aid was provided for (a) moving expenses and in some situations for temporary storage of household goods; (b) lump sum allowances (which were determined by the factory worker's average weekly pay) for the worker and his spouse and half that amount each for up to four dependents; and (c) temporary dual-household subsistence payments to enable workers to try a new job and to arrange housing before moving their families.

During the first year, relocation allowance costs were lower than expected, averaging under $300, with the average ranging by project from $100 to $800. The major reason was the discovery that few disadvantaged workers had household effects worth moving, but moves were also shorter, and there were fewer dependents than anticipated. The lump sum living allowances accounted for more than half the average cost; transportation and storage of household goods, 30 percent; and travel allowances, 20 percent. The highest costs were for skilled workers who moved longer distances and required higher average transportation allowances. Unskilled workers tended to move shorter distances (84 percent of all moves were less than 500 miles) but required more extensive supportive services.

The relocation projects encountered a number of difficulties which were resolved through experience. One was that potential relocatees sometimes accepted moving allowances and then failed to move. This problem was solved by parceling out reimbursements as or after expenses were incurred and by paying lump sum living allowances in part before and in part after the move was completed. A second was that the portion of the relocation allowances extended in loans was, in many cases, not repaid. Over half of the loans became delinquent, and when collection efforts were attempted, administrative costs ran about 64 cents on the dollar. Neither the employment service nor the private sponsors had experience or inclination as collection agencies, and they probably were reluctant to press those who had returned home or were struggling with high living costs in their new locations. After 1965, the use of loans was reduced and finally eliminated except for more highly skilled workers who could command salaries in excess of $7,500 per year.

Where large numbers of workers were involved, employers sent recruiters to the source of supply; they were unwilling to do so when the numbers were few and the area isolated, in part because of the expense of conducting the required personal interviews and physical examinations. Thus, in addition, the relocation allowances originally contemplated, it was necessary in many cases to pay travel expenses for interviews. The Mississippi STAR project found that for trips that could be concluded in one day, it was preferable for project personnel to fill an automobile with applicants and to transport them to potential employers for job interviews.

The California State Employment Service experimented with a bloc grant type of financial assistance. Rather than providing lump sum payments and moving expenses (either mileage costs or household transportation costs), a schedule of allowances based on the number of miles moved, size of family, and method of moving was developed. The program encouraged families to move their own effects with a rental truck or trailer. However, if they preferred to go first class with a moving van, they were responsible for any costs incurred above those provided by the scheduled grants. Using this schedule, average relocation costs fell from $657 to $457 per move.

Project sponsors met considerable opposition from local interests in supply areas. In rural areas, growers were often hostile to relocation of their potential labor supply, whether underemployed or unemployed during an off-season. In industrial areas, some companies refused to supply project sponsors with the names of laid-off workers. Resistance was particularly strong to attempts to relocate younger workers and those with skills, experience, or education. Other opposition came from politicians, civil rights organizations, and CAAs. The potential of MDTA to facilitate relocation was reduced in some cases by general opposition to training projects and local discrimination against minorities. Employment service sponsors proved most vulnerable to the local opposition because of their local and governmental connections.

An attempt has been made to minimize publicity concerning relocation activities because publicity sometimes created difficulties in project operations. As long as the projects have been experimental in nature, negative public reaction toward labor mobility has generally been fairly easy to mollify. It is likely that if larger operational programs are undertaken, a difficult public relations problem will be encountered.

As a part of the experimental design, relocation projects were funded through universities and other private, nonprofit contractors and through state employment services; a research-oriented group in the federal employment service coordinated state employment service activities and initiated projects. Though the largest number of individual projects funded were sponsored by the employment service, they tended to be smaller in size than the others and accounted for less than one-half of the money.

There appeared to be no clear superiority in individual project research or staff expertise between contractors and the employment services which proved themselves capable of rounding up large numbers of relocatees, testing and screening them, and referring them to other employment service offices in the receiving cities. However, the regular interarea placement procedures proved too slow and cumbersome, necessitating direct telephone and personal contact between employment service offices in supply and demand areas. The Iowa project utilized a successful television format; employers were brought from the demand area to make live broadcasts to the 12-county supply area and to conduct interviews with interested persons. The private institutions were involved in the more difficult and unusual situations, but they tended to be specialists in dealing with particular groups in narrowly restricted geographical areas.

Some employment service projects assigned personnel full time to relocation while others required regular interviewers to assume relocation duties on a part-time basis. Several project reports recommended a separate corps of relocation counselors, arguing that considerably greater client support and service were needed than were ordinarily supplied to employment service applicants. It would seem that if relocation assistance is to move from the special project level to become one among a variety of tools available within the employment service, regular counselors must have access to the full array of services. For these same reasons, it would seem that the employment service—given the flexibility to contract out where special groups or problems are involved—is the appropriate vehicle for a long-range program.

Evaluation and Policy Implications

Between 1965 and 1968, the relocation projects, after screening 40,000 eligible workers, assisted some 14,000 in actual moves. Ninety percent were men; 60 percent had dependents; one-half were between 25 and 44 years of age, and one-third under 25. One-fourth had no more than elementary education, but 50 percent had graduated from high school. Most had experienced extended unemployment or were farm workers earning less than $1,200 per year. Four out of five were white. Sixty percent of the moves were less than 300 miles; only 20 percent, mostly of skilled defense workers, were more than 500 miles. Nearly 60 percent of the moves were to cities under 250,000 population; only 10 percent were to major metropolitan areas.

Success for a relocation project requires that the relocated persons both remain in the new location and find a better life there. Available data leave the first outcome in doubt but are reassuring about the second. The Labor Department's follow-up system reported only 20 percent having returned home two months after the move. Twenty percent of those remaining changed jobs during the first two months. However, an independent examination of the 60-day follow-up data found about one-third to have returned to the point of origin, with one-third to one-fifth remaining on their original jobs.[9] The success of relocation clearly depends on economic conditions in the receiving areas. During the 1970–1971 period, for example, many of those who had been "successfully" placed lost their jobs.

All available sources appear to agree that the results were favorable for those who did remain in the demand area to which they were located.[10] They enjoyed more employment stability and higher earnings than control groups who remained behind. The costs for relocating those who remained in the demand area were soon recouped, but whether the gains for the successful were sufficient to offset the costs of moving the unsuccessful is doubtful. Education appeared to make little difference in success. Technical and skilled workers had a higher propensity to relocate than others and were most likely to stay with their new jobs. Unskilled workers found it difficult to obtain jobs and to take advantage of the program. When relocation was combined with basic education and skill training, willingness to move was higher and the return rate lower. MDTA graduates and those with larger numbers of dependents were more willing to move than others. Between 15 and 18 percent of all relocatees had participated in MDTA courses, with the number tending to increase as later efforts sought to combine basic education, skill training, and relocation.

Obstacles to relocation included factors in the depressed area (e.g., changed economic conditions) and factors in the demand area (e.g., depressed housing markets). Eligibility for unemployment insurance or public assistance discouraged relocation. So did the availability of special welfare programs not likely to be available as insurance in the demand area. The slightest improvement or promise of improvement in the local employment outlook, even though only temporary or seasonal, was enough to change the minds of potential relocatees. Obstacles to moving to a particular demand area were often impersonal ones affecting not the decisions of the potential relocatees but those of the sponsors. In some cases, minority workers were not moved for fear they would not be accepted in the demand area. Housing, particularly for minorities and large families, was a serious obstacle. High costs of living and lack of health and other social services in the demand area were others. A pervasive problem for those without skills was the lack of job opportunities for which they were.qualified.

The rate of return was primarily determined by such noneconomic factors as kinfolk ties, climate, school system, and general living problems. Layoffs, job losses, and declining employment opportunities in the demand areas often prompted a return to the home area. In general, the few high-skill workers tended to maintain their wage rates; those with industrial experience usually received higher pay than had been their supply area experience. Unskilled rural workers tended to receive the federal minimum wage. Sixty percent of the new jobs were in industrial production compared with only 30 percent of previous jobs held. Even the relocated technical and skilled defense workers tended to be placed in other vulnerable defense-related employment. All were under the threat of low seniority, and most were subject to high turnover.

The residents of the coal mining areas, especially West Virginia and Kentucky, were the most reluctant to move and also the most likely to return after moving. However, these were areas of long-term depression from which the more mobile had already moved. Over one-half of the relo-catees had been born in the community from which they were moving, sug-gesting that they were not highly mobile. Nevertheless, many of those who relocated had either moved to other areas before and returned or had worked away from home, leaving their families behind. In part, this was the result of the selection process. Only those sufficiently experienced for a firm job offer to be obtainable were eligible, and only the more mobile were willing to move. At the same time, there appeared to be no indication that significant numbers would have moved at that time without financial assis-tance. The defense workers would probably have obtained other, though lower skilled, jobs and remained where they were.

It is likely that the projects' major contribution was to affect the tim-ing and destination of the moves. In unaided moves, kinship and ethnic patterns are apparently more important as determining factors than is eco-nomic opportunity. Migrants tend to move to where others similar to them have already moved. The result is often increased concentration of low-skill workers where an oversupply already exists. The mobility projects, by requiring a firm job offer, increased the economic rationality of the moves. Many of the demand areas showed remarkable ability to absorb low skilled, though not "bottom of the barrel," workers.

Comparatively few eligible workers wanted to move, and those for whom the need for relocation was objectively the greatest were the most reluctant. Nevertheless the percentage of eligible unemployed persons who moved as a result of 1967 relocation projects is significant. Applied to all of those unemployed 15 weeks or more in the labor force, it indicates that 150,000 workers would have been relocated along with their families. Whether that many would have been found with both the skills to merit firm job offers and the willingness to move is unknown.

Apparently, the financial assistance did encourage mobility and was probably even more important in the retention rate. The lump sum living allowance bridged the difficult time until receipt of the first paycheck. The more desirable pattern of workers taking their families along could replace the familiar and more often unsuccessful pattern of working away from home, hoping to accumulate enough money to move families later. Where it was necessary to leave the family behind while family heads worked in the new area on a trial basis the dual-household subsistence payments and other financial assistance increased the possibility of successful relocation. As important as the financial assistance was, however, the availability of employment and guidance in surmounting the intricacies of moving and resettling were more crucial. A strong case was made for combining basic education, skill training, and relocation.

The experiences of mobility projects appear to justify modestly positive conclusions. Nothing definitive can be said about benefit-cost ratios. The successful programs had relatively low costs, but evaluation of the overall results requires more information on the proportions of retentions and returnees than is available. Because the projects, in effect, had quotas to fill, some who were actually reluctant and return-prone may have been encouraged to move. Such would not have been the case had relocation assistance been generally available for those who sought it. Some of those assisted might have moved on their own in the absence of the program, but the limited resources available to all but the more skilled groups make it doubtful that many could have supported their own relocation. The lack of financial reserves to pay living expenses until the first paycheck arrived was probably a more serious obstacle than the actual expenses of moving. Most of the skilled workers would probably have found other jobs but at lower skills and pay. However, their higher than average postrelocation wage rates, their low return rates, and the low administrative costs for these workers in all likelihood would give these projects the most favorable financial results. Judging from past experience, others who moved would have done so in a less rational pattern and with lower success rates.

Project results support the validity of the Labor Department's conclusion that a permanent and larger-scale mobility program is now justified. Such a program would provide no major solution to unemployment, but it would be important for those who chose to take advantage of it. The preliminary MDTA experience indicates that relocation assistance, financial and nonfinancial, is a useful and needed tool in the total kit of manpower policy measures. The disadvantaged as well as the advantaged should have some freedom to select the geographic areas in which they live and work. Their geographical mobility is currently high but often irrational; it could be made less random through a publicly supported program. Currently, the Labor Department is not pushing for renewal and refunding of special project authority. Rather, the hope is for inclusion of relocation assistance as one of the functional components of proposed comprehensive manpower legislation. With that approach, it is difficult to see how results could be other than positive.

CONCLUSION

We have explained the strong presumptive relationship between education and manpower programs and economic development. We say "presumptive" because many aspects of the causal relationships between these activities and economic development remain to be established. For example, no clear relationship has been discovered between expenditures on education, economic productivity, and incomes. Lack of precision in establishing these relationships is attributable both to the complexity of our problem and to the fact that education has noneconomic as well as economic objectives, and its effects are difficult to measure.

Nonetheless, considerable if not conclusive support exists for several conclusions. Fundamental is the realization that the development (recruiting, commitment, advancement, and maintenance) of industrial work forces is a prerequisite to economic development.

Second, the particular HRD strategy depends to some extent on the stage of economic development; for example, the emphasis on science and technology varies directly with the level of economic activity. However, at advanced stages, noneconomic HRD objectives become relatively more important because economic problems are less acute and people are concerned with the quality of life rather than with the struggle for survival. During this stage, the consumption aspects of education assume greater importance. Education in the arts and humanities again becomes important, as it was during the preindustrial period—with the difference that it is now available to the masses, not only the elite.

Before this stage is reached, however, there are likely to be urgent demands for equalizing the incomes of different groups and regions that have lagged during the industrial process. Minority groups are apt to demand that discrimination be ended and economic opportunities be enlarged, and people in low-income areas are apt to demand programs to reduce the gap between their incomes and those of more affluent regions. HRD programs can play important roles in all of these objectives. Measures will be demanded to provide jobs in lagging geographic and industrial areas and reduce the pressures on large metropolitan areas. This will require programs to create public or private employment opportunities in underdeveloped areas. Moreover, it will be necessary to prepare people for expanding job opportunities and redirect the flows of people to growth centers. Proper mixes of private and public programs also will be needed to facilitate the retraining and upgrading of people who already are in the labor force but whose skills have been made obsolete or those who want to acquire the necessary skills and education to upgrade themselves.

NOTES

1. Clark Kerr, John T. Dunlop, Frederick H. Harbison, and Charles A. Myers, *Industrialism and Industrial Man* (Cambridge, Mass.: Harvard University Press, 1960), p. 35.

2. Frederick Harbison and Charles A. Myers, *Education, Manpower, and Economic Growth* (New York: McGraw-Hill, 1964).

3. Max Lerner, "Humanistic Goals," in Paul R. Hannah, ed., *Education: An Instrument of National Goals* (New York: McGraw-Hill, 1962), p. 103.

4. Kerr, Dunlop, Harbison, and Myers, *op. cit.,* p. 167.

5. Walter Galenson, *Labor and Economic Development* (New York: John Wiley, 1959), p. 3.

6. Harbison and Myers, *op. cit.*, pp. 31–32.

7. Niles Hansen, "Growth Centers, Human Resources, and Rural Development," a paper written for the Rural Labor Market Strategies Project, the University of Texas (1971).

8. *Ibid.*

9. E. F. Shelley & Company, Inc., *Labor Mobility Study,* Progress Report Number 2 (New York: The Company, June 20, 1969).

10. Charles K. Fairchild, "Subsidized Relocation of the Rural Unemployed: Benefits and Costs," presented to the Southern Economic Association (November 14, 1969); Audrey Freedman, "Labor Mobility Projects for the Unemployed," *Monthly Labor Review* (June 1968).

Chapter 28
Comparative
Manpower
Policies

Explicit policies for the development and use of manpower resources have been a worldwide phenomenon since World War II. Useful perspective on U.S. manpower policies can be gleaned by comparing them with the approaches of other nations to related problems. Whether superior practices applicable to the U.S. can be found is another question. The democratic industrialized countries of western Europe and Canada have the most similar environments, yet provide sharp contrasts in policy and program. At the beginning of the 1960s, designers of the emerging U.S. manpower policies made pilgrimages to Europe in search of inspiration. There is now probably more to learn about manpower programs through a reverse flow, but the United States has much to learn about employment policy. The developing nations of the "third world" represent the greatest economic distance from the world's wealthiest nation; their manpower policies and practices have relevance to the U.S. only for our most depressed and under-developed areas. In between the western industrial nations and the primitive economies are a number of nations, with manpower policies that illustrate how various lands have made the transition from ancient to modern. The lessons to be drawn from such comparison are two: (a) that manpower policies and programs are a characteristic of modern nations and those which would become modern and (b) that those policies reflect the particular countries' economic environments and social value systems, with limited possibilities for effective transfer to contrasting settings.

MANPOWER IN THE WESTERN INDUSTRIAL DEMOCRACIES: A SOCIAL WELFARE ISSUE

Western Europe and Canada share with the United States certain social and political commitments to the supremacy of individual interests over those of the state. They differ in the demographic structure of the labor force, the degree of devotion to private decision-making, and the relative political balance between those most harmed by inflation and those more threatened by unemployment.

The Manpower Commitment in Historic Perspective

Prior to World War II, no country in western Europe or North America was specifically committed to the goal of full employment. Whatever labor market malfunctioning existed had been thought to be beyond control of man. Until the worldwide depression of the 1930s, public authorities did not seriously contemplate intervention, except through policies related to the protection of the worker on the job. The depression forced the issue into public consciousness and demonstrated that those at the mercy of the business cycle had adequate political clout to demand measures to alleviate the impact of unemployment.

Emerging from the war, a number of countries adopted legislation committing their governments to the pursuit of full employment. The laws adopted by Britain and Sweden were somewhat similar to the U.S. Employment Act of 1946, while other countries, notably France, the Netherlands, and Italy, adopted national planning policies along with the commitment to the goal of full employment. The recent experience of the Great Depression had provided the impetus, Keynesian thought had suggested the means, and the war had demonstrated the efficacy of public spending.

Using unemployment rates as evidence, one might conclude that most European governments kept those promises, while the United States did not. The average unemployment rate between 1965 and 1969 in this country, 3.8 percent, was about the same as in Italy, but it was substantially higher than in other western European nations. The rate in Great Britain was 3.2 percent; in France, 2.6 percent; in Sweden, 1.8 percent; and in West Germany, only 0.7 percent.

Illustrative is the meaning attached to the term "full employment," which has generally been interpreted by the last four U.S. Administrations as an unemployment rate of 4 percent, but was achieved only briefly by one of them. European countries, however, have generally endorsed the Swedish view that no percent of unemployment is acceptable. It has been a cornerstone of Swedish manpower policy that the provision of employment is always superior to unproductive financial maintenance of the unemployed. Political, social, and humanitarian considerations make it urgent to provide employment even for manpower of very low productivity.

The same factors that have encouraged labor governments have also required that they give highest priority to employment and manpower. European economies have faced greater, not lesser inflationary pressures than the United States over the years since World War II, but a different resolution of the tradeoff was required. Because political realities dictated policies generating labor shortages consequent to high economic growth rates, manpower policies became equilibrators of inflation rather than weapons against unemployment. Pressures on the price level have forced some relaxation of the European drive for rapid growth in recent years, but the philosophy remains unchanged. Continued tight labor markets have identified the margin of handicapped persons not employed even during stringent labor shortages. Added to the general policy of manpower programs to ease inflationary pressures through improved allocation of labor has been a specific attack on the employment obstacles faced by individuals.

Before giving excessive significant credit to European manpower policies, however, it is necessary to note significant differences in the economic and social environments, which would make it difficult for the United States to follow European patterns.

Demographic Factors and the Manpower Environment

The racial and ethnic heterogeneity of the American work force has no obvious counterpart in Europe. Repatriates from dispossessed colonies have encountered difficulties in gaining integration into the mainstream of social and economic life. The Algerians returning to France, the Indonesians to the Netherlands, and black immigrants from the West Indies and Africa to Great Britain are examples. The temporary importation of southeastern Europeans into labor-short central and northern Europe has produced social stresses. More persistent minorities are exemplified by the 300,000 nomads in West Germany and the much smaller number of gypsies in Sweden.

But none of these compare with the ethnic and racial conflicts of the United States, the long-standing and institutionalized racial separation, and the sharp differences in employment preparation. The Canadian labor market resembles the American in that the unsuccessful melting of the English-speaking and the French-speaking groups has prevented the emergence of a demographically homogeneous labor force. However, the consequence is a sharp division between one province and others rather than persistent resistance to widespread ethnic and racial pressures.

The populations and labor forces of western European countries are less comparable in size to the entire United States than to regions or individual states. For instance, the U.S. civilian labor force is more than three times as large as that of Great Britain or West Germany; four times as large as that of France or Italy; and twenty times as large as that of Sweden. Mobility is also higher in the United States, although differences are declining with the accelerating economic integration of Europe.

Of major significance is the larger World War II population losses and the proportionately smaller number of young people entering the labor force in European countries during the postwar period. In addition to higher losses among combatants, European nations, friend and foe, suffered widespread civilian casualties which the United States was spared. European birth rates were even lower than those of the United States during the depression and war years, while the postwar baby boom was shorter on the eastern side of the Atlantic. Rather than having to cope with the absorption of huge cohorts of new and inexperienced labor-force entrants, which proved to be the major manpower challenge to the United States during the 1960s, European nations actually suffered a shortage of young entrants. In fact, the major difference between the manpower and economic policies of the Western industrial nations has been the concern over labor shortages in Europe and potential surpluses in the United States, with Canada falling closer to its geographical neighbor than to its spiritual forebearers.

The U.S. technological base is considerably more complex, and the education and skill levels, the racial and ethnic mix, the geographical dispersion, and a variety of other factors make it much more difficult for the United States to adopt a set of manpower policies that are applicable for individuals who need employment assistance. The nature of government jurisdictions in the United States is also more complex. The federal-state-local relationships pose a major problem to the implementation of U.S. manpower policy that is not found in most European countries. Some of the more successful countries such as Sweden are able to maintain a strong central influence over their manpower activities, yet at the same time are blessed with very competent local government jurisdictions that are willing to assume the responsibility for operating activities and defer to the centralized government for policy direction and funding.

The United States is also more advanced into what promises to be a worldwide experience over time—the movement of jobs to the suburbs and concentrations of lower-skilled and hard-to-employ workers without adequate transportation to commute to the jobs for which their limited skills qualify them.

The Transition from School to Work

The familiar U.S. pattern in which teenage unemployment persists at triple the national average has been absent in western Europe. There, the hard to employ are primarily the physically, mentally, or socially handicapped and displaced older workers. This difference is attributable in large part to the persistence of high birth rates in the United States from 1946 through the late 1950s. The slower rates of economic growth generally experienced in the United States through the 1950s and the first half of the 1960s made it doubly difficult to absorb young job seekers. Most western European countries experienced shortages of manpower, making it relatively easy to find a job for those unwilling or unfit to continue their education or training. In addition, U.S. employment expansion came mainly in jobs requiring either advanced skill or adult reliability, reflecting the American lead in technological advancement and in the shift toward professional, technical, and public employment.

Differing attitudes toward the interface between the school and the workplace are also important. In the United States, 77 percent of a cohort of those entering the ninth grade will graduate from high school, 40 percent will enter college, and 20 percent will receive a bachelors degree. The standard European practice is to screen youth early and competitively to select the few who will be allowed to continue to higher education. Only a handful ever enter universities. The vast majority leave school at 14 to 16 years of age and enter upon a highly structured working career.

Americans have been constantly concerned that each year more than 500,000 teenagers drop out before high-school graduation; however, this proportion has been steadily decreasing. The difference in Europe is that over nine out of ten are already considered legitimately through with formal education by the time they reach the age where the small proportion of American youngsters are dropping out.

Employment Skills for Youth

Though apprenticeship has been the traditional method of skill development in most European countries, technological and social changes and the persistent labor shortages since World War II have encouraged formal policies to prepare youth for labor market entrance. The present English apprenticeship system emerged in response to severe criticisms of industrial training in the postwar period. Although the economy suffered from shortages of skilled manpower, the "bulge" of young people seeking to enter the labor force without higher education found inadequate training opportunities. Great Britain's desire to enter the Common Market led to a thorough study of apprenticeship and other industrial practices on the Continent. The Industrial Training Act of 1964 represents a mix of lessons from Continental Europe adapted to English conditions. This Act gives the Minister of Labor power to establish Industrial Training Boards (ITBs) which include representatives from employers and employees, the Ministry of Labor, and education. The ITBs are responsible for training in each industry and are financed by a training levy imposed on firms in that industry. The levy covers operating costs of the Board and any training conducted by or on behalf of the Board, as well as grants made by the Board to employers operating their own training programs. The functions of the Board comprise apprenticeship as well as adult retraining and upgrading of skills. The primary function of the ITB is to recommend appropriate training methods and the time required to complete each stage of the training process successfully.

In the Netherlands, the educational system has a definite technical bias. Whereas secondary schools in England and Germany, for example, primarily provide general education, the Dutch Junior Technical Schools provide predominantly skill training—for example, general metal-working, wood-working, painting, or masonry. Apprentices are drawn from these schools. A joint employee-employer board is responsible for directing apprenticeship in each industry. Apprenticeship in West Germany is also industry-oriented in that the apprentice is required to gain expertise in skills that are generally applicable to all types of firms within the industry, rather than be limited to a narrow set of skills required in a particular firm.

France, like Germany, began to consider the problem of adequate apprenticeship programs during the interwar period. Shortly after World War I, a tax was imposed on all industry to cover the cost of vocational training and education. During the 1930s, *centres d'apprentissage* (now renamed *colleges d'enseignement technique*) were established. The move to institutionalize apprenticeship appears to have resulted from the traditional size-structure of French firms. Small handicraft businesses did not provide a sufficient training base and require training institutions which are preferred to on-the-job training.

In Italy, apprenticeship got off to a late start. The Apprenticeship Act of 1955 represents the first central skill training policy. The local employment office is responsible for carrying out directives from the Ministry of Labor, which cooperates with other ministries in developing apprenticeship guidelines. All who wish to become apprentices must register with the employment office, and all firms must draw their apprentices from this register.

Sweden was without recognized training schemes since the abolition of the guild system in the midnineteenth century. Not until 1944 was the first national apprenticeship agreement concluded. Central guidance is now provided by the National Board of Vocational Education, a joint body of representatives from the Labor Market Board, the Board of Education, and various sectors of industry and commerce. Apprenticeship in artisan trades is under direct supervision by the Royal Vocational Training Board's field representatives, if such firms accept state subsidy, but a great deal of training remains independent.

The Role of Adult Retraining

The United States ventured tentatively into a retraining program to combat unemployment. The European policy was quite different. Aggressive economic policies made jobs plentiful; it was labor that was scarce. Retraining of adult European workers has had a dual purpose: First, economic, to help meet persistent shortages of skilled labor, particularly in the engineering and construction industries where an important contribution could be made to national economic growth and to reduce inflationary pressures from the labor market. Second, social, to help in the resettlement of the disabled, ex-servicemen, and unemployed people from rural and labor surplus areas.

In recent years, training has expanded to a greater variety of shortage occupations, and eligibility standards have been relaxed. As labor markets became increasingly tight, the supply of unemployed workers well-suited for vocational training tended to dry up. In addition, western Europe has experienced a shrinking recruitment base among the younger age groups. Therefore, vocational training programs for adults have increasingly catered to special hard-to-employ groups such as older workers and the physically and mentally handicapped.

Low training allowances and the relative overabundance of well-paying jobs may have made retraining an unattractive alternative for many western Europeans who might have benefitted from a refresher course or skill upgrading. Thus, tight labor markets may have favored the expansion of retraining for the disabled, while postponing the retraining of other groups. Increased training allowances along with greater variety in course offerings, both in curricula and duration of training, are policy changes aimed at luring the employed as well as unemployed to acquire new skills or upgrade old ones.

Sheltered Employment

Given the strong commitment to work as the socially accepted source of income and Western Europe's relatively greater political and social awareness of economic distress, a variety of forms of sheltered employment exist for workers who are difficult to place due to seasonal, regional, or structural shifts in the demand for particular skills, as well as for those with physical, mental, or social handicaps. Among these are special public works, sheltered workshops, homework, and outdoor projects. Special public works are primarily construction projects, scheduled for completion at some later date but accelerated to provide employment. Sheltered workshops and homework cater to persons with specific handicaps. Outdoor projects are considered to have special rehabilitative value for persons with social handicaps such as alcoholism.

Despite the relatively widespread use of sheltered employment, it is generally conceded in Europe that such policies should be considered as a last resort in pursuing the goal of full employment. While sheltered employment is still considered a legitimate solution to the employment problems of handicapped persons, high-cost public works have faded.

Relocation Measures

Governmentally assisted relocation of workers has never been politically popular in the United States and has been restricted to experimental pilot projects. European countries have pursued relocation in a more vigorous fashion. No doubt, general manpower scarcities in Europe explain part of the difference in attitudes.

Bringing workers to jobs or bringing jobs to workers are normally considered to be alternatives, but recent European experience supports the necessity of their being treated as complements. Regional development policies are gaining dominant public support, with manpower relocation policies being tailored to the growth-point strategy in developing stagnant regions. Such coordination of policies is sought both to arrest cumulative decay in depressed industrial regions and to prevent adding to the problems of already congested areas.

Among the financial incentives tried by the various countries have been refund of travel expenses to explore the new job location; assistance with moving costs, family allowances, and refund of travel expenses for home visits if the worker maintains two households for a limited period; assistance in securing housing; and per diem to cover incidental expenses associated with the relocation. However, the constraining element in implementing geographical mobility in Europe is less the financial incentives required than the shortage of housing in areas with ample job opportunities. Sample studies have shown that about 35 percent of those who were assisted to relocate returned to their former place of residence within two years, often due to dissatisfaction with new living accommodations.

As European countries exhausted every conceivable source of domestic labor supply in the face of rapid economic growth, immigration of foreign workers was actively encouraged. In recent years, these workers have come from labor surplus regions, notably in southern Italy and the islands, Spain, Portugal, Greece, Turkey, North Africa, and Yugoslavia. Prior to interposition of the Berlin Wall, heavy immigration to West Germany, particularly from eastern states, also took place, but not by inducement from the receiving country. Ambivalence toward these policies has grown, with the advantages of foreign labor for low-level jobs difficult to fill domestically offset by clashes among workers of different ethnic backgrounds and by associated social problems.

Conclusion

Postwar manpower policies in all the Western industrialized democracies have had a common objective: the social welfare of wage-earning families. They have differed only in demographic structure, degree of commitment, and technique. The task in the United States was made more difficult by the influx of youth into the labor market after 1963 and by racial and ethnic heterogeneity (accompanied by personal and institutionalized prejudice), but aided by geographical, social, and occupational mobility. European policies have placed a higher priority upon low unemployment as opposed to price stability. Despite rhetoric about workfare rather than welfare, European nations, as a rule, go to much greater public exertion and expense to provide employment opportunities for those who, in the United States, are more likely to receive public assistance without work. Such policies were made possible in all the western industrial democracies by the rise to political power of a working class, with a weaker class consciousness accounting for the greater ambivalence among U.S. policies.

But Western Europeans, too, find their homogeneity and ideological commitment lessening. Examples of racial and ethnic pressures were given earlier in the chapter. Perhaps more important, rising educational attainment produces the same kind of competition between the more and less educated the United States has experienced. European employers are not unlike their U.S. counterparts in preferring more to less education. As long as they prefer one set of workers over another for any reason, the inflationary consequences of a full-employment policy are increased. Employers are motivated to compete for those workers already in demand in preference to sopping up the pool of unemployed. And European workers, too, as they gain incomes, move to the suburbs, become property owners, and become ambivalent between high employment and inflation. A Tory government in the United Kingdom and a slight pullback from full employment to reduce inflation in other western European nations may, in part, be a response.

MANPOWER POLICY IN THE SOVIET UNION: ALLOCATING A SCARCE RESOURCE

In contrast to the Western concentration on social welfare objectives in manpower policy, the Soviet Union's concern is efficient utilization of a scarce economic resource. Manpower planning in the USSR is an integral part of the national economic plan prepared each year by the State Planning Commission (Gosplan). On matters related to labor and wages, including the economy's annual "manpower balance," the State Committee on Labor and Wages functions as an advisory committee to Gosplan. The "manpower balance" is constructed in traditional accounting fashion, with "resources" on the one hand and "utilization" on the other, to plan the organized deployment of the labor force in fulfillment of general economic objectives.

The Soviet Union practices its own unique version of a full-employment economy. Nearly half of the entire population is mobilized into the labor force, compared with about 40 percent in the United States. Due to the high level of labor-force participation and the socialistic nature of Soviet economic life, manpower policies differ substantially from those of Western countries. In market-oriented economies, manpower policies tend to be corrective in nature—that is, government intervention follows the recognition of maladjustments. The higher degree of acceptance of directed planning in the USSR makes their manpower system preventive in nature. Thus, the principle difference appears to be the mere existence of Gosplan, which coordinates the plans of all sectors of the economy relative to national priorities. In Western countries, the final coordination of most economic activity still awaits the test of the market.

A major policy objective has been to limit the supply of manpower going to the "nonproductive" sphere of the economy (trade, education, public health). This is a direct reflection of the Soviet development policy stressing maximum growth of "productive" work (industry, agriculture, construction, transport). The bulk of workers allocated by the central planning authorities in recent years to the major claimants came from two channels: some 50 percent from the "schools of vocational training" and 44 percent from the "organized recruitment of labor."

The School-to-Work Transition

The combining of work and study has expanded rapidly since 1955 when the specter of impending labor scarcity was widely recognized. In the School Reform of 1958, it became official Soviet manpower policy for all young people to participate in "socially useful work" while pursuing further training.

Because the training of professionals and technicians is at the expense of the state, graduates from such schools are obliged to work no less than three years in an assigned place of employment. Their assignment is under the control of the particular ministry or state committee that has jurisdiction over the educational institution in which they completed their course of study. Graduates of secondary vocational schools are similarly placed in mandatory job assignments for periods of two and four years by the State Committee for Vocational-Technical Training.

Students who choose to enter the labor force directly from schools of general education are placed by the Commission for the Labor Participation of Youths. Two points of exit are generally available: at age 15 after completion of 8 years compulsory schooling, or at the age of 18 after 11 years of classroom study. "Dropouts" are offered a choice between a job in a local enterprise, an assignment to a vocational school, or an assignment to an apprenticeship program.

Labor Mobility Measures

A major problem in the USSR's economy is the locational mismatch of workers and jobs. A variety of untapped resources, metal ores, fuel, timber, and water power are found in the eastern regions of the country, while

84 percent of the population and the labor force inhabits the European half of the country. The infrastructure needed for rapid development of the East is largely undeveloped, even while the European regions approach a high stage of development. Therefore, a principal feature of the Soviet manpower system is the transfer of large numbers of wage workers among specific job assignments, industrial sectors, regions of the country, or simply between rural and urban areas.

The placement system for voluntary job shifters in the USSR also differs from those of Western countries. Employment exchanges were abolished in the USSR in 1930 on the ideological pretext that, with socialism's abolishment of unemployment, there was no longer practical need for them. Nevertheless, a formal mechanism for the recruitment and transfer of wage-workers for high-priority economic activity has been in existence in the Soviet Union since 1931. However, the importance of organized recruitment has diminished, from about 3 million persons recruited annually in the 1930s to about 500,000 annually in recent years.

Also involved in the recruitment of voluntary job shifters has been the Union of Communist Youth (Komsomol). Beginning in 1954, Komsomol has been called upon by the party to "mobilize," on a regular basis, large numbers of "volunteers" to migrate to the labor-deficient eastern provinces. About 200,000 persons are permanently transferred each year through this mechanism, while an equally large number of students migrate to Siberia for seasonal jobs. Komsomol performs these recruiting tasks for the party without pay and in addition to the regular duties of members. More than 100,000 persons a year have voluntarily transferred permanently to Siberia in response to a variety of pecuniary incentives. Despite this technically stimulated inmigration, an offsetting outmigration has brought the actual growth of the labor force in these regions to below the natural rate of increase. As long as freedom of residential choice is possible, the incentives are apparently inadequate to offset the continued backwardness and the unfavorable living conditions.

Women in the Labor Force

The Soviet government is officially committed to transferring women from "unproductive housework" into "social labor." Among measures to draw women into the labor force are equal pay for equal work, liberal maternity leaves, and encouragement to pursue higher training in accordance with intellectual capabilities. Female labor predominates in such areas of employment as education (69 percent) and public health (85 percent). Women account for about 75 percent of all medical doctors. They also play a dominant part in scientific research, communications, retail trade, public catering, and public administration. Still the largest field of employment for the 33 million women wage-earners is manufacturing, where over 34 percent of the country's female labor is employed. The labor-force participation rate of those 16–54 years of age is 76 percent, compared with 51 percent in the United States.

Conclusion

All of these efforts to raise labor-force participation rates and allocate manpower in accord with official priorities had been largely motivated by the population deficit resulting from World War II. It is estimated that as many as 25 million workers were directly lost to the Soviet Union during that war, as well as another 7 to 10 million who would have entered the labor force, subsequently, had normal birth rates prevailed between 1940 and 1947.

It is this fact more than any other that has shaped postwar Soviet manpower policies. To the Western observer aware of this stringent demographic deficit, the discretion in occupational and residential choice left to the individual worker in a system not reputed to be overly concerned with the philosophical niceties of free choice is surprising.

MANPOWER POLICIES IN JAPAN:
POPULATION VS. LABOR FORCE

Japan was forced into manpower policy by the success of its economic growth and population policies. Concerned with the prospects for a population explosion in its limited land area, the nation undertook in the postwar period the most aggressive population-control program of any country. When this policy was accompanied by high and accelerating rates of economic growth, the ample supply of labor characteristic of the first postwar decade was absorbed by the late 1950s. As the overall rate of unemployment approached 1 percent, the imbalances between labor demand and supply by types of jobs, regions, industries, and age groups became acute. Further, birth rates were still falling and school years were increasing, which indicated a decreasing supply of new entrants for the years ahead.

These developments were complicated by the prevailing system of lifetime employment in Japan. Once hired, a worker rarely left his employer until retirement; each had a mutual responsibility to the other. Furthermore, the impact of technological change had begun to affect the occupational structure and the nature of demand for labor adjusted accordingly. A new, positive role for the government in manpower matters had two main objectives: first, to secure skilled manpower required for the growth of a dynamic economy; second, to prepare workers to engage in productive jobs corresponding to their aptitudes and abilities and utilize these optimally.

The Economic Setting for Manpower Policies

Postwar labor markets in Japan have been impacted by exceptionally high rates of economic growth. The economy grew only moderately during the first postwar decade, 1945–1955, as Japan returned to prewar levels of economic activity and released resources for civilian production needs. In the ten-year period 1955–1965 the rate of economic growth averaged 9.8 percent per annum in real terms. For 1961–1969, the growth rate was 13.7 percent.

Despite this rapid growth, employment in primary industries dropped from 41.0 percent of total employment in 1955 to only 24.6 percent in 1965. Heavy gains in employment were registered both in secondary and tertiary industries during that period. By 1960, the imbalances between labor demand and supply by types of jobs, regions, industries, and age groups was acute. Measures were needed to allocate labor efficiently, increase labor-force participation and productivity, and adjust to the impact of rapid change.

To create a balance between the benefits of economic concentration in big cities and diffusion of employment opportunities and social amenities throughout the country, the Japanese government undertook in 1950 a National Comprehensive Development Plan. Under it, several measures are taken to promote labor mobility and encourage technological change. Allowances are paid for retraining and job adaptability training. Information on job vacancies and applications is furnished by a Labor Market Center, and job placements are carried out over wide areas. To ensure that no hindrance should occur in the interregional movements of labor, a job reconversion benefit system is provided and each year about 10,000 houses are built and let for use by the unemployed to facilitate relocation.

Despite the rapid growth in productivity, as well as in GNP, output per employee in Japan on the average, is still substantially below that of West Germany, the United Kingdom, or France and far below that of the United States. Thus there is still a considerable margin for improvement in productivity through labor-saving technology and better utilization of labor generally. Given the demographic limitations on labor-force growth, active encouragement of technological change and increased productivity is necessary to sustain economic growth. The promotion of labor-saving devices meets little opposition because redundancy is not a serious problem, given intraenterprise transfer when jobs are eliminated. The rapid increase in employment due to high economic growth rates since 1953 has generally created a situation of more jobs than job seekers. For persons actually displaced because of changes in technology, job reconversion benefits, vocational training, and relocation housing, along with employment promotion efforts, facilitate adjustment.

Employment Measures for Special Groups

The U.S. differential between youth and adult unemployment rates does not exist in Japan. Generally, job openings for young persons far exceed job applications. In March 1967, there were over three times as many job orders for secondary-school graduates as there were graduates seeking employment. In 1967, 93 percent and 82 percent, respectively, of university and junior-college graduates had contracted for employment by March.

Women constitute about 30 percent of the Japanese labor force. Significant changes have occurred in the pattern of employment for women during the past 15 years. From being predominantly family workers in agriculture, most women are now engaged as paid workers in various industries. Married women increasingly seek employment, something they rarely did in the past. Several factors account for these changes: Modernization of the economy released manpower in rural areas and expanded job opportunities in urban industrial centers; the trend toward fewer children as well as rationalization of household work tended to free women from homebound duties; persistent shortages of labor made women an attractive alternative for job assignments previously reserved for men only. Policies to encourage female participation in the labor force include construction of nursing schools and increased training opportunities.

A survey in 1967 indicated that middle-aged workers and persons over 50 experience difficulties in Japanese job markets. Despite labor shortages, the ratio of job applicants to job openings was 1.3 for the 35 and over group as a whole, and 4.7 for those over 50.

A number of factors hinder persons in obtaining new jobs at an age that would not seem unduly advanced in the United States. The retirement age is 55 in most large enterprises, although public old-age pensions do not become effective until age 60. The system of life-time employment, even though it is eroding rapidly in the tight markets, is another deterrant to hiring anyone with relatively few productive years left. Among offsetting factors, the advent of rapid technological change in Japan in recent years has increased job mobility and tended to undermine the dominance of life-time employment. Length of service is becoming less of a prerequisite for performance. But due to the generally accepted opinion in Japan that as people become older they become increasingly unable to adjust to new work environments or skill requirements, the opening up of the labor market has mostly benefited the young who wish to change employment.

The government has initiated a variety of measures to alleviate the placement difficulties of middle-aged and older workers. Vocational guidance, job placement, vocational training and job adaptability training, and housing exist for middle-aged and older unemployed, as well as payment of various allowances. Removal funds, payments for interarea job-seeking activities, and job reconversion benefits are also paid to the employer. Talent banks designed mainly to take care of older persons and housewives and special facilities to handle employment of part-time workers were established in 1966 and 1967. Laws also provide for imposition of employment quotas for occupations suitable for middle-aged and older persons.

Special measures are provided for seasonal and migratory workers who find their employment opportunities concentrated in either summer or winter. Japanese manpower policy seeks to promote modernization of agriculture to insure selfsupporting farms. It also seeks to encourage regional development through industries suited to conditions in farming areas. The policy for summer workers seeks regular year-round employment through vocational training and the job reconversion benefit system. Employers who hire a large number of these workers are offered financial assistance to install the facilities and equipment necessary for year-round employment. Vocational counseling and measures designed to aid the seasonal worker to adjust to a steady environment have been expanded. In addition, construction companies located in areas with specified numbers of seasonal unemployment insurance beneficiaries are provided with a subsidy during the snow and cold season, if they employ such beneficiaries on a year-round basis.

The handicapped were recognized as a manpower resource when a 1965 survey found a little over 1 million disabled persons above 18 years of age, of whom only 40 percent were employed. Traditional methods for rehabilitation of the handicapped approached the task from a philanthropic standpoint. But because of the cost of providing special machines and equipment and the need for special care, there was little progress. Current efforts seek to develop jobs that are better suited for those with particular handicaps, and to adapt the handicapped person to such jobs. Less emphasis is being put in eliminating the actual handicaps. State and local public bodies, as well as private enterprises, are obligated by law to employ physically handicapped persons under a quota system. Entrepreneurs willing to employ the physically handicapped may obtain long-term low-interest loans for construction of facilities or for adapting the work assignment to the handicapped. Physically handicapped persons are encouraged to start their own business through a system of liability guarantees. For those wanting to purchase automobiles for commuting purposes, another system has been established to provide financial assistance.

Conclusion

Japan provides an example of manpower policies almost totally dedicated to the maximum utilization of the labor force. Given the context of rapid economic growth, reduced birth rates, and traditionally paternalistic employment system, the policy is not an inhumane one. There is some reason to think that the life-time employment system was better observed on behalf of key employees than those with less critical skills. Westernization of most aspects of Japanese life has added freedom of occupational choice. Yet, an intense demand for labor and a tradition of training within industry seem to provide worker security.

MANPOWER IN DEVELOPING NATIONS

In contrast to the economically advanced countries of the United States and western Europe, with their concentrations on the social welfare of workers, developing nations are typically preoccupied with coordinating aggregate flows of manpower to create the necessary preconditions for an economic "take off." Developing nations characteristically are faced with two kinds of manpower problems—shortages of persons with critical skills and surpluses of labor seeking entry into the modern sector. In this way, the industrialization process in developing countries differs more in degree than in kind from the industrialization of the depressed areas of modern countries (discussed in Chapter 26). This section identifies the general manpower problems of developing nations and illustrates them with the experiences and policies of specific nations.

The Dual Economy

Given a scarce supply of workers who are adequately prepared for modern, urbanized life, along with other constraints such as the availability of investment capital, a typical developing nation will choose an unbalanced approach toward sustained economic growth and development. Emphasis is given to industries and regions that have a higher probability of successful transformation. The resulting dual economy, one modern sector and one traditional, can be both a tool and a hurdle for the manpower specialist: a tool because the modern sector generates jobs and establishes the base for meeting the education and training needs of advanced production techniques; a hurdle because the modern sector tends to attract workers away from agriculture with no concern for their employability. Often the infrastructure of the modern sector is lagging relative to the main industrial pursuits, making the transition to modern life difficult for farmers and already "established" urbanites alike.

Typically, there are large numbers of workers whose marginal productivity is near zero in the traditional farming sector of developing nations. It should be possible to shift manpower to the modern sectors at close to zero social cost. However, this assumes that the remaining workers will work enough harder or longer to maintain the same production, yet will not increase their consumption patterns, thus leaving a surplus to be transferred to the modern sector to feed those workers who have been extracted from agricultural pursuits. However, this rarely happens unless consumption is forcefully restrained.

At the other end of the manpower transfer, the social costs are high because the migrants lack the vocational preparation needed by the more sophisticated production methods. It is common in developing nations to find that a very high proportion of the workers in the traditional farming sector are completely illiterate. These circumstances not only make the shift of workers to the modern sector more costly and time consuming; they also make introduction of new techniques in agriculture a mere theoretical possibility in the short run. Over time, however, given specific efforts to improve the education system, including remedial education and informal methods of training, such structural shifts of occupations take place. Expanding the primary and secondary-school enrollments of underdeveloped countries has been a high priority both for those countries and the developed nations seeking to aid them.

A further characteristic of the traditional society is the typically unfavorable attitude toward change. Thus, the manpower specialist, along with other scientists seeking an appropriate path of development for a particular country, must have a perceptive understanding of the history, culture, and geographic and climatic conditions that affect the traditional society.

The "Brain Drain"

A critical factor in the relative scarcity of high-level manpower, especially in professional and technical fields, is the so-called "brain drain." A relatively high number of educated nationals emigrate to more advanced countries for a variety of reasons. Of those who remain in their own countries, traditional attitudes encourage them to choose classical education in preparation for public administration rather than the more practically oriented technical, engineering, and managerial skills. The result is often a frustrated oversupply of the academically educated, despite critical shortages of practically educated manpower.

As an offset to the "brain drain" outflow of manpower, it is generally expected that a return flow will eventually take place. In the long run, the "brain drain" may actually turn out to be an advantage for further development because many of the returnees will have gained valuable experience in their jobs abroad. Of further relevance might be a short-term inflow of foreign technicians and professionals—the "brain gain." In the initial stages of development, it is not uncommon to find these two inflows of manpower combined in excess of the "brain drain" outflow. Nevertheless, with skilled manpower in short supply, significant leakages cannot be overlooked, whether or not offsetting flows exist.

Case Examples—Manpower Policies
in Colombia [1]

Colombia provides a typical example of the dual economy in developing nations. The high productivity component of the Colombian economy probably accounts for 80 percent of total Gross Domestic Product, but employs only about one-third of the total labor force. The employment out-look for the next few decades is also typical. On the basis of current trends, the rate of unemployment in the nonagricultural labor force should be expected to rise from about 14 percent in 1963 to anywhere between 20 and 40 percent in 1980.

Population has been growing at about 3.3 percent annually while the rate of economic growth has been slightly under 5 percent. Assuming constant technology, with both population growth and economic growth concentrated in the high-productivity component of the economy, a 5 percent rate of economic growth should be sufficient to generate enough jobs to at least prevent the current level of unemployment from worsening. However, this easy assumption ignores the age pyramid of the population, which is typical in countries experiencing a population explosion. The result is that the labor-force growth rate significantly exceeds the population growth rate, requiring a higher rate of economic growth to offset the employment pressure. Also, developing countries typically launch and expand their economic modernization by importing advanced technologies from the developed countries. The result is higher productivity advance in the growth sectors, easing manpower shortages there, but increasing the rate at which the total economy must grow to absorb available labor.

The popular assumption in Colombia is that children need to complete at least five years of primary schooling to compete successfully for urban employment. Steps have been taken to improve formal education and raise the general educational attainment of the labor force. For instance, between 1951 and 1963, primary-school enrollment increased from 50 percent to 76 percent of the 7–12 age group. Enrollment in secondary education more than doubled from 6 percent to 14 percent of the 13–18 year old group over the same period, while university enrollment increased from 0.9 percent of the 19–24 age group to 1.7 percent. However, the expansion of the primary-school system was neglected in rural areas, with two-thirds of all rural primary schools offering only two years of instruction.

Legal reforms changed the organizational structure of Colombian secondary education in 1962, with potentially far-reaching effects on the quality and flexibility of manpower preparation. Formerly, the coexistence of five separate branches—academic, normal (elementary teacher education), commercial, industrial, and agricultural—required a primary-school graduate to make an early and narrow occupational choice. This choice is now theoretically postponed until completion of a common four-year secondary school cycle, though few are retained long enough to enjoy that discretion.

Increased enrollment in Colombian universities, from about 11,300 students in 1951 to almost 35,000 in 1965, has been associated with a shift of matriculation away from the traditionally predominant fields, law and medicine, toward engineering, social sciences, education, and agriculture. Engineering now leads all other professions in total enrollments. In light of the previous emphasis on training physicians, it is interesting to note that the training of nurses and other paramedical personnel is still largely neglected.

In addition to expansion and improvement of the formal education system, two large-scale nationwide training programs have been established to upgrade manpower in the high-productivity component of the non-agricultural labor force. Training centers distributed among the major economic regions specialize in training for commerce, industry, and agriculture, with specialized facilities for textile, construction, nursing, and other types of vocational training, depending upon regional need. These training centers are typically well equipped with modern machinery and housed in newly built facilities, located in or near large cities or major enterprises. Training includes remedial training for unskilled laborers, three-year apprenticeships for young workers, and relatively short, specialized courses for older workers, the latter accounting for the highest proportion of enrollment. However, no more than 150,000 persons were trained between 1959 and 1965.

The only other sizable training program for blue-collar workers is provided by the military establishment. About 3000 recruits annually receive basic literacy training, if necessary, and many are trained as mechanics and construction workers.

In addition, the National Federation of Coffee Growers and the Catholic Church operate programs to spread literacy and basic health and agricultural knowledge throughout the rural area. A small number of fellowships and loans are available for postgraduate study abroad, and a few thousand government employees have received part-time instruction in public administration.

However, this apparently diversified training effort, representing a high level of investment for such a poor country, touches only a small fraction of the population and labor force. The picture is typical: There is neither the skilled manpower for growth, the growth to employ the manpower that exists, nor the wealth to invest in training for growth.

Case Example—India's Manpower Strategy [2].

To a Western observer, the most astonishing characteristic of India's manpower environment is the size and rate of growth of the labor force. Currently, the labor force is estimated in excess of 200 million, having grown at an annual rate of about 2–2.5 percent during the postwar period. India's economy must "run fast simply to stand still" in absorbing available workers.

Next in importance is the great variety of local languages, which pose serious obstacles to the employment of human resources. Although the education system uses a three-language formula—a local tongue and Hindi in primary schools and English in secondary school—language barriers effectively restrict mobility of manpower. The problem is most severely felt in agricultural extension work. The task of convincing the farmers, who make up over two-thirds of India's labor force, of the usefulness of new techniques is practically impossible unless the agricultural specialist is fluent in the local language.

India's initial manpower strategy was characterized by a supply-oriented "numbers game." The emphasis on manpower supply was a direct consequence of accepting as a basic postulate the existence of an automatic linkage between human resource development and economic growth. India's political forces were swayed to this faulty assumption by uncritical imitation of developed Western nations. Major emphasis on the number of graduates with various diplomas and degrees, without due regard to the quality of skills acquired, resulted from a critical shortage of high-level manpower during the early postwar years. But, as the economy failed to respond to the supply of educated manpower, India reached a relative surplus stage early in the 1960s, a position strongly influenced by structural maladjustments. As a result, policy shifted to a manpower requirements emphasis.

In most developing nations, manpower policies are made in the absence of reliable studies; India's manpower research compares favorably with advanced countries. An effective organization for manpower planning and coordination had been established both at the cabinet level and in state governments.

The development of a national apprenticeship scheme was judged impractical until the late 1950s, due to the absence of industrial firms with the capacity for in-plant training. In 1963, however, training began under a compulsory Apprenticeship Act. By December 1966, 30,000 apprentices were receiving training and a target of 100,000 apprentices was set for 1971.

Both public and private employers have training schemes to introduce new employees to a particular work environment. In some cases, graduate engineers and other technical personnel have been sent abroad to receive training in the appropriate industry in a developed country. Their training is usually phased so that the trainees return as a new plant begins operations. For instance, steel firms in both the United States and the Soviet Union trained Indian engineers as part of the assistance rendered in constructing plants in India. In addition, parent firms of large establishments typically overtrain to supply personnel to subsidiary units.

A serious shortcoming of Indian training programs has been the lack of emphasis on managerial training at the firm level. Managerial training sessions and seminars have been organized, but attendance by company training officials appears to have provided little feedback to their respective firms. When asked to describe his job, one training officer of a large establishment stated that for the most part he attended training seminars.

Throughout the postwar period, India has been committed to full-employment policies in a "plug the dike" fashion. All of the five-year plans have included schemes to foster the growth of small-scale, labor-intensive, village industries. The employment growth potential of such schemes appears drastically inadequate due to the smallness of the base. In 1961, the manufacturing sector employed only 11 percent of India's labor force, with over half of these workers in household industry. Other defensive policies range from assuring labor that mechanization and automation will be discouraged if they threaten reductions of the working force, to opposing moves by public sector industry to retrench employees.

The central government sponsors two nationwide programs to assist the unemployed in finding work: the National Employment Service and the Rural Works Program. However, it appears that beyond the mere registration of jobseekers India's employment service offers little help to the unemployed. During 1965, the employment service had 4 million job applicants registered and made 570,000 placements. The backlog of registrations is growing steadily; unskilled workers remain on the job-seeking lists as long as eight or nine years.

The Rural Works Program (RWP) was instituted in 1961 to provide large-scale employment opportunities for the rural underemployed during the slack agricultural season. Due to administrative difficulties, however, the program got off to a slow start. Many projects did not get off the ground because the technical supervisory personnel required could not be mobilized in the localities where they were needed. Others floundered because the projects were located too far away from the main source of surplus manpower. Although the projects were specifically designed to improve the infrastructure of the community, several projects failed because they had not been properly "sold" to the villagers. The RWP set a target of providing 250 million man-days of employment, not excessive considering the estimate of 16 million underemployed workers, but less than 14 percent of the target was achieved during the first five years of operation.

The "brain drain" is another element of India's manpower setting. ASSIST, a private nonprofit organization created in 1965 to repatriate Indian nationals working abroad, had returned only 25 to Indian jobs by mid-1967. There is need for an induced "brain gain" to return to the country exceptionally talented expatriates with the skills for India's particular problems. However, little appears to be known about the professional qualities of Indian manpower residing abroad, and about the price at which top talent could be induced to return to India.

CONCLUDING REMARKS

In the early 1960s, it was customary to lament the failure of the United States to develop manpower policies and programs equivalent to those in western Europe. Indeed, many lessons were learned that were helpful in the design of U.S. programs. No direct transfer was possible; social, political, and economic systems differed too greatly in tradition and structure. Now the shoe appears to be on the other foot. The United States made rapid manpower progress during the 1960s. Rather than the pilgrimages once made by Americans to Europe and elsewhere seeking to import manpower ideas, increasingly the United States is the exporter of experience. For the developed nations, such transfers of knowledge are possible and profitable.

A tragedy of manpower, as well as economic policies, is the fact that no developing nation has been launched into the modern industrial world in two generations, despite unprecedented effort and foreign assistance. A destroyed Europe was rebuilt within a decade after World War II. Israel is well on its way to establishing a modern industrial nation in a primitive setting. But both of these successful experiences were based on the availability of well-educated manpower with industrial traditions. The Soviet Union was the last nation to move successfully over the boundary between primitive agrarianism and modern industrialism. Those nations that have passed through the agrarian age into the industrial economy and now are approaching the threshhold of whatever is to follow have found no way to export the path they trod.

NOTES

1. This section draws heavily upon Dieter Zschock, *Manpower in Colombia* (Princeton, N.J.: Princeton University Press, 1967).

2. The material in this section is drawn from George Tobias and Robert S. Gallner, *India's Manpower Strategy Revisited 1947–67* (Bombay, N.M Tripathi Private, 1968).

Epilogue

Chapter 29
Issues
for the
1970s

What will be the critical human resource issues in the foreseeable future? Crystal gazing is a hazardous pursuit. For example, few foresaw the increasing importance of female workers over the last three decades, the "population explosion" that followed World War II, and the more abrupt decline in birth rates that occurred during the 1960s. Nonetheless, social institutions and trends are to a large extent shaped by past events. This review provides at least a tentative basis for pinpointing some of the major issues and indicating future directions of human resource development in the U.S.

PREPARING FOR WORK

In all likelihood, the declining rate of population growth will be sustained. Preoccupation with ecological balance, improved birth control technology, and the erosion of mores that hindered effective family planning will continue to reduce birth rates, conceivably to the point of stabilizing the population. As a result, more resources will be available for the development of each child, and radical changes are likely in the way this smaller number of American children are reared and educated. Educational facilities have been hard pressed during this century to expand as rapidly as population and the demand for higher education. Consequently, few institutional arrangements have been provided for the care of preschoolers, and in most communities no organized provision is made for children until they reach the normal school-entry age of 6. Despite the continuing and almost exclusive reliance upon home and mother to take care of children prior to their entering school, the number of working mothers continues to grow; the increasing millions of families with working mothers are likely to demand that society provide daycare for their children. The experience of other countries that have grown to rely upon female labor has been to expand preschool child-care facilities, as the United States did during World War II. The government already provides some facilities, particularly for the poor under the antipoverty programs, and the more affluent can purchase nursery care for their children, but universal coverage is needed. Child-care arrangements will also have to include educational and training components. This would involve the expansion of governmentally supported education facilities to age 3 or possibly earlier. In all likelihood, child care will became one of the greatest growth industries in the years ahead.

At the other end of the school-age spectrum, the continued growth of higher education during the past century is likely to be arrested. Already, three of every four young Americans continue their schooling until their eighteenth birthday, and almost one of five continues for four or more years. The need, wisdom, and practicality of prolonging school attendance is being increasingly questioned; too frequently the added school years have little relation to preparation for work or for life. Education throughout one's work life will probably emerge rather than further prolongation of the exclusively preparatory period during one's childhood, youth, and early adulthood. Changing technology and skill needs are likely to induce an increasing number of persons to undergo specific training periodically throughout their lifetime.

While mature and committed workers may occasionally turn to the educational system to recharge their intellectual batteries or their manual skills, youths and young adults may combine experience beyond their school walls with educational pursuits. This may lead to a restructuring of both educational facilities and labor market institutions to provide flexibility for the student-worker to enter and leave school and work. As greater specialization is required and more time is spent during one's lifetime in school, greater attention to counseling and exposure to work options will be necessary to facilitate successive occupational choices during the work career. Too often, career decisions are now being made on the basis of scholastic aptitude alone. Combining work experience with school attendance may lead to better informed and sounder career choices.

WORK ATTITUDES

Less tangible than the changing institutional arrangements for job preparation, but potentially of greater significance, will be the continued transformation of attitudes toward work. Much has been made of the alleged loss of pride in craftsmanship and the deterioration of the quality of services. These developments presumably reflect not only widespread job dissatisfaction but also a general antipathy to work, foresaking the traditional work ethic. Among youth, in particular, there is claimed to be a widespread rejection of the work ethic as the incentive of material rewards are becoming less important. To a large extent, these may be only youthful manifestations, and exaggerated at that. It is likely that the addiction to creature comforts that "hooked" their elders is also going to take hold of the current young as the responsibilities of family life induce them to maximize their incomes.

Nonetheless, real changes are taking place in work attitudes, and they will have a pervasive influence in the future. Workers are becoming increasingly concerned with the qualitative aspects of work—not just with wages, hour, and benefits, but also with opportunities, responsibilities, and freedom on the job. As wages increase, income may become a less potent incentive and other motivating forces will be needed to insure discipline in the work place. If economic prosperity and growth are sustained, the work ethic is likely to weaken as a generation of workers that has experienced nothing but relative affluence and job security takes its place.

WORK AND WELFARE

Apart from whatever changes are occurring in the work ethic, the inevitable growth of public income-support efforts will continue to erode the distinction between work and welfare. As the welfare floor is raised to help those nominally unable to work because of old age, infirmity, child-care responsibilities, or lack of jobs, and as supplements are extended to those who work but earn less than a socially acceptable minimum income, increasing numbers may opt for welfare instead of workfare, to borrow from President Nixon's rhetoric.

The challenge is to develop adequate work incentive schemes to insure that those who can support themselves will do so. But work incentives are of no help to the millions of poor who are unable to find or hold a job. Thus, maintaining a low guaranteed income and expecting the poor to supplement their welfare by earnings is not realistic.

MANPOWER PROGRAMS

As the overlap between welfare and work increases, manpower programs will have an expanded role. Opportunities must be provided for all individuals who will work but are unable to earn an adequate income. Artificial credential barriers can be broken down through subsidies, employer education, and governmental fiat; upgrading can be assisted through supplemental education and training; the employability of participants can be improved by training, counseling, education, and related services. However, those who believe that manpower programs can substitute employment for

welfare are likely to be disappointed. Only a minority of all welfare recipients can become self-supporting; manpower programs may have to
maintain the more modest aim of helping some recipients to supplement
their welfare income.

Furthermore, neither the scope nor the effectiveness of manpower
programs should be exaggerated. They can hardly instill a preference for
work over welfare; nor can they singlehandedly overcome the cumulative
disadvantages that are usually the case of low earnings. Even when applied
appropriately, manpower programs are hardly foolproof. The relatively
brief experience with manpower programs during the 1960s must be viewed
as experimental; hence, the limited success of these tools heretofore does
not preclude reliance on them in the future. From the many trials and failures experienced during the past decade, lessons were learned, services were
improved, and new options were provided for disadvantaged persons, especially blacks, to improve their abilities and thus gain entry into the mainstream economy. In many cases, manpower programs offer a second chance
to those who failed in, or were failed by, the educational system and for
those whose skills have been eroded by technological change. As more
knowledge is gained about the needs of particular individuals and about the
effectiveness of particular services or combination of services in meeting
these needs, the manpower programs may become an alternative for those
who do not succeed in the regular school system. The experience gained
from the manpower programs may also help the regular school system to
avoid many mistakes.

The combination of work and welfare is likely to be an increasingly
important, but hardly the sole, focus of manpower programs in the 1970s.
Other crucial tasks include assistance in retraining workers and offering
upward occupational mobility.

EQUAL EMPLOYMENT OPPORTUNITY

Manpower programs are closely related to combating discrimination
in employment. On the one hand, manpower programs are frequently
needed to help train the victims of discrimination in order to help them
compete for available employment opportunities. On the other hand, manpower programs can be effective only if discrimination in employment is
eliminated. Civil rights legislation and manpower programs have contributed to the substantial gains of blacks; pressures from women's liberation groups and action under civil rights legislation opened some doors for
women; the problems of Chicanos, Indians, and other minorities also have
been documented and some efforts have been made to alleviate them.
Nevertheless, discrimination remains a persistent and festering disease in the
American economy.

It is naïve to assume that progress toward equal employment opportunity is guaranteed or that freedoms achieved in the past will necessarily

persist. Other labor market problems may demand priority, or opposition may increase from those who are challenged by the gains of minorities. Also, if positive steps are not taken, the situation may deteriorate because of adverse developments in the labor market. An increasing number of educated blacks may demand entrance into better-paying or more responsible positions, while the value of a college education is declining as a guarantee of choice jobs. Constant vigil must, therefore, be exercised to insure that progress continues to be made.

It is the prime goal of manpower policy to insure that all human resources are fully developed and utilized. As long as discrimination exists and certain minorities are given fewer opportunities, assistance must be concentrated among these minorities. Manpower policy must, therefore, continue to focus on the victims of discrimination. Education must be improved, occupational training provided, and discriminatory barriers broken down. Both a push and a pull are required if those who are discriminated against are to get an equal chance in the work force.

THE ROLE OF GOVERNMENT

To achieve the expanded goals of human resource development, the government will have to assume an ever-increasing responsibility. In recent years, the government's role in education, manpower programs, and related efforts has drastically expanded. At the same time, there is a heightened awareness of the effect that a wide range of government actions has upon the development and utilization of our human resources. No longer viewed separately and in isolation, these actions more and more are being examined for their manpower implications.

A critical example is military manpower policies. Every war has had a profound impact upon manpower policy, and the latest war was no exception: Escalation and deescalation of the Vietnam conflict resulted in the critical reexamination of draft policies; the exemptions based on college attendance and marriage were questioned and redefined; the quality of the selection process was debated and new methods were implemented. As manpower shortages developed in tight labor markets, the military, as would any other employer, lowered entry qualifications to draw upon the pool of underutilized disadvantaged youths, especially blacks, who could not meet the more stringent entry requirements developed during peacetime. But as the military requirements declined with the withdrawal of American troops from Indochina, other manpower implications came to the fore. The interrelation between troop levels and aggregate unemployment rates became painfully evident with the rise of unemployment; the major impact of military service on the individual's employment prospects was manifested by the severe difficulties of veterans; and so few veterans took advantage of training and education opportunities that the adequacy of these benefits was questioned. Attention turned to the idea of establishing a volunteer armed forces, forcing the military to compete in the labor market.

Expanding governmental responsibilities have other broad implications for the development and utilization of human resources, not the least of which is the role of government as a civilian employer. In the past, neither the federal government nor the many state and local governments have acted as model employers. Pressures to eliminate discriminatory practices, to remove arbitrary credential barriers, and to expand training and advancement opportunities for the disadvantaged have resulted in some changes in governmental manpower practices. Yet much remains to be done, especially at the state and local levels, to make governments equal opportunity employers.

The government also plays a major role through such regulatory functions as the enforcement of antidiscrimination laws and wage and hours regulations. Perhaps most significantly, the federal government has assumed responsibility for the maintenance of a favorable economic climate. Because high employment is not the only goal, however, the Employment Act of 1946, which made it the policy of the federal government to sustain maximum employment, remains largely an exhortation. The consensus among economists, politicians, and informed citizens is that the unemployment rate can be lowered or raised almost at the public will. The problem is to achieve high employment without undue inflation, and the key issue, therefore, is the tradeoff between unemployment and inflation. At least in the short run, we can choose whatever employment level or price stability we are willing to pay for, but we cannot have both high employment and stable prices. In time, manpower programs and other structural measures such as aid to depressed areas may help to improve the terms of tradeoff, but there is no indication that both full employment and stable prices can be achieved in the immediate future. Given this dilemma, expedience dictates measures that will cushion the negative effects of inflation in order to sustain a high-employment economy. The progress made during the past three or four decades justifies optimism that increasingly sophisticated designs will ease the choice between inflation and unemployment.

THE EMERGENCE OF HUMAN RESOURCE POLICY

According to dictionary definitions, no policy for human resources now exists. At the federal level, most efforts have been a reaction to the special problems—real or imaginary—that caught public attention. Federal aid to elementary and secondary schools was initiated to help financially troubled areas, with little emphasis on educational innovations. Grants and loans to students were largely motivated by the Sputnik-induced fears of a technology gap. Manpower programs were funded in a haphazard fashion, in response to perceived needs. Military policies were promulgated to fight an unexpectedly difficult and unpopular war at what was thought to be the least political cost. Monetary and fiscal policies were geared to affect normal economic activity with little consideration of their impact on special groups or their relation to programs that focused on special needs.

It is not at all clear, however, that the impact of human resource programs would be more salubrious if a definite policy were selected to guide decisions. What would be the nature and scope of such a policy? From our examination of past and present developments, we cannot answer this vital question, but we can define the ingredients and objectives of a human resources policy. Such a policy must be capable of identifying problems, setting goals, designing programs, marshaling resources, and mounting activities encompassing the entire labor market. To achieve the dual objectives of efficient allocation of manpower resources and optimum choice for participants in the work force, a manpower system should allow each individual to plan a working career in full awareness of his own abilities and the alternatives open to him. A high and sustained level of economic activity is necessary to provide opportunities of sufficient number and range. Restrictions unrelated to productivity or equity—such as overcredentialization and discrimination based on age, race, or sex—must not be allowed to interfere with access to, and rewards for, these opportunities. The distribution of jobs must be open and flexible: Only the lack of potential competence should restrain preparation and access to individual occupation choice; lateral and upward mobility should be maintained; help in adapting to economic and technological change should be available. The reward structure—income, status, and job satisfaction—should be similarly unencumbered. All those able and willing to work should thus find both opportunities and rewards in the production of goods and services favored by society as reflected in the market place and the ballot box.

To what degree should policy be directed toward the achievement of these objectives? The supply of social energy is always limited and should be conserved for high-priority efforts. Interrelated with the development of human resources, as we have noted, are fiscal, monetary, education, housing, transportation, welfare, health, defense, and myriad other economic and social problems. Such linkages should be noted and policy makers in each arena should act consistently, but no single policy can comprehend all the others. Indeed, experience suggests the wisdom of leaving to unguided individual choice all those decisions that will cause no serious problems in the aggregate, for centralized decisions are not necessarily wiser and, if shortsighted, may cause more damage than a series of unwise individual decisions.

Public intervention is, in some cases, appropriate, but its limits must be understood. First, programs concerned with development of human resources can hope to solve only problems related to unemployment and earnings. A manpower program can contribute to the solution of poverty only for those families with present or potential workers; it can solve social discontent only for those whose problems relate to the lack of meaningful employment. Manpower policies are likely to affect only marginally problems connected with family break-ups, pollution, congestion, and other ills of a complex urban society. Second, public policy has only two sources of leverage: dollars and votes. Policies that do not affect the distribution of either are only pious declarations and have little influence.

Despite these limitations, important strides have been made toward more conscious and comprehensive action in human resource development. Insights have been gained by improved data and measurement techniques; one result has been a "cross-fertilization" showing the interdependence of problems and programs that had previously been dealt with independently. Educators are growing more aware of the need to prepare students for work, while manpower policy makers realize the difficulty and high cost of providing remedial attention where the schools have failed the first time around. The need to maintain full employment has been stressed by manpower analysts, and the possibility of making monetary and fiscal policies more effective through manpower programs has received increasing scrutiny. Interdependence of equal employment opportunity for minorities with education and manpower policies is clearly recognized; the relation of all these policies to overall economic growth is also being examined. The debate over the volunteer army has highlighted the manpower implications of military actions.

Recognizing the interdependence of various aspects of human resource development is a far cry from articulating a comprehensive human resources policy. But it is not clear that such a policy is necessary or even desirable. The importance of various problems fluctuates as priorities change; public policy is hammered out step by step; the full consequences of existing programs and newly discovered concerns unfold slowly. Hence, the trial-and-error approach may, in the long run, prove as effective as the most elaborate planning, possibly even more so. A comprehensive human resource policy may not be compatible with a pluralistic society such as ours, and perhaps the best that we can hope for is fragmented approaches to complex problems. The judgment of history may be that the search for a comprehensive manpower human resources policy is in line with the search for the holy grail.

RESPONDING TO CHANGE

Some of the probable directions of change have been outlined and their implications identified. But there is no certainty that these will bear out or that, even if they do, they will be the most significant developments of the coming years, for the only certain prediction about the future is that it will be different from the past. Clearly, changes lie ahead, and our policies and practices must be able to adapt.

Several steps can be taken to increase adaptability. Perhaps the most important is to expand the flow of information. Data and evaluative techniques must be improved, and the knowledge that is gained must be widely disseminated. This will facilitate the recognition of changing circumstances and the rapid replication of successful techniques for dealing with them.

Another ingredient of adaptability is experimentation. Research and development has been an important component of the manpower programs. Old approaches must be reexamined in light of changing circumstances and improved accordingly; new ideas must be generated and tested; the future must be projected and its implications incorporated as plans are developed. In the evolution of policy, one of the most difficult tasks is developing more orderly means of eliminating programs and practices that are no longer effective and of weeding out ideas and theories that have lost their relevance. But change for change's sake must be discouraged, and constant attention must be given to retaining what is useful from the past.

Finally, one of the most critical prerequisites to adaptability is an understanding of the historical context of change. Problems may gain sudden visibility, though they usually emerge gradually and are long undetected. To understand the present and to be able to cope with the future, we need to know what has gone before. In this sense, the knowledge contained in this volume will, hopefully, serve as a basis for more comprehensive analysis and action so that we can make more effective and rewarding use of our human resources.

Manpower
Bibliography

Manpower
Bibliography

BAKKE, E. WIGHT. *The Mission of Manpower Policy*. Studies in Employment and Unemployment Series. Washington, D.C.: Upjohn Institute for Employment Research, 1969.

The author argues that the *de facto* objective of present manpower policy (increasing the employability of the most disadvantaged) is too narrowly defined. He contends that manpower policy should deal with the entire supply of labor and should place more emphasis on the creation of particularized demand in the form of jobs geared to the available labor supply. His comparison of manpower policy in the United States and in western Europe is insightful.

BECKER, GARY. *Human Capital*. New York: National Bureau of Economic Research, 1964.

The author first constructs a general theoretical framework within which investment in human capital can be analyzed, and then illustrates the effect of human capital upon such economic variables as earnings and employment by a systematic analysis of on-the-job training. The second half of the book examines the empirical relationship between productivity and investment in human capital. Emphasis is on rates of return from investment in high-school and college education in the United States.

BERG, IVAR. *Education and Jobs: The Great Training Robbery*. New York: Praeger, 1970.

Ivar Berg, a sociologist, argues that education in the United States is becoming a formalized credentialing procedure which acts as a barrier to the advancement of the poor. He analyzes the educational requirements

585

for thousands of jobs along with Census Bureau reports on educational levels of the work force by occupation. His study examines the relationship between educational achievement and workers' performance and promotion expectations.

BLAU, PETER M., and OTIS DUDLEY DUNCAN. *The American Occupational Structure.* New York: John Wiley, 1967.

An empirical analysis of the determinants of the occupational position and mobility of American workers, using the tools of modern sociology. Of special interest is the readable summary of quantitative methodology and the special attention given to the effects of race, region, migration, and farm background on occupational status.

BOK, DEREK CURTIS, and JOHN T. DUNLOP. *Labor and the American Community.* New York: Simon & Schuster, 1970.

A comprehensive overview of the present state of the American labor movement, which explores the public attitude toward labor, reviews the growth of trade unions and assesses their internal government, and discusses the changing nature of collective bargaining and the political impact of labor.

BOWEN, WILLIAM G., and T. ALDRICH FINEGAN. *The Economics of Labor Force Participation.* Princeton: Princeton University Press, 1969.

A comprehensive and detailed analysis of the factors determining who is in the labor market and who is not working or seeking work. The effects on labor force participation of many individual characteristics and labor market conditions are analyzed for specific population groups. Also analyzed is the sensitivity of participation rates to the tightness of labor markets. Extensive appendices.

DOERINGER, PETER, and MICHAEL PEORE. *Internal Labor Markets and Manpower Analysis.* Lexington, Mass.: Heath, 1971.

Examines the nature of labor markets within which the pricing and allocation of labor are governed by administrative rules and procedures. Part I develops theoretical concepts of the internal labor market. In Part II these concepts are applied to a number of topics which are often of interest to manpower policy makers: manpower adjustment to labor market imbalances, technological change, racial discrimination, and the relationship of low-income employment to the disadvantaged labor force.

FERMAN, LOUIS A., JOYCE L. KORNBLUH, and J. A. MILLER, eds. *Negroes and Jobs.* Ann Arbor: University of Michigan Press, 1968.

This book of readings deals with the relationship of the black working man to the American labor market. The articles and excerpts, most of which appeared during the 1960s, encompass several different viewpoints. Topics treated include the economic status of blacks, background factors, institutional barriers, labor market structure, black experiences in the labor market, and the equalization of black-white employment opportunities.

FOLGER, JOHN, HELEN ASTIN, and ALAN BAYER. *Human Resources and Higher Education.* New York: Russell Sage Foundation, 1970.

A study of the processes involved in developing and utilizing professional workers. After analyzing the market for college graduates, the authors

587 Manpower Bibliography

discuss the problems faced by women, persons from the lower socioeconomic levels, and immigrants in obtaining access to higher education and to professional and specialized fields. The final section evaluates the effectiveness of manpower policies and suggests areas requiring additional research.

GREBLER, LEO, JOAN W. MOORE, and RALPH C. GUZMAN. *The Mexican American People*. New York: Free Press, 1970.

During the 1960s, Grebler and his colleagues conducted an interdisciplinary study of the socioeconomic position of Mexican Americans in selected southwestern urban areas. Utilizing research materials drawn from Census data, household surveys, interviews, and direct observation, the study team constructs an accurate picture of Mexican Americans as a national minority. The minority's interaction with the dominant system is emphasized.

GINZBERG, ELI. *Manpower Agenda for America*. New York: McGraw-Hill, 1968.

The papers in this volume identify the many barriers blocking the escape of people from poverty and unemployment, which must be considered in the formulation of public policy. Ginzberg concludes that "The final challenge to manpower policy . . . is to reduce waste in the acquisition and utilization of skill without jeopardizing other important values."

GINZBERG, ELI. *Career Guidance: Who Needs It, Who Provides for It, Who Can Improve It*. New York: McGraw-Hill, 1971.

A broad study of the role of both occupational and educational guidance in enhancing the ability of people to make optimum use of their options in acquiring an education and in pursuing a career. After establishing the social dimensions of career guidance, the author examines the institutions through which it operates. Recommendations are offered for the guidance profession and the public, and likely developments during the 1970s are discussed.

GORDON, R. A. *The Goal of Full Employment*. New York: John Wiley, 1967.

This monograph deals with full employment as a goal of national economic policy. The relationship of full employment to other, often conflicting, economic goals is discussed. In order to ascertain patterns of unemployment, the labor force is analyzed in terms of age, sex, color, education, industry, and occupation. The author concludes that with expanded and more effective manpower and public employment programs, along with a modified incomes policy, the United States could achieve a level of unemployment of around 3 percent.

HARBISON, FREDERICK, and CHARLES A. MYERS. *Education, Manpower, and Economic Growth*. New York: McGraw-Hill, 1969.

The authors, both economists, argue that human resource development is the most important determinant of economic growth. Seventy-five countries are ranked on the basis of a composite human resource development index and then grouped into four levels of development ranging from underdeveloped to advanced. Human resource development is analyzed qualitatively at each level and appropriate development strategies are suggested.

KREPS, JUANITA. *Sex in the Marketplace: American Women at Work,* Policy Studies in Employment and Welfare No. 11. Baltimore: Johns Hopkins, 1971.

After reviewing the literature on women's labor force activity—when women work, at what jobs, and under what arrangements, the author concludes that women are overeducated for most of the jobs they do.

LECHT, LEONARD A. *Manpower Needs for National Goals in the 1970's.* New York: Praeger, 1969.

An analysis of future manpower requirements from the perspective of an illustrative set of national goals to be achieved by 1975. The author warns that if we follow present patterns of employment, discrimination, training, and education we will face serious labor shortages in the future. The potential impact on the labor market of pursuing alternative goals is also discussed.

LEVITAN, SAR A., and GARTH L. MANGUM. *Federal Training and Work Programs in the Sixties.* Ann Arbor: University of Michigan Press, 1968.

The authors trace the development of programs for training the unemployed and the disadvantaged: the Manpower Development and Training Act, the Job Corps, the Neighborhood Youth Corps, the vocational education and rehabilitation programs, and the federal-state employment service. They describe and evaluate the major programs and recommend improvements in administration for more effective delivery of services.

LEVITAN, SAR A., and BARBARA HETRICK. *Big Brother's Indian Programs—With Reservations.* New York: McGraw-Hill, 1971.

A general review and critical evaluation of federal programs for the half million American Indians living on or near reservations. Programs in education, health, human and natural resources, and community structure are appraised. Problems in public policy and implications for the future are considered.

MANGUM, GARTH. *The Emergence of Manpower Policy.* New York: Holt, Rinehart & Winston, 1969.

A brief history of U.S. manpower policies to 1960 and a summary of the changing goals and methods of government manpower policies in the 1960s. Mangum discusses the relative success of the Job Corps, Neighborhood Youth Corps, and other training programs. The final chapters recommend changes in the administration and structure of federal manpower programs.

MARSHALL, RAY, and VERNON BRIGGS. *The Negro and Apprenticeship.* Baltimore: Johns Hopkins, 1967.

An analysis of the factors influencing the low participation rates of blacks in apprenticeship programs, and an evaluation of the measures being taken to promote equal apprenticeship opportunity. The authors examine black participation in apprenticeship programs in 10 major cities and make recommendations for increasing the number of black apprentices. Problems such as discrimination by unions and employers, the limited number of available apprenticeships, and low educational levels of black applicants are discussed.

MILLER, HERMAN P. *Rich Man, Poor Man.* New York: Thomas Y. Crowell, 1971.

The author, Chief of the Population Division of the U.S. Bureau of the Census, analyzes the social and economic aspects of income distribution. He demonstrates how personal income is correlated with such personal characteristics as race, sex, and educational attainment.

MILLER, S. M., and PAMELA ROBY. *The Future of Inequality.* New York: Basic Books, 1970.

This book analyzes six dimensions of inequality ranging from the distribution of personal income to inequality in active participation in educational and decision-making institutions. Issues and social policies involved in reducing inequalities are also discussed. A unique feature of this study is its emphasis on a number of social and psychological variables ordinarily neglected in analyses of inequality.

MYERS, CHARLES A. *The Role of the Private Sector in Manpower Development.* Baltimore: Johns Hopkins, 1971.

An evaluation of the private sector in recruiting, motivating, and developing manpower. Private training programs for managerial, technical, white-collar, skilled, production, and disadvantaged workers are examined. At the end of each chapter the author suggests some unanswered questions.

PATTEN, THOMAS H. *Manpower and the Development of Human Resources.* New York: John Wiley, 1971.

The author, previously an industrial relations executive with the Ford Motor Company, examines, in nonmathematical terms, manpower planning and development within businesses and organizations. Separate chapters are devoted to particular types of training—for example, programs for training apprentices, salesmen, foremen, and executives. Other chapters deal in general terms with the objectives and organization of manpower planning.

REUBENS, BEATRICE G. *The Hard-to-Employ: European Programs.* New York: Columbia University Press, 1970.

A detailed examination and evaluation of nine western European countries' programs and policies, including attempts to rehabilitate and place the hard-to-employ in the competitive labor market, efforts to create special jobs, subsidies for employers, and government intervention in the economies of depressed areas.

SOMERS, GERALD G., and J. KENNETH LITTLE, eds. *Vocational Education: Today and Tomorrow.* Madison: Center for Studies in Vocational and Technical Education, University of Wisconsin, 1971.

This collection of papers addresses the major issues confronting vocational education, including its relation with general education, training for specific occupations and industries, the labor market, individual needs, and the disadvantaged. Also explored are the role of counseling and placement activities; staffing; organization and administration; and research, evaluation, and experimentation.

SOMERS, GERALD G., and W. D. WOOD, eds. *Cost-Benefit Analysis of Manpower Policies*. Kingston, Ontario: Industrial Relations Centre, Queen's University, 1969.

This volume offers several papers presented at the North American Conference on Cost-Benefit Analysis. The first section deals with theoretical and methodological aspects of cost-benefit analysis; the final section considers the application of cost-benefit analysis to various types of manpower programs. Occupational training programs for adult workers, programs for disadvantaged workers, and the Canadian Manpower Mobility Program are examined.

STEIN, BRUNO. *On Relief: The Economics of Poverty and Public Welfare*. New York: Basic Books, 1971.

A survey and critical analysis of the historical evolution, politics, and economic logic of the major programs aiding the poor. The economic case for alternative programs is examined.

THUROW, LESTER C. *Poverty and Discrimination*. Washington, D.C.: Brookings Institution, 1969.

Utilizing econometric techniques and defining poverty and discrimination as problems of income distribution, this study examines their severity, the income differentials between whites and blacks, and factors that contribute to the persistence of poverty.

THUROW, LESTER. *Investment in Human Capital*. Belmont, Calif.: Wadsworth, 1970.

Emphasizes the need to integrate the concept of human capital into the main body of economic theory. Although much of the analysis is carried out within the framework of traditional investment theory, care is taken to describe the many peculiarities that differentiate human from physical capital. After dealing with the production and measurement of human capital, Thurow discusses investment decisions at the individual, firm, and government levels.

WOOL, HAROLD. *The Military Specialist*. Baltimore: Johns Hopkins, 1968.

Describes the problems involved in recruiting, training, and retaining specialized military personnel. The first half of the book deals with occupational requirements in the armed services; the second half focuses on the supply of specialized military manpower. Both economic and noneconomic factors affecting enlistment rates are examined.

Indexes

Index of Names

Index of
Subjects